에듀윌과 함께 시작하면,
당신도 합격할 수 있습니다!

편입 합격 후 대학에 진학했으나 학과 전공이 맞지 않아
휴학 후 다시 편입을 결심하여 서강대에 합격한 3학년 대학생

직장생활을 하며 2년간 편입공부를 해
인서울 대학에 당당히 합격한 30대 직장인

대학진학을 포기하고 20살 때 학점은행제 독학사를 통해 전문학사를 취득하고
편입을 준비하여 합격한 21살 전문학사 수험생

군복무 중 취업에 대해 고민하다 공대계열 학과로 편입을 결심하여
1년 만에 한양대에 합격한 복학생

누구나 합격할 수 있습니다.
시작하겠다는 '다짐' 하나면 충분합니다.

마지막 페이지를 덮으면,

**에듀윌과 함께
편입 합격이 시작됩니다.**

편입 교육 1위

업계 최고! 완벽한 교수 라인업
스타 교수진 대규모 입성

3년 연속 서성한반 100% 합격자 배출 에듀윌 교수진에
과목별 1타 교수진 대규모 입성

기본이론부터 문제풀이까지 6개월 핵심압축 커리큘럼

기본이론 완성	핵심유형 완성	기출심화 완성	적중실전 완성	파이널
기본이론 압축 정리	핵심포인트 집중 이해	기출문제 실전훈련	출제유력 예상문제 풀이	대학별 예상 모의고사

* 서성한반(P사) 교수진 전격입성 | 2019~2021년 서성한반(P사) 수강생 합격자 서울소재 20개 대학 기준 3년 연속 100% 합격자 배출
  (서울소재 20개 대학: 연세, 고려, 서강, 성균관, 한양, 중앙, 이화, 한국외, 경희, 서울시립, 건국, 국민, 동국, 숭실, 홍익, 숙명, 세종, 명지, 광운, 서울여)
* 1타 교수진 : W사 2022년 프리패스 수강 데이터 산출 (저스틴, 권윤아, 고하늬, 홍석기 2022.01~2022.12)

에듀윌 편입

에듀윌 편입 시리즈
전격 출간

3년 연속 100% 합격자 배출 교수진이 만든 교재로
합격의 차이를 직접 경험해 보세요.

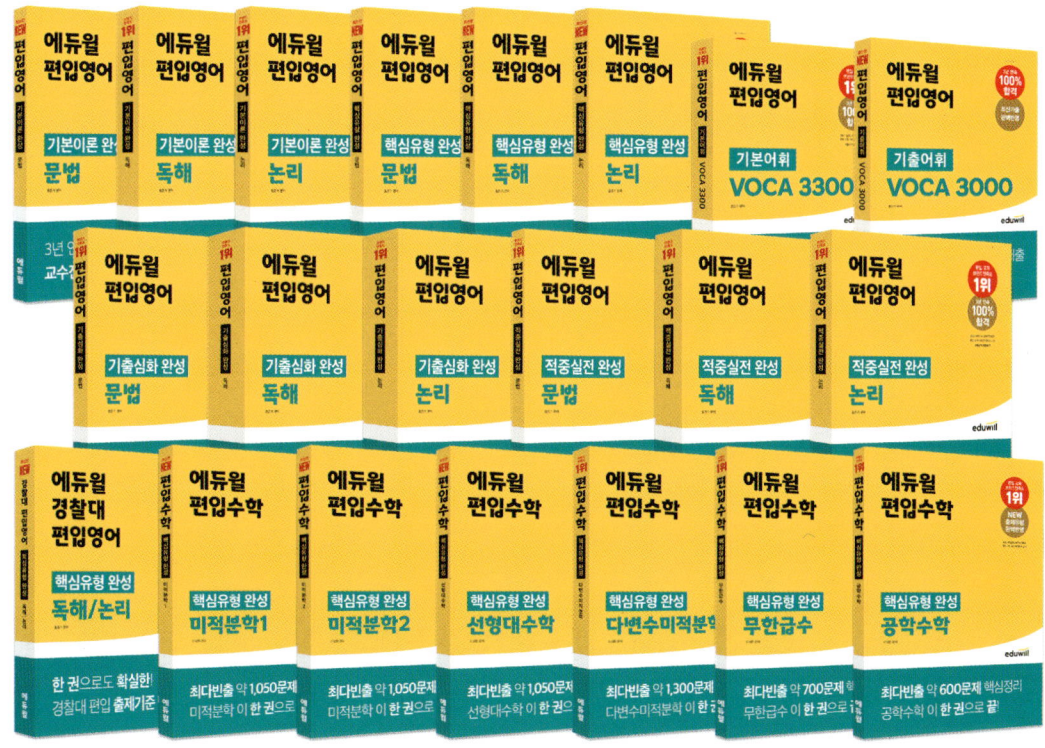

* 본 교재 이미지는 변동될 수 있습니다.
* 여러분의 합격을 도와줄 편입 시리즈 정보는 에듀윌 홈페이지(www.eduwill.net)에서 확인하세요.

* 서성한반(P사) 교수진 전격입성 | 2019~2021년 서성한반(P사) 수강생 합격자 서울소재 20개 대학 기준 3년 연속 100% 합격자 배출
  (서울소재 20개 대학: 연세, 고려, 서강, 성균관, 한양, 중앙, 이화, 한국외, 경희, 서울시립, 건국, 국민, 동국, 숭실, 홍익, 숙명, 세종, 명지, 광운, 서울여)

편입 교육 1위

노베이스 수험생을 위한
쌩기초 풀-패키지 무료배포

클라쓰가 남다른 1타 교수진으로 새롭게 탄생!
한 달이면 기초 탈출! 신규회원이면 누구나 신청 가능!

1타 교수진의 쉽고 알찬 쌩기초 입문 강의
- 1타 교수진 노하우 총 집합
- 기초 지식부터 입문 이론까지
- 초단기 쌩 노베이스 완벽 탈출

토익 베이직 RC/LC 강의
- 첫 토익부터 700+ 한 달이면 끝
- 편입 공인영어 성적 준비를 위한 토익 기초 지원
- 쉬운 토익 공식! 에듀윌 토익 강의

합격비법 가이드
- 대학별 최신 편입 전형 제공
- 최신 편입 관련 정보 모음
- 합격전략 및 합격자 수기 제공

기출어휘 체크북
- 편입생이 꼭 알아야 할 편입 어휘의 모든 것
- 최신 기출 어휘를 빈도순으로 구성
- 3,000개의 어휘를 한 권으로 압축

편입 합격!
에듀윌과 함께하면 현실이 됩니다.

쌩기초 풀패키지
무료 이벤트

* 1타 교수진 : W사 2022년 프리패스 수강 데이터 산출 (저스틴, 권윤아, 고하늬, 홍석기 2022.01~2022.12)
* 본 혜택과 경로는 예고 없이 변경되거나 대체될 수 있습니다.

에듀윌 편입 솔루션

독해 ADVANCED

편저자 에듀윌 편입 LAB

READING ADVANCED

독해가 어려워?

이 책을 봐!

편입 최초
프리미엄 해설 수록

eduwill

Preface 이 책의 **머리말**

안녕하세요, 에듀윌 편입 LAB입니다.

에듀윌 편입 솔루션 독해 Advanced는 대학 편입 시험에서 출제되는 다양한 주제의 독해 문항에 대비하기 위한 책입니다. 편입영어는 난이도 높은 입시영어이며 학교마다 다양한 주제의 영어 독해 문제들이 출제되기 때문에, 이 책에서는 이에 대비하여 다양한 실제 기출문제를 주제별로 제공해 드립니다.

에듀윌 편입 솔루션 독해 Advanced는 학생들이 자신의 영어 독해 능력을 크게 개선할 수 있도록 편입영어에 기출되는 독해 지문을 다양한 주제로 구성하였습니다. Part 1에서는 인문학을 테마로 7개의 하위 주제를 나누고 Part 2에서는 자연과학을 테마로 4개의 하위 주제를 분류하여 엄선된 문제들로만 구성하였습니다. 또한, 각 주제별로 문제를 풀이하는 데 도움이 되는 상세한 해설과 분석도 제공합니다.

에듀윌 편입 솔루션 독해 Advanced의 가장 큰 장점은 체계적이고 자세한 프리미엄 해설입니다. 편입교재 중 최초로 한글 해설에 정답과 오답의 근거를 표시하였을 뿐만 아니라 꼼꼼한 분석과 문제풀이에 도움이 될 만한 배경지식을 더하여 자습에 용이하도록 제작되었습니다.

에듀윌 편입 솔루션 독해 Advanced로 학습하여 편입 독해 문항의 고득점과 더불어 합격의 기쁨을 누리시길 기원합니다.

감사합니다.

Foreword 이 책의 **구성**

분야별 연습 문제

이 책은 최근 10년 동안의 편입 기출 문제를 분야별로 나누어 구성하였습니다. 각 분야의 내용을 파악하고 다양한 학교의 기출문제를 풀어 보세요.

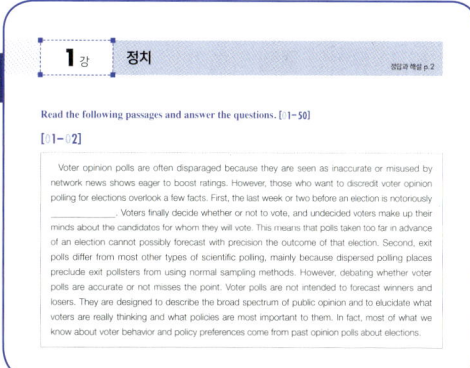

정답과 해설

이 책은 효율적인 학습을 위해 프리미엄 해설을 제공하고 있습니다. 자신의 문제 풀이 방법이 정확한지 해설지를 통해 확인해 보세요.

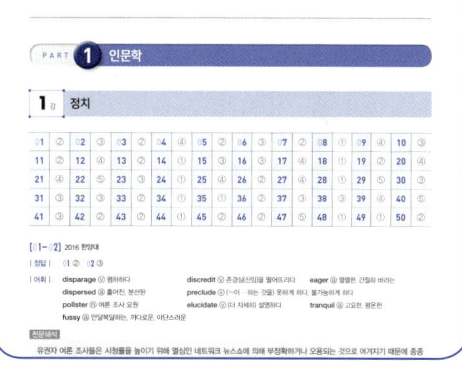

배경지식

이 책은 독해 지문을 이해하기 위해 필요한 배경지식을 제공합니다. 다양한 배경지식을 읽어보고 익히세요.

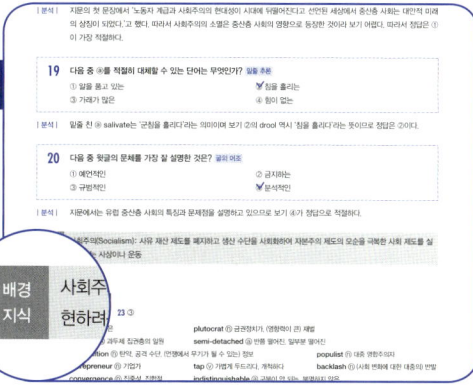

Guide 이 책의 **수준별 학습방법과 활용법**

1. 다양한 유형의 문제 익히기
이 책에 수록된 다양한 편입 독해 지문을 읽어 보고 여러 가지 유형의 문제를 풀어 보세요. 그리고 **자신이 자주 틀리는 문제 유형**을 정리하여 집중적으로 학습하세요.

2. 다양한 종류의 글 익히기
뉴스 기사, 에세이, 소설, 비평문, 학술 논문 등 다양한 종류의 지문을 읽고 **글의 종류에 따른 글의 핵심을 빠르게 파악**하는 연습을 하세요.

3. 배경지식 익히기
편입에 있어서 배경지식은 지문의 전반적인 이해를 도와 속독을 가능하게 하고 정답 확률을 증가시켜 줍니다. 문제를 풀면서 스스로 이해도가 높은 분야와 부족한 분야를 파악하고 약한 배경지식을 보충하여 **모든 분야를 강하게 만드세요.**

4. 다양한 어휘, 표현 익히기
이 책에 수록된 중장문의 지문들을 읽으면서 다양한 분야별 고급어휘와 표현들을 익히세요. **다양한 어휘의 학습**은 지문의 이해도를 높이고 독해의 정답률 또한 자연스럽게 향상시킬 것입니다.

Contents 이 책의 **차례**

PART 1　인문학

1강	정치	8
2강	경영 / 경제	34
3강	사회 / 문화	64
4강	언어 / 문학 / 예술	96
5강	역사 / 지리	132
6강	철학 / 종교	164
7강	교육 / 심리	194

PART 2　자연과학

8강	과학 / 기술	226
9강	우주 / 지구	254
10강	건강 / 의학	284
11강	환경 / 동식물	318

PART 1

에듀윌 편입
솔루션 독해 Advanced

Reading

인문학

- **1강** 정치
- **2강** 경영 / 경제
- **3강** 사회 / 문화
- **4강** 언어 / 문학 / 예술
- **5강** 역사 / 지리
- **6강** 철학 / 종교
- **7강** 교육 / 심리

1강 정치

Read the following passages and answer the questions. [01-50]

[01-02]

> Voter opinion polls are often disparaged because they are seen as inaccurate or misused by network news shows eager to boost ratings. However, those who want to discredit voter opinion polling for elections overlook a few facts. First, the last week or two before an election is notoriously _____. Voters finally decide whether or not to vote, and undecided voters make up their minds about the candidates for whom they will vote. This means that polls taken too far in advance of an election cannot possibly forecast with precision the outcome of that election. Second, exit polls differ from most other types of scientific polling, mainly because dispersed polling places preclude exit pollsters from using normal sampling methods. However, debating whether voter polls are accurate or not misses the point. Voter polls are not intended to forecast winners and losers. They are designed to describe the broad spectrum of public opinion and to elucidate what voters are really thinking and what policies are most important to them. In fact, most of what we know about voter behavior and policy preferences come from past opinion polls about elections.

01 윗글의 빈칸에 들어갈 말로 가장 적절한 것은?

① fussy
② volatile
③ elevated
④ tranquil

02 윗글의 내용과 가장 거리가 먼 것은?

① Media outlets are often believed to misuse voter opinion polls in order to increase their viewership.
② Voter opinion polls taken too early cannot predict the outcome of an election accurately.
③ The value of voter opinion polls resides in predicting winners and losers.
④ The discrepancy between exit polls and other types of polls is largely due to the fact that exit polls do not utilize normal sampling methods.

[03-04]

Neutrality is the absence of any form of partisanship or commitment; it consists of a refusal to 'take sides.' In international relations, neutrality is a legal condition through which a state declares its non-involvement in a conflict or war, and indicates its intention to refrain from supporting or aiding either side. As a principle of individual conduct, applied to the likes of judges, civil servants, the military and other public officials, it implies, strictly speaking the absence of political sympathies and ideological leanings. Neutral actors are thus _____. In practice, the less exacting requirement of impartiality is usually applied. This allows that political sympathies may be held as long as these do not intrude into, or conflict with, professional or public responsibilities.

03 Choose the one that best fills in the blank.

① powerful moguls
② political eunuchs
③ social pariahs
④ legal conduits

04 Which of the following can be inferred about "neutrality"?

① It renders agents accountable for their actions in a conflict.
② It is manifested differently across nations and cultures.
③ It is one of the basic principles of political parties.
④ It is a position in which skewing of judgement is avoided.

[05-06]

Over the past 15 years, my country has gone through a colossal political revolution. The traditional secular elite that identifies with the nation's modernist founder, Mustafa Ataturk, has been replaced by religious conservatives who, until recently, were largely powerless and marginalized. The religious conservatives have by now come to dominate virtually all institutions of the state, as well as the media and even much of the business sector.

This political revolution has had an inadvertent outcome. It has tested the ostensible virtues of these religious conservatives — and they have failed. They have failed the test so terribly that it raises the question of whether religiosity and morality really go hand in hand, as so many religious people like to claim. The religious conservatives morally failed because they ended up doing everything that they once condemned as unjust and cruel. For decades, they criticized the secular elite for nepotism and corruption, for weaponizing the judiciary and for using the news media to demonize and intimidate their opponents.

05 What does the underlined their opponents refer to?

① The secular elite
② The religious conservatives
③ The judiciary and the media
④ The followers of Mustafa Ataturk

06 Which of the following is true of the new political leaders?

① They are moral as well as conservative.
② They do not believe religious people are moral.
③ They are being accused of using their power unfairly.
④ They used to stand in the same political position as Mustafa Ataturk.

[07-09]

   Democratic theory is in a condition today akin to that of theoretical physics when Einstein began his speculations at the turn of the century. The accepted doctrine at that time was in the main what Newton had ⓐ enunciated two centuries earlier. Fundamental to his thinking were the concepts of space and time. Newton had conceived of each as distinct from the other. Both, in his view, were absolutes. Though 19th-century research had yielded results which Newtonian doctrine did not satisfactorily explain, Newton's image of the universe had not yet been reformulated. That reformulation was what Einstein achieved. His inspiration lay in treating space and time not as separate concepts, but as one, fused by him into space-time. Furthermore, this integrated concept was considered relative, not absolute. What space and time have been to physics, liberty and equality have been, and still are, to democratic theorists. More than any others, these _____Ⓐ_____ ideals serve as our basic concepts. If one tries to compress the ethos of democracy into the briefest summary, it will run something like this: democracy is the form of government which combines for its citizens as much freedom and as much equality as possible.

07 The author maintains that _____.

① liberty and equality are absolutes
② space and time were incompatible for Newton
③ there are differences between democratic theory and physics
④ Newton's theory is as much important as Einstein's

08 The meaning of the underlined word ⓐ is _____.

① announced
② denied
③ criticized
④ experimented

09 The most suitable word for Ⓐ is _____.

① different
② incompatible
③ false
④ twin

[10-11]

What is beyond doubt is that from first to last Hannah Arendt was irresistibly drawn to the activity of understanding, an endless and circular mental activity. Hannah Arendt had plenty of ideas and opinions, to be sure; hailed as both wanting change and desiring stability, she made new distinctions, contributed new concepts, and altered old categories of traditional political thought. Those are results, and they have proved useful to others. But, unlike most political thinkers, Arendt was not primarily concerned with solving problems; her ceaseless ventures in understanding were for her no more _____ than life itself. What is more difficult to grasp is that the activity of understanding afforded her a measure of reconciliation to the world in which she lived. If others came to understand, in her sense of understanding, then she was gratified and made to feel "at home." This does not mean she wanted or believed it possible to hand over her own thoughts to anyone else. That would have been sheer nonsense to Arendt, for whom thinking — understanding, endowing an event with meaning — was an engagement with oneself, solitary and private. She led an exemplary life, a life that has been told and retold, but ultimately the light shed on the world by her understanding of it is the only way to catch a glimpse of who Hannah Arendt was.

10 윗글의 빈칸에 들어갈 말로 가장 적절한 것은?

① intuitive
② intentional
③ instrumental
④ indeterminate

11 Hannah Arendt에 대한 설명으로 적절하지 <u>않은</u> 것은?

① By nature she could be considered to be either liberal or conservative.
② She was gradually cut off from the outside world in her later career.
③ Her activities cannot be defined in terms of traditional disciplinary categories.
④ The importance of understanding for her lay in understanding itself rather than in its results.

[12-14]

It is then only when suffering is considered from the standpoint of a politics of pity that the question of commitment appears as a problem. The reason for this is that a politics of pity must meet a double requirement. As a politics it aspires to generality. Its role is to detach itself from the local and so from those necessarily local situations in which events provoking compassion may arise. To do this politics may rely upon techniques for establishing equivalences, and on statistical techniques in particular. But in its reference to pity it cannot wholly free itself from the particular case. Pity is not inspired by generalities. So, for example, a picture of absolute poverty defined by means of quantitative indicators based upon existing conventions of equivalence may find its place in a macroeconomic treatise and may also help define a politics. It will not, however, inspire the sentiments which are indisputable for a politics of pity. To arouse pity, suffering and wretched bodies must be conveyed in such a way as to affect the sensibility of those more fortunate. Pity possesses the weakness of a lack of _____Ⓐ_____ : a suffering child fills our heart with sadness, but we greet the news of a terrible battle with indifference.

12 Which is true according to the passage?

① The death of a child is more tragic than a soldier's death.
② Statistics are irrelevant in the politics of pity.
③ Pity is less important than empathy.
④ The politics of pity requires detachment from local concerns.

13 What is the double requirement of the politics of pity?

① In order to develop an objective view of suffering, generality must not be tainted by subjective feelings.
② The politics of pity demands both a broad vision and an intimate affective response.
③ The spectator of suffering must not allow statistics to get in the way of heartfelt feelings.
④ In order to sympathize with those who suffer, one must limit statistical evidence in a way that creates empathy.

14 Choose the best word for blank Ⓐ.

① proportion   ② lassitude
③ temerity   ④ empathy

[15–17]

Years from now, historians will likely look back at this period in American history as one of heightened prejudice amongst a significant portion of the public and shortsightedness amongst many political leaders. [A] The consensus among serious observers of the Middle East is that the reasons for _____ in the region towards the United States are multifold, having to do with: the United States' unconditional support of Israel and its expansionary and oppressive policies against the Palestinians; propping up of a host of unrepresentative, corrupt and repressive dictatorships throughout the Middle East and North Africa; and widespread military intervention in the Muslim world, from drone attacks that have claimed tens of thousands of civilian lives to whole-scale invasions that have cost the lives of hundreds of thousands of Muslims. [B] Nearly 80 percent of the people living under the Palestinian Authority and Hamas qualify America as an "enemy." [C] Polls show that 7 of the top 10 countries that view the United States most unfavorably are Muslim countries, while only 1 of the top 10 countries that view America most favorably is Muslim. [D]

15 Choose the best word for the blank above.

① redolence
② comity
③ animosity
④ rapprochement

16 Choose the best location for the following statement.

"About 85 percent of Egyptians and Jordanians and 73 percent of Turks, all key U.S. allies in the Middle East, have an analogous opinion."

① [A]
② [B]
③ [C]
④ [D]

17 Select the statement most consistent with the passage.

① The antipathy between the U.S. and the Middle East is expected to decrease in the near future.
② Muslim countries have a pejorative feeling towards the U.S.
③ The U.S. lacks a strong confederate in the Middle East.
④ America's asymmetrical interference in the Middle East is one of the causes of stridency in the region.

[18-20]

In a world in which the modernity of the working class and of socialism have been declared obsolete, middle-class society has become the symbol of an alternative future. The developed countries of the North Atlantic are retrospectively dubbed middle-class — although this is an American notion which never really caught on in Europe. The core of this utopia is a dream of boundless consumption, of a middle class taking possession of the earth, buying cars, houses and a limitless variety of electronic goods, and sustaining a global tourist industry. While this globalized consumerism may be the stuff of nightmares for ecologically conscious people, it makes businessmen ⓐ salivate. Middle-class consumption also has the great advantage of accommodating the privileges of the rich while supplying a quiescent horizon of aspiration to the popular classes. The dark side of this dream is its inherent exclusivism. People who are not middle class — or rich — do not have any redeeming features or assets. They are just 'losers,' as the televised rant which ignited the U.S. Tea Party in 2009 put it. They are the 'underclass,' the 'chavs.' In the developing world, the 'cleansing' of public space is one manifestation of this sinister tendency, as the poor find themselves excluded from beaches, parks, streets and squares. An especially provocative example is the fencing of Jakarta's Independence Square with its phallic National Monument, turning it into 'a kind of exclusive middle-class theme park' and depriving the poor of their sole recreational area.

18 Which of the following, according to the above passage, is not a consequence brought forth by the spreading influence of middle-class society?

① demise of socialism
② growing class division
③ disappearance of public space
④ environmental hazard

19 Which of the following alternative words might fittingly replace ⓐ?

① brood
② drool
③ phlegmatic
④ enfeeble

20 Which of the following best illustrates the style of the above writing?

① predictive
② proscriptive
③ prescriptive
④ analytic

[21-23]

A slew of factors have combined in recent years to create the impression that the world is run by plutocrats, oligarchs and semi-detached politicians in the interests of the few not the many.

A quarter of a billion people are on the move around the world, providing more ammunition than ever before for right-wing populists who argue that political elites have failed to get a handle on the kind of immigration that they say threatens jobs, wages and social cohesion.

Meanwhile, the number of billionaires has jumped fivefold in the last 20 years, to more than 2,200, according to *Forbes*, as globalization opened up new markets for entrepreneurs to tap while at the same time making it possible to shield capital, assets and income from the taxman. The world's eight richest people own as much as the poorest 3.5 billion. The amount of money gained by the financial elite is put at as much as £10 trillion.

But there are also many non-economic factors that may offer partial explanations for populism's rise: a cultural backlash against elites, a technological revolution that has rewired our politics, a convergence of now indistinguishable left and right political parties on a technocratic centre.

21 The best title of the passage would be _____.

① How can you spot a populist?
② What is populism?
③ Who are the populists?
④ Why have the populists emerged now?
⑤ What's the opposite of a populist?

22 As a factor which has created a backdrop for populism, _____ is NOT mentioned in the passage.

① cultural elitism
② tax evasion
③ mass migration
④ soaring inequality
⑤ ideological confrontation

23 According to the passage, populism is against _____.

① political elites of the right
② political elites of the left
③ corrupt elites
④ he wicked businessmen
⑤ the ordinary masses

[24-26]

To free-market economists, public officers — politicians and government bureaucrats — pose a unique challenge. Their pursuit of self-interest cannot be ____Ⓐ____ to any meaningful degree because they are not subject to market discipline. Politicians do face some competition from each other, but elections happen so infrequently that their disciplinary effects are limited. ____Ⓑ____, there is plenty of scope for them to pursue policies that heighten their power and wealth, at the cost of national welfare. When it comes to the career bureaucrats, the scope for self-seeking is even greater. Even if their political masters, the politicians, try to make them implement policies that cater to electoral demands, they can always obfuscate and manipulate the politicians. ____Ⓒ____, unlike the politicians, these career bureaucrats have high job security, if not lifetime tenure, so they can wait out their political masters by simply delaying things.

24 Which is the most suitable word for Ⓐ?

① restrained
② available
③ recognized
④ sought
⑤ applied

25 Which are the most suitable expressions for Ⓑ and Ⓒ?

	Ⓑ	Ⓒ
①	In addition	For example
②	Moreover	Consequently
③	For example	As a result
④	Consequently	However
⑤	Moreover	Finally

26 According to the passage, which is correct?

① In a democratic society, the election system is a powerful means to challenge the greedy free-market.
② Politicians often abuse their powers to serve their own benefits, neglecting national interests.
③ Politicians tend to work hard to maximize the public interest in order to win election.
④ Bureaucrats are obliged to follow politician's demands in order to avoid being fired.
⑤ Public officers do not have authority to control the self-interest of the free-market.

[27–28]

Democracy has another merit. It allows criticism, and if there isn't public criticism there are bound to be hushed-up scandals. That is why I believe in the press, despite all its lies and vulgarity, and why I believe in Parliament. The British Parliament is often sneered at because it's <u>a talking shop</u>. Well, I believe in it because it is a talking shop. I believe in the private member who makes himself nuisance. He gets snubbed and is told that he is cranky or ill-formed, but he exposes abuses which would otherwise never have been mentioned, and very often an abuse gets put right just by being mentioned. Occasionally, too, in my country, a well-meaning public official loses his head in the cause of efficiency, and thinks himself God Almighty. Such officials are particularly frequent in the Home Office. Well, there will be questions about them in Parliament sooner or later, and then they'll have to mend their steps. Whether Parliament is either a representative body or an efficient one is very doubtful, but I value it because it criticizes and talks, and because its chatter get widely reported. So two cheers for democracy: one because it admits variety and two because it permits criticism. Two cheers are quite enough: there is no occasion to give three.

27 **Which has the closest meaning to the underlined part?**

① A space for diplomatic meetings
② A place for genuine and serious discussion
③ A space for healthy arguments
④ A noisy and boisterous place

28 **According to the passage, which is true?**

① One of the merits of democracy is to expose abuses.
② Too much talk interrupts the efficiency of a system.
③ Criticism is the only important ingredient of democracy.
④ Democracy should be based on the consideration of the others.

[29–30]

Viet Nam and Watergate greatly undermined the authority of American institutions. They encouraged people to pick and choose the parts they would play, the wars they would fight. <u>At the least, they handsomely legitimized a refusal to participate at all.</u> This moral individualism, an old and admirable American trait, has often been balanced in the past by a sense of duty to country. That sense has chipped and faded. The U.S. has become an appallingly self-contradicting collection of tribes. Lacking an extreme threat that the majority regard as real, Americans have demonstrated an us-against-us mentality. American pluralism has become an incoherence of individualism. The nation's social vision amounts to little more than an individual passion to be comfortable and secure. If sacrifices are required, it is a painful question whether any Americans are willing to give up some of their privilege for the common good: they will certainly never do so if they think that they are sacrificing even the slightest bit more than other Americans; in a period of scarcity, the nation will become even more litigious and niggling in its collection of grievances.

29 The underlined expression implies that _____.

① American attitudes toward the military draft have not changed since Vietnam and Watergate
② Americans were more willing to fight for their country after Vietnam and Watergate
③ Vietnam and Watergate made Americans believe that they needed a common enemy
④ Vietnam and Watergate made it more urgent for Americans to make the laws against the war
⑤ Vietnam and Watergate made it justifiable for Americans to refuse to fight for their own country

30 According to the passage, the author suggests that Americans are getting more _____.

① ambitious
② aggressive
③ narrow-minded
④ radical
⑤ patriotic

[31-32]

Few would deny that government is necessary to protect property rights and enforce contracts, and that it has a role to play in preserving markets and voluntary exchanges of goods. But it is the worst kind of slippery slope reasoning to maintain that government intervention to prevent theft and murder justifies, by being essentially the same thing as, government intervention to redistribute wealth from one person to another. In one case, so the founders of America thought, government acts to protect natural liberty and equality; in the other, it _____ upon that liberty and its underlying equality of rights. Rather than making an argument to defend the paradoxical aspects of the foundational principle, Cass Sunstein's book takes down a straw man. The position he opposes — that government intervention as such is always bad — is not intellectually respectable on either the Left or the Right. Those who hold that position are called anarchists, not originalists.

31 Which of the following is most appropriate for the blank?

① converges
② mitigates
③ infringes
④ draws

32 What can be inferred from the underlined phrase?

① Government is expected to protect its citizens.
② The idea of government is fundamentally contradictory.
③ Sunstein makes an argument by attacking weak opponents.
④ The founders of America wanted to defend individual rights.

[33-34]

Mosquitoes and politics have long been entwined in Florida — some counties elect dedicated mosquito commissioners — but this year, Zika and bugs that convey it have infected races across the ballot. Amid an epidemic of hyperactive credit-seeking and partisan blame, everyone criticizes congress for failing to pass emergency funding before its summer recess. Democrats assail Rick Scott, Florida's Republican governor, for previous state budget cuts. Patrick Murphy, victor in their senatorial primary on August 30th, lambastes Marco Rubio, his confirmed Republican opponent in November. Some Tampa-area politicians are agitating for the release of genetically modified mosquitoes, currently slated for a trial in the Keys, which might cut the Zika-spreading population.

As in actual war, however, the political grandstanding is a sideshow. The real combatants are the mosquito-control operatives, whose tools include _____. As Rob Kruger of the Pinellas squad recounts, one form of surveillance involves standing in a buzzy spot and seeing how many mosquitoes land on him in a minute. "You end up with a lot of mosquito bites," he says as his boss, Jason Stuck brings in the eggs from a reserve battalion of chickens. Many diseases are carried by Florida's numerous mosquito species, but Zika is the focus of anxiety because of its impact on tourism, plus the microcephaly it can cause in infants.

33. To win the election in Florida, you need _____.

① to be exposed to mosquito bites
② to know how to get rid of mosquitoes
③ to have a basic knowledge of biotechnology
④ to criticize other politicians in Florida
⑤ to be acquainted with as many residents as possible

34. The best expression for the blank would be _____.

① their own bodies
② mosquito's predators
③ animate weapons
④ harmful insecticides
⑤ genetic mutation

[35-36]

Today the difference between liberals and conservatives stems from their attitudes toward the purpose of government. Conservatives support the original purpose of government: to maintain social order. They are willing to use the coercive power of the state to force citizens to be orderly. But they would not stop with defining, preventing, and punishing crime. They tend to want to preserve traditional patterns of social relations — the domestic role of women and the importance of religion in school and family life, for example.

Liberals are less likely than conservatives to use government power to maintain order. Liberals do not shy away from using government coercion, but they use it for a different purpose: to promote equality. They support laws that ensure equal treatment of gays and lesbians in employment, housing, and education; laws that force private businesses to hire and promote women and members of minority groups; and laws that require public transportation to provide equal access to people with disabilities. Conservatives do not oppose equality, but they do not value it to the extent of using the government's power to enforce it. For liberals, the use of that power to promote equality is both valid and necessary.

35 The crucial difference between conservatives and liberals lies in their perspectives regarding _____.

① the values of equality and order
② the structure of government
③ the ways of preserving traditional values
④ the strategies for unifying state governments

36 According to the passage, which of the following is true?

① Promoting equality enhances traditional social relations.
② The traditional role of government is to keep society in order.
③ Private businesses are forced to hire minorities to reduce the crime rate.
④ Conservatives oppose using government coercion to maintain social order.

[37-39]

Political science, the rational analysis of systems of government, their organization, functions, and policies, first originated in the Western world with Niccolo Machiavelli, a citizen of the Italian city state of Florence in the late 15th century. At the time, the only school of political thought was that of the Church, which was highly idealistic and more concerned with theological musings and preserving the tenets of the faith than in the practical operation of government. Machiavelli rejected this approach, arguing that stability and order were more important than moral considerations. It was therefore justifiable for a ruler to use any means necessary to gain and maintain the power necessary to establish order. According to Machiavelli, rulers should not be constrained by traditional notions of morality and virtue. This gave rise to the famous quote "The ends justify the means." It is doubtful that Machiavelli ever actually uttered these words, but they sum up his views accurately.

37 **Which of the sentences below best expresses the essential information in the underlined part?**

① At the time only the Church taught highly idealistic politicians who were interested in their faith rather than the operation of government.
② At the time the only form of political thought was that of the Church, which offered practical solution to the operation of the government.
③ At the time the only political doctrine was that of the Church, which gave more thought to religious matters than the function of the state.
④ At the time the tenets of Church faith were highly idealistic and were an ineffective school of political thought.

38 **According to the passage, what did Machiavelli believe was the most important function of government?**

① The protection of the Christian faith
② The accumulation of greater power
③ The preservation of order and stability
④ The casting aside of traditional morality

39 **The word constrained in the passage in closest in meaning to _____.**

① chosen
② judged
③ educated
④ limited

[40-42]

Today, 147 countries have agreed to international standards for processing people who claim asylum at their borders, but Indonesia is not among them. It does not have laws distinguishing asylum seekers from illegal immigrants. In fact, while most of Europe, Africa and Latin America has signed the 1951 treaty, only a handful of Asian nations recognize global refugee rights, even though millions under the UNHCR(UN High Commissioner of Refugee)'s mandate are in the region. This year in Bangladesh, aid groups reported violent police crackdowns and widespread hunger in makeshift camps housing tens of thousands of Rohingya, an ethnic Muslim minority facing persecution in Burma, who have crossed into Bangladesh seeking protection. In 2009, human rights groups accused the Thai military of setting hundreds of Rohingya refugees adrift at sea without adequate supplies. Thailand — which like Indonesia and Bangladesh has not signed the 1951 Refugee Convention but generously hosted many refugees after the Vietnam War — came under scrutiny again in December when the government forcibly repatriated 4,000 Hmong asylum seekers to Laos. The same month, Cambodia bowed to economic pressure from its largest benefactor and sent 20 Uighur asylum seekers back to China after they had fled race riots — a move that sparked international outcry and has since prompted the US to cut off some aid to Phnom Penh. In Asia, "refugees are seen as political pawns," says Frelick of Human Rights Watch. "The idea that you would provide asylum to a person who is considered an enemy of another state is looked upon as an unfriendly act."

40 Which country was different from the others in treating the asylum seekers?

① Indonesia
② Bangladesh
③ Thailand
④ Cambodia
⑤ Laos

41 What does the underlined "its largest benefactor" refer to?

① UN
② Hmong
③ China
④ Uighur
⑤ US

42 According to the passage, _____ seems to be the main reason to produce asylum refugees.

① territorial feud
② racial discrimination
③ economic gap
④ difference in ideology
⑤ domestic violence

[43-44]

It was recognized early and has frequently been asserted that in totalitarian countries propaganda and terror present two sides of the same coin. This, however, is only partly true. Wherever totalitarianism possesses absolute control, it replaces propaganda with indoctrination and uses violence not so much to frighten people (this is done only in the initial stages when political opposition still exists) as to realize constantly its ideological doctrines and its practical lies. Totalitarianism will not be satisfied to assert, in the face of contrary facts, that unemployment does not exist; it will abolish ⓐunemployment benefits as part of its propaganda. Equally important is the fact that the refusal to acknowledge unemployment realized — albeit in a rather unexpected way — the old socialist doctrine: He who does not work shall not eat.

Or when, to take another instance, Stalin decided to rewrite the history of the Russian Revolution, the propaganda of his new version consisted in ⓑespousing, together with the older books and documents, their authors and readers. The publication in 1938 of a new official history of the Communist Party was the signal that ⓒthe superpurge which had decimated a whole generation of Soviet intellectuals had come to and end. Similarly, the Nazis in the Eastern occupied territories at first used chiefly anti-semitic propaganda to win firmer control of the population. They neither needed nor used terror to support this propaganda. When they ⓓliquidated the greater part of the Polish intelligentsia, they did it not because of its opposition, but because according to their doctrine Poles had no intellect, and when they planned to kidnap blue-eyed and blond-haired children, they did not intend to frighten the population but to save 'Germanic blood.'

43 윗글에서 논지의 흐름상 가장 적합하지 <u>않은</u> 것은?

① ⓐ   ② ⓑ
③ ⓒ   ④ ⓓ

44 윗글을 통해 추론할 수 있는 것으로 가장 적합한 것은?

① Totalitarian regimes will not need to use terror in conjunction with propaganda after seizure of power.
② Totalitarian regimes will need to use violence to achieve their ideological objectives after seizure of power.
③ Totalitarian regimes will not need to replace propaganda with indoctrination.
④ Totalitarian regimes will need to use terror to deter race propaganda after a stronger grip on power is established.

[45-47]

As Europe confronts a rapidly escalating migration crisis driven by war, persecution and poverty in an arc of strife from West Africa to Afghanistan, even high-level European officials are beginning to admit the obvious. The region's refugee management system is broken. In Western Europe, countries are dealing with the biggest wave of asylum-seekers and refugees since the 1990s. Hundreds of thousands of asylum-seekers are streaming through Europe's _____Ⓐ_____ borders, decamping from entry nations such as Italy to countries such as Germany, where they are creating new challenges and tensions. Germany is _____Ⓑ_____ to manage the largest number of asylum-seekers in the industrialized world.

Politicians in the country are, to varying degrees, confronting a public torn between being openhearted and wanting to close off entry for migrants. A good number of the newcomers are fleeing civil war in Syria or attacks by armed groups from South Sudan to Nigeria. But a large portion, officials say, are also arriving for economic reasons, rolling the dice that appeals processes may grant them an opportunity to build an immigrant life in some of the richest nations in the world. This nation of 82 million absorbed more asylum-seekers than any other in the region last year, sheltering 173,000. So many asylum-seekers are coming that Germany has now been forced to find accommodations for them in tiny communities like Tröglitz, nestled in an area that has become the epicenter of an anti-immigrant movement.

Last year, there were significant increases in anti-immigrant attacks, including 35 incidents of arson at refugee centers. "Germany was responsible for creating so many refugees in World War II," said Markus Nierth, the former mayor of Tröglitz. "Now it is upon us to take responsibility for the refugees coming in this new great wave." But even Nierth concedes that the refugee crisis is presenting towns like Tröglitz with something that locals, used to quiet and homogeneous village life, are not accustomed to.

45 What is the most appropriate title of the passage above?

① Persecution and Poverty in Europe
② New Crisis in Coping with Refugee Problems
③ The Rise of Migration Driven by War
④ Varying Reasons to Reject Asylum-Seekers in Europe
⑤ The Epicenter of Anti-Immigrant Movement

46 Which statement can be best inferred from the passage above?

① Before 1990s, most refugees in Europe arrived from West Africa and Afghanistan.
② Some refugees arrived in Germany for economic reasons.
③ There used to live diverse people in Tröglitz since World War II.
④ Germany has so far accepted 82 million asylum-seekers.
⑤ World War II caused a huge influx of refugees in Germany.

47 Which pair best fits Ⓐ and Ⓑ?

	Ⓐ	Ⓑ
①	closed	striving
②	divisive	opposing
③	stalwart	navigating
④	fluid	observing
⑤	porous	straining

[48-50]

Recently two presidents, Nicholas Sarkozy and Barack Obama, have taken up the issue of Muslim women's clothes in rather different ways. Sarkozy used Muslim dress as a nationalistic prop, seeing it as a threat to France's eternal values. In 2004, France banned head scarves from schools and public buildings. "In our country," said Sarkozy, "We cannot accept that women are prisoners behind netting, cut off from all social life, deprived of an identity. This is not the French republic's idea of dignity." Obama's speech in Cairo took a different tack. His concern was not the hijab — the Muslim woman's head covering — so much as a woman's right to wear it if she so chose. Western countries, Obama said, cannot dictate the dress of Muslim women. Obama avoided any sense that American values and Islamic ones were in conflict. Instead, he offered a more porous vision of both Islam and the West, one in which "Islam has always been a part of America's story." It may sound fine. But by talking only of women's dress, he ignored the many challenges Muslim women face, such as polygamy, early marriage and honor killings across the Muslim world. In the weeks since the two speeches, Iran has shown the world a different, more muscular image of Muslim women. The Tehran protesters, in their emerald hijabs, were not human signboards for imposed conservatism, as Sarkozy might think. But nor did they fit Obama's formulation of Muslim womanhood, one which needed legal protection for the freedom to wear what it likes. Iran's women are determinedly political actors, claiming fundamental rights, and deserving our support when they do so. When they risk their lives to claim such rights, what they wear is irrelevant. With Muslim women showing such involvement in basic political struggles, is it too much to hope that Western male leaders will find something more worthwhile to comment on than their clothes?

48 The best title of the passage would be _____.

① Far Bigger Challenges for Muslim Women
② Clothing as a Political Symbol in the Arab World
③ Discrimination against Muslim Women in the West
④ Obama's New Approach to U.S.–Muslim Relations
⑤ Growth of Secularism in Iran

49 According to the passage, Obama views the hijab as the matter of _____.

① personal choice
② cultural restraint
③ uncivilized tradition
④ male power
⑤ female resistance

50 The author argues that _____.

① the hijab is the essence of what a Muslim woman is
② the West should pay more attention to the political struggles of Muslim women
③ the education for Muslim women is far more important than Muslim women's clothes
④ talking about the hijab should be stopped because it prevents Muslim women from participating in politics
⑤ Obama's attitude to Muslim women's clothes is more flawed than Sarkozy's attitude

2강 경영 / 경제

Read the following passages and answer the questions. [01-52]

[01-03]

In most countries bereaved spouses or partners can expect only a fraction of the deceased's public pension, typically half, and it often comes with conditions attached, such as having dependent children or being close to retirement age themselves. In Brazil survivors of any age get almost the full sum for the rest of their lives. Even if the deceased person has not yet retired, the pension starts straight away. As a result, Brazil spends an unmatched 3% of GDP on survivors' pensions. Rich OECD countries on average spend less than 1%.

The pensioners themselves, too, do remarkably well. Men can retire at 65 and women at 60, on full pay up to a high cap, as long as they have contributed for 15 years. All but recently hired civil servants can retire on full pay with no cap. Men over 65 and women over 60 living in poor households get a pension equal to the minimum wage, currently 678 reais a month, even if they have never contributed. Rural workers, poor or not, enjoy the same privilege five years younger. Terms for early retirement are particularly generous. Greeks, whose pension system almost bankrupted their country, on average work on until they are 61. The average Brazilian draws a pension of 70% of final pay at 54.

01 The topic of the above passage is _____.

① Brazil's welfare system
② irrational pension system of Brazil
③ Brazil's ascension to a developed country
④ corruption of the Brazilian officers
⑤ average working hours of Brazilians

02 In Brazil, you can receive a full pay pension only if _____.

① you register for the pension
② you are born in Brazil
③ you work for 15 years
④ your spouse is dead
⑤ you are over working age

03 What does the underlined part "with no cap" mean?

① without any protection
② without any fund
③ without any clothes
④ without any limit
⑤ without any capability

[04-05]

The relevance of formal economic models to real-world policy has been a topic of some dispute. The economists R. D. Norton and S. Y. Rhee achieved some success in applying such a model _____Ⓐ_____ to the Korean economy over a fourteen-year period; the model's figures for output, prices, and other variables closely matched real statistics. The model's value in policy terms, however, proved less clear-cut. Norton and Rhee performed simulations in which, keeping long-term factors constant, they tried to pinpoint the effect of short-term policy changes. Their model indicated that rising prices for imported oil would increase inflation; reducing exports by five percent would lower Gross Domestic Product (GDP) and increase inflation; and slowing the growth of the money supply would result in slightly higher inflation. These findings are somewhat _____Ⓑ_____ Many economists have argued that reducing exports will lessen, not increase, inflation. And while most view escalating oil costs as inflationary, few would think the same of slower monetary growth. The Norton-Rhee model can perhaps be viewed as indicating the pitfalls of a formalist approach that stresses statistical "goodness of fit" at the expense of genuine policy relevance.

04 윗글의 목적으로 가장 적절한 것은?

① to propose a new type of economic analysis
② to suggest an explanation for Korean inflation
③ to determine the accuracy of Norton and Rhee's analysis
④ to describe the limitations of a formal economic model

05 윗글의 빈칸 Ⓐ, Ⓑ에 들어갈 말로 가장 적절한 것은?

	Ⓐ	Ⓑ
①	retrospectively	startling
②	reflectively	promising
③	prospectively	anticipating
④	intensively	disappointing

[06-07]

One phase of the business cycle is the expansion phase. This phase is a twofold one, including recovery and prosperity. ⓐ It is not prosperity itself but expectation of prosperity that triggers the expansion phase. During the recovery period there is ever-growing expansion of existing facilities, and new facilities for production are created. More businesses are created and older ones expanded. Improvements of various kinds are made. There is an ever-increasing optimism about the future of economic growth. Much capital is invested in machinery or heavy industry. More labor is employed. More materials are required. As one part of the economy develops, other parts are affected. ⓑ For example, a great expansion in automobiles results in an expansion of the steel, glass, and rubber industries. Roads are required; thus the cement and machinery industries are stimulated. ⓒ Demand for labor and materials results in greater prosperity for workers and suppliers of raw materials, including farmers. This increases purchasing power and the volume of goods bought and sold. Thus, prosperity is diffused among the various segments of the population. ⓓ This prosperity period may continue to rise and rise without an apparent end. However, a time comes when this phase reaches a peak and stops spiraling upwards. This is the end of the expansion phase.

06 윗글의 흐름상 가장 적합하지 않은 것은?

① ⓐ
② ⓑ
③ ⓒ
④ ⓓ

07 윗글을 통해 추론할 수 있는 것으로 가장 적합한 것은?

① When consumers lose their confidence in the market, a recession follows.
② In the expansion phase, many parts of the economy are mutually benefited.
③ Luxury goods such as jewelry are unaffected by industrial expansion.
④ The creation of new products is crucial in the prosperity period.

[08-09]

As economists deal with quantifiable objects, such as calories consumed or miles of cable laid, the models they use in their researches are almost always mathematical constructs. They can be stated in words, but mathematics is an enormously efficient way to express the structure of a model; more interestingly, for discovering the implications of a model. Applied mathematicians and physicists have known this for a long time, but it was only in the second half of the 20th century that economists brazenly adopted that research tactic; as have related disciplines, such as ecology. The art of good modelling is to generate a lot of understanding from focusing on a very small number of causal factors. I say 'art', because there is no formula for creating a good model. The _____Ⓐ_____ of a model is whether it discriminates among alternative explanations of a phenomenon. Those that survive empirical tests are accepted — at least for a while — until further evidence comes along that casts doubt on them, in which case economists go back to their drawing board to create better (not necessarily bigger!) models.

08 Which does NOT fit in the blank Ⓐ?

① acid test
② crucial test
③ ultimate test
④ arbitrary test

09 According to the passage, which is NOT true?

① Economic models can be described either verbally or mathematically.
② The objects of economic researches are those that can be measured in terms of quantity.
③ Mathematics came to be widely used in economics only in the second half of the 20th century.
④ A good economic model accommodates as many causal factors as possible in explaining a phenomenon.

[10-11]

The political economist Benjamin Friedman once compared modern Western society to a stable bicycle whose wheels are kept spinning by economic growth. Should that forward-propelling motion slow or cease, the pillars that define our society — democracy, individual liberties, social tolerance and more — would begin to teeter. Our world would become an increasingly ugly place, one defined by a scramble over limited resources and a rejection of anyone outside of our immediate group. Should we find no way to get the wheels back in motion, we'd eventually face total societal collapse.

Such collapses have occurred many times in human history, and no civilization, no matter how seemingly great, is immune to the vulnerabilities that may lead a society to its end. Regardless of how well things are going in the present moment, the situation can always change. Putting aside species-ending events like an asteroid strike, nuclear winter or deadly pandemic, history tells us that it's usually a plethora of factors that contribute to collapse. What are they, and which, if any, have already begun to surface? It should come as no surprise that humanity is currently on an unsustainable and uncertain path — but just how close are we to reaching the point of no return?

10 **According to the passage, which one does NOT lead our world to its collapse?**

① an interstellar collision
② the severe climatic change following a nuclear war
③ a volcanic eruption
④ the halt of economic growth
⑤ the worldwide spread of fatal epidemic disease

11 **The best topic of the passage would be _____.**

① the vulnerability of economic growth
② the eventual collapse of modern Western society
③ the potential doom of the ecological destruction
④ the possibility of the world collapse in the future
⑤ the sustainable model for the future society

[12-14]

I'm not sure why, but startups are very counterintuitive. Maybe it's just because knowledge about them hasn't permeated our culture yet. But whatever the reason, starting a startup is a task where you can't always _____Ⓐ_____. It's like skiing. When you first try skiing and you want to slow down, your instinct is to lean back. But if you lean back on skis, you fly down the hill out of control. So part of learning to ski is learning to suppress that impulse. Eventually you get new habits, but at first it takes a conscious effort. When you begin, there's a list of things you're trying to remember as you start down the hill. Startups are as unnatural as skiing, so there's a similar list for startups to remember. Startups are so weird that if you trust your instincts, you'll make a lot of mistakes. I often joke that my function is to tell founders things they would ignore. It's really true. Why do the founders not consider the advisor's advice seriously? Well, that's the thing about counterintuitive ideas: they are opposite to your instincts. You only need other people to give you advice that surprises you. That's why there are a lot of ski instructors and not many running instructors.

12 Startups are likened to skiing because they both _____.

① are easy to control
② contradict our intuitions
③ require intensive and extensive training
④ demand strategies like effective running

13 Which of the following best fits into Ⓐ?

① get new habits
② rely on your experience
③ make use of your expertise
④ trust your instincts

14 Which of the following does the author suggest the startup founders do?

① Listen to their advisors
② Take in-depth courses
③ Make a list of creative ideas
④ Observe successful startups first

[15-16]

One of the strategic principles for success in the stock market is to refrain from having knee-jerk reactions to possibly deceptive fluctuations in the market's or a particular stock's performance. Before reinvesting in a rapidly falling stock, analysts and investors will often wait for the passing of one or more small upward bumps, referred to as "dead cat bounces." The term reflects the somewhat crude idea that even a dead cat will bounce if it falls from a great height. Upticks in a plummeting stock can be caused by short selling, triggered sell-offs, or overly optimistic reactions to changes made by the company, such as replacing an unpopular CEO. Such a small, unimpressive rise is usually followed by another drop-off that surpasses the previous low. While almost exclusively related to the stock market, the term has found occasional use in describing other areas of misleading improvement. Poll numbers for a candidate losing ground near an election sometimes make a brief, _____ surge. In sports, losing teams that make mid season coaching changes sometimes experience a mild surge of energy that translates to one or more wins before the team reverts to form.

15 윗글의 내용과 가장 거리가 먼 것은?

① A "dead cat bounce" can be observed in sports and politics.
② A "dead cat bounce" refers to a small surge of a stock after a rapid decline.
③ Investors usually practice patience before reinvesting when a "dead cat bounce" occurs.
④ Replacing the unpopular CEO of a company can be a cause of a "dead cat bounce" in the stock market.
⑤ A fall of the stock can be expected after a "dead cat bounce," but it typically does not exceed the previous low point.

16 윗글의 빈칸에 들어갈 말로 가장 적절한 것은?

① sharp
② illusory
③ expected
④ impressive
⑤ inexplicable

[17-19]

In an experiment, Ms Tsay presented would-be investors with profiles of a group of fictional entrepreneurs, including attributes such as their leadership experience, management skills, IQ and the amount of capital they had raised. In the experiment, it was stated ⓐ explicitly that they were either naturals or strivers, though the investors were not told that this was the factor of most interest to the researcher. The study then calculated how much, on average, the investors would be willing to trade off any of the entrepreneur's other attributes in order to choose a natural or a striver.

The investors showed a clear preference for the supposed naturals. To gain backing from the investors, for example, a striver would need on average 4.5 more years of leadership experience, 9% better management skills, a 28-point higher IQ and nearly $40,000 more accrued capital than a natural. Yet before the experiment, most participants had expressed a proclivity for someone who could demonstrate ⓑ motivation and hard work. This suggests that the bias for ⓒ natural talent over ⓓ hard work is unconscious.

Achieving goals through ⓔ determination is a recurring cultural belief — think of the American dream, say, or the Protestant work ethic. So maybe it is not surprising that people parrot it as an ideal. When it comes to investing, however, the experiment suggests that such puritan values fall by the wayside.

17 Which is the closest in meaning to the underlined ⓐ**explicitly**?

① clearly
② secretly
③ cautiously
④ instantaneously

18 Which is NOT a characteristic of strivers according to the passage?

① ⓑ
② ⓒ
③ ⓓ
④ ⓔ

19 Which is the best title of the passage?

① Predisposed Bias for Strivers
② Gap between Research Findings and Reality
③ Investor's Choice: Natural Talent or Hard Work
④ Entrepreneur's Strategy: Preference for Potential

[20-22]

Bargaining may be defined as tacit or direct communication in an attempt to reach agreement on an exchange of value — that is, of tangible or intangible items that one or both parties value. Bargaining need not be explicit. Sometimes the content is communicated through actions rather than an exchange of words. A bargaining process has two or more participants and sometimes has mediators whose participation is nominally neutral. Participants have a direct stake in the outcome; mediators do not. There are one or more issues on which each participant hopes to reach agreement on terms favorable to itself, but the participants' interests diverge on these issues, creating conflicts. These conflicts define a bargaining space — one or more dimensions, each of which represents a distance between the positions of the participants concerning their preferred outcomes. The bargaining process disposes of these conflicts by achieving agreement on the distribution of the various items of value that are at stake. The end result is a position arrived at in the bargaining space. Such agreements do not necessarily represent a fair exchange of value; many agreements are manifestly one-sided and unfair. But in a broad sense, bargains whether fair or unfair contain an element of mutual gain. This is possible because the items of value being exchanged have different value to the different parties.

20 Which of the following can be inferred from the passage?

① Because disparate values are attached to the items being exchanged, inequality is frequent in negotiated outcomes.
② A bargain is accomplished only when all the parties concerned agree on fair, equitable gains.
③ The mediator usually takes a nominal sum in payment for modulating conflicting interests.
④ Bargaining can only be conducted on terms that are unfavorable to all the parties involved.

21 What is the best title of the passage?

① How to Avoid an Unfair Bargain
② The Secret of Seasoned Bargainers
③ Outwitting the Other Party
④ The Nature of Bargaining

22 Which of the following best defines "the bargaining space"?

① the combination of physical locations occupied by the bargaining parties and the mediator
② the metaphorical space created by distances between conflicting interests
③ the physical place where bargaining parties convene to conduct transactions
④ the range of monetary values that are targeted by the different parties

[23-24]

Of all the goods and services traded in the market economy, pharmaceuticals are perhaps the most contentious. Though produced by private companies, they constitute a public good, both because they can prevent epidemics and because healthy people function better as members of society than sick ones do. They carry a moral weight that most privately traded goods do not, for there is a widespread belief that people have a right to healthcare that they do not have for smartphones of trainers. Innovation accounts for most of the cost of production, so the price of drugs I much higher than cost of manufacture, making them unaffordable to many poor people. Firms protect the intellectual property that drugs represent and sue those who try to manufacture and sell patented drugs cheaply. For all these reasons, pharmaceutical companies are widely regarded as vampires who exploit the sick and ignore the sufferings of the poor. These criticisms reached a crescendo more than a decade ago at the peak of the HIV plague. When South Africa's government sought to legalise the import of cheap generic copies of patented AIDS drugs, pharmaceutical companies took it to court. The case earned the nickname "Big Pharma vs. Nelson Mandela." It was a low point for the industry, which wisely backed down.

23 According to the passage, which of the following is true?

① Pharmaceuticals are considered as a public good of moral significance.
② Many doubt that pharmaceutical firms spend much on innovation.
③ Pharmaceutical firms had conflicting views about intellectual property rights.
④ Sales of patented drugs exceeded the projections after the court ordeal.

24 Which of the following is true of "Big Pharma vs. Nelson Mandela"?

① Pharmaceutical firms filed a libel suit against Nelson Mandela.
② Nelson Mandela threatened pharmaceutical firms with court action.
③ Pharmaceutical companies finally retreated.
④ The court issued an injunction to ban pharmaceutical firms, from taking further action.

[25–27]

Think of the gigantic economic engine that China has become as it industrializes and its population becomes more affluent. More people mean larger markets, more workers, and efficiencies of scale in mass production of goods. _____Ⓐ_____, adding people boosts human ingenuity and intelligence that will create new resources by finding new materials and discovering new ways of doing things. Economist Julian Simon (1932–1998), a champion of this rosy view of human history, believed that people are the "ultimate resource" and that no evidence suggests that pollution, crime, unemployment, crowding, the loss of species, or any other resource limitations will worsen with population growth. In a famous bet in 1980, Simon challenged Paul Ehrlich, author of *The Population Bomb*, to pick five commodities that would become more expensive by the end of the decade. Ehrlich chose metals that actually became cheaper, and he lost the bet. Leaders of many developing countries share this outlook and insist that, instead of being _____Ⓑ_____ with population growth, we should focus on the _____Ⓒ_____ consumption of the world's resources by people in richer countries.

25 Which statement can be best inferred from the passage above?

① Population growth could bring benefits.
② Many factors determine population growth.
③ Population growth has already begun to slow.
④ Many people remain pessimistic about population growth.
⑤ The differences in population growth around the world are large.

26 Which expression best fits Ⓐ?

① Moreover
② On the other hand
③ Therefore
④ Meanwhile
⑤ Nevertheless

27 Which pair best fits Ⓑ and Ⓒ?

	Ⓑ	Ⓒ		Ⓑ	Ⓒ
①	temperate	overall	②	compulsive	gross
③	pessimistic	unnecessary	④	apathetic	elastic
⑤	obsessed	inordinate			

[28–30]

Capital and politics influence each other to such an extent that their relations are hotly debated by economists, politicians, and the general public alike. Ardent capitalists tend to argue that capital should be free to influence politics, but politics should not be allowed to influence capital. They argue that when _____Ⓐ_____ interfere in the _____Ⓑ_____, political _____Ⓒ_____ cause them to make unwise _____Ⓓ_____ that result in slower growth. For example, a government may impose heavy taxation on industrialists and use the money to give lavish unemployment benefits, which are popular with voters. But in the view of many business people, it would be far better if the government left the money with them. They would use it, they claim, to open new factories and hire the unemployed. In this view, the wisest economic policy is to keep politics out of the economy, reduce taxation and government regulation to a minimum, and allow market forces free rein to take their course.

28 The author's presentation is most like that of:

① A researcher offering a critique of how business and government policies can interrelate.
② A blogger writing to their network of readers offering advice on the best investments.
③ A bank manager writing a brochure to attract young clients to open a new bank account.
④ A politician giving a short election speech wooing business managers to vote for them.

29 Which of the following can <u>LEAST</u> be inferred from the passage?

① Industrialists are likely to vote for politicians adopting a low-tax approach to business.
② Capitalists will usually wish to see a marketplace untroubled by political interference.
③ Deregulated marketplaces give the best opportunity for businesses to turn a profit.
④ Keeping politics out of business ensures that there will always be jobs for everyone.

30 Choose the best set of words for the blanks.

	Ⓐ		Ⓑ		Ⓒ		Ⓓ
①	interests	–	investments	–	markets	–	governments
②	governments	–	markets	–	interests	–	investments
③	investments	–	interests	–	market	–	governments
④	markets	–	governments	–	interests	–	investments

[31-32]

Upper middle class — that's how I've always thought of myself. Upper middle class is the class into which I was born, the class to which I was always told I belonged, and the class with which, until this moment, I'd never had a problem. Upper middle class is a sneaky designation, however. It's a way of saying "I'm well-off" without having to say "I'm rich," even if, by most standards, you are. Upper-middle-classness has allowed me to feel like I'm not only competing in the same financial league as most Americans — I'm winning! Playing in the middle class, I have enjoyed huge success.

I now glimpsed the problem with upper-middle-classness: it isn't really a class. It's a space between classes. The space may once have been bridgeable, but lately it's become a chasm. Middle-class people fantasize about travel upgrades; upper-class people can't imagine life without a jet. Middle-class people help their children with their homework so they'll have a chance of getting into Princeton; upper-class people buy Princeton a new building. Middle-class people have homes; upper-class people have monuments. A man struggling to hold on to the illusion that he is upper middle class has become like a character in a cartoon earthquake: he looks down and sees his feet being dragged ever farther apart by a quickly widening fissure. His legs stretch, then splay, and finally he plunges into the abyss.

31 According to the passage, the author _____.

① regretted being a kid of upper middle class
② loved the life style of upper middle class
③ really wanted to be a part of upper class
④ didn't mind working with low-class people
⑤ finally fell down to the bottom of the social ladder

32 The underlined 'it's become a chasm' means that _____.

① people are getting apart more widely
② poverty cannot be solved by the system
③ there is no way to be a part of upper class
④ the upper class needs to be educated
⑤ America is now in big trouble due to economic inequality

[33-35]

'Form follows profit' is the aesthetic principle of our times. Thus, design skill is measured today by the architect's ability to build the largest possible enclosure for the smallest investment in the quickest time. The factors that now determine the design of a building are maximum economic efficiency in terms of rentable space to gross space, wall to floor ratios and minimum story height. The result is invariably a single-activity building in the form of a thin-skinned box — a shopping center, an office building or a block of flats — with no unprofitable public spaces, no expressive or innovative structural features and certainly no room to celebrate the art of Architecture. Arcades, gardens and balconies, even recessed windows, impinge on rentable space and are deemed incompatible with the profit principle. And because developers and their shareholders want a quick return on their investment — the horizons of stockbrokers and accountants do not extend to posterity — the cheapest materials must be used. Some clients refuse to plant even trees; no acorn will increase the rentable value of a property, and no investor, we are told, will wait for an oak. Most contemporary architecture is therefore the product of _____ rather than the work of a designer, it represents the logical product of a society which sees the environment in terms of profit.

33 Choose the one that best fills in the blank.

① one-size-fits-all tendencies
② user-friendly interfaces
③ environmental considerations
④ stark economic forces

34 What is the purpose of the passage?

① to accuse architects of being avant-garde
② to criticize external influences on architecture
③ to extol the contributions of architecture to society
④ to suggest architectural freedom should be restored

35 According to the passage, which aspect is associated with the contemporary design of buildings?

① cube-like shape
② multi-functionality
③ greenery
④ unique style

[36-38]

Ever since the 2008 financial crisis, predictions of the dollar's demise have come repeatedly. As the U.S. economy sank into recession, so too did confidence that the greenback could maintain its long-held position as the world's premier reserve currency. But here we are, several years after the crisis, and the dollar is showing just how _____Ⓐ_____ it is. The dollar index, which measures its value against other currencies, recently reached a four-year high. And the policymakers who criticized the dollar show little interest in dumping it. The buoyancy of the greenback reflects the fact that the U.S. is a rare bright spot among the world's major economies. American GDP in the third quarter grew an annualized 3.5%-far higher than what most other industrialized economies have been posting. The fact remains too that no other currency can truly _____Ⓑ_____ the dollar. The uncertain stability of the euro was exposed by its multiyear sovereign-debt crisis and the chaotic response that followed from Europe's leaders. How long the dollar's run lasts depends on everything from the future growth of U.S. GDP to the health of the global economy. There are plenty of factors that could undercut the dollar over the long term. Russia and China are settling more trade between the two nations in rubles and yuan. If other economic powerhouses follow suit, that could begin to chip away at the dollar's utility. ⓐ But for now, that's a very big if.

36 From the context, which of the following ordered pairs best fits into Ⓐ and Ⓑ?

	Ⓐ		Ⓑ
①	priceless	–	eliminate
②	improbable	–	supplement
③	sensitive	–	beat
④	almighty	–	rival

37 Which of the following is implied by ⓐ?

① The dollar's stability will last for a while.
② Other economic powerhouses will trade more in dollars.
③ The global economy will remain unhealthy.
④ Russia and China may threaten the dollar's utility.

38 Which of the following is NOT true of the passage?

① People have anticipated the fall of the American currency.
② There is potential for other currencies, such as ruble and yuan, to challenge the greenback.
③ The growth rate of the American GDP has outstripped those of its rivals recently.
④ Despite European debt, the euro has maintained its strong utility.

[39-41]

The First World War trailed in its wake a terrible crisis of confidence in _____Ⓐ_____. In the most developed economies of Europe, trade and retail distribution had long surpassed manufacturing as a means of value creation; things were ⓐ invariably made elsewhere. But in Britain, formerly the most ardent supporter of liberal trade, retail and financial services ⓑ slumped and, in response, the Government ⓒ ringfenced the economy in an attempt to boost internal products and markets. Other economies followed Britain's policy, causing free trade — formerly the engine of European expansion — to collapse, as national tariffs and trade barriers began to restrict the movement of things. It would take decades for the flows of capital, people and things to recover their former volumes; and Europe would never be able to resuscitate the ⓓ unbridled optimism it had enjoyed during the first modern period of material culture.

39 Which phrase would best fit Ⓐ?

① protection of the domestic market
② the interaction between economic and political factors
③ the global free-flow of materials
④ British superiority over European protectionism

40 Choose a statement that best describes the author's argument.

① National tariffs and trade barriers eventually served to reinstate European economic optimism.
② The global economy was boosted by the collapse of European free trade system.
③ The industrial base for mass production was considered the strongest factor in creating values before the First World War.
④ It was not until the outbreak of the First World War that European protective trade was launched.

41 Which one of the following expression may <u>not</u> replace each of the underlined words in the passage?

① ⓐ constantly
② ⓑ waned
③ ⓒ retaliated
④ ⓓ inordinate

[42-44]

Five years have passed since the onset of what is sometimes called the Great Recession. While the economy has slowly improved, there are still millions of Americans leading lives of quiet desperation: without jobs, without resources, without hope. Who was to blame? Was it simply a result of negligence, of the kind of inordinate risk-taking commonly called a "bubble," of an imprudent but innocent failure to maintain adequate reserves for a rainy day? ⓐ Or was it the result, at least in part, of fraudulent practices, of dubious mortgages portrayed as sound risks and packaged into ever more esoteric financial instruments, the fundamental weaknesses of which were intentionally obscured?

If it was the former, then the criminal law has no role to play in the aftermath. ⓑ For in all but a few circumstances, the fierce and fiery weapon called criminal prosecution is directed at intentional misconduct, and nothing less. If the Great Recession was in no part the handiwork of intentionally fraudulent practices by high-level executives, then to prosecute such executives criminally would be "scapegoating" of the most shallow and despicable kind. But if, ⓒ as a result, the Great Recession was the product of intentional fraud, the failure to prosecute those responsible must be judged one of the most egregious failures of the criminal justice system in many years. ⓓ Indeed, it would stand in striking contrast to the increased success that federal prosecutors have had over the past fifty years or so in bringing to justice even the highest-level figures who orchestrated mammoth frauds.

42 The passage is mainly about _____.

① the onset of the Great recession and its aftermath
② the source of the Great Recession and the role of criminal prosecution
③ how to prosecute those who are responsible for Great Recession
④ the lessons of the Great Recession that people should not forget

43 Which of the following is NOT an appropriate expression in its respective context?

① ⓐ
② ⓑ
③ ⓒ
④ ⓓ

44 Which of the following would best express the writer's main argument?

① Every effort should be made in all quarters of administration in order to prevent the possible onslaught of another form of financial crisis.
② Because so many people are still in trouble, it is urgent to question the exact cause of the Great Recession and heal the wounds it left behind.
③ The criminal justice system should be indicted on the ground that it has failed to prosecute those who drove the country into the predicament.
④ After investigating what caused the Great Recession, we should realize social justice by judging the people who are responsible for the case.

[45-47]

In the last days of 2019, as millions of Americans were contemplating their resolutions for the year ahead, the moving-and-storage company U-Haul set one for all of its future employees. The company announced that starting February 1, it will stop hiring people who use nicotine in the 21 states where such a prohibition is legal, including Texas, Florida, and Massachusetts. Seventeen of those states allow employers to administer drug test for nicotine.

_____Ⓐ_____ a new policy for U-Haul, this move is part of a larger trend toward "workplace wellness" programs, which encourage employees to pursue dietary changes and hit daily activity goals. Over the past decade, companies have become far more coercive in their insistence that employees optimize their bodies and behavior on their own time. ⓐ This cuts costs and, at least in theory, helps employees live healthier lives.

In a press release, U-Haul's chief of staff, Jessica Lopez, repeated some of the supposedly inspirational words that have embedded themselves into the workplace-wellness vernacular. "ⓑ We are deeply invested in the well-being of our team members. Nicotine products are addictive and pose a variety of serious health risks," she said. Lopez characterized the move as "a responsible step in fostering a culture of wellness at U-Haul, with the goal of helping our team members on their health journey."

According to U-Haul's announcement, the company plans to note its policy on job applications, question applicants about their nicotine usage in interviews, and require them to consent to nicotine testing in the seventeen states that allow it. The policy will apply to any nicotine use, which means that vapers and other users of smokeless tobacco will be excluded from the hiring pool, in addition to smokers. The policy won't apply to people already employed with the company. ⓒ People believe that the fundamental interests of employees and employers are necessarily hostile to each other.

Nicotine is, indeed, tied to some serious health risks. Globally, smoking cigarettes kills about 8 million people each year. But employers seeking to control ever more aspects of their employees' lives is already a troubling trend. ⓓ It's bleak when anyone's health is regarded as malfunctioning workplace machinery, but the problem becomes even worse when these expectations are foisted on the workers least equipped to fight back.

45 Which of the following best fits in the blank Ⓐ?

① Without
② While
③ Because
④ Whether

46 Which of the following is NOT appropriate?

① ⓐ
② ⓑ
③ ⓒ
④ ⓓ

47 Which of the following is true?

① Stopping hiring nicotine users is legal in some U.S. states.
② The smokers employed before February 1 must quit the company.
③ Each year, about 8 million Americans die because of smoking cigarettes.
④ Every U-Haul employee across the U.S. must take a nicotine test.

[48-50]

The neoliberal state should favor strong individual private property rights, the rule of law, and the institutions of freely functioning markets and free trade. These are the institutional arrangements considered essential to guarantee individual freedoms. The state must therefore use its monopoly of the means of violence to preserve these freedoms at all costs. By extension, the freedom of businesses and corporations (legally regarded as individuals) to operate within this institutional framework of free markets and free trade is regarded as a fundamental good. Private enterprise and entrepreneurial initiative are seen as the keys to innovation and wealth creation. Intellectual property rights are protected (for example through patents) so as to encourage technological changes.

Neoliberals are particularly assiduous in seeking the privatization of assets. Enclosure and the assignment of private property rights is considered the best way to protect against the so-called "tragedy of the commons". Sectors formerly run or regulated by the state must be turned over to the private sphere and be deregulated (freed from any state interference). Privatization and deregulation combined with competition, it is claimed, eliminate bureaucratic red tape, increase efficiency and productivity, improve quality, and reduce costs, both directly to the consumer through cheaper commodities and services and indirectly through reduction of the tax burden.

48 According to the passage, which of the following is NOT true?

① In situations where property rights are hard to define, it is not recommended that the state uses its power to impose or invent market systems.
② The assumption that individual freedoms are guaranteed by freedom of the market and of trade is a cardinal feature of neoliberal thinking.
③ The sanctity of contracts and the individual right to freedom of action, expression, and choice must be protected.
④ Competition—between individuals, between firms—is held to be a primary virtue.

49 Which of the following is NOT the characteristics of the neoliberal state?

① It seeks to transfer control of economic factors to the private sector from the public sector.
② It is a less regulatory state with regards to private life.
③ It emphasizes the efficiency of market competition and the role of individuals in determining economic outcomes.
④ It tries to protect social justice and redistribution at all costs.

50 What is the meaning of the "tragedy of the commons"?

① The tendency for markets to grow more imperfect, causing social inequality
② The tendency for individuals to irresponsibly exploit public property resources
③ The tendency for companies to ignore investing in quality-enhancing factors
④ The tendency for societies to self-protect against unregulated market exchange

[51-52]

[A] Stagflation is a combination of the words stagnation and inflation. It describes an economic condition characterized by slow growth and high unemployment (economic stagnation) mixed with rising prices (inflation). The term appeared as early as 1965, when British Conservative Party politician Ian Macleod in a speech to the House of Commons said: "We now have the worst of both worlds, not just inflation on the one side or stagnation on the other, but both of them together. We have a sort of 'stagflation' situation and history in modern terms is indeed being made."

[B] After all, unemployment and inflation rates generally move in opposite directions. However, as the "Great Inflation" period of the 1970s ultimately proved, stagflation is real, and it can have a devastating effect on the economy.

[C] Stagflation and inflation are related, but they shouldn't be confused. The term inflation refers to a sustained increase in the average price level of all goods and services, not just a few of them, in an economy over time. Inflation happens when the money supply grows at a faster rate than the economy can produce goods and services. Stagflation happens when inflation exists in tandem with slow economic growth and high unemployment. Typically, these economic conditions don't occur together. Unemployment and inflation tend to be inversely correlated. So, as unemployment rates increase, inflation usually decreases and vice versa. Of course, as the stagflation of the 1970s illustrated, this relationship isn't always stable or predictable.

[D] Stagflation is a perfect storm of economic ills: slow economic growth, high unemployment, and high prices. The two root causes of stagflation economists generally agree upon are supply shocks and fiscal and monetary policies. For households, stagflation means people are earning less money while spending more on everything from food and medicine to housing and consumer products. As consumer spending slows, corporate revenue declines, exacerbating the overall effect on the economy.

51 Which of the following is best for the sentence in the box?

> Initially, many economists believed stagflation wasn't possible.

① [A]
② [B]
③ [C]
④ [D]

52 Which of the following is NOT true?

① Slow growth and high unemployment with rising prices characterize stagflation.
② Stagflation is a made-up word describing a British economic situation in the 1960s.
③ During the stagflation, people tend to earn less money and spend even less.
④ The primary causes of stagflation are supply shocks and fiscal and monetary policies.

3강 사회 / 문화

정답과 해설 p.50

Read the following passages and answer the questions. [01-50]

[01-02]

Young people learn violence by living in situations containing violence. Such is the claim of Geoffrey Canada, who draws from his experience working with young people in Harlem. He argues that society should not concern itself with punishing youth violence so much as its members should work to prevent the circumstances that encourage it. Thus, he advocates a range of new programs that address the needs of young people before they commit violent or criminal acts. These include: creating a peace officer corps to keep gang-related flashpoints from escalating; reducing the demand for drugs by creating jobs for teens; preventing child and spouse abuse by training people with coping skills; reducing the amount of violence in the media; and requiring teens to take tests before buying handguns. These steps would ensure children and teens would not be exposed to violence, and therefore not learn it. Although he is a karate instructor, he trains young people to settle disagreements through dialog and mediation. He points out that violence costs over 5,000 American children their lives each year, and unless ⓐ things change, this number will increase.

01 According to the passage, which of the following is true?

① Seeing violence promotes violence in children.
② Limits on the ownership of pistols are unnecessary.
③ Prevailing approaches to youth drug use are credible.
④ Violent youths should face severe consequences.

02 Which of the following is closest to what ⓐ refers to?

① Disagreement among parents and teens
② The dire situation for youth in America at present
③ Creating a task force to prevent violent conflicts among gangs
④ Youth unemployment and drug use

[03-04]

When musing on cities over time and in our time, from the first to today, we must always remember that cities are artifacts. Forests, jungles, deserts, plains, oceans — the organic environment is born and dies and is reborn endlessly, beautifully, and completely without moral constraint or ethical control. But cities — despite the metaphors that we apply to them from biology or nature ("The city dies when industry flees"; "The neighborhoods are the vital cells of the urban organism") — are artificial. Nature has never made a city, and what nature makes that may seem like a city — an anthill, for instance — only seems like one. It is not a city.

Human beings made and make cities, and only human beings kill cities, or let them die. And human beings do both — make cities and unmake them — by the same means: by acts of choice. We enjoy deluding ourselves in this as in other things. We enjoy believing that there are forces out there completely determining our fate, natural forces that send cities through organic or biological phases of birth, growth, and decay.

03 **What would be the primary purpose of the passage?**

① To persuade the reader to change his behavior
② To illustrate the difference between cities and villages
③ To define the city as growing out of human intentions
④ To identify the sources of popular discontent with cities

04 **According to the passage, why is an anthill by definition unlike a city?**

① It is the vital cell of the urban organism.
② It exists on a far smaller scale than any city does.
③ It can be casually destroyed by human beings.
④ It is a work of instinct rather than of imagination.

[05-06]

    Among the central preoccupations of Durkheim is the question of what holds societies together. His answer points to the crucial role of law in promoting and maintaining this social _____Ⓐ_____. He shows how, as society advances from religion to secularism, and from collectivism to individualism, law becomes concerned less with punishment than compensation. But punishment performs a significant role in expressing the collective moral attitudes by which social solidarity is preserved. He distinguishes between what he calls mechanical solidarity and organic solidarity. The former exists in simple, homogeneous societies which have a uniformity of values and lack any significant division of labour. These uncomplicated communities tend to be collective in nature. In advanced societies, however, where there is division of labour, a high degree of _____Ⓑ_____ exists. There is substantial differentiation, and collectivism is replaced by individualism. These forms of social solidarity are, he argues, reflected in the law: classify the different types of law and you will find the different types of social solidarity to which it corresponds. According to Durkheim, while mechanical solidarity operates in traditional and small-scale societies, organic solidarity comes from individuals' reliance on each other to perform their specified tasks.

05 윗글의 제목으로 가장 적절한 것은?

① Types of Social Solidarity, Types of Society
② Coming Full Circle?: Law and Punishment
③ Division of Labor: How Societies Have Progressed
④ Making Room for Compromise: Solidarity & Individuality

06 윗글의 빈칸 Ⓐ, Ⓑ에 들어갈 말로 가장 적절한 것은?

	Ⓐ	Ⓑ
①	bond	diversity
②	cohesion	interdependence
③	solidarity	collectivism
④	homogeneity	distinctiveness

[07-08]

The Egyptians were certainly the first civilization to preserve food on a large scale. Those narrow fertile strips on either bank of the Nile were their principal source of food, and a dry year in which the Nile failed to flood could be disastrous. To be prepared, Egyptians put up food in every way they could, including stockpiling grain in huge silos. This fixation on preserving a food supply led to considerable knowledge of curing and fermentation. Were it not for their aversion to pigs, the Egyptians would probably have invented ham, for they salt-cured meat and knew how to domesticate the pig. But Egyptian religious leadership pronounced pigs carriers of leprosy*, made pig farmers social outcasts, and never depicted the animal on the walls of tombs. They tried to domesticate for meat the hyenas that scavenged** the edge of villages looking for scraps and dead animals to eat, but most Egyptians were revolted by the idea of eating such an animal. Other failed Egyptian attempts at an animal husbandry include antelope and gazelle. But the Egyptians did succeed in domesticating fowl-ducks, geese, quail, pigeon, and pelican. Ancient walls show fowl being splayed, salted, and put into large earthen jars.

* leprosy: 나병, 한센병   ** to scavenge: 쓰레기를 뒤지다

07 Which of the following does the passage mainly discuss?

① Preservation of food in Ancient Egypt
② Food and wall-painting in Ancient Egypt
③ Domestication of animals by the Egyptians
④ Importance of the Nile in Egyptian civilization

08 According to the passage, which of the following is true of the Egyptians?

① They managed to domesticate the hyenas.
② They knew how to preserve meat in salt.
③ They suffered from floods from the Nile.
④ They were the first civilization to invent ham.

[09-11]

Asian Americans have increasingly come to be viewed as a "model minority." They have been described in the media as "excessively, even provocatively" successful in gaining admissions to universities. Asian American shopkeepers have been congratulated, as well as criticized, for their ubiquity and entrepreneurial effectiveness. If Asian Americans can make it, many politicians and pundits ask, why can't African Americans? Such comparisons pit minorities against each other and generate African American resentment toward Asian Americans. The victims are blamed for their plight, rather than racism and an economy that has made many young African American workers superfluous, only to ⓐ exacerbate relations between them and Asian Americans.

The celebration of Asian Americans has obscured reality. For example, figures on the high earnings of Asian Americans relative to Caucasians are _____Ⓐ_____. Most Asian Americans live in California, Hawaii, and New York — states with higher incomes and higher costs of living than the national average. Furthermore, the "model minority" image _____Ⓑ_____ Asian Americans and hides their differences. For example, while thousands of Vietnamese American young people attend universities, others live in motels and hang out in pool halls in places like East Los Angeles; some join gangs.

09 Which of the following is the best for the title of the passage?

① The Diverse Success Strategies of Asian Americans
② The Differences between Asian Americans and African Americans
③ The Harmful Myths of Asian American Superiority
④ The Influences of Mass Media on Minorities

10 Which of the following is the closest in meaning to the underlined ⓐ**exacerbate**?

① enhance
② consolidate
③ complicate
④ worsen

11 Which of the following is most appropriate for the blanks Ⓐ and Ⓑ?

Ⓐ	Ⓑ
① unreliable	– discloses
② overwhelming	– represses
③ misleading	– homogenizes
④ negligible	– diversifies

[12-14]

Culture, or tradition — to use a less technical term — is not something that exists outside of or independently of individual human beings living together in society. Cultural values do not descend from heaven to influence the course of history. They are abstractions by an observer, based on the observation of certain similarities in the way groups of people behave, either in different situations or over time, or both. Even though one can often make accurate predictions about the way groups and individuals will behave over short periods of time on the basis of such abstractions, as such, they do not explain the behavior. To explain behavior in terms of cultural values is to engage in _____. If we notice that a landed aristocracy resists commercial enterprise, we do not explain this fact by stating that the aristocracy has done so in the past or even that it is the carrier of certain traditions that make it hostile to such activities: the problem is to determine out of what past and present experiences such an outlook arises and maintains itself. If culture has an empirical meaning, it is as a tendency implanted in the human mind to behave in certain specific ways acquired by man as a member of society.

12 What is the best title for the passage?

① Carrying out Tradition in the Face of Change
② How the Human Mind Is Dictated by Culture
③ Correlation of Cultural Values and Social Behavior
④ Cultural Values: Restoration and Preservation

13 Which of the following cannot be inferred about "culture"?

① It is interdependent with members of society.
② It is dominated by the values and beliefs of the majority.
③ It is manifested in the mind which in turn influences behavior.
④ It is composed of generalizations deduced by observers.

14 Choose the one that best fills in the blank.

① circular reasoning
② verbal sparring
③ heated debate
④ conservative rhetoric

[15-16]

Globalization is an uneven phenomenon. Its impact varies over space, through time, by social strata and by aspects of our life. We need to conceptualize globalization less as a wave sweeping all before it, and more like a leopard-spot pattern, with small islands of wealth and global connectivity interspersed with marginalized areas and populations. Marginalization may be occurring as much as globalization. The popular discourses of globalism have exaggerated the islands rather than the seas of poverty and marginalization.

The uneven nature of globalization occurs in three ways: geographical unevenness, social unevenness and sectoral unevenness. The uneven process of globalization in geographical terms can be observed in the disparity between developed and developing economies, booming and declining regions, and world and non-world cities. There have always been winners and losers in the regional development of capitalism, but now the inequality between winning and losing places (countries, regions and cities) is _____. Places which are more global have a much better chance to take advantage of globalization processes, while less global places are, relatively and sometimes absolutely losing ground.

15 Which of the following can be inferred from the passage?

① Due to globalization, resources are now shared among hitherto antagonistic sectors for a uniform betterment of both.
② Worsening poverty may give to previously marginalized regions an impetus and motivation to accelerate their development.
③ Globalization regulates the degrees of economic development in distant regions so that the quality of life may improve worldwide.
④ Discussions of globalization have often emphasized local concentrations of prosperity and progress, not extensive dispersions of cultural and economic disadvantages.

16 Choose the one that best fills in the blank.

① ameliorated
② eluded
③ aggravated
④ mollified

[17-18]

　　The misfortunes of human beings may be divided into two classes: first, those inflicted by the non-human environment, and, second, those inflicted by other people. As mankind have progressed in knowledge and technique, the second class has become a continually increasing percentage of the total. In olden times, famine, for example, was due to natural causes, and, although people did their best to combat it, large numbers of them died of starvation. At the present moment large parts of the world are still faced with the threat of famine, but although natural causes have contributed to the situation, the principal causes are human.

　　For a long time the civilized nations of the world devoted all their best energies to killing each other, and they find it difficult suddenly to switch over to keeping each other alive. It is now man that is _____Ⓐ_____. Nature, it is true, still sees to it that we are mortal, but with the progress in medicine it will become more and more common for people to live until they have had their fill of life. We are supposed to wish to live for ever and to look forward to the unending joys of heaven. But in fact, if you question any candid person who is no longer young, he is very likely to tell you that, having tasted life in this world, he has no wish to begin again as a "new boy" in another. For the future, therefore, it may be taken that much the most important evils that mankind have to consider are those which they inflict upon each other through stupidity or malevolence or both.

17 윗글의 빈칸 Ⓐ에 들어갈 말로 가장 적절한 것은?

① defender of nature
② man's worst enemy
③ environment's friend
④ creator of civilization

18 윗글의 내용과 맞지 <u>않는</u> 것은?

① Human problems created by humans themselves exceed all others.
② Though we must all die some time, medicine has made it possible for people to live longer than before.
③ There is no one who would refuse the opportunity, if offered, to begin a new life again in another world.
④ The most important problem for man in the future will probably be himself because of his maliciousness and lack of wisdom.

[19-20]

In the 19th century America had grown to dislike hanging, the usual method of executing condemned prisoners. Hanging often took place in public, frequently leading to riots and other unseemly behavior among spectators. Hangings also were often botched, resulting in slow strangulation or decapitation. Opponents of the death penalty gained adherents by arguing that hanging was cruel and barbaric. To restore respectability to executions, supporters of the death penalty came up with the idea of electrocution. Electricity was a new and glamorous technology. It was, above all, modern. At the same time, it made people nervous. America was just beginning to wire up its major cities, and although the benefits of electric light were obvious to everyone, no one was quite sure how safe it was. After surveying execution methods from the guillotine (too bloody) to morphine overdoses (too pleasant), a commission appointed by the New York state legislature recommended in 1888 the use of electrocution, which it promised would be instantaneous and painless and devoid of all barbarism. The man who had persuaded the commission of this was Thomas Edison, America's most famous inventor. Edison's primary interest in recommending electrocution was to discredit his chief rival in the race to wire America, George Westinghouse. Edison's company used direct current. Westinghouse's firm used alternating current. Edison not only argued that electrocution would be the best new way to kill condemned prisoners, but that Westinghouse's alternating current would be better at it than his own direct current. In other words, his support for electrocution was _____. Edison hoped that using alternating current for executions would indelibly associate it with death in the public mind, and give him an edge in the competitive industry.

19 According to the passage, which of the following is NOT a reason for the adoption of electrocution as the method of execution?

① it is humane
② it is quick
③ it is cheap
④ it is modern
⑤ it is clean

20 Which of the following is most appropriate for the blank?

① a religious decision
② a scientific reasoning
③ a political protest
④ a marketing strategy
⑤ a moral dilemma

[21-24]

The relationships and concerns of the typical metropolitan resident are so manifold and complex that, especially as a result of the ⓐ agglomeration of so many persons with such differentiated interests, their relationships and activities intertwine with one another into a many-membered organism. In view of this fact, the lack of the most exact punctuality in promises and performances would cause the whole to break down into an inextricable chaos. For this reason the technique of metropolitan life in general is not conceivable without all of its activities and reciprocal relationships being organized and coordinated in the most punctual way into a firmly fixed framework of time which transcends all subjective elements. But here too there emerge those conclusions which are in general the whole task of this discussion, namely, that every event, however restricted to this superficial level it may appear, comes immediately in contact with the depths of the soul, and that the most banal externalities are, in the last analysis, bound up with the final decisions concerning the meaning and style of life. Punctuality, calculability, and _____Ⓐ_____, which are required by the complications and extensiveness of metropolitan life are not only most intimately connected with its capitalistic and intellectualistic character but also color the content of life and are conducive to the exclusion of those irrational, instinctive, sovereign human traits and impulses which originally seek to determine the form of life from within instead of receiving it from the outside in general, schematically precise form.

21 According to the logic of the passage, what would least characterize metropolitan life?

① convection oven
② internet
③ subway
④ cell phone

22 According to the passage, what most characterizes metropolitan life?

① fierce competition
② capitalism
③ modern technology
④ punctuality

23 What is a synonym of ⓐagglomeration?

① cluster
② indoctrination
③ brainwashing
④ education

24 Choose the best word for blank Ⓐ.

① intransigence
② exactness
③ hirsute
④ reticence

[25-27]

What is likely to be the development of the family during the next two centuries? We cannot tell, but we can note certain forces at work which are likely, if unchecked, to have certain results. There are certain things in modern civilised communities which are tending to weaken the family; the chief of them is humanitarian sentiment toward children. More and more people come to feel that children should not suffer more than can be helped through their parents' misfortunes or even sins. In the Bible the lot of the orphan is always spoken of as very sad, and so no doubt it was; nowadays he suffers little more than other children. There will be a growing tendency for the state or charitable institutions to give fairly adequate care to neglected children, and consequently children will be more and more neglected by unconscientious parents or guardians. Gradually the expense of caring for neglected children out of public funds will become so great that there will be a very strong inducement for all who are not well off to avail themselves of the opportunities for giving their children over to the state; probably this will be done, in the end, as now with schooling, by practically all who are below a certain economic level.

25 According to the passage, humanitarian sentiment toward children _____.

① will weaken the family by making parents spend too much money on their children
② will eventually make children more and more neglected by parents or guardians
③ will lead the state to take children away forcefully from their poor or sinful parents
④ will cause a state financial crisis add even state bankruptcy.

26 The writer mentions the Bible to show _____.

① the similarity of the living conditions of orphans and of other children in the past
② the difference of the living conditions of orphans and of other children in the present
③ the similarity of the living conditions of orphans in the past and in the present
④ the difference of the living conditions of orphans in the past and in the present

27 Which of the following is implied in the passage?

① At present, the burden of child-caring is entirely borne by the state and public institutions.
② In the future, most parents will be so well educated as to give adequate care to their children.
③ At present, the state takes responsibility for the schooling of the children from families below a certain economic level.
④ In the future, practically all parents will give their children over to the state for their care as well as for their schooling.

[28-29]

To study social conformity, Philip Zimbardo and Craig Haney (1977) advertised in newspapers for volunteers to take part in a mock prison experiment. The volunteers were randomly assigned roles as "prisoners" and "guards." Both groups were placed in the basement of the Stanford University psychology building and given minimal instructions; they were told to assume their assigned roles and that the guards' job was to "maintain law and order." In only a few hours, the behavior of one group became sharply differentiated from the behavior of the other group. The guards adopted the behavior patterns and attitudes that are typical of guards in maximum security prisons, with most of them becoming abusive and aggressive. Most of the prisoners became passive, dependent, and depressed, although some became enraged at the guards. Suffering among the prisoners was so great that one had to be released in less than thirty-six hours; several other prisoners also had to be released before the intended two-week experiment was ended after six days.

Stereotypical social norms controlled the behavior of both groups. The guards adopted a manner they believed was necessary to simulate their role and maintain order. The prisoners, who were the targets of the guards' abuse, assumed attitudes that accorded with their image of prison life. As the groups became antagonistic, each reinforced the other's behavior. The prisoners expected the guards to be mean and vicious and treated them accordingly. The guards expected the prisoners to be rebellious and acted so as to prevent unruly behavior. A situation of pretense, by virtue of the participants' perceptions, had real effects on the feelings and behavior of everyone involved. As this experiment shows, conformity to social norms is not simply the result of social pressures from one's own group; the influence of other groups in society magnifies the pressure to conform.

28 윗글의 제목으로 가장 적절한 것은?

① Influence of Conformity on Social Behavior
② Behavior Change in a New Environment
③ Efficacy of Stereotypical Social Norms
④ Psychological Insecurity of Inmates

29 윗글의 내용과 일치하는 것은?

① Social pressure to conform within a group is mitigated by contact with other groups.
② The prisoner group pretended to be passive because of the instructions.
③ The participants behaved according to stereotypical social norms.
④ Conformity prevented the situation from getting worse.

[30-32]

The school system is viewed by Bourdieu as an institution for the reproduction of legitimate culture through the hidden linkages between scholastic aptitude and cultural heritage. He believes that, despite ideologies of equal opportunity and meritocracy, few educational systems are called upon by the dominant classes to do anything other than reproduce the legitimate culture as it stands and produce agents capable of manipulating it legitimately.

Bourdieu has argued that it is the culture of the dominant group, which is embodied in schools. Educational differences are thus frequently misrecognized as resulting from individual giftedness, rather than from class-based differences, ignoring the fact that the abilities measured by scholastic criteria often stem not from natural "gifts" but from "the greater or lesser affinity between class cultural habits and the demands of the educational system or the criteria which define success within it."

The notion of cultural capital was proposed by Bourdieu in the early 1960s to describe familiarity with bourgeois culture, the unequal distribution of which helps to conserve social hierarchy under the cloak of individual talent and academic meritocracy. This notion includes such things as acquired knowledge (educational or otherwise), cultural codes, manner of speaking and so forth, which are embodied as a kind of "habitus" in the individual and are also objectified in cultural goods.

30 According to the passage, which of the following is NOT true?

① Working-class students may feel like outsiders in the middle-class habitus of higher education.
② Individuals tend to possess innate intelligence based on their social class.
③ Educational institutions ensure the profitability of the cultural capital of the dominant.
④ The dominant culture, by making itself recognized as universal, legitimizes the interests of the dominant group.

31 Which of the following statements can be inferred from the passage?

① According to Bourdieu, every culture is equally valued and equally legitimate.
② According to Bourdieu, schooling produces certain entrenched ways of recognizing that foster existing class stratification.
③ According to Bourdieu, individuals' efficacy is most strongly influenced by mastery experiences throughout all phases of their lives.
④ According to Bourdieu, cultural reproduction is a trivial mechanism through which socioeconomic polarization takes place.

32 What would be the best title of the passage above?

① The importance of individual giftedness in schooling
② The significance of students' achievement in schooling
③ The social responsibility of dominant culture in schooling
④ The reproduction of inequalities in schooling

[33-35]

We're moving from an era of core competencies that differ from industry to industry to an age shaped by data and analytics and powered by algorithms. Strategies are shifting away from traditional differentiation based on cost, quality, and vertical expertise toward advantages like business network position, the accumulation of unique data, and the deployment of sophisticated analytics — all made possible by AI. Though it can unleash enormous growth, the removal of operating constraints isn't always a good thing. _____ are prone to instability and hard to stop once they're in motion. Think of a car without brakes. A digital signal — a viral meme, for instance — can spread rapidly through networks and can be impossible to halt, even for the organization that launched it in the first place or an entity that controls the key hubs in a network. If you have a message to send, AI offers a fantastic way to reach vast numbers of people and personalize that message for them. But the marketer's paradise can be a citizen's nightmare. Digital operating models can aggregate harm along with value. Even when the intent is positive, the potential downside can be significant. Algorithms, if left unchecked, can exacerbate bias and misinformation on a massive scale.

Digital scale, scope, and learning create a lot of new challenges. The institutions designed to keep an eye on business — regulatory bodies, for example — are struggling to keep up with all the rapid change. In an AI-driven world, once an offering's fit with a market is ensured, user numbers and revenues can skyrocket. Yet it's increasingly obvious that unconstrained growth is dangerous. The potential for businesses that embrace digital operating models is huge, but the capacity to inflict widespread harm needs to be explicitly considered. Navigating these opportunities and threats will be a real test of leadership for both businesses and public institutions.

33 윗글의 주제로 가장 적절한 것은?

① challenges and risks in the age of AI
② tech-driven dangers in globalized job markets
③ AI-centered companies' superiority over traditional firms
④ optimizing company culture by deploying sophisticated analytics
⑤ implementing new combinations of technologies and human skills

34 윗글의 빈칸에 들어갈 말로 가장 적절한 것은?

① Frictionless systems
② Outmoded technologies
③ Viral marketing strategies
④ Democratic decision-making processes
⑤ Government intervention and regulations

35 밑줄 친 "the marketer's paradise can be a citizen's nightmare"가 의미하는 바로 가장 적절한 것은?

① Data privacy must be prioritized.
② Customers may suffer from AI-powered growth.
③ Marketing strategies always need to take consumers' needs into account.
④ Productivity can be increased by human efforts as well as AI-enabled systems.
⑤ Advances in AI technology may create more high-skilled jobs but distort job markets.

[36-37]

    The depiction of a Polynesian character in a Disney film has prompted anger across the Pacific islands, with one New Zealand MP saying the portrayal of the god Maui as obese was "not acceptable." Jenny Salesa, who is of Tongan heritage, said Disney's rendering of Maui in the film *Moana* resembled a creature that was "half pig, half hippo."

    In Polynesian mythology Maui is a heroic figure who created the Pacific Islands by fishing them out of the sea. Will Illolahia told Waatea News that Disney's version of Maui did not fit with his heroic endeavors in Pacific creation myths. "He is depicted in the stories, especially in my culture, as a person of strength and magnitude, a person of a godly nature," Illolahia said. "This depiction of Maui being obese is typical American stereotyping. Obesity is a new phenomenon because of the first world food that's been stuffed down our throat."

    However, many people have commented on social media that Disney's Maui looks strong and powerful, and that his physique is not unusual among Polynesian men. Isoa Kavakimotu, a Tongan New Zealand man who identifies with being "a pretty big guy" created a YouTube video on the controversy, saying he had no problem with Disney's Maui. "I am fine with it," he said. "He doesn't look fat to me, he looks like a powerhouse who could do extraordinary labours. He is big for that reason. In the film they are sailing on a traditional waka, it is set before colonization, I highly doubt <u>a take-away store will pop up in the film</u>. To me, he looks ready for action."

36 The underlined "a take-away store will pop up in the film" means _____.

① the film uses speculative, fictional science-based depictions
② the time setting of the film is the modern period after colonization
③ the realistic depiction is strongly apparent in the film
④ the film focuses on everyday common life
⑤ the film is exploring the racial issue of a colony

37 According to the passage, which of the following is NOT correct?

① Most of Polynesian people are not overweight at present.
② Some expressed their approval of Disney's portrayal of Maui.
③ Portrayal of Maui prompted debate over stereotypes of Polynesian men on screen.
④ Disney's depiction of obese Polynesian god in the film sparked anger among Polynesian people.
⑤ The physical attributes of Maui were indicative of character in the Disney film.

[38-39]

Before we come to our main topic — the questions of what freedom means to modern man, and why and how he tries to escape from it — we must first discuss a concept which may seem to be somewhat removed from actuality. It is, however, a premise necessary for the understanding of the analysis of freedom in modern society. I mean the concept that freedom characterizes human existence as such, and furthermore that its meaning changes according to the degree of man's awareness and conception of himself as an independent separate being.

[A] In the life history of an individual we find the same process. A child is born when it is no longer one with its mother and becomes a biological entity separate from her. Yet, while this biological separation is the beginning of individual human existence, the child remains functionally one with its mother for a considerable period.

[B] The social history of man started with his emerging from a state of oneness with the natural world to an awareness of himself as an entity separate from surrounding nature and men. Yet this awareness remained very dim over long periods of history. The individual continued to be closely tied to the natural and social world from which he emerged; while being partly aware of himself as a separate entity, he felt also part of the world around him. The growing process of the emergence of the individual from his original ties, a process which we may call "individualism," seems to have reached its peak in modern history in the centuries between the Reformation and the present.

[C] To the degree to which the individual, figuratively speaking, has not yet completely severed the _____Ⓐ_____ cord which fastens him to the outside world, he lacks freedom; but these ties give him security and a feeling of belonging and of being rooted somewhere. I wish to call these ties that exist before the process of individuation has resulted in the complete emergence of an individual "primary ties." They are organic in the sense that they are a part of normal human development; they imply a lack of individuality, but they also give security and orientation to the individual. They are the ties that connect the child with its mother, the member of a primitive community with his clan and nature, or the medieval man with the Church and his social caste.

Once the stage of complete individuation is reached and the individual is free from these primary ties, he is confronted with a new task: to orient and root himself in the world and to find security in other ways than those which were characteristic of his _____Ⓑ_____ existence. Freedom then has a different meaning from the one it had before this stage of evolution is reached.

38 윗글의 단락을 논리적 흐름에 맞게 순서대로 배열한 것으로 가장 적합한 것은?

① [A] – [B] – [C]
② [A] – [C] – [B]
③ [B] – [A] – [C]
④ [C] – [B] – [A]

39 윗글의 빈칸 Ⓐ와 Ⓑ에 들어가기에 가장 적합한 것은?

	Ⓐ		Ⓑ
①	navel	–	egocentric
②	spinal	–	epistemological
③	funiculus	–	ontological
④	umbilical	–	preindividualistic

[40-41]

Having heard that Toronto was becoming one of the continent's noblest cities, we flew from New York to investigate. New Yorkers jealous of their city's reputation and concerned about challenges to its stature have little to worry about. After three days in residence, our delegation noted an absence of hysteria that was almost intolerable and took to consuming large portions of black coffee to maintain our normal state of irritability. The local people to whom we complained in hopes of provoking comfortably nasty confrontations declined to become _____Ⓐ_____. They would like to enjoy a gratifying big-city hysteria, they said, but believed it would seem ill-mannered in front of strangers. Extensive field studies — our stay lasted four weeks — persuaded us that this failure reflects the survival in Toronto of an ancient pattern of social conduct called "courtesy." "Courtesy" manifests itself in many quaint forms _____Ⓑ_____ to the New Yorker. Thus, for example, Yankee fans may be astonished to learn that at the Toronto baseball park it is considered a bad behavior to heave rolls of toilet paper and beer cans at players on the field. Official literature inside Toronto taxicabs includes a notification of the proper address to which riders may mail the authorities not only complaints but also _____Ⓒ_____ about the cabbie's behaviour.

40 윗글의 빈칸 Ⓐ, Ⓑ, Ⓒ에 들어가기에 가장 적합한 것은?

	Ⓐ	Ⓑ	Ⓒ
①	appalling	bellicose	compliments
②	different	compliant	apprehensions
③	compliant	pervasive	apprehensions
④	bellicose	unaccustomed	compliments

41 윗글을 통해 추론할 수 있는 것으로 가장 적합한 것은?

① New Yorkers could learn many things from Torontonians.
② New York is a good place to find many courteous people.
③ Torontonians consume large portions of coffee to relieve their stress.
④ Torontonians cannot bring the toilet paper and canned beers to the stadium.

[42-43]

Today, many people are worried that digital books and our increasingly screen-based culture herald the end of serious reading. This is nonsense. There are consequences, and sometimes drawbacks, to all new technologies, but human beings can't live without stories and poems. Young lovers will always read Sappho, Donne, and Keats. *Madame Bovary* and *The Great Gatsby* will remain irreplaceable commentaries on our proclivity for romantic illusion. Older folk, hoping to make some small sense of life before its end, will continue to study history and philosophy. Whether people turn pages or look at pixels on a screen is secondary.

But consider this: through social media, the young woman of today who discovers Sylvia Plath can quickly share her excitement with friends around the world. She might leave a comment about *Ariel* or *The Bell Jar* on Goodreads, or join an online discussion group, or post links to sites devoted to the poet's work and memory. Her enthusiasm might lead a dozen or a thousand more people to Plath.

That's just one advantage of our screen-based culture. Older and half-forgotten books are now readily available through Project Gutenberg. Entire libraries can be carried in your pocket. Digitized texts can be easily and quickly searched, or their font size enlarged for aging eyes.

_____Ⓐ_____, these real benefits create various pitfalls at the same time. Computers encourage skimming instead of focused attention and solitary engagement with a book's words and ideas. The buzzing Internet hive fosters meaningless chatter as well as meaningful dialogue. Screens themselves impose a factitious homogeneity: James Bond looks like Jane Austen and a smartphone blurs the difference in size between the Giant Bible of Mainz and a tiny miniature book.

42 Which expression best fits Ⓐ?

① Indeed
② Alarmingly
③ Consequently
④ In addition
⑤ Nonetheless

43 What is not inferable from the passage above?

① Despite the fast change in reading habits, people will not stop reading.
② Digitized texts will altogether replace printed books.
③ Reading on screen makes us unaware of the different material and generic traits individual printed books have.
④ Screen-based culture can expand the reader's active engagements with the book.
⑤ Not all comments and dialogues in online book clubs are meaningful.

[44-46]

　　Human beings find the most _____ⓐ_____ ways to protect their privacy, even under conditions of near-constant physical proximity to others. In many cultures, even minimal control over physical access can be hard to come by in the midst of communal and family life. Some villages have huts with walls so thin that sounds can easily be heard through them; others have no walls at all separating couples, or families. Many ways are then devised to create privacy. Villagers may set up private abodes outside the village to which they go for days or even months when they want to be alone or with just one or two others. Many cultures have developed strict rules of etiquette, along with means of dissimulation and hypocrisy that allow certain private matters to remain unknown or go unobserved. In such ways, _____ⓑ_____.

　　An _____ⓒ_____ example of how such control can be maintained is provided by the Tuareg men of North Africa who wear blue veils and long robes of indigo cotton, so that little of them shows except their hands, their feet, and the area around their eyes. The veil is worn at home as well as outside, even when eating or smoking. Some wear it even when asleep. It is raised to cover the face most completely in the presence of highly placed persons or family members granted special respect, such as in-laws. One observer noted that the veil protects ceremonial reserve and allows a "_____ⓓ_____." The veil, though providing neither isolation nor anonymity, bestows facelessness and the idiom of privacy upon its wearer and allows him to stand somewhat aloof from the perils of social interaction while remaining a part of it.

44 Which pair best fits Ⓐ and Ⓒ?

	Ⓐ		Ⓒ
①	impressive	–	aggregating
②	incontrovertible	–	appreciable
③	immediate	–	appetizing
④	ingenious	–	arresting
⑤	imaginative	–	apprehensive

45 Which best completes Ⓑ?

① it is benevolent to control the level of one's interaction with people from different social classes, educational backgrounds, and national origins

② it is possible to exercise some control over one's openness to others even in the midst of communal life or crowds

③ it is skeptical to exert one's control even over others who may not have antagonistic feelings about communal living

④ it is advisable to undermine the degree of one's control over others in collective relationships

⑤ it is mind-boggling to exert significant control over one's family life without abdicating one's personal rights

46 Which best suits the quote in Ⓓ?

① frequent interaction without subterfuge
② protective mechanism against one's potential advocates
③ questionable security from an unanticipated event
④ futile retreat from a potentially unpleasant and fatal encounter
⑤ symbolic withdrawal from a threatening situation

[47-50]

People born between 1946 and 1964 are called baby boomers in America. Many baby boomers are now over 50, but they still cling to their youth. Most continue to live a very active life. This group cherishes convenience, which has resulted in a growing demand for home delivery of large appliances, furniture, groceries, and other items. In addition, the spreading culture of convenience explains the tremendous appeal of prepared take-out foods, portable telephones, and the Internet.

Baby boomers' parents raised their children to think for and of themselves. Studies of child-rearing practices show that parents of the 1950s and 1960s consistently ranked "to think for themselves" as the number-one trait they wanted to nurture in their children. Postwar affluence also enabled parents to indulge their children as never before. They invested in their children's skills by sending them to college. They encouraged their children to succeed in a job market that rewarded competitive drive more than cooperative spirit and individual skills more than teamwork.

In turn, the sheer size of the generation encouraged businesses to play to the emerging individuality of baby boomers. Even before the oldest baby boomers started earning a living more than two decades ago, astute business people anticipated their profits that could come from giving millions of young people what they wanted. Business offered individualistic baby boomers a growing array of customized products and services.

47 Which of the following does properly characterize "Baby Boomers"?

① America's Mass Market
② Apocalypse Now
③ Walking Dictionary
④ Mission Impossible

48 What is the passage mainly about?

① economic principle
② demographic trends
③ common sense
④ competition and cooperation

49 Which of the following is true?

① Baby boomers are the results of generation of latchkey children.
② Baby boomers overestimate the value of competition and individual ability.
③ Some businessmen were wise enough to predict the future main customers.
④ To raise their children, baby boomers depended on cooperative teamwork.

50 Which of the following statements is likely to follow the final sentence?

① That is, houses, cars, furniture, appliances, and even beliefs.
② A large influx of new people into an area creates many new opportunities for all types of businesses.
③ Yet, today's mature consumers are wealthier, healthier, and better educated than those of earlier generations.
④ They choose products and services that meet traditional needs and interests.

4강 언어 / 문학 / 예술

정답과 해설 p.75

Read the following passages and answer the questions. [01–54]

[01–02]

Beethoven's compositional battles were hard fought, with certain works spending many years in labored gestation. Once fully formed, however, the majority of them were instantly successful. The growing middle-class enjoyed their immediacy, power, and dramatic virtuosity, while the cultural elite was equally impressed by the thorough absorption and subsequent transcending of 18th-century musical styles.

Although Beethoven's output is usually divided into three periods, a fourth, before his arrival in Vienna, should also be considered, as by then he had already composed a number of vocal and chamber works, and a very accomplished set of variations for piano. These early works are all catalogued with "WoO" numbers (*Werke ohne Opus* — works without opus). His early reputation and fame rested on his phenomenal gifts of improvisation at the keyboard — some said even greater than Mozart's — and it is therefore natural that most of his early compositions are for piano.

Beethoven's usually-designated "early" period began after his arrival in Vienna in 1792 at the age of 22. Here he assimilated — and then began to transform — the sonata principle from a balanced, arch-like structure to a more dynamic, urgent form, where the recapitulation (the third section after the exposition and the development sections) was a culmination rather than a repetition. At first tending towards exploration and elaboration of the initial musical ideas — and preferring four movements to the customary three — Beethoven's solo piano works were highly successful. But, as his accomplishment grew, his compositions became more expressive and concentrated. The *Pathétique* sonata, with its French name meaning "passionate" or "emotional" (given to it by Beethoven himself) is regarded as his first masterpiece.

01 윗글의 제목으로 가장 적절한 것은?

① Beethoven's Musical Improvisation
② Beethoven's Specialty in Piano Works
③ Beethoven's Early Life as a Composer
④ Beethoven's Passionate Sonata Masterpiece

02 윗글의 내용과 일치하는 것은?

① Some of Beethoven's works took many years for improvisation.
② Beethoven regarded the *Pathétique* as a misnomer for his masterpiece.
③ In fact, Beethoven's musical achievements can be divided into four periods.
④ Beethoven's early reputation is based on his balanced and arch-like structure in music.

[03-04]

Pidgins and creoles are the outcome of the need of people not sharing a language to communicate but differ from national and international languages in that a pidgin does not begin as an already existing language or dialect selected to serve this purpose; it is rather a particular combination of two languages. According to Loreto Todd, a pidgin is a _____ language which arises to fulfill certain restricted communication needs among people who have no common language. In the initial stages of contact the use of a pidgin is often limited to transactions where a detailed exchange of ideas is not required and where a small vocabulary, drawn almost exclusively from one language, suffices. Also, the syntactic structure of the pidgin is much less complex than the structures of the languages in contact, and though many pidgin features clearly reflect usages in the contact languages, others are unique to the pidgin. A creole arises when a pidgin becomes the mother tongue of a speech community. The simple structure that characterized the pidgin is carried over into the creole but since a creole, as a mother tongue, must be capable of expressing the whole range of human experience, the lexicon is expanded and frequently a more elaborate syntactic system evolves.

03 윗글의 내용과 가장 가까운 것은?

① A creole usually has simpler structures than a pidgin.
② The vocabulary of a pidgin is largely from two languages in contact.
③ A pidgin can be considered one of the pre-existing languages in contact.
④ A pidgin has its unique features other than the ones reflecting the usages in the contact languages.
⑤ A pidgin develops as a way to facilitate communication among the groups who used to speak a common language.

04 윗글의 빈칸에 들어갈 말로 가장 적절한 것은?

① poetic
② native
③ complicated
④ marginal
⑤ rhetorical

[05-07]

When Sir Salman Rushdie turned in the original manuscript of "Midnight's Children", which won many prizes in 1981, it contained an additional narrative voice. Luckily his sensible publisher took the view that this picaresque tale of modern India's birth was complicated enough already, and the superfluous character was removed. Sir Salman, who spent four years adapting his work for the screen, should have employed equal economy with his screenplay. The film is doggedly faithful to the novel, so much so that it is stuffed with plot and much of the story's lyrical beauty is lost along the way. Saleem and Shiva, both born at the precise moment of India's independence, are swapped at birth by a nurse eager to please a revolutionary. The presentation here is as ambitious as its theme, and in the first, more coherent half of the film there is much to admire. Deepa Mehta, a Canadian-Indian director, has conjured up a real feast of a film — with silks, saris and songs galore. Everything is bathed in a supernatural glow. But sumptuousness of this kind cannot make up for the episodic manner in which the story plays out on screen. Characters that viewers have come to be fond of are killed off in a single sentence. Even weighty performances, particularly from Satya Bhabha as the grown-up Saleem, fail to rescue the film from feeling both laboured and vague.

05 The best title of the passage would be _____.

① In Two Minds: A Biography of Salman Rushdie
② What Makes A Great Screenplay
③ Identity Crisis of A Great Writer
④ Film Adaptations in Decline
⑤ A Good Book that Makes A Bad Film

06 According to the passage, which of the following is true?

① The book publisher argued that the novel was too complex to be made into a film.
② The film director thought that the film could not express the lyrical beauty of the original novel.
③ The film suffers terribly from overly complicated plot lines.
④ Salman Rushdie's message was not successfully conveyed because the film was not faithful to the novel.
⑤ Salman Rushdie got rid of several characters for the film.

07 How is the tone of the passage?

① admiring
② ironic
③ critical
④ bewildering
⑤ poetic

[08-11]

Futurism was first announced on Feb. 20, 1909, when the Paris newspaper Le *Figaro* published a manifesto by the Italian poet and editor Filippo Tommaso Marinetti. Marinetti coined the word Futurism to reflect his goal of _____Ⓐ_____ the art of the past and _____Ⓑ_____ change, originality, and innovation in culture and society. Marinetti's manifesto glorified the new technology of the automobile and the beauty of its speed, power, and movement. Exalting violence and conflict, he called for the sweeping repudiation of traditional values and the destruction of cultural institutions such as museums and libraries. The manifesto's rhetoric was passionately bombastic; its aggressive tone was purposely intended to inspire public anger and arouse controversy. Marinetti's manifesto inspired a group of young painters in Milan to apply Futurist ideas to the visual arts. Like Marinetti, they glorified originality and expressed their _____©_____ for inherited artistic traditions. They wanted to depict visually the perception of movement, speed, and change. To achieve this, the Futurist painters adopted the Cubist technique of using fragmented and intersecting plane surfaces and outlines to show several simultaneous views of an object. Futurist paintings have brighter and more vibrant colours than Cubist works, and they reveal dynamic, agitated compositions in which rhythmically swirling forms reach ⓐ crescendos of violent movement.

08 윗글의 빈칸 Ⓐ와 Ⓑ에 들어갈 말로 가장 적절한 것은?

	Ⓐ	Ⓑ
①	discarding	celebrating
②	vindicating	defending
③	assimilating	modifying
④	validating	endorsing

09 윗글에 나타난 Futurism에 관한 설명 중 사실인 것은?

① Futurists were moderate in rejecting traditional art.
② Futurists presented segmented objects in their paintings.
③ Futurists disapproved of new perceptions of reality.
④ For Futurists, it is taboo to incite public sentiment.

10 윗글의 빈칸 ⓒ에 들어갈 말로 가장 적절한 것은?

① affection
② respect
③ disdain
④ admiration

11 윗글의 밑줄 친 ⓐcrescendos의 의미에 가장 가까운 것은?

① vacillation
② intensification
③ dissemination
④ publicity

[12-14]

Old-time (old-timey) refers to the oldest form of country music ever recorded. First recorded in the early '20s, its style and sound remained consistent through the 1800s. Though it encompassed a number of different influences, the music's roots lay in British folk songs that were played on stringed instruments, such as the fiddle. By the late 1800s, rural Americans had begun playing the folk songs on Spanish guitars and African banjos as well, adding other instruments — dobro, bass, washboards — to the mix. During the early 1900s, this country folk music incorporated some contemporary influences, particularly the blues and vaudeville comedy. This rurally <u>eclectic amalgamation</u> was the sound of country music during the '20s, and it would forever be identified as "old-time" country, because it was the music that evoked country's roots. Although the music began to evolve in the '30s, as Jimmie Rodgers brought country into the industrial age, there were groups that performed old-time into the end of the century, frequently without changing the conventions of the genre at all. One major style within old-time was bluegrass, which developed in the late '40s as a reaction to the increasing modernization of country music.

12 Which of the following cannot be inferred about "old-time" country music?

① It remained pure until the late 1900s.
② Jimmie Rodgers was a progressive old-time country singer.
③ It originated from British folk songs.
④ Americans broadened its instrumental repertory.

13 According to the passage, what is true about "bluegrass?"

① It preserved folk music in its original form.
② It tried to incorporate a mix of old-time country and pop music.
③ It developed from contemporary influences from the blues.
④ It was a backlash to the changing face of old-time country.

14 Choose the one closest in meaning to the underlined "eclectic amalgamation."

① absolute estrangement
② classical antiquity
③ selective hybridity
④ regional migration

[15-16]

Pidgins and creoles are the outcome of the need of people not sharing a language to communicate. They differ from national and international languages in that a pidgin does not begin as an already existing language or dialect selected to serve this purpose; it is rather a particular combination of two languages. Loreto Todd has the following to say about pidgins and creoles:

A pidgin is a marginal language which arises to fulfill certain restricted communication needs among people who have no common language. In the initial stages of contact the communication is often limited to transactions where a detailed exchange of ideas is not required and where a small vocabulary, drawn almost exclusively from one language, suffices. The syntactic structure of the pidgin is less complex and less flexible than the structures of the languages that were in contact, and though many pidgin features clearly reflect usages in the contact languages, others are unique to the pidgin.

A creole arises when a pidgin becomes the mother tongue of a speech community. The simple structure that characterized the pidgin is carried over into the creole but since a creole, as a mother tongue, must be capable of expressing the whole range of human experience, the lexicon is expanded, and frequently a more elaborate syntactic system evolves. Since creoles are often not regarded as "real" languages and consequently considered as inferior, it is worth noting that, for example, both French and English may be the outcome of pidgins — in the first case through contact between native Gauls and occupying Romans, and in the second through contact between the native Anglo-Saxons and the Danes who settled on the east coast of England.

15 윗글의 내용과 일치하지 <u>않는</u> 것은?

① A pidgin usually develops from two different languages.
② The vocabulary of the pidgin is typically drawn from the two languages that were in contact.
③ A creole can usually express a wider range of human experiences than a pidgin.
④ The structures of the languages that were in contact are generally more flexible than the structure of the pidgin.

16 윗글의 내용으로 추론할 수 있는 것은?

① French is possibly a creole.
② English is possibly a pidgin.
③ Pidgins develop to promote the exchange of philosophical ideas.
④ A creole becomes a pidgin when a speech community accepts it as its mother tongue.

[17-18]

Sound system of a language is broadly divided into two categories: consonant and vowel sounds (known as the segmental features) and more global aspects such as stress, rhythm, and intonation (known as suprasegmental features or prosody). Traditionally, the sound system has been described and taught in a building-block fashion: sounds > syllables > words > phrases > sentences > extended discourse. Although this makes sense from an analytical point of view, this is usually not how the language learners experience language. As speakers, we usually do not think about what we are saying sound by sound, or even syllable by syllable, _____ communication breaks down. So the bottom-up approach of mastering one sound at a time and eventually stringing sounds together has been replaced by a bit more top-down approach in which the sound system is addressed in the stream of speech.

17 Choose the best words or phrases for blank.

① lest
② unless
③ provided
④ as

18 Choose the statement LEAST consistent with the passage.

① Prosody is judged more important than segmental features in natural speech.
② Constants and vowels are building blocks in the analytical view of sounds.
③ Language description and language learning are considerably disparate.
④ Communication breakdown demonstrates the analytical nature of language.

[19-20]

James's first novels used conventional narrative techniques: explicit characterization, action which related events in distinctly phased sequences, settings firmly outlined and specifically described. But this method gradually gave way to a subtler, more deliberate, more diffuse style of accumulation of minutely discriminated details whose total significance the reader can grasp only by constant attention and sensitive inference. His later novels _____ scenes of abrupt and prominent action, and do not so much offer a succession of sharp shocks as slow piecemeal additions of perception. The curtain is not suddenly drawn back from shrouded things, but is slowly moved away. Such a technique is suit to James's essential subject, which is not human action itself but the states of mind which produce and are produced by human actions and interactions. James was less interested in what characters do, than in the moral and psychological antecedents, realizations, and consequences which attend their doings. This is why he more often speaks of "cases" than of actions. His stories, therefore, grow more and more lengthy while the actions they relate grow simpler and less visible; not because they are crammed with adventitious and secondary events, digressive relief, or supernumerary characters, as overstuffed novels of action are; but because he presents in such exhaustive detail every nuance of his situation. Commonly the interest of a novel is in the variety and excitement of visible actions building up to a climactic event which will settle the outward destinies of characters with storybook promise of permanence. A James novel, however, possesses its characteristic interest in carrying the reader through a rich analysis of the mental adjustments of characters to the realities of their personal situations as they are slowly revealed to them through exploration and chance discovery.

19 윗글의 빈칸에 들어갈 말로 가장 적절한 것은?

① draw on
② play down
③ underscore
④ juxtapose

20 윗글의 내용과 일치하지 <u>않는</u> 것은?

① James' later novels are characterized by the development of rising action to a climax.
② James' later novels differ from his earlier ones in their levels of moral and psychological complexity.
③ James' later novels became lengthy because he provided every nuance of his situation in exhaustive detail.
④ James' first novels utilize conventional narrative techniques which emphasize phased sequences in recounting actions.

21 다음 글의 내용과 일치하지 <u>않는</u> 것은?

> Cézanne's painting denies neither science nor tradition. He went to the Louvre every day when he was in Paris. He believed that one must learn how to paint and that the geometric study of planes and forms is a necessary part of this learning process. He inquired about the geological structure of his landscapes, convinced that these abstract relationships, expressed, however, in terms of the visible world, should affect the act of painting. The rules of anatomy and design are present in each stroke of his brush just as the rules of the game underlie each stroke of a tennis match.
>
> But what motivates the painter's movement can never be simply perspective or geometry or the laws governing color, or, for that matter, particular knowledge. Motivating all the movements from which a picture gradually emerges, there can be only one thing: the landscape in its totality and in. its absolute fullness, precisely what Cézanne called a "motif." He would start by discovering the geological foundations of the landscape; then, according to Cézanne, he would halt and look at everything with widened eyes, "germinating" with the countryside. Then he began to paint all parts of the painting at the same time, using patches of color to surround his original charcoal sketch of the geological skeleton. The picture took on fullness and density; it grew in structure and balance; it came to maturity all at once. "The landscape thinks itself in me," he said, "and I am its consciousness." Nothing could be farther from naturalism than this "intuitive science." Cézanne recaptures and converts into visible objects what would, without him, remain walled up in the separate life of each consciousness: the vibration of appearances which is the cradle of things.

① To Cézanne, the knowledge about geometry or the laws governing color was not the sole factor in motivating the painter's movements.
② Cézanne believed that the study of geological structure of the landscapes was a required part in learning how to paint pictures.
③ Cézanne's "motif" best reflects the contemporary naturalism view of painting which emphasized the role of visible world in painting.
④ Without Cézanne's contribution, the vibration of appearances would have not surfaced over the separate life of each consciousness.

[22-23]

For modern listeners, Debussy practically defines French music, by which I mean that the essential qualities of his music (not only his sensuous delicacy but also his aversion to the harmonic behavior characteristic of late-nineteenth-century German music, a dense chromatic motion that tends to constantly, restlessly build to orgiastic climaxes, as in Wagner and Strauss) have come to be seen as essentially "French" qualities. Walsh makes clear, however that Debussy, far from simply amplifying or exemplifying the dominant tendencies of his musical milieu, consciously and stubbornly swam against the current, especially when it came to the heavy influence of German music on French composers. Wagner was the unavoidable presence in late-nineteenth-century Paris, but Debussy traced the blame for that influence further back, to Gluck. Debussy was quietly radical in his preference for Rameau's "delicate and charming tenderness" over what he perceived as the Germanic "affectation of profundity or the need to double underline everything."

22 윗글의 제목으로 가장 적절한 것은?

① Further Back to Gluck: Root of Debussy's Music
② A Wizardly Gift: To Be Both French and German
③ What Makes Debussy's Music Fundamentally French
④ Rediscovering an Unsung Hero in the History of Music
⑤ Debussy's Alchemy: Textualizing Global Conflicts into Music

23 밑줄 친 "swam against the current"의 의미로 가장 적절한 것은?

① not to cater to the taste of his German audiences
② to control his own personal preferences for French music
③ to withdraw from the world and sink into the inner world of his art
④ not to imitate the formal logic and dense textures of German music
⑤ to curb the contemporary musical tendencies defined by delicacy and charm

[24-26]

An interesting aspect of graphic symbolism is the extent to which individual variations in letter formation can reliably be interpreted. The term graphology, which refers to the psychological study of handwriting, has been practised for over a century. It was the French abbot, Jean Hippolyte Michon, who first set this branch of scholarship in train. Graphologists claim that careful and detailed analysis of an individual's handwriting can reveal important information about an individual's personality and can indicate, for example, whether they are suitable for a particular job or not. In recent years they have been employed in several professional contexts and in forensic science, where questions of handwriting identity and imitation are critical. The subject plainly has the scope for scientific development, as variables such as letter size, shape, angle, line direction and consistency of stroke all lend themselves, in principle, to precise scientific description. _____ Graphology has suffered from scepticism generated by its popularity at agricultural shows and seaside resorts, where characters are described and fortunes foretold on the basis of little more than a scribbled signature. The subject has also been heavily biased towards the famous or infamous, discerning the basis of success in a signature — but without objective controls.

24. The best title of the passage would be _____.

① History of Handwriting Analysis
② Recent Popularity of Graphology among Job-seekers
③ Mythical Origin of graphic Symbolism
④ Digital Signatures as a Replacement for Handwriting
⑤ Use of Graphology in Criminal Investigation

25. Which of the following is most appropriate for the blank?

① Moreover
② Therefore
③ Obviously
④ Officially
⑤ Yet

26. According to the passage, which of the following is true?

① The government controlled handwriting practices because they often misled the general public.
② Michon was the first person to receive the research grant for the new field.
③ Identifying the difference between the famous and the infamous is the most important task for graphologists.
④ Graphology contributed to changing the superstitious minds of rural people.
⑤ Graphology was often regarded as a simple fortune-telling skill.

[27-29]

Thomas Hardy's impulses as a writer, all of which he indulged in his novels, were numerous and divergent, and they did not always work together in harmony. Hardy was to some degree interested in exploring his characters' psychologies, though impelled less by curiosity than by sympathy. Occasionally he felt the impulse to comedy (in all its detached coldness) as well as the impulse to farce, but he was more often inclined to see tragedy and record it. He was also inclined to literary realism in the several senses of that phrase. He wanted to describe ordinary human beings; he wanted to speculate on their dilemmas rationally (and, unfortunately, even schematically); and he wanted to record precisely the material universe. Finally, he wanted to be more than a realist. He wanted to transcend what he considered to be the banality of solely recording things exactly and to express as well his awareness of the occult and the strange.

In his novels these various impulses were sacrificed to each other inevitably and often. Inevitably, because Hardy did not care in the way that novelists such as Flaubert or James cared, and therefore took paths of least resistance. Thus, one impulse often surrendered to a fresher one and, unfortunately, instead of exacting a compromise, simply disappeared. A desire to throw over reality a light that never was might give way abruptly to the desire on the part of what we might consider a novelist-scientist to record exactly and concretely the structure and texture of a flower. In this instance, the new impulse was at least an energetic one, and thus its indulgence did not result in a relaxed style. But on other occasions Hardy abandoned a perilous, risky, and highly energizing impulse in favor of what was for him the fatally relaxing impulse to classify and schematize abstractly. When a relaxing impulse was indulged, the style — that sure index of an author's literary worth — was certain to become verbose. Hardy's weakness derived from his apparent inability to control the comings and goings of these divergent impulses and from his unwillingness to cultivate and _____Ⓐ_____ the energetic and risky ones.

27 **What is the most appropriate title of the passage above?**

① Divergent Impulses: The Issue of Unity in the Novel
② The Real and the Strange: Two Areas of Interest to Hardy
③ Hardy's Novelistic Impulses: The Problem of Control
④ The Role of Ordinary People in Hardy's Fiction
⑤ Verbosity: Hardy's Fatal Weakness

28 **Which expression best fits Ⓐ?**

① sustain
② subordinate
③ suppress
④ supplant
⑤ subsidize

29 **Which statement can not be inferred from the passage above?**

① The term "literary realism" is susceptible to more than a single definition.
② A writer's style is considered to be a reliable means by which to measure the writer's literary merit.
③ The indulgence of a relaxing impulse led Hardy into a wordy style.
④ Flaubert and James indulged more impulses in their novels than did Hardy in his novels.
⑤ Comedy appeared less frequently in Hardy's novels than did tragedy.

[30-32]

There have been various attempts to determine what literature is. You can regard it, for example, as 'imaginative' writing in the sense of fiction — writing which is not literally true. But even the briefest reflection on what people commonly include under the heading of literature suggests that this will not do. Seventeenth-century English literature includes Shakespeare, Webster, Marvell and Milton; but it also stretches to the essays of Francis Bacon, the sermons of John Donne, Bunyan's spiritual autobiography and whatever it was that Sir Thomas Browne wrote. It might even at a pinch be taken to encompass Hobbes's *Leviathan* or *Clarendon's History of the Rebellion*. French seventeenth-century literature contains, along with Corneille and Racine, La Rochefoucauld's maxims, Bossuet's funeral speeches, Boileau's treatise on poetry, Madame de Séignés letters to her daughter and the philosophy of Descartes and Pascal. Nineteenth-century English literature usually includes Lamb (though not Bentham), Macaulay (but not Marx), Mill (but not Darwin or Herbert Spencer).

A distinction between 'fact' and 'fiction', then, seems unlikely to get us very far, not least because the distinction itself is often a questionable one. It has been argued, for instance, that our own opposition between 'historical' and 'artistic' truth does not apply at all to the early Icelandic sagas. In the English late sixteenth and early seventeenth centuries, the word 'novel' seems to have been used about both true and fictional events, and even news reports were hardly to be considered factual. Novels and news reports were neither clearly factual nor clearly fictional: our own sharp discriminations between these categories simply did not apply. Gibbon no doubt thought that he was writing the historical truth, and so perhaps did the authors of *Genesis*, but they are now read as 'fact' by some and 'fiction' by others; Newman certainly thought his theological meditations were true but they are now for many readers 'literature.' Moreover, if 'literature' includes much 'factual' writing, it also excludes quite a lot of fiction. *Superman* comic and Mills and Boon novels are fictional but not generally regarded as literature, and certainly not as Literature. If literature is 'creative' or 'imaginative' writing, does this imply that history, philosophy and natural science are uncreative and unimaginative? Certainly not.

30 The above passage is <u>most</u> likely to be part of an essay whose topic is:

① The various usage of the word 'novel'
② The opposition between 'historical' and 'artistic'
③ The distinction between fact and fiction
④ The meaning and definition of literature

31 Which of the following is <u>most</u> likely to be inferred from the above passage?

① Literature can be thought of as fictional writing, that is, writing which is not literally true.
② History, philosophy and natural science cannot be imaginative because they are based on fact.
③ There were periods when the factual writing and the fictional writing were not clearly distinguished.
④ The distinction between 'fact' and 'fiction' is very helpful when one tries to identify what literature is.

32 According to the above passage, literature <u>cannot</u> be limited to 'fictional' writing because _____.

① people, who are not specialists on literature, commonly think that only fictional writings are included in literature
② factual writings, such as those in history, philosophy, and natural science are neither creative nor imaginative
③ seventeenth-century English literature include Shakespeare, Webster, Marvell and Milton
④ factual writings are often regarded as literature, and fictional writings are not always included in literature

[33-36]

[A] Words often have two types of meaning: denotation and connotation. Denotation refers to the actual dictionary definition of the word, without the attachment of an emotional response. For example, if you look up the word *aggressive*, you will find that it means "ⓐ unprovokedly offensive, ⓑ quite amicable, ⓒ vigorously energetic, and ⓓ boldly assertive." If used to describe a type of treatment for a deadly disease, *aggressive* carries a positive emotional response. On the other hand, if your friend complains that a salesperson is aggressive, the picture you get of that salesperson is not necessarily positive. Thus, the word *aggressive* evokes both positive and negative emotions depending on the context in which the word is used. Your connotations for words become part of your assumptions and thus influence your inferences.

[B] Writers and speakers consciously use connotative language to shape your inferences. They do this by choosing words with universal connotations. Thus, they expect you to respond emotionally in a certain way to the word choice. For example, imagine yourself in an art history class where the instructor is discussing some of the later paintings by the impressionist Claude Monet. The instructor carefully avoids including opinions about Monet because he wants his students to learn to evaluate paintings for form and style. _____Ⓐ_____, in commenting on a later Monet painting, he says that "the apparently random choice of reds and oranges is a departure from the more serene blues and greens that Monet used in earlier paintings of the same scene." *Random*, when used to refer to an artist's color choice, has a more negative connotation. On the other hand, *serene* holds a more positive connotation. The instructor's use of the words *random* and *serene* helps you infer that _____Ⓑ_____.

33 According to the paragraph [A], which has a positive connotation of *aggressive*?

① Aggressive behavior is a sign of emotional distress.
② People complain that salespersons are usually aggressive in today's competitive market.
③ My friend has been diagnosed with an aggressive form of cancer.
④ The doctor took an aggressive approach to treating the infection.

34 Identify the one underlined part that should be rewritten in the paragraph [A].

① ⓐ unprovokedly offensive
② ⓑ quite amicable
③ ⓒ vigorously energetic
④ ⓓ boldly assertive

35 Which is the most appropriate for the blank Ⓐ in the paragraph [B]?

① Thus
② However
③ Otherwise
④ Moreover

36 Which is the most appropriate for the blank ⓑ in the paragraph [B]?

① He preferred Monet's later paintings to his earlier ones.
② He is impressed with both Monet's later and earlier paintings.
③ He is not as impressed with Monet's later paintings as he is with his earlier ones.
④ He is not impressed with either Monet's earlier paintings or his later ones.

[37-39]

Literary fiction, you might think, is in wonderful health. Book festivals, from Edinburgh in Scotland to Bath in England, are flourishing.

Look at the facts, though, and a more worrying picture emerges. It is well known that financing for the arts in Britain suffered a great blow after the global financial crisis: public funding for cultural organizations took a hit and the art market was severely knocked. A decade on there have been some signs of a recovery, albeit patchy and fragile. But this is not so for sales of literary fiction, which have not recovered from the recession. The problem affects literary fiction in particular. Genre fiction is doing better, dominating digital sales. The arrival of the smartphone, offering a game or the latest headlines as a tempting alternative to a paperback when one is stuck on a train or waiting for a bus, has had an impact. Meanwhile, pricing of literary fiction has remained flat, so the value of the overall market has shrunk.

This matters to readers as well as to writers. Perhaps one should be content to regard the literary novel as an artform of the 19th and 20th centuries, and accept the probability that Dickens would have been pitching to Netflix had he been around now. But this is glib: of course the novel remains important. It unleashes universal truths through attention to the particular and the specific; it places the reader in other places, other times and other skins.

37 According to the paragraph, the popularization of the smartphone strikes the severest blow on the sale of _____ in particular.

① genre fiction
② paperbacks
③ historical novels
④ digital novels
⑤ hardcovers

38 The underlined "pitching to" means _____.

① making an appeal to
② pouring a curse on
③ setting up his own literary position against
④ making a great impact on
⑤ negotiating the benefit with

39 According to the passage, which of the following is correct?

① There have never been any meager signal of a recovery in art market until now.
② Genre fiction has a great benefit from digital sales.
③ The art market has dodged a great blow from the global financial crisis.
④ Pricing of literary fiction has jolted in accordance with the economic climate.
⑤ The importance of the novel form is now being replaced by that of the movie.

[40-41]

Let us recall that the Grimms first heard the tale of "Hansel and Gretel" told by Dortchen Wild some time between 1808 and 1810 and wrote it down in the Ölenberg manuscript of 1810 under the title "Das Brüderchen und das Schwesterchen" ("The Little Brother and the Little Sister"). It was very short and much different from the text that they published in the first edition of the Children and *Household Tales* in 1812. In a recent study Gerhard Neumann examines "Hansel and Gretel" as exemplary for the genre of the fairy tale and argues that Hansel and Gretel leave their home to undergo a psychological socialization in which they must realize that their mother and home are both loving and cruel and they must learn to come to terms with this ambivalence in order to survive. Neumann's study, however, disregarded the textual and intertexual development of the tale and overlooked important issues of poverty, abandonment, and patriarchy. A critical reading should focus on textual changes that the Grimms made to minimize the role of the father as victimizer and to depict a *stepmother* as aligned with a witch who wants to devour the children. Over the course of forty-seven years the Grimms kept changing the tale, adding some important motifs and incidents. Today the 1857 version, *Kinder- und Hausmarchen* (*Children's and Household Tales*) is considered to be the most definitive and "authentic." But how can any text that was first told by Dortchen Wild and that was written down, translated from the Grimms' perspective, and then edited and revised numerous times, be considered "authentic" or "original"? This question reveals a major problem — our non-recognition of translation. Translation is vital in the history of the oral folk tale. In some ways, translation is the overcoming of what Freud calls "das Unheimliche," the uncanny in life, so that which is strange becomes familiar and we feel comfortable with it. The translator takes that which is "um-*heimlich*," not homey, and transforms it into something "*heimlich*," homey, so that we are not threatened by what we otherwise cannot understand.

40 The author addresses Freud's concept of the uncanny in life to demonstrate that _____.

① "Hansel and Gretel" is an exemplary fairy tale that shows the process of children psychological socialization
② the Grimms minimize the role of the mother as victimizer in their translation of "Hansel and Gretel"
③ to translate is to interpret someone else's words as faithfully as possible according to the original intention
④ translation involves the interrogation and reiteration of a text into one's own language so that a foreign narrative becomes familiar

41 Choose the statement that can be BEST inferred from the passage.

① The Ölenberg manuscript includes the first version of "Hansel and Gretel," which is considered the most authentic text.
② Dortchen Wild told Wilhelm Grimm a story in which a mother attempts to devour her stepchildren.
③ Gerhard Neumanns study examines the middle-class attitudes regarding poverty and famine in nineteenth-century Germany.
④ The tale of "Hansel and Gretel" went through many editions in the first half of the nineteenth century.

[42-44]

The greatest invention of all must surely be writing. It is not just one of the foundations of civilization: it underpins the steady accumulation of intellectual achievement. By capturing ideas in ⓐ physical form, it allows them to travel across space and time without distortion, and thus slip the bonds of human memory and oral transmission, not to mention the whims of tyrants and the vicissitudes of history.

Its origins are prosaic: it was invented by accountants, not poets, in the 4th millennium BC, as a spur of the counting system with which farming societies kept track of agricultural goods. At first transactions were recorded by storing groups of shaped clay tokens — representing wheat, cattle or textiles — in clay envelopes. But why use tokens when pressing one into a tablet of wet clay would do instead? These impressions, in turn, were superseded by ⓑ symbols scratched or punched into the clay with a stylus. Tokens had given way to writing.

As human settlements swelled from villages to the first cities, writing was needed for administrative reasons. But it quickly became more flexible and expressive, capable of capturing the ⓒ subtleties of human thought, not just lists of rations doled out or kings long dead. And this allowed philosophers, poets and chroniclers to situate their ideas in relation to those of previous thinkers, to argue about them and elaborate upon them. Each generation could build on the ideas of its forebears, making it possible for there to be species-wide progress in philosophy, commerce, science and literature.

The amazing thing about writing, given how complicated its early systems were, is that anyone learned it at all. The reason they did is revealed in the ancient Egyptian scribal-training ⓓ texts, which emphasize the _____Ⓐ_____ of being a scribe over all other career choices, with titles like "Do Not Be Soldier, Priest or Baker", "Do Not Be a Husbandman" and "Do Not Be a Charioteer". This last text begins: "Set thine heart on being a scribe, that thou mayest direct the whole earth." The earliest scribes understood that literacy was power — a power that now extends to most of humanity, and has done more for human progress than any other invention.

42 Which of the following is different from the others?

① ⓐ physical form
② ⓑ symbols
③ ⓒ subtleties
④ ⓓ texts

43 Which of the following fits best in the blank Ⓐ?

① superiority
② flexibility
③ obscenity
④ simplicity

44 According to the passage, which of the following is true?

① People moved from villages to cities because of administrative problems.
② Early systems in the history of writing were easy for everyone to learn.
③ Most of the people in the world are illiterate these days.
④ Writing was invented for the purpose of record keeping.

[45-47]

Irish writer George Orwell's life and literature can be summarized by his faith in one thing: human decency. Although the definition can be ambiguous, it does contain a sense of fundamental dignity, and above all, honesty and tolerance. Orwell was opposed to dogma, ideological political doctrines, planned social reformation, and religious absolutism. He instead preferred to support the individual's right of expression, particularly the rights of minorities, and the freedom of press.

Orwell's sense of human decency was based on the idea of liberation and expression. It was not something that could be enjoyed passively, but must be worked for and sought after. The phrase "the secret of freedom is courage" implies that people have an obligation to be brave in their speech and courageous in their tolerance of other opinions. For Orwell, decency meant, above all else, communality, common sense, and respect for the common man. He was adamantly opposed to Marxism, which dictates that freedom is denied by equality. He believed true socialism was possible not by _____Ⓐ_____ power but by _____Ⓑ_____ fair and open discussions.

Orwell loathed abstract theories such as communism, which necessitated ideology. This can be seen in his anti-totalitarian work *Animal Farm* and his dystopia classic *1984*, in which he pursues an anti-dictatorial, anti-class, and anti-discriminatory society. Orwell believed that it was the obligation of human beings to fight against these systems not just for the sake of society, but for the progression of a society.

45 **Which of the following is the passage mainly about?**

① Literary techniques and craftsmanship of Orwell
② Philosophical viewpoints of Orwell's literature
③ Critical review of Orwell's personality
④ Development of Orwell's literary career

46 **Which of the following is LEAST likely to be opposed to by Orwell?**

① Need to limit the powers of government
② Choice of equality over freedom
③ Adherence to political ideology
④ Belief in religion without any doubts

47 **From the context, which of the following ordered pairs best fits into Ⓐ and Ⓑ?**

	Ⓐ		Ⓑ
①	relinquishing	–	encouraging
②	seizing	–	guaranteeing
③	capturing	–	restraining
④	renouncing	–	suppressing

[48-51]

One can think of literature less as some inherent quality or set of qualities displayed by certain kinds of writing than as a number of ways in which people relate themselves to writing. It would not be easy to isolate, from all that has been variously called 'literature', some constant set of inherent features. In fact, it would be as impossible as trying to identify the single distinguishing feature which all games have in common. There is no 'essence' of literature whatsoever. Any bit of writing may be read 'non-pragmatically', if that is what reading a text as literature means, just as any writing may be read 'poetically'. If I pore over the railway timetable not to discover a train connection but to stimulate in myself general reflections on the speed and complexity of modern existence, then I might be said to be reading it as literature. 'Literature' operates rather like the word 'weed'; weeds are not particular kinds of plant, but just any kind of plant which for some reason or another gardener does not want around. Perhaps 'literature' means something like the opposite: any kind of writing which for some reason or another somebody values highly. As the philosophers might say, 'literature' and 'weed' are functional rather than ontological terms: _____. 'Literature' is in this sense a purely formal, empty sort of definition. In any case, it is far from clear that we can discriminate neatly between 'practical' and 'non-practical' ways of relating ourselves to language. Reading a novel for pleasure obviously differs from reading a road sign for information, but how about reading a biology textbook to improve your mind? Is that a 'pragmatic' treatment of language or not? In many societies, 'literature' has served highly practical functions such as religious ones; distinguishing sharply between 'practical' and 'non-practical' may only be possible in a society like ours, where literature has ceased to have much practical function at all.

48 What would be the best title of the passage?

① What Is Literature?
② How to Read Literature
③ The Uses and Misuses of Literature
④ Significance of Literature

49 Choose the best expression for the blank.

① it is impossible to compare them from a linguistic point of view
② they operate as an index with which people gauge the meaning of life
③ they tell us about what we do, not about the fixed being of things
④ we cannot have direct access to their existence, regardless of their usefulness

50 According to the author, science textbooks can be read as literature when _____.

① they serve practical means of human life
② they give us valuable knowledge about the world
③ they are written in eloquent language
④ we treat them with a feeling of awe

51 Which of the following is NOT true, according to the passage?

① To some travellers, a railway timetable can be read as literature.
② Any bit of writing can be read pragmatically as well as non-pragmatically.
③ With proper efforts, the essence of literature can easily come out in the course of reading.
④ Literature has functioned differently from society to society

[52-54]

"Pidgin" and "creole" are two terms that are sometimes used interchangeably by the general public, but have specific meanings and differences in linguistics. "Pidgin" involves situations in which a population speaks several different languages and is required to communicate on a regular basis, but none of the languages of the population has primacy over the others. This situation is often found where multiple societies trade or where slave populations from multiple locations are brought into one area. The speakers create a mutual language using words from the speakers' mother tongues and an extremely flexible, simplified grammar. Most linguists do not consider a pidgin to be a _____Ⓐ_____ language, but something that is cobbled together due to circumstances and abandoned when it is no longer needed.

A creole language differs from a pidgin language by the fact that it is a native language for the majority of its speakers. Vocabulary is extensively borrowed from other languages, but the grammar often shares few traits with the languages that contributed vocabulary. Grammar and syntax are as _____Ⓑ_____ as any other long-established tongue.

If the situation that creates a pidgin endures, the first generation of children will learn pidgin as its mother tongue. There is argument about whether this immediately develops the pidgin into a creole, if it takes more than one generation to do so. Neurolinguists point out commonalities in how all humans learn language from birth and that the first generation of creole speakers create the aspects of language the pidgin was missing. Historians point out the frequent changes in vocabulary, syntax and pronunciation found in creole languages during their first 20 to 30 years, indicating that it takes more than one generation to stabilize.

Because both pidgins and creoles tend to be spoken by those in the lower echelons of a society, they are often held in contempt as degenerate forms of the parent tongue. Creole languages survive where the population of speakers retain their cultural and social identities apart from those who speak the parent languages natively. Creoles often survive even when government and economic forces work against them.

52 Which of the following fits best in the blanks Ⓐ and Ⓑ, respectively?

	Ⓐ	Ⓑ
①	fully developed	– rudimentary
②	rudimentary	– lasting
③	full-fledged	– fully developed
④	temporary	– fully understood

53 According to the passage, which of the following is NOT true?

① Pidgins are the result of contact between two or more languages.
② Neurolinguists and historians disagree about how pidgins develop to creoles.
③ People tend to have a negative attitude towards pidgins and creoles.
④ The use of creole languages will deteriorate the parent language.

54 According to the passage, which of the following is NOT true about pidgins?

① Pidgins have simpler grammar than ordinary languages.
② A pidgin language is a mother tongue for more than half of its speakers.
③ Pidgin speaker generally belong to the inferior social class.
④ A pidgin language borrows vocabulary from the contributing languages.

5강 역사 / 지리

Read the following passages and answer the questions. [01–53]

[01–02]

Reconquered by 1694, New Mexico settled into its place on the periphery of the Spanish Empire. The settlers of New Spain's northern frontier, the historian Oakah L. Jones has shown, developed a distinct culture, with basic institutions brought from Europe, yet modified to meet the challenge of different environmental conditions. The large majority of residents were neither soldiers nor missionaries, but civilian settlers — the farmer, day laborer, stockman, and artisan. With little beyond agriculture and ranching to attract settlers, New Mexico remained a remote, exposed, and isolated frontier .... similar to an island outpost. Still, with the bulk of population hard-working, individually employed small farmers and artisans, and with growing numbers of people, mixing of races and a blurring of class difference, New Mexico was anything but static. It was not the hypnotized, stagnant, sleepy backwater Anglo-Americans would later imagined it to be.

01 Which of the following is not biased view that the historian Oakah L. Jones attempts to correct?

① New Mexico had been static since it was a remote, isolated area.
② The majority of residents in the frontier of the Spanish Empire were soldiers and missionaries.
③ The settlers of New Spain's northern frontier developed a hybrid culture to adapt institutions from Europe into the area's environmental conditions.
④ Anglo-Americans thought of the New Mexico area as an empty, stagnant space.

02 Which of the following is most likely to be referred to as something "beyond agriculture and ranching to attract settlers"?

① horticulture
② gold
③ service
④ population

[03-04]

We historians have a responsibility to historical facts in general, and for criticizing the abuse of history in particular. I need to say little about the first of these responsibilities. I would not have to say anything, but for two developments. One is the current fashion for novelists to base their plots on recorded reality rather than inventing them, thus _____. The other is the rise of "postmodernist" intellectual fashions in universities, particularly in departments of literature and anthropology, which imply that all "facts" claiming objective existence are simply intellectual constructions — in short, that there is no clear difference between fact and fiction. But there is. And for historians, the ability to distinguish between the two is absolutely fundamental. We cannot invent our facts. Either Elvis Presley is dead or he isn't. The question can be answered unambiguously on the basis of evidence, in so far as reliable evidence is available.

03 윗글의 빈칸에 들어갈 말로 가장 적절한 것은?

① coming up with a new term, "historical novel"
② bridging the gap between history and literature
③ fudging the border between historical fact and fiction
④ proving that literary imagination is better than historical facts

04 윗글의 내용으로부터 유추할 수 <u>없는</u> 것은?

① The author does not like reading novels.
② The author is not favorable to postmodernism.
③ The author is certain that Elvis Presley is dead.
④ The author believes that historical facts can never be an intellectual construction.

[05-07]

　A rare, 60-page map of the world illustrated 430 years ago during the Renaissance era is finally on display. Historians know some basic details about the _____Ⓐ_____, Urbano Monte (1544–1613), who lived in Milan, Italy. Because of his family's affluence, Monte didn't have to work. Rather, he spent his time collecting books for his library and pursuing scholarly interests, including map-making. A visit to the first Japanese embassy in Europe piqued his interest in geography. So, he embarked on his map-making project to consolidate geographic knowledge. Relying on contemporary sources, he drew the map, which employs a unique Arctic perspective. This projection is very unusual but fairly accurate for its time. One of the places that seems the most distorted is Antarctica, because if you look from the top, it's going to be really big at ⓐ the bottom. In addition to drawing what he knew of the world's continents and islands, Monte speckled the map with illustrations of fantastic beasts, including unicorns, mermaids, griffins, and even a giant bird carrying an elephant. He also drew political leaders and their armed forces, including Philip II of Spain and several ships from his Spanish Armada dotting the Pacific and Atlantic oceans. Curiously, even though Monte had met with the Japanese delegation, he drew the Japanese islands horizontally instead of vertically. However, he made Japan quite large and filled in its geography, displaying his knowledge about the Land of the Rising Sun.

05 **Which of the following best fits into Ⓐ?**

① anthropologist
② geologist
③ oceanographer
④ cartographer

06 **Which of the following is closest to what ⓐ refers to?**

① The North Pole
② The South Pole
③ The Land of the Rising Sun
④ The Pacific and Atlantic oceans

07 **Which of the following is true of Monte's map?**

① It was designed for the convenience of those who would travel the world.
② It is based on field trips and is very accurate from today's standards.
③ It depicts a world populated by mythical creatures as well as prominent figures.
④ It shows a unique Antarctica-centered view of the world for the time.

[08-09]

　　In an absolute monarchy, all power comes from the King. In Versailles, Louis XIV was Master of his own house, just as he was Master of the kingdom that he governed through intermediaries that owed him everything. Excluded from affairs of government, the Nobility no longer held any real power, yet they nonetheless felt the need to appear at Court. It was there that the King dispensed favours: offices, land, titles, pension, etc. In this society founded on prestige and appearances, emulation was constant, luxury compulsory, life extravagant. In this way, Louis XIV _____Ⓐ_____. It was he who had to dominate in every way; in his eyes, the exercise and outward signs of power were one and the same thing. His residence had to be the biggest and the most beautiful and its decor loaded with symbols to his glory. The number of servants, in the noble sense of the term, assembled in the King's House, had to be the greatest and his Court had to be attended by the most people; between 3,000 and 10,000 courtiers, depending on the day. This huge crowd had to be strictly regulated. Etiquette and its constraints — who had access to the King, who had the right to sit down in his presence, who was ranked above whom, etc. — may seem pointless to us today.

　　_____Ⓑ_____, etiquette was essential, since it served to confirm ranks, the primacy of the King, in short the hierarchy within the Court. It applied to the Sovereign's most private moments — getting up in the morning, going to bed at night, mealtimes, going for walks — which were perceived as acts of State when acts of State appeared to be the King's personal acts. Another specific feature of Versailles, and something which naturally astonished foreigners, was that both gardens and the inside of the Chateau were largely open to the public. Anyone, be they a member of the Court or otherwise, could see the King when he crossed his State Apartments to go to the Chapel. All these functions — representation, government, accommodation and service — explain the layout of the place. But it was not built in a day.

08 윗글의 빈칸 Ⓐ와 Ⓑ에 들어가기에 가장 적절한 것은?

	Ⓐ	Ⓑ
①	had a hold over his courtiers	– However
②	exercised his authority on the Court	– Hence
③	had his subjects under firm control	– Moreover
④	provided dwellings for the poor	– Nevertheless

09 윗글의 제목으로 가장 적절한 것은?

① The Dwelling Place of All Power
② The Making of a Stylish Nobility
③ The King's Grand Garden and Its Vicinity
④ The Intricacy of Etiquette and Its Constraints in Court

[10-12]

History, at least in its state of ideal perfection, is a compound of poetry and philosophy. It impresses general truths on the mind by a vivid representation of particular characters and incidents. But, in fact, the two hostile elements of which it consists have never been known to form a perfect amalgamation; and at length, in our own time, they have been completely and professedly separated. Good histories, in the proper sense of the word, we have not. But we have good historical romances, and good historical essays. The imagination and the reason have made partition of a province of literature and now they hold their respective portions in severalty, instead of holding the whole in common.

To make the past present, to bring the distant near, to place us in the society of a great man or on the eminence which overlooks the field of a mighty battle, to invest with the reality of human flesh and blood beings whom we are too much inclined to consider as personified qualities in an allegory, to call up our ancestors before us with all their peculiarities of language, manners, and garb, to show us over their houses, these parts of the duty which properly belongs to the historian have been appropriated by the historical novelist. On the other hand, to extract the philosophy of history, to direct on judgement of events and men, to trace the connection of cause and effect, and to draw from the occurrences of former time general lessons of moral and political wisdom, has become the business of a distinct class of writers.

10 Which is the primary mode of composition of the passage?

① historical narration
② process analysis
③ comparison and contrast
④ cause and effect

11 In the first paragraph, which is NOT described as the two hostile pairs?

① severalty and history
② imagination and reason
③ romances and essays
④ poetry and philosophy

12 Which is the purpose of the second paragraph?

① To argue for the superiority of historical romances and what they can offer
② To describe what historical romances and historical essays each offer
③ To explain the process of making "the past present" and bringing "the distant near"
④ To evaluate which type of history is superior, leaving the answer up to the reader

[13-14]

Nestled along the northern border of Mongolia, Tuva is easy to miss. There are no direct flights from Moscow; the only ways in are turbo-prop planes from nearby Siberian cities or a long drive through the surrounding mountains. Most of the region's 308,000 people are native Tuvans, a Turkic people some of whom still practise a traditional nomadic lifestyle. [A] Shamanism and Buddhism remain more widespread than Orthodox Christianity, Russia's dominant religion. [B] As Oksana Tyulyush, artistic director of the Tuvan National Orchestra, quips, "God is a long way up and Moscow is a long way away." [C] Russians typically know little of the region, which lived under Mongol or Chinese rule for most of its history. [D] Between 1921 and 1944 Tuvans enjoyed a brief run of *de jure* independence as Tannu Tuva, or the Tuvan People's Republic, which delighted philatelists by issuing a series of oddly shaped stamps. [E] After the end of the second world war, the Soviet Union moved in, making Tuvan an official protectorate at the request of local authorities. [F] For most outsiders, Tuva is best known for its music: *khoomei*, or throat singing, a trance-inducing drone created when one singer hits several notes simultaneously. *Khoomei* is inspired by nature, as performers seek to channel the waters, winds and beasts of their surroundings. In Tuva harking back to tradition has helped fill the void left after the Soviet collapse.

13 Which one is NOT true of Tuva?

① It is surrounded by mountains.
② It used to be ruled by China and Mongolia.
③ It once was an independent country.
④ It is famous for its traditional throat singing.
⑤ It was invaded by Russia after the second world war.

14 When the passage is divided into three paragraphs, which would be most appropriate boundary?

① [A] and [C]
② [B] and [E]
③ [C] and [E]
④ [C] and [F]
⑤ [D] and [F]

[15-16]

When Queen Victoria died in 1901, a reaction developed against many of the achievements of the previous century; this reinforced the sense that the Victorian age was a distinct period. In the earlier decades of the twentieth century writers took pains to separate themselves from the Victorians. It was then the fashion for most literary critics to treat their Victorian predecessors as somewhat absurd creatures, stuffily complacent prigs with whose way of life they had little in common. Writers of Georgian period (1911–36) took great delight in puncturing overinflated Victorian balloons, as Lytton Strachey did in Eminent Victorians. Their witty descriptions not only identify a distinguishing quality of Victorian life and literature but reveal the author's distaste for its smothering profusion.

The Georgian reaction against the Victorians is now only a matter of the history of taste, but its aftereffects still sometimes crop up when the term Victorian is employed in an exclusively pejorative sense, as prudish or old-fashioned. Contemporary historians and critics now find the Victorian period an example of a richly multi-faceted society struggling with the issues and problems we identify with modernism. So, to give the period the single designation Victorian _____. For a period almost seventy years in length, we can hardly expect generalizations to be uniformly applicable.

15 What is the best expression for the blank?

① ignores its problems
② reduces its complexity
③ elicits sympathetic reflections
④ wipes out historical consciousness

16 Which of the following is NOT true according to the passage?

① Victorians were the people who deserve a harsh criticism.
② Victorians had their own peculiar attitudes and behaviors.
③ The term Victorian had a pejorative nuance to many writers of Georgian period.
④ Most critics of early 20th century distanced themselves from their Victorian predecessors.

[17-18]

For centuries the idea of two men facing each other in a duel has seemed anachronistic. Guy de Maupassant, a 19th-century writer, declared it to be "the last of our unreasonable customs". Two centuries before that Louis XIV, king of France, tried to outlaw it as a feudal archaism. Yet despite this, the literature of the 19th and even the early 20th century is peppered with accounts of swashbuckling men. Why? In the early 18th century many writers depicted men who fought duels as hot-headed. By the 19th century, although it still seemed to spring from an older, medieval age, duelling was regarded as quite glamorous. In "The Memoirs of Barry Lyndon, Esq"(1844) by William Makepeace Thackeray the hero rails against "cowardly pistols" and harks back to the "honourable and manly weapon of gentlemen". And compared with the burgeoning violence at the start of the 20th century, duels could also seem remarkably measured. A character in a G.K. Chesterton novel from 1908 prevents a suspected anarchist from exploding a bomb by challenging him to a duel. After two world wars, though, the glamour had begun to fade. In Evelyn Waugh's "Officers and Gentlemen" (1955) one character admits he would laugh if he was challenged to a duel.

17 The best title of the passage would be _____.

① Modern Parallels to Duel
② Duel in Literature
③ Origin of Duel
④ Duel as an Old-fashioned Folly
⑤ History of Violence

18 The underlined expression implies that the duel _____.

① has been legalized
② has almost disappeared
③ is a random act of anarchism
④ is a lower form of aggression
⑤ is a form of ordered violence

[19-21]

Home to a traumatic but rich history, stunning scenery, and some of the continent's most welcoming people, Colombia is ⓐ a natural draw for travellers to South America. Despite its four-decade-long civil war, improved security conditions have led to a sharp increase in tourism. Foreigners and Colombians alike are now far more able to explore this thrilling paradise of cloud-forested mountains, palm-fringed beaches, and gorgeous colonial cities. The only country in South America to border both the Pacific and the Caribbean, Colombia offers a huge range of ecosystems, from the Amazon rainforest to snowcapped mountains to tropical islands. From gilded Caribbean coasts and cobblestoned colonial charm to clusters of coffee plantations, Colombia encapsulates Latin America in a single country. Don't miss the rejuvenated metropolis, Gabriel Garcia Marquez's magical Cartagena. Even more shrouded in mystery is San Agustin, where more than 500 life-sized ancient sculpted statues dot the surrounding countryside. Colombia's varied terrain is fertile ground for outdoor adventurers to dive, climb, raft, and trek. Some of South America's most iconic trekking is here. Ciudad Perdida is a multiday jungle walk to the ancient ruins of the Tayrona civilization, while numerous ascents inside national parks place fearless hikers on the highest reaches of the Andes. Providencia's world-class reef spells aquatic heaven for scuba divers, and whale-watchers on the Pacific coast can see majestic humpback whales in the wild.

19 Which of the following is NOT an example of ⓐ?

① Four-decade-long civil war
② A cluster of coffee plantations
③ The Amazon rainforest
④ A jungle walk to ancient ruins

20 Which of the following is the passage mainly about?

① Natural history of Colombia
② Places to visit in Colombia
③ Colombian national security
④ Sporting opportunities in Colombia

21 Which of the following is NOT stated or implied by the passage?

① Colombia used to be an unsafe place to travel.
② Colombia has little in common with its neighbors.
③ You can hike up to the top of the Andes.
④ Colombia is both a Caribbean and Pacific country.

[22-24]

　　In the seven-year battle since 2001 to set Afghanistan back on its feet after more than two decades at war, the country's historical sites have been ignored. Its ancient heritage has fallen victim to an epidemic of pillaging on par with the depredations of Genghis Khan's army that in 1220 left the city of Balkh in ruins. Unauthorized excavation on the scale of organized crime is carried out by professional gangs supported by local warlords and even government officials, with ties to the international black market in antiquities. While estimates of this illicit trade vary widely, government authorities put it at as high as $4 billion, roughly on par with the country's drug trade. This hurts historians and archaeologists who are just starting to understand the country's important role in the development of Central Asian civilization. The mid-20th century blossoming of archaeological research in Afghanistan uncovered treasures of unimaginable value. Those findings also ignited gold fever in the country, inspiring hundreds of freelance "archaeologists" to dig for treasures of their own, with a black market value that far exceeded a farmer's annual earnings. Then, starting in 1979, war uprooted the fragile government protections and thousands of priceless artifacts were spirited out of the country. But it was the fall of the Taliban in December 2001, and the subsequent power vacuum, that unleashed the most devastating rape of Afghanistan's heritage to date. _____ poverty and war are what kept these sites safe. In times of conflict, civilians were afraid to leave home, and the fear of land mines kept many from digging. Now that a nationwide campaign to clear the mines is bearing fruit, looters are returning to sites that have been untouched for years, and are even discovering new ones.

22 The best title of the passage would be _____.

① Decline of Illicit Trades in Afghanistan
② History of Treasure Hunt in Afghanistan
③ Afghanistan's Nationwide Campaign against Land Mines
④ Historians and Afghanistan's Cultural Heritage
⑤ Afghanistan's Ongoing War on Militancy

23 Which of the following is most appropriate for the blank?

① Consequently
② Still
③ Ironically
④ By contrast
⑤ Predictably

24 According to the passage, which of the following is true?

① The farmers sustained the most damage from the professional looters.
② The decline of Taliban forces had positive effects on the national efforts to preserve historical artifacts.
③ The successful campaign to clear land mines encouraged the looters to strike again.
④ Unlike amateur archaeologists, professional looters were supported by drug trades in the nation.
⑤ The government officials did their best to prevent unauthorized excavation.

[25-26]

By the time Nazism arose in Germany in the 1930s, anti-Semitism was nothing new — not by a long shot. The Jewish people had suffered a long history of prejudice and persecution. And although Nazis perpetuated centuries-old lies, this time those lies would have their most devastating effects. Like never before, anti-Semitism was manifested in a sweeping national policy known as "the Final Solution," which sought to eliminate Jews from the face of the Earth.

To accomplish this, Adolf Hitler and his minister of propaganda, Joseph Goebbels, launched a massive campaign to convince the German people that the Jews were their enemies. Having taken over the press, they spread lies blaming Jews for all of Germany's problems, including the loss of World War I. One of them was an outrageous lie dating back to the Middle Ages, which claimed that Jews engaged in the ritual killings of Christian children and used their blood in the unleavened bread eaten at Passover.

Using Jews as the scapegoat, Hitler and his cronies orchestrated what they called "the big lie." This theory states that no matter how big the lie is (or more precisely, because it's so big), people will believe it if you repeat it enough. Everyone tells small lies, Hitler reasoned, but few have the guts to tell colossal lies. In other words, because a big lie is so unlikely, people will come to accept it.

25 Which of the following would be the best title for this passage?

① The Nazi's Big Lie
② The Jews and World War I
③ Emergence of Nazism
④ History of Racism

26 Which of the following is NOT stated about Hitler and the Nazis?

① They believed that the bigger the lie, the more likely it would be accepted.
② They invented many new lies in order to intensify hatred against the Jews.
③ They recycled falsehoods that had been widely circulating for centuries.
④ They claimed Jews killed Christian children and mixed their blood in bread.

[27-28]

Osiris, also called Usir, is one of the most important gods of ancient Egypt. The origin of Osiris is obscure; he was a local god of Busiris, in Lower Egypt, and may have been a personification of underworld fertility. By about 2400 BCE, however, Osiris clearly played a double role: he was both a god of fertility and the embodiment of the dead and resurrected king. This dual role was in turn combined with the Egyptian concept of divine kingship: the king at death became Osiris, god of the underworld; and the dead king's son, the living king, was identified with Horus, a god of the sky. Osiris and Horus were thus father and son. The goddess Isis was the mother of the king and was thus the mother of Horus and consort of Osiris. The god Seth was considered the murderer of Osiris and adversary of Horus.

Osiris was not only ruler of the dead but also the power that granted all life from the underworld, from sprouting vegetation to the annual flood of the Nile River. From about 2000 BCE onward it was believed that every man, not just the deceased kings, became associated with Osiris at death. This identification with Osiris, however, did not imply resurrection, for even Osiris did not rise from the dead. Instead, it signified the renewal of life both in the next world and through one's descendants on Earth. In this universalized form, Osiris's cult spread throughout Egypt, often joining with the cults of local fertility and underworld deities.

The oldest known depiction of Osiris dates back to about 2300 BCE, but representations of him are rare before the New Kingdom (1539–1075 BCE), when he was shown in an archaizing form as a mummy with his arms crossed on his breast, one hand holding a crook, the other a flail. On his head was the crown, composed of the white crown of Upper Egypt and two ostrich feathers.

27 Which of the following would be best for the title?

① The Familial Lineage of Osiris
② The Death of Osiris
③ The Mummification of Osiris
④ The Cult of Osiris in Ancient Egypt

28 Which of the following is NOT true?

① Osiris first appeared as one of the local gods in Lower Egypt.
② Seth murdered Osiris, who was succeeded by Horus.
③ As a symbol for resurrection, Osiris came back to life from the dead.
④ One form of the representations of Osiris was that of a mummy in the New Kingdom.

[29-30]

Perhaps the single most startling fact about America is that, alone among the modern nations that have become world powers, it did so while butted up against three thousand miles of howling wilderness populated by Stone-Age tribes. From King Philip's War in the 1600s until the last Apache cattle raids across the Rio Grande in 1924, America waged an ongoing campaign against a native population that had barely changed, technologically, in 15,000 years. Over the course of three centuries, America became a booming industrial society, while the Indians lived communally in mobile or semi-permanent encampments.

The proximity of these two cultures over the course of many generations presented both sides with a stark choice about how to live. It may say something about human nature that a surprising number of Americans — mostly men — wound up joining Indian society rather than staying in their own. They emulated Indians, married them, were adopted by them, and on some occasions even fought alongside them. And the opposite almost never happened: Indians almost never ran away to join white society. Emigration always seemed to go from the civilized to the tribal, and it left Western thinkers flummoxed about how to explain such an apparent rejection of their society.

"When an Indian child has been brought up among us, taught our language and habituated to our customs," Benjamin Franklin wrote to a friend in 1753, "[yet] if he goes to see his relations and make one Indian ramble with them, there is no persuading him ever to return." On the other hand, Franklin continued, white captives who were liberated from the Indians _____Ⓐ_____: "Tho' ransomed by their friends, and treated with all imaginable tenderness to prevail with them to stay among the English, yet in a short time they become disgusted with our manner of life ... and take the first good opportunity of escaping again into the woods."

29 What is the main idea of the passage above?

① Americans succeeded in building a great civilization in a wilderness occupied by hostile Indians.
② Indians treated white Americans with great deal of sympathy and kindness.
③ Americans who happened to live among Indians were repulsed by their uncivilized customs.
④ Many Americans made a choice of leaving civilization to live among Indians.
⑤ The repudiation of civilized life was a cause for concern among cultural elites in America.

30 Which expression best completes Ⓐ?

① showed a curious tendency to be aggressive
② were happy to come back
③ were almost impossible to keep at home
④ slowly embraced their restored life
⑤ were hard to please

[31-33]

When and why did things start to change? The latter half of the 17th century saw the start of a backlash against extreme Puritanism, particularly among the upper classes who observed the louche goings on at court, led by the libidinous Charles II. But the reasons for the first sexual revolution were complex and varied. The migration of people to big cities had made the bonds of traditional morality much harder to enforce, while the explosion of mass-printed media both spread ideas and exploited prurient interest in sexual shenanigans. Exploration also had an influence, as travellers returned with tales of very different sexual cultures. But the key driver was the spread of nonconformity, which eroded the church's authority. Samuel Johnson, a high Tory Anglican, spoke for many in 1750 when he opined that "every man should regulate his actions by his own conscience." The upper-middle-class members of the Beggar's Benison club in Scotland, founded in 1732, apparently thought nothing of arranging meetings where they could drink, sing and fondle naked women. Yet it would be wrong to view late-18th-century attitudes towards sex as a prototype of our own. Sexual liberation was largely confined to the ranks of well-to-do chaps. It was generally assumed that while it was "natural" for men to pursue sexual opportunity, women were instinctively more virtuous.

31 The best title of the above passage would be _____.

① Sexual Persecution in Early Modern England
② Sex and Punishment in the 18th century England
③ How Morality Became Personal in the 18th century England
④ Sexual Freedom of Women in the 18th century England
⑤ How to Police Sexuality in the 18th century England

32 According to the passage, which of the following is NOT a factor contributing to the first sexual revolution?

① urbanization
② religious tolerance
③ circulation of ideas
④ corruption of women
⑤ decline of the Puritanism

33 The sexual liberation in the late 18th century was limited to _____.

① the working class
② urban people
③ wealthy men
④ educated men
⑤ politicians

[34-36]

The history of cosmetics spans at least 6,000 years and is present in almost every society on Earth. Archaeological evidence of cosmetics dates from ancient Egypt and Greece. It is known that some women in ancient Rome invented makeup formulas to whiten the skin. During the 1900s, makeup was not popular because it was still mostly used by the 'ladies of the night'. Around 1910, makeup became fashionable in the United States and Europe owing to the influence of ballet and theater stars. During World War II, cosmetics were in short supply because their basic ingredients were diverted into war supply. _____Ⓐ_____, at this time when they were restricted, lipstick, powder, and face cream were most desired, and most experimentation was carried out for the postwar period. This is because cosmetics developers rightly predicted that the war would result in a phenomenal boom afterwards. During the 1960s and 1970s, many women influenced by feminism _____Ⓑ_____ to cosmetics' role in the second-class status of women, making them mere sex objects. Although modern makeup has been used mainly by women, an increasing number of men are using cosmetics to enhance their own facial features. Cosmetics brands are releasing products such as concealers especially created for men. There is some controversy over this, however, as many feel that men who wear makeup are neglecting traditional gender roles. But others view this as a sign of ongoing gender equality since they feel that _____Ⓒ_____.

34. Which one of the following ordered pairs best fits into Ⓐ and Ⓑ?

	Ⓐ		Ⓑ
①	Ironically	–	objected
②	In fact	–	adhered
③	Sadly	–	yielded
④	Naturally	–	corresponded

35. Which of the following best fits into Ⓒ?

① men should purchase cosmetics for women
② men are free to buy cosmetics as long as they remain masculine
③ men have long purchased their own cosmetics
④ men also have the right to use cosmetics if women do

36. According to the passage, which of the following is NOT true?

① Actors contributed to the popularity of makeup in the 1910s.
② Formulas to whiten the skin first appeared in Greece.
③ There are concealers exclusively produced for men.
④ There came a boom in cosmetics after World War II.

[37-39]

The north Quebecois town of Tadoussac is caught between mountain and ragged shoreline, just where the fresh Saguenay Fjord runs into the warm, salty waters of the St. Lawrence River. Each year, from May to October, it swells with tourists hoping to glimpse the baleen whales that gather to gorge on the krill that thrive at this aquatic intersection.

Those who deign to drift inland, however, will meet with a wildlife-watching experience of a different kind — intimate, inexpensive and decidedly Canadian. For toiling away in Tadoussac's forgotten backwoods is the humble beaver, face of the 5-cent piece. Without him, the history of this former French trading post, founded in 1600 by reason of a fur monopoly, would hardly be the same.

Neither would the rowdy, red-roofed Maison Majorique, the town's only youth hostel. Free beaver-watching tours leave from its reception every day at 5 p.m., when the web-footed rodents wake to work through the night. For 21 years, the excursions have been led by the same woodsman. His face capped with a nest of frenzied white hair reaches down into a matching beard. Coco is as coarse and weather-beaten as the wetlands he knows so well. "I prefer the forest to the sea," he offers up in thorny French. (He'll translate into an even thornier English upon request.) Partakers begin at L'Anse-à-l'Eau, a still lake ringed by dense firs and five log-heaped beaver homes. The wearying walk around the water takes about two hours with stops. Alone, Coco hikes the trail in 45 minutes.

37 What would be the main topic of the above passage?

① A Remote Place in Canada
② Splendor of Baleen Whales
③ Forest vs. Shoreline
④ Beaver Watching
⑤ How to Enjoy Wild Life

38 Which is NOT true of the above passage?

① Many tourists gather to see baleen whales.
② There is only one hostel in this town.
③ Beavers are more popular than whales.
④ The picture of beaver is on the Canadian 5-cent coin.
⑤ Coco is a bilingual guide.

39 What does the underlined part imply?

① Maison Majorique hostel is not that old.
② The hostel was not built for French fur traders either.
③ The youth hostel building is another pleasure to look at.
④ Without beaver, there wouldn't be many hostel guests.
⑤ The Place was not forgotten either by the hostel guests.

[40-42]

The mummified body of an ancient Egyptian pharaoh has been studied for the first time in millennia after being _____Ⓐ_____ "unwrapped." The mummy of Amenhotep I, who ruled from 1525 to 1504 BC, was found at a site in Deir el-Bahari 140 years ago. But archaeologists have refrained from opening it in order to preserve the exquisite face mask and bandages. Computed tomography (CT) scans have now revealed previously unknown information about the pharaoh and his burial. "We got to see the face of the king that has been wrapped for more than 3,000 years," Dr. Sahar Saleem, professor of radiology at Cairo University, told the BBC. She said the first thing that had struck her was how Amenhotep I's facial features resembled those of his father Ahmose I, the first pharaoh of ancient Egypt's 18th Dynasty, with a narrow chin, a small narrow nose, curly hair, and mildly protruding upper teeth.

The researchers also established that Amenhotep I was approximately 169 centimeters tall and that he was about 35 years old when he died. Dr. Saleem said the scans showed he was in very good physical condition and in good health at the time of his death, with no signs of any wounds or disfigurement due to disease. That suggested he died as a result of an infection or a virus.

The researchers were able to gain insights about the mummification and burial of Amenhotep I, including that he was the first pharaoh to have his forearms folded across his chest and that, unusually, his brain was not removed. They also concluded that his mummy was "lovingly repaired" by priests of the 21st Dynasty, which ruled about four centuries after this death. The scans showed that the mummy suffered from multiple post-mortem injuries that were likely to have been inflicted by grave robbers.

40 Which of the following best fits in Ⓐ?

① digitally
② forcefully
③ expectedly
④ artistically

41 Which of the following is true?

① The mummy of Amenhotep I was first discovered four hundreds years ago.
② Researchers did not open the mummified body right after the discovery.
③ The brain of Amenhotep I was removed and well preserved.
④ Amenhotep I had been suffering from serious health problems.

42 Which of the following is best for the title?

① The List of Unknown Egyptian Mummies
② The Discovery of Mummified Amenhotep I
③ The History of Pharaoh Burial Sites
④ The Revealed Information of Amenhotep I

[43-46]

[A] During Queen Victoria's sixty-four year reign (1837–1901), the British Empire, led by an array of great statesmen and supported by great industrial expansion, grew to a size so vast that "the sun never sets upon it." Victoria's long reign saw many changes in British institutions and the British "way of life." Her rejection of the amusements and life of the aristocracy enabled the common people to identify themselves with this simple wife and widow, which led to a revival of popular support for the monarchy. Above all, her essentially middle-class views and life-style, combined with the rise of the middle classes themselves, led to an affirmation of values — the paternalistic integrity and discipline of the family, the sobriety and puritanism of public life — which in later years came to be known as "Victorian values" to which the Thatcher government of the 1980s wished to return.

[B] At the same time as the middle classes were expanding in Victorian Britain, so were the working classes. The Industrial Revolution had now entered its second stage: new industries were developed, new factories were built, Britain's products were exported all over the world, and Britain became known as "the workshop of the world."

[C] Life in the new factories and towns was one of terrible hardship. Men, women, and children worked fifteen or sixteen hours a day in dangerous, unhealthy conditions for poor wages and lived in dirty, dreary slums, so vividly described by Charles Dickens in the novel *Bleak House*.

[D] Meanwhile the working classes were becoming organized. While the ideas of Karl Marx never won much support among British workers (even though Marx himself studied and wrote most of his works while living in London), the idea of socialism was nevertheless a potent force in late Victorian Britain. In the last quarter of the century there was a massive increase in trade unionism and in 1893 the founding of the Labour Party, led by Keir Hardie, gave the proletariat a greater voice in Parliament.

43 According to paragraph [A], which of the following can be inferred as being the value to which the Thatcher government of the 1980s wished to return?

① sexual liberation
② the dignity of human rights
③ political emancipation
④ gender equality
⑤ the temperance of public life

44 Which of the following can the underlined word dreary in paragraph [C] be best replaced with?

① dried
② gloomy
③ diminished
④ opaque
⑤ flustered

45 According to paragraph [C], the novel *Bleak House*, by Charles Dickens, is mentioned because _____.

① it triggered the middle classes to fight against the injustices and wrongdoings of being practiced against them by the ruling capitalist classes, based upon the ideas of Karl Marx
② it vividly described the terrible hardship of the working classes, whose size drastically decreased in late Victorian Britain
③ it admirably exposed the terrible working and living conditions of the working classes in Victorian Britain
④ it portrayed the collaborative relationship between the middle classes and the working classes in the early period of the Industrial Revolution
⑤ it embodied the pride of Great Britain as "the workshop of the world," while also focusing on the horrible labor conditions of the working classes in late Victorian Britain

46 According to the above passage, which of the following is true?

① Karl Marx was an insightful researcher of the British economy although he had never studied and lived in London.
② The ideas of Karl Marx were enthusiastically embraced by British workers in the 19th century.
③ Queen Victoria attempted to strengthen her royal authority by simultaneously practicing the aristocratic way of life and identifying herself with the middle class.
④ The Industrial Revolution originated in late Victorian Britain.
⑤ The idea of socialism was highly influential in late Victorian Britain.

[47-50]

[A] Progress in knowledge was painfully slow as long as the racial memory was transmitted only by oral tradition. For example, some primitive man or woman discovered long ago that the great enemy, fire, could be forced to obey and to make life better. Without any organized means of communication, it may have taken many generations for this new knowledge to become universal. With the invention of writing, the process of building up a body of knowledge available, especially, to all human beings accelerated. Today, devices for storing and recalling the accumulated knowledge of the human race, such as computers, are themselves subject to progressive efforts to improve them.

[B] These things being so, the history of mankind is the history of the progress and developments of human knowledge. Universal history, at least, which deals not so much with the deeds of individuals or even of nations ⓐ as with the accomplishments and the failures of the race as a whole, is no other than an account of how mankind's knowledge has grown and changed over the ages.

[C] Universal history, thus conceived as the history of knowledge, is not a chronology of every discovery and invention ever made. Many of them are ultimately ⓑ of little value. Instead, it is and must be the story, told in the broadest and most general terms, of the significant new knowledge that humanity has acquired at various epochs and added to the growing store. It is also the story of how knowledge has changed more than it has grown, and how major elements of knowledge have been given up or lost completely because these seemed irrelevant to a ⓒ succeeding age.

[D] For example, the fall of the Roman Empire was a nearly universal _____Ⓐ_____, resulting in misery and suffering everywhere in the European world. Despite that, or perhaps because of it, new kinds of knowledge emerged in the following centuries. Most of that new knowledge has not ⓓ endured, but it remains as an example of a remarkable way of life that we have discarded, but ⓔ which it is possible that we may some day return.

47 Which of the following would be the best title for the above passage?

① The Definition of Universal History
② The Significance of the Roman Empire
③ The Unremitting Progress in Knowledge
④ Obstacles to Transmission of Knowledge
⑤ The Importance of Written Language

48 Which of the following can be inserted into the blank Ⓐ in paragraph [D]?

① capitalism
② cataclysm
③ historicism
④ salvation
⑤ catalyst

49 Choose the underlined word or phrase that must be changed for the sentence to be correct.

① ⓐ as with
② ⓑ of little value
③ ⓒ succeeding age
④ ⓓ endured
⑤ ⓔ which

50 According to the above passage, which of the following is true?

① Universal history has accumulated every form of knowledge since the invention of written language.
② Universal history is different from one nation to another even though they sometimes overlap.
③ European people constructed their own unique universal history following the fall of the Roman Empire.
④ The invention of writing accelerated the transmission of knowledge, which helps the West dominate.
⑤ Even though a certain kind of knowledge lost its power on the world, it is possible for it to regain its power generations later.

[51-53]

Set high in a remote Himalayan mountain range stands the Pangboche Buddhist monastery. During heavy snowstorms, it can be found only by travelers who listen for the monks' ceremonial horns. The walls are lined with traditional Nepalese paintings depicting the treacherous tracks to the monastery.

And among them are pictures of the legendary ape-like creature we refer to as the Yeti. This might seem fanciful until you learn that, for many years, a shriveled hand (about the size of an adult human's, with long, fat fingers and curling nails) was also on display in the monastery — and revered by the monks, who believed it protected them from bad luck.

I would know nothing about this story were it not for the fact that while walking around a collection of human and primate skeletons at the Royal College of Surgeons in London three years ago, I came across a withered finger which had only recently been found in the vaults of the College's Hunterian Museum. It was labeled "a Yeti finger from Pangboche hand." What was the story behind this finger, I wondered, and how did it end up in London? Where was the rest of the "Pangboche hand?" And what truth was there behind the label's claim that this finger belonged to the Yeti of ancient legend? The myth has _____Ⓐ_____ that the Yeti, or Abominable Snowman, is a vast creature which inhabits the Himalayan regions of Nepal and Tibet, where tales about Yetis have been passed down through generations.

Fossil remains found there from the Pleistocene age (2,500,000 to 11,700 years ago) reveal skeletons of a creature called the Gigantopithecus, or great ape, which became extinct 300,000 years ago. These ⓐ towering primates reached about 10ft in height and weighed half a ton. It is possible they lived alongside our human ancestors in what are now China, India and Vietnam. Yet the scientific community generally regards this species simply as a large, extinct ape — and the Yeti as nothing more than a legend.

51 Which of the following fits best in the blank Ⓐ?

① this
② that
③ it
④ them

52 Which of the following is closest in meaning to ⓐ towering?

① big
② hairy
③ heavy
④ robust

53 According to the passage, which of the following is NOT true?

① Pangboche is hard to reach in inclement weather.
② One of the Yeti's fingers is on display in London.
③ The Yeti is arguably a distant relative to humans.
④ The fossil remains prove the Yeti's current existence.

6강 철학 / 종교

Read the following passages and answer the questions. [01-52]

[01-02]

In rapidly modernizing societies, if the traditional religion is unable is adapt to the requirements of modernization, the potential exists for the spread of Western Christianity and Islam. In these societies the most successful protagonists of Western culture are not neo-classical economists or crusading democrats or multinational corporation executives. They are and most likely will continue to be Christian missionaries. Neither Adam Smith nor Thomas Jefferson will meet the psychological, emotional, moral, and social needs of urban migrants and first-generation secondary school graduate. Jesus Christ may not meet them either, but He is likely to have a better chance. In the long run, however, Mohammed wins out. Christianity spreads primarily by conversion, Islam by conversation and _____. The percentage of Christians in the world peaked at about 30 percent in the 1980s, leveled off, is now declining, and will probably approximate about 25 percent of the world's population by 2025. As a result of their extremely high rates of population growth, the proportion of Muslims in the world will continue to increase dramatically, amounting to 20 percent of the world's population about the turn of the century, surpassing the number of Christians some years later, and probably accounting for about 30 percent of the world's population by 2025.

01 Choose the one that best fills in the blank.

① modernization
② degeneration
③ education
④ reproduction

02 Which of the following CANNOT be inferred according to the passage above?

① Christianity and Islam are likely to play an important role in rapidly modernizing societies
② The social needs of urban migrants will probably be met by multinational corporation executives.
③ The percentage of Christians in the world was higher in the 1980's than in the 2000's.
④ By 2025, the number of Muslims in the world will have surpassed that of Christians.

[03-04]

Ramadan is the ninth month of the Islamic calender, and is observed by Muslims worldwide as a month of fasting _____ Ⓐ _____ the first revelation of the Quran to Muhammad according to Islamic belief. This annual observance is regarded as one of the Five Pillars of Islam. The month lasts 29-30 days based on the visual sightings of the crescent moon, according to numerous biographical accounts compiled in the hadiths. The word, Ramadan, means scorching heat or dryness. Fasting is obligatory for adult an illness, travelling, elderly, pregnant, breastfeeding, diabetic, chronically ill or menstruating. Muslims who live in regions with a natural phenomenon such as the midnight sun or polar night should follow the timetable of Mecca, but the more commonly accepted opinion is that Muslims in those areas should follow the timetable of the closest country to them in which night can be distinguished from day. While fasting from dawn until sunset, Muslims refrain from consuming food, drinking liquids, smoking, and engaging in sexual relations. Muslims are also instructed _____ Ⓑ _____ sinful behavior that may negate the reward of fasting, such as false speech (insulting, cursing, lying, etc.) and fighting except in self-defense.

03 윗글의 빈칸 Ⓐ, Ⓑ에 들어갈 말로 가장 적절한 것은?

	Ⓐ	Ⓑ
①	to observe	– to reflect on
②	to overlook	– to leave off
③	to celebrate	– to stand for
④	to disregard	– to get around
⑤	to commemorate	– to refrain from

04 윗글의 내용과 일치하지 <u>않는</u> 것은?

① There is a relation between Ramadan and the visibility of the crescent moon.
② Fasting during Ramadan can be optional under certain conditions.
③ The timetable of Mecca has been respected by Muslims in other countries.
④ Cursing and fighting are prohibited during Ramadan, but in some cases, they are permitted.
⑤ Muslims must not take food or liquids after sunset during Ramadan.

[05-06]

The dispute between rationalism and empiricism takes place within epistemology, the branch of philosophy devoted to studying the nature, sources and limits of knowledge. We can form true beliefs just by making some lucky guesses. How we can gain warranted beliefs is unclear. Moreover, to know the world, we must think about it, and it is not clear how we gain the concepts we use in thought or what assurance, if any, we have that the ways in which we divide up the world using our concepts correspond to divisions that actually exist.

Rationalists claim that there are significant ways in which our concepts and knowledge are gained independently of sense experience. Empiricists claim that sense experience is the ultimate source of all our concepts and knowledge. Rationalists argue that there are cases where <u>the content of our knowledge outstrips the information that sense experience can provide</u>. Empiricists present complementary lines of thought. They develop accounts of how experience provides the information that rationalists cite, insofar as we have it in the first place.

05 Choose the one closest in meaning to the underlined part.

① experience is bound to produce information that distorts knowledge
② we may attain knowledge that surpasses the data garnered from experience
③ experience alone is sufficient to yield knowledge
④ it becomes impossible to acquire knowledge from raw experience

06 According to the passage, which of the following is not a question asked in epistemology?

① what kinds of knowledge are valuable
② how we can ascertain the truth of a belief
③ how valid our categorization of the world is
④ where our conceptual tools come from

[07-08]

In the fifth century B.C., the Greek philosophers tried to overcome the sharp contrast between the views of Parmenides and Heraclitus. In order to reconcile the idea of unchangeable Being of Parmenides with that of eternal Becoming of Heraclitus, they assumed that the Being is manifest in certain invariable substances, the mixture and separation of which gives rise to the changes in the world. This led to the concept of the atom, the smallest invisible unit of matter, which found its clearest expression in the philosophy of Democritus. The Greek atomists drew a clear line between spirit and matter, picturing matter as being made of several basic building blocks. These were purely passive and intrinsically dead particles moving in the void. The cause of their motion was not explained, but was often associated with external forces which were assumed to be of spiritual origin and fundamentally different from matter. In subsequent centuries, this image became an essential element of Western thought, of dualism between mind and matter, between body and soul.

07 What is the passage mainly about?

① The origin of Western dualism
② The main problem of Western thought
③ The relationship between sprit and matter
④ The uncanny world of the Greek philosophers

08 Which of the following is NOT true, according to the passage?

① Parmenides and Heraclitus were two opposing poles of the Greek thought.
② Parmenides and Heraclitus once worked together to reconcile their ideas.
③ The Greek atomists believed in the two different worlds of spirit and matter.
④ The tradition of Western thought has been largely embedded in the dualistic world view.

[09-10]

It is 400 years since Galileo published his *Sidereus Nuncius*, the starry messenger or astronomical message, a book which gravely downgraded humanity's place in the universe and at the same time revealed to it some of the mysteries previously hidden by the blindfold of doctrine. In that small volume he showed that the firmament was crowded with stars invisible to the naked eye, that the moon was rugged rather than the smooth, ludicrously perfect object of the churchmen, and that the Earth was not unique in having a moon and had therefore become a candidate for demotion from its cosmic egotism. The explosive little volume was the only book Galileo wrote in Latin. Everything else was in Tuscan. In his wittily challenging *Galileo: Watcher of the Skies*, David Wootton argues that Galileo was (or said he was) primarily concerned with what his fellow Florentines thought about him. And when his works came to be banned, Galileo feared they would be forgotten in Italy, whether or not they were being read in Latin elsewhere in Europe. Tuscan was a language which could be read by the educated laity throughout northern Italy; Latin was the language of the universities, where Aristotelian thinking ruled.

09 **Which of the following would best replace the underlined word in the passage?**

① diversion
② relegation
③ accretion
④ rudiment

10 **Which of the following CANNOT be inferred from the above passage?**

① *Sidereus Nuncius* debunked the idea of human supremacy in the universe.
② Galileo was afraid of being overlooked by his contemporary Florentines.
③ The publication of *Sidereus Nuncius* rejuvenated the Aristotelian conceptions of the universe.
④ Latin was the primary medium for scholarly research and writing in Galileo's age.

[11-12]

Not too many Koreans would answer "Yes" if they were asked whether they think Confucianism is a religion. Koreans do not regard it as religion. However, if you were to shift the question a bit and ask whether they would practice filial piety, the most integral part of Confucianism, almost all Koreans would not hesitate to answer "Yes." For Koreans, Confucianism is their life itself, rather than a particular teaching that is separate from their daily activities. This is true even in the younger generations of today. They strongly dislike Confucianism, and believe it is quite pre-modern. In their heads, Confucianism is an ideology of the past dynasty that _____Ⓐ_____ no relevance to modern generations. However, delve a bit into their life, and one can find that they are still living deep in the value system of Confucianism. In Korea, for example, almost everyone follows the age-hierarchy protocol. When meeting a person for the first time, Koreans compare their age to decide who is higher or lower in ranking. In schools, there is no need to compare their age since the school year is already a/an _____Ⓑ_____ of age. Hence, the students of lower school year address the higher school-year students in familial terms, such as "older brother," or "older sister," and use a respectful register when speaking to them.

11 Which best fits into the blanks Ⓐ and Ⓑ?

	Ⓐ		Ⓑ
①	shows	–	donator
②	hides	–	director
③	bears	–	indicator
④	contains	–	moderator

12 Which is the best title of the passage?

① Importance of Age in Social Relationship
② Deep-Rooted Confucianism in the Korean Value System
③ Ever Reducing Influences of Confucianism on Korean Society
④ Young Generations' Antagonism to Confucianism in Korea

[13-15]

In Russia, several religions coexist, including Christianity, Judaism, Islam, and animism. The most common religion is Christianity, and most Christians are members of the Russian Orthodox Church. The Church has existed for over 1,000 years, surviving even the official atheism of the Soviet era and the agnosticism that may have been even more prominent at the time.

During the communist years, many Russians who practiced Orthodoxy sacrificed career and educational opportunities. The tenacity of Russian Orthodoxy may explain why even nonreligious Russians are inclined to call themselves Russian Orthodox. That same staying power drives the Church today, which is run by Aleksey II of Moscow. Born Aleksey Mikhailovich Ridiger, the future patriarch was from a very _____ family. As a boy, Aleksey was often taken by his parents on their annual pilgrimages, when he most certainly began contemplation of the religious ways of life he was to choose. As patriarch, Aleksey is exalted in the Church governance, but he is not deified. He has published articles on Church history and peacemaking in both the ecclesiastical and secular press, broadening the Church's image both in Russia and abroad.

13 Which of the following best expresses the essential information of this passage?

① The Russian Orthodox Church was banned under Soviet control.

② Few Russians believe in a god.

③ Aleksey II has expanded the church's members.

④ The Russian Orthodox Church has a long history of strong membership in Russia.

14 According to the passage, Aleksey II of Moscow is _____.

① a historian

② a high church official

③ a secular leader

④ an atheist

15 Which of the following best fits in the blank?

① pious

② opulent

③ slant

④ appalling

[16-18]

Cardinal Jorge Mario Bergoglio became the first pope from Latin America, the continent which accounts for 40% of the world's 1.2 billion baptized Catholics. The conclave, the assembly of 115 cardinals that elected the pope, had looked set to be the scene for a showdown between a faction led by Vatican insiders, and a party of mainly English- and German-speaking cardinals pressing for thorough reform of the central administration of the church, the Curia. The conclave's members eventually solved the problem by choosing a compromise candidate they already knew. At the age of 76, Francis is old enough to be considered another transitional leader, but vigorous enough to leave an enduring mark on the world's largest Christian church. Like predecessor Pope Benedict XVI, the new pope regards evangelization as a priority: his chosen name signals that, recalling both the inspirational St Francis of Assisi and St Francis Xavier, the first Jesuit missionary. "Go out," he told Argentina's priests last year, "and share your testimony." A controversial but more positive hallmark of his time in Argentina has been a focus on the interests of the poor. In 2009 he upbraided the government of Argentina's then president Nestor Kirchner for failing to stem the spread of poverty, asserting that human rights were not only violated by terrorism, but also by _____. Yet Francis is no liberal. He had no truck with liberation theology, the popular movement in Latin America which links the church's work to radical social change, even though many of its supporters have been Jesuits. Not Francis. He has staunchly defended church teaching on abortion, euthanasia and adoption by same-sex couples. He clashed with Argentina's president, Cristina Fernandez, calling her approval of gay marriage "an attempt at destruction of God's plan."

16 Which of the following is most appropriate for the blank?

① kidnapping and torture
② the teaching of dogmatic religion
③ political assassination
④ unfair economic structures
⑤ the lack of religious belief

17 The underlined expression "Not Francis" means that Francis _____.

① was not popular at that time
② was not a supporter of the Jesuits
③ was not involved in politics
④ did not want to ignore social problems
⑤ refused to be associated with liberation theology

18 According to the passage, which of the following is true?

① Francis was elected a new pope because he was completely unknown to the public.
② Francis realizes his limitation as a temporary leader.
③ Francis chose his name because it could distinguish himself from the predecessors.
④ The pope is elected in the Curia, the administrative body of the church.
⑤ The pope's style and origins are new but his ideas are conservative.

[19-20]

If you have ever made a list of pros and cons to help you make a decision, you have used the utilitarian method of moral reasoning. One of the main ethical theories, utilitarianism posits that the key to deciding that makes an act morally right or wrong is its consequences. Whether our intentions are good or bad is irrelevant; what matters is whether the result of our actions is good or bad. To utilitarians, happiness is the ultimate goal of human beings and the highest moral good. Thus, if there is great unhappiness because of an act, then that action can be said to be morally wrong. If, on the other hand, there is great happiness because of an action, then that act can be said to be morally right. Utilitarians believe that we should carefully weigh the potential consequences of an action before we take it. Will the act lead to things that will make us, or others, happy? Will it make us, or others, unhappy? According to utilitarians, we should choose to do what creates the greatest amount of good (happiness) for the greatest number of people. This can be difficult to determine, though, because sometimes an act can create short-term happiness but misery in the long term. Another problematic aspect of utilitarianism is that it deems it acceptable — indeed, even necessary — to use another person as a means to an end and sacrifice the happiness of one or a few for the happiness of many.

19 According to the definition of utilitarianism in the passage, stealing bread to feed hungry children would be _____.

① morally wrong because stealing is illegal.
② morally right because it has good intentions.
③ morally wrong because it violates another's rights.
④ morally right because it has positive consequences

20 윗글의 내용과 가장 어울리는 견해는?

① Great good often comes at a great price.
② Using utilitarianism to make a moral decision is not always easy.
③ Long-term consequences are more important than short-term consequences.
④ A pro/con list is the most effective technique for making an important decision.

[21-24]

Philosophy, like all other studies, aims primarily at knowledge. The knowledge it aims at is the kind of knowledge which gives unity and system to the body of the sciences, and the kind which results from a critical examination of the grounds of our convictions, prejudices, and beliefs. But it cannot be maintained that philosophy has had any very great measure of success in its attempts to provide definite answers to its questions. If you ask a mathematician, a mineralogist, a historian, or any other man of learning, what definite body of truths has been ascertained by his science, his answer will last as long as you are willing to listen. But if you put the same question to a philosopher, he will, if he is ⓐ candid, have to confess that his study has not achieved positive results such as those achieved by other sciences. It is true that ⓑ this is partly accounted for by the fact that, as soon as definite knowledge concerning any subject becomes possible, this subject ceases to be called philosophy and becomes a separate science. The whole study of the heavens, which now belongs to astronomy, was once included in philosophy; Newton's great work was called 'the mathematical principles of natural philosophy'. _____Ⓐ_____, the study of the human mind, which was a part of philosophy, has now been separated from philosophy and has become the science of psychology. Thus, to a great extent; the uncertainty of philosophy is more apparent than real: those questions which are already capable of definite answers are placed in the sciences, while those only to which, at present, no definite answer can be given, remain to form the residue which is called philosophy.

21 The main topic of this passage is _____.

① the difficulty in defining the goal and the object of philosophy
② the relation between astronomy, psychology and philosophy
③ the joy and happiness of investigating knowledge in philosophy
④ the measure of successful investigation in philosophy

22 Which can be used instead of ⓐ?

① terrific
② insincere
③ discontented
④ forthright

23 What is ⓑ this referring to?

① The critical investigation of the grounds of our prejudices, convictions, and beliefs made by philosophy
② The definite body of truths ascertained by various types of sciences including philosophy
③ The lack of definite answers to the knowledge philosophy aims at
④ The fact that subjects with concrete answers become a separate science such as astronomy and psychology

24 Which is most suitable for Ⓐ?

① In contrast
② Similarly
③ Therefore
④ Nevertheless

[25-26]

René Descartes was a French philosopher, mathematician, physicist, and writer. He has been dubbed the "Father of Modern Philosophy," and much subsequent Western philosophy is a response to his writings which have been studied closely to this day. In particular, his *Meditations on First Philosophy* continues to be a standard text at most university philosophy departments. In addition, *Discourse on the Method*, became and remains one of the most influential books in all philosophy. In Part IV of that book, Descartes proposed the famous philosophical statement "*Cogito ergo sum*," meaning "I think, therefore I am." Another phrase, "*de omnibus dubitandum*" (we must doubt everything) often used by Descartes, also well expresses the crux of the Cartesian method. This statement may seem strangely ____Ⓐ____ advice from a religious man; and, indeed, it did not make him popular with the clergy of his day. Yet, when Descartes used the method of doubt, he reached a religious position somewhat by paradox. His aim in using the method was always clear. Unlike Michel de Montaigne and other skeptics against whom he wrote, Descartes had no interest in a modish attitude of doubt for the sake of doubting. His aim was by way of doubt to reach down to what can be shown with ____Ⓑ____. This was essentially the scientific procedure of seventeenth-century physics, in which doubt played a constant part: 'to accept nothing as true' until it was established, as far as possible, beyond doubt.

25 윗글의 빈칸 Ⓐ, Ⓑ에 들어갈 말로 가장 적절한 것은?

Ⓐ	Ⓑ
① sagacious	– disbelief
② skeptical	– coercion
③ rational	– deduction
④ cynical	– certainty

26 윗글의 내용과 일치하는 것은?

① Descartes and Montaigne were different in their attitude toward the method of doubt.
② Descartes's philosophical statements sometimes convey paradoxical messages.
③ Descartes had many staunch supporters among religious men.
④ Descartes made an even bigger contribution to the field of mathematics than to that of physics.

[27–28]

It's safe to say that no civilization has ever been more obsessed with miracles than late antique and medieval Christendom. For more than a thousand years, until the Protestant Reformation, miracles stood as the unquestioned benchmark of religious credibility — and credulity — in the Christian world. The familiar exaltation of the other-worldly at the expense of the worldly was expressed with remarkable consistency, from the timeless frozen purity of Byzantine iconography to the writings of figures such as the Venerable Bede — who salts his eighth-century history of the English church with thrilling miracles on nearly every page, and who praises Caedmon, the first poet to write in English, as having "stirred the hearts of many folk to despise the world and aspire to heavenly things." This was, quite simply, the highest praise a medieval critic could offer. Medieval society's insistent supernaturalism — enforced by a powerful church that constantly policed the thinking of philosophers and didn't hesitate to burn _____ — amounts to nothing less than a wholesale cultural denial of nature's regularity. It went hand-in-hand with the demotion of nature itself.

27. Which of the following is most appropriate for the blank?

① heretics
② haberdashers
③ seamstresses
④ chroniclers

28. Which would be the best title for the passage?

① History and Iconography
② Aftermaths of the Protestant Revolution
③ Religion and Civilization
④ Miracles and Christianity

[29-31]

For centuries the Roman Catholic Church maintained an ⓐ Inquisition, which sent many people with deviant ideas to their deaths and banned or burned books; some books are banned by the Roman Catholic Church even today. In Iran, A. R. Khomeini, shortly before his death in 1989, banned the book *The Satanic Verses* by Salman Rushdie and invited all believers to kill the author and his publishers. It is somewhat amazing that many people in Christian countries were so shocked by this action, in view of their own countries' histories of religious intolerance. With some exceptions, and Khomeini's action is one of them, Islam in history has been _____ than has Roman Catholic Christianity. The medieval Crusades, which cost hundreds of thousands of lives, were a product of Christian, not of Muslim, intolerance. In the Muslim Turkish Empire, People of the Book were tolerated and could exercise their religion, as long as they paid a special tax. On the other hand, even Protestant Christians, generally considered to be more broad-minded, have made victims of religious intolerance. Protestant nations have also in past centuries burned supposed witches. In the early 21st century, fundamentalist Christian preachers denounced *Harry Potter* series as a work of the devil.

29 Choose the one that best fills in the blank.

① more flourished
② less tolerant of other religions
③ more tolerant of other religions
④ less flourished

30 It can be inferred from the passage that an ⓐ"Inquisition" here means _____.

① a former tribunal of the Roman Catholic Church created to discover and suppress heresy
② the illegitimate legacy of Roman Catholic Church which caused many fanciful ideas and thoughts.
③ a general term for a severe mental interrogation
④ a situation of violating the rights or privacy of individuals

31 Which of the following is NOT true according to the passage?

① Salman Rushdie's book was forbidden to read in Iran.
② Protestants generated the victims of intolerance as Roman Catholics did.
③ *Harry Potter* series were negatively appreciated by some Christians.
④ *The Satanic Verses* was banned for its vanity and intolerance.

[32-34]

　　Mr. Makari's highly engaging story begins with René Descartes. Ever since Greek philosophy had merged with Christianity, the soul had been regarded as the "unifying link between nature, man and God," Mr. Makari writes. By the 17th century, however, Christendom was in crisis, and many found it hard to reconcile the notion of an incorporeal soul with a mechanical world that was increasingly understood as made up of matter. Descartes tried to satisfy the demand of skeptical naturalists by narrowing the concept of the soul to a "thing that thinks," yet that was separate from the body. The French philosopher thus breathed new life into the Christian belief in an immortal soul. At the other end of the _____Ⓐ_____ stood Thomas Hobbes, who thought there was no such thing as "immaterial substance." In his view the soul, rather than being rational and Godlike, was "material, prone to illness and errors." _____Ⓑ_____. And they were to demonstrate the importance of Mr. Makari's narrative as more than just an intellectual exercise. After Hobbes concluded that men were controlled by animal feelings that inevitably produced conflict, his proposed solution was to hand over power to an absolute monarch.

32 Select the statement most consistent with the passage.

① European philosophy became increasingly religious in the seventeenth century.
② Mr. Makari charts the rise of modern secular philosophy.
③ Hobbes advocated modern forms of demagoguery based on humans' tendency to "illness and errors."
④ Descartes emphasized the insignificance of the mechanical world.

33 Choose the best sentence that fits blank Ⓑ above.

① Hobbes's views were consistent with those of Descartes but extrapolated them one step further.
② Hobbes corroborated Descartes's ideas by translating his notion of the immaculate soul into material terms.
③ The disparate views on the nature of the "thing that thinks" were to have monumental implications.
④ Rather than "I think, therefore I am," Hobbes famously posited, "I think, therefore I am," but "I am, therefore I think, too."

34 Choose the best word for blank Ⓐ above.

① diaspora
② bulwark
③ obscurity
④ gamut

[35-37]

What makes people do things that are wrong? This question has puzzled philosophers since Plato who famously asked: If you found a magic ring that let you do whatever you wanted: rob a bank, take over the world, or enslave your enemies, would you? Plato postulated that if the price of exploiting this wrong, was not worth the reward, morality would be vindicated. Plato assumed that people stray from ⓐ the straight and narrow path due to temptation for personal gain. However, there is another school of thought that hypothesizes the inverse: people act immorally because they want to conform to society, even when it opposes their own core values. In other words, people _____Ⓐ_____. For most people, doing the wrong thing is not embezzling millions of dollars or usurping political power in a coup, it is joining in when a person is being disparaged or laughing at a racist joke. We do this because we do not want any trouble. Immanuel Kant calls this sort of excessively deferential attitude 'servility.' Rather than downgrading the values and commitments of others, servility involves downgrading your own values and commitments relative to those of others. The servile person is thus the mirror image of the conventional, self-interested immoral person found in Plato. To Kant, servile people deny themselves the same moral equality and respect as anyone else. They do this so as not to appear arrogant, untoward, or rude and thereby allow themselves to be socialized into doing the wrong thing.

35 According to the passage, which of the following is closet in meaning to ⓐ?

① A road that does not bend
② Behaving honestly and ethically
③ working towards an academic goal
④ The shortest path to your destination

36 Which of the following best fits into Ⓐ?

① think conforming to others is an evil behavior
② try too hard to reject society and promote their values
③ are too concerned about how others view them
④ become obsessed with doing the right thing

37 According to the passage, which of the following is NOT true?

① Plato thought that people did wrong acts for personal gain.
② Kant thought servile people act immorally because they want to conform.
③ Plato felt morality would be vindicated if immorality's cost was too high.
④ Kant felt that servile people often usurped political power.

[38–40]

An argument often advanced for the encouragement of religion is that, to paraphrase St. Mathew's report of Jesus's words, it leads people to love their neighbors as themselves. That would be a powerful point were 'it' true. But is it? This was the question Jean Decety, a developmental neuroscientist at the University of Chicago, asked in a study just published in *Current Biology*.

Dr. Decety is not the first to wonder, in a scientific way, about the connection between religion and _____. He is, though, one of the first to do it without recourse to that standard but peculiar laboratory animal beloved by psychologists, the undergraduate student. Instead, he collaborated with researchers in Canada, China, Jordan, South Africa and Turkey, as well as with fellow Americans, to look at children aged between 5 and 12 and their families.

38 What does the underlined 'it' mean?

① Most people are religious.
② The object of belief is not important.
③ Jesus emphasized the love of people.
④ Science and religion are not different.
⑤ Religion makes people help others.

39 Choose one that is most appropriate for the blank.

① altruism
② individualism
③ egoism
④ capitalism
⑤ narcissism

40 According to the passage, psychologists' favorite subject of experiment is _____.

① children
② college students
③ Americans
④ animals
⑤ researchers

[41-42]

The division of Europe into a Catholic and a Protestant camp affected even the art of small countries like the Netherlands. The southern Netherlands, which today we call Belgium, had remained Catholic, and we have seen how Rubens in Antwerp received innumerable commissions from churches, princes and kings to paint vast canvases for the glorification of their power. The northern provinces of the Netherlands, however, had risen against their Catholic overlords, the Spaniards, and most of the inhabitants of their rich merchant towns adhered to the Protestant faith. The taste of these Protestant merchants of Holland was very different from that prevailing across the border. These men were rather comparable in their outlook to the Puritans in England: devout, hard-working, parsimonious men, most of whom disliked the exuberant pomp of the southern manner. Though their outlook mellowed as their security increased and their wealth grew, these Dutch burghers of the 17th century never accepted the full Baroque style which held sway in Catholic Europe. Even in architecture they preferred a certain sober restraint. When, in the middle of the 17th century, at the peak of Holland's successes, the citizens of Amsterdam decided to erect a large town hall which was to reflect the pride and achievement of their new-born nation, they chose a model which, for all its grandeur, looks simple in outline and sparing in decoration.

41 Rubens was a painter who _____.

① was supported by the wealthy Protestant merchants of Holland
② had a liking for huge canvases to decorate churches and palaces
③ felt no inclination towards the exuberant style of the southern Netherlands
④ made a profound impact on the 17th-century northern Netherlands paintings

42 According to the passage, which of the following is true?

① The large town hall of Amsterdam was built in the full Baroque style.
② The victory of Protestantism was conspicuous in the southern Netherlands paintings.
③ The Protestant merchants of Holland wanted to demonstrate the pride of their nation.
④ The painters of Protestant Holland produced numerous paintings for the Spanish patrons.

[43-46]

Not many years after the French philosopher Rousseau promulgated the idea of the 'noble savage', which embodied his belief that man in his natural state was innately good, there walked out of the woods a living specimen who, it was hoped, would prove the point. It happened at the village of Saint-Sernin in southern France on January 9, 1800. A strange creature from the forest was caught scavenging for food, and though it appeared to be a wild animal, it walked erect. As soon as those who captured the creature realized it was human, a boy of about 12 years in fact, they attempted to care for him. The 'Wild Boy of Aveyron', as he became known, could not speak and had no apparent awareness that he was human. Offered white bread, he spat it out immediately and bit anyone who approached too close. It was time to alert the scientists. Here, apparently, was the noble savage in person.

Over the next few months, attempts were made to bring the boy back into the human race. With some optimism, he was given the name Victor and he had the benefit of a patient tutor and a woman who grew to love him with a mother's devotion. But the experiments to which this poor wretch was subjected met with repeated defeat, while he longed to return to his freedom and his woods. Invited to dinner, he stole everything small enough to grab and clambered up a tree, which left the astonished guests resentful that Rousseau was not alive to see his theories disproved. But were they disproved? Theft is a transgression against a specific moral rule, but does not, in itself, denote badness if the rule has no significance for the thief. What was more telling was the fact that Victor was never able to see the world through the eyes of anyone but himself and had no capacity for empathy. He certainly learned how people could hurt, but he never learned to recognize that other people existed except as satisfiers of his need. The boy didn't prove that the primitive state was one of essential goodness, but he did prove that it was selfish. Which is not to say that it was not also innocent: the boy showed no malice or cruelty, did not seek to revenge, did not direct hostility against individuals. He was not so much _____Ⓐ_____ as _____Ⓑ_____.

43 The best title of the passage would be _____.

① How to Distinguish Right from Wrong
② Importance of Human Education
③ The Survival of the Fittest
④ Moral Codes in the Primitive State
⑤ Decline of Human Capacity for Empathy

44 According to the passage, which of the following is true?

① When the boy was first found, he was mistaken for the lost son of a French nobleman.
② Victor was provided with proper education and motherly affection.
③ The boy's captors handed him over to the police because of his violent nature.
④ What surprised the scientists most was that the boy had a great capacity for understanding other people.
⑤ The scientists found that the boy had been mistreated by his rescuers.

45 Which of the following is most appropriate for the blanks Ⓐ and Ⓑ?

	Ⓐ	Ⓑ
①	human	inhuman
②	inhuman	human
③	immoral	pre-moral
④	pre-moral	immoral
⑤	amoral	immoral

46 According to the passage, the story of Victor eventually suggests that man is innately _____.

① violent
② dishonest
③ good
④ evil
⑤ self-centered

[47-49]

Kant's cleavage between analytic and synthetic truths was foreshadowed in Hume's distinction between relations of ideas and matters of fact, and in Leibniz's distinction between truths of reason and truths of fact. Leibniz spoke of the truths of reason as true in all possible worlds. Picturesqueness aside, this is to say that the truths of reason are those which could not possibly be false. In the same vein we hear analytic statements defined as statements whose denials are self-contradictory. But this definition has small explanatory value; for the notion of self-contradictoriness, in the quite broad sense needed for this definition of analyticity, stands in exactly the same need of clarification as does the notion of analyticity itself. The two notions are the two sides of a single dubious coin.

Kant conceived of an analytic statement as one that attributes to its subject no more than is already conceptually contained in the subject. This formulation has two shortcomings: it limits itself to statements of subject-predicate form, and it appeals to a notion of containment which is left at a metaphorical level. But Kant's intent, evident more from the use he makes of the notion of analyticity than from his definition of it, can be restated thus: a statement is analytic when it is true by virtue of meanings and without any consideration of fact. Pursuing this line, let us examine the concept of meaning which is presupposed.

47 Which of the following is the most likely to be the main topic of the passage?

① Hume's distinction between truths of reason and truths of facts
② Leibniz's truths of reason and Kant's analytic statement
③ The relation between possible worlds and the truths of fact in Leibniz's philosophy
④ The importance of statements of subject-predicate form in Kant's philosophy

48 According to the passage, which of the following CANNOT be inferred?

① Leibniz's notion of truths of reason can be comparable with Kant's analytic truths.
② Kant thought that an analytic statement is always true because of its meaning by itself.
③ Kant's distinction between analytic and synthetic truths precedes Hume and Leibniz's philosophy.
④ Leibniz thought that a statement which is true by reason should be true in every possible world.

49 Which of the following is the most likely to follow the passage?

① The depiction of the notion of containment
② The critique of the definition of analyticity
③ The description of the concept of truth
④ The discussion of the notion of meaning

[50-52]

At the start of it all there is He: the classical ideal of 'Man', formulated first by Protagoras as 'the measure of all things', later renewed in the Italian Renaissance as a universal model and represented in Leonardo da Vinci's Vitruvian Man. An ideal of bodily perfection which, in keeping with the classical dictum *mens sana in corpore sano*,* doubles up as a set of mental, discursive and spiritual values. Together they uphold a specific view of what is 'human' about humanity. Moreover, they assert with unshakable certainty the almost boundless capacity of humans to pursue their individual and collective perfectibility. That iconic image is the emblem of Humanism as a doctrine that combines the biological, discursive and moral expansion of human capabilities into an idea of teleologically ordained, rational progress. Faith in the unique, self-regulating and intrinsically moral powers of human reason forms an integral part of this high-humanistic creed, which was essentially predicated on eighteenth- and nineteenth-century renditions of classical Antiquity and Italian Renaissance ideals.

This model sets standards not only for individuals, but also for their cultures. Humanism historically developed into a civilizational model, which shaped a certain idea of Europe as coinciding with the universalizing powers of self-reflexive reason. The mutation of the Humanistic ideal into a hegemonic cultural model was canonized by Hegel's philosophy of history. This self-aggrandizing vision assumes that Europe is not just a geo-political location, but rather a universal attribute of the human mind that can lend its quality to any suitable object. This is the view espoused by Edmund Husserl in his celebrated essay "The Crisis of European Sciences", which is a passionate defence of the universal powers of reason against the intellectual and moral decline symbolized by the rising threat of European fascism in the 1930s. In Husserl's view, Europe announces itself as the site of origin of critical reason and self-reflexivity, both qualities resting on the Humanistic norm.

* a sound mind in a sound body

50 Which of the following is NOT associated with the other three views of humanity?

① a doctrine that asserts the boundless human capabilities

② the Vitruvian Man

③ the measure of all things.

④ the moral decline symbolized by the threat of fascism

51 Why does the author mention Edmund Husserl's essay in the passage?

① To argue that he is the last successor to European humanism

② To illustrate the influence of the classical ideals on a modern standard

③ To provide an example of the qualities of critical reason and self-reflexivity

④ To give an explanation for an iconic image of humanism

52 According to the passage, which of the following is true?

① Leonardo da Vinci inherited a universal model of 'Man' from classical antiquity.

② Italian Renaissance ideas are opposed to classical antiquity.

③ Hegel is not related to the mutation of the Humanistic ideal into a hegemonic model.

④ Humanism has nothing to do with the universalist norms.

7강 교육 / 심리

Read the following passages and answer the questions. [01-51]

[01-03]

As social beings, it's in our nature to get along with others; our survival and success depend on it. However, there is a fine line between healthy social behavior and the experience of emotional depletion caused by chronic people-pleasing. There are common signs of chronic people-pleasing and some ways to overcome it. [A]

People-pleasers want everyone around them to be happy, and they will do whatever is asked of them to keep it that way, according to Susan Newman, a social psychologist.

People-pleasers often feel like they have to say _____Ⓐ_____ when someone asks for their help. This makes them feel important and like they're contributing to someone else's life. They worry how others will view them when they say _____Ⓑ_____. People don't want to be seen as lazy, selfish, or totally egocentric. They fear they'll be disliked and cut from the group, whether it's friends, family or co-workers. [B]

People-pleasers yearn for outside validation. Their personal feeling of security and self-confidence is based on getting the approval of others, said Linda Tillman, a clinical psychologist. Thus, at the core, people-pleasers lack confidence, she said. [C]

What many people-pleasers don't realize is that people-pleasing can have serious risks. Not only does it put a lot of pressure and stress on them, but essentially they can make themselves sick from doing too much. [D]

01 Which of the following is most suitable for Blanks Ⓐ and Ⓑ?

① yes : no
② yes : yes
③ no : no
④ no : yes

02 Which is the most appropriate place for the paragraph below?

> Here's a slew of strategies to help you stop being a people-pleaser. Remember that you always have a choice to say no whenever someone asks you for a favor. Set your priorities. Knowing your priorities and values helps you put the brakes on people-pleasing.

① [A]
② [B]
③ [C]
④ [D]

03 Which of the following can be inferred from the passage?

① People-pleasing is one of the healthy social behaviors of humans as social-beings.
② Susan Newman offered some tips to keep people-pleasers happy.
③ According do Linda Tillman, low self-confidence is the only reason to cause chronic people-pleasing.
④ People-pleasers tend to put much pressure and stress on themselves.

[04-05]

New York state is calling on schools to get tough against bullying and, judging from local school districts, the call is being heeded. In fact, many anti-bullying efforts have been in practice for years. But administrators and educators say it's difficult, if not impossible, to gauge their effectiveness. "This is hard to _____ because it is difficult to track instances that have been averted due to these programs," said Tom Phillips. "What we can say is the climate of the school through use of discipline referral data has been much more positive in that a smaller percentage of the student population is being dealt with through the formal discipline procedure. This also speaks to the commitment of staff to deal with student issues as they arise rather than to simply write up a student and refer it to the school administration. The impact of teacher intervention and involvement cannot be overstated," he said in an e-mail.

04 Which title does best describe the passage above?

① Discipline and Punishment
② The Bully, the Bullied, and the Bystander
③ Bullying Changes a School, One Child at a Time
④ How to Make Anti-Bullying Efforts Successful
⑤ The Necessity of Making a Report about Students in Writing

05 What would be the most appropriate expression in the blank?

① modify
② proceed
③ quantify
④ renounce
⑤ signify

[06-08]

Learning is commonly thought to be a relatively permanent change in behavior resulting from experience and training, and interacting with biological processes. One of the problems teachers have in directing learning processes and in assessing learning is that learning cannot be directly observed. Learning can only be inferred from a person's behavior or performance. Performance is observable, whereas learning is not. This creates difficulty for teachers, because sometimes students have learned and are not performing according to what they have learned, and sometimes they have not learned, but perform as though they have. For example, a student may demonstrate a motor skill when you are observing him or her but may not be able to produce that skill in any consistent way again. _____Ⓐ_____, a student may have learned the skill but may be fatigued and not demonstrate the motor skill. That is why the idea of consistent observable performance is important in determining whether learning has taken place. If students cannot demonstrate an ability consistently, they probably have not learned it.

06 Which best fits into the blank Ⓐ?

① Likewise
② Consequently
③ Surprisingly
④ Notwithstanding

07 What is the passage mainly about?

① How to assess learning
② Ways to define motor skills
③ Consistency of human performance
④ Characteristics of motor skill learning

08 Which is NOT mentioned in the passage?

① We cannot directly observe learning.
② Teachers are inconsistent in measuring students' performance.
③ Learning results from experience, training, and interaction with biological processes.
④ Students sometimes fail to perform motor skills that they have successfully learned.

[09-10]

Schooling is primarily a linguistic process, and language serves as an often unconscious means of evaluating and differentiating students. [A] Inasmuch as content and disciplinary knowledge are constituted and presented through language, learning an academic subject means reading and writing texts that are organized linguistically to accomplish particular communicative purposes. [B] In school, students are expected to use language to demonstrate what they have learned and what they think in ways that can be shared, evaluated, and further challenged or supported. [C] Their attention is typically on the content of the texts they read and respond to but not on the ways language construes that content. In addition, teachers' expectations for language use are seldom made explicit, and much of what is expected regarding language use in school tasks remains couched in teachers' vague admonitions to "use your own words" or to "be clear." Writing tasks are assigned without clear guidelines for students about how a particular text type is typically structured and organized. [D] For these reasons Christie (1985) has called language the "hidden curriculum" of schooling. Judgments about students' abilities are often based on how they express their knowledge in language. The testing, counseling, and classroom interactions that inform these judgments perpetuate and maintain values that are often not made explicit. This suggests that a careful analysis of the linguistic challenges of learning is important for understanding the difficulties students face and the limitations they demonstrate in talking and writing about topics they have studied.

09 Choose the most appropriate place for the sentence below.

> But language patterns themselves are rarely the focus of attention of students and teachers.

① [A] ② [B]
③ [C] ④ [D]

10 What is the LEAST appropriate title for the passage above?

① The Language of Schooling
② The Hidden Curriculum of Schooling
③ The Linguistic Challenges of Learning
④ The Disciplinary Knowledge of Schooling

[11-13]

When the eighteenth century concerned itself with constituting for the child, with educational rules that followed his development, a world that would be adapted to him, it made it possible to form around children an unreal, abstract, archaic environment that had no relation to the adult world. The whole development of contemporary education, with its irreproachable aim of preserving the child from adult conflicts, accentuates the distance that separates, for a man, his life as a child and his life as an adult That is to say, by sparing the child conflicts, it exposes him to a major conflict, to the contradiction between his childhood and his real life. If one adds that, in its educational institutions, a culture does not project its reality directly, with all its conflicts and contradictions, but that it reflects it indirectly through the myths that excuse it, justify it, and idealize it in a(n) _____Ⓐ_____ coherence; if one adds that in its education a society dreams of its golden age, one understands that fixations and pathological regressions are possible only in a given culture, that they multiply to the extent that social forms do not permit the assimilation of the past into the present content of experience.

11 Choose the best word for the blank Ⓐ above.

① genuine
② consistent
③ extant
④ chimerical

12 According to the passage, why does childhood cause a major conflict?

① Children are not as innocent as they pretend to be.
② Childhood creates a cleavage between the past and present.
③ Childhood is no different from adulthood.
④ Children are full of pathological regressions

13 Which statement is NOT consistent with the passage?

① Eighteenth-century educational institutions separated childhood from adulthood.
② Childhood became associated with an ancient golden age.
③ Adulthood is presumed to be more real than childhood.
④ Childhood inherently lacks conflict.

[14-15]

In *The Act of Creation*, the psychologist Arthur Koestler summarized his own extensive research into the human creative process by introducing the term bisociation to convey the coincidence of discontinuous ideas. He described the creative act as the perceiving of a situation or idea, L, in two self-consistent but habitually incompatible frames of reference. The event L, in which the two intersect, is made to vibrate simultaneously on two different wavelengths, as it were. While this situation lasts, L is not merely linked to one associative context, but bisociated with two. What we value in creative ideas is not just their apparent novelty. Novelty in itself induces excitement because it has the effect of opening up new connective paths, or fields, in the cognitive medium, and this may require an exceptional discharge of energy. But having had this experience the excitement may be short-lived — once opened the paths cannot be opened in the same way again. Richer creative acts lie in opening complex and far-reaching new pathways that connect disparate concepts, the more of them the greater the level of excitement; in Koestler's terms, one multiplies bisociations. If our sense of being relies, at least in part, on the presence of active mental states, it follows that more active mental states create a more expansive sense of awareness or being. And the more diverse and complex the mental states are at any one time the more corresponding energy is required to traverse them, and hence the greater the sense of physical exhilaration.

14 What would be the best title of the passage above?

① The negative impact of bisociated exhilaration
② The birth of novelty and excitement
③ The cognitive medium and associative context
④ The complex physical features of energy

15 What can be inferred from the passage above?

① Human ability to connect discontinuous ideas has its own limit.
② Creativity does not necessarily consist in the production of anything that is completely new.
③ Destruction is the opposite pole of creation.
④ Creative thoughts themselves are of little use unless scientifically measured.

[16-17]

　　Sigmund Freud never set out to be a psychologist. Much less did he see himself — until quite late in life — as contributing to the field of social psychology. He was simply a Viennese physician specializing in ⓐ the treatment of nervous disorders. That ⓑ this activity would lead him to fundamentally new ways of ⓒ conceiving social behavior was little imagined by Freud when he took up ⓓ this work.

　　In fact, Freud was already thirty years old before he began his private practice; and his reasons for doing so were originally more financial than scientific. After an engagement of four years, Freud married Martha Bernays in the fall of 1886. He needed to provide support for his parents as well as the new family he and his wife would be starting. It was at this time that Sigmund Freud, in search of improved financial security, embarked on his career as a private physician.

16 Which does NOT have the same meaning as the others?

① ⓐ
② ⓑ
③ ⓒ
④ ⓓ

17 Which is true according to the passage?

① In a way his financial situation forced Freud to be a private physician.
② Freud never saw himself as a contributor to the field of social psychology.
③ From the start Freud determined to be a pioneer in understanding human psyche.
④ Unfortunately Freud's marriage made him give up significant psychological researches.

[18-19]

In many ways persistence brings us back full circle to regulation. When a toy becomes too predictable, it is no longer fun. If a parent comes every time the infant makes a sound, calling the parent would require no effort. What engages learners best is a challenge whose solution is possible but not simple. In order to see such a challenge through to solution, the infant or toddler must be able to tolerate some frustration. The adult partner assists in this by helping the child stay focused and excited as well as able to pause and gather more information. In an intriguing twist, researchers wondered whether the child's competence affected the mother's investment and satisfaction in supporting her child. They looked at children at 6 and 18 months to measure their ability to complete physical and social tasks through some frustration. They also measured the mother's satisfaction and sense of competence as a parent. Competent infants had confident mothers. Less competent infants had less satisfied mothers. This might have been because the mothers had expectations that were too high or fewer skills to support their children's efforts. Either way, it suggests the possibility of a(n) _____ nature to this approach to learning.

18 윗글의 빈칸에 들어갈 말로 가장 적절한 것은?

① biological
② humanistic
③ irreversible
④ transactional

19 윗글의 내용과 일치하지 <u>않는</u> 것은?

① The more expected a toy is, the less amused a child is.
② Children's competence is related to the level of mothers' satisfaction.
③ Tolerating frustration is required for learners to find a possible but not simple solution.
④ The adult partner needs to immediately help infants or toddlers find an answer for the challenge

[20-21]

Researchers have long been intrigued as to whether an ability to avoid, or defer, gratification is related to outcomes in life. The best-known test is the "marshmallow" experiment, in which children who could refrain from eating the confection for 15 minutes were given a second one. Children who could not wait tended to have lower incomes and poorer health as adults. Dr David Lindahl of Stockholm University used data from a Swedish survey in which more than 13,000 children aged 13 were asked whether they would prefer to receive $140 now or $1,400 in five years' time. About four-fifths of them said they were prepared to wait. Unlike previous researchers, Dr Lindahl was able to track all the children and account for their parental background and cognitive ability. He found that the 13-year-olds who wanted the smaller sum of money at once were 32% more likely to be convicted of a crime during the next 18 years than those children who said they would rather wait for the bigger reward. Individuals who are impatient, he believes, prefer instant benefits and are therefore less likely to be deterred by potential punishments. But those who fret that a person's criminal path is set already as a teenager should not despair. Dr Lindahl offers a remedy. When the respondents' education was included in the analysis, he found that higher educational attainment was linked to a preference for delayed gratification. "I therefore suspect that schooling can deter people from crime by making them value the future more," explains Dr Lindahl.

20 The best title of the above passage would be _____.

① Temptation and Punishment
② Human Behavior and Legal Loopholes
③ How to Educate Impatient Children
④ Time Preferences and Criminal Behavior
⑤ Limitations of Higher Education

21 According to the passage, Dr Lindahl's research argues _____.

① educational background and patience are not related
② the "marshmallow" test does not serve any longer as an effective measure of children's self-control
③ kids who delay rewards are more likely to become criminals later
④ patience is not always a virtue
⑤ schooling could make people more likely to postpone rewards

[22-24]

Most modern phenomenologists have recognized that self-reports may not reveal everything important about behavior and may not give a complete picture of personality. Persons may be conscious of the reasons for their behavior but be unable or unwilling to report them, for example, if they are uncomfortable or ashamed about aspects of their own feelings, perceptions, and behaviors. Or they may not be conscious of all of their experiences, in which case they cannot communicate them no matter how hard they try. Rather than considering that as a limitation, phenomenologists such as Rogers focus on the person's frame of reference as an important vantage point for understanding him or her.

The psychologist's task is to provide conditions that are _____Ⓐ_____ to growth and that facilitate free exploration of feelings and self in a therapeutic context. This is because one cannot expect people to be honest about themselves when they fear that their statements may incriminate them or lead to negative decisions about their future. In order to become more aware of and articulate private feelings, one needs an unthreatening atmosphere that reduces anxieties and inhibitions, and _____Ⓑ_____ self-disclosure. Phenomenologically oriented psychologists therefore try to create conditions of acceptance, warmth, and empathy in which the individual may feel more at ease for open self-exploration. These conditions of acceptance are illustrated vividly in "client-centered" therapy. Rogerians use the interview to observe how the individual interprets himself and his experiences, _____Ⓒ_____ the validity of the data he provides.

22 Choose a statement that may be inferred from the passage above.

① Self-reports reveal everything important about personality characteristics.
② Persons are conscious of all of their experiences.
③ Meditation is a method to enhance self-awareness.
④ Healthy personality is attained by concealing personal genuineness.
⑤ Psychologists use the interview to explore the person's self-concepts.

23 Which pair best fits Ⓐ and Ⓑ?

	Ⓐ	Ⓑ
①	concrete	encourages
②	conductive	discourages
③	conducive	fosters
④	helpful	precludes
⑤	modal	daunts

24 Which best fits Ⓒ?

① according to
② at the cost of
③ in spite of
④ regardless of
⑤ with respect to

[25-26]

People often confuse what is easily noticed when it is expected with what should be noticed when it is unexpected. The procedures frequently used in hospitals when reviewing radiographs are affected by the illusion of attention; doctors themselves also assume that they will notice unexpected problems in an image, even when they are looking for something else. To reduce the effects of inattentional blindness, one can deliberately reexamine the same images with an eye toward the unexpected. When participants in our studies know that something unexpected might happen, they consistently see the gorilla (the unexpected object in the experiment) — the unexpected has become the target of focused attention. Devoting attention to the unexpected is not a cure-all, however. We have limited attention resources, and devoting some attention to unexpected events means that we have less attention available for our primary task. It would be imprudent to ask radiologists to take time and resources away from detecting the expected problem in an x-ray to focus instead on things that are unlikely to be there. A more effective strategy would be for a second radiologist, unfamiliar with the case and the tentative diagnosis, to examine the images and to look for secondary problems that might not have been noticed the first time through.

So it turns out that even experts with a decade of training in their medical specialty can miss unexpected objects in their domain of expertise. Although radiologists are better able than laypeople to detect unusual aspects of radiographs, they suffer from the same limits on attention as everyone else. Their expertise lies not in greater attention, but in more precise expectations formed by their experience and training in perceiving the important features of the images. Experience guides them to _____, and in most cases, that strategy is wise.

25 윗글의 빈칸에 들어갈 말로 가장 적절한 것은?

① look for common problems rather than rare anomalies
② reexamine the same images with a fresh eye
③ detect both expected and unexpected problems
④ listen to another radiologist's diagnosis

26 윗글을 통해 추론할 수 있는 것으로 가장 적절한 것은?

① We are less likely to detect the unexpected when we are engaged in a familiar task.
② Familiarity can free our attention resources from a primary task.
③ One experienced radiologist is sufficient in reaching an accurate diagnosis.
④ Our attention resources can be extended by intensive training.

[27-28]

In a comprehensive report released recently by the Association for Psychological Science, the authors closely examine 10 learning tactics and rate each from high to low utility on the basis of the evidence they've amassed. Here is a quick guide to the report's conclusions.

Highlighting and underlining led the authors' list of ineffective learning strategies. Although they are common practices, studies show they offer no benefit beyond simply reading the text. Some research even indicates that highlighting can get in the way of learning; because it draws attention to individual facts, it may hamper the process of making connections and drawing inferences. Nearly as bad is the practice of rereading, a common exercise that is much less effective than some of the better techniques you can use. Lastly, summarizing, or writing down the main points contained in a text, can be helpful for those who are skilled at it, but again, there are far better ways to spend your study time. Highlighting, underlining, rereading and summarizing were all rated by the authors as being of "low utility."

_____Ⓐ_____ familiar practices like highlighting and rereading, the learning strategies with the most evidence to support them aren't well known outside the psych lab. Take distributed practice, for example. This tactic involves spreading out your study sessions, rather than engaging in one marathon. Cramming information at the last minute may allow you to get through that test or meeting, but the material will quickly disappear from memory. It's much more effective to dip into the material at intervals over time. And the longer you want to remember the information, whether it's two weeks or two years, the longer the intervals should be.

The second learning strategy that is highly recommended by the report's authors is practice testing. Yes, more tests — but these are not for a grade. Research shows that the mere act of calling information to mind strengthens that knowledge and aids in future retrieval. Both spaced-out learning, or distributed practice, and practice tests were rated as having "high utility" by the authors.

27 Which of the following best fits in Ⓐ?

① In place of
② In addition to
③ In contrast to
④ On behalf of

28 Which of the following is NOT true?

① The authors' list of ineffective learning strategies includes the most popular ones among people.
② The most effective learning strategies are well known to the general public.
③ Practice testing aids in future retrieval of the information.
④ Short-term intensive efforts are less efficient for retaining knowledge than long-term extensive efforts.

[29-30]

Have you ever come out of a stressful exam or interview and thought that you could devour a whole tub of ice-cream? Or maybe it was an emotional movie that left you drained. Why do many people who endure a stressful experience want a stiff drink or to raid the fridge in search of comfort foods that are high in fat and sugar? One intriguing idea is that when we succumb to these temptations, we are experiencing ego depletion.

Ego depletion comes from American psychologist Roy Baumeister, who believes that enduring something stressful exhausts our capacity for willpower to the extent that we give in to temptations that we would rather avoid. In one of his studies, he made hungry students eat bitter radishes rather than delicious chocolate cookies. Even people who like a bit of radish in their salad would find that task difficult. However, Baumeister was not interested in eating habits. He was really interested in how long the students would preserve on an insoluble geometry task. The students who had been allowed to eat the cookies stuck at the geometry task on average for about twenty minutes, whereas those who were forced to eat the radishes gave up after only eight minutes. They had used up all the willpower to eat the radishes so they were left with less reserve to cope with another situation of completing a difficult problem.

Performance on one task that requires effort can therefore have unforeseen consequences for a subsequent situation that is completely unrelated except that it requires effort. This is why Baumeister regards willpower as _____.

29 Choose the one that best fills in the blank.

① a ubiquitous lubricant in human relationships
② an essential element in avoiding stress
③ the sole ingredient for healthy diet recipes
④ a mental muscle that can become exhausted

30 Choose the best title for the passage.

① Ego Depletion as a Culprit for Food Craving on Stressful Days
② Ongoing War between Emotional Pain vs. Physical Hunger
③ Get Even with Your Inner Radishes through Balanced Diet Habits
④ Task Difficulty: a Superficial Excuse for Weight Gain

[31-34]

Experiments have shown that in selecting personnel for a job, interviewing is at best a hindrance and may even cause harm. These studies have disclosed that the judgments of interviewers differ markedly and bear little or no relationship to the adequacy of job applicants. Of the many reasons why this should be the case, three in particular stand out. The first reason is related to an error of judgment known as the halo effect. If a person has one noticeable good trait, their other characteristics will be judged as better than they really are. Thus, an individual who dresses smartly and shows self-confidence is likely to be judged capable of doing a job well regardless of his or her real ability. The horns effect is ⓐ essentially the same error, but focuses on one particular bad trait. Here the individual will be judged as incapable of doing a good job.

Interviewers are also prejudiced by an effect called the primacy effect. This error occurs when interpretation of later information is distorted by earlier connected information. Hence, in an interview situation, the interviewer spends most of the interview trying to confirm the impression given by the candidate in the first few moments. Studies have repeatedly demonstrated that such an impression is unrelated to the aptitude of the applicant.

The phenomenon known as the contrast effect also skews the judgment of interviewers. A suitable candidate may be underestimated because he or she contrasts with a previous one who appears exceptionally intelligent. Likewise, an average candidate who is preceded by one who gives a weak showing may be judged as more suitable than he or she really is.

Since interviews as a form of personnel selection have been shown to be inadequate, other selection procedures have been devised that more accurately predict candidate suitability. Of the various tests devised, the predictor that appears to do this most successfully is cognitive ability as measured by a variety of verbal and spatial tests.

31 What does the author mean by the phrase "ⓐ essentially the same error"?

① The effect of the error is the same.
② The error is based on the same kind of misjudgment.
③ The effect focuses only on negative traits.
④ The individual is considered less capable of the job.

32 **Which of the following applicants would probably be hired for the job based on an interview in which the typical interview errors are made?**

① A well-dressed, confident person following someone who appears very intelligent
② An unconfident, well-dressed person following someone who is well-dressed and confident
③ A well-dressed, confident person following someone who has apparent flaws
④ A confident person following a well-dressed, confident person

33 **Which of the following statements would the author most likely agree with concerning the actions of an interviewer looking for the best applicant for a job?**

① The interviewer should spend time trying to confirm a first impression.
② The interviewer should be confident and well-dressed.
③ The interviewer should be aware that this process is a hindrance to finding the right person.
④ The interviewer should look for other ways to choose the best applicant.

34 **The paragraphs following the passage most likely discuss which of the following?**

① Other reasons for misjudgments about applicants
② More information on the kinds of judgmental effects
③ More information on tests measuring cognitive ability
④ Other selection procedures included in interviewing

[35-36]

A recent paper by Uma Karmarkar of Harvard Business School and Bryan Bollinger of Duke Fuqua School of Business finds that shoppers who bring their own bags when they buy groceries like to reward themselves for it. For two years the authors tracked transactions at a supermarket in America. Perhaps unsurprisingly, shoppers who brought their own bags bought more green products than those who used the store's bags. But the eco-shoppers were also more likely to buy sweets, ice cream and crisps.

Psychologists call this sort of behaviour "moral licensing." Although this example may seem harmless, the results can be perverse. A study from 2011 on water-conservation in Massachusetts shows how. In the experiment, some 150 apartments were divided into two groups. Half received water-saving tips and weekly estimates of their usage; the other half served as a control. The households that were urged to use less water did so: their consumption fell by an average of 6% compared with the control group. The hitch was that their electricity consumption rose by 5.6%. The moral licensing was so strong, in other words, that it more or less outweighed the original act of virtue.

Moral licensing seems to occur when _____. In one study, participants imagined themselves doing community service. Then they were asked to pick between two rewards: an indulgent one (a pair of designer jeans) and a practical one (a vacuum cleaner). If they were told to imagine that they had been sentenced to community service for a driving violation, they were much less likely to choose the jeans than if they pictured themselves as volunteers.

35 **The underlined expression, "moral licensing," means a tendency _____.**

① to act morally in front of others
② to feel morally superior to others
③ to indulge yourself for doing something good
④ to give yourself permission to do something virtuous
⑤ to punish yourself for doing something bad

36 **Which of the following is most appropriate for the blank?**

① people feel bad about others
② people violate the laws
③ people are not willing to make sacrifices
④ virtuous conduct is not obligatory
⑤ the consumption patterns change

[37-39]

Broadly speaking, individuals who score highly on measures of extraversion tend to seek stimulation, whereas those who score low tend to avoid it. When asked to describe a typical extrovert, most people tend to think of the lively "party animal," equating extraversion with a preference for social interactions. However, individuals who score highly for extraversion seek more than just social stimulation; they also tend to gravitate toward other stimulating situations, including active leisure, travel, and even celebrity.

Introverts, on the other hand, have a generally lower affinity for stimulation. They find too much stimulation, of whatever type, ⓐ rather than ⓑ . Contrary to popular belief, introverts are not necessarily shy or fearful about social situations, unless they also score highly on measure of social anxiety and neuroticism.

On this basis, one might assume that extroverts would be drawn to extreme environments where they could satisfy their desire for stimulating situations, whereas introverts would find them unattractive. And yet, extreme environments may also expose people to monotony and solitude — experiences that extroverts would find aversive, but which are tolerated or even enjoyed by well-balanced introverts.

37 According to the author, extroverts are most likely to enjoy an extreme activity if _____.

① it is stimulating enough
② it is very popular among people
③ it helps to cultivate leadership
④ it attracts many celebrities

38 From the context, which of the following ordered pairs best fits into Ⓐ and Ⓑ?

	Ⓐ		Ⓑ
①	exciting	–	boring
②	threatening	–	restraining
③	beneficial	–	harmful
④	draining	–	energizing

39 Which of the following is stated about introverts in the passage?

① They are eager for intellectual stimulation.
② They are vulnerable to neuroticism.
③ They are considered as shy in general.
④ They are fearful of solitary activities.

[40-42]

B. F. Skinner, who transformed the landscape of modern psychology, ⓐ coined the term operant conditioning to explain the acquisition of learning. Operant conditioning is the process by which organisms learn to behave in ways that produce desirable outcomes. The behavior itself is called an "operant" because it is designed to operate on the environment. In other words, in contrast to classical conditioning — which involves the learning of associations between stimuli resulting in a passive response — operant conditioning involves the learning of an association between a spontaneously emitted action and its consequences.

Skinner also used the term reinforcement instead of *reward* or *satisfaction*. Objectively defined, a reinforcer is any stimulus that _____ⓐ_____ the likelihood of a prior response. There are two types of reinforcers: positive and negative. A *positive reinforcer* strengthens a prior response through the presentation of a positive stimulus. In contrast, a *negative reinforcer* strengthens a response through the removal of an aversive stimulus.

Skinner was quick to point out that Skinner was quick to point out that punishment is not a form of negative reinforcement. Although the two are often confused, punishment has the opposite effect: It _____ⓑ_____ the likelihood of a prior response. There are two types of punishment. A *positive punisher* weakens a response through the presentation of an aversive stimulus to weaken specific behaviors. In contrast, a *negative punisher* weakens behaviors through the removal of a stimulus typically characterized as positive.

40 Which is closest in meaning to the underlined ⓐ coined?

① induced
② invented
③ referred
④ repeated

41 Which pair best fits in the blanks Ⓐ and Ⓑ?

	Ⓐ	Ⓑ		Ⓐ	Ⓑ
①	remits	repeals	②	denies	approves
③	rejects	receives	④	increases	decreases

42 According to the passage, which is true?

① A positive punisher is a stimulus encouraging a behavior.
② A negative reinforcer is a stimulus reducing a behavior.
③ Positive reinforcement improves the probability of a behavior.
④ Negative punishment is the same as negative reinforcement.

[43–44]

Education is both an uplifting and integrating force. It uplifts, as people acquire the skills and knowledge to lead dignified lives, fulfil their aspirations and contribute to society. It is also an integrating force, because as people improve their lives through education, we have better chances of narrowing the gaps of inequality. The uplifting and integrating forces strengthen each other. Both objectives are being _____Ⓐ_____ today. Rapid technological advancements put a shorter expiry date on the skills and knowledge we acquired in schools and higher education, and globalization has widened social inequality. Recently, I have spoken extensively in Parliament on what we have done and will be doing to strengthen the integrative aspect of education. Today, I will not talk about inequality. Today, I will talk about the changes we need to make to ensure that education continues to uplift lives and prepare our young for the future. This is the central question every educator in the world is asking — how to prepare our young for the future?

43 The targeted audiences of the speech are _____.

① congressmen
② news reporters
③ educators
④ diplomats
⑤ parents

44 What is most appropriate for the blank Ⓐ?

① maintained
② achieved
③ pursued
④ challenged
⑤ promoted

[45-47]

The false smile, a ubiquitous social lubricant, has been unmasked by new research that has differentiated the specific muscle patterns in smiles reflecting true delight from those masking displeasure. Psychologist Dr. Ekman and his colleagues have developed a technique for analyzing more than 100 muscle patterns of the face as a person changes expression. With their method, they have been able to determine precisely which of those muscles is at play when the face takes on a given emotional expression.

In a study on lying, real smiles differed from those that hid unhappy feelings on two counts. In spontaneous smiles, the cheeks move up and the muscles around the eyes tighten, making the lines that extend from the corners of the eyes — crow's feet, and the skin around the eyebrow droops down a bit toward the eye. In the false smile, however, the face reveals traces of unhappy feelings behind the smile that can be seen apart from the supposed expression of pleasure — for instance, a slight furrowing of the muscle between the eyebrows. The eyes will not develop crow's feet unless the smile is especially broad. And even then, the tell-tale droop of skin around the eyebrow, which is difficult to feign, will not emerge. This research may be of particular importance to those who sometimes need to rely on subtle cues to know when a person is trying to hide physical pain, emotional anguish, or evil intention behind the mask of a smile.

45 Which of the following would be the best title for the passage?

① The Anatomy of Real and Fake Smiles
② Facial Expressions and Muscle Movements
③ Reading the Facial Expression of Emotion
④ How to Tell if Someone Is Lying

46 According to the passage, which of the following is a sign of a real smile?

① Wrinkled eyelids
② Furrowed eyebrows
③ Extended eyebrow lines
④ Droopy eyebrows

47 Which of the following is NOT stated or implied in the passage?

① The cheeks move up in the real smile.
② There are more than 100 facial muscles.
③ This research can be used for criminal investigations.
④ Smiling falsely is a common practice.

[48-51]

[A] Although many people use the two words "guilt" and "shame" interchangeably, from a psychological perspective, they actually refer to different experiences. Guilt and shame sometimes go hand in hand; the same action may give rise to feelings of both shame and guilt, where the former reflects how we feel about ourselves and the latter involves an awareness that our actions have injured someone else. In other words, shame relates to self; guilt to others.

[B] According to Dictionary.com, guilt involves the awareness of having done something wrong; it arises from our actions (even if it might be one that occurs in fantasy). Shame may result from the awareness of guilt but apparently is not the same thing as guilt. It's a painful feeling about how we appear to others (and to ourselves) and doesn't necessarily depend on our having done anything. I once said something hurtful at a dinner party, and on some level, I intended it to be hurtful. Afterward, I felt guilty because I could see that I had hurt my friend. More painfully, I also felt ashamed that I was the sort of person who would behave that way. Guilt arose as a result of inflicting pain on somebody else; I felt shame in relation to myself.

[C] In order to feel guilt about the harm you may have done to somebody else, you must recognize him or her as a distinct individual, to begin with. Thus, a person who struggles with separation and merger issues might not feel true guilt even if he or she were to use that word to describe a feeling. Many people who display narcissistic behavior often suffer from profound feelings of shame but have little authentic concern for other people; they don't tend to feel genuinely guilty. The lack of empathy to be found in narcissistic personality disorder makes real guilt unlikely since guilt depends upon the ability to intuit how someone else might feel.

[D] When shame is especially pervasive, it can preclude feelings of genuine concern and guilt from developing; the sense of being damaged is so powerful and painful that it crowds out feelings for anyone else. In such cases, idealization often comes into play: other people are then viewed as perfect, the lucky ones who have the ideal shame-free life we crave; powerful envy may be the (unconscious) result. In those cases, we might take pleasure in hurting the person we envy rather than feeling guilty about it.

48 According to the above passage, which of the following is NOT true about guilt?

① Guilt interferes with an other-oriented connection.
② Guilt involves a condemnation of a specific behavior.
③ Guilt-proneness is positively associated with empathy.
④ Guilt requires more sophisticated cognitive abilities than shame.
⑤ The capacity to feel guilt depends on the psychological growth to view other people as separate.

49 Which of the following would be the best title for paragraph [C]?

① The Self in Shame and Guilt
② Shame, Guilt, and Psychoanalysis
③ Authentic Shame and Genuine Guilt
④ Shame and Guilt as Moral Emotions
⑤ The Link between Shame and Interpersonal Sensitivity

50 Which of the following is the best summary of paragraph [D]?

① Shame-free state is the cause of envy.
② Shame can lead to idealization of others.
③ Shame-proneness is often caused by envy.
④ The self-focus of shame can impede sensitivity to others.
⑤ The feelings of shame are induced by the sense of being damaged.

51 Which of the following is the best summary of the author's argument in the above passage?

① Shame and guilt induce different emotions.
② Shame and guilt relate to interpersonal empathy.
③ The self-focus of shame can impede the development of guilt.
④ The difference between shame and guilt can be examined in the role of the self.
⑤ Shame involves negative evaluations of the self while guilt involves positive evaluations of the self.

PART 2

에듀윌 편입
솔루션 독해 Advanced

Reading

자연과학

8강 과학 / 기술

9강 우주 / 지구

10강 건강 / 의학

11강 환경 / 동식물

8강 과학 / 기술

Read the following passages and answer the questions. [01–49]

[01–02]

Perhaps the most significant problem with the media hyperbole concerning cloning is the easy assumption that humans simply are a product of their genes — a view usually called "genetic essentialism." Television hosts and radio personalities have asked whether it would be possible to stock an entire basketball team with clones of Michael Jordan. In response, philosophers, theologians, and other experts have reiterated wearily that, although human behavior undeniably has a genetic component, a host of other factor — including uterine environment, family dynamics, social setting, diet, and other personal history — play important roles in an individual's development. Consequently, a clone produced from the DNA of an outstanding athlete might not be interested in sports. What's more, the cloning issue reveals the way in which the mass media foster attitudes of technological and scientific determinism by implying that scientific 'progress' cannot be halted. Of course, many scientists share these attitudes, and, too often, they refuse to accept moral responsibility for their participation in research that may contribute to human suffering.

01 The best title of the passage would be _____.

① Benefits of Scientific Progress
② Media and the Ethics of Cloning
③ Media's Contribution to Anti-cloning Campaigns
④ Sports and Scientific Determinism
⑤ Regulation of Cloning through Laws

02 According to the passage, which of the following is true?

① Scientists are entitled to adopt the objective attitude towards moral controversy.
② The media seem to be obsessed with the idea of DNA as fate.
③ Most scientists admit that cloning research needs to be limited.
④ Most theologians have very little knowledge of science.
⑤ There has been too much negative media attention on human cloning.

[03-04]

　　Creativity for the scientist does have certain characteristics that are unique. To begin with, the scientist picks his problem because he knows enough about it to know that no one knows very much about it — except that there are _____Ⓐ_____ there. Out of insight or inspiration, he suggests a possible answer to one of the questions: for example, what is a possible structure for the atom? What does bind the atoms together to form molecules? By what means does the living cell store the chemical energy released within its walls? The creative moment occurs when the suggested answer is being formed. Naturally, the scientist would like to be proved right, and so the performance of the deciding experiment can never be the _____Ⓑ_____ it is popularly thought to be. Experiment carries all the emotion of a contest. Objectivity lies in the scientist's willingness to accept, however reluctantly, evidence that his brilliant conception is wrong. Once Nature gives its decision, there is no appeal. In fairly short order, the scientist is ruthlessly informed whether his creation is valid or not.

03 윗글에서 내용의 흐름상, 빈칸 Ⓐ와 Ⓑ에 들어가기에 가장 적절한 것은?

	Ⓐ		Ⓑ
①	infinite orders	–	adverse trial
②	assumed hypotheses	–	fervent experience
③	creative possibilities	–	supportive task
④	unanswered questions	–	dispassionate exercise

04 윗글을 통해 추론할 수 있는 것으로 가장 적절한 것은?

① Objectivity is the most important quality for a scientist in suggesting a possible answer.
② The world of science needs to be restricted to researching on testable phenomena.
③ Scientists exert creativity in their quest for scientific problems.
④ Inspirational conception plays a crucial role in interpreting the results of an experiment.

[05-07]

The phenomenon of simultaneous discovery-what science historians call "multiples" — turns out to be _____. The law of the conservation of energy, so significant in science and philosophy, was formulated four times independently in 1847, by Joule, Thomson, Colding and Helmholz. They had been anticipated by Robert Mayer in 1842. The sheer number of multiples could mean only one thing: scientific discoveries must, in some sense, be inevitable. They must be in the air, products of the intellectual climate of a specific time and place. It should not surprise us, then, that calculus was invented by two people at the same moment in history. Leibniz and Newton may never have actually sat down together and shared their work in detail. But they occupied a common intellectual milieu.

Of course, that is not the way Newton saw it. He had done his calculus work in the mid-1660s, but never published it. And after Leibniz came out with his calculus, in the 1680s, people in Newton's circle accused Leibniz of stealing his work, setting off one of the great scientific scandals of the 17th century. That is the inevitable human response. We're reluctant to believe that great discoveries are in the air. We want to believe that great discoveries are in our heads.

05 Choose the one that best fills in the blank.

① relatively timed
② bafflingly mysterious
③ extremely common
④ absolutely novel

06 Which of the following can be inferred about "multiples"?

① They do not transcend time and place.
② They happen without prior knowledge of one another.
③ They enhance the reputation of the discoverer.
④ They add importance to an already made discovery.

07 What is the main idea of the passage?

① Plagiarism of ideas is rampant among rivals.
② Credit must be given to multiple scientists for the same discovery.
③ Multiples are evidence that scientific discoveries are predestined.
④ Science historians must record multiples objectively.

[08-09]

The greatest scientific example of the sensing type was Sir Isaac Newton. He convinced three centuries of science to look first at the facts and only then to draw cautious inferences. The real world was neither what we wanted it to be, nor influenced in any way by our wishes. We must humbly reflect God-given realities on the pupils of our eyes and not let our beliefs or conceits stand in the way. Only after we have made sure of all the facts should we start to draw inferences. Yet science moves on, and theoretical physics is quite another challenge, needing intuition to disentangle its puzzling anomalies. Albert Einstein was famed for his intuitive powers and would cut himself shaving if an exciting intuition struck him. But none of this means that he ignored the available facts. Having gained his intuitions, he proceeded to test them — an example of how one type helps to verify the conjecture of another.

08. What would be the best title of the passage above?

① the tedious development of scientific analysis
② sensing versus intuiting
③ the cautious progress of big data
④ the decreasing tendency of anomalies and uncertainty

09. Which of the following is true according to the passage above?

① Newton analyzed the situation and looked hard at facts. These speak for themselves, needing no general theorization.
② Einstein gained deep insights into the meaning of the issue. These speak for themselves, needing no factual support.
③ Einstein gained deep insights into the meaning of the issue. Facts are dependent on context. Once he grasped the context, he did not need to think about facts themselves.
④ Newton analyzed the situation and looked hard at the fact, but then he started to draw inferences until the meaning of this issue became clear.

[10-11]

Blockchain is an enormous digital record open for anyone with internet access to see. This record is not maintained by any individual or organization, but by approximately 9,000 computers in a distributed network. The computers' owners volunteer to add their machines to the network because, in exchange for their computer's services, they sometimes receive payment. All the information in the record is permanent. It cannot be changed because each of the computers keeps a copy of the record. If you wanted to hack the system, you would have to hack every computer on the network which has so far proved impossible, despite many trying. The collective power of all these computers is greater than the world's top 500 supercomputers combined. New information is added to the record every few minutes, but it can be added only when all the computers signal their approval, which they do when they receive satisfactory proof that the new information is correct. Everybody knows how the system works, but nobody can change how it works because it is _____Ⓐ_____.

10 According to passage, which of the following is true of blockchain?

① Its information is secure.
② It consists of 500 supercomputers.
③ Owners can delete its information.
④ People pay to become part of it.

11 From the context, which of the following best fits into Ⓐ?

① uncontrolled
② fully automated
③ regularly updated
④ freely available

[12-13]

Science is not, on the whole, a glamorous enterprise. A single set of data points routinely represents months in the lab or years out in the field. Even the most productive researchers are constantly getting stuck and having to dig their way out. Meanwhile, most researchers' labors end up wasted, lost on hypotheses that were ill-conceived or simply unlucky. And yet they keep at it, now and then with fatal consequences. The difficulty of the work is essential to it; the true subject of science, one could argue, is _____.

And what goes for science also goes for science writing, or at least for the best of it. It is less about answers than about questions: why does time move only in one direction? How did life begin? What happened to the Neanderthals? The stories are exciting but also demanding. They take us to places that — in some cases literally, in some metaphorically — are hard to get to. They ask us to look at the world in a new way.

12 Which of the following cannot be inferred from the passage?

① For meaningful outcomes scientists often spend more time and energy than they originally plan to.
② Fruits of scientific research can be earned through perseverance.
③ Research success depends on expeditious experiments.
④ Even the best of science writing does not necessarily provide definitive explanations.

13 Choose the one that best fills in the blank.

① the amazing human intellect
② the obduracy of reality
③ the origin of the universe
④ our vulnerability to pain

[14-15]

Accustomed to living with almost routine scientific breakthroughs, we have yet to come to terms with the fact that the most compelling 21st-century technologies pose a different threat than the technologies that have come before. Each of these technologies also offers untold promise: The vision of near immortality that Kurzweil sees in his robot dreams drives us forward; genetic engineering may soon provide treatments, if not outright cures, for most diseases; and nanotechnology and nanomedicine can address yet more ills. Together they could significantly extend our average life span.

_____Ⓐ_____, with each of these technologies, a sequence of small, individually sensible advances leads to an accumulation of great power and, concomitantly, great danger. The 21st-century technologies — genetics, nanotechnology, and robotics — are so powerful that they can spawn whole new classes of accidents and abuses. Most dangerously, for the first time, these accidents and abuses are widely within the reach of individuals or small groups. They will not require large facilities or rare raw materials. Knowledge alone will enable the use of them. _____Ⓑ_____ we have the possibility not just of weapons of mass destruction but of knowledge-enabled mass destruction, this destructiveness hugely amplified by the power of self-replication. I think it is no exaggeration to say we are on the cusp of the further perfection of extreme evil, an evil whose possibility spreads well beyond that which weapons of mass destruction bequeathed to the nation-states, on to a surprising and terrible empowerment of extreme individuals.

14 윗글의 빈칸 Ⓐ, Ⓑ에 들어갈 말로 가장 적절한 것은?

	Ⓐ		Ⓑ
①	But	–	However
②	Yet	–	Thus
③	Therefore	–	Nevertheless
④	Accordingly	–	Likewise

15 윗글에 드러난 필자의 어조로 가장 적절한 것은?

① critical
② satirical
③ duplicitous
④ declarative

[16-18]

 A preview of Christmas toys for 2012 has ignited a new debate over nature, nurture, toys and sex. Hamleys, the 251-year-old London toy store, recently discarded its pink "girls" and blue "boys" sections in favor of gender-neutral displays. Replacing floors dedicated to Barbie dolls and action figures, merchandise is now organized by types (Soft Toys) and interests (Outdoor). Toy-maker Lego, however, has launched a line of Friends, which features pastel-colored blocks that allow a girl to build herself a cafe or a beauty salon.

 So who has it right? Should gender be systematically removed from playthings? ⓐ Or is Lego merely being realistic, meeting girls half way in an attempt to spark their interest in engineering? The new Friends collection, Lego says, was based on research revealing that the sexes play differently and that preschool girls prefer playthings that are pretty and allow them to tell stories. ⓑ In order to be gender-fair, Lego insists, they have to be gender-specific.

 These findings are offset by other studies of preschoolers which show that the environment in which children play can encourage new attitudes. Encouraging gendered play patterns may negatively impact kids' potential, while promoting a variety of play styles may be beneficial. The rebellion against gender apartheid may have begun and Hamleys is perhaps on to something.

16 In the underlined part ⓐ, the author asks readers to consider whether gender should be _____ in playthings.

① definitely preserved
② partially accommodated
③ completely removed
④ strongly reinforced

17 What is the best interpretation of the underlined part ⓑ?

① To be socially responsible, toy companies should offer more toys which cater to girls' preferences.
② Toy companies should develop products which incorporate gender preferences.
③ Boys and girls should be encouraged to play with toys designed for the opposite sex.
④ Toy companies should clearly label their products, indicating whether they are for boys or for girls.

18 What would be the best title for this passage?

① Favorite Toys of Young Children
② Toy Stores Preparing for 2012 Christmas Sales
③ Will Boys and Girls Ever Get Along?
④ Should the World of Toys Be Gender-Free?

[19-20]

To understand why introverts and extroverts might react differently to the prospect of rewards, you have to know a little about brain structure. Our limbic system, which we share with the most primitive mammals and which Dorn calls the "old brain," is emotional and instinctive. It comprises various structures, including the amygdala, and it's highly interconnected with the nucleus accumbens, sometimes called the brain's "pleasure center." The old brain, according to Dorn, is constantly telling us, "Yes, yes, yes! Eat more, drink more, take lots of risk, go for all the gusto you can get, and above all, do not think!" The reward-seeking, pleasure-loving part of the old brain is what Dorn believes spurred people to treat their life savings like chips at the casino. We also have a "new brain" called the neocortex, which evolved many thousands of years after the limbic system. The new brain is responsible for thinking, planning, language, and decision-making — some of the very faculties that make us human. Although the new brain also plays a significant role in our emotional lives, it's the seat of rationality. It's job, according to Dorn, includes saying, "No, no, no! Don't do that, because it's dangerous, makes no sense, and is not in your best interests, or those of your family, or of society." The old brain and the new brain do work together, but not always efficiently. Sometimes they're actually in _____, and then our decisions are a function of which one is sending out stronger signals.

19 Choose the one that best fills in the blank.

① equilibrium
② balance
③ conflict
④ turmoil

20 Which of the following CANNOT be inferred according to the passage?

① The new brain plays an important role in our emotional lives.
② The old brain seeks reward and pleasure, which often makes people reckless.
③ We share both the old brain and the new brain with the primitive mammals.
④ Genetically, the new brain is what makes human distinctively different from other animals.

[21-23]

One may object that I exaggerate the artificiality of our world. Man must obey the law of gravity as surely as does a stone, and as a living organism man must depend for food, and in many other ways, on the world of biological phenomena. I shall plead guilty to overstatement, while protesting that the exaggeration is slight. To say that an astronaut, or even an airplane pilot, is obeying the law of gravity, hence is a perfectly natural phenomenon, is true, but its truth calls for some sophistication in what we mean by obeying a natural law. Aristotle did not think it natural for heavy things to rise or light ones to fall; but presumably we have a deeper understanding of natural than he did. So too must be careful about equating biological with natural. A forest may be a phenomenon of nature; a farm certainly is not. The very species upon which we depend for our food — our corn and our cattle — are artifacts of our ingenuity. A plowed field is no more part of nature than an asphalted street — and no less. These examples set the terms of our problem, for those things we call artifacts are not apart from nature. They have _____. At the same time they are adapted to human goals and purposes. They are what they are in order to satisfy our desire to fly or to eat well.

21 Which of the following is the most appropriate for the blank?

① no dispensation to ignore or violate natural law
② dispensation to ignore or violate natural law
③ no dispensation to ignore or violate artificial law
④ dispensation to ignore or violate artificial law

22 What would be the best title of the passage above?

① the complex nature of the natural law
② the complex nature of the artifact
③ the pejorative nature of natural science
④ the pejorative traits of the artificiality

23 How would you describe the author's attitude to artificiality?

① surprised   ② ridiculous
③ joyful   ④ inquisitive

[24-26]

 Since Hitler's day the armory of technical devices at the disposal of the would-be dictator has been considerably enlarged. As well as the radio, the loud-speaker, the moving picture camera and the rotary press, the contemporary propagandist can make use of television to broadcast the image as well as the voice of his client, and can record both image and voice on spools of magnetic tape. Thanks to technological progress, Big Brother can now be almost as omnipresent as God. Nor is it only on the technical front that the hand of the would-be dictator has been strengthened. Since Hitler's day a great deal of work has been carried out in those fields of applied psychology and neurology which are the special province of the propagandist, the indoctrinator and the brain-washer. In the past these specialists in the art of changing people's minds were empiricists. By a method of trial and error they had worked out a number of techniques and procedures, which they used very effectively without, however, knowing precisely why they were effective. Today the art of mind-control is in process of becoming _____. The practitioners of this science know what they are doing and why. They are guided in their work by theories and hypotheses solidly established on a massive foundation of experimental evidence. Thanks to the new insights and the new techniques made possible by these insights, the nightmare that was "all but realized in Hitler's totalitarian system" may soon be completely realizable.

24 Which is the most appropriate for the blank?

① a dream
② a fantasy
③ a science
④ a mystery

25 According to the passage, which is true?

① The totalitarianism like Hitler's is impossible in the age of technology.
② People are not easily manipulated by the technology of propaganda.
③ Hitler used all kinds of propaganda technology including television.
④ The technology of brain-washing has developed to the level of science.

26 Which is the topic of the passage?

① Hitler and propaganda
② Dictatorship and mass manipulation
③ Technology and empiricism
④ Hitler and new techniques of neurology

[27-29]

Longer battery life and miniaturization are making tracking cheaper and more practical. The easiest way is to use smartphones. Many mobile operators offer child-tracking at extra cost, but the number of free tracking applications is growing fast. These services and devices can provide children's location, or send alerts about their behaviour. Parents in Japan and America are the keenest on such gizmos. Europeans, seemingly more relaxed about child safety and with more complex privacy laws, are less enamoured. Enthusiasts say tracking means more freedom, not less. Parents who know they can easily find their children may be happier to let them roam. Teenagers are spared annoying phone calls. Critics say _____. Savvy kidnappers will dispose of phones or alert trackers. And strangers rarely attack children anyway: parents are the most likely murderers, and accidents are a far graver danger than assault. Location tracking won't stop children falling into a river. The same technology also enables snooping on adults. In America mobile subscribers can buy location-tracking services for all users of a family phone plan. Some survivors of domestic violence say this makes it harder to escape. Parents use webcams to keep an eye on their children's carers. A Saudi government agency that sends men text messages if their children leave the country also helps track wives.

27 **The best title of the passage would be _____.**

① New Families?: Change in Modern Relationships
② Positive Side for Technology and Children
③ Ethics of State Surveillance
④ Tracking Children: Nice for Parents, Not for Privacy
⑤ Technology: Unreliable Servant

28 **Which of the following is most appropriate for the blank?**

① tracking devices can also be used by kidnappers
② tracking does not really protect children
③ tracking devices are too expensive
④ teenagers do not like to carry tracking devices
⑤ smartphones are more efficient than tracking devices

29 **According to the passage, which of the following is true?**

① High cost of tracking applications deters wider use of tracking devices.
② Tracking devices may promote a dehumanizing tendency.
③ Europeans are not very keen on tracking devices because they trust each other more.
④ Mobile tracking services help prevent domestic violence in Saudi Arabia.
⑤ Children are more prone to surveillance than adults.

[30-31]

Is the bitcoin boom about to turn into one of history's biggest busts? The digital currency's massive surge this year — it's up more than 1,400% — has all the hallmarks of a huge _____Ⓐ_____ bubble, according to people such as Warren Buffett. And if it bursts, the results are likely to be _____Ⓑ_____. "In terms of how it ends, bubble history suggests it will be with a bang, rather than a whimper," said Sharon Zoller, an economist at ANZ. [A] "I can't think of any reason why this time would be different." To better understand what may lie ahead, here's the lowdown on one famous financial bubble in history: Tulip mania. In the early 17th century, speculation helped drive the value of tulip bulbs in the Netherlands to previously unheard of prices. [B] Newly imported from Turkey, tulips were a big novelty at the time. Hard data from those days is _____Ⓒ_____, so it's difficult to gauge exactly how much prices soared. [C] But people were putting up their homes as collateral. like many bubbles, prices, were driven by greed or the fear of missing out. Speculators were buying bulbs in the hope that they could sell them on at an even higher price. [D] Again, it didn't last. A flurry of sales caused a domino effect, and prices collapsed. [E] "Prices will become so out of reach of the common man that ultimately demand fades," he said.

30 다음 주어진 표현이 들어갈 위치로 가장 적절한 곳은?

> Stephen Innes, head of Asian trading at currency broker Oanda, believes bitcoin bubble could go the same way.

① [A] ② [B]
③ [C] ④ [D]
⑤ [E]

31 윗글의 빈칸 Ⓐ, Ⓑ, Ⓒ에 들어갈 말로 가장 적절한 것은?

	Ⓐ	Ⓑ	Ⓒ
①	scarce	spectacular	speculative
②	speculative	spectacular	scarce
③	scarce	speculative	scarce
④	speculative	scarce	spectacular
⑤	spectacular	scarce	speculative

[32–33]

Despite evidence of innate hedonic responses to basic tastes, the vast majority of specific food likes and dislikes are not ⓐ predetermined — no one is born liking blue cheese, for example. This is not to suggest that basic sensory qualities are ⓑ unimportant. On the contrary, relatively fixed hedonic responses to sweet, salty, bitter, and umami (glutamate taste) tastes, and almost certainly fat, are present at or shortly after birth, and continue to exert an influence on food preferences. The strong affinity that children show for very sweet foods, and the persistence of the early development of liking for the taste of salt and salty foods throughout life appear to be ⓒ universal. A majority in many Western societies also choose a diet that is high in fat. However, innate responses do not account for the broad range of food likes and dislikes that develop beyond infancy. For instance, humans and many other mammals can detect bitterness at low levels and find it ⓓ palatable because it is a potential sign of toxicity. Yet, while coffee and beer are typically rejected on first tasting, they are ultimately the strongest contenders for being the global beverages. The pungency of spicy foods is also initially rejected. Worldwide, though, chili is second only to salt as a food spice. Thus, although innate influences are clearly important in food selection, these are ⓔ modified by our experience with foods (although both physiological makeup and culture will partly determine the extent to which experience is allowed to operate). Then, what is more important than our innate preferences is the fact that _____.

32 윗글의 밑줄 친 ⓐ~ⓔ 중 문맥상 낱말의 쓰임이 적절하지 않은 것은?

① ⓐ
② ⓑ
③ ⓒ
④ ⓓ
⑤ ⓔ

33 윗글의 빈칸에 들어갈 말로 가장 적절한 것은?

① foods may be rejected for a variety of reasons
② we are predisposed to learn to like or dislike foods
③ we have access to a wide range of potential nutrients
④ food's hedonic values can vary significantly across cultures
⑤ food preferences are strongly influenced by cultural contexts

[34-35]

What do 'neural network,' 'machine learning,' and 'deep learning' actually mean? These are the three terms you're most likely to have heard lately. Neural networks are a type of computer architecture onto which artificial intelligence is built. These networks are a way of structuring a computer so that it looks like a cartoon of the brain, comprised of neuron-like nodes connected together in a web. Individually these nodes are dumb, answering extremely basic questions, but collectively they can tackle difficult problems. More importantly, with the right algorithms, they can be taught. Machine learning is a program you might run on a neural network, training computers to look for certain answers in pots of data. Deep learning is a particular type of machine learning that's only become popular over the past decade, largely thanks to two new resources: cheap processing power and abundant data (otherwise known as the internet). If a deep learning system is looking at a picture, each layer is essentially tackling a different magnification. The bottom layer might look at just a 5 x 5 grids of pixels, answering simply "yes" or "no" as to whether something shows up in that grid. If it answers yes, then the layer above looks to see how this grid fits into a larger pattern. Is this the beginning of a line, for example, or a corner? This process gradually builds up, allowing the software to understand even the most complicated data by breaking it down into constituent parts.

34 According to the passage, which is true?

① In a deep learning system, the most complicated data can be understood from the bottom layer.
② Deep learning is a type of computer architecture which makes machine learning possible.
③ Cheap processing power and abundant data enabled a neural network system to be developed.
④ In a neural network system, individual nodes collectively tackle difficult problems.

35 Which is indicated by the underlined part?

① processing complicated data at the bottom layer
② collectively tackling difficult problems
③ answering simple questions at the lower layer
④ breaking complicated data into constituent parts

[36-37]

This simple observation leads to a test for AI consciousness that _____Ⓐ_____ AIs with PC* from those that merely have features of cognitive consciousness, such as working memory and attention. The test would challenge an AI with a series of increasingly demanding natural language interactions to see how readily it can grasp and use concepts based on the internal experiences we associate with consciousness. A creature that merely has cognitive abilities, yet is a zombie, will lack these concepts, at least if we make sure that it does not have _____Ⓑ_____ knowledge of consciousness in its database. At the most elementary level, we might simply ask the machine if it conceives of itself as anything other than its physical self. We might also run a series of experiments to see whether the AI tends to prefer certain kinds of events to occur in the future, as opposed to in the past. Time in physics is _____Ⓒ_____, and a nonconscious AI should have no preference whatsoever, at least if it is boxed in** effectively. In contrast, conscious beings focus on the experienced present, and our subjective sense presses onto the future. The "AI Consciousness Test," or "the ACT Test" for short, may serve as a first step toward making machine consciousness accessible to objective investigations.

* Phenomenal Consciousness (PC): the felt quality of one's inner experience—what it feels like, from the inside, to be you
** boxing-in: making an AI unable to get information about the world or act outside of a circumscribed domain.

36 Which statement CANNOT be inferred from the passage?

① The ACT Test is designed to identify the AI's cognitive consciousness.
② Biological creatures with PC can imagine a state of afterlife.
③ An AI zombie has cognitive consciousness and may not behave as phenomenally conscious systems do.
④ Working memory and attention are two architectural features of cognitive consciousness.

37 Choose the BEST set of words for blanks Ⓐ, Ⓑ, and Ⓒ.

	Ⓐ	Ⓑ	Ⓒ
①	differentiates	proleptic	systemic
②	singles out	antecedent	symmetric
③	isolates	ancillary	centrifugal
④	separates	analeptic	centripetal

[38-39]

The 1600s were not, on the face of it, an obvious candidate for the description of the "age of genius." It was a world in which everyone was God-fearing and when everything from floods to comets was seen as the inscrutable will of a jealous, stern deity. [A] Yet it was from this unpromising soil that the modern, scientific world-view bloomed. The crowning achievement of the age — Isaac Newton's *Philosophiæ Naturalis Principia Mathematica* — is among the most influential books ever written; those with the mathematical fortitude to make sense of its deliberately obscure diagrams are struck dumb with admiration. The equations derived by the eccentric genius are still used to design cars, build bridges and send spacecraft into the cosmos. [B] But the legacy of the age is more than just a set of useful theories. The intuition of men like Newton and Johannes Kepler that, beneath the apparent chaos of everyday life, the universe is a regular, ordered machine that can be described with a few simple equations proved amazingly to be correct. [C] It is this idea of universality that is the true legacy of the scientific revolution. [D] The standard account tells us that the new science broke the stranglehold that the church and a few of its favoured pagan thinkers had exerted for centuries on Western thought. That is broadly true, but the reality was a good deal more complicated. [E] The proto-scientists did not spring into being as paid-up believers in modern materialism and rationality. [F] Newton divided his time between pursuits that today we would recognize as science and older, much more arcane disciplines such as alchemy and an obsessive search for numerological codes in the Bible. Newton intended his great system of the world as a tribute to a dazzlingly deft geometer-god. When others took it to suggest that, once the universal clockwork was wound up there would be no further need for divine intervention to keep the planets in their orbits, he was dismayed. In a sense, he was not the first of the scientists, but the last of the sorcerers.

38 When the above passage can be divided into three paragraphs, which would be the best boundary?

① [A] and [C]
② [B] and [D]
③ [B] and [F]
④ [C] and [E]
⑤ [D] and [F]

39 The underlined expression implies that _____.

① his conviction that the universe was an orderly place sprang from his religious belief
② he believed that the universe was something that could be comprehended by mortal minds
③ his scientific achievement was diminished by his belief in alchemy
④ he was neither a scientist nor a sorcerer
⑤ his scientific achievement kept his sorcerer persona hidden

[40-42]

    The conservation of energy means that the total energy in the world is kept the same. But in the irregular jigglings that energy can be spread about so uniformly that, in certain circumstances, there is no way to make more go one way than the other — there is no way to control it any more, I think that by an analogy I can give some idea of the difficulty, in this way. Imagine you are sitting on the beach with several towels, and suddenly a tremendous downpour comes. You pick up the towels as quickly as you can, and run into the bathhouse. Then you start to dry yourself, and you find that this towel is a little wet, but it is drier than you are. You keep drying with this one until you find it is too wet — it is wetting you as much as drying you — and you try another one; and pretty soon you discover a horrible thing — that all the towels are damp and so are you. There is no way to get any drier, even though you have many towels, because there is _____ Ⓐ _____ . I could invent a kind of quantity which I could call 'ease of removing water.' The towel has the same ease of removing water from it as you have, so when you touch yourself with the towel, as much water comes off the towel on to you as comes from you to the towel. It does not mean there is the same amount of water in the towel as there is on you — a big towel will have more water in it than a little towel — but they have the same dampness. When things get to the same dampness then there is nothing you can do any longer.

40 **Choose the best title for this passage.**

① Recognizing the Connection between Energy and Water
② Using Water to Analyse the Necessity for Energy Conservation
③ Saving Water Saves Energy
④ Understanding the Way Energy is Recycled

41 **Choose the best ending for Ⓐ.**

① no difference between the wetness of the towels and the wetness of yourself
② a big difference between drying yourself with a wet towel and a dry towel
③ no difference because you will get wet when you go back outside
④ a big difference between a wet towel and a dry towel

42 **The purpose of the analogy in this passage is to show that:**

① energy that is equally divided can function similar to water.
② energy is like water, in that its distribution fluctuates and its quantity remains the same.
③ towels, when wet, distribute an equal amount of water to the body's surface.
④ by constantly drying yourself, the water dried up can be reused in another towel.

[43–46]

Until the beginning of the 19th century, light was modeled as a stream of particles emitted by a source that stimulated the sense of sight on entering the eye. The chief architect of the particle theory of light was Newton. Most scientists accepted Newton's particle theory of light. During Newton's lifetime, however, another theory was proposed. In 1678, the Dutch physicist and astronomer Christiaan Huygens showed that a wave theory of light could also explain the laws of reflection and refraction.

The wave theory _____Ⓐ_____ for several reasons. First, all the waves known at the time traveled through some sort of medium, but light from the Sun could travel to Earth through empty space. Further, it was argued that if light were some form of wave, it would bend around obstacles; hence, we should be able to see around corners.

The first clear demonstration of the wave nature of light was provided in 1801 by Thomas Young, who showed that under appropriate conditions, light exhibits interference behavior. Light waves emitted by a single source and traveling along two different paths can arrive at some point and combine and cancel each other by _____Ⓑ_____. Such behaviour couldn't be explained at that time by a particle model, because scientists couldn't imagine how two or more particles could come together and cancel each other.

In 1905, Einstein published a paper that formulated the theory of light quanta and explained the photoelectric effect. He reached the conclusion that light was composed of corpuscles, or discontinuous quanta of energy. These corpuscles or quanta are now called photons to emphasize their particle-like nature. Electron interacts with one photon of light as if the electron had been struck by a particle. Yet the photon has wavelike characteristics, as implied by the fact that a frequency is used in its definition.

43 Which of the following is most appropriate for the blank Ⓐ?

① never refracted the essential aspects of light
② received immediate acceptance
③ explained the essential aspects of light
④ did not receive immediate acceptance

44 The main theme of the passage would be _____.

① the quality of energy
② the nature of light
③ the measurement of light
④ total internal reflection

45 Fill in the blank Ⓑ with suitable words.

① constructive guidance
② destructive interference
③ inappropriate manipulation
④ appropriate manipulation

46 We may infer from the passage that _____.

① Classical electromagnetic wave theory disregards the effects of interference.
② The cardinal aspects of lights are best understood through the wave model.
③ In the final analysis of light, Newton's vision is right.
④ Light has a number of physical properties; some associated with waves and others with particles.

[47-49]

The paradox that had troubled Einstein for a decade was this. In the mid-1800s, after a close study of the experimental work of the English physicist Michael Faraday, the Scottish physicist James Clerk Maxwell succeeded in uniting electricity and magnetism in the framework of the electromagnetic field. If you've ever been on a mountaintop just before a severe thunderstorm or stood close to a Van de Graaf generator, you have a visceral sense of what an electromagnetic field is, because you've felt it. In case you haven't, it is somewhat like a tide of electric and magnetic lines of force that permeate a region of space through which they pass. When you sprinkle iron filings near a magnet, for example, the orderly pattern they form traces out some of the invisible lines of magnetic force. When you take off a wool sweater on an especially dry day and hear a crackling sound and perhaps feel a momentary shock or two, you are witnessing evidence of electric lines of force generated by electric charges swept up by the fibers in your sweater. Beyond uniting these and all other electric and magnetic phenomena in one mathematical framework, Maxwell's theory showed — quite unexpectedly — that electromagnetic disturbances travel at a fixed and never-changing speed, a speed that turns out to equal that of light. From this, Maxwell realized that visible light itself is nothing but a particular kind of electromagnetic wave, one that is now understood to interact with chemicals in the retina, giving rise to the sensation of sight. Moreover (and this is crucial), Maxwell's theory also showed that all electromagnetic waves — visible light among them — are the epitome of the peripatetic traveler. They never stop. They never slow down. Light always travels at light speed.

All is well and good until we ask: what happens if we chase after a beam of light, at light speed? Intuitive reasoning, rooted in Newton's laws of motion, tells us that we will catch up with the light waves and so they will appear stationary; light will stand still. But according to Maxwell's theory, and all reliable observations, there is simply no such thing as stationary light: no one has ever held a stationary clump of light in the palm of his or her hand. Hence the problem. Luckily, Einstein was unaware that many of the world's leading physicists were struggling with this question (and were heading down many a spurious path) and pondered the paradox of Maxwell and Newton largely in the pristine privacy of his own thoughts.

47 According to the above passage, which of the following is not an instance of experiencing the electromagnetic field?

① The feeling one can have on a mountaintop just before a severe thunderstorm.
② The pattern iron filings show when they are spread near a magnet.
③ The cracking sound one can hear when taking off a wool sweater in a dry day.
④ The recognition that light travels at a fixed and never-changing speed.

48 According to the above passage, which of the following is the problem Einstein faced?

① The pattern of iron filings near a magnet is different from that which can be found on a wool sweater.
② Even though one would chase after a beam of light at light speed, the light can never be stationary.
③ Light is just a kind of electromagnetic wave, but it can interact with chemicals in the retina.
④ Light can permeate a region of space as a tide of electric and magnetic lines of force.

49 Which of the following is least likely to be inferred from the above passage?

① Both Maxwell and Newton recognized the paradox between the laws of motion and the speed of light.
② Maxwell managed to unite electricity and magnetism via a thorough investigation of Faraday's experiment.
③ According to Maxwell's theory, the prediction on light speed based on Newton's laws of motion is not borne out.
④ Both the pattern of iron filings near a magnet and the sound of a wool sweater can be explained by the electromagnetic field.

9강 우주 / 지구

Read the following passages and answer the questions. [01–47]

01 Select the statement most consistent with the passage.

Meet ANITA. Strictly, ANITA III — for she is the third iteration of the Antarctic Impulsive Transient Antenna. Her job, when she is launched sometime in the next few days, will be to float, suspended from a giant balloon, over Antarctica's ice, in order to record radio waves which that ice is giving off. These radio waves are generated by neutrinos passing through the ice, making Antarctica the biggest neutrino-detection laboratory in the world. The particular neutrinos that ANITA seeks are of extremely high energy. Where they come from, no one knows — nor, strictly speaking, is it actually known that they exist, for ANITAs I and II, which were smaller devices, failed to find them. But theory says they should be there, generated in whatever giant explosions also create cosmic rays. Cosmic rays are high-velocity protons, sprinkled with a smattering of heavier atomic nuclei, that fly through space until they hit something such as Earth's atmosphere, when they disintegrate into a shower of other particles. They have been known for a century, but their origin remains mysterious because, being electrically charged, their paths are bent by the galaxy's magnetic field. That means the directions they come from do not point to whatever created them. Neutrinos, however, are electrically neutral, as their name suggests. Their paths should thus point back towards their origins.

① ANITAs I and II failed because they were smaller devices than ANITA III.
② ANITA is the acronym of the name of a device used to study neutrinos.
③ Neutrinos have not been detected because they are electrically neutral.
④ Cosmic rays are low-velocity protons.

[02-03]

The effects of an earthquake are strongest in a broad zone surrounding the epicenter. Surface ground cracking often occurs, with horizontal and vertical displacements of several yards. Such movement does not usually occur during a major earthquake: slight periodic movements called 'fault creep' can be accompanied by microearthquakes, too small to be felt. The extent of earthquake vibration and subsequent damage to a region is partly dependent on characteristics of the ground. For example, earthquake vibration last longer and are of greater wave amplitudes in unconsolidated surface material. _____Ⓐ_____ poorly compacted fill or river deposits: bedrock areas receive fewer effects. The worst damage occurs in _____Ⓑ_____ populated urban areas where structures are not built to withstand intense shaking.

02 Which of the following is NOT TRUE for the above passage?

① During a major earthquake, horizontal and vertical earthquake usually occur.
② The characteristics of the ground partly affect the extent of earthquake vibration.
③ Densely populated urban areas could have the worst damage.
④ Horizontal and vertical earthquake do not usually occur during a major earthquake.
⑤ Earthquake vibrations may last shorter in consolidated surface material than unconsolidated one.

03 Which would be the most appropriate pair for the blank Ⓐ and Ⓑ?

	Ⓐ	Ⓑ
①	such as	clearly
②	such as	rarely
③	as for	scarcely
④	for instance	scarcely
⑤	such as	densely

[04-06]

Further encouragement for the existence of black holes came in 1967 with the discovery by a research student at Cambridge, Jocelyn Bell-Burnell, of objects in the sky that were emitting regular pulses of radio waves. At first Bell and her supervisor, Antony Hewish, thought they might have contact with an alien civilization in the galaxy. In the end, however, they came to the less romantic conclusion that these objects, which were given the name pulsars, were in fact rotating neutron stars that were emitting pulses of radio waves because of a complicated interaction between their magnetic fields and surrounding matter. This was bad news for writers of space westerns, but very hopeful for the small number of us who believed in black holes at that time: it was the first positive evidence that neutron stars existed. A neutron star has a radius of about ten miles, only a few times the critical radius at which a star becomes a black hole. If a star could collapse to such a small size, it is not reasonable to expect that other stars could collapse to even smaller size and become black holes. How could we hope to detect a black hole, as by its very definition it does not emit any light? It might seem a bit like looking for a black cat _____. Fortunately, there is a way. As John Michell pointed out in his pioneering paper in 1783, a black hole still exerts a gravitational force on nearby objects.

04 The passage above is mainly about _____.

① the legacy of black hole
② the function of black hole
③ the discovery of black hole
④ the latent power of black hole

05 Choose the one that best fills in the blank.

① in a coal cellar
② in an inflated ballon model
③ through a triangular-shaped piece of glass
④ with concave lens telescope

06 Which of the following is true?

① Bell and Hewish contacted with an alien civilization in the galaxy.
② A star can be enlarged to a gigantic size and become a black hole.
③ The existence of black holes was fully known in 1967.
④ A black hole can exercise a gravitational force on nearby matters.

[07-08]

"When we say "potentially habitable' exoplanets, that's a term that refers to measurable qualities of a planet that are necessary for habitable conditions," says Prof. Abel Mendez, from the University of Puerto Rico at Arecibo.

These are, then, promising targets where nothing is guaranteed. But two criteria dominate popular discussions of planetary habitability: first, whether it is within Earth's general size range (and therefore has a chance of being rocky) and, second, whether it resides in what's known as the habitable zone.

This is the range of distances around a host star where there's just enough starlight to keep water in liquid form on a planet's surface. Too close to the star, and the heat will cause water to boil off; too far away and any water will freeze.

These are useful rules of thumb, but a host of factors influence how hospitable planets are. And some are excluded from the conversation because of limitations in technology.

07 '_____' is NOT included in necessary conditions for a habitable exoplanet.

① Water
② Size
③ Distance
④ Starlight
⑤ Sun

08 The underlined "rules of thumb" means _____.

① standards based on practical experience
② procedures drawn by theoretical inference
③ best rules induced from scientific observations
④ prime standards built on the expenditures
⑤ easy procedures made by elaborate calculation

[09-10]

Water covers approximately 75% of the Earth's surface, yet only 3% of it is drinkable; the rest is salt water. Of the little that is fresh, a staggering 99% is inaccessible, buried deep beneath the world's glaciers. According to Kummu et al. (2010), roughly a third of the world's population is at risk from water scarcity, and population growth is only exacerbating the issue. Not only does our species need water to survive, we also rely heavily on it to water our crops and sustain our livestock — people typically drink around five liters of water per day, while agriculture accounts for the majority of global fresh water consumption. In some parts of the world, water scarcity severely limits food production capabilities. Coumou and Rahmstorf (2012) have also forecast that climate change will increase precipitation variability (i.e., rain _____), raising the risk of flooding and drought that blight food production. So, what solutions are available to ensure a consistent and stable freshwater supply?

09 윗글의 빈칸에 들어갈 말로 가장 적절한 것은?

① volume
② scarcity
③ surplus
④ fluctuation

10 윗글의 내용과 일치하지 <u>않는</u> 것은?

① We cannot drink 99% of the water on the Earth.
② Population growth worsens the shortage of water.
③ Farming requires more water than human consumption.
④ Rain shortages will aggravate agriculture in the future.

[11-12]

Given what is at stake it is worth pressing the notion of ultimate knowledge, or explanation, to its logical conclusion. To put it brutally: knowing the ultimate nature of the universe (or, if you prefer, the 'Theory of Everything' or the 'Final Theory') would actually imply knowing everything about the universe, everything that has happened and everything that will happen. One cannot restrict a theory of everything to an arbitrarily disjointed branch of study, e.g. physics, even if it produces a startlingly elegant unifying formula for the behaviour of all known forces. [A] On top of this one would be required to attend to the outstanding question of, for example, how we know what we know about the forces. [B] In other words, how are we conscious of the universe at all? How would such a theory of unified forces help us to understand the nature of war, or global poverty, or jokes? One cannot propose a theory of everything that is only a theory of some things, for as long as just one thing remains unknown our knowledge of the universe remains partial, incomplete and, therefore, not ultimately explained. [C] Which further points to a paradox: science itself proceeds on the very assumption that there is more to be known about the world, that in fact we are grossly ignorant of many aspects of natural phenomena and, indeed, it is this very state of affairs that scientists often highlight when pressing for funds. [D] But how would we know what we don't know?

11 What would be the best title of the passage above?

① The emergence of science on the edge of order
② The emergence of knowledge
③ The fallacy of ultimate knowledge
④ The illusion of cause and effect in science

12 Find the best place for the following passage.

So it would seem to be a requirement of any theory of everything that it is able to tell us that there is nothing else we don't know.

① [A]   ② [B]
③ [C]   ④ [D]

[13-15]

The one great question left unanswered by the manned landings of the Apollo Project in the 1960s was the moon's origin. Now a growing consensus among astronomers favors the "giant impact" theory, an idea that was discounted by most when it was first put forward in 1975. The Moon may have gotten its start four and half billion years ago when, according to the theory, a planetary projectile about one-seventh the earth's mass collided with the earth. The energy of collision crushed and vaporized major parts of the two globes, sending out a high-velocity jet of material at temperatures as high as 12,000 degrees F. Within just a few hours, some of it came back together far enough away from the earth to remain in orbit. The earth itself re-formed as a combination of the old planet and the bulk of the projectile. One reason for the appeal of the giant-impact scenario is that it seems to explain all the chemical findings from Apollo. For example, the moon rocks lack water, sodium and other volatile materials — precisely the substances that would boil away in the rapid _____ after impact.

13 Which of the following is most appropriate for the blank?

① vaporization
② condensation
③ sedimentation
④ transformation

14 According to the "giant impact" theory, which of the following is the best description of the moon?

① A part of the earth which was separated from it.
② A planetary projectile which collided with the earth.
③ A part of the earth and a planetary projectile which collide with it.
④ A planetary projectile which came close to the earth and remained in orbit.

15 Which of the following is true of the Apollo Project according to the passage?

① It did not answer the question of the moon's origin.
② It established the framework of "giant impact" theory.
③ It succeeded in putting the moon into orbit for the first time.
④ It did not attract as much attention as the "giant impact" theory.

[16-17]

Let us suppose that I am looking at a star, Sirius say, on a dark night. If physics is to be believed, light waves which started to travel from Sirius many years ago reach (after a specified time which astronomers calculate) the earth, impinge upon my retinas and cause me to say that I am seeing Sirius. Now the Sirius about which they convey information to me is the Sirius which existed at the time when they started. This Sirius, may, however, no longer exist; it may have disappeared in the interim. To say that one can see what no longer exists is absurd. It follows that, whatever it is that I am seeing, it is not Sirius. What in fact I do see is a yellow patch of a particular size, shape and intensity. I infer that this yellow patch had an origin (with which it is connected by a continuous cain of physical events) several years ago and many million miles away. But this inference may be mistaken; the origin of the yellow patch, which I call a star, may be a blow on the nose, or a lamp hanging on the mast of a ship.

Nor is this the only inference involved. It is true that I think I am seeing a yellow patch, but am I really justified in holding this belief? So far as physics and physiology are concerned, all that we are entitled to say is that the optic nerve is being stimulated in a certain way, as a result of which certain events are being caused in the brain. Are we really justified in saying any more than this? Directly we go beyond the bare statement "the optic nerve is being stimulated in such and such a way" and conclude from this fact "therefore I am seeing an object of such and such a character." We are drawing an inference and _____.

16 윗글의 빈칸에 들어갈 말로 가장 적절한 것은?

① are liable to fall into error
② are led to the world that really exists
③ confirming it by actually seeing its origin
④ perceiving that the world exists only outside our brain

17 윗글의 내용과 가장 거리가 <u>먼</u> 것은?

① Sirius may no longer exist in the universe.
② The outside world is the same as what we perceive.
③ What we see is caused by certain events taking place in our own brains.
④ The existence of the outside world is not itself known but only inferred.

[18-19]

A NASA study revealed that during twelve gravity-free weeks in space, astronauts grow an average of two inches. Why does rapid growth occur in a weightless environment? One way to answer the question is to observe _____. Between morning and night, everyday weight-bearing activities made possible by gravity such as sitting, standing, or walking cause compression in the spine. This compression squeezes fluid out of the spinal discs into nearby soft tissue. By the end of the day, the moisture gone from the disc causes a person to grow shorter by one-half to three-quarters of an inch. During sleep, where the body does not have to bear its own weight, the fluid soaks back into the spinal discs, lengthening the body to its former height. In space, moisture from the bloodstream collects in the discs of the spine, just as it does on Earth, but because there is no gravitational pull, no compression occurs. Moisture is not squeezed out of the discs. It remains, making the discs plumper and consequently making a person taller. Most people probably wouldn't mind being an inch or two taller so that they could more easily reach things on high shelves. However, the height increase and spinal pull that occur in zero-gravity environments are frequently accompanied by concurrent negative effects, such as backaches and nerve irritation. In addition, on Earth the human skeleton and musculature must remain strong in order to do the work it takes to hold the body upright against the counterpull of gravity. In gravity-free environments, muscles and bones tend to weaken because they are not used. Astronauts combat this by maintaining a rigorous exercise routine while in space.

18 윗글의 빈칸에 들어갈 말로 가장 적절한 것은?

① how soft tissue surrounding the spinal disc develops to bear weight
② the relationship between everyday activities and weight
③ how musculature works to counter the pull of gravity
④ the effect of gravity on the spine column

19 윗글의 내용과 일치하지 않는 것은?

① In space, astronauts turn back to their former heights after sleep.
② Astronauts grow in height in space because their spinal discs retain moisture.
③ A person is taller in the morning than in the evening on Earth.
④ Zero-gravity environments often cause some negative effects on the human body.

[20-21]

The Universe's gravitational force played an important role in the formation of the Earth. Gas and dust in the solar nebula were formed by the pull of gravity. This force continued to pull the clumps of gas and dust together until they grew larger and larger, and then the nebula began to shrink into itself. The center of the cloud became very dense and hot. Nuclear reactions within the core of the cloud soon gave birth to a star. The Sun was formed this way, and the energy that the Sun possesses allowed planets to form.

Most scientists believe that another star may have passed close to the Sun and caused matter from the Sun to tear away. The matter was large enough so that when the pieces cooled and became solid, they began to draw near each other as they orbited around the Sun. This is called the planetesimal theory and the masses are called planetesimals. The planetesimals absorbed each other and subsequently formed planets. [A] This theory is highly likely because the composition of the inner planets — Earth, Mars, Venus and Mercury — is rock, while that of the outer planets is mostly gas. [B] Farther away from the Sun, however, temperatures were cold enough to allow the gases to accumulate and form the Jovian Planets — Jupiter, Saturn, Uranus and Neptune. [C]

The planetesimal Earth went through long stages of development before becoming a planet. Heavier matter sank to the center, and the lighter material rose to the surface. [D] We call this movement of layering differentiation. As a result, the Earth formed in layers: a core, a mantle and a crust. Furthermore, volcanic activities released large amounts of water vapour, which condensed into oceans.

20 What does the author imply about the origin of the Earth?

① The planetesimal theory is reasonable.
② Scientists can only guess how the Earth formed.
③ Astronomers disagree on the Earth's origin.
④ It is less important than the origin of the Sun.

21 Where could the following sentence be added to the passage?

Composed of silicate rocks, these astronomical bodies were too hot to condense into volatile gases and formed into the planets.

① [A] ② [B]
③ [C] ④ [D]

[22–23]

Up until the 1920s, everyone thought the universe was essentially static and unchanging in time. Then it was discovered that the universe was expanding. Distant galaxies were moving away from us. This meant they must have been closer together in the past. If we extrapolate back, we find we must have all been on top of each other about 15 billion years ago. This was the Big Bang, the beginning of the universe. But was there anything before the Big Bang? If not, what created the universe? Why did the universe emerge from the Big Bang the way it did? We used to think that the theory of the universe could be divided into two parts. First, there were the laws like Maxwell's equations and general relativity that determined the evolution of the universe, given its state over all of space at one time. And second, there was no question of the initial state of the universe. We have made good progress on the first part, and now have the knowledge of the laws of evolution in all but the most extreme conditions. But until recently, we have had little idea about the initial conditions for the universe. However, this division into laws of evolution and initial conditions depends on time and space being separate and distinct. Under extreme conditions, general relativity and quantum theory allow time to behave like another dimension of space. This removes the distinction between time and space, and means the laws of evolution can also determine the initial state. The universe can spontaneously create itself out of nothing. Moreover, we can calculate a probability that the universe was created in different states. These predictions are in excellent agreement with observations by the WMAP satellite of the cosmic microwave background, which is an imprint of the very early universe. We think we have solved _____. Maybe we should patent the universe and charge everyone royalties for their existence.

22 Choose the sentence that best fills in the blank.

① the chance of spreading out into space
② the mystery of creation
③ the future of the human race
④ the question of the universe through observation

23 Which of the following is true?

① It is undeniable that galaxies are moving closer to us.
② The evolutionary law cannot be applied to the initial state of the universe.
③ The distinction between time and space can disappear in an extreme condition.
④ The calculation of the age of the universe is not supported by any empirical observation.

[24-25]

An earthquake is what happens when two blocks of the earth suddenly slip past one another. The surface where they slip is called the fault or fault plane. The location below the earth's surface where the earthquake starts is called the hypocenter, and the location directly above it on the surface of the earth is called the epicenter.

Sometimes an earthquake has foreshocks. These are smaller earthquakes that happen in the same place as the larger earthquake that follows. Scientists cannot tell that an earthquake is a foreshock until the larger earthquake happens. The largest, main earthquake is called the mainshock. Mainshocks always have aftershocks that follow. These are smaller earthquakes that occur afterwards in the same place as the mainshock. Depending on the size of the mainshock, aftershocks can continue for weeks, months, and even years after the mainshock!

Then, what causes earthquakes and where do they happen? The earth has four major layers: the inner core, outer core, mantle and crust. The crust and the top of the mantle make up a thin skin on the surface of our planet. But this skin is not all in one piece. It is made up of many pieces like a puzzle covering the surface of the earth. Not only that, but these puzzle pieces keep slowly moving around, sliding past one another and bumping into each other. We call these puzzle pieces tectonic plates, and the edges of the plates are called the plate boundaries. The plate boundaries are made up of many faults, and most of the earthquakes around the world occur on these faults. Since the edges of the plates are rough, they get stuck while the rest of the plate keeps moving. Finally, when the plate has moved far enough, the edges unstick on one of the faults and there is an earthquake.

24 Which of the following is true?

① Most earthquakes occur on the faults of the plate boundaries.
② The epicenter of an earthquake is located directly beneath the starting point.
③ Mainshocks precede foreshocks but sometimes are not followed by aftershocks.
④ An earthquake happens because the earth has multiple layers in one piece.

25 Which of the following determines the duration of an earthquake?

① the time of its breakout
② the size of its mainshock
③ the number of its foreshocks
④ the size of the faults

[26-29]

At a time when Earth faces grim news on climate change, slow growth and fraught politics, space might seem to offer a surprising reason for optimism. But it is neither a panacea nor a bolthole. [A] The big problem is developing the rule of law. The Outer Space Treaty of 1967 declares space to be "the province of all mankind" and forbids claims of sovereignty. That leaves lots of room for interpretation. Who would have the best claim to use the ice at the poles of the moon for life support? Should Martian settlers be allowed to do what they like to the environment? Who is liable for satellite collisions? [B] Such uncertainties magnify the dangerous risk: the use of force in space. America's unparalleled ability to project force on Earth depends on its extensive array of satellites. Other nations, knowing this, have built anti-satellite weapons. And military activity in space has no well-tested protocols or rules of engagement. [C]

It is a mistake to promote space as a romanticized Wild West, an anarchic frontier where humanity can throw off its fetters and rediscover its destiny. For space to fulfill its promise, governance is required. [D] At a time when the world cannot agree on rules for the terrestrial trade of steel bars and soybeans, that may seem like a big ask. But without it the potential of all that lies beyond Earth will at best have to wait another 50 years to be fulfilled. At worst space could add to Earth's problems.

26 What is the author's main purpose in writing this passage?

① to explain the roles of the Outer Space Treaty of 1967
② to discuss the necessity of military protocols in space
③ to describe the bright future of space resources
④ to inform potential problems related to space development

27. Which is the most appropriate place for the sentence below?

> And to realize its promise, a big problem has to be resolved and a dangerous risk avoided.

① [A]
② [B]
③ [C]
④ [D]

28. Which is the most appropriate tone of the passage regarding the development of space?

① dubious
② hopeful
③ concerned
④ detestable

29. According to the passage, which of the following is true?

① The ice of the moon may be properly used to support the space force.
② The Outer Space Treaty of 1967 will not be sufficient to handle space problems.
③ Satellite collisions will hinder the peaceful settlement of Martians.
④ Space will be Earth's problem if the world agrees on terrestrial trade.

[30-32]

It took humans thousands of years to explore our own planet and centuries to comprehend our neighboring planets, but nowadays new worlds are being discovered every week. To date, astronomers have identified more than 370 "exoplanets," worlds orbiting stars other than the sun. Many are so strange as to confirm the biologist J. B. S. Haldane's famous remark that "the universe is not only queerer than we suppose, but queerer than we can suppose." There's an Icarus-like "hot Saturn" 260 light-years from Earth, whirling around its parent star so rapidly that a year there lasts less than three days. Circling another star 150 light-years out is a scorched "hot Jupiter," whose upper atmosphere is being blasted off to form a gigantic, comet-like tail. Three benighted planets have been found orbiting a pulsar — the remains of a once mighty star shrunk into a spinning atomic nucleus the size of a city — while untold numbers of worlds have evidently fallen into their suns or been flung out of their systems to become "floaters" that wander in eternal darkness.

Amid such exotica, scientists are eager for a hint of the familiar: planets resembling Earth, orbiting their stars at just the right distance — neither too hot nor too cold — to support life as we know it. No planets quite like our own have yet been found, presumably because they're _____. To see a planet as small and dim as ours amid the glare of its star is like trying to see a firefly in a fireworks display; to detect its gravitational influence on the star is like listening for a cricket in a tornado. Yet by pushing technology to the limits, astronomers are rapidly approaching the day when they can find another Earth and interrogate it for signs of life.

30 According to the context, Earth's <u>parent star</u> would be _____.

① the sun
② Saturn
③ the moon
④ a planet
⑤ comet

31 The best expression for the blank would be _____.

① too large
② floating around
③ inconspicuous
④ transparent
⑤ transient

32 The best title of the passage would be _____.

① Our Own Planet: Earth
② Icarus-like "hot Saturn"
③ Queer Universe
④ The Floaters
⑤ Seeking New Earths

[33-35]

Of what materials is the earth composed, and in what manner are these materials arranged? These are the first inquiries with which Geology is occupied, a science which derives its name from the Greek *ge*, the earth, and logos, a discourse. Previously to experience we might have imagined that investigations of this kind would relate exclusively to the mineral kingdom, and to the various rocks, soils, and metals, which occur upon the surface of the earth, or at various depths beneath it. But, in pursuing such researches, we soon find ourselves led on to consider the successive changes which have taken place in the former state of the earth's surface and interior, and the causes which have given rise to these changes; and what is still more singular and unexpected, we soon become engaged in researches into the history of the animate creation, or of the various tribes of animals and plants which have, at different periods of the past, inhabited the globe.

All are aware that the solid parts of the earth consist of distinct substances, such as clay, chalk, sand, limestone, coal, slate, granite, and the like; but previously to observation it is commonly imagined that all these had remained from the first in the state in which we now see them — that they were created in their present form, and in their present position. The geologist soon comes to a different conclusion, discovering proofs that the external parts of the earth were not all produced in the beginning of things in the state in which we now behold them, nor in an instant of time. On the contrary, he can show that they have acquired their actual configuration and condition gradually, under a great variety of circumstances, and at successive periods, during each of which distinct races of living beings have flourished on the land and in the waters, the remains of these creatures still lying buried in the crust of the earth.

33 Which of the following modes of writing is included in the first paragraph?

① criticism
② narration
③ classification
④ definition

34 Which is the closest in meaning to the underlined part?

① channel
② trajectory
③ mutation
④ shape

35 According to the passage, which is true?

① Although geology was first thought to be a study of earth changes, further study shows that the history of animals and plants are part of the subject as well.
② Although geology was first thought to be a study of minerals, further study shows that animals and plants are part of the subject as well.
③ Although geology was first thought to be a study of the earth's surface, further study shows that the depths beneath the surface are part of the subject as well.
④ Although geology was first thought to be a study of the history of creation, further study shows that animals and plants are part of the subject as well.

[36-37]

Astronomers all over the world were waiting in excitement as August 1993 approached. Mars Observer, the American spacecraft, was scheduled to move into orbit around Mars and begin sending new information back to Earth. In addition to mapping the planet, Mars Observer was going to study the Martian atmosphere and surface. ⓐ Unfortunately, scientists lost contact with Mars Observer on August 24. The Mars Observer mission, which cost $845 million, failed.

In contrast, the United States' ⓑ previous mission to Mars was a great success. In 1976, two American spacecraft landed on Mars in order to search for signs of life. The tests that the Viking landers performed had negative results. However, scientists still had questions about our close neighbor in space. They wanted to investigate further into the possibility of life on Mars. This was the purpose of the Mars Observer mission.

Scientists were ⓒ satisfied with the Viking mission. The two sites where the spacecraft landed provided safe landing places, but they were not particularly interesting locations. Scientists believe there are other areas on Mars that are similar to specific places on Earth that support life. For example, an area in Antarctica, southern Victoria Land, which is not covered by ice, ⓓ resembles an area on Mars.

In the dry valleys of southern Victoria Land, the temperature averages below zero, yet biologists found simple life forms in rocks and frozen lakes. Perhaps this is also true of places on Mars.

Scientists want another investigation of Mars. They want to map the planet's surface and land a spacecraft in a more promising location. They want to search for fossils, the ancient remains of life. If life ever existed on Mars, scientists believe that future missions might find records of it under sand, or in the ice. They are very ⓔ disappointed in the failure of the Mars Observer mission and want to start a new mission.

36 윗글의 밑줄 친 ⓐ~ⓔ 가운데, 문맥상 낱말의 쓰임이 적절하지 <u>않은</u> 것은?

① ⓐ
② ⓑ
③ ⓒ
④ ⓓ
⑤ ⓔ

37 윗글의 제목으로 가장 적절한 것은?

① Missions to Find Life on Mars
② The Disaster of Mars Observer
③ Astronomers' Challenge in Mars
④ How Earth and Mars are Similar
⑤ Future Spacecraft for Space Travel

[38-40]

European and U.S. astronomers Thursday announced the discovery of two solar systems with planets in orbits similar to our own, a finding that boosts the odds that they house extraterrestrial life. In all, astronomers announced they had found 27 previously unknown planets, bringing the number of known planets orbiting nearby stars to more than 100.

One group led by Geoffrey Marcy of the University of California-Berkeley and Paul Butler of the Carnegie Institution of Washington, D.C., released details of 15 planets. A European team led by Swiss astronomer Michael Mayor of the University of Geneva unveiled details of 12 more, several days ahead of a planned announcement at a science meeting.

"There must be billions of planetary systems like our own within our Milky Way galaxy," Marcy says. His team found that the star 55 Cancri hosts a Jupiter-like planet occupying a near-circular orbit, much like Jupiter's. The planet, a giant ball of gas, takes about 14 years to circle 55 Cancri, a star 41 light-years away in the constellation Cancer.

Marcy's team calculates that a planet like Earth could safely orbit 55 Cancri without disturbance from planets orbiting the star. The European team also reports on a different solar system with a planet that resembles Jupiter in size and its circular orbit.

Astrobiologists say solar systems whose outlying gas giants follow near-circular orbits might be more likely to have planets with life. In theory, the Jupiter-like objects would screen smaller, Earth-like planets closer into their star from comet impacts, as Jupiter apparently has done over the history of our own solar system. Plus, a planet with a circular orbit has less chance of disturbing the orbital stability of other planets. Astrophysicist David Spergel of Princeton University says, "Now we have the first report that suddenly our solar system _____."

38 What is the topic of the passage?

① Calculation of the circular orbit of an unknown planet
② The distance among planets in star systems
③ An announcement of a science meeting
④ Star systems similar to ours found
⑤ A planet resembling Jupiter found

39 Which one is true of the passage?

① The planet which 55 Cancri hosts takes about 41 years to circle 55 Cancri.
② A different solar system which European team of astronomers found has a planet resembling Jupiter.
③ The number of previously unknown planets which the astronomers found is more than 100.
④ Theoretically, Jupiter-like objects are believed to screen greater planets.
⑤ A planet with a circular orbit has less chance of promoting other planet's orbital stability.

40 What is most appropriate for the blank?

① is not important
② is in danger
③ is much like Jupiter
④ is too far from 55 Cancri
⑤ is not special

[41-43]

The earth's motion has two components. It *rotates* on its axis, the imaginary line about which the earth is spinning, and it *revolves* around the sun in its orbit. As for the earth's rotation, there are lots of evidence and arguments. The sun, planets, and stars rise in the east and set in the west because the earth rotates. Also observers in the Northern Hemisphere can see that the northern stars move counterclockwise in circles centered on the North Star. These observations, however, could be explained not only by a rotating earth but also by a stationary earth with a moving sky. Hence, we need stronger arguments such as the following.

First, the earth is not exactly spherical; the distance through the earth at its equator is 12,756 km while the distance from one pole to the other is only 12,713 km. So the earth has a bulging shape, and scientists explain it by using the idea of *inertia*, the tendency of moving matter to continue moving in the same direction. If the matter making up the planet were not held in place by the planet's gravity, it would fly out from the rotating planet, like mud from a spinning wheel. The earth's surface is moving fastest at its equator where its matter bulges out against the inward pull of gravity. Hence the bulge at the equator results.

Another piece of evidence comes from the earth's wind patterns. If the earth were not spinning but it retained the same atmospheric heat distribution, the wind patterns would be much simpler; the heated air at the equator would move toward the poles, and the cold air from the higher latitudes would move back toward the equator. The motion would be straight north and south. However, we actually observe a curved wind pattern because the earth's rotation deflects the wind.

Finally, we know by direct observation that the earth is rotating: Astronauts on the moon saw the earth's entire surface in each twenty-four-hour day. The moon does not revolve around the earth once each day. Therefore, _____.

41 Fill in the blank with the best expression.

① the earth must be rotating
② other plants must not be revolving, either
③ the earth not only rotates but also revolves
④ the reports from the astronauts should be revised

42 What is the best title for the passage?

① The Distinction between Rotation and Revolution
② Evidence for the Earth's Rotation
③ Methods of Astronomical Observations
④ The Interaction between Inertia and Gravity on Earth

43 Which of the following is the undeniable argument for the earth's rotation?

① The sun and stars rise in the east and set in the west.
② The earth's wind patterns are not straight but curved.
③ The northern stars move counterclockwise in circles centered on Polaris.
④ The distance from one pole to the other is equivalent to the distance through the earth at the equator.

[44-45]

Galileo attempted to use Copernican astronomy as a mathematician's means of subverting Aristotelian cosmology. He trampled on the usual _____Ⓐ_____ between physics and mathematics by stressing that the natural philosopher had to take into account the discoveries of the mathematical astronomer, since they directly affected the content of the natural philosopher's theorizing — the astronomer told the physicist what the phenomena were that required explanation. In his Italian work known as *Letters on Sunspots* (1613), Galileo made this point strongly in arguing for the presence of variable blemishes on the Sun's surface.

The Aristotelian heavens were held to be perfect and substantively unchanging; all they did was to wheel around eternally, exhibiting no generation of new things. The marks first seen on the face of the Sun by Galileo and others in 1611 did not appear to show the permanence and cyclicity characteristic of _____Ⓑ_____ bodies, and Galileo took the opportunity to argue that they were, in fact, dark blemishes that appeared, changed, and disappeared irregularly on the surface of the Sun. It was important to the Aristotelian argument that the spots should be located precisely on the Sun's surface itself. The Jesuit Christoph Scheiner, Galileo's main rival for the glory of their discovery, at first thought that the spots were actually composed of small bodies akin to moons, which orbited around the Sun in swarms so numerous as to elude, thus far, reduction to proper order.

Accordingly, Galileo presented careful, geometrically couched observational reasoning to show, first of all, that there was an apparent shrinkage of the spots' width as they moved across the face of the Sun from its centre towards the limb (and corresponding widening as they appeared from the other limb and approached the centre); and second, that this effect, interpreted as foreshortening when the spots were seen near the edges of the Sun's disc, was consistent with their having a location on the very surface of the Sun itself. The precise appearances, he argued, would be noticeably different if these necessarily flat patches were any distance above the Sun.

Galileo's argument leads to the following point: if it is established that the Sun's surface is _____Ⓒ_____ by dark patches that manifestly appear from nothing and ultimately vanish, then it becomes undeniable that there is, contrary to Aristotelian doctrine, generation and corruption in the heavens. Galileo thereby moved from a 'mathematical' explication of the external properties of things (here, the apparent size, shape, and motion of the sunspots) to a properly *physical* conclusion about the matter of the heavens.

44 윗글의 빈칸 Ⓐ, Ⓑ, Ⓒ에 들어가기에 가장 적절한 것은?

	Ⓐ		Ⓑ		Ⓒ
①	classification	–	glacial	–	demised
②	demarcation	–	celestial	–	blemished
③	ramification	–	terrestrial	–	smudge
④	discrimination	–	heavenly	–	perished

45 윗글을 통해 추론할 수 없는 것은?

① Aristotelians believed that heavens were eternally wheeling around, showing no generation of something new.

② For Galileo, Copernican astronomy was a useful mathematical means to change the traditional idea of Aristotelian cosmology.

③ Following Aristotelian way of using physics and mathematics, Galileo employed the two natural disciplines to explicate the matter of the heavens.

④ The careful observation of the dark marks changing on the Sun's surface led Galileo to argue that Aristotelian cosmology was wrong.

[46-47]

Most astronomy data today are gathered automatically through robotic systems that collect far more information than the world's roughly 10,000 professional astronomers could ever evaluate in their lifetimes. However, there are at least one million amateur astronomers, who now have a way to get in on the action and make real contributions. [A] In 2007, a group of astronomers wrote a web-based application called Galaxy Zoo, which created a clever, gamelike user interface for a database of astronomical information collected by the Sloan Digital Sky Survey. [B] It turns out that people can do certain kinds of galaxy classifications visually that computers are not yet very good at. So the project made it fun for the public to participate in the classifications, which also helped the astronomers test a theory that spiral galaxies tended to rotate clockwise. [C] Galaxy Zoo was launched with a data set made up of a million galaxies imaged with a robotic telescope. Participants looked at the images and classified the galaxies as "right-handed" (meaning they rotated clockwise) or "left-handed" (rotating counterclockwise). With so many galaxies, the team thought it might take at least two years for the site's visitors to work through them all. Within 24 hours of its launch, however, the site was receiving 70,000 classifications an hour, and more than 50 million classifications were received by the project during its first year, from almost 150,000 people. The effort refuted the idea that most spiral galaxies were right-handed. It turns out that only half of them were. [D] Even more amazing, a Dutch schoolteacher participating in the project found a strange galaxy that so baffled astronomers it ended up getting the attention of the Hubble telescope. [E] In 2008, Microsoft introduced the WorldWide Telescope (WWT) and gave astronomers and the general public access to interactive 3-D images of the sky, planets, and galaxies. Visitors can view the images through a standard browser and visualize the same data that professional astronomers use. WWT incorporates the Galaxy Zoo classifications and more. Visualization tools such as the WWT can actually transform scientists' ability to gain insights from data, sometimes with the help of ordinary citizens.

— adapted from an article by Tony Hey

46 Where would the best points be to divide this essay into paragraphs?

① at points [A], [B], and [D]
② at points [A], [C], and [D]
③ at points [B], [C], and [D]
④ at points [A], [C], and [E]
⑤ at points [B], [D], and [E]

47 Which of these sentences incorrectly paraphrases an idea from the passage?

① As a result of the Galaxy Zoo project, astronomers discovered that there was no special tendency of galaxies to rotate either clockwise or counterclockwise.
② There is so much information available for astronomers to analyze that there are not enough professional astronomers to analyze all the information.
③ Computers are not as good as people at some kinds of astronomy tasks, such as deciding whether a galaxy is "right handed" or "left handed."
④ When astronomers created the Galaxy Zoo program they did not expect to get results as quickly as they actually got them.
⑤ Visualization tools on the internet mean that amateur astronomers in modern times can do better work than professional astronomers could do in the past.

10강 건강 / 의학

정답과 해설 p.223

Read the following passages and answer the questions. [01-51]

[01-02]

> Here are some tips for healthy aging, which you may need to decrease the risk of chronic illness in your later life. Men in their 30s and 40s often injure themselves by engaging in contact sports of exercising improperly, while men in their 50s and 60s are often too _____Ⓐ_____. One of the secrets of healthy aging is knowing how to evaluate the riskiness of your behavior. Another is being willing to let go of behaviors more suited to younger bodies.
>
> Obviously you will not have a chance to experience healthy aging if you succumb to one of the common diseases that strike people in mid-life, such as a heart attack or a cancer. To avoid these, you must be aware of your personal health risks, and one of the best ways to keep track of them is to have a regular physical checkup every year.

01 윗글의 빈칸 Ⓐ에 들어갈 말로 가장 적절한 것은?

① impudent
② destitute
③ sedentary
④ courteous

02 윗글의 제목으로 가장 적절한 것은?

① Most Dangerous Chronic Illness
② How to Avoid Common Diseases
③ Importance of Regular Physical Checkups
④ What You Have to Do for Healthy Aging

[03-04]

　　Among scientists who study how our DNA affects our weight, a gene called FTO stands out. "It's the _____Ⓐ_____ for the genetics of obesity," said Struan F. Grant, an associate professor of pediatrics at the University of Pennsylvania School of Medicine. In 2007, researchers discovered that people with a common variant of FTO tend to be heavier than those without it. Since then, studies have repeatedly confirmed the link. On average, one copy of the risky variant adds up to 3.5 extra pounds of weight. Two copies of the gene bring 7 extra pounds and increase a person's risk of becoming obese by 50 percent. But the gene doesn't seem to have always been a problem. If scientists had studied FTO just a few decades ago, ⓐthey would have found no link to weight whatsoever. A new study shows that FTO became a risk only in people born after World War II. The research reuses questions that extend far beyond obesity. Genes clearly influence our health in many ways, but so does our environment; often, it is the interplay between them that makes the difference in whether we develop obesity, cancer, or another ailment.

03 Which of the following best fits into Ⓐ?

① antithesis
② poster child
③ flip side
④ memorandum

04 Which of the following is the most likely reason for ⓐ?

① FTO was discovered after World War II.
② Scientific studies were not conducted back then.
③ The environment was very different back then.
④ FTO did not exist in people a few decades ago.

[05-06]

Not to be confused with the common cold, which is generally milder, the flu is a contagious viral infection of the respiratory tract, and can affect anyone from toddlers to expectant mothers and seniors. [A] This same group, pending other existing health conditions, are also the most susceptible to flu-related complications that may lead to death. [B] Traditionally, fighting the flu has largely been within the domain of Western medicine. [C] The ubiquitous flu vaccination remains the frontline between the flu bug and body resistance; each shot essentially contains a small dose of flu viruses that the body learns to develop antibodies against. [D] After symptoms show themselves, people turn to their GPs or the pharmacy for help. [E] GPs generally prescribe a range of symptoms-easing drugs, which may include paracetamol (for fever and aches), codeine (for coughs), danzen (to sooth throat inflammation) and antihistamines (to unblock stuffy noses or stop the sniffles). Meanwhile, antiviral drugs like Tamiflu and Relenza help shorten the time you have flu symptoms by stopping the spread of the virus in your body.

05 When the above passage is divided into three paragraphs, which would be the best boundaries?

① [A] and [C]
② [A] and [D]
③ [B] and [D]
④ [B] and [E]
⑤ [C] and [E]

06 Which one is NOT true of the above passage?

① Flu is different from cold.
② Catching flu can be critical to some patients.
③ Flu is transmitted by a sort of virus.
④ Flu vaccine eliminates the flu viruses.
⑤ There's no cure for flu.

[07-08]

There are two types of people in the world: those who believe in the Myers-Briggs Type Indicator (MBTI) Personality Test and those who don't. The MBTI is simultaneously the most popular personality test in the world and the most frequently debunked. About 1.5 million people take the test each year, and more than 88% of *Fortune 500* companies, as well as hundreds of universities, use it for hiring and training. Even fictional characters, from Disney princesses to Darth Vader, have been assigned an MBTI type. Despite the popularity of the test, many psychologists criticize it. Some research suggests that the MBTI is unreliable because the same person can get different results when retaking the test. Some of the test's limitations, however, are inherent in its conceptual design, such as the MBTI's black-and-white categories: You are classified, for instance, as either an extrovert (E) or an introvert (I), and as either a judger (J) or a feeler (F). This is a shortcoming because many people don't fall neatly into two categories on any personality dimension. Instead, people have many degrees of the dimension. In fact, people are close to the average, and relatively few people are at either extreme. By placing people into tidy boxes, we are separating people who are in reality more similar to each other than they are different.

07 Which of the following is the major topic of the passage?

① Corporate uses of the MBTI
② Reasons for the MBTI's popularity
③ Controversies surrounding the MBTI
④ Explanations of the various MBTI categories

08 According to the passage, which of the following is NOT true?

① There can be different degrees of introversion in people.
② The MBTI categorizes people as either judgers or feelers.
③ Many companies use the MBTI to assess job applicants
④ The same person will always get the same results on the test

[09-10]

  In poring over medical journals, he was struck by how many findings of all types were refuted by later findings. Of course, medical-science "never minds" are hardly secret. And they sometimes make headlines, as when in recent years large studies or growing consensuses of researchers concluded that mammograms, colonoscopies, and PSA tests were far less useful cancer-detection tools than we had been told; or when widely prescribed antidepressants such as Prozac, Zoloft, and Paxil were revealed to be no more effective than a placebo for most cases of depression; or when we learned that staying out of the sun entirely can actually increase cancer risks; or when we were told that the advice to drink lots of water during intense exercise was potentially fatal; or when, last April, we were informed that taking fish oil, exercising, and doing puzzles doesn't really help fend off Alzheimer's disease, as had long been claimed. Peer-reviewed studies have come to opposite conclusions on whether using cell phones can cause brain cancer, whether sleeping more than eight hours a night is healthier or dangerous, whether taking aspirin every day is more likely to save your life or cut it short, and whether routine angioplasty works better than pills to unclog heart arteries.

09 The underlined "never minds" refers to the articles that _____.

① don't consider patients' conditions
② have nothing to do with medicine
③ are not medical researches
④ are not different from the doctors' advice
⑤ are not concerned whether their claims are correct

10 According to the passage, _____.

① most doctors take aspirin every day
② many of medical findings are controversial
③ Prozac is more effective than a placebo
④ the use of cell phones does not cause brain cancer
⑤ most people get medical information from the Internet

[11-12]

It's not uncommon for young women like Maya to be repeatedly misdiagnosed. Because autism is at least three times as common in boys as in girls, scientists routinely include only boys in their research. The result is that we know shockingly little about whether and how autism might be different in girls and boys. What we do know is grim: on average, girls who have mild symptoms of autism are diagnosed two years later than boys. There's some debate about why this might be so. From the start, girls' restricted interests seem more socially acceptable — dolls or books, perhaps, rather than train schedules — and may go unnoticed. But the fact that diagnostic tests are based on observations of boys with autism almost certainly contributes to errors and delays.

As they enter teens, girls struggle to keep up with the elaborate rules of social relationships. Cribbing notes on what to say and how to say it, many try to blend in, but at great cost to their inner selves. Starting in adolescence, they have high rates of depression and anxiety. A few studies have also found an intriguing overlap between autism and eating disorders such as anorexia, although the studies are too small to estimate how many women have both.

11 The autism in girls is not well-known because _____.

① there were not many autistic girls
② parents of autistic girls hide their kids
③ it is not different from that in boys
④ autistic girls only stay at home
⑤ girls' autism didn't get much attention

12 Which one is NOT a symptom of autism in teenage girls?

① depression
② anxiety
③ gaining weight
④ thin figure
⑤ eating little

[13-14]

Antidepressants were found by chance. In the 1950s, drugs being used to treat schizophrenia and tuberculosis showed antidepressant properties by increasing the level of brain chemicals called monoamines (including serotonin). This led to the first antidepressant drugs — TCAs (tricyclic antidepressants) and MAOIs (monoamine oxidase inhibitors).

All commercially available antidepressants still work by increasing monoamines. Current drugs are safer than the earlier examples and are effective in many cases, but side effects such as anxiety, nausea, loss of appetite and sleep disturbances exits. Also, up to 50 per cent of people don't respond to treatment and, for those who do, effects are only seen after several weeks of treatment. Antidepressants have also shown only a small advantage over placebos in some drug trials.

The current lack of a gold standard antidepressant is probably because depression can be difficult to define. Scientists are even considering whether hormones such as oestrogen or stress hormones are involved.

All too often, depression can be a natural reaction to life's events. But beyond chemicals and hormones, there are complex emotional, psychological and social factors, so antidepressants are unlikely to be a total cure. Exercise, talking therapy and diet can all help.

13 Which is NOT the side effect of antidepressants?

① immunity to antidepressants
② inability to get a sound sleep
③ involuntary impulses to vomit
④ uneasiness and psychological tension

14 Which is NOT true according to the passage?

① It takes time for antidepressants to have their effects.
② Depression cannot be explained away as a matter of chemicals and hormones.
③ Current antidepressants function roughly the same way a the earlier ones.
④ Placebos are more effective than normal antidepressants in dealing with depression.

[15-17]

For nearly a century, surgical residency had been a period of both intensive experience and increasing responsibility. More recent research has affirmed that approach, demonstrating the strong link between a surgeon's operative skill, the number of operations performed and patient outcomes. For the past decade, with limits set on their time at the hospital, young surgeons-in-training had fewer opportunities to scrub in on operations. While previous generations of trainees participated in at least one operation a day, new trainees had only enough time to be involved in two or maybe three operations each week. Calculating the number of hours "lost" by cutting back on in-hospital time, surgical leaders estimated that young surgeons-to-be were now missing out on as much as a year's worth of experience. Surgery itself was also changing, and the number of skills surgeons now needed was expanding. The discovery of new medications rendered once standard operations less common, but not entirely obsolete; so surgeons still had to know how to perform all the operations without getting to practice them as often.

Surgical training programs scrambled to make up for less time and cover the ever-expanding body of knowledge by creating online educational tools and offering trainees experiences in simulated operating rooms and trauma resuscitations using electronic mannequins. But as The Annals of Surgery study reveals, even the best-equipped simulation labs cannot replace a year's worth of lost experience.

15 What is the main idea of the passage?

① In surgical training, diversity in pedagogical methods is needed.
② Non-text book knowledge can be obtained through apprenticeship in surgery.
③ Nothing can compensate for first-hand experience in surgical training.
④ Online courses can be an effective means of acquiring surgical skills.

16 What is the tone of the passage?

① pedantic
② laudatory
③ sardonic
④ critical

17 According to the passage, what is true about "trainees"?

① Cutting-edge technology has made them almost immune to making mistakes.
② They can conduct virtual operations through simulated training.
③ The amount of time spent in lectures has reduced the time spend in hospitals.
④ They tend to choose majors that do not require complex surgeries.

[18-20]

In 1999, the Institute of Medicine reported that American health care was decidedly dangerous for patients. One in every few hundred was hurt, and one in every few thousand was killed by medical misadventures. The cause was not malfeasant individuals; it was inadequately designed and operated systems of care delivery. Since then, health care providers have invested in a variety of initiatives aimed at improving safety. However, according to findings published recently in *The New England Journal of Medicine*, things have not improved. Researchers looked at performance changes in North Carolina hospitals supposedly doing the right things — and therefore assumed to be representative of organizations on the cutting edge in improving quality and safety. Their findings: The needle on patient well-being had moved insignificantly.

The only reasonable explanation for this disparity between _____ Ⓐ _____ is that health care leaders are not investing in the right operational changes to achieve excellence in safety, affordability, and capacity. Unfortunately, many health care organizations continue to cling to the view that improvement can be achieved by purchasing one-off interventions. Their thinking: If they implement enough best-practice bundles here or there to remove the problem and hire enough outsiders to lead improvement projects, things should get good enough. But the sad reality is while this approach will generate improvements, they will not be significant and sustainable.

18 윗글의 제목으로 가장 적절한 것은?

① How Best Practices Improve Health Care
② The New Trend in the Modern Hospital
③ The Future Sustainable Hospital Project
④ Why Best Practices Haven't Fixed Health Care

19 글의 흐름상 빈칸 Ⓐ에 들어갈 말로 가장 적절한 것은?

① income and outcome
② cost and service
③ service and health care
④ effort and outcome

20 What should hospitals do for improvement according to the passage?

① to find more significant and sustainable approaches
② to purchase one-off interventions
③ to implement best practices in the hospital
④ to hire experts to deliver cutting edge health care

[21-23]

If you're someone who has trouble sleeping, somebody has probably already suggested white noise to you. For better or worse, our brains continue to process sensory stimuli when we're asleep, meaning that our partner's snoring, dog's barking, and even our leaky sinks can easily make us victims of restless nights. The reason noise wake us up at night is not exactly because of the noise itself, but rather the sudden change in noise. White noise works by masking these changes and allowing our brains the benefit of a more consistent sonic environment. Aside from the benefit of a better night's sleep, white noise has shown promising results related to memory and concentration. Lots of studies on sound therapy have focused on specific sonic hues like white, pick, and brown, so what exactly is the difference between them? White noise, probably the most familiar of these, sounds like a radio turned to an unused frequency. Similar to the way white light contains all the wavelengths of the visible spectrum at equal intensity, white noise has equal power across all frequencies _____Ⓐ_____ to the human ear. Pink noise is white noise, but with reduced higher frequencies. It resembles the sounds of steady rainfall or wind, and it is often considered to be more soothing than white noise. Several studies on pink noise have shown that sleeping with it can improve our memories the following day, and potentially even long-term. Brown noise lowers the higher frequencies even more. It's a bit 'rougher' than pink noise and resembles the roar of a river current or strong wind. Common benefits associated with brown noise are relaxation, improved focus, and of course, sleep improvement.

21 **Which of the following is the best title for the passage?**

① Differences Among White, Pink, and Brown Noise
② Why We Overlook White, Pink, and Brown Noise
③ Pros and Cons of Sound Therapy
④ How to Sleep Better at Night

22 **According to the passage, which of the following is true?**

① Our brains stop processing sensory stimuli while we sleep.
② Noise change, rather than noise itself, wake us at night.
③ Pink noise is white noise with increased higher frequencies.
④ Brown noise can improve focus but not sleep.

23 **Which of the following best fits into Ⓐ?**

① irrelevant
② audible
③ applied
④ invisible

[24-26]

During the COVID-19 pandemic, countries have been scrambling to create vaccine passports to _____Ⓐ_____ the virus from crossing the border or entering indoor facilities like restaurants or gyms. People often have to prove that they have been vaccinated, recently tested negative, or previously had COVID-19 and recovered. Governments are not alone as tech companies and industry associations are getting involved.

The problem with vaccine passports is that the passes are not interoperable. Most appear to look the same with a QR code on a smartphone or a piece of paper, but scanning the codes can be an issue. Various verifier apps read various passes. Once the codes are scanned, varying information is revealed depending on the national or local health systems or stances on privacy. Some vaccine passports such as the CommonPass issued in the U.S. share raw data on the status of vaccinations. Others, like the one used by the UK's National Health Service (NHS), show only a tick, a cross, or a symbol. Also, the rules of vaccine passports are not fixed. For instance, during the surge of infections in Israel, the government pulled its "green pass" from about two million people who had not yet received the booster shot.

What is even more difficult is a unified system for checking for digital signatures of health authorities. Creating a database of all trusted signatures is a costly and politically complicated task. Countries with a national health service, like the U.K., have just one issuer, but in the U.S. there are about 300, including hospitals, pharmacies, and state governments.

24 Which one CANNOT fill Ⓐ?

① halt
② block
③ prevent
④ facilitate

25 Which one is TRUE?

① The CommonPass is not issued in the U.S.
② In the U.S., there is a single issuer of health service.
③ Vaccine passports issued by the NHS can show a symbol.
④ Vaccine passports are a problem because they can protect people's privacy.

26 Which one is NOT a problem with vaccine passports?

① The passes are not interoperable.
② The rules of vaccine passports are subject to change.
③ Tech companies are getting involved with vaccine passports.
④ It is expensive to manage all the different digital signatures from various authorities.

[27-29]

Modern medicine has developed the God-like power to stabilize the vital signs that spiral out of control as a person approaches death, and to then keep that person alive despite her inability to breathe, eat or drink. It wields this power liberally. As an intensive-care unit (ICU) nurse, I am haunted by memories of patients who were stabilized in intensive care so that their catastrophic injuries or diseases did not kill them, but who were left unable to communicate or do anything but receive medical care. When I am face-to-face with a patient like this — someone who will never again be able to communicate, and who has been placed on the treadmill of continuous medical care — I feel the same type of shame as when I walk by a cold, crippled homeless person on the sidewalk. The wrongness is just as obvious. When I stick a needle into his arm, it feels as though I am kicking a homeless person.

It's a moral crisis hiding in plain sight, yet the people involved claim to be mere cogs in the machine. When I asked an ICU attending physician why families aren't given data and clear explanations of probable outcomes rather than best-case scenarios and "only time will tell" conversations, he said, "palliative care unit (PCU) people can do that. In the ICU, we don't really have time." Another physician mentioned the "_____Ⓐ_____ of the system." It falls to the general public — the patients — to take the initiative in reforming the excesses of modern medical care.

You can determine your fate by completing an advance directive. This is a legal document in which you can explain what measures should be undertaken if you are unable to communicate; name a health care proxy who can communicate your wishes to medical providers; and lay out how you envision the end of your life. If you don't want to be kept alive on life support, you can indicate as much in your advance directive. If you want the longest life possible no matter what, you can affirm this wish. Either way, families and care providers should know. It will help move our medical system toward a more humane approach to end-of-life care.

27 What is the occupation of the author?

① physician
② surgeon
③ nurse
④ pharmacist

28 Which of the following best fits in Ⓐ?

① privilege
② advantage
③ flexibility
④ inertia

29 Which of the following is true?

① ICU is the perfect unit for patients.
② Homeless people are also patients.
③ An advance directive is mandatory.
④ People should make end-of-life care decisions.

[30-31]

A fundamental principle of pharmacology is that all drugs have multiple actions. Actions that are desirable in the treatment of disease are considered therapeutic, while those that are undesirable or pose risks to the patient are called "effects." Adverse drug effects range from the trivial, e.g., nausea or dry mouth, to the serious, e.g., massive gastrointestinal bleeding; and some drugs can be lethal, Therefore, an effective system for the detection of adverse drug effects is _____ of any advanced nation. Much of the research conducted on new drugs aims at identifying the conditions of use that maximize beneficial effects and minimize the risk of adverse effects. The intent of drug labeling is to reflect this body of knowledge accurately so that physicians can properly prescribe the drug; or, if it is to be sold without prescriptions, so that consumers can properly use the drug. The current system of drug investigation in the U.S. has proved very useful and accurate in identifying the common side effects associated with new prescription drugs. By the time a new drug is approved by the Food and Drug Administration, its side effects are usually well described in the package insert for physicians. The investigational process, however, cannot be counted on to detect all adverse effects because of the relatively small number of patients involved in premarketing studies and the relatively short duration of the studies. Animal toxicology studies are, of course, done prior to marketing in an attempt to identify any potential for toxicity, but negative results do not guarantee the safety of a drug in humans, as evidenced by such well known examples as the birth deformation due to thalidomide.

30 윗글의 빈칸에 들어갈 말로 가장 적절한 것은?

① a denouement of public health education
② an important component of health care system
③ the realistic remedy for illegal drug prescription
④ the obligatory consequences of overlooking health care

31 윗글을 통해 추론할 수 있는 것으로 가장 적절한 것은?

① Most physicians are not aware that prescription drugs have side effects.
② Drugs with therapeutic effects are seldom approved for distribution.
③ Consumers are seldom able to understand directions for proper use of a drug.
④ Some rare adverse drug effects are not discovered with the limited testing.

[32-34]

Gene therapy, also called human gene transfer, is a medical field which focuses on the utilization of the therapeutic delivery of nucleic acids into a patient's cells as a drug to treat disease. The first attempt at modifying human DNA was performed in 1980 by Martin Cline, but the first successful nuclear gene transfer in humans, approved by the US National Institutes of Health, was performed in May 1989. The first therapeutic use of gene transfer as well as the first direct insertion of human DNA into the nuclear genome was performed by French Anderson in a trial starting in September 1990. It is thought to be able to cure many genetic disorders or treat them over time.

Between 1989 and 2018, over 2,900 clinical trials were conducted, with more than half of them in phase I. As of 2017, Spark Therapeutics' Luxturna and Novartis' Kymriah are the FDA's first approved gene therapies to enter the market. Since that time, drugs such as Novartis' Zolgensma and Alnylam's Patisiran have also received FDA approval, in addition to other companies' gene therapy drugs.

The concept of gene therapy is _____Ⓐ_____. If, for instance, in an (usually recessively) inherited disease, a mutation in a certain gene results in the production of a dysfunctional protein, gene therapy could be used to deliver a copy of this gene that does not contain the deleterious mutation, and thereby produces a functional protein. This strategy is referred to as gene replacement therapy and is employed to treat inherited retinal diseases.

While the concept of gene replacement therapy is mostly suitable for recessive diseases, novel strategies have been suggested that are capable of also treating conditions with a dominant pattern of inheritance.

The introduction of CRISPR gene editing has opened new doors for its application and utilization in gene therapy, as, instead of pure replacement of a gene, it enables correction of the particular genetic _____Ⓑ_____. Solutions to medical hurdles, such as the eradication of latent human immunodeficiency virus (HIV) reservoirs and correction of the mutation that causes sickle cell disease, may be available as a therapeutic option in the next couple of years.

32 Which of the following best fits in Ⓐ?

① to extract genetic information from patients
② to fix a genetic problem at its source
③ to generate mechanism to erase functional protein
④ to identify genetic patterns common to humans

33 Which of the following best fits in Ⓑ?

① solution
② diagnosis
③ advantage
④ defect

34 Which of the following is NOT true?

① Martin Cline was the first scientist who attempted to modify human DNA.
② The first gene transfer for therapeutic purpose was conducted in 1990.
③ More than half of the clinical trials during 1989–2018 were performed in phase I.
④ Novartis' Zolgensma and Alnylam's Patisiran were approved by FDA before 2017.

[35-38]

Until recently, pioneers of _____Ⓐ_____ health innovation had remained at the margins of our biomedical research and regulatory establishment. Yet in the last two months alone, two individuals widely shared videos in which they injected themselves with unregulated gene therapies. Josiah Zayner is one of the self-experimenters and the CEO of the Odin, a start-up that sells gene-editing kits for home use. [A] is self-experimentation with gene-editing techniques something we should herald as a new form of "permissionless" innovation? Or will self-proclaimed biohackers, by testing the regulatory framework, harm the emerging ecosystem of citizens who contribute to biomedical innovation? [B] _____Ⓑ_____ banning the sale of gene-editing kits is only a weak, temporary solution. What we need is to foster an ethos of responsible innovation outside of traditional research institutions. We must recognize the urgent need to build legitimacy, but also tailored regulatory support for new forms of health research. [C] The path forward is not to promote radical, unregulated science, but to develop engagement channels that force citizens, patients, ethicists and regulators to rethink and design an adaptive oversight system. [D]

35 Choose the words that fit best for blanks Ⓐ and Ⓑ.

	Ⓐ		Ⓑ
①	transnational	–	Furthermore
②	democratized	–	Yet
③	ecological	–	For instance
④	optimal	–	Nevertheless

36 The author's presentation is most like that of a _____.

① researcher offering a scholarly analysis
② daily journalist reporting on a news story
③ motivational speaker giving an inspiring talk
④ public intellectual presenting an opinion on an ethical dilemma

37 Which of the following cannot be inferred from the passage?

① Biotechnologies have progressed to a point where individuals can experiment with gene therapies at home.
② The U.S government recently approved self- experimentation by a practitioner outside of a traditional research institution.
③ A recent development in health research involves entrepreneurship.
④ Despite the potential for citizens to take a proactive role outside of medical practices, many ethical issues remain unresolved.

38 Which would be the best place for the following sentence?

> Self-experimentation with gene therapies raises troubling safety and ethical questions, from the potential for infections and immunological reactions to lack of understanding of the risks involved and unrealistic expectations from patients.

① [A]
② [B]
③ [C]
④ [D]

[39-41]

There are several pro tips for long and healthy life. First, diet. Weight loss likely explains many of the positive changes, such as lower blood pressure and better blood-sugar levels. But some experts speculate that fasting also makes the body more resistant to stress, which can have beneficial effects at the cellular level. One expert says, "Diet is by far the most powerful intervention to delay aging and age-related diseases."

In the past couple of years, scientists have shown that _____Ⓐ_____ behavior, like sitting all day, is a risk factor for earlier death. They found that hours spent sitting are linked to increased risks of Type 2 diabetes and nonalcoholic fatty liver disease. You can't exercise away all the bad effects of sitting too much. But the good news is that doing anything but sitting still-even fidgeting counts — can add up. People who logged the least physical activity had the highest risk of a heart event in the next ten years, which isn't shocking. But to the surprise of the researchers, moving just a little bit more during the day — like doing chores around the house — was enough to lower the risk of a heart event.

By now it's clear to scientists that our emotions affect our biology. Studies have shown for years that anger and stress can release stress hormones like adrenaline into our blood, which trigger the heart to beat faster and harder. Stress may even have an effect on how well our brains hold up against Alzheimer's disease. The researchers found that people who held more negative views of aging earlier in life had greater loss in the volume of their hippocampus, a region of the brain whose loss is linked to Alzheimer's disease. This is not the first time research has suggested that _____Ⓑ_____.

39 Which best fits in the blank Ⓐ?

① active
② abrupt
③ sedentary
④ vociferous

40 According to the passage, which is NOT one of the pro tips for long and healthy life?

① not sitting still for long
② doing excessive exercise
③ keeping to a regimen of diet
④ having an optimistic attitude

41 Which best fits in the blank Ⓑ?

① how we feel about aging can affect how we age
② stress and exercise are interrelated with each other
③ Alzheimer's disease is linked to positive views of aging
④ anger and stress have no direct bearing on Alzheimer's disease

[42-43]

Immunology is the study of the body's defense against infection. We are continually exposed to microorganisms, many of which cause disease, and yet become ill only rarely. How does the body defend itself? When infection does occur, how does the body eliminate the invader and cure itself? And why do we develop long-lasting immunity to many infectious diseases encountered once and overcome? These are the questions addressed by immunology, which we study to understand our body's defenses against infection at the cellular and molecular levels.

[A] Jenner had observed that the relatively mild disease of cowpox, or vaccinia, seemed to confer protection against the often fatal disease of smallpox, and in 1796, he demonstrated that inoculation with cowpox protected the recipient against smallpox. His scientific proof relied on the deliberate exposure of the inoculated individual to infectious smallpox material two months after inoculation. This scientific test was his original contribution.

[B] The beginning of immunology as a science is usually attributed to Edward Jenner for his work in the late 18th century. The notion of immunity — that surviving a disease confers greater protection against it later — was known since ancient Greece. Variolation — the inhalation or transfer into superficial skin wounds of material from smallpox pustules — had been practiced since at least the 1400s in the Middle East and China as a form of protection against that disease and was known to Jenner.

[C] Jenner called the procedure vaccination. This term is still used to describe the inoculation of healthy individuals with weakened or attenuated strains of disease-causing agents in order to provide protection from disease. Although Jenner's bold experiment was successful, it took almost two centuries for smallpox vaccination to become universal. This advance enabled the World Health Organization to announce in 1979 that smallpox had been eradicated, arguably the greatest triumph of modern medicine.

42 윗글의 단락을 논리적 흐름에 맞게 순서대로 배열한 것으로 가장 적절한 것은?

① [B] – [A] – [C]
② [B] – [C] – [A]
③ [C] – [A] – [B]
④ [C] – [B] – [A]

43 윗글의 내용과 일치하는 것은?

① Edward Jenner was not aware of the existence of smallpox pustules.
② The occurrence of smallpox cannot be prevented by variolation.
③ Cowpox can be prevented by using vaccination.
④ Edward Jenner was informed of variolation practiced in the past.

[44-45]

People worldwide are living longer. Today most people can expect to live into their sixties and beyond. Every country in the world is experiencing growth in both the size and the proportion of older persons in the population.

By 2030, 1 in 6 people in the world will be aged 60 years or over. At this time the share of the population aged 60 years and over will increase from 1 billion in 2020 to 1.4 billion. By 2050, the world's population of people aged 60 years and older will double (2.1 billion). The number of persons aged 80 years or older is expected to triple between 2020 and 2050 to reach 426 million.

While this shift in distribution of a country's population towards older ages, known as population aging, started in high-income countries (for example in Japan 30% of the population is already over 60 years old), it is now low- and middle-income countries that are experiencing the greatest change. By 2050, two-thirds of the world's population over 60 years will live in low- and middle-income countries.

The United Nations General Assembly declared 2021–2030 the Decade of Healthy Aging and asked WHO to lead the implementation. The Decade of Healthy Aging is a global collaboration bringing together governments, civil society, international agencies, professionals, academia, the media and the private sector for 10 years of concerted, catalytic and collaborative action to foster longer and healthier lives.

The Decade builds on the WHO Global Strategy and Action Plan and the United Nations Madrid International Plan of Action on Aging, and supports the realization of the United Nations Agenda 2030 on Sustainable Development and the Sustainable Development Goals.

The Decade of Healthy Aging seeks to reduce health inequities and improve the lives of older people, their families and communities through collective action in four areas: changing how we think, feel and act towards age and ageism; developing communities in ways that foster the abilities of older people; delivering person-centered integrated care and primary health services responsive to older people; and providing older people who need it with access to quality long-term care.

44 **Which of the following is true by 2030?**

① More than 30% of people in the world will be 60 years and older.
② The number of 60 years and older people will be around 2.1 billion.
③ Japan will implement an international plan of Action on Aging.
④ Older people will be provided with better access to quality care.

45 **What do you expect to happen by 2050?**

① Those who are 60 years old and over will triple.
② Two thirds of people over 60 will live in high-income countries.
③ The number of 80 years and older people will be 426 million.
④ The number of old and young people will be in a good balance.

[46-48]

Our conceptions of human nature affect every aspect of our lives, from the way we raise our children to the political movements we embrace. Yet just as science is bringing us into a golden age of understanding of human nature, many people are hostile to the very idea. They fear that discoveries about innate patterns of thinking and feeling may be used to justify inequality, to subvert social change, to dissolve personal responsibility, and to strip life of meaning and purpose.

In *The Blank Slate*, Steve Pinker explores the idea of human nature and its moral, emotional, and political colorings. He shows how many intellectuals have denied the existence of human nature by embracing three linked dogmas: The Blank Slate (the mind has no innate traits), the Noble Savage (people are born good and corrupted by society), and the Ghost in the Machine (each of us has a soul that makes choices free from biology). Each dogma carries a moral burden, so their defenders have engaged in desperate tactics to discredit the scientists who are now challenging them.

Pinker injects calm and rationality into these debates by showing that equality, progress, responsibility, and purpose have nothing to fear from discoveries about a rich human nature. He disarms even the most menacing threats with clear thinking, common sense, and pertinent facts from science and history. Despite its popularity among intellectuals during much of the twentieth century, he argues, the doctrine of the Blank Slate may have done more harm than good.

46 **Why do many people disapprove of scientific efforts to understand human nature?**

① They want their theories to contribute to new scientific discoveries.

② They feel science is not adequate to explore the human mind.

③ They believe the human mind is something to be studied more rigorously.

④ They worry that the results of such endeavors may be abused.

47 **Pinker believes that _____.**

① the mind has no innate traits

② people are born good and corrupted by society

③ the doctrine of the Ghost in the Machine is correct

④ science deepens our understanding of human nature

48 **Which of the following is NOT stated or implied in the passage?**

① The way we rear children depends on our idea of human nature.

② We now have a better understanding of the innate patterns of thinking.

③ Some thinkers believe that people are born bad and improved through education.

④ The Blank Slate is a theory of the human mind which was influential in the 20th century.

[49-51]

Forensic science helps us understand the past, whether in terms of studying the spread of a disease or investigating the site of an ancient massacre. And, of course, it is important to the legal system when it comes to solving crimes. Across all of these fields, the microscope is an important tool, used to help reconstruct past events. Microscopes are essential for many investigative purposes, because they can magnify an object to such great detail.

Forensic epidemiology investigates how diseases spread usually for legal reasons. For example, forensic epidemiologists may be assigned to discover the source of dangerous bacteria, such as E. coli or salmonella. To do so, they will use microscopes to study food for contamination. Under a microscope, the presence of certain strains of bacteria may point a scientist to the source of contamination. This can prove pivotal in stopping more people from being infected as well as pinpointing the individuals or group responsible for the outbreak.

In forensic anthropology, microscopes are used to study tissue, bone or other remains to determine factors of a death. For example, scanning electron microscopes can be used to identify the long-liquified remains of a person that have left behind a deposit in the soil. Microscopes in this field are additionally used in looking at the residue found on the teeth. Tissue, cells or other remains may coat the teeth after death, helping researchers determine a person's habits, ailments or even cause of death.

Forensic pathologists are responsible for determining the manner in which a person has died. If the person died from a certain disease, forensic pathologists may use a microscope to identify the deadly bacteria or virus. A microscope may be beneficial when it comes to more closely examining the tissue around a wound and determining what sort of object — be it a bullet, a knife or something else — caused the damage.

49 What would make the best title for the passage?

① Forensic Science and Its Legal Backgrounds
② Uses of Microscopes in Forensic Science
③ Early Development of Forensic Science
④ Needs for Forensic Science in the Future

50 According to the passage, which of the following CANNOT be inferred?

① Forensic science deals with understanding of the past by reconstructing past events.
② Forensic epidemiology contributes to stopping the spread of dangerous diseases.
③ Remains on teeth of the dead body can hint at the person's habit.
④ Deadly bacteria and virus cause difficulties in forensic pathologists' examining tissues.

51 Which of the following is closest to the way in which the passage is organized?

① Spatial order
② Chronological order
③ Question and answer
④ Main idea with supporting lists

11강 환경 / 동식물

Read the following passages and answer the questions. [01-52]

[01-03]

At a distance a fish school resembles a large organism. Its members, numbering anywhere from two or three into the millions, swim in tight formations, wheeling and reversing in near unison. Either dominance systems do not exist or they are so weak as to have little or no influence on the dynamics of the school as a whole. There is, moreover, _____. When the school turns to the right or left, individuals formerly on the flank assume the lead. The average school size varies according to species, as does the spacing of its members, its average velocity, and its three-dimensional shape. Although the fish are usually aligned with military precision while the group is on the move, they assume a more nearly random orientation while resting or feeding. Their alignments also shift in particular ways when the fish are attacked by predators. Spacing within the moving school is evidently determined to a large extent by hydrodynamic force. Individual fish tend to seek positions in which they can be as close as possible to their neighbors without suffering serious loss of efficiency due to turbulence created by the other fish.

01 According to the passage, what does not influence school size?

① the direction of the fish
② the proximity of the fish
③ the type of the fish
④ the speed of the fish

02 Choose the one that best fills in the blank.

① an opportunity to swim solo
② no consistent leadership
③ little room for autonomy
④ a strong sense to diverge

03 Which of the following cannot be inferred about a "fish school"?

① Its main role is to provide safety to its members.
② Predators affect the alignment of the fish.
③ It refers to a group of more than two fish.
④ Feeding is an exception to uniform formation.

[04-05]

We have big decisions to make and little time to make them if we are to provide stability and greater prosperity to the world's growing population. Top of the priority list is climate change. All around the world, it is plain that climate change is happening and that human activities are the principal cause. Climate change is affecting agriculture, water resources, human health, and ecosystems on land and in the oceans. [A] It poses sweeping risks for economic stability and the security of nations. [B] We can avert those risks if we take bold, decisive action now. An increasing number of government leaders, policymakers, businesses, investors, and concerned citizens are beginning to comprehend the costs of climate change. [C] More crucially, they are also learning that affordable solutions exist or are in the pipeline to reduce greenhouse gas emissions and support resilience. [D] That means investment, and it means global co-operation, especially in the areas of finance and technology. [E] That is why it is important that governments complete their work on a new universal climate agreement in the near future.

04 윗글의 요지로 가장 적절한 것은?

① Human activities are the principal cause of climate change.
② We have to join forces to act on climate change with no delay.
③ It is important to confirm the widespread effects of climate change.
④ Listing our tasks in the order of priority makes us stable and prosperous.
⑤ Affordable solutions were developed to reduce greenhouse gas emissions.

05 다음 주어진 문장이 들어가기에 가장 적절한 곳은?

We need to deploy these solutions at a scale commensurate to the challenge.

① [A]
② [B]
③ [C]
④ [D]
⑤ [E]

[06-07]

While some scientists explore the surface of Antarctica, others are learning more about a giant body of water 4 km beneath the ice pack. Scientists first discovered Lake Vostock in the 1970s by using radio waves that penetrate the ice. Since then they have used sound waves and even satellites to map this massive body of water (14,000 sq. km). How does the water in Vostock remain liquid beneath an ice sheet? The thick glacier above acts like an insulating blanket and keeps the water from freezing, says Martin Siegert, a glaciologist from the University of Wales in Great Britain. In addition, geothermal heat from deep within the Earth may warm the hidden lake. The scientists suspect that microbes may be living in Lake Vostock, closed off from the outside world for more than 2 million years. Anything found there will be totally _____ to what's on the surface of Earth, says Siegert. Scientists are trying to find a way to drill into the ice and draw water samples without causing contamination. Again, robots might be the solution. If all goes as planned, a drill-shaped cryorobot (*cryo* means cold), will melt through the surface ice. When it reaches the lake, it will release a hydrorobot (*hydro* means water) that can swim in the lake, take pictures, and look for signs of life.

06 윗글의 내용과 일치하지 않는 것은?

① Robots could be used to draw water samples from the lake without contamination.
② It was possible for scientists to discover Lake Vostock in the 1970s by means of sound waves.
③ The water in Lake Vostock has not been exposed to the outside world for more than 2 million years.
④ Both the thick glacier and geothermal heat from the Earth prevented the water in Vostock from freezing.

07 윗글의 빈칸에 들어갈 말로 가장 적절한 것은?

① alien
② familiar
③ similar
④ dangerous

[08-09]

They're counting sheep in Scotland, and not because of an outbreak of Celtic insomnia. For the past few decades, researchers have been keeping close tabs on the wild Soay sheep in the St. Kilda archipelago off the western coast of Scotland. Recently they noticed something odd: the Soays had shrunk. This was surprising because bigger is generally better for sheep. They fatten up on grass during the fertile, sunny summer; when the harsh Scottish winter comes, the grass disappears, and the smallest, scrawniest sheep tend to die off while their heftier, fitter cousins survive to reproduce in the spring.

But in just 25 years, Soay sheep have gotten 5% smaller, on average, according to a new study led by Tim Coulson of Imperial College London. It's not that evolution has been repealed in Scotland; rather, global warming has simply made it easier for smaller, less fit Soay sheep to survive. And plenty of other species are quickly adapting to the changing climate in similar ways. It seems global warming, which by one forecast could threaten up to one-third of the world's species by midcentury if left unchecked, is emerging as Darwin's new enforcer. "We're definitely seeing evolutionary change connected to climate change," says Arthur Weis, an evolutionary biologist at the University of Toronto.

08 The shrinking of Soay sheep was caused by _____.

① their insomnia
② global warming
③ lack of grass
④ evolutionary mutation
⑤ spread of the disease

09 The wild Soay sheep case supports the idea of "_____."

① endangered species
② green revolution
③ butterfly effect
④ relativity
⑤ survival of the fittest

[10-11]

Earlier this month a nuclear power station at Oskarshamn, Sweden, had to shut down because a swarm of jellyfish had clogged the pipes it uses to extract cooling water from the Baltic Sea. Such incidents are becoming more common, for the world's jellyfish population is increasing. Some blame climate change. Some point the finger at overfishing, which both removes species that eat jellyfish and reduces competition for food. And some think the culprit is the run-off into the ocean of fertilisers, for jellyfish can outcompete real fish in such nutrient-rich, oxygen-poor water.

Whatever the reasons (and all may contribute) may be, they not only affect power stations but also disrupt desalination plants, interfere with fishermen and — sometimes with fatal consequences — sting people taking a dip at the seaside. Using fishing boats to net and remove jellyfish is possible, but slow and costly. Myung Hyun of the Korean Advanced Institute of Science and Technology, in Daejeon, thinks he has a better answer: a fleet of killer robots that turn jellyfish into ⓐ mush. Dr. Myung and his colleagues have been testing their robo jellyfish-hunters in a series of trials around South Korea's coast. The machines float on a pair of booms propelled through the water by thrusters. They are designed to follow a lead robot and work together in formation.

10 What word can replace the word in ⓐ?

① something sticky
② something harsh
③ something alive
④ something soft

11 Which is NOT true, according to the passage above?

① Overfishing results in the shrink of species that eat jellyfish.
② A swarm of jellyfish can expose a danger to nuclear power stations or desalination plants as well as to people at the seaside.
③ It is only due to climate change that jellyfish population has increased.
④ Korean scientists have devised robots killing jellyfish with no use of nets.

[12-13]

Biologist Charles Brown discovered that some birds actually establish "information centers" where they can learn where to go for food. Observing cliff swallows on the plains of Nebraska for several years, he noted that the birds, on returning to their nests from a food hunt, would "rock back and forth" if their hunts were successful. When they left their nests to search for more food, they were followed by their neighbors only if their body language indicated success.

This bird dance, however, hardly compares to the well-documented dance of the honey bee. When scouts locate a source of food, they return to their hive and inform others of its whereabouts. Their scent declares what they've found; their dance gives directions and more. If the food is nearby, they perform a "round dance" — they run around in circles — which simply announces the find. When the location is far away, they perform a "waggle dance." The waggle dance is extraordinary in its detail. The movements tell the other bees how far away the food is, its precise location, and even how much there is.

12 Which of the following would be the best title of the passage?

① Bird Dance
② Information Centers
③ Animal Communication
④ Two Types of Bee Dance

13 Which of the following is NOT true of the passage?

① Some birds dance when their hunt for food is successful.
② Honey bees waggle to indicate that the food is located far away.
③ Through dance honey bees can show the amount of food they found.
④ Cliff swallows fly in groups when they leave their nests to search for food.

[14-15]

Scientists long believed that gradual changes in global climate caused the extinction of the dinosaurs. In 1979, however, a team from Berkeley discovered in Italy a layer of clay from about the time of the dinosaurs' disappearance, with an iridium level some thirty times greater than that of the clays in the adjacent strata. Since iridium settles fairly evenly over time and is extraterrestrial in origin, the researchers concluded that the high iridium level of this clay must have resulted from a sudden, catastrophic event. Scientists differ over the exact nature of the event. The possibility that a stellar explosion caused the deposition has been discounted because certain radioactive isotopes are largely absent from the clay. If the material had originated within the solar system, the earth must have collided with an astral body large enough to distribute the iridium-rich material around the globe. There is no geological evidence of the impact of such massive objects, but Grieve argues that the clay layers could have settled as fallout after an atmospheric explosion. Kyte asserts that a comet, disrupted by the earth's gravitational field, would have produced a deluge of falling debris without creating major craters. The Berkely group suggests that an asteroid may have landed in the sea. Whatever the type of event, the Berkely team argues that it disrupted the planetary ecology by suspending vast clouds of matter in the stratosphere. The effects of the impact would have increased as the blockage of sunlight impeded photosynthesis, causing a massive disruption at the base of the global food chain.

14 저자의 의도로 가장 적절한 것은?

① rebutting a traditional assumption
② discussing the implications of a discovery
③ suggesting a new course of investigation
④ summarizing and assessing differing theories

15 "The Berkely Group"의 주장을 뒷받침할 수 있는 근거로 가장 알맞은 것은?

① a drop in the number of plant fossils in the strata above those studied in Italy
② a discovery of dinosaur fossils in the strata older than the iridium-rich clay layer in Italy
③ a discovery of elevated levels of iridium in the rocks above and below the clay strata in Spain
④ a development of a consensus among scientists on the probability of a comet's impact with the earth.

[16-18]

In Toyama Bay, Japan, visitors idling on a pier overlooking the water were greeted by a 12-foot-long red-and-white giant squid. Despite its massive size, this squid was a juvenile. Dead specimens have been measured as long as 43 feet. The giant squid spends its life in the abyssal depths of the open ocean. These gigantic, solitary predators feast upon other deep sea fish or squid and are themselves hunted by sperm whales in what must unfold into epic battles of giants in the blackness of the deep ocean. They have been found dead washed up ashore or tangled in fishermen's nets for centuries, but have only been captured on film alive twice before. In 2004, researchers snapped the first images of a live giant squid, and in 2012, an expedition filmed a live giant squid for the first time ever; it was wrangling with their iridescent lures thousands of feet below the surface of the ocean. But the video of the Toyama Bay visitor is the most detailed and up-close viewing of a live giant squid yet. The animal was filmed with a submersible camera by Akinobu Kimura. This was ⓐ either a bold or foolish move considering there was no way of knowing how a large predator unaccustomed to human interaction would react to his presence. The juvenile giant squid apparently moseyed around in the bay for a couple of hours before receding back into the deep.

16 Which of the following is implied by ⓐ?

① Kimura was undecided about his course of action.
② The animal might consume Kimura.
③ The predator may wish to flee.
④ There could be dangerous undercurrents.

17 Which of the following is NOT stated or implied by the passage?

① Sperm whales battle giant squid.
② Squid are attracted to glowing objects.
③ Squid hunt for sperm whales alone.
④ The squid in Toyama Bay was not fully mature.

18 According to the passage, giant squid _____.

① frequently entertain onlookers
② eat seaweed in the deep ocean
③ are usually found dead
④ typically hunt near the surface

[19-21]

While the size of the brain certainly has some relation to smarts, much more can be learned from its structure. Higher thinking takes place in the cerebral cortex, the most evolved region of the brain and one many animals lack. Mammals are members of the cerebral-cortex club, and as a rule, the bigger and more complex that brain region is, the more intelligent the animal. But it's not the only route to creative thinking. Consider tool use. Humans are magicians with tools, apes dabble in them, and otters have mastered the task of smashing mollusks with rocks to get the meat inside — which, through primitive, counts. But if creativity lives in the cerebral cortex, why are corvids, the class of birds that includes crows and jays, better tool users than nearly all non-human species?

Crows, for example, have proved themselves adept at bending wire to create a hook so they can fish a basket of food from the bottom of a plastic tube. More remarkably, last year a zoologist at the University of Cambridge — the aptly named Christopher Bird — found that the rook, a member of the crow family, could reason through how to drop stones into a pitcher partly filled with water in order to raise the level high enough to drink from it. _____, the rooks selected the largest stones first, apparently realizing they would raise the level faster. Aesop wrote a tale about a bird that managed just such a task more than 2,500 years ago, but it took 21st century scientists to show that the feat is no fable.

19 **According to the passage, many animals are not intelligent because they _____.**

① live a simple life
② have a very small brain
③ didn't have to use the tools
④ were never trained to use their brain
⑤ don't have cerebral cortex

20 **Which is most appropriate for the blank?**

① On the contrary
② Nevertheless
③ What's more
④ Ironically
⑤ On the one hand

21 **What does the underlined "the feat" mean?**

① animals' use of language
② otters' use of rocks
③ chimpanzee's mastery of sign language
④ Christopher Bird's reasoning
⑤ birds' use of tools to achieve their goal

[22-24]

For years, attention has focused on the role of China, the largest emitter of greenhouse gases, and the United States, one of the largest emitter of per capita emitters. In November 2014 the two nations promised substantial limits on greenhouse gas emissions for the first time; China has pledged that its carbon dioxide output would fall after 2030, while the US has vowed to cut its output by more than a quarter in about the same time frame. Indeed, China's emissions have fallen so fast in the past year that many believe it may achieve its target ahead of time — the biggest stride yet in the fight against the climate change.

India's carbon output, _____, is growing faster than any other country's. Should that trend continue — and there is reason to think that it will — India could surpass China in 25 years to become the world's greatest emitter. Conceivably, its increasing emissions could offset all the efforts at curtailment in the rest of the world, leading to catastrophe. "India is the biggest piece of the puzzle," says John Coequyt, Sierra Club's director of international climate campaigns. "Is there a way for that rapid growth to happen quickly and pull people out of poverty using more renewable energy than has ever been used before? Or will they build more of what they have with almost no pollution controls?" The latter of course, he says, would be "a disaster for everyone."

22 According to the passage, _____.

① China is reluctant to keep the promise with the US
② the US pressed China to obey the global rule
③ India will be the largest emitter of gases
④ the US had to compete with China
⑤ India will follow the Chinese way

23 The most appropriate expression for the blank would be _____.

① by contrast
② however
③ on the one hand
④ in fact
⑤ by the way

24 Which one would be an example of "what they have"?

① solar energy
② wind power
③ hydrogen energy
④ coal plants
⑤ reforestation project

[25-28]

Dr. Pickett, a Canadian entomologist, and his associates struck out on a new road instead of going along with other entomologists who continued to pursue the will-o'-the-wisp of the ever more toxic chemical. [A] Recognizing that they had a strong ally in nature, they devised a program that makes maximum use of natural controls and minimum use of insecticides. Whenever insecticides are applied only minimum dosages are used — barely enough to control the pest without avoidable harm to beneficial species. Proper timing also enters in. [B]

How well has this program worked? Nova Scotia orchardists who are following Dr. Pickett's _____Ⓐ_____ spray program are producing as high a proportion of first-grade fruit as are those who are using _____Ⓑ_____ chemical applications. They are also getting as good production. They are getting these results, moreover, at a substantially lower cost. [C]

More important than even these excellent results is the fact that Dr. Pickett's program is not doing violence to nature's balance. [D] It is well on the way to realizing the philosophy stated by G. C. Ullyett a decade ago: "We must change our philosophy, abandon our attitude of human superiority and admit that in many cases in natural environments we find ways of limiting populations of organisms in a more economical way than we can do it ourselves."

25 Which of the following is most suitable for the blanks Ⓐ and Ⓑ?

	Ⓐ	Ⓑ
①	prolific	resilient
②	unvaried	varied
③	indiscreet	discreet
④	modified	intense

26 Which is the most appropriate place for the sentence below?

> Thus, if nicotine sulphate is applied before rather than after the apple blossoms turn pink one of the important predators is spared, probably because it is still in the egg stage.

① [A]
② [B]
③ [C]
④ [D]

27 What are the two most important factors in applying insecticides in Dr. Pickett's program?

① maximum dosages and proper timing
② proper dosages and early timing
③ sufficient dosages and early timing
④ minimum dosages and proper timing

28 Which of the following can NOT be inferred from the passage?

① Dr. Pickett and his associates believed that they had a strong ally in nature.
② One of the advantages of the Dr. Pickett's program was that it produced positive results at a lower cost.
③ G. C. Ullyett and Dr. Pickett saw eye to eye about ways to use nature.
④ Dr. Pickett and his associates did not believe in the need to limit populations of organisms.

[29-30]

The nervous system of vertebrates is characterized by a hollow, dorsal nerve cord that ends in the head region as an enlargement, the brain. Even in its most primitive form this cord and its attached nerves are the result of evolutionary specialization, and their further evolution from lower to higher vertebrate classes is a process that is far from fully understood. Nevertheless, the basic arrangements are similar in all vertebrates, and the study of lower animals gives insight into the form and structure of the nervous system of higher animals. Moreover, for any species, the study of the embryological development of the nervous system is indispensable for an understanding of adult morphology. In any vertebrate two chief parts of the nervous system may be distinguished. These are the central nervous system consisting of the brain and spinal cord, and the peripheral nervous system, consisting of the cranial, spinal, and peripheral nerves, together with their motor and sensory endings. The term "autonomic nervous system" refers to the parts of the central and peripheral systems that supply and regulate the activity of cardiac muscle, smooth muscle, and many glands. The nervous system is composed of many millions of nerve and glial cells, together with blood vessels and a small amount of connective tissue. The nerve cells, or "neurons," are characterized by many processes and are specialized in that they exhibit to a great degree the phenomena of irritability and conductivity. The glial cells of the central nervous system are supporting cells collectively termed "neuroglia." They are characterized by short processes that have special relationships to neurons, blood vessels, and connective tissue. The comparable cells in the peripheral nervous system are termed "neurilemmal" cells.

* vertebrate: 척추가 있는, 척추동물

29 윗글의 주제로 가장 적절한 것은?

① the evolution of nerve cells
② the advancement of bioengineering
③ the nervous system of vertebrates
④ the functions of the automatic nervous system

30 The author implies that a careful investigation of a biological structure in an embryo may lead to _____.

① improved research of the same structure in other species
② a better understanding of the fully developed structure
③ a method by which scientists can diagnose nervous disease
④ discovering ways in which poor development can be corrected

[31-32]

> In the 19th century, the UK government nearly surrendered to a powerful foe — the smell of human excrement. By that summer, the River Thames had become such a large repository of human waste that the stench drove all of London to its knees.

[A] Then came the great heat wave of 1858. That summer was a scorcher in England. It boiled the waste in the Thames, which released noxious odors of increasing pungency. The situation grew so desperate that everyone agreed that something had to be done. Figuring out the solution was the next challenge, and after debates and arguments, Disraeli finally passed a bill in July 1858 authorizing the construction of a system of embankments and tunnels that would lead the sewage out of the city.

[B] For all the suffering it caused, the Great Stink of 1858 eventually became a blessing for London. Not only was the Thames cleansed over the next decade but the whole city was infrastructurally and visibly improved by Thames embankments, which carried the sewage while at the same time easing road traffic from the congested thoroughfare, embracing the new underground railway system and enhancing the look of London above ground.

[C] The problem had been decades in the making. Since experts at the time believed the spread of contagious disease was solely airborne, little thought was given to the dangers of disposing of London's sewage in the Thames. Media outlets like the *Times* had editorialized for years about the need to clean up the river, but nothing changed.

[D] As work got underway, Joseph Bazalgette, the chief engineer who led the project, spoke publicly about its problems. "It was tremendously hard work," Bazalgette said. Despite the difficulties, the embankment project gradually became part of the crafting of a more modern city. A new underground-railway system was also built as part of the effort. The embankment wasn't completed until 1874, but by 1861 residents were raving about the transformation.

31 Choose the best order between the boxes.

① [C] – [A] – [B] – [D]
② [B] – [C] – [A] – [D]
③ [C] – [A] – [D] – [B]
④ [A] – [C] – [D] – [B]

32 Choose the best title for the passage.

① The Great Stink, the Hidden Foe of the UK
② The Great Stink, a Blessing in Disguise
③ The Making of a Modern City in the 19th century
④ Joseph Bazalgette, the Man Who Saved London from the Great Stink

[33-35]

A glacier is a huge mass of ice that moves slowly over land. The term "glacier" comes from the French word glace which means ice. Glaciers are often called "rivers of ice." Glaciers begin forming in places where more snow piles up each year than _____Ⓐ_____. Soon after falling, the snow begins to compress, or become denser and tightly packed. It slowly changes from light, fluffy crystals to hard, round ice pellets. New snow falls and buries this granular snow. The hard snow becomes even more compressed. It becomes a dense, grainy ice called firn. The process of snow compacting into glacial firn is called firnification.

As years go by, layers of firn build on top of each other. When the ice grows thick enough — about 50 meters — the firn grains fuse into a huge mass of solid ice. The glacier begins to move under its own weight. It is so heavy and exerts so much pressure that the firn and snow melt without any increase in temperature. The meltwater makes the bottom of the heavy glacier slicker and more able to spread across the landscape.

Glaciers melt when ice melts more quickly than firn can accumulate. Earth's average temperature has been increasing dramatically for more than a century. Glaciers are important indicators of global warming and climate change in several ways. Melting ice sheets contribute to rising sea levels. As ice sheets in Antarctica and Greenland melt, they raise the level of the ocean. Tons of fresh water are added to the ocean every day. In March 2009, a 160-square-mile piece of the Wilkins Ice Shelf broke off of the Antarctic Peninsula. Large icebergs created by such an event create hazards for shipping.

Large additions of fresh water also change the ocean ecosystem. Organisms, such as many types of corals, depend on salt water for survival. Some corals may not be able to adjust to a more freshwater habitat. The loss of glacial ice also reduces the amount of fresh water available for plants and animals that need fresh water to survive. Glaciers near the Equator, such as those on the tropical island of Papua or in South America, are especially at risk.

33 Which of the following best fits in Ⓐ?

① arrives
② falls
③ gathers
④ melts

34 Which of the following is NOT true?

① Firn is the product of a long-term hardening process of snow.
② The heavy glacier causes temperature to rise in the firn.
③ Iceberg is created when a large mass of glacier breaks off.
④ Some corals are vulnerable to the dilution of sea water.

35 Which of the following has nothing to do with firnification?

① cold weather
② snow pile-up
③ icebergs
④ grainy ice

[36-38]

Hydraulic fracturing — a method by which oil and gas service companies provide access to domestic energy trapped in hard-to-reach geologic formations — has been the subject of increasing environmental and health concerns in recent years. Hydraulic fracturing creates access to more natural gas supplies, but the process requires the use of large quantities of water and fracturing fluids, which are injected underground at high volumes and pressure. The composition of these fluids varies by formation, ranging from a simple mixture of water and sand to more complex mixtures with a multitude of chemical additives. The companies may use these chemical additives to improve the flow of the fluid, or kill bacteria that can _____Ⓐ_____ fracturing performance. Some of these chemicals, if not _____Ⓑ_____ safely or allowed to leach into the drinking water supply, could damage the environment or pose a risk to human health. Federal Law, however, contains no public disclosure ⓐ provision for oil and gas producers or service companies involved in hydraulic fracturing, and state disclosure provision vary greatly. While the industry has recently announced that it soon will create a public database of fluid components, reporting to this database is strictly voluntary, and there is no way to determine if companies are accurately reporting information for all wells. _____Ⓒ_____.

36 Which pair best fits Ⓐ and Ⓑ?

	Ⓐ	Ⓑ
①	enhance	– disarrayed
②	reduce	– disposed of
③	augment	– deprived of
④	mitigate	– disheveled
⑤	animate	– dismantle

37 Which expression may not replace ⓐ?

① stipulation
② directive
③ requirement
④ admonition
⑤ terms

38 Which of the following best suits ⓒ?

① Any risk to the environment and human health posed by fracturing fluids depends in large part on their contents
② As a result of hydraulic fracturing, natural gas production in the United States reached the highest level since 1974
③ Such an informational void leaves the public unable to access any impact the use of these fluids may have on its health
④ Although some fracturing fluids are removed from the well at the end of the fracturing process, a substantial amount remains underground
⑤ Oil and gas service companies design fracturing fluids to transport sand or other granular substances to prop open the fractures

[39-41]

Ponderosa pine* forests in the American West will die at an increasing rate as the world grows warmer, becoming less and less resilient when they are weakened by higher temperatures, according to new projections.

Although these forests now withstand short droughts, warming temperatures increasingly stress the forests, which means they will no longer survive the shorter droughts they once endured. And future droughts will be hotter as the planet warms.

"We're saying that if the climate warms a little more, things don't get _____Ⓐ_____ different, they get _____Ⓑ_____ different," said Henry Adams, a plant biologist at Oklahoma State University and lead author of a new paper, "Focus on Tree Mortality in a Warming World," published in *Environmental Research Letters*. "You get an acceleration in the rate of mortality."

"Long droughts are what it takes to kill trees," Dr. Adams said. "As you crank up the heat though, the time it takes to kill trees is less and less."

This study is significant because rather than looking at the effects of a single temperature increase, it examines the effects of multiple increases that provide a more realistic forecast.

"The confidence we've developed about our forests being at great risk is really high now," said David D. Breshears, a professor of natural resources at the University of Arizona and co-author of the paper. "Warming makes droughts more lethal."

Dr. Breshears said that the research shows that warming temperatures and drought alone could cause 9 or 10 additional forest die-offs during this century by killing seedlings. "It's not sustainable if you knock out a forest every ten or twelve years," Dr. Breshears said. "We are at a big risk of losing lots and lots of forest." The researchers also say that they believe the results of this study apply to many other types of forests around the world.

Such die-offs can lead to a state change, a radical shift in which the forest disappears and becomes a different type of _____Ⓒ_____, perhaps a grassland or shrub land.

*ponderosa pine: 소나무의 일종

39 Which of the following sets best fits in Ⓐ and Ⓑ?

	Ⓐ		Ⓑ
①	very	–	a little
②	a little	–	very
③	partially	–	totally
④	totally	–	partially

40 Which of the following best fits in Ⓒ?

① ecosystem
② forest
③ geography
④ shift

41 Which of the following is true?

① A ponderosa pine forest disappears every year.
② Dr. Breshears has high confidence in the sustainability of forests.
③ Warming and droughts are destructive combination for forest loss.
④ Drought alone could cause 9 or 10 additional deforestation during this century.

[42-44]

The production of food is the most basic of all human needs. It is based upon the extraction of materials from the natural environment. In principle, food production is a renewable activity, although over-production, soil erosion and water shortages can, in effect, make agriculture impossible under certain conditions. Having changed relatively slowly over long periods of time, the production, distribution and consumption of food have been transformed during the past four decades. They have become increasingly industrialized. In addition, although for millions of people basic subsistence is still the norm and starvation is always imminent, for millions of others food has become as much a statement about lifestyle as about survival. Abundance amidst scarcity is a glaring paradox of today's world.

In some respects, therefore, the modern agro-food industries may seem little different from other manufacturing industries. But, _____Ⓐ_____ the industrialization of much food production, this greatly oversimplifies what are highly complex and geographically differentiated activities. The basic fact remains that food production is fundamentally different from other manufacturing industries in one particular way: it is literally grounded in biophysical processes.

Food production remains an intensely local process, bound to specific climatic, soil and often socio-cultural conditions. At the same time, certain kinds of local production, notably _____Ⓑ_____ foods, have become increasingly global in terms of their distribution and consumption. For affluent consumers, with access to the overflowing cornucopias of supermarket shelves, the seasons have been displaced by permanent global summertime. But such apparently idyllic circumstances for affluent consumers have a dark and contentious side.

Producing food for a global market requires huge capital investment and gives immense power to the transnational food producers and the big retailers. It creates serious problems — as well as opportunities — for food suppliers as they become increasingly locked into transnational agro-food production networks. Global food production and distribution create huge environmental _____Ⓒ_____ in terms of excessive exploitation of sensitive natural ecosystems, the application of chemical fertilizers and pest controlling agents, the increasing attempts to genetically modify seeds, plants and even animals and to 'patent life,' and the transportation of high-value foods over vast geographical distances. These processes make agro-food an intensely sensitive industry, raising the fundamental question of 'who owns nature.'

42 윗글의 빈칸 Ⓐ, Ⓑ, Ⓒ에 들어가기에 가장 적절한 것은?

	Ⓐ	Ⓑ	Ⓒ
①	despite	– high-value	– disturbances
②	due to	– industrialized	– revolutions
③	similar to	– global	– shifts
④	albeit	– cultural	– transformation

43 윗글의 내용과 일치하지 <u>않는</u> 것은?

① The rich can enjoy abundant foods all year around thanks to modern agro-food industries.
② The global market makes it easier for food producers to supply their products worldwide.
③ Excessive exploitation of ecosystems can be settled by efficient transnational network systems.
④ Food production is a renewable activity in spite of some serious environmental problems.

44 윗글을 통해 추론할 수 있는 것으로 가장 적절한 것은?

① Food production is unique in that it cannot be industrialized.
② Agro-food industries come to invent new ecosystems unlike other manufacturing industries.
③ The highly complex activities of agro-food industries have become free from the biophysical processes over long periods of time.
④ The consumption of global food somehow has contributed to exacerbating the sensitive natural ecosystem.

[45-47]

A "charismatic little fish" declared extinct in the wild has been reintroduced to its native Mexico after being bred in an aquarium at Chester zoo. Named after the Tequila volcano, which looms north of its native habitat, the Tequila fish was discovered in 1990 in the Teuchitlan River. Recent studies have confirmed that the fish are thriving and already breeding in the Teuchitlan. Experts say it has created a blueprint for future reintroductions of other highly endangered fish species, with a rescue mission for another, the golden skiffia, now under way. Prof. Omar Dominguez said: "This is the first time an extinct species of fish has ever been successfully reintroduced in Mexico and so it's a real landmark for conservation. It's a project which has now set an important precedent for the future conservation of the many fish species in the country that are threatened or even extinct in the wild but which rarely take our attention. " In preparation for the reintroduction, 40 males and 40 females from the colony were released into large, artificial ponds at the university. This exposed them to a semi-natural environment where they would encounter fluctuating resources, potential competitors, parasites, and predators such as birds, turtles and snakes. After four years, this population was estimated to have increased to 10,000 individuals and became the source for the reintroduction to the wild.

A long-term monitoring program was established involving local people trained to assess water and habitat quality. Dr. Gerardo Garcia, Chester zoo's curator of lower vertebrates and invertebrates, said the successful reintroduction was an important moment in the battle for species conservation. "With nature declining globally at rates unprecedented in human history and the rate of extinction accelerating, this is a rare success story. We now have a blueprint for what works in terms of recovering these delicate fish species in Mexico and already we're on to the next one, a new rescue mission for the golden skiffia is already well under way."

45 Which of the following is best for the title?

① The Name of "Charismatic Little Fish"
② The Cost of New Breeding Method
③ How to Revive the Golden Skiffia
④ The Reintroduction of Near-extinct Fish

46 Which of the following is NOT true about the Tequila fish in artificial ponds?

① They were safe from predators.
② They competed to find their food.
③ They found their mates to reproduce.
④ They were released to the wild.

47 Which of the following is true?

① The Tequila fish was named after those who discovered it.
② The extinction of the Tequila fish proved true.
③ Experiment in reintroduction lasted for years.
④ The rescue of the golden skiffia was completed.

[48-50]

  Komodo dragons have lived on some of Indonesia's islands for thousands of years. One story tells that the Komodo dragon was first discovered during World War I, when an airplane crash landed in the waters around Komodo Island. The story tells how the pilot swam to the island, where he was surrounded by terrifying, huge lizards. It sounds like something out of an action movie; however, the story is actually a myth. We don't know exactly when Komodo dragons were first discovered, but the existence of the Komodo dragon was confirmed in 1926. This was the year that the explorer Douglas Burden led an expedition to Komodo. He was working for the American Museum of Natural History. He returned from his trip with twelve dead specimens and two living Komodo dragons.

  The Komodo dragon is the largest living lizard in the world. Some Komodo dragons can be 3 m long and can weigh more than 130 kg. This means that Komodo dragons are the heaviest lizards on Earth. They have long heads with short snouts, scaly skin, short legs, and big, strong tails. The largest dragon ever found was 3.13 m long and weighed 166 kg! Komodo dragons are the top predators on the islands where they live. They will eat nearly anything, including carrion, smaller dragons, wild horses and pigs, large water buffalo and sometimes unlucky humans! Although the Komodo dragon can run briefly at 20 km per hour, the reptiles usually hunt using camouflage and patience. They can spend hours in one place, waiting for their prey. When their unfortunate victim passes, the dragons attack and rip it to pieces. Their saliva has more than fifty types of bacteria. If the prey animal is bitten and escapes, it usually dies of blood poisoning quite quickly. If this happens, the dragons follow and locate the dead or dying animal by using their excellent sense of smell. Many large carnivores, such as tigers, do not eat 25 to 30 per cent of their prey. They leave the stomach, hide, bones, and feet. However, Komodo dragons are less wasteful and leave only about 12 per cent of their prey. They eat bones, feet, fur and skin — they even eat the stomach! A Komodo dragon can eat 80 per cent of its own body weight. However, when they feel scared or nervous, Komodo dragons can throw up the contents of their stomachs. This makes them lighter so they can escape more easily.

48 The existence of Komodo dragons was known to the world by _____.

① a pilot who swam to Komodo Island after his plane crashed in the waters
② an expedition team leader from the American Museum of Natural History
③ a rescue team who went to search for a missing pilot in Komodo Island
④ a fisherman who captured a huge lizard in Komodo Island

49 Which of the following is a characteristic of Komodo dragons?

① Komodo dragons can run fast for long.
② Komodo dragons are wasteful of their food.
③ Komodo dragons can vomit when they need to.
④ Komodo dragons do not eat dead animals.

50 How does a Komodo dragon find its prey that is bitten and escapes?

① By tracing the prey's blood drops
② By following the dying prey's smell
③ By waiting in camouflage for the prey to die
④ By dropping its own saliva on the prey's way

[51-52]

Mercury pollution is a global problem. Emissions from gold mining, coal burning, and other industrial processes travel through the atmosphere, eventually falling to Earth as rain or snow. The poison can make its way to fish and the humans who eat them, where it can damage the developing nervous system, causing problems with memory and language in children exposed in the womb.

When mercury lands in wetlands and lake sediment, microbes change the metallic element into a dangerous compound called methylmercury that builds up in food webs. Concentrations are highest in larger, predatory fish. Public health agencies regularly test such fish in many lakes, sometimes leading to warnings to limit consumption.

[A] To get a clear understanding, a large research project began an experiment in 2001 using a kind of chemical tracer: enriched stable isotopes of mercury. These forms of the element behave the same way chemically, but they can be distinguished from typical mercury in the environment. For 7 years, the researchers added one isotope of mercury to the water of Lake 658, part of a remote Canadian research station called the Experimental Lakes Area where 58 lakes and their watershed have been reserved for science. They also sprayed different isotopes from an airplane onto the surrounding wetland and upland to study how it moves into the lake.

[B] Since the 1980s, regulations to control air pollution have gradually lowered emissions of mercury in North America and Europe, but sources elsewhere are still increasing, particularly small-scale gold mining in Latin America and coal burning power plants in Asia. In 2013, nations agreed to an international treaty, called the Minamata Convention on Mercury, that requires signers to ban mercury in products such as light bulbs and batteries, as well as reducing industrial emissions.

[C] But how quickly do these measures have an effect? One hurdle to answering that question has been the complicated behavior of mercury in ecosystems, which makes it hard to figure out how much of a given decline in mercury concentrations in fish is due to reductions in air pollution rather than to factors such as excessive nutrients, invasive species, and other ecological changes.

Soon after the experiment began, isotopically labeled methylmercury began to accumulate in invertebrates living in the lake, such as zooplankton. It also rose in yellow perch and other small fish that eat the zooplankton, and increased by about 40% in larger fish such as pike, which eat smaller fish. After the first 7 years of the experiment, the researchers stopped adding the isotopic mercury and continued to check the concentrations in the animals living in the lake. During the next 8 years of the study, concentrations of isotopic mercury dropped by up to 91% in the small fish. Concentrations also fell in populations of the larger fish. Only a small amount of the mercury that was added to the surrounding land ended up in fish, and these levels also fell quickly.

The exact benefits to particular lakes will be difficult to predict, researchers say, because local conditions, such as the size of the surrounding watershed and rates of methylation, influence how much mercury ends up in fish. And even if all atmospheric emissions cease, some mercury — the legacy of past air pollution — will continue to enter lakes from the surrounding watershed.

51 윗글의 단락을 논리적 흐름에 맞게 순서대로 배열한 것으로 가장 적합한 것은?

① [B] – [A] – [C]
② [B] – [C] – [A]
③ [C] – [A] – [B]
④ [C] – [B] – [A]

52 윗글의 요지로 가장 적합한 것은?

① The long-term experiment was supported by the international authorities to prevent mercury contamination.
② Researchers analyzed the factors of raising the concentrations of mercury.
③ Lengthy experiment demonstrated environmental recovery by cutting mercury contamination.
④ Local conditions yielded the different results in terms of the concentrations of mercury.

여러분의 작은 소리
에듀윌은 크게 듣겠습니다.

본 교재에 대한 여러분의 목소리를 들려주세요.
공부하시면서 어려웠던 점, 궁금한 점,
칭찬하고 싶은 점, 개선할 점, 어떤 것이라도 좋습니다.

에듀윌은 여러분께서 나누어 주신 의견을
통해 끊임없이 발전하고 있습니다.

에듀윌 도서몰 book.eduwill.net
- 부가학습자료 및 정오표: 에듀윌 도서몰 → 도서자료실
- 교재 문의: 에듀윌 도서몰 → 문의하기 → 교재(내용, 출간) / 주문 및 배송

에듀윌 편입 솔루션 독해 Advanced

발 행 일	2023년 11월 1일 초판
편 저 자	에듀윌 편입 LAB
펴 낸 이	양형남
펴 낸 곳	(주)에듀윌
등록번호	제25100-2002-000052호
주　　소	08378 서울특별시 구로구 디지털로34길 55
	코오롱싸이언스밸리 2차 3층

* 이 책의 무단 인용 · 전재 · 복제를 금합니다.

www.eduwill.net
대표전화 1600-6700

꿈을 현실로 만드는
에듀윌

고객의 꿈, 직원의 꿈,
지역사회의 꿈을 실현한다

에듀윌 편입 학원의
독한 관리 시스템

전문 학습매니저의 독한 관리로
빠르게 합격할 수 있도록 관리해 드립니다.

독한 담임관리

· 진단고사를 통한 수준별 학습설계
· 일일 진도율부터 성적, 멘탈까지 관리
· 밴드, SNS를 통한 1:1 맞춤 상담 진행
· 담임 학습매니저가 합격할 때까지 독한 관리

독한 학습관리

· 학습진도 체크 & 학습자료 제공
· 데일리 어휘 테스트
· 모의고사 성적관리 & 약점 보완 제시
· 대학별 배치상담 진행

독한 생활관리

· 출석 관리
· 나의 학습량, 일일 진도율 관리
· 월별 총 학습시간 관리
· 슬럼프 물리치는 컨디션 관리
· 의무 자습 관리

에듀윌
편입 솔루션

독해 ADVANCED 정답과 해설

편저자 에듀윌 편입 LAB

READING ADVANCED

독해가 어려워?

이 책을 봐!

편입 최초
프리미엄 해설 수록

eduwill

에듀윌 편입 솔루션

독해 ADVANCED 정답과 해설

에듀윌 편입 솔루션

독해 ADVANCED 정답과 해설

READING ADVANCED

독해가 어려워?

이 책을 봐!

편입 최초
프리미엄 해설 수록

eduwill

PART 1 인문학

1강 정치

01	②	02	③	03	②	04	④	05	②	06	③	07	②	08	①	09	④	10	③
11	②	12	④	13	④	14	①	15	③	16	③	17	④	18	①	19	②	20	④
21	④	22	⑤	23	②	24	②	25	④	26	②	27	④	28	③	29	⑤	30	③
31	②	32	④	33	②	34	④	35	①	36	①	37	③	38	③	39	④	40	⑤
41	③	42	②	43	②	44	①	45	②	46	②	47	⑤	48	③	49	①	50	②

[01-02] 2016 한양대

| 정답 | 01 ② 02 ③

| 어휘 | **disparage** ⓥ 폄하하다　**discredit** ⓥ 존경심(신임)을 떨어뜨리다　**eager** ⓐ 열렬한, 간절히 바라는
dispersed ⓐ 흩어진, 분산된　**preclude** ⓥ (~이 …하는 것을) 못하게 하다, 불가능하게 하다
pollster ⓝ 여론 조사 요원　**elucidate** ⓥ (더 자세히) 설명하다　**tranquil** ⓐ 고요한, 평온한
fussy ⓐ 안달복달하는, 까다로운, 야단스러운

전문해석

유권자 여론 조사들은 시청률을 높이기 위해 열심인 네트워크 뉴스쇼에 의해 부정확하거나 오용되는 것으로 여겨지기 때문에 종종 폄하된다. 하지만, 선거를 위한 유권자 여론 조사를 신뢰하지 않으려는 사람들은 몇 가지 사실을 간과한다. 첫 번째로, 선거 전 마지막 1~2주는 악명 높을 정도로 상황이 변덕스럽다. 유권자들은 마침내 투표의 여부를 결정하고, 결정을 내리지 못한 유권자들은 그들이 투표할 후보자들에 대한 그들의 마음을 결정한다. 이것은 선거 전에 너무 앞서서 행해진 여론 조사가 그 선거의 결과를 정확하게 예측할 수 없다는 것을 의미한다. 두 번째로, 출구 조사는 다른 대부분의 과학적인 여론 조사와 다른데, 그 주된 이유는 분산된 투표소들이 출구 조사관들로 하여금 일반적인 샘플링 방법을 사용하는 것을 배제하기 때문이다. 하지만 유권자 여론 조사가 정확한지 아닌지에 대한 논쟁은 핵심을 놓치고 있다. 유권자 여론 조사는 승자들과 패자들을 예측하기 위한 것이 아니다. 그것들은 광범위한 여론을 설명하고 유권자들이 정말로 무슨 생각을 하고 있고 그들에게 가장 중요한 정책이 무엇인지를 설명하기 위해 고안된 것이다. 사실, 우리가 유권자들의 행동과 정책 선호에 대해서 알고 있는 것들의 대부분은 선거에 대한 과거의 여론 조사들로부터 나온 것이다.

01 윗글의 빈칸에 들어갈 말로 가장 적절한 것은? 빈칸 추론

① 까다로운　　✓② 변덕스러운
③ 고상한　　　④ 평온한

| 분석 | 빈칸이 포함된 문장과 바로 뒷 문장에서 유권자들은 선거 1~2주 전에야 투표 여부를 결정하고 투표할 후보자들에 대한 그들의 마음을 결정한다는 내용으로부터 빈칸에 들어갈 단어를 추론할 수 있다. 이렇게 변수가 많은 상황을 "변덕스럽다"고 추론하는 것이 가장 적절하다.

02 윗글의 내용과 가장 거리가 먼 것은? 내용 불일치

① 언론 매체들은 종종 그들의 시청률을 높이기 위해 유권자들의 여론 조사를 오용한다고 여겨진다.
② 너무 일찍 실시된 유권자 여론 조사는 선거 결과를 정확하게 예측할 수 없다.
✓③ 유권자 여론 조사의 가치는 승자와 패자를 예측하는 데 있다.
④ 출구 조사와 다른 유형의 여론 조사 간의 차이는 출구 조사가 일반적인 샘플링 방법을 사용하지 않기 때문에 발생한다.

| 분석 | 유권자 여론 조사의 목적은 선거에서 승자와 패자를 예측하는 것이 아니라 유권자들의 생각과 그들이 선호하는 정책을 알아내는 것이다.

[03-04] 2014 고려대

| 정답 | 03 ② 04 ④

| 어휘 |
neutrality ⓝ 중립
take side 편들다
eunuch ⓝ 환관, 내시, 거세당한 사람
mogul ⓝ 거물, 실력자
skew ⓥ 왜곡하다, 비스듬히 움직이다
partisanship ⓝ 당파심, (맹목적) 가담
refrain ⓥ 삼가다, 참다, 자제하다
exacting ⓐ 힘든, 까다로운
pariah ⓝ (사회에서) 버림받은 사람
render ⓥ (어떤 상태가 되게) 하다
commitment ⓝ 약속, 전념, 헌신
civil servant 공무원
impartiality ⓝ 공평무사, 공명정대
conduit ⓝ 도관, 전선관, (정보 등의) 전달자

전문해석
중립성은 어떤 형태의 당파심이나 헌신이 부재하는 상태이다; 그것은 편들기를 거부하는 것으로 구성되어 있다. 국제 관계에서 중립성은 국가가 분쟁이나 전쟁에 관여하지 않음을 선언하는 법적 조건이며, 어느 한쪽을 지지하거나 돕는 것을 자제할 의사를 나타낸다. 개인 행위의 원칙으로서, 재판관이나 공무원, 그리고 군과 기타 공직자들에게 적용되는 중립성은 엄격히 말해 정치적인 공감과 이념적 성향이 없는 것을 의미한다. 따라서 중립적인 행위자는 정치적 내시이다. 실제로, 공정성에 대한 덜 엄격한 요구사항이 일반적으로 적용된다. 04 ④ 이를 통해 정치적 공감은 전문적 또는 공공적 책임에 개입하거나 충돌하지 않는 한 유지될 수 있다.

03 빈칸을 가장 잘 채우는 것을 고르시오. 빈칸 추론
① 정치적 거물
✓② 정치적 내시
③ 사회에서 버림받은 사람
④ 법률 전달자

| 분석 | 빈칸 직전 문장에서 중립성을 '이념적 성향이 없는 것'으로 서술했고 빈칸이 포함된 문장에서 주어는 '중립적인 행위자'로 한쪽에 치우지지 않는 사람을 뜻한다. 따라서 정치적으로는 일종의 '거세된 사람', 즉 '정치적 내시'가 빈칸에 가장 적절하다.

04 다음 중 "중립성"에 대해 유추할 수 있는 것은? 세부 내용 추론
① 중립성은 정부 관리들이 갈등 상황에서 수행한 작업에 대해 책임을 지게 한다. 중립성은 공공적 책임에 개입하지 않을 때 유지됨
② 중립성은 국가와 문화에 따라 다르게 나타난다. 언급 안 함
③ 중립성은 정당의 기본 원칙 중 하나다. 중립성은 당파심이 부재하는 상태
✓④ 중립성은 판단의 왜곡을 피할 수 있는 태도이다.

| 분석 | 지문에 따르면 중립성이란 개인 행위의 원칙으로서 판단에 있어서 한쪽으로 치우치는 것을 피하는 태도이다.

[05-06] 2018 서울여대

| 정답 | 05 ② 06 ③

| 어휘 |
colossal ⓐ 거대한, 엄청난
replace ⓥ (다른 것의 기능을) 대신[대체]하다
marginalize ⓥ 사회에서 소외하다
virtually ⓐⓓ 사실상
inadvertent ⓐ 부주의한, 의도하지 않은, 불의의
religiosity ⓝ 독실함, 지나치게 종교적임
criticize ⓥ 비판하다, 비난하다
weaponize ⓥ 무기화하다
intimidate ⓥ 겁을 주다

secular ⓐ 세속적인, 현세의, 비종교적인
dominate ⓥ (불쾌한 방식으로) 지배하다, 군림하다
institution ⓝ 기관, 시설, 제도
morality ⓝ 도덕, 윤리
nepotism ⓝ 친족 등용, 족벌주의
judiciary ⓝ 사법부, 사법제도
opponent ⓝ 상대, 반대자

founder ⓝ 창립자, 설립자
conservative ⓝ 보수주의자, 보수적인 사람
sector ⓝ 부문, 분야
ostensible ⓐ 표면상의 겉보기만의
condemn ⓥ 비난하다
corruption ⓝ 타락, 부패
demonize ⓥ 악마로 만들다[묘사하다]

전문해석

지난 15년 동안, 나의 국가는 거대한 정치 혁명을 겪었다. 국가의 근대적 창시자인 무스타파 아타튀르크(Mustafa Ataturk)와 동일시하는 전통적인 세속적 엘리트들은 최근까지 대부분 무력하고 소외되었던 종교적 보수주의자들로 대체되었다. 종교적 보수주의자들은 언론과 심지어 비즈니스 부문의 많은 부분뿐만 아니라 국가의 거의 모든 기관들을 지배하게 되었다.

이 정치혁명은 의도치 않은 결과를 낳았다. 그것은 이러한 종교적 보수주의자들의 표면적인 미덕을 시험했고, 그들은 실패했다. 그들은 그 시험에서 너무 끔찍할 정도로 실패했기 때문에, 많은 종교인들이 주장하는 것처럼 종교성과 도덕성이 정말로 일치하는지에 대한 의문을 제기한다. 종교적 보수주의자들은 한때 그들이 부당하고 잔인하다고 비난했던 모든 것들을 결국은 그들도 했기 때문에 도덕적으로 실패했다. 수십 년 동안, 그들은 세속적 엘리트들을 족벌주의와 부패, 사법부를 무기화하고 언론 매체를 이용하여 <u>그들의 적수</u>를 악마화하고 위협했다고 비판했다. 06 ③

---

05 밑줄 친 <u>그들의 적수</u>가 의미하는 것은? 밑줄 추론
① 세속적인 엘리트들
✓② 종교적 보수주의자들
③ 사법부와 언론
④ 무스타파 아타튀르크의 추종자들

| 분석 | 지문 마지막 문장에 따르면 종교적 보수주의자들이 비판하는 행위(족벌주의, 부패, 사법부 무기화 등)를 하는 주체는 '세속적 엘리트 계층'이다. 밑줄 친 부분은 '그들의 적'으로 표현되었고 결국 세속적 엘리트 계층의 적인 '종교적 보수주의자들'을 지시하고 있음을 추론할 수 있다.

06 다음 중 새로운 정치 지도자에 대한 설명으로 옳은 것은? 세부 내용 일치
① 그들은 보수적일 뿐만 아니라 도덕적이다. 종교 보수주의자들은 도덕적으로 실패함
② 그들은 종교적인 사람들이 도덕적이라고 믿지 않는다. 언급 안 함
✓③ 그들은 부당하게 권력을 사용했다는 비난을 받고 있다.
④ 그들은 무스타파 아타튀르크와 같은 정치적 위치에 서 있다. 무스타파 아타튀르크와 동일시하는 것은 세속적 엘리트

| 분석 | 지문 두 번째 문장에 따르면 새로운 정치 지도자는 '종교적 보수주의자들'이다. 지문 두 번째 단락의 네 번째 문장에서 '종교적 보수주의자들이 한때 그들이 부당하고 잔인하다고 비난했던 모든 것들을 결국은 그들도 했기 때문에 도덕적으로 실패했다'고 했으므로 그들도 부당하게 권력을 사용했을 것이다. 따라서 보기 ③이 올바른 진술이다.

| 배경 지식 | 보수주의(Conservatism): 급격한 변화를 반대하고 현 체제를 유지하려는 사상이나 태도
족벌주의(Nepotism): 자신의 일족을 우선하는 태도 |

[07-09] 2015 동덕여대

| 정답 | 07 ② 08 ① 09 ④

| 어휘 | akin ⓐ ~와 유사한, 같은 종류의　　speculation ⓝ 추측, 짐작, 사색, 심사숙고　　enunciate ⓥ (생각을 명확히) 밝히다
reformulate ⓥ 새로 만들다[준비하다]　　ethos ⓝ 기풍, 정신

전문해석

민주주의 이론은 오늘날 아인슈타인이 세기의 전환기에 그의 추측을 시작했던 이론 물리학의 그것과 비슷한 상태에 있다. 그 당시에 받아들여진 교리는 주로 뉴턴이 두 세기 전에 ⓐ 선언했던 것이었다. 그의 사고의 근본은 공간과 시간의 개념들이었다. 뉴턴은 시간과 공간을 서로 구별되는 것으로 생각했다. 그가 보기에, 둘(시간과 공간)은 모두 절대적이었다. 비록 19세기의 연구가 뉴턴의 이론이 만족스럽게 설명하지 못한 결과를 낳았지만, 뉴턴의 우주에 대한 이미지는 다시 새롭게 구성되지 않았다. 그 개혁은 아인슈타인이 성취한 것이었다. 그의 영감은 공간과 시간을 별개의 개념으로 취급하는 것이 아니라 그에 의해 시공간으로 융합된 하나로 취급하는 데 있었다. 게다가, 이 통합된 개념은 절대적인 것이 아니라 상대적인 것으로 간주되었다. 물리학에서 시간과 공간의 관계는 민주주의 이론가들에게 자유와 평등의 관계와 유사하다. 다른 어떤 것보다도, 이 Ⓐ 쌍둥이 이념들은 우리의 기본적인 개념들의 역할을 한다. 만일 민주주의 정신을 가장 간단한 요약으로 압축한다면, 그것은 다음과 같을 것이다: 민주주의는 시민들을 위해 가능한 한 많은 자유와 평등을 결합하는 정부의 형태이다.

---

07 저자는 _____ 라고 주장한다.　내용 일치

① 자유와 평등은 절대적이다
✓② 공간과 시간은 뉴턴에게는 양립할 수 없었다
③ 민주주의 이론과 물리학 사이에는 차이점이 있다
④ 뉴턴의 이론은 아인슈타인의 이론만큼 중요하다

| 분석 | 지문에 따르면 뉴턴은 시간과 공간을 서로 구별되는 것으로 보았다. 따라서 ②가 옳은 진술이다.

---

08 밑줄 친 단어 ⓐ의 의미는 _____ 이다.　빈칸 추론

✓① 공지된　　　　　　　② 거부된
③ 비판을 받은　　　　　④ 실험된

| 분석 | enunciate는 '(학설이나 이론 등을) 발표하다'의 의미가 있으므로 보기 중 ①이 가장 유사한 뜻을 가진다.

---

09 Ⓐ에 가장 적합한 단어는 _____ 이다.　빈칸 추론

① 다른　　　　　　　② 호환되지 않는
③ 가짜의　　　　　　✓④ 쌍둥이의

| 분석 | 빈칸 Ⓐ의 직전 두 문장에 따르면, 아인슈타인은 시간과 공간을 별개가 아닌 '시공간으로 융합된 하나로 취급'했다는 것을 알 수 있다. 따라서 빈칸 Ⓐ에는 시간과 공간의 이러한 관계를 나타내는 단어가 와야 한다. 보기 ④가 정답으로 가장 적절하다.

| 배경지식 | 민주주의(Democracy): 국민이 권력을 가지고 그 권력을 스스로 행사하는 제도나 그런 정치를 지향하는 사상 |

[10-11] 2017 한양대

| 정답 | 10 ③ 11 ②

| 어휘 |
hail ⓥ 환호하여 맞이하다, ~라고 부르다   distinction ⓝ 구별, 구분   ceaseless ⓐ 끊임없는
venture ⓥ (위험을 무릅쓰고) 모험하다, 조심스럽게 하다[말하다]   reconciliation ⓝ 화해, 조화
gratify ⓥ 기쁘게 하다, 충족시키다   feel at home 마음이 편안하다   sheer ⓐ 순전한, 완전한, 순수한
endow ⓥ 기부하다   engagement ⓝ 약혼, (업무상의) 약속   exemplary ⓐ 모범적인, 훌륭한
shed on ~을 비추다

전문해석

의심의 여지가 없는 것은 처음부터 끝까지 한나 아렌트(Hannah Arendt)가 끝없는 순환적인 정신 활동인 이해라는 활동에 거부할 수 없이 이끌렸다는 것이다. 한나 아렌트는 확실히 많은 아이디어와 의견을 가지고 있었고, 변화를 원하면서도 안정을 바란다는 것으로 환영받았으며, 새로운 구별을 만들었고, 새로운 개념에 기여했으며, 전통적인 정치적 사고의 오래된 범주들을 변경했다. 그것들은 (그녀의 이해 활동의) 결과들이었고, 다른 사람들에게 유용한 것으로 증명되었다. 그러나 대부분의 정치적 사상가들과 달리, 아렌트는 주로 문제들을 해결하는 것에는 관심이 없었다; 끊임없는 이해에 있어서의 모험은 그녀에게 삶 그 자체처럼 <u>도구적인</u> 것이 아니었다. 이해하기 더 어려운 것은 이해의 활동이 그녀에게 그녀가 살았던 세상과의 어느 정도의 화해를 제공했다는 점이다. 만약 다른 사람들이 이해하게 된다면, 그녀는 만족감을 느꼈고 마음에 편안함을 느꼈다. 이것은 그녀가 자신의 생각을 다른 사람에게 전달하는 것이 가능하다고 믿거나 그것을 원했다는 것을 의미하지 않는다. 그것은 생각하는 것—즉 이해하고 사건에 의미를 부여하는 것—은 자신에게만 관련되는 고독하고 사적인 일이었던 아렌트에게 순전히 말도 안 되는 소리였을 것이다. 그녀는 모범적인 삶을 살았고, 반복해서 이야기되어 온 삶을 살았지만, 결국 그녀의 이해로 세상을 비추어 보는 것이 한나 아렌트가 누구였는지 엿볼 수 있는 유일한 방법이다.

10 윗글의 빈칸에 들어갈 말로 가장 적절한 것은? 빈칸 추론

① 직관적인   ② 의도적인
✓③ 도구적인   ④ 불확실한

| 분석 | 빈칸이 포함된 문장에서 '대부분의 정치적 사상가들과 달리 아렌트는 문제들을 해결하는 것에는 관심이 없었다'고 했다. 그렇다면 문제를 해결하기 위해 필요한 무언가가 그녀의 삶의 특징이 될 수 없으므로 문제 해결과 관련된 표현 중에서 정답을 찾도록 한다. 보기 ③이 정답으로 가장 적절하다.

11 한나 아렌트에 대한 설명으로 적절하지 않은 것은? 세부 내용 불일치

① 그녀는 천성적으로 자유주의자이거나 보수주의자로 여겨질 수 있다.
✓② 그녀는 이후의 경력에서 점차 외부 세계와 단절되었다.
③ 그녀의 활동은 전통적인 규율 범주의 관점에서 정의될 수 없다
④ 그녀에 대한 이해의 중요성은 결과보다는 그 자체를 이해하는 데 있었다.

| 분석 | 지문의 다섯 번째 문장에서 '그녀의 이해의 활동이 그녀에게 그녀가 살았던 세상과의 어느 정도의 화해를 제공했다'고 서술했다. 따라서 그녀는 세상과 화해하고 세상을 이해한 사람이고 외부 세계와 단절된 사람은 아니었음을 알 수 있다. 보기 ②가 적

절하지 않은 진술이다.

> **배경 지식** 한나 아렌트(Hannah Arendt): 사회적 악과 폭력의 본질에 대해 깊이 연구한 독일 태생의 유대인 철학사상가

[12-14] 2018 서강대

| 정답 | 12 ④ 13 ② 14 ①

| 어휘 |
pity ⓝ 연민, 동정(심)
commitment ⓝ 약속, 전념, 헌신
aspire ⓥ 열망[염원]하다
generality ⓝ 일반론, 대부분, 보편성
provoke ⓥ (특정한 반응을) 유발하다, 화나게 하다
compassion ⓝ 동정, 연민
equivalence ⓝ 등가, 동량
quantitative ⓐ 양적인, 분량상의
macroeconomic ⓐ 거시 경제의
treatise ⓝ 논문
indisputable ⓐ 논의의 여지가 없는, 명백한
wretched ⓐ 몸이 안 좋은, 비참한, 형편없는

전문해석

고통을 연민의 정치학이라는 관점에서 고려할 때 헌신의 문제가 문제점으로 나타난다. 그 이유는 **연민의 정치학은 두 가지 요건을 충족시켜야 하기 때문이다.** 정치학으로서 그것은 보편성을 열망한다. 연민의 정치학의 역할은 국부적인 것으로부터, **동정심을 자극하는 사건들이 발생할 수 있는 필연적인 지역 상황들로부터 스스로 벗어나는 것이다.** 이렇게 하기 위해 정치학은 동등성을 확립하는 기술, 특히 통계적 기법에 의존할지도 모른다. 그러나 연민과 관련해서 그것은 **특정 사례에서 완전히 벗어날 수 없다.** 동정심은 보편성에서는 불러일으켜지지 않는다. 예를 들어, 현존하는 동등성의 관습에 기초한 양적 지표에 의해 정의되는 절대 빈곤에 대한 묘사는 거시 경제학 논문에서 찾을 수 있고 정치학을 정의하는 데 도움이 될 것이다. 그러나 그것은 연민의 정치학에서 논쟁의 여지가 없는 감정들을 자극하지는 못할 것이다. 연민을 불러일으키려면 고통과 비참한 인간들이 더 운이 좋은 사람들의 감성에 영향을 미치는 방식으로 전달되어야 한다. 연민은 Ⓐ <u>비례성</u>이 부족하다는 약점을 가지고 있다. 고통받는 아이의 모습은 우리의 가슴을 슬픔으로 가득 채우지만 우리는 끔찍한 전투의 소식을 무관심으로 대한다.

---

12 윗글에 따르면 다음 중 사실인 것은? 〔내용 일치〕

① 아이의 죽음은 군인의 죽음보다 더 비극적이다. 〔언급 안 함〕
② 연민의 정치에서 통계는 무관하다. 〔통계적 기법에 의존할 가능성 있음〕
③ 연민은 공감보다 덜 중요하다. 〔언급 안 함〕
✓ ④ 연민의 정치는 지역적 관심사들로부터 분리될 필요가 있다.

| 분석 | 지문에 따르면 정치학의 측면에서 연민의 정치학은 '동정심을 자극하는 사건들이 발생할 수 있는 지역 상황들로부터 스스로 벗어나는 것'이라 했다. 따라서 보기 ④는 지문의 내용과 일치한다.

---

13 연민의 정치의 이중적 요건은 무엇인가? 〔세부 내용 일치〕

① 고통에 대한 객관적인 관점을 발전시키기 위해서는, 일반성이 주관적인 감정에 의해 더럽혀져서는 안 된다. 〔언급 안 함〕
✓ ② 연민의 정치는 넓은 시야와 친밀한 감정적 반응을 모두 요구한다.
③ 고통의 관중은 통계가 진심 어린 감정을 방해하게 해서는 안 된다. 〔통계가 감정을 방해한다는 진술은 없음〕
④ 고통받는 사람들에 공감하기 위해서는, 공감을 일으키는 방식으로 통계적 증거를 제한해야만 한다. 〔통계적 증거를 제한해야만 한다는 주장은 없음〕

| 분석 | 지문에 따르면 연민의 정치학은 보편성과 특수성이라는 두 가지 요소를 모두 충족시켜야 한다. 따라서 지역적 상황으로부터 스스로 벗어날 수 있는 폭넓은 관점과 더불어 고통과 비참함에 대한 감정적 반응을 불러일으킬 수 있어야 할 것이다. 따라서 보기 ②가 정답이다.

---

14 빈칸 Ⓐ에 가장 적절한 단어를 고르시오. `빈칸 추론`

① ✓ 비례성 ② 노곤함
③ 무모함 ④ 공감

| 분석 | 지문 마지막 문장에서 '고통받는 아이의 모습은 우리의 가슴을 슬픔으로 가득 채우지만 우리는 끔찍한 전투의 소식을 무관심으로 대한다'고 했다. 고통의 크기는 끔찍한 전투 희생자들의 고통이 한 아이의 고통보다 더 크겠지만 연민은 아이의 고통에서 더 많이 느낀다는 뜻이다. 따라서 연민은 꼭 고통의 크기에 비례하지 않는다고 할 수 있으므로 빈칸에는 보기 ① '비례성'이 가장 적절하다.

[15-17] 2016 서강대

| 정답 | 15 ③ 16 ③ 17 ④

| 어휘 | expansionary ⓐ 확장[확대/팽창]성의   military intervention 군사적 개입
claim ⓥ 주장하다, (재해·병 등이 인명을) 빼앗다   comity ⓝ 예의(= courtesy)
rapprochement ⓝ (특히 국가·단체 사이의) 화해, 관계 회복   ally ⓝ 동맹국
analogous ⓐ 유사한   antipathy ⓝ 반감   pejorative ⓐ 경멸적인, 비난 투의
confederate ⓐ 동맹을 맺고 있는, 연합한   asymmetrical ⓝ 비대칭   stridency ⓝ 삐걱거림

전문해석

지금으로부터 몇 년 후, 역사가들은 미국 역사에서 지금 이 시기를, 많은 대중들 사이의 높아진 편견과 많은 정치 지도자들의 근시안적 시각에 사로잡혀 있던 시대로 되돌아볼 것이다. [A] 중동지역에 대한 진지한 관찰자들 사이의 합의는 이 지역에서 미국에 대한 적대감에 대한 이유가 다면적이라는 것이다: 이는 이스라엘에 대한 미국의 무조건적인 지지와 팔레스타인들에 대한 확장적이고 억압적인 정책들, 중동과 북아프리카 전역에 걸친 부패하고 억압적인 많은 독재 정권들에 대한 지원; 수만 명의 시민들의 목숨을 앗아 간 드론 공격에서부터 수십만 명의 무슬림들의 목숨을 앗아 간 전면적인 침략에 이르는 이슬람 세계에 대한 광범위한 군사 개입. [B] 팔레스타인 자치정부와 하마스 통치하에 사는 사람들의 거의 80%가 미국을 "적"으로 여기고 있다. [C] 〈중동 지역 내 미국의 우방이라고 할 수 있는, 이집트인과 요르단인의 약 85% 그리고 터키인의 73%도 유사한 의견을 가지고 있다.〉 여론 조사에 따르면 미국을 가장 비우호적으로 보는 상위 10개국 중 7개국이 이슬람 국가인 반면, 미국을 가장 호의적으로 보는 상위 10개국 중 오직 1개국만이 이슬람 국가이다. [D]

---

15 빈칸에 가장 적절한 단어를 고르시오. `빈칸 추론`

① 적막감 ② 사교성
③ ✓ 적대감 ④ 화해

| 분석 | 빈칸 이후로 미국이 중동 지역에 저지른 일들이 나열되었으므로 이를 토대로 중동 지역이 미국에 대해 어떤 태도를 가지고 있을지 추론해 본다. 또한 지문의 마지막 문장의 통계를 확인해 보면 중동 지역 내 미국의 적대심을 확인할 수 있다. 따라서 정답은 ③이다.

16 다음 문장의 가장 적절한 위치를 고르시오. 문장 삽입

"중동지역 내 미국의 우방이라고 할 수 있는, 이집트인과 요르단인의 약 85% 그리고 터키인의 73%도 유사한 의견을 가지고 있다."

① [A] ② [B]
✓ ③ [C] ④ [D]

분석 | 주어진 문장의 마지막 부분에 '유사한 의견을 가지고 있다'고 했으므로 직전 내용에서 동의할 만한 의견이 언급되어야 할 것이다. 따라서 '팔레스타인 사람의 80%가 미국을 적으로 여기고 있다'고 언급한 다음인 [C]에 주어진 문장을 삽입해야 한다.

17 윗글의 내용과 가장 일치하는 문장을 고르시오. 내용 일치

① 미국과 중동 사이의 반감은 가까운 미래에 줄어들 것으로 예상된다. 언급 안 함
② 이슬람 국가들은 미국에 대해 경멸적인 감정을 가지고 있다. 적대감과 경멸은 다름
③ 미국은 중동에서 강력한 연합국이 부족하다. 중동 지역 내 미국의 우방에 대한 설명은 있으나 강력한 연합국은 언급 안 함
✓ ④ 중동에 대한 미국의 비대칭적인 간섭은 이 지역의 긴장의 원인 중 하나이다.

분석 | 지문에 따르면 미국이 중동에서 무조건적으로 이스라엘을 지지하고 팔레스타인에 대해서는 확장적이고 억압적인 정책들을 썼다는 것을 알 수 있으므로 보기 ④가 정답으로 가장 적절하다.

[18-20] 2013 경희대

정답 | 18 ① 19 ② 20 ④

어휘 |
obsolete ⓐ 더 이상 쓸모가 없는, 구식의   alternative ⓐ 대안의
retrospectively ⓐⓓ 회고조로, 과거를 회상하며
dub ⓥ 별명을 붙이다, (영화 등을 다른 언어로) 재녹음하다   catch on 인기를 얻다, (~을) 이해하다
core ⓝ 핵심   ecologically ⓐⓓ 생태학적으로, 환경적으로   salivate ⓥ 침을 흘리다
quiescent ⓐ 조용한, 잠잠한   horizon ⓝ 수평선, 지평선   aspiration ⓝ 열망
exclusivism ⓝ 배타주의, 당파주의   redeeming ⓐ (결점·실망을) 보충하는, 벌충하는
rant ⓝ 호언장담, 허풍   ignite ⓥ 불이 붙다, 점화하다
chav ⓝ 하류층 젊은이, (저급한 패션과 취향을 즐기는) 일탈 청소년들 또는 그 문화   manifestation ⓝ 징후, 나타남
sinister ⓐ 사악한, 불길한   provocative ⓐ 도발적인, 자극적인   phallic ⓐ 남근 숭배의
brood ⓥ (새가 알을) 품다, 숙고하다   drool ⓥ (탐이 나거나 좋아서) 침을 흘리다   phlegmatic ⓐ 침착한, 가래의
enfeeble ⓥ 약화시키다, 쇠약하게 만들다   proscriptive ⓐ 금지하는, 추방하는   prescriptive ⓐ 지시하는, 규정하는
analytic ⓥ 분석적인

전문해석

노동자 계급과 사회주의의 현대성이 시대에 뒤떨어진다고 선언된 세상에서 중산층 사회는 대안적 미래의 상징이 되었다. 비록 중산층이 유럽에서는 한 번도 유행한 적이 없는 미국적인 개념이지만, 북대서양의 선진국들은 회고적으로 중산층이라고 불린다. 이 유토피아의 핵심은 땅을 소유하고 차와 집을 사고 제한 없는 다양한 전자제품들을 구입하고 세계적인 관광산업을 유지하는 중산층의 무한한 소비에 대한 꿈이다. 이 세계화된 소비주의는 생태학적으로 의식이 있는 사람들에게 악몽의 대상이 될 수 있지만, 그것은 사업가들이 ⓐ 군침을 흘리게 만든다. 중산층 소비는 또한 부유층의 특권을 수용하면서 대중들에게 열망의 조용한 지평을 제공하는 큰 이점을 가지고 있다. 이 꿈의 어두운 측면은 내재된 배타주의이다. 중산층이 아니거나 부자가 아닌 사람들은 어떤 상황 기능이나

자산도 가지고 있지 않다. 그들은 2009년 미국 티 파티에 불을 지핀 TV의 고함 소리처럼 그저 '패배자'일 뿐이다. 그들은 '하층계급', '하층민'이다. 개발도상국에서, 공공장소의 '정리'는 가난한 사람들이 해변, 공원, 거리, 광장에서 배제된 자신들을 발견하기 때문에 이러한 사악한 경향의 명백한 표현이다. 특히 도발적인 예는 자카르타의 남근 숭배 국가 유물이 있는 독립광장에 울타리를 침으로써 그곳을 '일종의 배타적인 중산층 테마파크'로 만들고 가난한 사람들에게서 유일한 여유 공간을 빼앗은 것이다.

---

18 윗글에 따르면 다음 중 중산층 사회의 영향력이 확산되어 야기된 결과가 <u>아닌</u> 것은? `세부 내용 불일치`

✓① 사회주의의 소멸
② 증가하는 계급 분열
③ 공공 공간의 소멸
④ 환경적 위험

| 분석 | 지문의 첫 문장에서 '노동자 계급과 사회주의의 현대성이 시대에 뒤떨어진다고 선언된 세상에서 중산층 사회는 대안적 미래의 상징이 되었다.'고 했다. 따라서 사회주의의 소멸은 중산층 사회의 영향으로 등장한 것이라 보기 어렵다. 따라서 정답은 ①이 가장 적절하다.

---

19 다음 중 ⓐ를 적절히 대체할 수 있는 단어는 무엇인가? `밑줄 추론`

① 알을 품고 있는   ✓② 침을 흘리는
③ 가래가 많은   ④ 힘이 없는

| 분석 | 밑줄 친 ⓐ salivate는 '군침을 흘리다'라는 의미이며 보기 ②의 drool 역시 '침을 흘리다'라는 뜻이므로 정답은 ②이다.

---

20 다음 중 윗글의 문체를 가장 잘 설명한 것은? `글의 어조`

① 예언적인   ② 금지하는
③ 규범적인   ✓④ 분석적인

| 분석 | 지문에서는 유럽 중산층 사회의 특징과 문제점을 설명하고 있으므로 보기 ④가 정답으로 적절하다.

배경지식 사회주의(Socialism): 사유 재산 제도를 폐지하고 생산 수단을 사회화하여 자본주의 제도의 모순을 극복한 사회 제도를 실현하려는 사상이나 운동

[21-23] 2019 성균관대

| 정답 | 21 ④ 22 ⑤ 23 ③

| 어휘 |
a slew of 많은
plutocrat ⓝ 금권정치가, (영향력이 큰) 재벌
oligarch ⓝ 과두제 집권층의 일원
semi-detached ⓐ 반쯤 떨어진, 일부분 떨어진
ammunition ⓝ 탄약, 공격 수단, (논쟁에서 무기가 될 수 있는) 정보
populist ⓝ 대중 영합주의자
entrepreneur ⓝ 기업가
tap ⓥ 가볍게 두드리다, 개척하다
backlash ⓝ (사회 변화에 대한 대중의) 반발
convergence ⓝ 집중성, 집합점
indistinguishable ⓐ 구분이 안 되는, 분명하지 않은

> **전문해석**

최근 몇 년 동안 많은 요소들이 결합되어 세계가 다수가 아닌 소수의 이익을 위해 재벌, 과두제 집권층, 정경 유착한 정치인들에 의해 운영된다는 인상을 만들었다.

2억 5천만 명의 사람들이 전 세계를 돌아다니며, 정치적 엘리트들이 일자리, 임금, 사회적 결속력을 위협한다고 그들이 말하는 이민 관리에 실패했다고 주장하는 우파 대중주의 정치인들에게 그 어느 때보다 더 많은 공격수단을 제공하고 있다.

한편, 포브스(Forbes)에 따르면, 세계화로 인해 기업가들이 새로운 시장을 개척함과 동시에 자본, 자산 및 소득을 세무사로부터 보호할 수 있게 됨에 따라 억만장자의 수는 지난 20년 동안 5배 증가하여 2,200명 이상으로 증가했다. 세계에서 가장 부유한 8명의 사람들이 가진 부는 가장 가난한 35억 명이 소유한 것과 같다. 금융 엘리트들이 벌어들인 돈은 무려 10조 파운드에 달한다.

그러나 포퓰리즘의 부상에 대한 부분적인 설명을 제공할지도 모르는 많은 비경제적 요인들도 있다. 엘리트들에 대한 문화적 반발, 우리의 정치를 재조직한 기술 혁명, 이제 서로 구별할 수 없는 좌파와 우파 정당의 기술관료주의 중심에서의 수렴 등이다.

---

21 윗글의 가장 좋은 제목은 _____.이다. 제목

① 포퓰리즘을 어떻게 발견할 수 있는가? 포퓰리즘의 발견은 키워드가 아님
② 포퓰리즘이란 무엇인가?
③ 포퓰리스트들은 누구인가?
④ ✓ 포퓰리스트들은 왜 이제 나타났는가? 포퓰리즘이나 포퓰리스트에 대한 정의는 키워드가 아님
⑤ 포퓰리즘의 반대는 무엇인가?

| 분석 | 지문에서는 최근 몇 년 동안의 대중주의의 등장 배경을 경제적, 비경제적 요인으로 나눠서 설명하고 있다. 따라서 제목으로는 보기 ④가 적절하다.

---

22 포퓰리즘의 배경이 된 요인으로 _____ 는 지문에 언급되어 있지 않다. 세부 내용 불일치

① 문화적 엘리트주의
② 탈세
③ 대규모 이주
④ 불평등의 심화
⑤ ✓ 이데올로기적 대결

| 분석 | 지문의 마지막 문장에서 포퓰리즘의 부상에 대한 비경제적 요인으로 '좌파와 우파 정당의 기술관료주의 중심에서의 수렴'을 들었다. 이는 두 이데올로기의 충돌보다는 융합이기 때문에 보기 ⑤가 지문에서 언급되지 않은 정보이다.

---

23 윗글에 따르면 포퓰리즘은 _____ 에 대항한다. 세부 내용 일치

① 우파의 정치적 엘리트들
② 좌파의 정치적 엘리트들
③ ✓ 부패한 엘리트들
④ 사악한 기업인들
⑤ 일반 대중들

| 분석 | 지문 첫 번째 단락에서는 최근 등장한 포퓰리즘의 원인이 '재벌, 과두제 집권층, 정경 유착한 정치인'에게 있음을 언급했다. 따라서 포퓰리즘은 ③의 '부패한 엘리트'에 대해 반대한다고 볼 수 있다.

| 배경지식 | 포퓰리즘(Populism): 대중의 의견을 대변하고 대중을 중시하는 정치사상 또는 활동 |

[24-26] 2022 숙명여대

| 정답 | 24 ①   25 ④   26 ②

| 어휘 |
bureaucrat ⓝ 관료, 관료주의자, 독선자
pursuit ⓝ 추구
self-interest ⓝ 사리사욕, 이기주의
disciplinary ⓐ 징계의
scope ⓝ (~할) 기회, (활동 등의) 여지
pursue ⓥ 추구하다, (일 등을) 밀고 나가다
at the cost of ~의 비용을 지불하고, ~을 희생하고
self-seeking ⓐ 사기 본위의, 이기적인
obfuscate ⓥ 애매하게 만들다
manipulate ⓥ (교묘하게) 조종하다, (사물을 능숙하게) 다루다
tenure ⓝ 재임 기간, 거주권

전문해석

자유 시장 경제학자들에게, 정치인과 정부 관료들인 공무원들은 독특한 도전을 제기한다. 그들의 사리사욕 추구는 시장 규율의 대상이 아니기 때문에 의미 있는 수준으로 Ⓐ 억제될 수 없다. 정치인들은 서로의 경쟁에 직면하기는 하지만, 선거는 너무 드물게 일어나기 때문에 징계 효과가 제한적이다. Ⓑ 결과적으로, 그들이 국가 복지를 희생하면서 권력과 부를 높이는 정책을 추진할 여지가 충분하다. 직업 관료에 관한 한 자기 이익 추구의 범위는 더욱 넓다. 그들의 정치적 상관인 정치인들이 선거의 요구에 부응하는 정책을 펼치도록 하여도, 그들은 항상 정치인들을 혼란스럽게 하고 조종할 수 있다. Ⓒ 그러나, 정치인들과 달리 이들 직업 관료들은 종신 재직권은 아니더라도 높은 직업 안정성을 가지고 있어서 단순히 일을 지연시킴으로써 정치적 상관의 임기가 끝날 때까지 기다릴 수 있다.

---

24 Ⓐ에 가장 적절한 것은 무엇인가? 　빈칸 추론

✓ ① 억제된
② 이용할 수 있는
③ 인정된
④ 추구된
⑤ 적용된

| 분석 | 빈칸 뒤 because절에서 '그들의 사리사욕 추구는 시장 규율의 대상이 아니기 때문에'라고 언급했고 여기서 그들은 'public officers'를 가리킨다. 따라서 그들의 사적 이익 추구는 의미 있는 수준으로 '억제되기' 힘들 것임을 추론할 수 있다. 보기 ①이 정답이다.

---

25 Ⓑ와 Ⓒ에 가장 적절한 표현은 무엇인가? 　연결사

① 게다가 – 예를 들면
② 더욱이 – 결과적으로
③ 예를 들면 – 결과적으로
✓ ④ 결과적으로 – 그러나 　→ 유일한 역접 표현이므로 Ⓒ부터 해결하는 것도 좋은 방법
⑤ 더욱이 – 마침내

| 분석 | 빈칸 (Ⓑ)의 직전 문장에서 '선거는 너무 드물게 일어나기 때문에 징계 효과가 제한적이다.'라고 했고 빈칸 Ⓑ 뒤로는 그 결과에 해당하는 내용이 이어지므로 빈칸에는 Consequently가 적절하다. 또한 빈칸 Ⓒ 직전 문장에서 '그들은 항상 정치인들을 혼란스럽게 하고 조종할 수 있다.'라고 했으나 빈칸 Ⓒ 뒤에서는 그들이 '높은 직업 안정성을 가지고 있어서 단순히 일을 지연시킴으로써 정치적 상관의 임기가 끝날 때까지 기다릴 수 있다.'고 했으므로 빈칸 Ⓒ에는 역접의 부사가 와야 한다. 따라서 보

기 ④가 정답으로 가장 적절하다.

> **26** 윗글에 따르면, 어느 것이 올바른가? 내용 일치
>
> ① 민주주의 사회에서 선거 제도는 탐욕스러운 자유 시장에 도전할 수 있는 강력한 수단이다. 선거는 드물게 일어나서 징계 효과가 제한적임
> ✓ ② 정치인들은 종종 국익을 무시한 채 자신들의 이익을 위해 권력을 남용한다.
> ③ 정치인들은 선거에서 이기기 위해 대중의 이익을 극대화하기 위해 열심히 일하는 경향이 있다. 대중의 이익이 아닌 자신의 이익 추구함
> ④ 관료들은 해고되는 것을 피하기 위해 정치인의 요구를 따를 의무가 있다. 관료들은 높은 직업 안정성을 가짐
> ⑤ 공무원들은 자유 시장의 사익을 통제할 권한이 없다. 언급 안 함

| 분석 | 지문에서는 정치인들이 '국가 복지를 희생하면서 권력과 부를 높이는 정책을 추진할 여지가 충분하다.'고 했으므로 보기 ②는 옳은 진술이다.

[27-28] 2019 단국대

| 정답 | 27 ④ 28 ①

| 어휘 | be bound to *do* 반드시 ~하다   hushed-up ⓐ 은폐된   vulgarity ⓝ 상스러움, 음란물
sneer ⓥ 비웃다, 조롱하다   private member (영국 정치에서 정부 각료가 아닌) 일반 의원
nuisance ⓝ 성가신 존재, 골칫거리   snub ⓥ 모욕하다, 무시하다, 거절하다   cranky ⓐ 기이한, 짜증을 내는
ill-formed ⓐ 모양이 갖추어지지 않은, 부적격한, 비문법적인   well-meaning ⓐ 선의에서 하는
Home Office (영국의) 내무성   mend ⓥ 수리하다, (문제를) 해결하다   doubtful ⓐ 확신이 없는, 의심스러운

전문해석

민주주의에는 또 다른 장점이 있다. 그것은 비판을 허용하고, 만약 대중의 비판이 없다면, 스캔들은 은폐될 수밖에 없다. 그것이 내가 언론의 모든 거짓말과 저속함에도 불구하고 언론을 믿는 이유이며, 의회를 믿는 이유이다. 영국 의회는 말만 무성한 곳이기 때문에 자주 조롱을 받는다. 글쎄, 나는 그곳이 말만 무성한 곳이기 때문에 그것을 믿는다. 나는 스스로를 성가신 존재로 만드는 일반 의원을 믿는다. 그는 무시당하고 그가 성격이 나쁘거나 부적격하다는 말을 듣지만, 그렇지 않았다면 결코 언급되지 않았을 권력의 남용을 폭로하고, 남용이 언급되는 것만으로도 바로잡히는 경우가 매우 많다. 우리나라에서도 가끔 선의를 가진 공무원이 효율성을 위해 자제력을 잃고 <u>스스로를 전능한 하나님이라고 생각한다.</u> 이러한 공무원들은 내무부에서 특히 빈번하게 있다. 조만간 의회에서 그들에 대한 질문이 있을 것이고, 그러고 나서 그들은 그들의 행동을 고쳐야 할 것이다. 의회가 대의 기구인지 효율적인 기구인지는 매우 의심스럽지만, 의회가 비판하고 이야기하기 때문에, 그리고 그 말이 널리 보도되기 때문에 나는 그것을 중요하게 생각한다. 그래서 민주주의를 두 번 찬양한다: 하나는 민주주의가 다양성을 인정하기 때문이고 다른 하나는 비판을 허용하기 때문이다. 두 번의 찬양으로 충분하다: 세 번 찬양해 줄 이유는 없다.

> **27** 밑줄 친 부분과 가장 가까운 의미는 무엇인가? 밑줄 추론
>
> ① 외교 회의를 위한 장소
> ② 진실하고 진지한 토론을 위한 장소
> ③ 건전한 토론을 위한 장소
> ✓ ④ 시끄럽고 떠들썩한 장소

| 분석 | 지문의 밑줄 친 a talking shop은 '(행동으로 옮기는 것은 없고) 말만 무성한 곳'이라는 의미의 표현이다. 따라서 보기 ④가 밑줄 친 표현과 가장 유사한 의미를 가진다.

| **28** | 윗글에 따르면, 다음 중 사실인 것은? 내용 일치

✓① 민주주의의 장점 중 하나는 권력 남용을 폭로하는 것이다.
② 너무 많은 이야기는 시스템의 효율성을 방해한다. 언급 안 함
③ 비판은 민주주의의 유일하게 중요한 요소이다. 다양성 인정, 비판의 허용 두 가지가 민주주의를 찬양하는 이유로 비판이 유일한 요소 아님
④ 민주주의는 다른 것을 고려하는 것에 기초해야 한다. 민주주의의 기초에 대한 언급 안 함

| 분석 | 지문의 저자는 민주주의의 장점으로 권력의 남용이 폭로되고 언급되는 것만으로도 바로잡히는 것을 들었다. 따라서 보기 ①이 정답이다.

[29–30] 2011 성균관대

| 정답 | 29 ⑤ 30 ③

| 어휘 | Watergate ⓝ 워터게이트(1974년 Nixon 대통령 사임의 직접적 원인이 된 도청 사건), 정치적 부정행위
undermine ⓥ (자신감·권위 등을) 약화시키다   authority ⓝ 지휘권, 권위
handsomely ⓐⓓ 멋지게, 훌륭하게   refusal ⓝ 거절, 거부   individualism ⓝ 개인주의
admirable ⓐ 존경할 만한   trait ⓝ 특성   chip ⓥ 이가 빠지다, (도구를 써서) 깎다
fade ⓥ (색깔이) 바래다, 희미해지다   self-contradicting ⓐ 자기모순적인   passion ⓝ 열정
sacrifice ⓝ 희생   privilege ⓝ 특권   common good ⓝ 공익, 공동선
litigious ⓐ 소송을 일삼는   niggling ⓐ 하찮은 일에 골몰하는, 옹졸한   grievance ⓝ 불만, 고충

전문해석

베트남(전쟁)과 워터게이트(사건)는 미국 기관의 권위를 크게 약화시켰다. 그것들은 국민에게 그들이 행할 역할과 그들이 싸울 전쟁을 고르고 선택하도록 장려했다. 적어도, 그들은 참여 자체를 거부하는 것을 훌륭하게 정당화했다. 이 도덕적 개인주의는 오래되고 존경받는 미국적 특성으로, 과거에는 종종 국가에 대한 의무감과 균형을 이루었다. 그 감각은 줄어들고 희미해졌다. 미국은 놀랄 만큼 자기모순적인 무리들의 집합체가 되었다. 대다수가 현실로 간주하는 극단적인 위협이 부족한 미국인들은 서로를 배척하는 사고방식을 보여 주었다. 미국의 다원주의는 개인주의의 모순이 되었다. 미국의 사회적 비전은 편안하고 안전하기 위한 개인의 열정에 불과하다. 만약 희생이 필요하다면, 미국인들이 공동의 이익을 위해 그들의 특권 일부를 기꺼이 포기할 것인지는 고통스러운 질문이다. 만약 그들이 다른 미국인들보다 조금이라도 자신이 더 희생하고 있다고 생각한다면, 그들은 절대 그렇게 하지 않을 것(자신의 특권을 포기하지 않을 것)이다. 결핍의 시대에, 국가는 불만을 수집하는 데 있어 훨씬 더 소송하고 불만을 가지는 데 있어서 옹졸해질 것이다. 30③

| **29** | 밑줄 친 표현은 _____ 을 의미한다. 밑줄 추론

① 베트남과 워터게이트 이후 징병제에 대한 미국인들의 태도는 변하지 않았다 ─ 두 사건으로 미국 기관의 권위 크게 약화, 국가에 대한 의무감 희미해짐
② 미국인들은 베트남과 워터게이트 이후 그들의 나라를 위해 더 기꺼이 싸웠다
③ 베트남과 워터게이트는 미국인들이 공동의 적이 필요하다고 믿게 만들었다 미국인들은 현실로 간주하는 극단적인 위협이 부족
④ 베트남과 워터게이트는 미국인들이 전쟁에 반대하는 법을 만드는 것을 더 긴급하게 만들었다 언급 안 함
✓⑤ 베트남과 워터게이트는 미국인들이 그들의 나라를 위해 싸우는 것을 거부하는 것을 정당화했다

| 분석 | 지문의 첫 두 문장을 통해 베트남 전쟁과 워터게이트 사건을 통해 미국인들은 전쟁을 고르고 선택하게 되었다는 것을 알 수 있다. 밑줄 친 부분에서의 '참여'는 앞 내용으로 미루어 보아 '전쟁에 참여'하는 것으로 추론할 수 있으므로 보기 ⑤가 정답으로 가장 적절하다.

30	윗글에 따르면, 저자는 미국인들이 점점 _____라고 암시한다. 세부 내용 일치
	① 야심 있는 ② 공격적인
	✓ 편협한 ④ 과격한
	⑤ 애국적인

| 분석 | 지문에서 미국의 다원주의는 개인주의의 모순이 되어 미국인들은 공동의 이익을 위해 자신의 특권을 포기하지 않으며 더 많이 소송하며 옹졸해질 것이라고 했다. 따라서 미국인들은 보기 ③과 같이 점점 '편협해'지고 있다고 볼 수 있다.

| 배경 지식 | 다원주의(Pluralism): 개인이나 개인으로 이루어진 집단이 기본으로 삼는 원칙이나 목적이 서로 다를 수 있음을 인정하는 태도 |

[31-32] 2011 서강대

| 정답 | 31 ③ 32 ③

| 어휘 |
property right 재산권 enforce ⓥ (법률 등을) 집행하다, 강요하다 contract ⓝ 계약
voluntary ⓐ 자발적인, 임의적인 exchange ⓝ 교환 theft ⓝ 도둑질
justify ⓥ 정당화하다 intervention ⓝ 개입 redistribute ⓥ 재분배하다
founder ⓝ 건국자, 창립자 paradoxical ⓐ 역설적인 take down ~을 공격하다[때려눕히다]
straw man (허수아비 등의) 밀짚 인형, 하찮은 사람[물건/논의] position ⓝ 입장, 견해
respectable ⓐ 존경할 만한, 훌륭한 anarchist ⓝ 무정부주의자
originalist ⓝ 원전주의자, 근원주의자(헌법을 입법할 당시의 의도대로 해석해야 한다고 주장하는 사람)
converge ⓥ 모여들다, 집중되다 mitigate ⓥ 완화시키다 infringe ⓥ 위반하다, (법적 권리를) 제한하다

전문해석

정부가 재산권을 보호하고 계약을 집행하기 위해 필요하며, 시장을 보존하고 자발적인 상품 교환에 역할을 한다는 것을 부인하는 사람은 거의 없을 것이다. 하지만 절도와 살인을 막기 위한 정부의 개입이 한 사람에게서 다른 사람으로 부를 재분배하는 정부의 개입과 본질적으로 동일하기 때문에 정당화된다고 주장하는 것은 비탈길 추론 중에서도 최악의 종류이다. 미국의 건국자들의 생각에 따르면 어떤 경우에는, 정부가 천부적인 자유와 평등을 보호하기 위해 행동하는 한편, 다른 경우에는 그것이 자유와 그 자유에 내재하는 근본적인 평등권을 침해한다. 카스 선스타인(Cass Sunstein)의 책은 기본 원리의 역설적인 측면을 옹호하는 주장을 하기보다는 허수아비를 쓰러뜨린다. 그가 반대하는 입장―즉 정부의 개입은 항상 나쁘다는 입장―은 좌파나 우파 모두에서 지적으로 존중받지 못한다. 이런 입장을 가진 사람들은 근원주의자가 아니라 무정부주의자라고 불린다.

31	빈칸에 가장 적절한 것은 무엇인가? 빈칸 추론
	① 수렴한다 ② 완화한다
	✓ 침해한다 ④ 끌어당긴다

| 분석 | 빈칸 앞의 in the other는 상충되는 의견이나 상황 사이에 쓰는 표현이다. 빈칸 앞 절에서는 정부가 천부적 자유를 보호한다고 했기 때문에 바로 다음 내용 앞에 in the other가 있다면 앞 내용과 상충되도록 '그 자유를 침해한다'는 내용이 와야 한다. 따라서 정답은 보기 ③이다.

32 밑줄 친 문구에서 유추할 수 있는 것은? 밑줄 추론

① 정부는 시민들을 보호할 것으로 기대된다.
② 정부의 생각은 근본적으로 모순된다.
☑ 선스타인은 약한 상대들을 공격하여 주장을 펼친다.
④ 미국의 설립자들은 개인의 권리를 보호하기를 원했다.

| 분석 | 지문에서 선스타인의 책은 '허수아비를 쓰러뜨린다'고 했는데 '허수아비'란 '하찮은 사람'이나 '약자'를 뜻한다. 따라서 보기 ③의 '선스타인은 약한 상대들을 공격함으로써 주장을 펼친다'가 적절한 추론이다.

| 배경지식 | 미끄러운 비탈길 논증(Slippery slope reasoning): 개인이나 단체가 상대적으로 사소한 것을 허용했는데 연쇄적인 과정을 통해 엄청난 부정적 결과를 가져올 것이라는 예측에 사용되는 논증

[33-34] 2018 성균관대

| 정답 | 33 ②   34 ①

| 어휘 |
entwine ⓥ 꼬다, 뒤엉키다, 얽히다
ballot ⓝ 무기명 투표
partisan ⓐ 편파(당파)적인, 열렬한 지지자
senatorial a. 상원(의원)의
agitate ⓥ 주장하다, 요구하다, (마음을) 뒤흔들다
grandstanding ⓝ 사람들의 눈길을 끌려는 행위
surveillance ⓝ 감시, 감독
end up with 결국 ~하게 되다
microcephaly ⓝ 소두증

dedicated ⓐ 전념하는, 헌신적인
amid prep ~ 가운데[중]에, ~로 둘러싸여
recess ⓝ (의회·위원회 등의) 휴회 기간
primary ⓝ (미국) 예비 선거

buzzy ⓐ 윙윙거리는, (장소나 분위기가) 활기 넘치는, 신명 나는
battalion ⓝ 대대, (특정 목적을 위해 조직된 사람들) 부대

commissioner ⓝ 위원, 경찰국장, 장관
hyperactive ⓐ 활동 과잉의
assail ⓥ 공격을 가하다, 괴롭히다

slate ⓥ (특히 신문·잡지 등에서) 혹평하다
sideshow ⓝ 부차적인 일

전문해석

플로리다에서는 모기와 정치가 오랫동안 얽혀 있었다—몇몇 카운티에서는 전담 모기 위원들을 선출한다—하지만 올해는 지카(바이러스)와 지카(바이러스)를 옮기는 벌레들이 투표를 통해 인종들을 감염시켰다. 과도한 이익 추구와 당파적 비난이 만연한 가운데, 모든 시민들은 의회가 여름 휴회 전에 긴급 자금 지원법을 통과시키지 못했다고 비난한다. 민주당원들은 이전 주 정부의 예산 삭감을 이유로 플로리다의 공화당 소속 주지사 릭 스콧(Rick Scott)을 공격한다. 8월 30일 상원 예비 선거에서 승리한 패트릭 머피(Patrick Murphy)는 11월 공화당 후보로 확정된 마르코 루비오(Marco Rubio)를 맹비난한다. 탬파 지역 몇몇 정치인들은 현재 키스 지역에서 실험이 예정되어 있는 유전자 변형 모기들을 풀어놓기 위해 선동하고 있으며, 이는 지카를 확산시키는 모기의 수를 줄일 수도 있다.

그러나, 실제 전쟁에서와 마찬가지로, 정치적으로 눈길을 끌려는 행위는 부차적인 것이다. 실제 전투원들은 모기를 통제하는 요원들인데, 그들의 도구는 <u>그들 자신의 몸</u>을 포함한다. 피넬라스 팀의 롭 크루거(Rob Kruger)가 다시 이야기하듯이, 감시 행동의 한 가지 형태는 번잡한 장소에 서서 1분에 얼마나 많은 모기가 그에게 착륙하는지 보는 것을 포함한다. "당신은 결국 모기에 많이 물리게 됩니다."라고 그의 상사인 제이슨 스턱(Jason Stuck)이 비축용 닭들에게서 알을 가져오면서 말했다. 많은 질병들이 플로리다의 수많은 모기 종들에 의해 옮겨지지만, 지카는 유아들에게 소두증을 유발하는 것에 더하여 관광업에 미치는 영향 때문에 걱정의 대상이다.

33 플로리다에서 선거에서 이기려면, 당신은 _____ 이 필요하다. 　세부 내용 추론

① 모기에 물리는 것에 노출되는 것
✓ 모기를 없애는 방법을 알고 있는 것
③ 생명 공학에 대한 기본 지식을 가지고 있는 것 　지카바이러스나 유전자변형 모기와 생명공학을 관련시킨다면 너무 포괄적
④ 플로리다의 다른 정치인들을 비판하는 것
⑤ 가능한 한 많은 주민들과 친해지는 것

| 분석 | 지문에서 플로리다주는 모기와 정치의 관계가 복잡하게 얽혀 있고 시민들은 모기를 퇴치하는 데 긴급 자금지원법을 통과시키지 못한 의회를 비난하고 있는 상황이므로 플로리다주에서 선거에 이기기 위해서는 보기 ②와 같이 모기를 없애는 방법을 알고 있을 필요가 있다.

34 빈칸에 가장 좋은 표현은 _____ 이다. 　빈칸 추론

✓ 그들 자신의 몸
② 모기의 포식자
③ 왕성한 무기
④ 해로운 살충제
⑤ 유전자 돌연변이

| 분석 | 빈칸 이후 내용에서 모기를 통제하는 요원들의 '감시 행동의 한 가지 형태는 번잡한 장소에 서서 1분에 얼마나 많은 모기가 그에게 착륙하는지 보는 것을 포함한다.'고 했다. 따라서 이들이 도구로 사용하는 것은 바로 보기 ① '그들 자신의 몸'이라고 할 수 있다.

[35-36] 2015 서울여대

| 정답 | 35 ① 36 ②

| 어휘 | **liberal** ⓝ 진보주의자　　**conservative** ⓝ 보수주의자　　**stem from** ~에서 기인하다
coercive ⓐ 강압적인　　**shy away from** ~을 피하다　　**perspective** ⓝ 관점, 시각
crucial ⓐ 중요한

전문해석

오늘날 진보주의자와 보수주의자의 차이는 정부의 목적에 대한 그들의 태도에서 비롯된다. 보수주의자들은 정부의 원래 목적인 사회 질서를 유지하는 것을 지지한다. 그들은 시민들이 질서를 지키도록 강요하기 위해 국가의 강압적인 힘을 기꺼이 사용하려 한다. 하지만 그들은 범죄를 정의하고, 예방하고, 처벌하는 것으로 멈추지 않을 것이다. 예를 들어, 그들은 사회적 관계의 전통적인 패턴, 즉 여성의 가정적 역할과 학교와 가족생활에서 종교의 중요성 같은 사회적 관계의 전통적인 패턴들을 보존하고자 하는 경향이 있다. 진보주의자들은 보수주의자들보다 질서를 유지하기 위해 정부 권력을 사용할 가능성이 적다. 진보주의자들은 정부의 강압을 이용하는 것을 피하지는 않지만, 그것을 평등을 촉진하는 것과 같은 다른 목적을 위해 사용한다. 그들은 고용, 주택, 교육에서 게이와 레즈비언에 대한 동등한 대우를 보장하는 법, 민간 기업들이 여성과 소수 집단의 구성원을 고용하고 승진시키도록 하는 법, 그리고 장애를 가진 사람들에게 대중교통이 동등한 접근을 제공하도록 요구하는 법을 지지한다. 보수주의자들은 평등을 반대하지는 않지만, 정부의 힘을 이용해 강제하는 정도로 평등을 중시하지는 않는다. 진보주의자들에게 있어서, 평등을 촉진하기 위한 (정부) 권력의 사용은 유효할 뿐 아니라 필수적이다.

35 보수와 진보의 결정적인 차이는 ＿＿＿＿＿＿에 대한 그들의 관점에 있다. 세부 내용 일치
☑ 평등과 질서의 가치관
② 정부의 구조
③ 전통적인 가치를 보존하는 방법들
④ 주 정부를 통합하기 위한 전략

| 분석 | 지문에 따르면 진보주의자와 보수주의자는 평등과 질서를 위한 정부 권력의 사용에 대한 입장이 다르다. 따라서 보기 ①이 정답이다.

36 윗글에 따르면, 다음 중 옳은 것은? 내용 일치
① 평등을 촉진하는 것은 전통적인 사회관계를 향상시킨다. 평등을 촉진하는 것은 전통적인 사회적 패턴들을 변화시킴
☑ 정부의 전통적인 역할은 사회를 질서 있게 유지하는 것이다.
③ 개인 사업자들은 범죄율을 줄이기 위해 소수자들을 고용할 수밖에 없다. 언급 안 함
④ 보수주의자들은 사회 질서를 유지하기 위해 정부의 강요를 사용하는 것에 반대한다. 보수주의자들은 국가의 강압적 힘을 기꺼이 사용함

| 분석 | 지문 두 번째 문장에서 '보수주의자들은 정부의 원래 목적인 사회 질서를 유지하는 것을 지지한다.'고 했으므로 보기 ②가 올바른 진술이다.

[37-39] 2011 인천대

| 정답 | 37 ③ 38 ③ 39 ④

| 어휘 | rational ⓐ 합리적인, 이성적인
school of thought 학설, 학파
theological ⓐ 신학의, 신학적인
tenet ⓝ 교리, 신조
approach ⓝ 접근법, 처리방법
moral ⓐ 도덕적인, 도의상의
justifiable ⓐ 정당하다고 인정되는, 이치에 맞는
maintain ⓥ 유지하다
constrain ⓥ ~하게 만들다, 강요하다
morality ⓝ 도덕
utter ⓥ 발언하다
accurately ⓐⓓ 정확하게
organization ⓝ 구조
idealistic ⓐ 이상적인
musing ⓝ 사색
practical ⓐ 실용적인
stability ⓝ 안정
consideration ⓝ 고려
necessary ⓐ 필요한, 불가피한
traditional ⓐ 전통적인
virtue ⓝ 미덕
sum up 요약하다, 합치다
originate ⓥ 생겨나다
concerned ⓐ 관여한, 관계된
preserve ⓥ 보존하다
operation ⓝ 운영
order ⓝ 질서, 명령, 주문
therefore ⓐⓓ 그러므로
means ⓝ 수단, 방법
establish ⓥ 설립하다
notion ⓝ 개념
end ⓝ 목적
view ⓝ 관점

전문해석

정부의 체계, 그들의 조직, 기능, 그리고 정책에 대한 합리적 분석인 정치학은 15세기 후반 이탈리아 피렌체의 시민인 니콜로 마키아벨리(Niccolo Machiavelli)와 함께 서구에서 처음 시작되었다. <u>그 당시, 정치사상의 유일한 학파는 매우 종교적인 것으로, 정부의 실질적인 운영보다는 신학적 사색과 신앙의 교리 보존에 더 관심이 있었다.</u> 마키아벨리는 이 접근법을 거부했고, 도덕적 고려보다 안정성과 질서가 더 중요하다고 주장하였다. 따라서 통치자가 질서를 확립하는 데 필요한 권력을 얻고 유지하기 위해 필요한 모든 수단을 사용하는 것은 정당했다. 마키아벨리에 따르면, 통치자들은 도덕과 미덕에 대한 전통적인 개념에 <u>구속되어서는</u> 안 된다. 이것은 "목적은 수단을 정당화한다"라는 유명한 인용구를 낳았다. 마키아벨리가 실제로 이런 말을 한 적이 있는지는 의심스럽지만, 이 말은 그의 견해를 정확하게 요약한다.

37 다음 문장 중에서 밑줄 친 부분의 필수 정보를 가장 잘 표현한 것은? 재진술

① 그 당시에는 오직 교회만이 정부의 운영보다는 그들의 신앙에 관심이 있는 매우 이상주의적인 정치인들을 가르쳤다.
② 그 당시 정치적 사고의 유일한 형태는 정부의 운영에 대한 실질적인 해결책을 제공한 교회의 그것이었다.
③ ✓ 그 당시 유일한 정치적 교리는 국가의 기능보다 종교적 문제에 더 많은 사색을 하는 교회의 교리였다.
④ 그 당시에 교회 신앙의 교리는 매우 이상적이었고 비효율적인 정치적 사고의 학파였다.

| 분석 | 지문의 밑줄 친 부분에서는 당시의 정치학이 종교적인 것으로 실제적 정치기능보다는 종교적인 것에 더 관심이 있었음을 설명했다. 따라서 보기 ③이 정답으로 가장 적절하다.

38 윗글에 따르면, 마키아벨리는 정부의 가장 중요한 기능이 무엇이라고 믿었는가? 세부 내용 일치

① 기독교 신앙의 보호
② 더 큰 힘의 축적
③ ✓ 질서와 안정성의 보존
④ 전통적인 도덕성을 버리는 것

| 분석 | 지문에서 마키아벨리에 따르면 '통치자가 질서를 확립하는 데 필요한 권력을 얻고 유지하기 위해 필요한 모든 수단을 사용하는 것은 정당했다.'고 했다. 따라서 보기 ③이 정답으로 적절하다.

39 윗글의 밑줄 친 단어 '강제적인'에 가장 가까운 의미를 가지는 단어는? 밑줄 추론

① 선택된
② 판단된
③ 교양 있는
④ ✓ 한정된

| 분석 | 밑줄 친 단어 constrained에는 '강제적인, 강요된, 굳어진, 경직된'의 의미가 있다. 따라서 보기 ④가 가장 가까운 의미를 가진다.

| 배경 지식 | 니콜로 마키아벨리(Niccolò Machiavelli): 16세기 르네상스 시대 이탈리아의 역사학자이자 정치이론가

[40-42] 2013 성균관대

| 정답 | 40 ⑤ 41 ③ 42 ②

| 어휘 |
asylum ⓝ 망명
UNHCR 유엔난민고등판무관[사무소]
makeshift @ 임시변통의
scrutiny ⓝ 정밀 조사, 철저한 검토
benefactor ⓝ (자선단체 등의) 후원자
pawn ⓝ 담보물, 볼모, 인질

treaty ⓝ 조약
mandate ⓝ 권한, 위임, 통치 기간
adrift @ 표류하는, 방황하는
repatriate ⓥ 본국으로 송환하다
race riot 인종 폭동

refugee ⓝ 난민
crackdown ⓝ 엄중 단속, 강경 탄압
Refugee Convention 난민협약
bow ⓥ 굴복하다
outcry ⓝ (대중들의) 격렬한 반응, 항의

전문해석

오늘날, 147개국이 국경에서 망명을 주장하는 사람들을 처리하기 위한 국제 표준에 동의했지만, 인도네시아는 그들 중 하나가 아니다(포함되지 않는다). 인도네시아는 망명 신청자와 불법 이민자를 구별하는 법이 없다. 사실, 대부분의 유럽, 아프리카, 라틴 아메리카가 1951년 조약에 서명했지만, UNHCR(유엔난민고등판무관)의 위임하에 수만 명이 이 지역에 있음에도 불구하고 소수의 아시아 국가들만이 전 세계적인 난민의 권리를 인정하고 있다. 올해 방글라데시에서 구호단체들은 폭력적인 경찰의 진압과 버마에서 박해를 받고 있는 소수 무슬림 민족인 수만 명의 로힝야족이 살고 있는 임시 수용소에서의 광범위한 굶주림을 보고했다. 2009년, 인권 단체들은 태국 군부가 수백 명의 로힝야 난민들을 충분한 보급품 없이 바다로 떠내려가게 했다고 비난했다. 인도네시아나 방글라데시처럼 1951년 난민협약을 체결하지 않았지만, 베트남전 이후 많은 난민을 관대하게 수용했던 태국은 정부가 12월 몽족 망명 신청자 4,000명을 라오스로 강제 송환하면서 다시 감시를 받게 되었다. 같은 달, 캄보디아는 <u>가장 큰 후원자</u>의 경제적 압력에 굴복하고 인종 폭동에서 도망 온 20명의 위구르 난민을 중국으로 돌려보냈다—이는 전 세계적인 비난을 촉발시켰고 그 이후 미국이 프놈펜에 대한 지원을 중단하도록 자극했다. Human Rights Watch의 프레릭(Frelick)은 아시아에서 "난민들은 정치적 볼모로 간주된다"고 말한다. "다른 국가의 적으로 간주되는 사람에게 망명을 제공하겠다는 생각은 비우호적인 행동으로 간주된다."

---

40 망명 신청자들을 대하는 데 있어서 어느 나라가 <u>다른</u> 나라들과 달랐는가? [세부 내용 일치]

① 인도네시아 ② 방글라데시
③ 태국 ④ 캄보디아
✓⑤ 라오스

| 분석 | 지문에 따르면 인도네시아, 방글라데시, 태국, 캄보디아 모두 난민들에게 피난처를 제공하는 데 있어 비슷한 입장을 보이고 있는 나라들이다. 그러나 라오스의 경우 태국이 난민을 강제 송환시킨 나라로 언급되었기 때문에 보기 ⑤가 정답으로 가장 적절하다.

---

41 밑줄 친 "가장 큰 후원자"가 의미하는 것은? [밑줄 추론]

① 유엔 ② 몽족
✓③ 중국 ④ 위구르족
⑤ 미국

| 분석 | 캄보디아는 이 '가장 큰 후원자'의 압력에 굴복하고 난민을 중국으로 돌려보냈으므로 중국을 후원자로 추론할 수 있다.

---

42 윗글에 따르면, _____이 망명 난민을 양산하는 주된 이유인 것으로 보인다. [세부 내용 추론]

① 영토 분쟁
✓② 인종 차별
③ 경제적 격차
④ 이념의 차이
⑤ 가정 폭력

| 분석 | 지문에 따르면 '폭력적인 경찰의 진압과 버마에서 박해를 받고 있는 소수 무슬림 민족인 수만 명의 로힝야족'이 난민의 사례로 언급된다. 따라서 보기 중 ②가 이유로 가장 적절하다.

[43-44] 2022 중앙대

| 정답 | 43 ②   44 ①

| 어휘 |
totalitarianism ⓝ 전체주의
terror ⓝ 공포, 공포정치, 공포시대
frighten ⓥ 겁을 주다
espouse ⓥ 지지하다
decimate ⓥ (전쟁 따위가) 많은 사람을 죽이다, 훼손하다
liquidate ⓥ (부채를 갚기 위해 사업체를) 청산하다, 팔다
propaganda ⓝ (정치 지도자나 정당 등에 대한 허위·과장된) 선전, 선동
absolute ⓐ 완전한, 완벽한
abolish ⓥ 폐지하다
superpurge ⓝ 대대적 숙청
indoctrination ⓝ 세뇌, 주입
socialist ⓐ 사회주의의
intelligentsia ⓝ 지식계급, 지식인들

전문해석

전체주의 국가에서 선전과 테러가 동일한 동전의 양면을 나타낸다는 주장은 일찍 인식되었고 자주 주장되었다. 그러나 이것은 부분적으로만 사실이다. 전체주의는 절대적인 통제권을 가진 곳이라면 어디서든 선전을 세뇌로 대체하고 사람들을 겁주기 위해 폭력을 사용하지 않고(이것은 정치적 반대가 여전히 존재하는 초기 단계에서만 행해진다) 끊임없이 이념적 교리와 현실적 거짓말을 실현한다. 전체주의는 반대되는 사실에도 불구하고 실업이 존재하지 않는다고 주장하는 것에 만족하지 않을 것이다; 그것은 선전의 일환으로 ⓐ 실업 수당을 폐지할 것이다. 마찬가지로 중요한 사실은 실업을 인정하지 않는 것이 비록 다소 예상치 못한 방식이긴 하지만 오래된 사회주의 교리를 실현했다는 사실이다: 일하지 않는 자는 먹지 말아야 한다.

아니면, 또 다른 예로, 스탈린이 러시아 혁명의 역사를 다시 쓰기로 결정했을 때, 그의 새 버전의 선전은 오래된 책과 문서, 그들의 저자와 독자들을 ⓑ 지지하는 것에 있었다. 1938년 공산당의 새로운 공식 역사에 대한 출판은 전 세대의 소련 지식인들을 파괴했던 ⓒ 대대적인 숙청이 끝났다는 신호였다. 마찬가지로, 동유럽의 점령지의 나치는 처음에는 인구에 대한 더 확고한 통제를 얻기 위해 주로 반유대주의 선전을 사용했다. 그들은 이 선전을 지지하기 위해 테러를 필요로 하지도, 사용하지도 않았다. 그들이 폴란드 지식인의 대부분을 ⓓ 제거했을 때, 그들은 지식인들의 반대 때문이 아니라, 나치의 교리에 따라 폴란드인들이 지성이 없었기 때문에 그렇게 했으며, 그들이 파란 눈과 금발의 아이들을 납치할 계획을 세웠을 때, 그들은 국민들을 겁주려고 한 것이 아니라 '독일인의 혈통'을 구하기 위한 것이었다.

---

43 윗글에서 논지의 흐름상 가장 적합하지 않은 것은? 무관한 단어

① ⓐ
② ⓑ ✓
③ ⓒ
④ ⓓ

| 분석 | 보기 ② ⓑ의 경우 오래된 책과 문서 그리고 옛 저자와 독자를 지지하면 러시아 혁명의 새로운 역사를 쓰지 못할 것이다. 따라서 이것들을 지지하는 것이 아니라 '파괴'나 '제거'한다고 언급해야 흐름상 자연스러울 것이다. ⓑ의 espousing을 destroying으로 고쳐야 한다.

---

44 윗글을 통해 추론할 수 있는 것으로 가장 적합한 것은? 내용 추론

✓ ① 전체주의 정권은 권력 장악 후에는 선전과 함께 공포정치를 사용할 필요가 없을 것이다.
② 전체주의 정권은 권력 장악 후에 이념적 목표를 달성하기 위해 폭력을 사용해야 할 것이다. 통제권을 가진 후에는 폭력을 사용하지 않음
③ 전체주의 정권은 선전을 세뇌로 대체할 필요가 없을 것이다. 선전을 세뇌로 대체함
④ 전체주의 정권은 권력 장악이 강화된 후 선전을 저지하기 위해 공포정치를 사용할 필요가 있다. 선전을 세뇌로 대체하고 폭력은 사용하지 않음

| 분석 | 지문의 세 번째 문장에서 '전체주의는 절대적인 통제권을 가진 곳이라면 어디서든 선전을 세뇌로 대체하고 사람들을 겁주기 위해 폭력을 사용하지 않고(이것은 정치적 반대가 여전히 존재하는 초기 단계에서만 행해진다) 끊임없이 이념적 교리와 현실적 거짓말을 실현한다.'고 했다. 따라서 보기 ①이 정답으로 적절하다.

| 배경 지식 | 전체주의(Totalitarianism): 개인의 모든 활동은 민족이나 국가와 같은 전체의 존립과 발전을 위하여서만 존재한다는 이념 아래 개인의 자유를 억압하는 사상

[45-47] 2018 이화여대

| 정답 | 45 ② 46 ② 47 ⑤

| 어휘 |
escalate ⓥ 확대[증가/상승]하다
arc ⓝ 호, 둥근 활 모양
stream ⓥ 흘러나오다
varying ⓐ 바뀌는, 변화하는
entry ⓝ 입장, 출입, 가입
emigrant ⓝ (다른 나라로 가는) 이민자
grant ⓥ 주다, 수여하다
shelter ⓥ (비·위험 등으로부터) 막아 주다, 보호하다
epicenter ⓝ (지진의) 진원지, 진앙
homogeneous ⓐ 동종의, 동질의

migration ⓝ 이주, 이전
strife ⓝ (개인이나 집단 간의) 갈등, 불화
border ⓝ 국경, 경계(지역)
confront ⓥ ~에 직면하다
roll the dice 주사위를 던지다, ~에 모험을 걸다
portion ⓝ 일부, 부분
absorb ⓥ 흡수하다
significant ⓐ 중요한, 상당한
accustomed ⓐ 익숙한, 평상시의

persecution ⓝ (특히 종교적) 박해
asylum ⓝ 망명, 정신병원
decamp ⓥ 서둘러 떠나다, 도주하다
openhearted ⓐ 숨김없는, 솔직한

appeal ⓥ 호소하다

accommodation ⓝ 숙박시설, 합의, 협상
concede ⓥ 인정하다, 허락하다

전문해석

유럽이 서아프리카에서 아프가니스탄으로 이어지는 활 모양의 분쟁지역에서 전쟁, 박해, 빈곤으로 인해 급격히 증가하는 이주 위기에 직면함에 따라, 심지어 유럽의 고위 관리들도 명백한 사실을 인정하기 시작했다. 그 지역의 난민 관리 시스템은 붕괴되었다. 서유럽 국가들은 1990년대 이후 가장 많은 망명 신청자들과 난민들의 유입에 대처하고 있다. 수십만 명의 망명 신청자들이 유럽의 ⓐ 허술한 국경을 통과하여 이탈리아와 같은 입국 국가에서 독일과 같은 국가로 몰려들어 새로운 도전과 긴장을 조성하고 있다. 독일은 산업화된 세계에서 가장 많은 수의 망명 신청자들을 관리하느라 ⓑ 몹시 애쓰고 있다.

그 나라의 정치인들은, 다양한 정도로, 대중들이 개방적인 쪽과 이민자들의 입국을 막으려는 쪽으로 나누어지는 상황에 직면해 있다. 시리아 내전이나 남수단에서 나이지리아에 이르는 무장단체의 공격을 피해 달아나는 이들도 적지 않다. 하지만 관계자들의 말에 따르면, 많은 난민들이 경제적인 이유로 도착하고 있으며, 난민 지위 청구 절차가 세계에서 가장 부유한 국가 중 일부에서 이민자의 삶을 구축할 수 있는 기회를 줄 수 있다는 모험을 건 사람들이다. 8천2백만 명의 인구를 가진 이 나라는 작년에 173,000명을 수용하면서 이 지역의 다른 어떤 나라보다 더 많은 망명 신청자들을 흡수했다. 망명 신청자들이 너무 많이 와서, 독일은 이제 반이민 운동의 진원지가 된 지역에 자리 잡은 트뢰글리츠와 같은 작은 공동체에서 그들을 위한 수용시설을 찾아야 했다.

지난해에, 난민 센터에서의 35건의 방화 사건을 비롯해 반이민 공격이 크게 늘었다. "독일은 제2차 세계대전에서 많은 난민들을 만든 것에 책임이 있습니다."라고 트뢰글리츠의 전 시장 마르쿠스 니에르스(Markus Nierth)가 말했다. "이제 우리는 이 새로운 큰 물결 속에서 오는 난민들에 대한 책임을 져야 합니다." 하지만 니에르스조차도 난민 위기가 트뢰글리츠와 같은 도시들에 조용하고 동질적인 마을 생활에 익숙지 않은 무언가를 제공하고 있다는 것을 인정한다.

45 윗글의 제목으로 가장 적절한 것은? 제목

① 유럽의 박해와 빈곤 키워드(난민 문제) 없음
✓ 난민 문제에 대처하는 새로운 위기
③ 전쟁으로 인한 이민의 증가 이민의 증가로 인한 문제가 언급되어야 함
④ 유럽에서 망명 신청자들을 거부하는 다양한 이유 언급 안 함
⑤ 반이민 운동의 진원지 키워드(난민 문제) 없음

| 분석 | 지문 두 번째 문장에서 유럽의 난민 관리 시스템이 붕괴되었다고 했으며 마지막 단락에서도 독일의 난민 센터에서의 35건의 방화 사건을 비롯해 반이민 공격이 크게 늘었다고 밝혔다. 따라서 제목으로는 보기 ②가 가장 적절하다.

46 윗글에서 가장 잘 유추할 수 있는 진술은 무엇인가? 내용 추론

① 1990년대 이전에, 유럽의 난민 대부분이 서아프리카와 아프가니스탄에서 왔다. 1990년대 이전 상황 언급 안 함
✓ 몇몇 난민들은 경제적인 이유로 독일에 왔다.
③ 트뢰글리츠에는 제2차 세계대전 이후 다양한 사람들이 살고 있었다. 반이민 운동의 진원지인 작은 공동체이므로 다양한 사람들이 살고 있을 가능성 적음
④ 독일은 지금까지 8천2백만 명의 망명 신청자를 받아들였다. 173,000명을 수용함
⑤ 제2차 세계 대전은 독일에 엄청난 난민 유입을 야기했다. 독일은 제2차 세계 대전에서 많은 난민을 만든 책임이 있음

| 분석 | 지문 두 번째 단락에서 '많은 난민들이 경제적인 이유로 도착하고 있으며, 난민 지위 청구 절차가 세계에서 가장 부유한 국가 중 일부에서 이민자 삶을 구축할 수 있는 기회를 줄 수 있다는 모험을 건 사람들이다'라고 했다. 따라서 ②가 추론 가능하다.

47 Ⓐ와 Ⓑ에 들어가기에 가장 적절한 것은? 빈칸 추론

① 폐쇄된 – 노력 중인 ② 불화를 일으키는 – 반대하고 있는
③ 튼튼한 – 조종하고 있는 ④ 유동적인 – 관찰하고 있는
✓ 허점이 많은 – 안간힘을 쓰고 있는

| 분석 | 빈칸 Ⓐ가 포함된 문장의 직전 내용에서 '서유럽 국가들은 1990년대 이후 가장 많은 망명 신청자들과 난민들의 유입에 대처하고 있다'고 했으므로 유럽의 국경은 난민이 유입되기에 관리 상태가 허술하다고 할 수 있을 것이다. 따라서 빈칸 Ⓐ에는 '허술한, 허점이 많은'의 의미를 가진 단어를 삽입해야 할 것이다. 빈칸 Ⓑ가 포함된 문장에서는 '독일은 산업화된 세계에서 가장 많은 수의 망명 신청자들을 관리'하므로 관리에 애쓰고 있을 것임을 추론할 수 있다. 따라서 보기 ⑤가 정답이 된다.

[48-50] 2012 성균관대

| 정답 | 48 ① 49 ① 50 ②

| 어휘 |
nationalistic ⓐ 민족주의의, 국수주의적인 prop ⓝ 지주, 버팀목 threat ⓝ 위협, 협박
eternal ⓐ 영원한 ban ⓥ 금지하다 netting ⓝ 그물
deprived of ~을 박탈당한 dignity ⓝ 위엄, 품위, 존엄성 dictate ⓥ 명령하다, 지시하다
porous ⓐ (구멍이 많은) 다공성의, 투과성의 honor killing 명예 살인 muscular ⓐ 근육의, 강력한
signboard ⓝ 간판, 게시판 fundamental ⓐ 근본적인, 핵심적인 irrelevant ⓐ 무관한
comment ⓥ 논평하다

전문해석

최근 두 대통령 니콜라스 사르코지와 버락 오바마는 다소 다른 방식으로 이슬람 여성의 복장 문제를 다뤘다. 사르코지는 무슬림 복장을 민족주의적 지지로써 그것을 영원한 프랑스적 가치에 대한 위협으로 여겼다. 2004년에, 프랑스는 학교와 공공건물에서 이슬람식 두건을 금지했다. 사르코지는 "우리나라에서 여성들이 모든 사회생활과 단절되고 정체성을 박탈당한 그물 뒤의 죄수라는 것을 받아들일 수 없습니다. 이것은 프랑스 공화국의 존엄성에 대한 생각이 아닙니다."라고 말했다. 카이로에서 오바마의 연설은 다른 방침을 취했다. 그의 관심사는 히잡—무슬림 여성의 머리를 덮는 것—이 아니라 여성이 원한다면 히잡을 착용할 권리였다. 오바마는 서양 국가들은 이슬람 여성들의 복장을 지시할 수 없다고 말했다. 오바마는 미국의 가치관과 이슬람의 가치관이 충돌하고 있다는 어떠한 느낌도 주는 것을 피하려 했다. 그 대신, 그는 이슬람과 서구 모두에 대한 더 구멍이 많은(개방적인) 비전을 제시했는데, 그중 하나는 "이슬람은 항상 미국 역사의 일부였습니다."이다. 그 말은 듣기 좋은 것 같다. 하지만 여성복에 대해서만 이야기함

으로써, 그는 이슬람 세계 전역에서 일부다처제, 조혼, 명예 살인과 같은 이슬람 여성들이 직면한 많은 도전들을 무시했다. 두 번의 연설 이후 몇 주 동안, 이란은 세계에 이슬람 여성들에 대한 다른, 더 강력한 이미지를 보여 주었다. 에메랄드 히잡을 쓴 테헤란 시위대는 사르코지가 생각하는 것처럼 강요된 보수주의의 인간 간판이 아니었다. 그러나 그들은 또한 좋아하는 옷을 입을 수 있는 자유를 위해 법적 보호가 필요한 무슬림 여성이라는 오바마의 공식에도 맞지 않았다. 이란의 여성들은 기본적인 권리를 주장하고 있으며, 그렇게 할 때 우리의 지원을 받을 자격이 있는 단호한 정치적 행위자이다. 그들이 그러한 권리를 주장하기 위해 목숨을 걸었을 때, 그들이 무엇을 입는지는 무관하다. 이슬람 여성들이 기본적인 정치적 투쟁에 그렇게 관여하는 것을 보여 주면서, 서구 남성 지도자들이 그들의 옷보다 더 언급할 가치가 있는 것을 찾기를 바라는 것은 너무 지나친 희망일까?

48 ① 50 ②

48 윗글의 가장 좋은 제목은 _____ 일 것이다. 제목
① 이슬람 여성들을 위한 훨씬 더 큰 도전들 ✓
② 아랍 세계의 정치적 상징으로서의 의복 키워드(이슬람 여성을 위한 정치적 도전) 아님
③ 서구의 이슬람 여성에 대한 차별 너무 포괄적
④ 미국–이슬람 관계에 대한 오바마의 새로운 접근법 너무 지엽적
⑤ 이란의 세속주의 성장 키워드 아님

| 분석 | 지문의 마지막 문장은 의문문으로 작성되었는데 질문의 의도가 있다기보다는 강조의 표현으로 이해하도록 한다. 지문의 저자는 서구의 두 대통령이 이슬람 여성의 의복보다 그들이 직면한 더 기본적인 권리와 관련된 문제들을 찾아야 한다고 강조했다. 따라서 보기 ① '이슬람 여성들을 위한 훨씬 더 큰 도전들'이 제목으로 가장 적절하다.

49 윗글에 따르면, 오바마는 히잡을 _____ 의 문제로 보고 있다. 세부 내용 일치
① 개인적인 선택 ✓
② 문화적 구속
③ 미개한 전통
④ 남성의 힘
⑤ 여성의 저항

| 분석 | 지문에서 오바마는 이슬람 여성의 의복 문제를 여성 개인의 선택의 문제로 보고 있으므로 정답은 보기 ①이다.

50 저자는 _____ 라고 주장한다. 요지
① 히잡은 이슬람 여성의 본질이다 언급 안 함
② 서구는 이슬람 여성들의 정치적 투쟁에 더 많은 관심을 기울여야 한다 ✓
③ 이슬람 여성들을 위한 교육은 이슬람 여성들의 옷보다 훨씬 더 중요하다 언급 안 함
④ 히잡에 대한 이야기는 무슬림 여성들이 정치에 참여하는 것을 방해하기 때문에 중단되어야 한다 언급 안 함
⑤ 이슬람 여성복에 대한 오바마의 태도는 사르코지의 태도보다 더 결함이 있다 두 지도자의 비교는 언급 안 함

| 분석 | 48번 제목 문제를 해결하기 위한 단서와 같은 단서로 작가의 주장을 추론해 본다. 지문의 마지막 문장에서 '이슬람 여성들이 기본적인 정치적 투쟁에 그렇게 관여하는 것을 보여 주면서, 서구 남성 지도자들이 그들의 옷보다 더 언급할 가치가 있는 것을 찾기를 바라는 것은 너무 지나친 희망일까?'라는 작가의 말을 통해 그의 주장에 가까운 보기가 ②임을 알 수 있다.

배경지식 민족주의(Nationalism): 민족의 독립과 통일을 가장 중시하는 사상

2강 경영 / 경제

01	②	02	③	03	④	04	④	05	①	06	①	07	②	08	④	09	④	10	③
11	④	12	②	13	④	14	①	15	⑤	16	②	17	①	18	②	19	③	20	①
21	④	22	②	23	①	24	③	25	①	26	①	27	⑤	28	①	29	④	30	②
31	②	32	③	33	④	34	②	35	①	36	④	37	①	38	④	39	③	40	④
41	③	42	②	43	③	44	④	45	②	46	③	47	①	48	①	49	④	50	②
51	②	52	③																

[01-03] 2014 성균관대

| 정답 | 01 ② 02 ③ 03 ④

| 어휘 |
bereaved ⓐ 사별한, 뒤에 남겨진   fraction ⓝ 파편, 단편, 분수, 아주 조금   deceased ⓐ 죽은, 고인의
pension ⓝ 연금, 양로 연금, 부조금   unmatched ⓐ 비할 데 없는, 상대가 없는   pensioner ⓝ 연금 수령자
cap ⓝ 정상, 한도   high cap 최고한도   civil servant 공무원
real ⓝ 헤알(브라질의 화폐 단위) (pl. reais)   privilege ⓝ 특권, 특전   generous ⓐ 후한, 풍부한, 관대한
irrational ⓐ 불합리한, 이성이 없는   ascension ⓝ 오름, 상승, 즉위, 승천   corruption ⓝ 타락, 퇴폐, 부패, 위법행위

전문해석

대부분의 나라에서, 배우자를 사별한 배우자나 동거인들은 사망자의 공적 연금의 극히 일부, 전형적으로는 절반만 받을 것을 기대하며, 그리고 그것도 대개 부양할 자녀들이 있거나 그들 자신이 퇴직 연령에 가까워야 하는 것과 같은 조건들이 있다. 브라질에서는 유족의 나이와 상관없이 자신의 남은 인생 동안 거의 총액을 받게 된다. 사망자가 아직 퇴직 연령에 이르지 못하였더라도 연금은 바로 지급되기 시작한다. 그 결과 브라질은 유례가 없는, 국가의 GDP 3%에 해당하는 액수를 유족 연금으로 지출한다. 부유한 OECD 국가들은 평균 약 1%를 지출한다.

연금 수령자 자신들도 상황이 놀랍게도 좋다. 남자들은 65세에 여자들은 60세에 15년 동안 회사에 기여했다면 최고상한액 제한 없이 연금 전액을 수령하면서 퇴직할 수 있다. 최근에 공무원이 된 사람들을 제외하고는 모든 공무원들이 최고상한액 제한 없이 퇴직할 수 있다. 가난한 가정에서 65세가 넘은 남자나 60세가 넘은 여자는, 전혀 기여를 한 바가 없더라도 최소임금과 같은 액수, 현재로는 매달 678헤알(reais)을 받게 된다. 시골의 노동자들은 부자든 가난하든 똑같은 혜택을 도시 사람들보다 5년 먼저 누리게 된다. 조기퇴직의 조건은 특히 관대하다. 연금제도로 국가를 거의 부도나게 한 그리스인들은 평균 61세가 될 때까지 일한다. 평균적으로 브라질 사람들은 54세의 마지막 급여의 70%를 수령한다.

---

01 윗글의 주제는 _____ 이다. 주제

① 브라질의 복지제도 너무 포괄적
✓ ② 브라질의 불합리한 연금제도
③ 브라질의 선진국 등극 지문과 불일치
④ 브라질 공무원들의 부패 언급 안 함
⑤ 브라질 사람들의 평균 노동 시간 너무 지엽적

| 분석 | 지문의 핵심 주제는 브라질의 연금제도를 다루고 있는데, 첫 번째 단락 마지막 부분에서도 브라질의 연금은 부유한 국가보다 지출이 크다고 했으며, 두 번째 단락 마지막에서도 연금제도로 국가가 거의 부도나게 한 그리스보다도 브라질은 더 관대하다고 했으므로 비합리적인(irrational) 브라질의 연금제도가 글의 주제로 가장 적절하다.

02 브라질에서는, 오직 _____는 조건하에, 당신은 전액 연금을 받을 수 있다. 세부 내용 파악
① 당신이 연금에 등록했다
② 당신이 브라질에서 태어났다
✔ 당신이 15년 기간 동안 일했다
④ 당신의 배우자가 사망했다
⑤ 당신이 일할 나이를 넘었다

| 분석 | 전액 연금을 받을 수 있는 조건을 묻는 문제이다. 지문의 두 번째 단락에서 15년 동안 회사에 기여했다면 최고상한액 제한 없이 연금 전액을 수령할 수 있다고 했다.

03 밑줄 친 "with no cap"의 의미는 무엇인가? 숙어, 표현
① 아무런 보호도 받지 않고
② 무일푼으로
③ 아무 옷도 입지 않고
✔ 무제한으로
⑤ 아무 능력도 없이

| 분석 | 밑줄 친 표현은 '최고상한액 제한 없이'라는 뜻이며, cap의 의미를 묻는 문제이다. cap은 '(액수의) 한도'를 나타낸다.

| 배경지식 | 복지제도(Welfare system): 행복한 생활을 누릴 수 있는 상태를 복지라고 한다. 국민의 인간다운 삶을 위한 제도로 거기에는 국민연금, 건강 보험, 국민 기초 생활 보장 제도, 아동 복지, 장애인 복지들을 통틀어 복지제도라 할 수 있다.

[04-05] 2015 한양대

| 정답 | 04 ④ 05 ①

| 어휘 | relevance ⓝ (당면한 문제와의) 관련성, 적절함, 타당성   output ⓝ 생산량, 산출량
variable ⓝ 변수   clear-cut ⓐ 명백한, 명쾌한   simulation ⓝ 모의실험, 시뮬레이션
constant ⓝ 상수 ⓐ 불변의, 일정한   pinpoint ⓥ 정확히 보여 주다, 정확히 찾아내다
Gross Domestic Product 국내총생산 (GDP)   inflationary ⓐ 물가 상승의
monetary growth 통화 팽창   pitfall ⓝ (눈에 안 띄는) 함정, 위험   formalist approach 형식주의적 접근 방법
goodness of fit 적합도   retrospectively ⓐⓓ 소급하여, 과거로 거슬러 올라가
startle ⓥ 깜짝 놀라게 하다, 깜짝 놀라다   reflectively ⓐⓓ 반성하여, 반사적으로   prospectively ⓐⓓ 장래에 관하여
intensively ⓐⓓ 집중적으로, 집약적으로

| 전문해석 |
형식적인 경제 모델과 현실의 정책 사이의 적절성이 일부 논쟁의 주제가 되어 왔다. 경제학자 R. D. 노턴(R. D. Norton)과 S. Y. 리(S. Y. Rhee)는 그런 모델을 지난 14년간의 한국 경제에 ⓐ 소급하여 적용하는 데 어느 정도의 성공을 이루었다; 즉 생산량, 가격 그리고 다른 변수들에 대한 그 모델의 수치들이 실제 통계수치와 거의 일치했다. 하지만, 정책 측면에서 그 모델의 값은 덜 명확한 것으로 판명되었다. 노턴과 리는 모의실험을 실행하여, 장기적인 요소들은 고정값으로 두고, 단기적인 정책 변화의 효과를 정확히 보여 주려고 했다. 그들의 모델은 수입 석유 가격 상승은 인플레이션을 증가시킬 것이며, 수출을 5% 줄이면 GDP가 감소할 것이고 인플레이션은 증가하게 될 것이며, 통화 공급의 증가를 줄이는 것은 약간 더 높은 물가 상승을 초래할 것이라고 보여 주었다. 이러한 연구 결과들은 다소 ⓑ 놀라웠다. 많은 경제학자들은 수출을 줄이는 것이 인플레이션을 증가시키는 것이 아니라 감소시킬 것이라고 그동안 주장해 왔다. 그리고 대부분의 경제학자들은 유가 상승을 인플레이션으로 간주하는 반면, 조금 더 느려진 통화 팽창에 대하여 똑같이 생각하는 경제학자들은 거의 없다. 노턴-리(Norton-Rhee)의 모델은 아마도 진정한 정책 관련성을 희생하여 통계적 적합성을 강조하는 형식주의적 접근방법의 함정을 보여 주는 것으로 아마도 여겨질 수 있다.

04 윗글의 목적으로 가장 적절한 것은? 글의 목적

① 경제 분석의 새로운 종류를 제안하기 위하여 키워드 없음
② 한국의 인플레이션에 대한 설명을 제시하기 위하여 키워드 없음
③ Norton과 Rhee의 분석의 정확성을 결정하기 위하여 키워드 없음
④ ✓ 형식적 경제 모델의 한계점을 설명하기 위하여

| 분석 | 이 글은 노턴과 리가 기존의 형식적인 경제 모델이 실제 현실과 맞아떨어지는지 실험을 통해 검증해 보니 일부 맞는 부분도 있었지만 정책 측면에서는 기존 경제 모델이 현실과 동떨어져 있다고 문제를 지적하는 글이다. 따라서 글의 목적으로는 ④가 가장 적절하다.

05 윗글의 빈칸 Ⓐ, Ⓑ에 들어갈 말로 가장 적절한 것은? 빈칸 추론

① ✓ 소급하여 – 깜짝 놀라는
② 반사하여, 반영하여 – 유망한, 촉망되는
③ 유망하여, 장래에 관하여 – 예상하는
④ 집중적으로 – 실망스러운

| 분석 | 빈칸 Ⓐ는 빈칸 뒤의 over a fourteen-year period가 단서가 될 수 있다. 지난 14년 동안의 한국 경제에 적용하였으므로 이는 '과거로 소급하여', 과거를 '반영하여' 적용했다고 할 수 있다. 따라서 빈칸 Ⓐ에는 retrospectively와 reflectively가 적절하다. 그리고 빈칸 Ⓑ는 빈칸 앞뒤를 보면 빈칸 앞에서 언급한 노턴과 리의 실험값이 빈칸 뒤에 나온 기존 전문가들이 주장한 수치와 다르다는 것을 알 수 있다. 따라서 노턴과 리의 실험 결과는 기존의 주장과 다른 수치이므로 그 결과값은 기존과는 다른 깜짝 놀랄 결과일 것이다. 그러므로 빈칸 Ⓑ는 startling이 적절하다.

[06-07] 2017 중앙대

| 정답 | 06 ① 07 ②

| 어휘 | **phase** ⓝ 국면, 단계 **two-fold** ⓐ 이중적인 **optimism** ⓝ 낙관주의
heavy industry 중공업 **raw material** 원자재 **volume** ⓝ 부피, 총량
diffuse ⓥ 뿌리다; 확산하다, 보급시키다 **segment** ⓝ 구획, 부분 **apparent** ⓐ 명백한, 외견상의
spiraling ⓐ 상승하는 **recession** ⓝ 경기후퇴

전문해석

경기순환의 한 국면은 확장 국면이다. 이 단계는 회복과 번영을 포함한 이중적인 국면이다. ⓐ 확장 국면을 촉발하는 것은 번영 그 자체가 아니라 번영에 대한 기대이다. 회복기에는 기존 설비가 계속 확장되고 새로운 생산설비가 생겨난다. 더 많은 사업체들이 생겨나며 기존의 사업체들은 확장된다. 다양한 분야에서의 개선이 이루어진다. 경제 성장의 미래에 대한 낙관론이 점점 증가한다. 많은 자본이 기계 산업이나 중공업에 투자된다. 더 많은 고용이 이루어진다. 더 많은 원자재가 필요하게 된다. 경제의 한 부문이 발전함에 따라 다른 부문들이 영향을 받는다. ⓑ 예를 들어, 자동차 산업에서의 대규모 성장은 철강, 유리, 고무산업의 확장을 가져온다. 07 ② 도로가 필요하게 되며, 따라서 시멘트와 기계 산업이 활기를 띠게 된다. ⓒ 노동력과 원자재에 대한 수요는 농민을 포함한 원자재 공급자들과 노동자에게 더 큰 번영을 유발한다. 이것이 구매력과 사고 팔리는 상품량을 증가시킨다. 따라서 번영이 전체 인구의 다양한 부문들로 확산된다. ⓓ 이러한 번영 기간은 명백한 끝도 없이 아마도 계속 상승을 이어간다. 하지만 이 단계가 정점에 달하고 나선형의 상승을 멈추는 시기가 찾아온다. 이때가 바로 확장 국면의 끝이다.

06 윗글의 흐름상 가장 적합하지 않은 것은? 글의 흐름 파악
① ⓐ ✓
② ⓑ
③ ⓒ
④ ⓓ

| 분석 | 글의 앞부분에서 확장 국면은 이중적이어서 회복과 번영이라는 두 가지로 나뉜다는 포괄적인 진술을 했다. 따라서 그 뒤 문장은 상술로서 회복기에 대한 설명과 번영에 관한 설명이 차례로 나와야 자연스러운데 ⓐ 문장을 삭제해 보면 회복기에 대한 설명이 언급되고 있고 글의 마지막 부분에서 번영에 관한 설명이 이어지고 있어서 자연스럽다. 하지만 ⓐ의 내용은 번영과 관련된 내용이므로 뒤에 나오는 회복기보다 앞부분에 나올 수 없으므로 ⓐ를 삭제해야 자연스럽다.

07 윗글을 통해 추론할 수 있는 것으로 가장 적합한 것은? 내용 추론
① 소비자들이 시장에 대한 신뢰를 잃어버리면, 경기 후퇴가 뒤따른다.
② 확장 국면에서 경제의 많은 부문들이 서로 간에 이익을 준다. ✓
③ 보석과 같은 사치품들은 산업 확장에 영향을 받지 않는다.
④ 번영의 시기에는 새로운 상품의 개발이 중요하다.

| 분석 | 지문의 중간에서 경제의 한 부문이 발달하면 다른 부문들도 영향을 받는다(As one part of the economy develops, other parts are affected.)고 언급했으므로 보기 ②는 지문에서 추론 가능한 내용인데 나머지 보기는 지문에 언급한 적이 없으므로 추론할 수 없다.

배경지식 경기순환 (Business cycle): 경기는 일정한 패턴을 가지고 주기적으로 반복하게 된다. 즉, 국민경제의 활동이 활발하여 경기가 상승할 때도 있고 경제 활동이 위축되어 불황에 빠지기도 한다. 이렇게 경제 활동이 적정 수준 이상으로 활발한 경기 상승과 그 반대인 경기하강이 반복되는 현상을 '경기순환(business cycle)'이라고 한다.

[08-09] 2019 국민대

| 정답 | 08 ④ 09 ④

| 어휘 |
quantifiable ⓐ 수량화할 수 있는, 계량화할 수 있는
mathematical ⓐ 수학의, 수리적인
efficient ⓐ 능률적인, 효과적인
brazenly ⓐd 버젓이, 뻔뻔스럽게
ecology ⓝ 생태학
formula ⓝ 공식; (일정한) 방식, 방법
alternative ⓐ 양자택일의; 대체되는
evidence ⓝ 증거
construct ⓝ 구조물, 건조물; 구성개념
implicate ⓥ 관련시키다; 함축하다
tactic ⓝ 작전; 방책, 전략
causal ⓐ 원인의, 원인이 되는
discriminate ⓥ 판별하다, 구별하다; 차별하다
phenomenon ⓝ 현상
go back to the drawing board 처음부터 다시 시작하다. 백지로 돌리다
consume ⓥ 소비하다; 소모하다
enormously ⓐd 대단히, 막대하게
physicist ⓝ 물리학자
discipline ⓝ 훈련; 규율; 학과, 학문, 분야
factor ⓝ 요소, 요인
empirical ⓐ 경험[실험]에 의한, 실증적인

전문해석
경제학자들은 소비된 열량이나 케이블이 깔린 거리와 같이 수량화할 수 있는 대상을 다루기 때문에, 그들이 연구에서 사용하는 모델은 거의 항상 수학적인 구조물이다. 그것들(모델)을 말로 표현할 수 있긴 하지만, 수학은 모델의 구조를 표현하는 데 있어서, 그리고 더 흥미로운 것은, 모델 속에 들어 있는 의미를 발견하는 데 있어서 대단히 효율적인 방법이다. 응용 수학자들과 물리학자들은 이것을 오랫동안 알고 있었지만, 생태학 같은 관련 분야들이 그랬던 것처럼 경제학자들이 그 연구 전략을 버젓이 받아들인 것은 비로소 20세기 후반이 되어서였다. 훌륭한 모델링을 만들어 내는 기술은 매우 적은 수의 인과 요소들에 집중하고 그것으로부터 많은

이해를 이끌어 내는 것이다. 내가 '기술'이라고 말하는 것은 훌륭한 모델을 만드는 데는 정해진 공식이 없기 때문이다. 모델에 대한 Ⓐ 엄밀한 검사는 그것이 어떤 현상에 대한 여러 대체 가능한 설명들을 판가름할 수 있는지 여부이다. 경험적 검사에서 살아남은 모델들은—적어도 잠시 동안은—의문을 제기하는 추가적인 증거가 나올 때까지는 옳은 것으로 받아들여지며, 의심의 증거가 나올 경우에 경제학자들은 (반드시 더 큰 것은 아니더라도) 더 나은 모델을 만들어 내기 위해 처음부터 다시 시작한다.

08 다음 중 빈칸 Ⓐ에 적절하지 <u>않은</u> 것은? 빈칸 추론
① 엄밀한 검사
② 결정적 시험
③ 궁극의 시험
✓ ④ 임의적인 시험

| 분석 | 어떤 현상에 대한 대체 가능한 여러 가지 설명들을 구별하고 판별한다고 했으므로 그 시험의 성격은 엄격하고, 결정적이고, 궁극적이라 할 수 있으며, 모두 다 같은 동의적 개념인데, ④ arbitrary test는 '임의적인 시험'이란 의미이므로 빈칸 Ⓐ에 적절하지 않다.

09 윗글에 의하면, 다음 중 옳지 <u>않은</u> 것은? 내용 일치
① 경제 모델은 말 또는 수학적으로 설명될 수 있다.
② 경제 연구의 대상은 양으로 측정할 수 있는 것들이다.
③ 수학은 20세기 후반에서야 경제학에서 널리 사용되기 시작했다.
✓ ④ 좋은 경제 모델은 현상을 설명할 때 가능한 한 많은 인과적 요인을 수용한다.

| 분석 | 지문에서 훌륭한 모델링을 만들어 내는 기술은 매우 적은 수의 인과 요소들에 집중하고 그것으로부터 많은 이해를 이끌어 내는 것이다(The art of good modelling is to generate a lot of understanding from focusing on a very small number of causal factors.)라고 언급했는데 이것은 ④와 일치하지 않는 진술이다.

[10-11] 2018 성균관대

| 정답 | 10 ③ 11 ④

| 어휘 | propel ⓥ 추진하다, 나아가게 하다 cease ⓥ 멈추다, 중지하다 pillar ⓝ 기둥, 대들보, 기본적인 부분[특징]
teeter ⓥ 비틀거리다, 동요하다 scramble ⓝ 쟁탈 seemingly ⓐⓓ 외견상으로, 겉보기에는
be immune to ~의 영향을 받지 않다 vulnerability ⓝ 상처받기 쉬움; 취약함 put aside 무시하다, 제쳐놓다
asteroid ⓝ 소행성 pandemic ⓝ 전국[전 세계]적인 유행병 surface ⓥ 나타나다[드러나다], 표면화되다
come as no surprise 놀라운 일이 아니다 unsustainable ⓐ 유지[지지]할 수 없는

전문해석

정치 경제학자인 벤저민 프리드먼(Benjamin Friedman)은 한때 현대 서구 사회를 경제 성장에 의해 바퀴가 계속 굴러가는 안정된 자전거에 비유했다. 앞으로 나아가는 움직임이 느려지나 멈춘다면 우리 사회를 특징짓는 기둥—민주주의, 개인의 자유, 사회적 관용 등—이 흔들리기 시작할 것이다. 우리의 세계는 점점 한정된 자원을 놓고 싸우고 가까운 사람들 집단 밖의 그 누구도 받아들이지 않는 추한 곳이 될 것이다. 만약 바퀴를 다시 움직일 방법을 찾지 못한다면, 우리는 결국 총체적인 사회적 붕괴에 직면하게 될 것이다.

그러한 붕괴는 인류 역사상 여러 번 일어났으며, 아무리 훌륭해 보일지라도, 그 어떤 문명도 한 사회를 종말로 이끌 수 있는 그러한

취약성에 저항할 수 있는 문명은 없다. 현시점에서 상황이 얼마나 잘 돌아가는지와 관계없이, 이 상황은 언제나 바뀔 수 있다. 소행성 충돌, 핵겨울 또는 치명적인 유행병과 같이 종의 멸종을 일으키는 사건은 제쳐놓더라도, 붕괴의 원인이 되는 많은 요인들이 항상 있음을 역사는 우리에게 말해 준다. 그 요인들은 무엇인가? 이미 표면화되기 시작한 요인들이 혹 있다면 어떤 요인들인가? 인류가 지금 현재 지속 불가능하고 불확실한 길을 가고 있다는 것은 전혀 놀라운 일이 아니다. 그렇다면 돌아올 수 없는 지점에 우리는 얼마나 근접해 있는 것인가?

10 윗글에 따르면, 다음 중 우리의 세계를 멸망에 이르게 하지 않는 것은? 〔세부 내용 파악〕
① 행성 간의 충돌
② 핵전쟁으로 인한 심각한 기후 변화
✓ ③ 화산 폭발
④ 경제 성장의 멈춤
⑤ 치명적인 전염병의 전 세계적 확산

| 분석 | 첫 번째 단락에서 만약 바퀴가 멈추어 다시 움직일 방법을 찾지 못한다면 총체적인 사회 붕괴에 직면하게 될 것이라고 했으므로, ④ '경제 성장의 멈춤'은 세계를 멸망에 이르게 하는 요소로 언급했다. 두 번째 단락에서 '① 소행성 충돌, ② 핵겨울, ⑤ 치명적인 유행병과 같은 종의 멸종을 일으키는 사건' 또한 세계를 멸망에 이르게 하는 요소로 언급되어 있다. '화산 폭발'은 지문에서 언급한 적이 없다.

11 윗글의 주제는 _____ 이다. 〔주제〕
① 경제 성장의 취약성
② 현대 서구 사회의 궁극적인 붕괴 〔너무 지엽적〕
③ 생태 파괴로 인한 잠재적인 재앙
✓ ④ 미래의 세계 붕괴 가능성
⑤ 미래 사회를 지속할 수 있는 모델

| 분석 | 첫 번째 단락에서 사회를 종말로 이끌 수 있는 요인에 대해 소개하고, 두 번째 단락에서 세계를 붕괴시키는 요소에 대해 설명했다. 이 내용을 모두 포괄하는 글의 주제로는 '미래의 세계 붕괴 가능성'이 적절하다.

[12-14] 2018 한국외대

| 정답 | 12 ② 13 ④ 14 ①

| 어휘 | startup ⓝ 스타트업(설립한 지 오래되지 않은 신생 벤처기업)
counterintuitive ⓐ 반직관적인, 직관에 어긋나는
instinct ⓝ 본능
impulse ⓝ 충격, 자극; 충동
founder ⓝ 창립자, 설립자
lean back 상체를 뒤로 젖히다
conscious ⓐ 의식하고 있는; 의식적인
opposite ⓐ 정반대의; 맞은편의
permeate ⓥ 스며들다, 침투하다
suppress ⓥ 억압하다; 억누르다, 참다
weird ⓐ 수상한, 불가사의한, 기묘한
instruction ⓝ 훈련, 교육, 가르침

〔전문해석〕
이유를 확실히는 모르겠지만, 스타트업(벤처기업)은 매우 직관에 반한다. 그것은 아마도 스타트업에 대한 지식이 아직 우리 문화에 침투하지 않았기 때문일 것이다. 그러나 그 이유가 무엇이든, 스타트업을 시작하는 것은 Ⓐ 당신의 본능을 항상 믿을 수는 없는 그런 일이다. 그것은 스키를 타는 것과 비슷하다. 처음 스키를 타려 할 때 속도를 줄이고 싶으면, 당신은 본능적으로 상체를 뒤로 젖히

30 _ 에듀윌 편입 솔루션 독해 Advanced

게 된다. 그러나 스키를 타고서 상체를 뒤로 하면, 통제력을 잃고 빠른 속도로 언덕 아래를 향해 내려가게 된다. 그래서 스키를 배우는 것의 일부는 그러한 충동을 억제하는 법을 배우는 것이다. 결국 당신은 새로운 습관을 들이게 되지만, 처음에는 의식적인 노력을 필요로 한다. 스키에 입문할 때에는, 언덕을 내려가기 시작하면서 잊지 않고 하려 하는 여러 가지 것들이 있다. 스타트업도 스키만큼이나 부자연스러운 것이기 때문에, 스타트업 역시 잊지 않고 해야 할 일들이 있다. 스타트업은 너무나도 기묘해서 본능을 믿으면 많은 실수를 하게 될 것이다. 나는 종종 나의 역할은 창업자들에게 그들이 무시할 것들을 말해 주는 것이라는 농담을 하곤 한다. 그것은 실제로 사실이다. 창업자들은 왜 조언자의 조언을 진지하게 새기지 않는 것일까? 글쎄, 그것은 바로 직관과 어긋나는 견해들에 관한 것이다. 이 견해들은 당신의 본능과 상반된다. 당신은 당신을 놀라도록 하는 조언을 당신에게 해 줄 다른 사람들이 필요할 뿐이다. 그것이 스키 강사는 많고 달리기 강사는 많지 않은 이유이다.

14 ①

12 스타트업을 스키에 비유하는 이유는 둘 다 _____ 이기 때문이다. 세부 내용 파악
① 통제가 쉽기
✓ ② 우리의 직관과 모순되기
③ 집중적이고 광범위한 훈련이 요구되기
④ 효율적인 달리기와 같은 전략을 요하기

| 분석 | 지문의 앞부분에서 '스타트업과 스키 모두 우리가 가진 직관과 어긋나며 본능을 억눌러야 한다는 공통점이 있음'을 언급했다.

13 다음 중 Ⓐ에 들어가기에 가장 적절한 것은? 빈칸 추론
① 새로운 습관을 얻다
② 당신의 경험에 의존하다
③ 당신의 전문지식을 이용하다
✓ ④ 당신의 본능을 믿다

| 분석 | 빈칸 뒤에서 스키를 스타트업에 비유하면서 속도를 줄이려면 본능적으로 상체를 뒤로 하지만, 그렇게 하는 경우에는 통제력을 잃고서 언덕을 내려오게 됨을 언급했다. 따라서 스타트업의 경우에도 '본능에 의지해서는 안 된다'는 것을 의미하므로, 빈칸에는 본능에 관한 문장이 필요하다.

14 다음 중 저자가 스타트업 창업자들에게 권하는 것은 무엇인가? 세부 내용 파악
✓ ① 조언자들에게 귀를 기울이라.
② 심화 과정을 수강하라.
③ 창조적 생각의 목록을 만들라.
④ 성공적인 스타트업기업들을 먼저 관찰하라.

| 분석 | 지문의 마지막 부분에서 '스타트업 창업자들이 조언자들의 조언을 진지하게 받아들이지 않는 것은 그들의 본능에 어긋나기 때문인데, 사실은 이런 사람들이 그들에게 필요함'을 언급했다. 따라서 이것은 저자가 창업자들에게 조언자들이 해 주는 조언에 귀를 기울일 것을 권한다고 할 수 있다.

[15-16] 2019 한양대
| 정답 | 15 ⑤ 16 ②

| 어휘 |
refrain ⓥ 삼가다, 참다
bump 융기
short selling 공매도(개인 혹은 단체가 주식, 채권 등을 보유하지 않은 상태에서 매도하는 행위)
sell-off n (구조조정을 위한) 자산매각
illusory ⓐ 눈을 속이는, 현혹시키는
knee-jerk ⓐ 자동적으로 나오는, 반사적인
uptick ⓝ 상향
drop-off ⓝ 급경사면, 낭떠러지
revert[return] to form 본래 상태로 돌아가다
fluctuation ⓝ 변동, 오르내림
plummet ⓥ 수직으로 떨어지다
misleading ⓐ 오해하게 하는

전문해석

주식시장에서 성공하기 위한 중요한 전략적 원칙들 가운데 하나는 시장의 실적이나 특정 주식의 실적에 있어서 거짓 변동에 대한 자동 반사 반응을 삼가는 것이다. 급속히 가격이 떨어지는 주식에 재투자하기 전에, 분석가들과 투자자들은 한 번 혹은 그 이상의 소폭 상승, 즉 "dead cat bounces"라 불리는 과정이 지나가기를 기다린다. 이 용어는 죽은 고양이조차 아주 높은 곳에서 떨어지면 튀어 오른다는 약간은 조잡한 생각을 반영한다. 급락하는 주식이 반등하는 것은 공매도, 긴급한 자산매각, 혹은 인기 없는 CEO의 교체와 같은 회사 조치에 대한 과도한 낙관적 반응에 의해 생긴다. 그러한 약간의 인상적이지 못한 상승 뒤에는 통상적으로 이전 저점을 뛰어넘는 가파른 하락이 뒤따른다. 거의 주식시장과 관련해서만 사용되지만, 이 용어는 다른 영역에서도 오해를 낳는 개선에 대해 가끔 사용된다. 선거를 앞두고 지지도가 떨어지고 있는 어떤 후보자에 대한 여론 조사 결과가 단기간의 남들을 속이는 급등을 보일 때가 있다. 스포츠에서도, 하위권의 팀들이 시즌 도중 코치진을 교체할 때 가끔 완만한 상승세를 보이면서 한두 번 승리를 거두지만 곧 본래 상태로 돌아간다.

15 윗글의 내용과 가장 거리가 먼 것은? 내용일치
① "dead cat bounces"는 스포츠와 정치에서 관찰될 수 있다.
② "dead cat bounces"는 급속한 하락 이후 어떤 주식이 약간 오르는 것을 가리킨다.
③ 투자자들은 "dead cat bounces"가 발생하면 재투자하기 전에 보통 참고 기다린다.
④ 주식시장에서 회사의 인기 없는 CEO를 교체하는 일은 "dead cat bounces"의 원인이 될 수 있다.
✓ "dead cat bounces" 이후 주식의 하락이 예상될 수 있지만, 전형적으로 이전 저점보다 더 낮아지지는 않는다.

| 분석 | 지문에서 그러한 약간의 인상적이지 못한 상승 뒤에는 통상적으로 이전 저점을 뛰어넘는 가파른 하락이 뒤따른다(Such a small, unimpressive rise is usually followed by another drop-off that surpasses the previous low)고 하였으므로, ⑤는 지문의 내용과 일치하지 않는다.

16 윗글의 빈칸에 들어갈 말로 가장 적절한 것은? 빈칸 추론
① 날카로운
③ 예상된
⑤ 불가해한
✓ 남을 속이는
④ 인상적인

| 분석 | 빈칸은 dead cat bounces의 특징을 넣는 자리이므로, 글에서 언급한 deceptive, misleading과 같은 의미를 전달하는 표현이 들어가야 한다. 따라서 정답으로는 '남을 속이는', '환영의', '착각의'의 의미를 갖는 'illusory'가 가장 적절하다.

[17-19] 2016 국민대

| 정답 | 17 ① 18 ② 19 ③

| 어휘 |
would-be ⓐ ~이 되려고 하는, 지망하는
accrued capital 누적된 자본
parrot ⓥ 앵무새처럼 되풀이하다, 되풀이하여 말하다
natural ⓝ 타고난 사람
recurring ⓐ 되풀이되는
striver ⓝ 노력하는 사람
fall by the wayside 도중에 실패하다

전문해석

한 실험에서 Ms 체이(Tsay)는 예비 투자자들에게, 리더십 경험, 경영 스킬, 지능 그리고 그들이 모금할 수 있는 자본의 양 등과 같은 특징을 포함하고 있는, 가상의 기업가들 집단의 프로필을 제공했다. 비록 투자자들에게는 말하지 않았지만, 이 실험에서 연구들이 가장 큰 관심을 가지고 있는 요소가 가상 기업가들이 타고난 기업가들 아니면 노력형 기업가들이 사실이라는 점이 분명하게 명시되었다. 그리고 그 연구는, 투자자들이 타고난 기업가 아니면 노력형 기업가를 선택하기 위해서, 평균적으로 얼마나 많이 가상 기업가들의 어떠한 특징들을 검토하고자 하는지를 따져 보았다.

투자자들은 타고난 것처럼 보이는 기업가들에 대한 명백히 선호를 보여 주었다. 예를 들어, 투자자들로부터 지지를 얻기 위해서 노력형 기업가는 타고난 기업가보다, 평균 4.5년의 리더십 경험, 9% 더 좋은 경영 스킬, 28포인트 더 높은 지능 그리고 4만 달러 이상의 누적 자본이 필요로 했다. 그러나 실험 전에는, 대부분의 참여자들은 의욕이 넘치고 열심히 일하는 모습을 보여 주는 사람을 선호한다는 의견을 제시했었다. 이 실험은 노력보다 타고난 재능을 선호하는 것이 무의식적이라는 것을 암시한다.

결심을 통해서 목적을 성취하는 것은 반복되는 문화적 믿음이다—예를 들어, 아메리칸드림 혹은 개신교 직업 윤리 등을 생각해 보자. 따라서 사람들이 그것을 이상향으로써 앵무새처럼 되풀이하는 것은 놀랄 일이 아니다. 그러나 투자에 관한 한, 실험은 그와 같은 청교도적 가치들이 실패하고 만다는 것을 보여 준다.

17 밑줄 친 ⓐexplicitly과 가장 가까운 의미는? 표현
☑① 명백하게
② 비밀리에
③ 신중하게
④ 즉시

| 분석 | explicitly는 '명백하게, 분명하게'의 의미를 갖는다.

18 윗글에 따르면 다음 중 노력형인 사람의 특징이 아닌 것은? 세부 내용 파악
① ⓑ
☑② ⓒ
③ ⓓ
④ ⓔ

| 분석 | 지문에서 ⓑ 동기부여, ⓓ 성실함, ⓔ 결단력 등은 노력형 인간의 특징으로 언급되었지만, ⓒ 타고난 재능은 천재형 인간의 특징으로 언급되었다.

19 윗글의 제목으로 가장 적절한 것은? 제목
① 노력형 인간을 선호하는 편견 너무 지엽적
② 연구 결과와 현실 사이의 큰 격차 지문의 주된 내용이 아님
☑③ 투자자의 선택: 타고난 재능 혹은 성실함
④ 기업인의 전략: 잠재력에 대한 선호 너무 지엽적

| 분석 | 지문은 예비 투자자를 대상으로 한 연구, 실험의 글이다. 투자자들이 노력형 기업가보다는 타고난 기업가를 더 선호한다는 내용이므로 ③이 제목으로 가장 적절하다.

[20-22] 2015 고려대

| 정답 | 20 ① 21 ④ 22 ②

| 어휘 | bargaining ⓝ 교섭, 협상, 흥정   tacit ⓐ 무언의 침묵의   tangible ⓐ 유형의

explicit ⓐ 명백한
at stake 성패가 달려 있는, 위태로운
manifest ⓐ 분명한
convene ⓥ 모으다, 소집하다
mediator ⓝ 중재자
disparate ⓐ 서로 다른, 이질적인
mutual ⓐ 서로의, 상호 관계가 있는
modulate ⓥ 조정하다, 조절하다
nominally ⓐᵈ 명목상으로
diverge ⓥ 갈라지다, 다르다, 분기하다
monetary ⓐ 금전의, 화폐의, 통화의

전문해석

협상은 가치의 교환을 위한 합의에 도달하려 시도하는 암묵적이거나 직접적인 의사소통이라고 정의될 수 있는데, 가치는 합의 과정에 참여하고 있는 한쪽 혹은 양쪽 모두가 가치가 있다고 여기는 유형 혹은 무형의 아이템이다. 협상은 명백할 필요는 없다. 때때로 협상의 내용은 말의 교환이 아니라 행동을 통한 의사소통일 수도 있다. 협상 과정은 두 명이나 혹은 그 이상의 참가자를 가지며 때로는 명목상 중립적인 중재인이 개입하는 경우도 있다. 참가자들은 결과에 대해서 직접적인 이해관계를 갖는 반면 중재자들은 그렇지 못하다. 각 참여자가 자신들에게 유리한 조건으로 합의에 도달하기를 바라는 하나 혹은 더 많은 문제점들이 있지만, 참여자들의 이해관계는 이러한 문제들에서 서로 갈리고 갈등을 초래한다. 이러한 갈등은 협상 공간을 정의하게 된다—(협상 공간)이란 하나 또는 그 이상의 영역으로, 각 영역은 자신들이 선호하는 결과에 대한 참여자들의 입장 차이를 나타낸다. 협상 과정은 성패가 달린 가치를 지닌 다양한 항목들의 분배에 합의하는 것을 통해서 이러한 갈등을 해결한다. 최종 결과는 협상 공간 속에서 도달하게 되는 어떤 위치이다. 이러한 합의가 반드시 가치의 공정한 교환을 나타내는 것은 아니다. 많은 합의는 명백히 일방적이며 불공정하다. 그러나 보다 넓은 의미에서 공정하든 불공정하든 협상은 상호 이익이라는 요소를 포함한다. 이것은 거래되는 가치를 지닌 항목들이 각기 다른 상대방에게 서로 다른 가치를 지니기 때문에 가능해지게 된다.

20 ①
22 ②

---

20 다음 중 윗글로부터 추론 가능한 것은? 내용추론

✓ ① 교환되는 품목에 각기 다른 가치가 부여되기 때문에 협상 결과가 불공정한 경우는 빈번하다.
② 협상은 오직 모든 관련 당사자들이 공정하고 정당한 이득에 합의할 때에만 이루어진다.
③ 중재자는 상반되는 이해관계를 조정한 것에 대해 일반적으로 명목상의 금액을 받는다.
④ 협상은 관련된 모든 집단에 불리한 조건에서만 수행될 수 있다.

| 분석 | 지문의 후반부에서 협상을 통해 교환되는 가치를 가진 품목들이 당사자끼리 각각 다른 가치를 지니기 때문에 협상 결과가 불공정하게 나타나는 경우가 많다고 언급했다.

---

21 윗글의 제목으로 가장 적절한 것은? 제목

① 불공정한 협상을 피하는 방법 언급 안 함
② 경험 많은 협상자들의 비결 언급 안 함
③ (협상) 상대측 속이기 언급 안 함
✓ ④ 협상의 속성

| 분석 | 이 글은 협상의 개념을 정의하고, 협상 당사자들, 중재자, 그리고 협상 공간 등 협상의 각종 특징들에 관하여 다루고 있으므로 글 전체를 담을 수 있는 ④ '협상의 속성'이 제목으로 적절하다.

---

22 다음 중 "협상 공간"에 대해 가장 잘 정의한 것은 무엇인가? 세부 내용 파악

① 협상 당사자들과 중재자에 의해 점유된 물리적 장소들의 조합
✓ ② 상반된 이해관계 사이의 거리로 만들어진 비유적 공간
③ 협상 당사자들이 협상을 수행하기 위해 모이는 물리적인 장소
④ 각기 다른 협상 당사자들이 목표로 하는 금전적 가치

| 분석 | 지문에 언급된 협상 공간(bargaining space)의 정의를 찾아보면 '협상 공간이란 하나 또는 그 이상의 영역으로, 각 영역은

자신들이 선호하는 결과에 대한 참여자들의 입장 차이를 나타낸다.'고 언급했다. 이는 실제 물리적 공간이 아닌 상반된 이해 관계 차이를 말하는 비유적인 공간을 가리키므로 ②가 정답으로 적절하다.

[23-24] 2015 한국외대

| 정답 | 23 ①   24 ③

| 어휘 |
contentious ⓐ 논쟁을 일으키는; 논쟁을 좋아하는
epidemic ⓝ 전염병
healthcare ⓝ 의료, 건강관리
patented ⓐ 특허받은
reach a crescendo 최고조에 달하다
low point ⓝ 최악의 상태
exceed ⓥ 초월하다, 능가하다
file a suit against ~을 상대로 소송을 걸다
function ⓥ 기능하다, 역할을 하다
unaffordable ⓐ 감당할 수 없는 가격의
vampire ⓝ 흡혈귀
plague ⓝ 전염병
significance ⓝ 의미, 중요성
projection ⓝ 예상
libel ⓝ 명예훼손
a public good 공공재
weight ⓝ 책임; 무게, 힘, 중요성
intellectual property 지적 재산권
exploit ⓥ 착취하다
generic ⓐ 상표 등록이 되어 있지 않은
conflicting ⓐ 대립되는, 상충하는, 충돌하는
ordeal ⓝ 시련, 힘든 일
injunction ⓝ 명령, 경고 명령

전문해석

시장경제에서 거래되는 모든 상품과 서비스 중에서, 아마도 가장 논쟁이 되는 것은 의약품일 것이다. 비록 민간 기업에 의해 생산되지만, **의약품은 전염병을 막아 주기 때문에, 그리고 건강한 사람들이 아픈 사람들보다 사회 구성원으로서 더 잘 기능하기 때문에, 의약품은 공공재의 구성요소이다.** 의약품은 사적으로 거래되는 대부분의 제품들이 가지고 있지 않은 도덕적 책임을 갖는데, 스마트폰이나 헬스 트레이너에 대해서는 권리를 가지지 않지만, 의료에 대해서는 권리를 가진다는 일반적인 믿음 때문이다. 기술 혁신이 대부분의 생산비를 차지하기 때문에, 약값은 제조비보다 훨씬 더 높아서 가난한 많은 사람들에게는 감당할 수 없을 정도로 너무 비싼 것이 된다. 기업들은 약이 대표하는 지적 재산권을 보호하며 특허받은 약을 값싸게 제조하고 팔려는 사람들에게 소송을 건다. 이러한 모든 이유들 때문에, 제약 회사들은 아픈 사람들을 착취하고 가난한 사람들의 고통을 무시하는 흡혈귀로 널리 평가받는다. 이런 비난은 HIV 전염병이 절정에 이르렀던 10여 년 전에 최고조에 이르렀다. 남아프리카공화국 정부가 특허받은 에이즈 약의 저렴한 복제 의약품을 수입하는 것을 합법화하려고 했을 때, 제약회사들은 사건을 법정으로 가져갔다. 그 사건은 "대규모 제약회사 대 넬슨 만델라(Nelson Mandela)"라는 별명을 얻었다. **그 사건이 제약업계로서는 최악의 상태였지만, 제약업계는 현명하게도 물러났다(소송을 취하했다).**

23 다음 중 윗글의 내용과 일치하는 것은? 내용 일치

✓ ① 의약품은 도덕적으로 중요한 공공재로 간주된다.
② 많은 사람들이 제약회사가 기술 혁신에 많은 돈을 쓴다는 것을 의심한다.
③ 제약회사들은 지적 재산권에 대해 상반되는 의견을 가지고 있었다.
④ 특허받은 약의 판매는 소송 이후에 예상을 초월했다.

| 분석 | 지문의 두 번째 문장에서 '의약품은 전염병을 막아 준다'고 했으며 또한 세 번째 문장에서 '다른 제품들이 갖고 있지 않은 도덕적 책임(a moral weight)을 갖고 있다'고 했으므로 의약품은 도덕적으로 중요한 공공재이다.

24 "거대 제약회사 vs. 넬슨 만델라"와 관련하여 일치하는 것은 무엇인가? 세부 내용 파악

① 제약회사들은 넬슨 만델라(Nelson Mandela)를 상대로 명예훼손으로 고소했다.
② 넬슨 만델라(Nelson Mandela)는 제약회사들에 법적 조치를 취하겠다고 위협했다.
✓ ③ 제약회사들은 결국 물러섰다.
④ 법원은 제약회사들에 더 이상의 조치를 금지하는 명령을 내렸다.

| 분석 | 지문의 마지막에서 It was a low point for the industry, which wisely backed down.이라고 언급했는데 back down은 '뒤로 물러서다'라는 표현으로 retreat과 같은 말이다.

[25-27] 2016 이화여대

| 정답 | 25 ①   26 ①   27 ⑤

| 어휘 |
gigantic ⓐ 거대한
boost ⓥ 북돋우다, 신장시키다
moreover ⓐⓓ 더욱이, 게다가
meanwhile ⓐⓓ 한편
overall ⓐ 전반적인
pessimistic ⓐ 비관적인
elastic ⓐ 탄력 있는, 신축적인
industrialize ⓥ 산업[공업]화되다
ingenuity ⓝ 독창성, 기발함
on the other hand 한편, 반면에
nevertheless ⓐⓓ 그럼에도 불구하고
compulsive ⓐ 강박적인; 상습적인
unnecessary ⓐ 불필요한
affluent ⓐ 부유한
ultimate ⓐ 궁극적인, 최종적인; 최고의
therefore ⓐⓓ 그러므로
temperate ⓐ 온건한
gross ⓐ 총 ~, 전체의
apathetic ⓐ 무관심한, 냉담한

전문해석

중국이 산업화되고 중국인들이 부유해지면서 중국이 거대한 경제 엔진이 된 것을 생각해 보라. 사람들이 더 많아진다는 것은 더 커진 시장과 더 많은 노동자들 그리고 상품의 대량 생산에 있어서의 규모의 효율성을 의미한다. Ⓐ 더욱이, 늘어난 인구는 새로운 물질을 찾아내고 여러 가지 일을 하는 새로운 방법들을 발견함으로써 새로운 자원을 창조해 내는 독창성과 지능을 증가시킨다. 이러한 인간 역사에 대한 장밋빛 견해의 지지자인 경제학자 줄리안 사이먼(Julian Simon, 1932~1998)은 사람들이 궁극적인 자원이고, 오염, 범죄, 실업, 과밀, 생물 종의 손실, 혹은 다른 자원의 제한들이 인구 증가와 더불어 악화될 것이라는 어떤 증거도 없다고 믿었다. 1980년의 유명한 내기에서, 사이먼은 인구 폭탄(The Population Bomb)의 저자 폴 에를리히(Paul Ehrlich)에게 10년 이내 더 비싸질 상품 다섯 개를 골라 보라고 요구했다. 에를리히는 금속들을 골랐는데 그것들은 실제로는 값이 더 싸졌고, 에를리히는 내기에 졌다. 많은 개발도상국들의 지도자들은 이런 관점을 공유하고 있으며 인구 증가에 Ⓑ 집착하는 대신에 부유국 사람들에 의한 전 세계 자원의 Ⓒ 지나친 소비에 초점을 맞춰야 한다고 주장한다.

25 어떤 진술이 윗글로부터 추론될 수 있는가? 내용 추론

✓① 인구 증가는 이점을 가져올 수도 있다.
② 많은 요소들이 인구 증가를 결정한다.
③ 인구 증가는 이미 둔화되기 시작했다.
④ 많은 사람들은 여전히 인구 증가에 대해 비관적이다.
⑤ 전 세계에서 인구 증가 차이는 크다.

| 분석 | 이 글의 요지는 인구 증가가 경제에 부담을 주는 것이 아니라 오히려 여러 가지 다양한 이점을 가져올 수 있다는 것이다.

26 Ⓐ에 들어가기에 가장 적절한 표현은? 연결어

✓① 게다가, 더욱이
② 다른 한편으로는, 반면에
③ 따라서
④ 그 동안에
⑤ 그럼에도 불구하고

| 분석 | 빈칸 Ⓐ의 앞 문장과 뒤 문장 모두 인구 증가가 가져올 이로운 부분에 관하여 기술하고 있으므로 순접의 연결어가 필요하며, 인과의 관계는 아니므로 ③ Therefore는 적절하지 않다. 따라서 첨가의 의미를 갖는 ① Moreover가 적절하다.

27 ⓑ, ⓒ에 들어갈 말이 알맞게 짝지어진 것은? 빈칸 추론

① 온건한 – 전반적인
② 강박적인 – 총, 전체의
③ 비관적인 – 불필요한
④ 무관심한 – 탄력 있는
☑ ⑤ 집착하는 – 지나친

| 분석 | 이 글은 인구 증가가 경제에 항상 문제가 되는 것이 아니라 이점들도 가져올 수 있다는 내용의 글이며, 빈칸 ⓑ 앞에서 개발 도상국 지도자들도 이런 관점을 공유한다고 했으므로, 인구 증가라는 문제에 '집착'할 필요가 없다고 표현하는 것이 적절하다. 따라서 빈칸 ⓑ에는 '~에 집착하다'라는 의미를 갖는 be obsessed with가 적절하다. 그리고 빈칸 ⓒ에는 '부유국 사람들의 세계 자원의 소비'를 수식하는 자리이므로 '과도한, 지나친'이라는 의미를 갖는 inordinate가 적절하다.

[28-30] 2019 서강대

| 정답 | 28 ① 29 ④ 30 ②

| 어휘 |
capital ⓝ 자본; 수도
extent ⓝ 정도; 범위, 한계
economist ⓝ 경제학자, 경제 전문가
argue ⓥ 논하다; 주장하다
impose ⓥ (의무·세금·벌 따위를) 지우다, 부과하다; 강요[강제]하다
industrialist ⓝ 경영자, 사주, 실업가
claim ⓥ 요구하다, 청구하다; 주장하다
market forces 시장의 힘, 자유 시장 방식

politics ⓝ 정치; 정치학
relation ⓝ 관계, 관련
ardent ⓐ 열렬한
interfere ⓥ 간섭하다(in); 방해하다(with)
lavish ⓐ 아끼지 않는, 후한; 낭비벽이 있는
regulation ⓝ 규칙, 규정; 단속
rein ⓝ 고삐; 구속 (pl.) 통제권, 제어력

influence ⓥ ~에 영향을 미치다; 좌우하다
debate ⓥ 토의하다, 논의하다
capitalist ⓝ 자본가, 자본주의자
taxation ⓝ 과세, 징세
unemployment benefits 실업 수당
minimum ⓝ 최소, 최소한도

전문해석

자본과 정치가 서로에게 너무나 큰 영향을 미치다 보니 그 결과, 자본과 정치의 관계는 경제학자, 정치인, 일반 대중 모두에게 뜨거운 논쟁거리가 되고 있다. 열렬한 자본주의자들은 자본이 자유롭게 정치에 영향을 미쳐야 하지만 정치는 자본에 영향을 미치게 해서는 안 된다고 주장하는 경향이 있다. ⓐ 정부가 ⓑ 시장에 간섭하면, 정치적 ⓒ 이해관계로 인해 현명하지 못한 ⓓ 투자를 하게 되고, 이것은 성장의 둔화를 초래한다고 그들은 주장한다. 예를 들어, 정부는 기업가들에게 무거운 세금을 부과하고 (세금으로 걷은) 그 돈을 유권자들에게 인기 있는 실업 수당을 후하게 지급하는 데 사용할 수도 있을 것이다. 그러나 많은 기업인들이 보기에는, 정부가 그 돈을 (세금으로 걷지 말고) 자신들에게 남겨 주는 것이 훨씬 나을 것이다. 그들은 자신들이라면 그 돈을 새로운 공장을 지어 실업자들을 고용하는 데 사용할 거라고 주장한다. 이런 관점에서는, 가장 현명한 경제 정책은 경제가 정치의 영향을 받지 않도록 하고, 세금과 정부 규제를 최소한으로 줄이고, 시장의 힘이 자유롭게 제 갈 길을 갈 수 있도록 해 주는 것이다.

28 저자의 발표 내용은 _____의 그것과 가장 유사하다. 내용 파악

☑ ① 기업과 정부의 정책이 어떻게 서로 연관 있는지에 대해 논평하는 연구원
② 연락망 속의 독자들에게 글을 쓰면서 최고의 투자에 대한 조언을 제공하는 블로거
③ 젊은 고객들을 끌어들여 새로운 계좌를 개설하도록 안내책자를 쓰는 은행장
④ 자신들에게 투표할 것을 기업 경영자들에게 호소하는 내용의 짧은 선거 연설을 하는 정치인

| 분석 | 이 글의 전체 내용은 '자본과 정치와의 관계'를 분석하는 글이므로 이 글을 쓴 저자는 ① '기업과 정부의 정책이 어떻게 서로 연관 있는지에 대해 논평하는 연구원'이라 할 수 있다.

29 다음 중 윗글을 통해 가장 추론할 수 없는 것은? 〔내용 추론〕

① 기업가들은 기업에 낮은 세금을 부과하는 정치인들에게 투표할 가능성이 있다.
② 자본주의자들은 주로 정치적 간섭에도 흔들리지 않는 시장을 보고 싶어 할 것이다.
③ 규제가 완화된 시장은 기업이 이익을 낼 수 있는 최고의 기회를 제공한다.
✓④ 정치가 기업에서 벗어나게 하는 것은 모든 사람을 위한 일자리가 언제나 있게 되는 것을 보장한다.

| 분석 | 기업이 정치로부터 자유로워지면, 기업가가 공장을 세워 실업자들이 일자리를 가질 수 있는 기회를 제공할 수 있는 것은 맞지만, 그렇다고 해서 모든 사람이 일할 수 있는 일자리가 언제나 있다고 할 수는 없다. 또한 보기 ④의 always나 everyone의 표현은 일반화의 오류라고 할 수 있다.

30 빈칸에 가장 적절한 단어로 짝지어진 것을 고르시오. 〔빈칸 추론〕

	Ⓐ	Ⓑ	Ⓒ	Ⓓ
①	이해관계	투자	시장	정부
✓②	정부	시장	이해관계	투자
③	투자	이해관계	시장	정부
④	시장	정부	이해관계	투자

| 분석 | 앞 문장에서 '정치가 자본에 영향을 미쳐서는 안 된다'고 하고 나서 이어지는 문장이므로 그것과 같은 말을 만들면 빈칸 Ⓐ와 Ⓑ에는 각각 Ⓐ '정부(governments)'와 Ⓑ '시장(markets)'이 들어가야 적절하다. 그리고 예시 문장에서 언급한 '정부가 기업가들에게 무거운 세금을 부과하고 그 돈을 유권자들에게 인기 있는 실업 수당을 후하게 지급하는 것'과 같은 말을 만들면 정치적 Ⓒ '이해관계(interests)'로 인해 현명하지 못한 Ⓓ '투자(investments)'를 하게 되는 상황을 보여 준다고 할 수 있다.

[31-32] 2016 성균관대

| 정답 | 31 ② 32 ③

| 어휘 |
sneaky ⓐ 몰래[가만히] 하는; 비열한
bridgeable ⓐ 가교[연락]할 수 있는
fissure ⓝ 터진[갈라진] 자리, 틈, 균열
designation ⓝ 지시; 지명, 명칭, 칭호
chasm ⓝ (지면·바위 등의) 깊게 갈라진 틈; 깊은 구렁; 빈틈(= gap), 간격; 차이
splay ⓥ (팔꿈치·다리 등을) 벌리다
glimpse ⓥ 얼핏 보다, 흘끗 보다
abyss ⓝ 심연; 끝없이 깊은 구렁

〔전문해석〕
상위 중산층—그것은 항상 나 자신에 관해 생각해 온 방식이다. 상위 중산층은 내가 태어난 계층이고 내가 속해 있다고 항상 들어왔던 계층이며, 그리고 내가, 이 순간까지도, 이 계층에서 결코 문제가 없었던 계층이었다. 하지만, 상위 중산층은 비열한 호칭이다. 그것은 대부분의 기준에서 당신이 부자임에도 불구하고 "나는 부자이다."라고 말해야 한다는 필요성을 느끼지 않고, "나는 풍요롭다."라고 말하는 방식이다. 상위 중산층이라는 의식으로 인해, 나는 대부분의 미국인들처럼 동일한 경제적인 부류에서 경쟁하고 있을 뿐만 아니라, 그 경쟁에서 내가 이기고 있는 것 같은 느낌이 들게 했다. 중산층에서 경쟁하며 나는 큰 성공을 누려 왔다. 〔31②〕
이제 나는 상위 중산층 의식의 문제점을 약간 보게 되었다. 그것은 실제로 계층이 아니다. 그것은 계층 사이에 존재하는 공간이다. 그 공간은 한때는 서로 연결될 수 있었을지도 모르겠지만, 이제 그 공간은 깊게 갈라진 틈이 되어 버렸다. 중산층 사람들은 업그레이드된 여행을 꿈꾼다. 상류층 사람들은 자기 소유 비행기가 없는 삶은 생각할 수 없다. 중산층 사람들은 아이들이 Princeton 대학에 들어갈 기회를 잡을 수 있도록 아이들의 숙제를 도와준다. 상류층 사람들은 Princeton 대학에 새 건물을 사 준다. 중산층 사람들은 집을 소유하고 있다. 상류층 사람들은 기념물(기념비적인 건물)을 소유한다. 그가 상위 중산층이라는 환상을 붙들려고 하는 사람은 지진 장면이 나오는 만화 속 등장인물과 같다. 그는 내려다보면서 자신의 다리가 빠르게 갈라지는 균열에 의해 더 멀리 떨어져 끌려가는 것을 보게 된다. 그의 다리는 늘어나고 벌어져 결국 그는 깊은 수렁에 빠지게 되는 것이다.

31. 윗글에 따르면 저자는 _____. 내용 일치

① 상위 중산층의 아이인 것을 후회했다
☑ ② 상위 중산층의 생활 방식을 좋아했다
③ 정말로 상위층의 일원이 되기를 원했다
④ 하위층 사람들과 일하는 것을 꺼려 하지 않았다
⑤ 결국 사회 계층 사다리의 밑바닥으로 떨어졌다

| 분석 | 보기의 동사의 시제를 보면 과거 동사라는 것을 알 수 있는데, 따라서 이 글의 저자가 과거에 어땠는지를 묻는 문제이다. 과거에 대한 내용은 첫 번째 단락에 언급되어 있는데 첫 번째 단락은 상위 중산층으로 의식하고 살면서 누린 이점을 진술하고 있으므로 지문과 가장 일치하는 것은 ②라고 할 수 있다.

32. 밑줄 친 'it's become a chasm'의 의미는 _____ 이다. 밑줄 의미 추론

① 사람들이 점점 더 멀리 떨어지고 있다
② 가난은 시스템으로 해결될 수 없다
☑ ③ 상류층의 일원이 될 방법은 없다
④ 상류층은 교육받을 필요가 있다
⑤ 미국은 현재 경제적 불평등 때문에 큰 어려움을 겪고 있다

| 분석 | 밑줄 친 문장의 뒤를 보면 중산층과 상류층의 생활 방식이 너무나도 차이가 나서 둘 간의 간격이 더욱더 멀어져 좁힐 수 없다는 내용이 이어지고 있으므로 문맥상 '틈(chasm)'은 깊게 갈라져서 좁힐 수 없는 틈을 말하는 것이며 결국 중산층이 상위층의 일원이 될 방법이 없다는 의미가 된다. ①은 사람들 사이의 거리가 멀어진다는 의미로 상류층과 중산층이 멀어진다는 의미가 아니다.

[33-35] 2011 고려대

| 정답 | 33 ④ 34 ② 35 ①

| 어휘 |
aesthetic ⓐ 미적인, 심미적인
deem ⓥ 생각하다, ~로 간주하다
contemporary ⓐ 동시대의, 현대의
accuse ~ of ... ~을 …로 고발하다
extol ⓥ 칭찬하다
greenery ⓝ 푸른 잎, 푸른 나무

enclosure ⓝ 구내, 공간
shareholder ⓝ 주주(株主)
one-size-fits-all ⓐ 널리 적용되도록 만든
avant-garde ⓝ (예술상의) 전위파, 아방가르드; 선구자
cube ⓝ 입방체, 정육면체

rentable ⓐ 임대할 수 있는
posterity ⓝ 자손, 후세
stark ⓐ 순전한, 완전한
functionality ⓝ 기능성

전문해석

'형태가 수익을 따라간다'는 것이 우리 시대 미학적 원리이다. 그래서 설계 능력은 가장 빠른 시간에 가장 적은 투자로 가능한 가장 큰 내부 공간을 만들어 내는 건축가의 능력으로 평가된다. 현재 빌딩의 설계를 결정하는 요인들은, 총면적 대비 임대 가능 면적으로 환산할 경우, 최대의 경제적 효과, 벽과 바닥의 비율, 그리고 최소의 충고이다. 그 결과는 변함없이 껍질이 얇은 상자의 형태로 된 쇼핑센터, 사무실 빌딩, 아파트 건물들과 같은 단일 활동의 건물인데, 이런 건물에는 비영리적인 공공의 면적이 없고, 표현적이거나 혁신적인 구조상의 특징도 없으며, 그리고 확실히 건축술을 기념하는 공간도 없다. 아케이드, 정원, 그리고 발코니, 심지어는 움푹 들어간 창들은 임대 가능한 면적을 침해하고, 수익의 원칙과 양립할 수 없는 것으로 간주된다. 그리고 개발업자들과 그들의 주주들은 자신들의 투자에 대한 빠른 회수를 원하기 때문에—증권 중개사들과 회계사들의 시야는 후대까지 미치지 않는다—가장 저렴한 자재들을 사용해야 한다. 일부 고객들은 심지어 나무를 심는 것도 거절한다. 도토리 열매는 재산의 임대 가능한 가치를 증가시키지

정답과 해설_ 39

못할 것이다. 그리고 어떤 투자자도 참나무를 기다리지 않을 것이라는 이야기를 우리는 듣는다. 그러므로 대부분의 현대 건축물은 디자이너의 작품이라기보다는 엄격한 경제적 요소들의 산물이다. 현대의 건축은 수익의 측면에서 환경을 바라보는 사회가 만들어낸 논리적인 산물을 나타낸다.

---

33 빈칸에 들어갈 말로 가장 적절한 것을 고르시오. 빈칸 추론
① 어디에나 맞는 경향
② 사용자 친화적인 인터페이스
③ 환경적 고려 사항들
✓ 엄격한 경제적 요소들

| 분석 | 지문에서 현대건축은 그 설계의 특징이 최대의 경제적 효율성에 집중하고 있다. 이는 곧 현대건축은 엄격한 경제적 수익의 관점에서만 설계되는 것이므로 정답은 ④ '엄격한 경제적 요소들'이 적절하다.

---

34 윗글의 목적은 무엇인가? 글의 목적
① 건축가들이 전위적으로 된 것을 비난하기 위해
✓ 건축에 미치는 외부의 영향을 비판하기 위해
③ 건축의 사회에 대한 기여를 극찬하기 위해
④ 건축학적 자유가 되살아나야 한다고 제안하기 위해

| 분석 | 이 글은 현대건축에 영향을 준 경제적 요소에 대해 말하는데 이는 곧 건축이 경제와 같은 외부 요소에 영향을 받는다는 것이다. 그로 인해 값싼 재료를 쓴다든가, 의미 있고 혁신적이며, 예술적인 특징을 가진 건축은 부족하다는 것을 말하고 있으므로 ②가 정답으로 적절하다.

---

35 윗글에 의하면, 현대 건물의 설계와 관련된 측면은 어느 것인가? 세부 내용 파악
✓ 정육면체 모양
② 다양한 기능성
③ 친환경적인
④ 독특한 스타일

| 분석 | 지문에서 '현재 빌딩의 설계를 결정하는 요인들은, 총면적 대비 임대 가능 면적으로 환산할 경우, 최대의 경제적 효과, 벽과 바닥의 비율, 그리고 최소의 층고이다'라고 했다. 그것의 결과물은 '변함없이 껍질이 얇은 상자의 형태로 된 쇼핑센터, 사무실 빌딩, 아파트 건물들과 같은 단일 활동의 건물'이라고 했으므로 현대 건물의 설계와 관련된 측면은 ① '정육면체 모양'이 정답으로 적절하다.

[36-38] 2016 한국외대

| 정답 | 36 ④　37 ①　38 ④

| 어휘 | **demise** ⓝ 종말, 죽음, 사망　　　　**greenback** ⓝ 녹색 지폐(미국 달러)　　　　**premier** ⓐ 최고의, 제1의
reserve currency 기축통화　　　　**dump** ⓥ 버리다　　　　**buoyancy** ⓝ 부력; 상승
bright spot 밝은 부분, 괜찮은 부분　　　　**GDP** ⓝ 국내 총생산 (Gross Domestic Product)

annualized ⓐ 연간으로 환산한
chaotic ⓐ 혼란[혼돈] 상태의
powerhouse ⓝ 강국
chip away at ~을 조금씩 깎아 먹다
post ⓥ 게시하다, 발표하다
undercut ⓥ 약화시키다
follow suit 방금 나온 패와 같은 패를 내다, 선례를 따르다
sovereign debt 국가 부채
settle ⓥ 지불하다, 정산하다

전문해석

2008년 금융 위기 이후로, 달러화의 종말에 대한 예측들이 반복적으로 나오고 있다. 미국 경제가 불황에 빠졌듯이, 미국 달러화가 세계 제일의 기축통화로서의 오래된 지위를 유지할 수 있으리라는 확신 또한 가라앉았다. 그러나 금융위기 이후 몇 년이 지난 이제 달러화는 그것이 얼마나 ⓐ 전능한지를 보여 주고 있다. 다른 통화와 비교해 달러화의 가치를 측정하는 달러 지수는 최근에 4년 만의 최고치에 도달했다. 그리고 달러화를 비난했던 정책담당자들은 달러화를 내다 파는 것에는 거의 관심이 없다. 달러화의 상승은 세계의 주요 경제국들 가운데 미국이 드물게 (경제적으로) 좋은 상황이라는 것을 반영하는 것이다. 3분기에 미국의 국내 총생산(GDP)은 연간으로 환산한 3.5퍼센트 증가했는데, 이것은 대부분의 다른 선진국들이 발표하고 있는 것보다 훨씬 더 높은 수치이다. 다른 어떤 통화도 달러와 ⓑ 필적할 수 없다는 사실 또한 여전하다. 유로화의 불확실한 안정성은 수년간의 국가 부채 위기와 유럽 지도자들로부터 나오는 혼란스러운 대처에 의해 드러났다. 달러화의 추세가 얼마나 지속될지는 미국 국내 총생산의 미래 성장에서부터 세계 경제의 건강성에 이르기까지 모든 것에 달려 있다. 장기적으로는 달러화를 약화시킬 수 있는 요소들이 많다. 러시아와 중국은 양국 간의 무역을 루블화와 위안화로 더 많이 지불하고 있다. 만약 다른 경제 강국들이 따라한다면, 그것은 달러화의 유용성을 깎아 먹기 시작할 수도 있다. ⓐ 그러나 현재로서는, 그것은 너무 큰 가정이다.

36 문맥상 다음 중 빈칸 ⓐ와 ⓑ에 가장 적절한 단어로 짝지어진 것은? 빈칸 추론

① 매우 귀중한 – 제지하다
② 있음 직하지 않은 – 보충하다/추가하다
③ 민감한 – 이기다
✓ 전능한 – ~에 필적하다

| 분석 | 앞부분에서 달러화에 대한 전망이 안 좋다고 했는데 역접의 접속사 But을 썼으므로 빈칸 ⓐ에는 달러화에 대해 '긍정적'인 표현이 적합하다. 그리고 빈칸 ⓑ의 앞뒤 내용은 미국 경제가 다른 선진국보다는 좋은 편이며, 유로화의 불확실한 안정성이 노출되었다고 했으므로, 빈칸 ⓑ에는 다른 어떤 통화도 달러화와 '필적'할 수 없다고 표현하는 것이 올바르다.

37 다음 중 ⓐ가 함축하는 것은? 문맥상 의미 추론

✓ 달러화의 안정성은 한동안 지속될 것이다.
② 다른 경제 강국들은 달러화로 더 많은 무역을 할 것이다.
③ 세계 경제는 여전히 건강하지 못할 것이다.
④ 러시아와 중국은 달러화의 유용성을 위협할 것이다.

| 분석 | 밑줄 친 표현은 '그것은 아주 큰 가정이다', 즉 그리될 가능성이 희박하다는 의미이다. if가 명사로 쓰일 경우 '가정'이라는 의미이다. 그리고 대명사 that이 가리키는 것은 앞부분에서 다른 경제 강국들이 러시아와 중국처럼 달러가 아닌 통화로 무역을 하면 달러의 유용성을 약화시킬 수도 있다는 내용이다. 따라서 달러화의 유용성이 약화될 가능성이 현재로서는 희박하다는 것이므로 '달러화의 안정성은 한동안 지속될 것'이라는 의미로 보아야 한다.

38 다음 중 윗글의 내용과 일치하지 않는 것은? 내용 일치

① 사람들은 미국 통화의 몰락을 예상하고 있다.
② 루블화나 위안화 같은 다른 통화가 미국 달러화에 도전할 가능성이 있다.
③ 미국 국내 총생산의 성장률은 최근에 경쟁국들을 앞질렀다.
✓④ 유럽의 부채에도 불구하고, 유로화는 강한 유용성을 유지하고 있다.

| 분석 | 지문에서 '유로화의 불확실한 안정성은 수년간의 국가 부채 위기와 유럽 지도자들부터 나오는 혼란스러운 대처로 인해 드러났다.'고 했으므로, ④는 이 글의 내용과 일치하지 않는다.

배경지식
기축통화(Key Currency): 국제 외환시장에서 금융 거래 또는 국제 결제의 중심이 되는 통화. 대표적으로 미국 달러가 이에 속한다. 기축통화로서 기능을 수행하기 위해서는 군사적으로 지도적인 입장에 있어 전쟁으로 국가의 존립이 문제시되지 않아야 하며, 기축통화 발행국은 다양한 재화나 서비스를 생산하고, 통화 가치가 안정적이며, 고도로 발달한 외환시장과 금융·자본시장을 갖고 있어야 하며, 대외 거래에 대한 규제도 없어야 한다.

[39-41] 2011 이화여대

| 정답 | 39 ③ 40 ④ 41 ③

| 어휘 |
- **trail** ⓥ 뒤쫓다, 추적하다
- **surpass** ⓥ 능가하다, 뛰어나다
- **slump** ⓥ (물가 등이) 급락하다, 쇠퇴하다
- **boost** ⓥ 격려하다, 후원하다; 경기를 부양시키다
- **barrier** ⓝ 장벽, 방해물
- **unbridled** ⓐ 억제되지 않은
- **wane** ⓥ 작아지다; 적어지다, 약해지다
- **wake** ⓝ 여파, 자국
- **invariably** ⓐⓓ 변함없이, 일정불변하게
- **ringfence** ⓥ (특정한 용도용으로 보호하기 위해) 제한하다
- **resuscitate** ⓥ 소생시키다; 의식을 회복시키다
- **outbreak** ⓝ 발생, 발발
- **retaliate** ⓥ 보복하다
- **retail distribution** 소매유통
- **ardent** ⓐ 열렬한, 격렬한
- **national tariff** 국정관세율
- **launch** ⓥ 시작하다, 일으키다

전문해석

제1차 세계 대전은 그 여파로 인해 Ⓐ 물류의 전 세계적인 자유로운 흐름에서 끔찍한 자신감의 위기를 초래했다. 유럽의 선진화된 경제 국가들에서, 무역과 소매유통이 가치 창출의 수단으로서 제조업을 오랫동안 능가했고, 제품들이 ⓐ 끊임없이 도처에서 만들어졌다. 그러나 영국에서는, 이전에 가장 열정적인 자유무역의 버팀목이었던 소매와 금융서비스가 ⓑ 침체되었고, 이에 대응해서, 영국 정부는 내수시장과 물류를 부양하기 위한 시도로 경제에 ⓒ 보호조치를 가했다. 다른 경제대국들도 영국의 정책을 따르면서, 이전에 유럽 팽창의 원동력이었던 자유무역을 붕괴시켰다. 즉, 관세와 무역장벽으로 인해 물류의 흐름이 제한되었다. 자본, 인력, 물류의 흐름이 이전의 크기로 회복하는 데는 수십 년이 걸렸다. 그리고 유럽은 최초의 현대 물질문명의 기간에 만끽했던 ⓓ 무한한 낙관론을 회복시킬 수는 없었다.

39 빈칸 Ⓐ에 들어가기에 가장 적절한 것은? 빈칸 추론

① 국내 시장의 보호
② 경제적 요인과 정치적 요인 사이의 상호 작용
✓③ 물류의 전 세계적인 자유로운 흐름
④ 유럽 보호주의에 대한 영국의 우월성

| 분석 | 빈칸 Ⓐ 뒤에서 제1차 세계 대전 이전에 무역과 소매유통이 제조업을 능가하고 제품이 끊임없이 생산되었다는 것과 자유무역(free trade)이 성행했다는 것이므로 이와 같은 말인 ③ '물류의 전 세계적인 자유로운 흐름'이 빈칸에 적절하다.

| 40 | 작가의 주장을 가장 잘 기술한 진술을 고르시오. 내용 파악

① 국가 관세와 무역 장벽은 결국 유럽의 경제적 낙관주의를 회복하는 데 도움이 되었다.
② 유럽 자유무역 체제의 붕괴로 세계 경제가 활성화되었다.
③ 대량 생산을 위한 산업 기반은 제1차 세계 대전 이전에 가치를 창출하는 가장 강력한 요소로 여겨졌다.
✓④ 제1차 세계 대전이 발발하고 나서야 유럽의 보호무역이 시작되었다.

| 분석 | 지문에서 제1차 세계 대전을 계기로 영국에서 경제 제한 조치를 취한 것이 유럽 전역에 퍼져 나갔다고 했다. 따라서 ④ '제1차 세계 대전이 발발하고 나서야 유럽의 보호무역이 시작되었다.'가 정답으로 적절하다.

| 41 | 다음 중 윗글의 밑줄 친 단어를 대체하지 못하는 것은 무엇인가? 동의어

① ⓐ 지속적으로   ② ⓑ 쇠약해진
✓③ ⓒ 보복하다   ④ ⓓ 과도한

| 분석 | ⓒ의 ringfence는 일정 액수의 돈을 특정 목적을 위해서만 쓰이도록 용도를 한정하는 것을 의미하고 retaliate는 '보복하다'이므로 대체할 수 없다.

| 배경 지식 | 보호무역(Protective Trade): 국가가 관세 또는 수입 할당제 및 그 밖의 수단으로 외국의 무역에 간섭하여 외국과의 경쟁에서 국내산업을 보호할 목적으로 하는 무역정책을 이야기한다. 국가권력이 보호정책을 취하는 것을 '보호무역제도'라고 하며, 이러한 주장을 하는 일련의 사상을 '보호무역주의'라고 한다. 국가권력을 배제하여 자유로운 외국무역을 하는 '자유무역'과 반대되는 입장에 있다.

[42-44] 2014 가톨릭대

| 정답 | 42 ② 43 ③ 44 ④

| 어휘 | desperation ⓝ 필사적임, 절망, 자포자기   negligence ⓝ 태만, 등한, 부주의, 무관심, 단정치 못함
Inordinate ⓐ 지나친, 과도한, 난폭한, 무절제한, 불규칙한   imprudent ⓐ 경솔한, 무모한, 경망스러운
fraudulent ⓐ 사기의, 사기를 치는   dubious ⓐ 의심하는, 불확실한   mortgage ⓝ 담보대출금 ⓥ 저당잡히다
esoteric ⓐ 비법의, 내밀한   obscure ⓐ 불분명한, 모호한, 잘 알려져 있지 않은 ⓥ 보기 어렵게 하다, 모호하게 하다
aftermath ⓝ 여파, 후유증   fierce ⓐ 몹시 사나운, 모진   fiery ⓐ 불의, 불길의, 불같은, 열띤
prosecution ⓝ 실행, 속행, 고소, 구형   fraudulent ⓐ 사기의, 부정한, 속이는   despicable ⓐ 야비한, 비열한
egregious ⓐ 엄청난, 터무니없는   fraud ⓝ 사기, 사기꾼, 가짜, 엉터리
orchestrate ⓥ 관현악용으로 편곡하다; 편성하다, 조직화하다, 획책하다
mammoth ⓝ 매머드(멸종한 코끼릿과의 포유동물) ⓐ 거대한, 엄청난   recession ⓝ (경기) 후퇴, 불경기, 물러남
onslaught ⓝ 돌격, 맹공격, 습격   predicament ⓝ 곤경, 궁지, 상태, 상황

전문해석
대불황이라고 간혹 부르는 그 시기의 시작점으로부터 5년이 지났다. 경제가 서서히 나아지기는 했지만 아직도 직업도 없고, 자원도 없고, 희망도 없이, 조용한 좌절 속에 삶을 살아가고 있는 미국인들이 수백만 명 있다. 누구의 탓인가? 그저 태만의 결과인가? 흔히 버블이라고 부르는 부적절한 모험의 결과인가? 어려운 때를 위해 적절한 보유량을 유지하지 못한, 경솔하지만 순진한 잘못의 결과인가? ⓐ 혹은, 최소한 부분적으로는 부정행위들의 결과인가? 건전한 모험인 양, 또 그 근본적인 약점이 의도적으로 가려져 있던 매우 비밀스러운 회계 도구들로 포장한 의심스러운 저당의 결과인가?

만일 전자의 경우라면, 이 후폭풍에서 형법은 역할을 할 것이 없다. ⓑ 왜냐하면 몇 가지 경우를 빼고서는 형법상의 입건이라고 부르는 엄정하고 무서운 무기는 의도적으로 잘못된 행위만 겨냥할 수 있고 그 이하에는 해당이 되지 않기 때문이다. 만일 대불황이 윗선의 집행부의 의도적인 사기 행각의 결과가 아니라면, 그러한 집행부를 형사법으로 처벌하는 것은 가장 천박하고도 경멸할 만한 '희생양 만들기'가 될 것이기 때문이다. 그러나 만일, ⓒ 결과적으로, 대불황이 의도적인 사기의 산물이라면, 책임 있는 사람들을 처벌하지 않는 것은 수년간 형법 사법제도의 매우 심각한 잘못임에 틀림없다. ⓓ 실제로, 그것은 연방 검찰이 거대한 사기를 배후 조종한 가장 높은 단계의 인물들까지도 법의 심판을 받게 했던, 지난 50여 년 동안 점점 더 성공해 왔던 것과는 명백한 대조가 될 것이다.

42 윗글은 주로 _____ 에 관한 내용이다. 제목
① 대불황의 시작과 그 여파
✓ ② 대불황의 근원과 형사 기소의 역할
③ 대불황에 책임이 있는 사람들을 기소하는 방법
④ 사람들이 잊지 말아야 할 대불황의 교훈

| 분석 | 이 글은 첫 번째 단락에서는 경제 대불황의 원인을 기술하고, 두 번째 단락에서는 형법의 역할에 관하여 기술하고 있다. 따라서 적절한 주제는 ② '대불황의 근원과 형사 기소의 역할'이라 할 수 있다.

43 다음 중 각각의 맥락상 적절하지 않은 표현은? 연결사
① ⓐ   ② ⓑ
✓ ③ ⓒ   ④ ⓓ

| 분석 | 문맥으로 보아 ⓒ의 앞부분에서는 의도적으로 잘못된 행위를 한 게 아니라면 형사법이 할 수 있는 역할이 없다고 했는데, ⓒ의 뒤에서는 의도적인 행위였다면 형사법의 잘못이라고 하고 있으므로 서로 상반된 내용이 나온다는 것을 알 수 있다. 따라서 '결과적으로'의 순접이 아닌 역접의 연결사 '대조적으로(by contrast)'로 바꾸어야 한다.

44 다음 중 자자의 주요 주장을 가장 잘 표현한 것은 무엇인가? 글의 요지
① 또 다른 형태의 금융위기의 발발을 막기 위해 행정부의 모든 영역에서 모든 노력이 이루어져야 한다.
② 아직도 많은 사람들이 어려움에 처해 있기 때문에, 대불황의 정확한 원인을 묻고 그것이 남긴 상처를 치유하는 것이 시급하다.
③ 형사사법제도는 나라를 곤경에 빠뜨린 사람들을 기소하는 데 실패했으므로 형사사법제도는 반드시 비난받아야 한다.
✓ ④ 대불황의 원인을 규명한 뒤 사건의 책임자를 판단해 사회 정의를 실현해야 한다.

| 분석 | 이 글 저자의 입장은 경제 대불황이라는 문제의 원인을 찾아서 사회적 정의를 실현해야 한다는 것이다. ① '재발 방지 노력을 촉구하자', ② '원인 규명이 시급하다', ③ '형사제도를 비난하자'는 저자의 생각이라 볼 수 없다.

[45-47] 2020 숭실대
| 정답 | 45 ② 46 ③ 47 ①

| 어휘 | contemplate ⓥ 고려하다, 생각하다   resolution ⓝ (굳은) 다짐 결심   hire ⓥ 고용하다
prohibition ⓝ 금지법, 금지 규정   coercive ⓐ 강압[강제적]인   insistence ⓝ 고집, 주장, 강조

optimize ⓥ 최대한 좋게[적합하게] 만들다	press release 보도 자료	supposedly ⓐⓓ 추정상, 아마
embed ⓥ (마음·기억에) 깊이 새겨 두다	vernacular ⓝ 말, 토착어, 전문어, 은어	be invested in ~에 관심이 있다
announcement ⓝ 발표, 공표	note ⓥ 언급하다	job application 구직
vaper ⓝ 전자담배를 피우는 사람	smokeless tobacco 씹는담배	pool ⓝ 이용 가능 인력
in addition to ~에 더하여, ~일 뿐 아니라	hostile ⓐ 적의 있는	troubling ⓐ 골치 아픈, 귀찮은
bleak ⓐ 암울한, 절망적인	malfunctioning ⓐ (기계 따위가) 제대로 기능하지 못하는	
foist ⓥ 억지로 떠맡기다, 속여 팔다	equip ⓥ 갖추게 하다, 수여하다	fight back 저항하다, 가로막다

전문해석

2019년 마지막 시기에, 수백만 명의 미국인들이 새해의 결심을 사전에 생각하고 있었을 때인데, 이사와 보관 회사인 U-Haul은 미래의 모든 직원들을 위해 한 가지를 설정했다. 그 회사는 2월 1일부터 21개 주에서 니코틴을 사용하는 사람들을 고용하지 않을 것이라고 발표했는데, 21개의 주는 그러한 금지가 합법이며, 거기에는 텍사스, 플로리다, 매사추세츠 등이 포함된다. 이들 주 중에서 17개의 주에서는 고용주들이 니코틴에 대한 약물검사를 실시할 수 있도록 허가한다.

U-Haul에게 이러한 조치가 새로운 방침인 Ⓐ 반면, 이러한 조치는 직원들이 식생활 변화를 추구하고 일상 활동의 목표를 달성하도록 격려하는 '직장 건강' 프로그램으로 향한 더 큰 트렌드의 일부이다. 지난 수십 년 동안 회사들은 직원들이 스스로 시간을 내서 몸과 행동을 최적화해야 한다고 주장을 펼치며, 훨씬 더 강압적으로 변했다. ⓐ 적어도 이론적으로 이것은 비용을 줄이고, 직원들이 더 건강한 삶을 살 수 있도록 도와준다.

보도 자료에서 U-Haul의 인사부장인 제시카 로페즈(Jesica Lopez)는 이제는 직장에서의 건강과 관련한 전문어가 되어 버린 몇 마디 영감을 주는 말을 반복했다. "ⓑ 우리는 우리 팀원들의 건강에 대해 깊이 관심을 두고 있습니다. 니코틴 제품은 중독성이 있고 여러 가지 심각한 건강상의 위험이 됩니다"라고 그녀는 말했다. 로페즈는 이 조치를 "우리 팀원들이 건강해지도록 돕는 것을 목표로 하여 U-Haul의 웰빙 문화를 조성하기 위한 중요한 조치'라고 생각했다.

U-Haul의 발표에 따르면, 회사는 입사 지원서에 회사의 방침을 공지하고, 면접에서 지원자의 니코틴 사용량에 대해 질문하며, 니코틴 테스트를 허가하는 17개 주에서는 니코틴 검사에 응하는 것을 동의하도록 요구할 계획이다. 그 방침은 모든 형태의 니코틴 사용에 적용될 것인데, 이는 흡연자들뿐만 아니라 전자담배 흡연자들과 또 다른 씹는담배 사용자들이 고용 가능한 인력 대상에서 제외될 것이라는 것을 의미한다. 그 방침은 회사에 이미 고용된 사람들에게는 적용되지 않을 것이다. ⓒ 사람들은 직원과 고용주의 근본적인 이해관계가 필연적으로 서로 적대적이라 생각한다.

니코틴은, 실제로 심각한 건강상의 위험과 결부되어 있다. 전 세계적으로 흡연은 매년 약 8백만 명의 사람들을 사망에 이르게 한다. 그러나 고용주들이 직원들의 삶의 더 많은 부분을 통제하려고 하는 것은 이미 문제를 유발하는 추세이다. ⓓ 누군가의 건강이 직장의 고장 난 기계로 간주될 때는 암울하지만, 이러한 기대들을 대항할 준비가 거의 되지 않은 노동자들에게 억지로 할 때 문제는 훨씬 더 악화된다.

45 빈칸 Ⓐ에 들어가기에 가장 적절한 것은? 연결사

① ~ 없이
☑ ~인 반면
③ 왜냐하면
④ ~이든 아니든

| 분석 | 빈칸 다음에 명사가 와서 전치사 Without이 적절한 것처럼 보이지만 '~이 없이'라는 의미는 내용상 적합하지 않다. 또한 주절이 뒤에 있고 콤마 앞에 넣는 것이므로 부사절을 이끄는 종속접속사인 Whether, While, Because가 가능한데, Whether는 뒤에 A or B의 형태가 나와야 하기 때문에 적합하지 않다. Because는 부사절이지만 S와 be동사를 생략한 분사구문의 형태로 사용할 수 없기 때문에 적합하지 않다. While (this move is) a new policy for U-Haul에서 주어인 this move와 be동사 is를 생략한 형태이며, 내용상으로도 자연스럽다.

46 다음 중 적절하지 않은 것은? 글의 흐름 파악

① ⓐ
② ⓑ
✓ ⓒ
④ ⓓ

| 분석 | 네 번째 단락 마지막에서 그 방침은 회사에 이미 고용된 사람들에게는 적용되지 않는다고 했는데, ⓒ에서는 고용주와 직원들이 적대적이라고 나와 있다. 직원은 이미 고용된 사람이므로 회사의 새로운 조치에 적용되지 않으므로 직원과 고용주가 적대적일 이유는 없다. 따라서 ⓒ가 문맥상 적절하지 않다.

47 다음 중 옳은 것은 무엇인가? 내용 일치

✓ 니코틴을 사용하는 사람들을 고용하지 않는 것은 미국의 일부 주에서는 합법적이다.
② 2월 1일 전에 고용된 흡연자들은 회사를 그만두어야 한다.
③ 매년 약 8백만 명의 미국인들이 흡연으로 인해 사망한다.
④ 미국 전역의 모든 U-Haul 직원은 니코틴 검사를 받아야 한다.

| 분석 | 첫 번째 단락에서 '2월 1일부터 21개 주에서 니코틴을 사용하는 사람들을 고용하지 않을 것이라고 발표했는데, 21개의 주는 그러한 금지가 합법이며, 거기에는 텍사스, 플로리다, 매사추세츠 등이 포함된다.'고 언급했으므로 ①이 지문과 일치한다.

[48-50] 2020 홍익대

| 정답 | 48 ① 49 ④ 50 ②

| 어휘 | neoliberal ⓐ 신자유주의의 ⓝ 신자유주의자
private property rights 사유재산권
arrangement ⓝ 배열; 준비; 조절
preserve ⓥ 보전하다, 유지하다; 보존하다
initiative ⓝ 진취적 기상, 기업심
patent ⓝ 특허, 특허권
asset ⓝ 자산; 재산
assignment ⓝ 할당; 지정
deregulate ⓥ (경제·가격 등의) 공적 규제를 해제하다
bureaucratic ⓐ 관료정치의; 관료적인

the rule of law 법치주의
guarantee ⓥ 보증하다; 보장하다
by extension 더 나아가
innovation ⓝ 혁신
assiduous ⓐ 근면한, 주도면밀한
enclosure ⓝ 울타리를 침(특히, 공유지를 사유지로 만들기 위해서)
regulate ⓥ 통제하다; 조절하다

red tape 관료적 형식주의

favor ⓥ 호의를 보이다; 찬성[지지]하다
institution ⓝ 학회, 협회; 제도, 관례
monopoly ⓝ 독점; 독점권
entrepreneurial ⓐ 실업가의, 기업가의
intellectual property right 지적재산권
privatization ⓝ 민영화, 사유화
sphere ⓝ (활동) 영역, (세력) 범위
interference ⓝ 방해, 훼방; 간섭
commodity ⓝ 일용품, 필수품; 상품

전문해석

신자유주의 국가는 강력한 개인의 사유재산권, 법치주의, 자유롭게 작동하는 시장과 자유무역 제도를 지지해야만 한다. 이것들은 개인의 자유를 보장하기 위해 필수적인 것으로 여겨지는 제도적 장치이다. 그러므로 국가는 모든 대가를 치르서라도 이러한 자유를 지키기 위해 국가가 독점하고 있는 폭력 수단을 사용해야 한다. 더 나아가, 자유시장과 자유무역이라는 이와 같은 제도적 틀 안에서 사업체나 기업(법적으로는 개인으로 간주됨)이 영업을 할 수 있는 자유는 근본적으로 좋은 것으로 간주된다. 민간 기업과 기업가적 진취성은 혁신과 부의 창출에 있어서 핵심적인 요소로 여겨진다. 지적재산권은 기술 변화를 촉진하기 위해 (예를 들어 특허를 통해) 보호된다.

신자유주의자들은 자산의 사유화를 추구하는 데 특히 주도면밀하다. 공유지를 사유지로 만드는 것과 사유재산권의 지정은 소위 "공유지의 비극"을 막아 내기 위한 최고의 방법으로 여겨진다. 이전에 국가가 운영하거나 규제한 부문은 민간 영역으로 이관하고

규제를 철폐해야 한다(국가의 그 어떤 간섭으로부터도 자유로워야 한다). 그들은 경쟁과 결합된 사유화와 규제철폐가 관료적 형식주의를 없애고, 효율성과 생산성을 높이고, 품질을 향상시키며, 직접적으로는 보다 값싼 상품과 서비스를 통해, 간접적으로는 세금 부담의 완화를 통해 소비자들의 비용을 줄여 준다고 주장된다.

48 윗글에 따르면, 다음 중 옳지 않은 것은? 내용 일치

① ✓ 재산권을 규정하기 어려운 상황에서는, 국가가 권력을 사용하여 시장 경제 체제를 강제하거나 만드는 것은 바람직하지 않다.
② 개인의 자유가 시장과 무역의 자유에 의해 보장된다는 가정은 신자유주의적 사고의 주된 특징이다.
③ 계약의 신성함과 행동 표현, 선택의 자유에 대한 개인의 권리는 보호되어야 한다.
④ 개인 간의, 기업 간의 경쟁은 중요한 미덕으로 간주된다.

| 분석 | 지문에 따르면 신자유주의 국가는 강력한 개인재산권, 법치주의, 자유무역 제도를 지지해야 하며, 이것들이 개인의 자유를 보장하기 위해 필수적으로 여긴다고 했다. 또한 국가는 그것을 지키기 위해 권력을 사용해야 한다고 했다. 따라서 '권력을 사용하는 것이 바람직하지 않다'는 ①은 이와 상반되는 진술이므로 지문과 일치하지 않는다.

49 다음 중 신자유주의 국가의 특징이 아닌 것은? 세부 내용 파악

① 경제 요인에 대한 통제를 공공 부문에서 민간 부문으로 옮기려 노력한다.
② 사생활에 관해 규제가 덜한 국가다.
③ 시장 경쟁의 효율성과 경제적 성과를 결정하는 데 있어서 개인의 역할을 강조한다.
④ ✓ 사회적 정의와 재분배를 어떤 대가를 치르더라도 보호하려 한다.

| 분석 | 첫 단락에서 신자유주의는 '그러므로 국가는 모든 대가를 치러서라도 이러한 자유를 지키기 위해 국가가 독점하고 있는 폭력 수단을 사용해야 한다.'고 언급했는데 이것은 자유를 지켜야 한다는 개념으로 ④의 사회적 정의와 재분배와 반대되는 말이다. 따라서 ④는 지문과 불일치한다.

50 "공유지의 비극"은 어떤 의미인가? 문맥상 의미, 표현

① 시장이 더 불완전해져서 사회적 불평등을 초래하는 경향
② ✓ 개인이 공공재를 무책임하게 이용하는 경향
③ 품질 향상 요인에 대한 투자를 기업들이 외면하는 경향
④ 규제받지 않는 시장교류에 대해 사회가 스스로를 보호하는 경향

| 분석 | 공유지의 비극은 '주인이 따로 없는 공동 방목장에선 농부들이 경쟁적으로 더 많은 소를 끌고 나오는 것이 이득이므로 그 결과 방목장은 곧 황폐화되고 만다'는 개념으로 그 의미는 누구나 자유롭게 사용할 수 있는 공공재는 사람들의 남용으로 쉽게 고갈될 수 있다는 것이다.

| 배경지식 | 신자유주의 (Neoliberalism): 자본주의 경제의 근본적 불안정성을 전제로 정부의 적극적 개입을 내세운 케인즈주의가 쇠퇴하면서 재등장한 신고전파 경제학 전통을 이어받은 이념으로 개방화, 자유화, 민영화, 탈규제, 탈복지 등을 내세운다. 신자유주의 이론은 1970년대 후반부터 국민경제에서든 국제경제에서든 국가나 정부 차원의 모든 인위적인 개입을 공격하면서 '자유 시장'의 논리를 설파하는 데에 성공했다.

[51-52] 2022 숭실대

| 정답 | 51 ② 52 ③

| 어휘 | combination ⓝ 조합, 결합 stagnation ⓝ 정체; 부진, 불경기 devastating ⓐ 대단히 파괴적인
inflation ⓝ 인플레이션, 통화 팽창; (물가 등의) 폭등
sustained ⓐ 지속된, 일관된 in tandem with (~와) 동시에[나란히] vice versa ⓐⓓ 반대로; 역 또한 같음
stable ⓐ 안정된 predictable ⓐ 예측할 수 있는
perfect storm (한꺼번에 여러 가지 안 좋은 일이 겹쳐) 더할 수 없이 나쁜 상황 root cause 근본 원인
household ⓝ 가정, 가구

전문해석

[A] 스태그플레이션(stagflation)은 스태그네이션(stagnation)과 인플레이션(inflation)이라는 단어의 합성어이다. 스태그플레이션은 물가 상승(인플레이션)과 더불어 느린 성장과 높은 실업률(경기 침체)로 특징지어지는 경제 상태를 설명한다. 이 용어는 1965년 초에 처음 등장했는데, 그때 영국 보수당 정치인인 이안 매클로드(Ian Madeod)가 하원에서 한 연설에서 다음과 같이 말했다: "우리는 현재 한쪽의 인플레이션이나 다른 쪽의 스태그네이션만을 겪고 있는 것이 아니라 둘 모두가 함께 있어 양쪽 세계 모두의 최악을 겪고 있습니다. 우리는 일종의 '스태그플레이션' 상황을 겪고 있고 현대적 용어들에서 역사가 실제로 만들어지고 있습니다."
[B] 〈처음에는, 많은 경제학자들은 스태그플레이션이 불가능하다고 믿었다.〉 결국 실업률과 인플레이션은 일반적으로 서로 반대 방향으로 움직이는 것이다. 그러나 1970년대의 '대 인플레이션' 시대가 결국 증명한 것처럼, 스태그플레이션은 현실에 존재하며 경제에 파괴적인 영향을 가할 수 있다.
[C] 스태그플레이션과 인플레이션은 관련이 있지만, 그것들을 혼동해서는 안 된다. 인플레이션이라는 용어는 시간이 지남에 따라 경제에서 일부가 아닌 모든 재화 및 용역의 평균 가격 수준이 지속적으로 상승하는 것을 일컫는다. 인플레이션은 통화 공급량이 경제가 재화 및 용역을 생산할 수 있는 것보다 더 빠른 속도로 증가할 때 발생한다.
스태그플레이션은 느린 경제 성장과 높은 실업률과 함께 인플레이션이 존재할 때 발생한다. 일반적으로 이런 경제 상황들은 함께 발생하지 않는다. 실업률과 인플레이션은 반비례로 연결되는 경향이 있다. 따라서 실업률이 증가하면 인플레이션은 대개 감소하고 그 반대의 경우도 사실이다. 물론 1970년대의 스태그플레이션이 보여 줬듯이, 이 관계가 항상 안정적이거나 예측 가능한 것은 아니다.
[D] 스태그플레이션은 경제적 병폐들의 완벽한 폭발이다: 느린 경제 성장, 높은 실업, 그리고 높은 물가. 경제학자들이 동의하는 스태그플레이션의 두 가지 근본 원인은 공급 충격과 재정 및 통화 정책이다. 가계에 있어서, 스태그플레이션은 사람들이 더 적은 돈을 벌면서 반면에, 음식과 의약품에서부터 주택과 소비재에 이르는 모든 것에 더 많은 돈을 소비한다는 것을 의미한다. 소비자 지출이 감소함에 따라, 경제에 가하는 전반적 효과를 악화시키면서 기업의 수익은 감소한다.

51 주어진 문장이 들어가기에 가장 적절한 곳은? 문장 삽입

처음에는, 많은 경제학자들은 스태그플레이션이 불가능하다고 믿었다.

① [A] ✓② [B]
③ [C] ④ [D]

| 분석 | 주어진 문장은 "경제학자들은 스태그플레이션이 불가능하다고 믿었다."는 내용인데, 이와 같은 내용이 나오는 부분에 삽입하는 것이 적절하다. [B] 다음에 스태그네이션과 인플레이션은 서로 반대 방향으로 움직인다고 했으므로, 경제학자들이 '스태그플레이션이 불가능하다고 생각한다'와 일맥상통하는 말이다. 따라서 주어진 문장은 [B]에 들어가야 적절하다.

52 다음 중 일치하지 않는 것은?? 내용 일치

① 물가 상승과 더불어 느린 성장과 높은 실업률은 스태그플레이션을 특징짓는다.
② 스태그플레이션은 1960년대 영국의 경제 상황을 설명하려고 만든 단어이다.
✓ ③ 스태그플레이션 동안 사람들은 더 적은 돈을 벌고 훨씬 더 적은 돈을 쓰는 경향이 있다.
④ 스태그플레이션의 주요 원인은 공급 충격과 재정 및 통화 정책이다.

| 분석 | 마지막 단락에서 "가계의 경우, 스태그플레이션은 사람들이 더 적은 돈을 벌지만 음식과 의약품에서부터 주택과 소비재에 이르는 모든 것에 더 많은 돈을 소비한다는 것을 의미한다."고 했으므로, 사람들이 더 적은 돈을 버는 것은 맞지만 지출은 늘어나게 되는 상황에 놓이게 되므로 ③이 글의 내용과 일치하지 않는다.

3강 사회 / 문화

01	①	02	②	03	③	04	④	05	①	06	②	07	①	08	②	09	③	10	④
11	③	12	③	13	②	14	①	15	④	16	③	17	②	18	③	19	③	20	④
21	①	22	④	23	①	24	②	25	②	26	④	27	③	28	①	29	③	30	②
31	②	32	④	33	①	34	①	35	②	36	②	37	①	38	③	39	④	40	④
41	①	42	⑤	43	②	44	④	45	②	46	⑤	47	①	48	②	49	③	50	①

[01-02] 2016 한국외대

| 정답 | 01 ① 02 ②

| 어휘 | **contain** ⓥ ~이 들어 있다   **encourage** ⓥ 격려[고무]하다, 용기를 복돋우다
commit ⓥ (죄·과실 따위를) 범하다   **flashpoint** ⓝ 인화점; 일촉즉발의 상황   **escalate** ⓥ 확대[증가]시키다
disagreement ⓝ 의견 충돌, 다툼, 불일치

전문해석

젊은이들은 폭력이 포함된 상황에서 살면서 폭력을 배운다. 할렘에서 젊은이들과 함께 일한 경험을 바탕으로 한 제프리 캐나다(Geoffrey Canada)의 주장은 이렇다. 그는 구성원들이 젊은이들의 폭력을 처벌하는 것 자체에 관심을 가지기보다는 사회 구성원들이 폭력을 조장하는 상황들을 예방하기 위해 노력해야 한다고 주장한다. 따라서, 그는 젊은이들이 폭력적이거나 범죄적인 행동을 하기 전에 그들의 욕구를 다루는 다양한 새로운 프로그램들을 옹호한다. 여기에는 갱단과 관련된 일촉즉발의 상황이 확대되는 것을 막기 위한 치안 경찰단을 만드는 것, 십 대들을 위한 일자리를 만들어 마약에 대한 수요를 줄이는 것, 대처 기술을 가진 사람들을 훈련시켜 아동과 배우자 학대를 예방하는 것, 언론에 나오는 폭력의 양을 줄이는 것, 그리고 십 대들이 권총을 사기 전에 시험을 보도록 하는 것이 포함된다. 이러한 방법들은 어린이들과 청소년들이 폭력에 노출되지 않도록 보장할 것이고, 따라서 폭력을 배우지 않을 것이다. 그는 가라테 강사지만, 대화와 중재를 통해 의견 차이를 해결하도록 젊은이들을 훈련시킨다. 그는 폭력이 매년 5,000명 이상의 미국 어린이들의 생명을 앗아 가고 있으며, ⓐ 상황이 바뀌지 않는 한, 이 숫자는 증가할 것이라고 지적한다.

01 윗글에 따르면, 다음 중 옳은 것은? 내용 일치

✓ 폭력을 보는 것은 아이들의 폭력을 조장한다.
② 권총의 소유권에 대한 제한은 불필요하다. 십 대들이 권총을 사기 전에 시험을 보는 등의 제한이 필요함
③ 젊은이들의 약물 사용에 대한 일반적인 접근 방식은 신뢰할 수 있다. 마약 수요를 줄여야 한다고만 언급함
④ 폭력적인 젊은이들은 심각한 결과에 직면해야 한다. 젊은이들을 처벌하는 것보다는 폭력을 조장하는 상황의 예방이 필요함

| 분석 | 본문 첫 문장에서 '젊은이들은 폭력이 포함된 상황에서 살면서 폭력을 배운다'고 했다. 게다가 본문에서 젊은이들의 욕구를 다루는 새로운 프로그램들을 소개했는데 그중 '언론에 나오는 폭력의 양을 줄이는 것'이 있었다. 따라서 폭력을 보는 것이 폭력을 조장하는 것과 관련이 있다는 것을 알 수 있으므로 보기 ①이 정답이다.

02 다음 중 ⓐ가 가리키는 것과 가장 가까운 것은? 밑줄 추론

① 부모와 청소년 사이의 의견 불일치
✓② 현재 미국 젊은이들이 심각한 상황
③ 갱단 간의 폭력충돌 방지 대책위원회 구성
④ 청년 실업과 약물 사용

| 분석 | 밑줄 친 ⓐ가 포함된 문장에서 매년 5천 명 이상의 미국 어린이들이 폭력 사건으로 목숨을 잃고 있다고 했으므로, things는 '미국의 어린이들이 처한 심각한 상황'으로 보는 것이 가장 적절하다. 정답은 보기 ②이다.

[03-04] 2011 단국대

| 정답 | 03 ③ 04 ④

| 어휘 |
muse on ~을 곰곰이 생각하다
organic ⓐ 유기(화학)의, 유기체[생물]의
metaphor ⓝ 은유
flee ⓥ 달아나다, 도망하다
artificial ⓐ 인공[인조]의, 거짓된
delude ⓥ 속이다
artifact ⓝ 인공물, 인공 유물
reborn ⓐ 다시 활발해진
apply ⓥ 적용하다, 응용하다
neighborhood ⓝ 근처, 인근, 이웃
anthill ⓝ 개미총[탑]
decay ⓝ 부패, 부식, 쇠퇴
plain ⓝ 평원, 평지
constraint ⓝ 제한, 통제
biology ⓝ 생물학
vital ⓐ 필수적인, 활력이 넘치는
unmake ⓥ 망치다, 부수다, 파괴하다

전문해석

과거부터 현재에 이르기까지 초기 도시들과 현재의 도시에 대해 생각할 때, 우리는 항상 도시가 인공물이라는 것을 기억해야 한다. 숲, 정글, 사막, 평원, 바다—유기적 환경은 태어나고 죽고 끝없이, 아름답게, 그리고 완전히 도덕적 제약이나 윤리적 통제 없이 다시 태어난다. 하지만 도시들은—우리가 생물학이나 자연으로부터 그들에게 적용하는 "산업이 달아나면 도시가 죽는다"; "이웃은 도시적 유기체의 필수 세포이다"와 같은 은유에도 불구하고—인공적이다. 자연은 절대로 도시를 만들어 본 적이 없고, 자연이 만들어 낸 도시처럼 보이게 하는 것—예를 들어, 개미집—은 단지 도시처럼 보일 뿐이다. 그것은 도시가 아니다. 인간은 (과거에) 도시를 만들었고, (지금도) 만들고, 오직 인간만이 도시를 죽이거나 죽게 한다. 그리고 인간은 도시를 만드는 것과 죽이는 것을 같은 방법으로—선택의 행위에 의해—한다. 우리는 다른 것들처럼 이것에 우리 자신을 속이는 것을 즐긴다. 우리는 우리의 운명을 완전히 결정하는 힘, 즉 도시가 탄생, 성장, 부패의 유기적 또는 생물학적 단계를 거치게 하는 자연적인 힘이 존재한다고 믿는 것을 즐긴다.

03 윗글의 주요 목적은 무엇인가? 글의 목적

① 독자가 자신의 행동을 바꾸도록 설득하는 것 행동보다는 인식의 변화를 설득하고 있음
② 도시와 마을의 차이를 설명하는 것 언급 안 함
✓③ 도시를 인간의 의도를 벗어나 성장하는 것으로 정의하는 것
④ 도시에 대한 대중의 불만의 원인을 파악하는 것 언급 안 함

| 분석 | 지문 첫 문장에서 저자는 '항상 도시가 인공물이라는 것을 기억해야 한다'고 서술했으며 글을 전개하며 그 이유에 대해 상세하게 설명하고 있다. 따라서 글의 주요 목적은 보기 ③이 가장 적절하다.

04 윗글에 따르면 왜 개미집은 도시와 다르게 정의되는가? 세부 내용 일치

① 그것은 도시 유기체의 필수 세포다.
② 그것은 어느 도시보다 훨씬 작은 규모로 존재한다.
③ 그것은 인간에 의해 무심코 파괴될 수 있다.
✓ ④ 그것은 상상력보다는 본능의 작품이다.

| 분석 | 지문에서 개미집은 '자연이 만들어 낸 도시처럼 보이게 하는 것'으로 서술했으므로 인공물인 도시와 다르다. 따라서 개미집은 도시와 달리 개미들이 '자연적' 혹은 '본능적'으로 만든 것이며 보기 ④가 정답으로 가장 적절하다.

[05-06] 2018 한양대

| 정답 | 05 ① 06 ②

| 어휘 |
preoccupation ⓝ 선점; 몰두[열중]해 있는 문제
secularism ⓝ 세속주의
collectivism ⓝ 집산주의(모든 농장이나 산업을 정부나 집단이 소유하는 정치 제도)
compensation ⓝ 보상
collective ⓐ 집단의
solidarity ⓝ 연대, 결속
homogeneous ⓐ 동종[동질]의
uniformity ⓝ 획일성, 균일성
division of labour 분업
substantial ⓐ (양·크기 등이) 상당한, 충분한
differentiation ⓝ 차별(의 인정), 구별
specify ⓥ (구체적으로) 명시하다
cohesion ⓝ 화합, 결합
interdependence ⓝ 상호 의존

전문해석

뒤르켐(Durkheim)의 중심 관심사 중 하나는 무엇이 사회를 하나로 결속시키는지에 대한 문제이다. 그의 대답은 이 사회적 ⓐ 응집력을 촉진하고 유지하는 데 있어 법의 중요한 역할을 지적한다. 그는 사회가 종교에서 세속주의로, 그리고 집단주의에서 개인주의로 발전함에 따라 법이 보상보다는 처벌에 덜 관심을 갖는다는 것을 보여 준다. 그러나 처벌은 사회적 연대가 유지되게 하는 집단의 도덕적 태도를 표현하는 데 중요한 역할을 한다. 그는 자신이 기계적 연대와 유기적 연대라고 부르는 것들을 구분한다. 전자는 가치관의 균일성을 가지고 있고 그 어떤 중요한 분업도 없는 단순하고 동질적인 사회에 존재한다. 이러한 복잡하지 않은 공동체들은 본질적으로 집단적인 경향이 있다. 그러나 노동 분업이 있는 선진 사회에는, 높은 수준의 ⓑ 상호 의존성이 존재한다. 거기에는 상당한 차별화가 있고, 집산주의는 개인주의로 대체된다. 그는 이러한 형태의 사회적 연대가 법에 반영되어 있다고 주장한다: 다양한 유형의 법을 분류하면 그것에 해당하는 다양한 유형의 사회적 연대를 찾을 수 있다. 뒤르켐에 따르면, 기계적 연대는 전통적이고 작은 규모의 사회에서 작동하지만, 유기적 연대는 개인들이 그들의 특정한 과업을 수행하기 위해 개인들이 상호의존하는 것에서 비롯된다.

05 ①

05 윗글의 제목으로 가장 적절한 것은? 제목

✓ ① 사회 연대의 유형, 사회의 유형
② 돌고 도는 것?: 법과 처벌 키워드 아님
③ 분업: 사회는 어떻게 발전해 왔는가 키워드 아님
④ 타협의 여지 마련: 연대와 개성 키워드 아님

| 분석 | 지문에서 뒤르켐은 무엇이 사회를 결속시키는지에 대한 문제에 관심을 가졌으며 '사회적 연대'를 '사회의 유형'에 따라 '기계적 연대'와 '유기적 연대'로 구분하여 그 차이를 설명했다. 따라서 글의 제목으로는 '사회 연대의 유형들과 관련된 사회의 유형들'이라고 볼 수 있으므로 보기 ①이 정답으로 가장 적절하다.

06 윗글의 빈칸 ⓐ, ⓑ에 들어갈 말로 가장 적절한 것은? 빈칸 추론

① 결합 – 다양성
② 응집력 – 상호 의존성 ✓
③ 연대 – 집산주의
④ 동질성 – 차별성

| 분석 | 빈칸 ⓐ 앞 지시사 'this'는 직전 내용에서 무엇을 지시하는지 추론할 수 있다. 빈칸이 포함된 문장의 직전 내용은 '무엇이 사회를 하나로 결속시키는지'에 관한 것으로 빈칸 ⓐ에는 보기 ①, ②, ③이 모두 정답으로 가능하다. 빈칸 ⓑ가 포함된 문장은 앞 문장과 역접되어 있으므로 직전 내용인 '기계적 연대'에 관련한 설명이 끝나고 역접되어 '유기적 연대'에 관한 설명이 이어짐을 확인할 수 있다. 빈칸 ⓑ에는 '유기적 연대'에 높은 수준의 무엇이 존재하는지를 추론하기 위해 빈칸 ⓑ 이후 문장들을 확인해 보면 지문의 마지막 문장에서 '유기적 연대는 개인들이 그들의 특정한 과업을 수행하기 위해 개인들이 상호 의존하는 것에서 비롯된다.'고 했다. 따라서 빈칸 ⓑ에는 '상호 의존성'이 들어가는 것이 가장 적절하다. 정답은 보기 ②이다.

| 배경지식 | 에밀 뒤르켐(Durkheim, Emile): 프랑스의 철학자이자 사회학자로, 사회학의 연구 방법에 대해 최초로 지시하고 적극적인 통계 사용을 통해 현대 사회학의 실증론적 기조를 창시

[07-08] 2019 서울여대

| 정답 | 07 ① 08 ②

| 어휘 |
preserve ⓥ 보존하다, 유지하다
fertile ⓐ (땅이) 비옥한, 기름진
strip ⓝ 길고 가느다란 조각[땅]
bank ⓝ 둑, 제방
flood ⓥ 물에 잠기다, 침수되다
stockpile ⓥ (대량으로) 비축하다
silo ⓝ 사일로(큰 탑 모양의 곡식 저장고)
cure ⓥ (병을) 고치다, (건조나 염장으로 육류 등을) 보존하다, 말리다
fermentation ⓝ 발효 (작용)
aversion ⓝ 반감, 혐오
domesticate ⓥ (동물을) 길들이다, 사육하다
pronounce ⓥ 발음하다, (공개적으로) 선언하다
carrier ⓝ 보균자, (병원체의) 매개체
leprosy ⓝ 나병, 한센병
social outcast 인생의 낙오자
tomb ⓝ 무덤
scavenge ⓥ (먹을 것 등을 찾아) 쓰레기 더미를 뒤지다
scraps ⓝ 먹다 남은 음식, 찌꺼기
revolt ⓥ 반란[봉기]을 일으키다, 들고일어나다
animal husbandry 축산[가축]학
antelope ⓝ 영양
fowl ⓝ 닭, 가금류
quail ⓝ 메추라기 (고기)
splay ⓥ (팔꿈치·다리 등을) 펼치다, 벌리다

전문해석

이집트인들은 확실히 음식을 대규모로 보존한 최초의 문명이었다. 나일강 양쪽 제방의 좁고 비옥한 지역은 그들의 주요 식량 공급원이었고, 나일강이 범람하지 못한 건조한 해는 재앙이 될 수 있었다. 이에 대비하기 위해, 이집트인들은 거대한 곡식 저장고에 곡물을 비축하는 것을 포함하여 그들이 할 수 있는 모든 방법으로 음식을 저장했다. 식량을 저장하는 것에 대한 이러한 집착은 절임과 발효에 대한 상당한 지식으로 이어졌다. 이집트인들이 돼지에 대한 혐오감이 없었다면, 아마도 이집트인들이 햄을 발명했을 것이다. 소금에 절인 고기와 돼지를 사육하는 방법을 알았기 때문이다. 그러나 이집트 종교 지도자들은 돼지를 나병의 매개체로 선언했고, 양돈 농부들을 사회적으로 왕따로 만들었고, 무덤 벽화에 그 동물을 절대로 묘사하지 않았다. 그들은 먹다 남은 음식들과 죽은 동물들을 먹기 위해 마을 주변을 뒤지는 하이에나들을 식육으로 사육하기 위해 노력했지만, 대부분의 이집트인들은 그런 동물을 먹는 생각에 분개했다. 이집트인들이 동물 사육에 실패한 다른 동물에는 영양과 가젤이 있다. 하지만 이집트인들은 오리, 거위, 메추라기, 비둘기, 펠리컨 등을 사육하는 데 성공했다. 고대의 벽화들은 새를 벌려서, 소금에 절이고, 큰 토기 항아리에 넣는 것을 보여 준다.

07 다음 중 윗글에서 주로 다루는 것은 무엇인가? 주제

☑ ① 고대 이집트의 식량 보존
② 고대 이집트의 음식과 벽화 '음식'은 너무 포괄적, '음식의 저장이나 보존'이 키워드
③ 이집트인의 동물 사육 키워드 아님
④ 이집트 문명에서 나일강의 중요성 키워드 아님

| 분석 | 지문에서는 '이집트인들의 식량 저장'을 소재로 하여 이집트에서 식량 저장의 기술이 왜 필요했는지를 서술하고 있다. 보기 ①의 '고대 이집트의 식량 보존'이 주제로 가장 적절하다.

08 윗글에 따르면 다음 중 이집트인에 대한 설명으로 옳은 것은? 세부 내용 일치

① 그들은 하이에나를 길들일 수 있었다. 하이에나를 사육하기 위해 노력했지만 그 동물을 먹는 것은 혐오감을 유발했기 때문에 실패함
☑ ② 그들은 고기를 소금에 절이는 방법을 알고 있었다.
③ 그들은 나일강의 홍수로 고통받았다. 건조한 해가 재앙이었음
④ 그들은 햄을 발명한 최초의 문명이었다. 돼지에 대한 혐오감이 없었다면 햄을 발명했을 것으로 가정함, 사실은 아님

| 분석 | 지문의 마지막 문장에서 고대 벽화를 통해 이집트인들이 고기를 소금에 절였다는 것을 확인할 수 있으므로 보기 ②가 정답이다.

[09-11] 2018 가천대

| 정답 | 09 ③   10 ④   11 ③

| 어휘 | minority ⓝ 소수, 소수집단, 미성년
ubiquity ⓝ (동시에) 도처에 존재함, 편재
pundit ⓝ 박식한 사람, 전문가
resentment ⓝ 분개, 분노
superfluous ⓐ 남는, 여분의, 과잉의
relative ⓐ 비교상의, 상대적인
disclose ⓥ 들추어내다, 폭로하다
homogenize ⓥ 균질화하다

provocatively ⓐⓓ 약이 올라서, 도발적으로
entrepreneurial ⓐ 기업가의
pit against ~와 맞붙이다, ~에 대항하게 하다
plight ⓝ 곤경, 궁지
exacerbate ⓥ 악화시키다
Caucasian ⓝ 백인
overwhelming ⓐ 압도적인
negligible ⓐ 무시해도 좋은, 사소한

shopkeeper ⓝ 가게 주인, 소매상인
make it (자기 분야에서) 성공하다
racism ⓝ 인종[민족] 차별주의
obscure ⓥ 보이지 않게 하다
hang out (~에서) 많은 시간을 보내다
misleading ⓐ 오해하기 쉬운
diversify ⓥ 다양화하다, 다채롭게 하다

전문해석

아시아계 미국인들은 점점 더 "모범적 소수민족"으로 간주되고 있다. 그들은 언론에서 대학 입학에 "지나치게, 심지어 도발적으로" 성공한 것으로 묘사되어 왔다. 아시아계 미국인 상점 주인들은 그들의 편재성과 기업가적 효율성에 대해 비판뿐만 아니라 칭찬도 받았다. 만약 아시아계 미국인들이 성공할 수 있다면, 많은 정치인들과 전문가들은 왜 아프리카계 미국인들은 성공할 수 없느냐고 묻는다. 이러한 비교들은 소수민족들을 서로 적대시하고 아시아계 미국인들에 대한 아프리카계 미국인들의 분노를 불러일으킨다. 희생자들이 인종 차별과 많은 젊은 아프리카계 미국인 노동자들을 불필요하게 만든 경제보다는 그들과 아시아계 미국인들 사이의 그들의 곤경에 대해 비난을 받고 있고, 결과적으로 그들과 아시아계 미국인들 사이의 관계를 ⓐ 악화시켰다. 09 ③
아시아계 미국인들에 대한 찬양은 현실을 가려 왔다. 예를 들어, 백인과 비교한 아시아계 미국인의 높은 수입에 대한 수치는 Ⓐ 오해의 소지가 있다. 대부분의 아시아계 미국인들은 캘리포니아, 하와이, 뉴욕—전국 평균보다 소득이 높고 생활비가 비싼 주들—에 살고 있다. 게다가, "모범적 소수민족"은 아시아계 미국인들을 Ⓑ 균질화하고 그들의 차이점을 숨긴다. 예를 들어, 수천 명의 베트남계 미국인 젊은이들이 대학에 다니는 반면, 다른 사람들은 모텔에서 살고 이스트 로스앤젤레스와 같은 곳의 당구장에서 놀고, 일부는 갱단에 가입한다.

09 다음 중 윗글의 제목으로 가장 적절한 것은? 제목

① 아시아계 미국인들의 다양한 성공 전략 성공 전략은 소개되지 않음
② 아시아계 미국인과 아프리카계 미국인의 차이 언급 안 함
③ ✓ 아시아계 미국인의 우월성이라는 해로운 통념
④ 대중 매체가 소수민족에 미치는 영향 언급 안 함

| 분석 | 지문에서는 "모범적 소수민족"으로 간주되는 아시아계 미국인들에 대한 묘사가 아프리카계 미국인들의 분노를 일으키는 한편 아시아계 미국인들의 관련한 수치에 오해의 소지가 있음을 서술하고 있다. 따라서 이 글의 제목으로는 보기 ③이 적절하다.

10 다음 중 밑줄 친 ⓐexacerbate와 의미가 가장 가까운 것은 무엇인가? 밑줄 추론

① 높이다, 향상시키다
② 강화하다, 통합하다
③ 복잡하게 하다
④ ✓ 악화시키다

| 분석 | 밑줄 친 단어 'exacerbate'는 '악화시키다'라는 의미가 있으므로 유사한 뜻으로는 보기 ④가 적절하다.

11 빈칸 Ⓐ와 Ⓑ에 들어갈 말로 가장 적절한 것은? 빈칸 추론

① 믿을 ~ 없는 – 공개하다
② 압도적인 – 억제하다
③ ✓ 오해의 소지가 있는 – 균질화하다
④ 무시할 수 있는 – 다양화하다

| 분석 | 지문 두 번째 단락의 첫 문장에서 '아시아계 미국인들에 대한 찬양은 현실을 가려 왔다.'고 서술한 뒤 그 예시로 빈칸이 포함된 문장이 왔다. 따라서 아시아계 미국인들의 높은 수입에 대한 수치도 현실을 가리는, 즉 오류나 오해의 소지가 있을 것이다. 따라서 빈칸 Ⓐ에는 보기 ①이나 ③이 적절하다. 이어서 빈칸 Ⓑ는 빈칸 이후의 and로 연결된 진술을 통해 추론이 가능한데, "모범적인 소수민족"이라는 이미지가 그들 사이의 차이를 가렸다면 그들은 그 이미지로 '균질화' 혹은 '동일시'되었을 것이다. 따라서 두 빈칸의 조건을 모두 만족시키는 보기 ③이 정답이다.

[12-14] 2011 고려대

| 정답 | 12 ③   13 ②   14 ①

| 어휘 |
descend ⓥ 내려오다, 내려가다
abstraction ⓝ 추상 (작용), 추상 개념
aristocracy ⓝ 귀족 (계급); 귀족 사회
empirical ⓐ 경험의, 경험적인, (이론보다는) 실제 관찰에 의한
dictate ⓥ 구술하다; 명령[지시]하다
manifest ⓥ (감정이나 태도를) 분명히 나타내다
generalization ⓝ 일반화, 보편화, 귀납
deduce ⓥ (결론이나 진리 등을) 연역하다, 추론하다
circular reasoning 순환 논증
sparring ⓝ 논쟁
rhetoric ⓝ 수사, 수사학, 화려한 문체

전문해석

문화, 혹은—덜 전문적인 용어로—전통은 사회에서 함께 사는 개인들의 외부에 혹은 그들로부터 독립적으로 존재하는 것이 아니다. 문화적 가치는 역사의 흐름에 영향을 주기 위해 하늘에서 내려오는 것이 아니다. 그것들은 관찰자에 의한 추상화로, 사람들의 집단들이 다른 상황에서나 시간이 지남에 따라 또는 둘 다에 따라 행동하는 방식의 특정 유사성에 대한 관찰에 기초한다. 비록 어떤 사람이 종종 그러한 추상화에 기초하여 짧은 시간 동안 집단과 개인이 행동하는 방식에 대해 정확한 예측을 할 수 있지만, 그들은 그 추상화 자체로 그 행동을 설명하지 않는다. 문화적 가치의 관점에서 행동을 설명하는 것은 순환 논증에 관여된 것이다. 만약 우리가 지주 귀족들이 상업적인 사업에 저항한다는 것을 알게 된다면, 우리는 귀족들이 과거에도 그렇게 했다거나 심지어 그러한 활동에 적대적이게 만드는 것은 특정 전통을 가졌기 때문이라고 진술함으로써 이 사실을 설명하지 않는다: 문제는 어떤 과거와 현재의 경험에서 그런 관점이 생겨나고 유지되는가를 결정하는 것이다. 만약 문화가 경험적인 의미를 갖는다면, 그것은 인간이 사회의 일원으로서 획득한 특정한 방식으로 행동하는 경향으로서 인간의 정신에 심어진 것이다.

12 ③

---

12 윗글의 제목으로 가장 적절한 것은? `제목`

① 변화에 직면한 전통 수행 `키워드 아님`
② 인간의 정신은 문화에 의해 어떻게 좌우되는가 `너무 포괄적`
✓ ③ 문화적 가치와 사회적 행동의 상관관계
④ 문화적 가치: 복원 및 보존 `키워드 아님`

| 분석 | 지문에서는 문화적 가치가 사람들이 집단에서 행동하는 방식의 유사성과 관련이 있음을 서술하고 있다. 따라서 정답은 보기 ③이다.

---

13 다음 중 "문화"에 대해 추론할 수 <u>없는</u> 것은? `세부 내용 비추론`

① 그것은 사회 구성원들과 상호 의존적이다.
✓ ② 그것은 다수의 가치와 믿음에 의해 지배된다.
③ 그것은 행동에 영향을 미치는 마음에서 나타난다.
④ 그것은 관찰자들에 의해 추론된 일반화로 구성되어 있다.

| 분석 | 지문에 따르면 문화적 가치는 사람들이 행동하는 방식의 유사성을 관찰자가 추상화시킨 것이다. 따라서 ②는 추론할 수 없는 진술이다.

---

14 빈칸을 가장 잘 채우는 것을 고르시오. `빈칸 추론`

✓ ① 순환 논증
② 말싸움
③ 열띤 토론
④ 보수적인 미사여구

| 분석 | 빈칸 뒤에 언급되는 지주 귀족들의 예시에서 추론의 근거를 찾도록 한다. 문화적 가치란 사람들의 행동의 유사성을 관찰하고 그것을 추상화한 개념이며 이 추상화한 개념에 따라 행동을 설명한다면 판단의 원인과 결과가 같은 것이 된다. 증명하고자 하는 결론을 다시 전제로 하여 결론을 증명하는 것을 이른바 '순환 논증'이라 한다. 따라서 정답은 ①이다.

[15-16] 2015 고려대

| 정답 | 15 ④ 16 ③

| 어휘 | intersperse ⓥ 흩뿌리다, (~ 속에) 배치하다　　　　　　　　　　marginalize ⓥ 무시하다
sectoral ⓐ 부채꼴의, 구역의　　　disparity ⓝ 불일치, 격차
lose ground 지지[인기]를 잃다, 약세를 보이다　　　　　　　　　take advantage of ~을 이용하다

전문해석

세계화는 고르지 못한 현상이다. 그것의 영향은 공간, 시간, 사회 계층, 그리고 우리 삶의 측면들에 따라 다르다. 우리는 세계화를 모든 것을 휩쓰는 파도가 아니라, 몇몇 부유한 일부 지역들 그리고 소외된 지역과 사람들로 퍼져 있는 세계적 차원의 연결망을 가진 마치 표범의 점 패턴처럼 개념화할 필요가 있다. 주변화는 세계화만큼 발생할 수 있다. 세계주의에 대한 대중적인 담론은 가난과 소외의 바다보다는 (부유한) 섬들을 과장했다.

세계화의 불균등한 본질은 지리적 불균등, 사회적 불균등, 부문별 불균등의 세 가지 방식으로 발생한다. 지리적 측면에서 세계화의 불균등한 과정은 선진국과 개발도상국, 호황 지역과 쇠퇴 지역, 세계적 도시와 및 비세계적인 도시 간의 격차에서 관찰될 수 있다. 자본주의의 지역적 발전에는 항상 승자와 패자가 있었지만, 지금은 승자와 패자 사이의 불평등(국가, 지역, 도시)이 <u>악화되고 있다</u>. 더 세계화된 곳은 세계화 과정을 이용할 수 있는 훨씬 더 나은 기회를 가지고 있는 데 반하여, 덜 세계화된 곳은 상대적으로 그리고 때로는 절대적으로 그 입지를 잃고 있다.

15 다음 중 윗글에서 유추할 수 있는 것은 무엇인가? 　내용 추론

① 세계화로 인해 지금까지 적대적인 부문 간에 자원을 공유하여 두 부문의 일관된 개선을 도모하고 있다.　언급 안 함
② 빈곤의 악화는 이전에 소외되었던 지역에 발전을 가속화하는 자극과 동기를 부여할 수 있다.　호황 지역과 쇠퇴 지역의 불균형이 관찰되며 지역 발전 가속화 언급 안 함
③ 세계화는 세계적으로 삶의 질이 향상될 수 있도록 먼 지역의 경제 발전 정도를 규제한다.　규제에 관한 언급 안 함
✔ 세계화에 대한 논의는 종종 문화적, 경제적 불이익의 광범위한 분산이 아니라 번영과 진보의 지역 집중을 강조했다.

| 분석 | 지문은 '불균등한 본질을 가진 세계화'를 소재로 세계화의 부정적인 측면을 서술하고 있다. 이어서 두 번째 단락에서도 3가지 방식으로 발생하는 세계화의 불균등한 본질에 대해 자세히 설명하고 있다. 따라서 정답은 보기 ④이다.

16 빈칸을 가장 잘 채우는 것을 고르시오. 　빈칸 추론

① 개선된
② 제외된
✔ 악화된
④ 유화된

| 분석 | 빈칸 직후 문장, 즉 지문의 마지막 문장에서는 더 세계화된 곳과 덜 세계화된 곳의 불균등한 상황을 설명하고 있으므로 빈칸에는 승자와 패자 사이의 불평등에 대해 부정적 표현이 들어가야 할 것이다. 따라서 보기 ③이 정답이다.

| 배경 지식 | 세계화(Globalization): 정치, 경제, 문화 등의 사회 여러 분야에서 국가 간의 교류가 증대하여 개인과 사회 집단이 하나의 지구인 공동체로 나아가는 것

[17-18] 2018 중앙대

| 정답 | 17 ②   18 ③

| 어휘 | misfortune ⓝ 불운, 불행, 재난
combat ⓥ ~와 싸우다
candid ⓐ 정직한, 솔직한
inflict ⓥ (타격이나 상처를) 주다, 입히다
see to it that 반드시 ~하도록 조처하다
stupidity ⓝ 우둔, 어리석음
progress ⓥ 진전을 보이다, 나아가다
mortal ⓐ 죽음을 면할 수 없는, 치명적인
malevolence ⓝ 악의, 적의, 해칠 마음

전문해석

인간의 불행은 두 부류로 나눌 수 있다: 첫째는, 비인간적인 환경에 의해 야기되는 것이고, 둘째는 다른 사람들에 의해 야기되는 것이다. 인류의 지식과 기술이 발전함에 따라, 두 번째 부류의 불행은 지속적으로 전체에서 차지하는 비율이 증가했다. 예를 들어, 옛날에는, 기근은 자연적인 원인에 의한 것이었고, 사람들이 그것과 싸우기 위해 최선을 다했지만, 그들 중 많은 수가 기아로 죽었다. 현재 세계의 많은 부분이 여전히 기근의 위협에 직면해 있지만, 비록 자연적인 원인이 그 상황에 기여했더라도, 주요 원인은 인간이다.

오랫동안 세계의 문명국들은 서로 죽이기 위해 최선의 에너지를 쏟아 왔기 때문에, 그들이 갑자기 서로를 살려 두는 것으로 전환하는 것이 어렵다는 것을 알게 되었다. ⓐ 인간의 최악의 적은 이제 인간이다. 자연은, 사실, 여전히 우리가 죽을 수밖에 없게 하지만, 의학의 발전과 함께 사람들이 삶을 충분히 누릴 때까지 사는 것이 점점 더 흔해질 것이다. 우리는 영원히 살기를 바라고 하늘의 끝없는 기쁨을 기대한다. 하지만 사실, 만약 당신이 더 이상 젊지 않은 솔직한 사람에게 질문을 한다면, 그는 이 세상의 삶을 맛본 후, 다른 세상에서 "새로운 소년"으로 다시 시작하고 싶지 않다고 말할 가능성이 매우 높다. 따라서 미래를 위해, 인류가 고려해야 할 가장 중요한 악은 어리석음이나 악의 또는 둘 다를 통해 서로에게 가하는 악이라고 생각할 수 있다.

---

17 윗글의 빈칸 ⓐ에 들어갈 말로 가장 적절한 것은? [빈칸 추론]

① 자연의 수호자
☑ ② 인간의 최악의 적
③ 환경의 벗
④ 문명의 창조자

| 분석 | 지문 두 번째 단락의 첫 문장에서 '오랫동안 세계의 문명국들은 서로 죽이기 위해 최선의 에너지를 쏟아 왔기 때문에, 그들이 갑자기 서로를 살려 두는 것으로 전환하는 것이 어렵다'고 했다. 이 문장에 따르면 인간들은 서로를 죽이려 하는 적으로 여긴다. 따라서 정답은 보기 ②이다.

---

18 윗글의 내용과 맞지 않는 것은? [내용 불일치]

① 인간 스스로가 만들어 낸 인간의 문제는 다른 모든 문제를 능가한다.
② 비록 우리 모두가 언젠가는 죽어야 하지만, 의학은 사람들이 전보다 더 오래 사는 것을 가능하게 했다.
☑ ③ 다른 세상에서 새로운 삶을 다시 시작할 수 있는 기회가 주어진다면 거절할 사람은 없다.
④ 미래의 인간에게 가장 중요한 문제는 아마도 그의 악의와 지혜의 부족 때문에 그 자신일 것이다.

| 분석 | 지문 두 번째 단락의 다섯 번째 문장에서 '만약 당신이 더 이상 젊지 않은 솔직한 사람에게 질문을 한다면, 그는 이 세상의 삶을 맛본 후, 다른 세상에서 "새로운 소년"으로 다시 시작하고 싶지 않다고 말할 가능성이 매우 높다.'고 했다. 따라서 보기 ③은 글의 내용과 일치하지 않는다.

[19-20] 2020 성균관대

| 정답 | 19 ③   20 ④

| 어휘 |
condemned ⓐ 비난받은, 유죄를 선고받은, 사형수의
hanging ⓝ 교수형
strangulation ⓝ 교살(목을 졸라서 죽임)
respectability ⓝ 존경할 만함, 존경할 만한 사회적 지위
glamorous ⓐ 매혹적인
barbarism ⓝ 야만, 미개, 만행
indelible ⓐ 지울 수 없는, 씻을 수 없는
unseemly ⓐ (모양이) 보기 흉한
decapitation ⓝ 목 베기, 참수
instantaneous ⓐ 즉시[즉석]의, 순간적인
direct current ⓝ (전기의) 직류
edge ⓝ 가장자리, 우위, 유리함
execute ⓥ 처형하다, 실행하다
botch ⓥ (서투른 솜씨로) 망치다
electrocution ⓝ 감전사
devoid ⓐ ~이 전혀 없는
alternating current ⓝ (전기의) 교류

전문해석

19세기에 미국은 사형수를 처형하는 일반적인 방법인 교수형에 반감을 가지게 되었다. 교수형은 종종 공공장소에서 집행되었고, 구경꾼들 사이에서 폭동과 다른 꼴사나운 행동을 자주 이끌었다. 교수형은 또한 종종 서툴게 집행되어 천천히 목이 졸리거나 목이 잘리는 결과를 낳았다. 사형제도에 반대하는 사람들은 교수형이 잔인하고 야만적이라고 주장함으로써 지지자들을 얻었다. 사형 집행에 대한 사회적 지위를 회복하기 위해, 사형 제도의 지지자들은 전기사형의 아이디어를 생각해 냈다. <mark>전기는 새롭고 매혹적인 기술이었다. 그것은 무엇보다도 현대적이었다.</mark> 동시에, 그것은 사람들을 불안하게 만들었다. 미국은 이제 막 주요 도시들의 전력망을 연결하기 시작했고, 비록 전등의 이점이 모두에게 명백했지만, 아무도 그것이 얼마나 안전한지 확신하지 못했다. <mark>단두대(너무 피투성이인)</mark>에서 모르핀 과다복용(너무 쾌락적인)까지 처형 방법을 조사한 후, 뉴욕주 의회에 의해 임명된 위원회는 1888년에 <mark>즉각적이고 고통이 없으며 모든 야만성이 없을 것이라고 기대되는 전기사형의 사용을 권고했다.</mark> 전기사형에 대하여 위원회를 설득한 사람은 미국의 가장 유명한 발명가인 토머스 에디슨(Thomas Edison)이었다. 에디슨이 전기사형을 추천한 것에 있어서 주된 관심사는 미국의 전력망을 구축하는 데 그의 주요 경쟁자인 조지 웨스팅하우스(George Westinghouse)의 평판을 떨어뜨리는 것이었다. 에디슨의 회사는 직류를 사용했다. 웨스팅하우스의 회사는 교류를 사용했다. 에디슨은 사형수를 죽이는 가장 좋은 새로운 방법이 전기사형이라고 주장했을 뿐만 아니라, 웨스팅하우스의 교류가 자신의 직류보다 더 나을 것이라고 주장했다. 즉, 그의 전기사형에 대한 지지는 <mark>마케팅 전략</mark>이었다. 에디슨은 사형 집행을 위해 교류를 사용하는 것이 대중의 마음속에서 교류를 죽음과 영원히 연관시키고, 경쟁 산업에서 우위를 점할 수 있기를 바랐다.

---

19 윗글에 따르면, 다음 중 사형 집행 방법으로 전기사형을 채택한 이유가 아닌 것은? 세부 내용 불일치

① 인간적이다
② 빠르다
✓③ 저렴하다
④ 현대적이다
⑤ 깨끗하다

| 분석 | 지문에서 전기사형을 하는 이유로 사형수들을 전기사형 방법으로 처형해야 하는 이유가 '즉각적이고 고통이 없으며 모든 야만성이 없을 것'이라 했다. 그러나 집행 비용과 관련한 이유는 지문에 열거되지 않았으므로 보기 ③이 정답이다.

---

20 다음 중 빈칸에 들어갈 말로 가장 적절한 것은? 빈칸 추론

① 종교적 결정
② 과학적 추론
③ 정치적 항의
✓④ 마케팅 전략
⑤ 도덕적 딜레마

| 분석 | 빈칸이 포함된 문장의 직후 내용, 즉 지문의 마지막 문장에서 '에디슨은 사형 집행을 위해 교류를 사용하는 것이 대중의 마음 속에서 교류를 죽음과 영원히 연관시키고, 경쟁 산업에서 우위를 점할 수 있기를 바랐다'고 서술했다. 이것은 미국의 전력망을 구축하는 데 있어서 자신의 경쟁사인 웨스팅하우스의 교류 전기를 대중에게 죽음을 유발할 수 있는 것으로 인식시켜 자사의 직류 전기를 더 사용하도록 하기 위한 전략으로 보인다. 따라서 '사업상의 이익'과 관련된 보기 ④가 정답이다.

[21-24] 2013 서강대

| 정답 | 21 ① 22 ④ 23 ① 24 ②

| 어휘 |
manifold ⓐ (다종)다양한, 여러 가지의
punctuality ⓝ 시간[기간] 엄수
reciprocal ⓐ 상호의, 호혜적인
externality ⓝ 외부적임, 형식주의
be conducive to ~에 공헌[이바지]하다
seek ⓥ 구하다, 추구하다
brainwashing ⓝ 세뇌
reticence ⓝ 과묵, 말수가 적음

agglomeration ⓝ 덩어리, 응집
break down 고장나다, 실패하다
superficial ⓐ 표면상의, 피상적인
be bound up with ~와 밀접한 관계가 있다, ~에 의존하다
exclusion ⓝ 제외, 배제
schematically ⓐ 개략적으로, 도식적으로
intransigence ⓝ 타협하지 않음

intertwine ⓥ (~와) 얽히다
inextricable ⓐ 탈출할[헤어날] 수 없는
banal ⓐ 평범한, 진부한
sovereign ⓐ 주권이 있는, 독립적인
indoctrination ⓝ 주입, 세뇌
hirsute ⓐ 털이 많은

전문해석

전형적인 대도시 거주자들의 관계와 관심사는 매우 다양하고 복잡해서, 특히 그러한 차별화된 관심사를 가진 많은 사람들의 ⓐ 집합체의 결과로, 그들의 관계와 활동은 서로 얽히고설켜 다원적인 유기체로 이어진다. 이러한 사실을 고려할 때, 약속과 수행에서 가장 정확한 시간 엄수의 부족은 사회 전체를 헤어날 수 없는 혼란으로 붕괴시킬 것이다. 이러한 이유로 도시 생활의 기술은 일반적으로 모든 활동과 상호 관계가 모든 주관적 요소를 초월하는 확고하게 고정된 시간의 틀 안에서 가장 정확한 방식으로 조직되고 조정되지 않는다고 상상할 수 없다. 그러나 여기에도 일반적으로 이 논의의 전체 과제인 결론이 나온다. 즉, 아무리 표면적인 수준으로 제한되어 있더라도 모든 사건은 깊이 있는 영혼과 즉시 접촉하며, 가장 진부한 외부적인 것들도 결국 삶의 의미와 스타일에 관한 최종 결정과 결부되어 있다. 도시 생활의 복잡성과 확장성에 의해 요구되는 시간 엄수, 예측 가능성, 그리고 ⓑ 정확성은 그것의 자본주의적이고 지적인 특성과 가장 밀접하게 연관되어 있을 뿐만 아니라 삶의 내용에 영향을 주고 비합리적이고 본능적이며 독립적인 인간적 특성 그리고 삶의 형태를 일반적으로 외부에서 도식적으로 정확한 형태에서 받아들이려 하는 대신에, 내부에서부터 삶의 형태를 결정하는 것을 추구하는 충동들을 배제하는 데 도움이 된다.

21 윗글의 논리에 따르면, 도시 생활을 가장 덜 특징짓는 것은 무엇인가? 세부 내용 불일치
☑ 대류 오븐 시간 엄수, 예측 가능성, 정확성과는 관련 없음
② 인터넷
③ 지하철
④ 휴대 전화

| 분석 | 지문의 마지막 문장에서 도시 생활의 복잡성과 확장성에 의해 요구되는 것들은 '시간 엄수, 예측 가능성, 그리고 정확성'이 있다. 보기 중 이러한 특징에 해당되지 않는 것은 ①이다.

22 윗글에 따르면, 도시 생활을 가장 잘 특징짓는 것은 무엇인가? 세부 내용 일치
① 치열한 경쟁
② 자본주의
③ 현대의 기술
☑ 시간 엄수

| 분석 | 지문의 두 번째 문장에서 '약속과 수행에서 가장 정확한 시간 엄수의 부족은 사회 전체를 헤어날 수 없는 혼란으로 붕괴시킬 것이다.'라고 했다. 따라서 시간이나 기간을 엄수하는 것이 대도시 생활의 가장 중요한 특징이므로 보기 ④가 정답이다.

---

23 ⓐ 'agglomeration'의 동의어는 무엇인가? 밑줄 추론

☑ ① 무리　　② 세뇌
③ 세뇌　　④ 교육

| 분석 | 밑줄 친 ⓐ agglomeration은 '덩어리' 혹은 '응집'이라는 의미를 가진다. 따라서 보기 ①이 정답으로 가장 적절하다.

---

24 빈칸 Ⓐ에 가장 적절한 단어를 고르시오. 빈칸 추론

① 비타협적인 태도　　☑ 정확성
③ 털이 많은　　　　　④ 말수가 적음

| 분석 | 지문에서 빈칸 Ⓐ는 주어 자리로 앞선 두 명사와 순접으로 연결되어 있다. 따라서 punctuality나 calculability와 유사한 의미의 표현이 들어가야 할 것이므로 보기 ②가 정답이다.

[25-27] 2014 서울여대

| 정답 | 25 ②　26 ④　27 ③

| 어휘 |
unchecked ⓐ 억제[저지]되지 않은　　humanitarian ⓐ 인도주의의, 박애주의의　　sentiment ⓝ 감정, 정서
misfortune ⓝ 불운, 불행　　charity ⓝ 자애, 자비, 자선　　neglected ⓐ 방치된, 도외시된
unconscientious ⓐ 비양심적인, 지조가 없는　　guardian ⓝ 관리인, 감시인, 보호자

전문해석

다음 2세기 동안 가족은 어떻게 발전될 것 같은가? 우리는 말할 수 없지만, 억제하지 않으면 특정한 결과를 가져올 가능성이 있는 특정한 힘에 주목할 수 있다. 현대 문명 사회에는 가족을 약화시키는 경향이 있는 특정한 것들이 있다. 그들 중 가장 중요한 것은 아이들에 대한 인도주의적 정서이다. 점점 더 많은 사람들이 아이들이 부모의 불행이나 심지어 죄로 인해 고통을 받기보다는 도움을 받아야 한다고 느끼게 되었다. 성경에서 많은 고아들은 항상 매우 슬프고, 그래서 의심의 여지가 없이 과거에도 그랬지만 요즘은 그(고아)는 다른 아이들처럼 고통을 거의 겪지 않는다. 국가나 자선 기관이 방치된 아이들에게 상당히 적절한 보살핌을 제공하는 경향이 증가할 것이고, 결과적으로 아이들은 비양심적인 부모나 보호자들에 의해 점점 더 방치될 것이다. 점차 공적 자금에서 소외된 아이들을 돌보는 비용이 너무 커져서 형편이 좋지 않은 모든 사람들이 그들의 아이들을 국가에 맡기는 기회를 이용할 수 있는 매우 강력한 유인책이 될 것이다. 아마도 이것은 학교 교육과 마찬가지로 사실상 특정 경제 수준 이하의 모든 사람들에 의해 결국 이루어질 것이다.

---

25 윗글에 따르면, 어린이에 대한 인도주의적 정서는 _____. 세부 내용 일치

① 부모들이 그들의 아이들에게 너무 많은 돈을 쓰게 함으로써 가족을 약화시킬 것이다 (형편이 좋지 않은 부모들이 아이들을 국가에 맡김)
☑ ② 결국 부모나 보호자들에 의해 아이들을 점점 더 방치하게 만들 것이다
③ 국가가 가난하거나 죄 많은 부모로부터 아이들을 강제로 빼앗도록 이끌 것이다 (강제로 빼앗는 것은 언급 안 함)
④ 국가 재정 위기를 야기할 것이고 심지어 국가 파산을 초래할 것이다 (국가 파산은 언급 안 함)

| 분석 | 지문의 여섯 번째 문장에서 저자는 '국가나 자선 기관이 방치된 아이들에게 상당히 적절한 보살핌을 제공하는 경향이 증가할

것이고, 결과적으로 아이들은 비양심적인 부모나 보호자들에 의해 점점 더 방치될 것이다.'라고 했다. 즉 국가의 보살핌이 역설적으로 아이들의 방치를 부추길 수도 있으므로 보기 ②가 정답이다.

---

26 저자는 _____을 보여 주기 위해 성경을 언급한다. 세부 내용 일치
① 과거 고아와 다른 아이들의 생활 환경의 유사성
② 현재 고아들과 다른 아이들의 생활 조건의 차이
③ 과거와 현재 고아들의 생활 환경의 유사성
✓ ④ 과거와 현재 고아들의 생활 환경의 차이

| 분석 | 지문에서 언급한 성격에 묘사된 고아들은 과거 고아들의 모습을 설명하기 위해 인용되었다. 그러나 이어지는 서술에서 내용이 역접되며 요즘 고아들의 고통은 경감된 것으로 서술했으므로 성경을 인용한 목적은 과거와 현재 고아들의 환경 차이를 보여 주기 위한 것이다. 따라서 보기 ④가 정답으로 가장 적절하다.

---

27 다음 중 윗글에서 암시하는 것은 무엇인가? 내용 추론
① 현재 육아 부담은 전적으로 국가와 공공기관이 부담하고 있다. 전적으로 부담하는 것은 아님
② 미래에, 대부분의 부모들은 그들의 아이들에게 적절한 보살핌을 줄 정도로 교육을 잘 받을 것이다. 언급 안 함
✓ ③ 현재, 국가는 일정한 경제 수준 이하의 가정에서 아이들을 교육하는 것에 대한 책임을 진다.
④ 미래에는, 실질적으로 모든 부모들이 그들의 교육뿐만 아니라 그들의 보살핌을 위해 그들의 아이들을 국가에 넘겨줄 것이다. 모든 부모들로 일반화할 수 없음

| 분석 | 지문 마지막 문장에서 현재 국가가 공적 자금에서 소외된 아이들을 돌보고 있고 미래에 그 비용이 계속 커질 것을 예상하고 있음을 알 수 있다. 마지막 부분에서 '아마도 이것은 학교 교육과 마찬가지로 사실상 특정 경제 수준 이하의 모든 사람들에 의해 결국 이루어질 것이다.'라고 했으므로 현재 국가가 소외된 아이들의 교육에 책임을 지고 있다는 보기 ③이 추론 가능한 진술이다.

[28-29] 2013 중앙대

| 정답 | 28 ① 29 ③

| 어휘 |
conformity ⓝ (규칙·관습 등에) 따름, 순응(성)
instruction ⓝ 설명, 지시
norm ⓝ 기준, 규범
vicious ⓐ 사악한, 악덕한, 사나운
magnify ⓥ (렌즈 등으로) 확대하다, 크게 보이게 하다; 과장하다
abusive ⓐ 모욕적인, 폭력적인, 학대하는
simulate ⓥ 가장하다, 흉내 내다
unruly ⓐ 제멋대로 구는, 제어하기 어려운
mock ⓐ 모의의, 가짜의
enrage ⓥ 격분하게 만들다
accord ⓥ 일치하다, (권위 등을) 부여하다
pretense ⓝ 구실, 핑계, 거짓

전문해석

사회적 순응을 연구하기 위해, 필립 짐바르도(Philip Zimbardo)와 크레이그 해니(Craig Haney)는 1977년 신문에 모의 감옥 실험에 참여할 지원자들을 모집하는 광고를 냈다. 지원자들은 무작위로 "죄수"와 "교도관" 역할을 할당받았다. 두 그룹 모두 스탠퍼드 대학 심리학 건물의 지하에 배치되어 최소한의 지시를 받았다. 그들은 할당된 역할을 맡도록 지시받았고, 교도관의 일은 "법과 질서를 유지하는 것"이었다. 불과 몇 시간 만에, 한 그룹의 행동은 다른 그룹의 행동과 극명하게 구별되었다. 교도관들은 최대의 보안시설이 있는 감옥의 교도관들의 전형적인 행동 패턴과 태도를 채택했고, 그들 대부분은 폭력적이고 공격적이 되었다. 비록 죄수들의 일부는 교도관들에게 화를 냈지만, 대부분의 죄수들은 수동적이고, 의존적이며, 우울해졌다. 죄수들 사이의 고통이 너무 커서 한 명은 36시간 이내에 석방되어야 했고, 다른 몇몇 죄수들도 6일 후 2주간의 실험이 끝나기 전에 석방되어야 했다.

전형적인 사회 규범이 두 집단의 행동을 통제했다. 교도관들은 그들이 역할을 모방하고 질서를 유지하기 위해 필요하다고 믿는 방식을 채택했다. 교도관들의 학대 대상이었던 재소자들은 교도소 생활에 대한 이미지와 일치하는 태도를 취했다. 두 그룹들이 서로 적대적이 되면서, 각각은 상대방의 행동을 강화했다. 죄수들은 교도관들이 비열하고 악랄하기를 기대하고 그에 따라 그들을 대했다. 교도관들은 죄수들이 반항적이라고 예상했고, 제멋대로 행동을 하는 것을 막기 위해 행동했다. 가식적인 상황은 참여자들의 지각을 통해 관련된 모든 사람들의 감정과 행동에 실질적인 영향을 미쳤다. 이 실험이 보여 주듯이, 사회 규범에 순응하는 것은 단순히 자신의 집단으로부터 오는 사회적 압력의 결과가 아니다. 사회의 다른 집단의 영향은 순응하는 압력을 증가시킨다.

29 ③
28 ①

28 윗글의 제목으로 가장 적절한 것은? 제목
① 순응이 사회적 행동에 미치는 영향 ✓
② 새로운 환경에서의 행동 변화 키워드 없음
③ 정형화된 사회 규범의 유효성
④ 수감자들의 심리적 불안 키워드 없음

| 분석 | 지문의 도입부에서 '사회적 순응'의 실험 연구가 글의 소재임을 확인할 수 있다. 또한 지문 마지막 문장에 이르기까지 실험 결과를 상세하게 서술하고 있으므로 보기 ①이 가장 적절한 제목이다.

29 윗글의 내용과 일치하는 것은? 내용 일치
① 집단 내에서 순응해야 하는 사회적 압력은 다른 집단과의 접촉에 의해 완화된다. 다른 집단과의 접촉에 의해 각각은 상대방의 행동을 강화함
② 죄수 그룹은 지시 때문에 수동적인 척했다. 죄수들은 실제로 수동적, 의존적, 우울해짐
③ 참가자들은 전형적인 사회 규범에 따라 행동했다. ✓
④ 순응은 상황이 악화되는 것을 막았다. 순응으로 인한 죄수들 사이의 고통이 너무 컸음

| 분석 | 두 번째 단락의 첫 문장에서는 '전형적인 사회 규범이 두 집단의 행동을 통제했다.'고 했다. 따라서 보기 ③이 정답으로 적절하다.

[30-32] 2020 홍익대

| 정답 | 30 ② 31 ② 32 ④

| 어휘 | **institution** ⓝ 기관, 단체; (특정 집단 사이에서 오랫동안 존재해 온) 제도, 관습
legitimate ⓐ 합법의, 적법의
heritage ⓝ 상속재산, 유산, 전통
dominant ⓐ 지배적인, 유력한
manipulate ⓥ (교묘하게 사람·여론을) 조종하다, 조작하다
giftedness ⓝ 영재성
affinity ⓝ 친밀감
conserve ⓥ 보존하다, 보호하다
habitus ⓝ 습관, 버릇; 체질
scholastic ⓐ 학교[대학]의
meritocracy ⓝ 실력[능력]주의, 실력자[엘리트]층
reproduce ⓥ 재생하다, 재현하다, 재연하다
criterion ⓝ (판단이나 결정을 위한) 기준
familiarity ⓝ 친밀, 친숙, 친교
hierarchy ⓝ (사회나 조직 내의) 계급 제도, 지배층, 체계
objectify ⓥ 객관화하다, 구체화하다, 구상화하다
reproduction ⓝ 재생, 재생산, 재현
aptitude ⓝ 경향, 습성, 소질, 재능
embody ⓥ (사상·감정 등을) 구체화하다
stem ⓥ 일어나다, 생기다, 유래하다
distribution ⓝ 분배, 배분

전문해석

부르디외(Bourdieu)는 학교 시스템을 학문적 적성과 문화적 유산 사이의 숨겨진 연결고리를 통해 적법한 문화를 재생산하는 제도로 본다. 그는 평등한 기회와 능력주의의 이념에도 불구하고, 지배 계급에 의해 적법한 문화를 있는 그대로 재현하고 그것을 합법적으로 조작할 수 있는 행위자들을 생산하는 것 외에 다른 것을 하도록 요구되는 교육 시스템은 거의 없다고 믿는다.

부르디외는 그것이 학교에서 구체화된 지배적인 집단의 문화라고 주장해 왔다. 따라서 교육적 차이는 종종 계급에 따른 차이가 아닌 개인의 재능에 기인하는 것으로 잘못 인식되고 있으며, 학문적 기준에 의해 측정된 능력들이 종종 천부적인 "재능"에서 비롯되는 것이 아니라 "계급 문화적 습관과 교육 시스템의 요구 또는 그 안에서 성공을 정의하는 기준 사이의 더 크거나 작은 친화력"에서 비롯된다는 사실을 무시한다.

문화 자본이 개념은 부르주아 문화에 대한 친숙함을 설명하기 위해 부르디외에 의해 1960년대 초에 제안되었다. 부르주아 문화의 불평등한 분배는 개인의 재능과 학문적 성과주의의 위장 아래 사회 계급을 보존하는 데 도움이 된다. 이 개념은 획득된 지식(교육적이든 그 밖의 다른 것이든), 문화적 코드, 말하는 방식 등을 포함하며, 이는 개인에서 일종의 "습관"으로 구체화되고 문화 상품에서도 구체화된다.

---

30 윗글에 따르면, 다음 중 사실이 아닌 것은? 〔내용 불일치〕

① 노동자 계층 학생들은 중산층의 고등교육 관습에서 외부자처럼 느낄 수 있다.
✓② 개인은 사회적 계층을 바탕으로 하는 타고난 지능을 소유하는 경향이 있다.
③ 교육 제도는 지배계층 문화 자본의 수익성(유용성)을 보장한다.
④ 지배 문화는 그 자체를 보편적인 것으로 인식되게 함으로써 지배 집단의 이익을 정당화시킨다

| 분석 | 지문 두 번째 단락의 두 번째 문장에서 '교육적 차이는 종종 계급에 따른 차이가 아닌 개인의 재능에 기인하는 것으로 잘못 인식되고 있다'고 서술했다. 그렇다면 실제로는 교육적 차이가 개인이 가진 선천적인 요인에 의해 발생하는 것이 아니므로 보기 ②는 틀린 진술이다.

---

31 다음 중 윗글에서 유추할 수 있는 진술은 무엇인가? 〔내용 추론〕

① 부르디외에 따르면, 모든 문화는 동등하게 평가되고, 동등하게 기준에 맞다. 〔언급 안 함〕
✓② 부르디외에 따르면, 학교 교육은 기존의 계급 계층화를 더욱 조장하는 고착된 특정 인식 방법을 만들어 낸다.
③ 부르디외에 따르면, 개인의 효율성은 삶의 모든 단계에 걸친 숙달 경험의 영향을 가장 강하게 받는다. 〔개인의 효율성은 계급 문화적 습관과 교육 시스템의 요구의 영향을 받음〕
④ 부르디외에 따르면, 문화적 재생산은 사회경제적 양극화를 일어나게 하는 사소한 기제이다. 〔언급 안 함〕

| 분석 | 부르디외는 학교 제도를 지배계급의 정통 문화를 있는 그대로 재현하기 위한 제도로 간주하고 있으므로, ②가 정답으로 적절하다.

---

32 윗글의 제목으로 가장 적절한 것은? 〔제목〕

① 학교 교육에서의 개인적 재능의 중요성
② 학교 교육에서의 학생 성적의 중요성 ── 〔'불평등' 혹은 '불평등의 분배' 등의 키워드 없음〕
③ 학교 교육에서의 지배 문화의 사회적 책임
✓④ 학교 교육에서의 불평등의 재생산

| 분석 | 지문의 첫 단락에서 부르디외는 학교 시스템이 '지배 계급에 의해 적법한 문화를 있는 그대로 재현하고 그것을 합법적으로 조작할 수 있는 행위자들을 생산하는 것'만을 목표로 하고 있다고 했다. 이것은 학교 교육에서 계급에 따른 불평등이 있음을

의미하기 때문에 제목으로는 ④가 적절하다.

> **배경지식** 피에르 부르디외(Pierre Bourdieu): 프랑스의 세계적 사회학자, 철학자, 문화비평가로 사회학을 '구조와 기능의 차원에서 기술하는 학문'으로 파악함

[33-35] 2022 한양대

| 정답 | 33 ①　34 ①　35 ②

| 어휘 |
competency ⓝ 적성, 자격, 능력
differentiation ⓝ 차별(의 인정)
accumulation ⓝ 누적, 축적
sophisticated ⓐ 정교한
constraint ⓝ 제약(이 되는 것), 구속
meme ⓝ 밈(특정 메시지를 전하는 문구, 사진, 영상, 또는 그것을 퍼뜨리는 문화 현상)
entity ⓝ 실재, 존재
unchecked ⓐ 저지[억제]되지 않은, 검사받지 않은
keep up with 유행을 따르다, ~에 정통하다, ~에 뒤지지 않다
inflict ⓥ (타격·상처·고통 따위를) 주다, 입히다

algorithm ⓝ 알고리즘, 연산법
vertical ⓐ 수직의
deployment ⓝ (부대의) 전개, (병력 장비의) 배치
unleash ⓥ (강력한 반응이나 감정 등을) 촉발시키다
friction ⓝ (두 물체의) 마찰, 불화
aggregate ⓥ 모으다, 종합하다

shift ⓥ (자리를) 옮기다, 이동하다
expertise ⓝ 전문가의 의견
halt ⓥ 정지하다
downside ⓝ 불리한 면[예측]
exacerbate ⓥ 악화시키다
skyrocket ⓥ 급히 상승하다[시키다]

> **전문해석**
우리는 산업마다 핵심 역량이 다른 시대에서 데이터와 분석으로 인해 형성되고 알고리즘에 의해 구동되는 시대로 전환하고 있다. 전략은 비용, 품질 및 수직적 전문지식을 기반으로 하는 전통적인 차별화에서 벗어나 비즈니스 네트워크 위치, 고유한 데이터 축적, 정교한 분석 배치와 같은 이점으로 전환되고 있다—이 모든 것이 인공지능에 의해 가능해졌다. 비록 엄청난 성장을 촉발할 수 있지만, 운영 제약을 제거하는 것이 항상 좋은 것은 아니다. 마찰 저항이 없는 시스템은 불안정해지기 쉽고 일단 작동하면 멈추기가 어렵다. 브레이크가 없는 차를 생각해 보라. 디지털 신호—예를 들어, 밈과 같은—는 네트워크를 통해 빠르게 확산될 수 있으며, 애초에 디지털 신호를 시작한 조직이나 네트워크의 주요 허브를 제어하는 조직에서도 중지시키는 것이 불가능할 수 있다. 만약 당신이 보낼 메시지가 있다면, 인공지능은 방대한 수의 사람들에게 접근하고 그들을 위해 그 메시지를 개인화할 수 있는 환상적인 방법을 제공한다. 하지만 마케터의 천국은 시민들에게는 악몽이 될 수 있다. 디지털 운영 모델은 가치와 함께 피해를 통합할 수 있다. 의도가 긍정적인 경우에도 잠재적인 단점은 상당할 수 있다. 확인하지 않은 채로 두면 알고리즘은 대규모로 편견과 잘못된 정보를 엄청난 규모로 악화시킬 수 있다. 디지털 규모, 범위 및 학습은 많은 새로운 과제를 만든다. 기업을 감시하는 기관들—예를 들어 규제 기관들—은 모든 빠른 변화를 따라잡기 위해 고군분투하고 있다. 33① 인공지능 중심의 세계에서, 일단 제품이 시장에 적합한지 확인되면, 사용자 수와 수익이 급증할 수 있다. 그러나 제한 없는 성장이 위험하다는 것은 점점 더 분명해지고 있다. 디지털 운영 모델을 채택하는 기업의 잠재력은 크지만, 광범위한 피해를 입힐 수 있는 능력을 분명히 고려해야 한다. 이러한 기회와 위협을 탐색하는 것은 기업과 공공 기관 모두에게 진정한 리더십의 시험대가 될 것이다.

33 윗글의 주제로 가장 적절한 것은? 주제

✓ ① 인공지능 시대의 도전과 위험
② 세계화된 고용 시장에서 기술 주도의 위험 키워드(인공지능 시대) 없음
③ 인공지능 중심 기업의 전통 기업에 대한 우위 우위에 관한 언급 안 함
④ 정교한 분석 기능 구축에 의한 기업 문화 최적화 키워드(인공지능 시대) 없음
⑤ 기술과 인간 기술의 새로운 조합 구현 키워드(인공지능 시대) 없음

| 분석 | 지문 첫 단락에서 '인공지능 시대'로의 전환을 소개한 뒤 내용이 역접되어 그 역기능에 대해 서술하고 있다. 두 번째 단락의 다섯 번째 문장에 이르기까지 '디지털 운영 모델을 채택하는 기업의 잠재력은 크지만, 광범위한 피해를 입힐 수 있는 능력을 분명히 고려해야 한다.'는 언급을 통해 인공지능 시대에 관한 문제제기와 함께 해결책을 제안하고 있다. 따라서 주제로는 보기 ①이 가장 적절하다.

34 윗글의 빈칸에 들어갈 말로 가장 적절한 것은? 빈칸 추론

☑ ① 마찰 저항이 없는 시스템
② 구식 기술
③ 입소문 마케팅 전략
④ 민주적인 의사결정 과정
⑤ 정부의 개입과 규제

| 분석 | 빈칸 뒤에서 예시로 '브레이크 없는 차를 생각해 보라'고 서술된 것을 기준으로 빈칸을 추론해 본다. 브레이크는 '마찰 저항을 활용하여 운동하고 있는 기계의 속도를 감속하거나 정지시키는 장치'를 의미하므로 예시로 '브레이크 없는 차'를 언급했다면 멈추기 어려운 이유가 '마찰 저항의 부족'임을 알 수 있다. 따라서 보기 ①이 정답으로 가장 적절하다.

35 밑줄 친 "마케터의 천국은 시민들의 악몽이 될 수 있다"가 의미하는 바로 가장 적절한 것은? 밑줄 추론

① 개인정보 보호가 최우선시되어야 한다.
☑ ② 고객은 AI 기반 성장으로 인해 고통을 겪을 수 있다.
③ 마케팅 전략은 항상 소비자의 요구를 고려해야 한다.
④ 생산성은 AI 지원 시스템뿐만 아니라 인간의 노력에 의해 증가될 수 있다.
⑤ AI 기술의 발전은 더 많은 고급 직업을 창출할 수 있지만 고용 시장을 왜곡할 수 있다.

| 분석 | 밑줄 친 부분에서 marketer는 '인공지능을 활용하는 기업'을 의미하고 paradise는 '인공지능으로 인해 기업이 얻게 될 막대한 이익'을 가리킨다. 반면, 시민이 겪게 될 수도 있는 nightmare는 '악몽 같은 경험'이라는 부정적 의미를 가진 표현이다. 따라서 인공지능의 성장과 고객의 고통을 관련시킨 보기 ②가 정답으로 가장 적절하다.

| 배경지식 | 인공지능(Artificial intelligence): 인간 지능이 가지는 학습, 추리, 적응, 논증 등의 기능을 갖춘 컴퓨터 시스템

[36-37] 2017 성균관대

| 정답 | 36 ② 37 ①

| 어휘 |
depiction ⓝ 묘사
MP ⓝ 하원 의원(= Member of Parliament)
heritage ⓝ 유산, 전통
fish ⓥ 물고기를 잡다, 끌어내다, 꺼내다
powerhouse ⓝ 유력[실세] 집단
take-away ⓝ 사서 들고 가는 요리[음식]
prompt ⓥ 촉발하다, 불러일으키다
rendering 묘사, 연출
endeavor ⓝ 노력
stuff ⓥ (빽빽히) 채워 넣다, 쑤셔 넣다
pop up 불쑥 나타나다, 갑자기 일어나다
portrayal ⓝ 묘사
mythology ⓝ 신화
magnitude ⓝ (엄청난) 규모, 중요도
extraordinary ⓐ 대단한, 비상한

전문해석

디즈니 영화에서 폴리네시아인 등장인물의 묘사는 태평양 섬 전역에 분노를 불러일으켰으며, 한 뉴질랜드 하원 의원은 마우이 신을 비만으로 묘사한 것을 "받아들일 수 없다"고 말했다. 통가 혈통의 제니 살레사(Jenny Salesa)는 디즈니가 영화 '모아나'에서 마우이 신을 묘사한 것이 "반은 돼지, 반은 하마"인 생물과 닮았다고 말했다.

폴리네시아 신화에서 마우이는 바다에서 태평양 섬들을 끌어올려 태평양 제도를 만든 영웅적인 인물이다. 윌 일로라히아(Will Illolahia)는 와테아 뉴스와의 인터뷰에서 디즈니 영화의 마우이는 태평양 창조 신화에 나오는 그의 영웅적인 노력과 맞지 않는다고 말했다. 일로라히아는 "신화에서, 특히 우리 문화에서, 그는 힘이 세고 중요성을 가진 사람, 신성한 본성을 가진 사람으로 묘사됩니다."라고 말했다. "마우이가 비만이라는 이 묘사는 전형적인 미국인의 고정관념입니다. 비만은 우리의 목구멍으로 채워진 선진국의 음식 때문에 생긴 새로운 현상입니다."

하지만, 많은 사람들이 소셜 미디어에 디즈니의 마우이는 강하고 힘이 있어 보이고, 그의 체격은 폴리네시아 남성들 사이에서 특이하지 않다고 언급했다. 자신을 '꽤 큰 남자'라고 밝힌 통가 뉴질랜드 남성 이소아 카바키모투(Isoa Kavakimotu)는 디즈니의 마우이에 대한 묘사가 아무 문제가 없다며 논란에 대한 유튜브 영상을 만들었다. "저는 그것에 대해 괜찮습니다."라고 그가 말했다. "제가 보기에 그는 뚱뚱해 보이지 않고, 비범한 일을 할 수 있는 정력적인 사람처럼 보입니다. 그는 그런 이유로 몸집이 큽니다. 그들이 전통적인 와카(카누)를 타고 항해하는 영화에서, 그것은 식민지 시대 이전을 배경으로 하고 있습니다. 저는 영화에 테이크아웃 가게가 갑자기 등장할지에 대해 매우 의심스럽습니다. 제가 보기에, 그는 행동할 준비가 되어 있는 것처럼 보입니다."라고 그는 말했다.

---

36 밑줄 친 "영화에 테이크아웃 가게가 갑자기 나타날 것이다"는 _____를 의미한다. 〔밑줄 추론〕

① 그 영화는 추리, 허구적인 과학에 기초한 묘사를 한다
✓ 이 영화의 시간적 배경은 식민지 시대 이후의 근대기이다
③ 이 영화에서는 현실적인 묘사가 매우 분명하다
④ 이 영화는 평범한 일상생활에 집중한다
⑤ 이 영화는 식민지 시대의 인종 문제를 분석하고 있다

| 분석 | 밑줄 친 부분의 테이크아웃 가게는 '구입하여 가게에서 먹거나 사용하지 않고 들고 가는 가게'를 의미한다. 이는 식민지 시대 이후에 생겨났다고 볼 수 있으므로 이것이 영화에 등장한다는 것은 영화의 시대적 배경이 식민지 시대 이후라는 말이 된다. 따라서 밑줄 친 부분의 의미는 보기 ②이다.

---

37 윗글에 따르면, 다음 중 올바르지 않은 것은? 〔내용 불일치〕

✓ 대부분의 폴리네시아 사람들은 현재 뚱뚱하지 않다.
② 몇몇 사람들은 디즈니에서 마우이를 묘사한 것에 대해 동의를 표했다.
③ 마우이에 대한 묘사는 영화에서 폴리네시아 사람의 고정관념에 대한 논쟁을 불러일으켰다.
④ 영화 속에서 폴리네시아 신을 비만으로 묘사한 디즈니는 폴리네시아 사람들 사이에서 공분을 불러일으켰다.
⑤ 마우이의 신체적인 특징들이 디즈니 영화 속의 등장인물을 나타내 준다.

| 분석 | 지문의 두 번째 단락에서 윌 일로라히아는 "마우이가 비만이라는 이 묘사는 전형적인 미국인의 고정관념입니다. 비만은 우리의 목구멍으로 채워진 선진국의 음식 때문에 생긴 새로운 현상입니다."라고 말했다. 그것은 현재의 폴리네시아인들은 비만인 상태임을 암시하므로 보기 ①은 틀린 진술이다.

[38-39] 2022 중앙대

| 정답 | 38 ③ 39 ④

| 어휘 |
actuality ⓝ 실재, 현실, 사실
considerable ⓐ 상당한, 많은
individualism ⓝ 개인주의
sever ⓥ 자르다, 절단하다, 단절하다
clan ⓝ 씨족, (대)가족
egocentric ⓐ 자기중심의, 이기적인
funiculus ⓝ 탯줄
entity ⓝ 실재, 존재, 실체
emerge ⓥ 나오다, 드러나다, 생겨나다
figuratively speaking 비유적으로 말하자면
umbilical cord 탯줄, 생명줄
caste ⓝ (힌두교 사회의) 계급, 계층
spinal ⓐ 척추의
ontological ⓐ 존재론적인
functionally ⓐⓓ 기능적으로
tie ⓝ 끈, 유대, 구속
individuation ⓝ 개별화, 개별적 존재, 개성
navel ⓝ 배꼽, 중심, 중앙
epistemological ⓐ 인식론(상)의

전문해석

우리가 우리의 주요 주제—자유가 현대인에게 무엇을 의미하는지, 그리고 그가 왜, 그리고 어떻게 그것으로부터 탈출하려고 하는지에 대한 질문—에 이르기 전에 우리는 먼저 현실에서 다소 벗어난 것처럼 보일 수 있는 한 개념에 대해 논의해야 한다. 그러나 그것은 현대 사회의 자유 분석에 대한 이해에 필요한 전제이다. 나는 자유가 인간의 존재를 그렇게 특징짓고, 더 나아가 인간이 독립적인 별개의 존재로서 자기 자신에 대한 인식과 관념의 정도에 따라 그 의미가 변한다는 개념을 의미한다.

[B] 인간의 사회적 역사는 그가 자연계와 일체가 된 상태에서 벗어나 주변 자연과 인간으로부터 분리된 존재로서 자신을 인식하는 것으로 시작되었다. 그러나 이러한 인식은 오랜 역사 동안 매우 희미하게 남아 있었다. 그 개인은 그가 등장한 자연적이고 사회적인 세계에 계속해서 밀접하게 묶여 있었다. 그는 부분적으로 그 자신을 별개의 실체로 인식하면서도, 또한 그를 둘러싼 세계의 일부라고 느꼈다. 우리가 "개인주의"라고 부를 수 있는 원래 유대에서 개인이 벗어나는 점차적인 과정은 종교 개혁과 현재 사이의 세기에 현대 역사에서 정점에 도달한 것으로 보인다.

[A] 개인의 삶의 역사에서도 우리는 같은 과정을 발견한다. 아이는 더 이상 엄마와 하나가 아닐 때 태어나 엄마와 분리된 하나의 생물학적 실체가 된다. 그러나, 이러한 생물학적 분리가 개별적인 인간 존재의 시작이지만, 아이는 상당한 기간 동안 엄마와 기능적으로 하나인 상태에 있다.

[C] 비유적으로 말해서, 개인이 아직 외부 세계에 자신을 고정시키는 Ⓐ 탯줄을 완전히 끊지 않은 정도로, 그는 자유가 부족하다. 그러나 이러한 유대는 그에게 안정감과 소속감과 어딘가에 뿌리박혀 있다는 느낌을 준다. 나는 개인화의 과정이 개인의 완전한 출현을 초래하기 전에 존재하는 이러한 유대를 "1차적 유대"라고 부르고 싶다. 그 유대는 정상적인 인간 발달의 일부라는 점에서 유기적이다. 그 유대는 개성의 부족을 의미하지만, 또한 개인에게 안정감과 방향성을 제공한다. 그 유대는 아이와 그 어머니, 그의 씨족과 자연을 가진 원시 공동체의 구성원, 또는 중세의 인간을 교회와 그의 사회적 계급과 연결시키는 유대이다.

일단 완전한 개별화의 단계에 도달하고 개인이 이러한 1차적인 유대로부터 자유로워지면, 그는 새로운 과제에 직면하게 된다: 자신을 방향으로 잡고 세상에 뿌리를 내리고 그의 Ⓑ 개인주의 이전의 존재의 특징이었던 것들이 아닌 다른 방법으로 안정을 찾는 것이다. 그러면 자유는 이 진화의 단계에 도달하기 전에 가졌던 것과는 다른 의미를 가진다.

38
윗글의 단락을 논리적 흐름에 맞게 순서대로 배열한 것으로 가장 적합한 것은? 문장 배열

① [A] – [B] – [C]　　　　② [A] – [C] – [B]
✓③ [B] – [A] – [C]　　　　④ [C] – [B] – [A]

| 분석 | 지문의 두 번째 단락부터 올바른 순서로 배열해야 하는 문제이므로 첫 단락의 내용이 이어지는 단락이 시작되는 내용과 연결되어야 할 것이다. 첫 단락에서는 현대 사회의 자유 분석의 전제로 '인간이 독립적인 별개의 존재로서 자기 자신에 대한 인식과 관념의 정도에 따라 그 의미가 변한다는 개념'을 소개했다. 따라서 이어지는 단락은 사회적 역사에서 개인화 과정을 다룬 단락 [B]가 와야 하며 이후로는 개인의 삶의 역사에서도 같은 과정이 일어남을 설명한 단락 [A]가 이어져야 할 것이다. 다음으로 단락 [C]의 내용이 '개인의 1차적 유대'를 소개했기 때문에 지문 마지막 단락에서 이러한 1차적 유대로부터 자유로워진 후 개인이 직면하는 새로운 과제에 대한 설명이 자연스럽게 연결된다. 따라서 보기 ③이 논리적 흐름에 가장 적합하다.

39 윗글의 빈칸 Ⓐ와 Ⓑ에 들어가기에 가장 적합한 것은? 빈칸 추론

① 배꼽 – 자기중심적인
② 척추 – 인식론적인
③ 탯줄 – 존재론적인
✓ ④ 탯줄 – 개인주의 이전의

| 분석 | 세 번째 단락의 마지막 문장에서 '아이는 상당한 기간 동안 엄마와 기능적으로 하나인 상태에 있다.'고 했다. 이러한 유대를 다음 단락에서 비유적으로 말한다면 빈칸 Ⓐ에는 어머니와 아이를 이어 주는 '탯줄'을 추론할 수 있으며 빈칸 Ⓑ의 경우 1차적 유대로부터 자유로워진 후 개인이 안정을 찾는 방식은 개인화 이전과 달라야 할 것이므로 '개인주의 이전의'라는 표현이 가장 적절하다. 따라서 보기 ④가 정답이다.

[40-41] 2012 중앙대

| 정답 | 40 ④ 41 ①

| 어휘 |
jealous ⓐ 질투심 많은, (소중하게 여기는 것을) 지키려고 애쓰는
residence ⓝ 주거, 거주
intolerable ⓐ 견딜 수 없는, 애타는
nasty ⓐ 불쾌한, 싫은, 더러운
extensive ⓐ 광범위한
manifest ⓥ 명시하다, 증명하다, 나타내다
literature ⓝ 문학, 인쇄물
complaint ⓝ 불평
appalling ⓐ 섬뜩하게 하는, 지독한, 형편없는
compliment ⓝ 칭찬
unaccustomed ⓐ ~에 익숙지 않은[숙달되지 않은]
delegation ⓝ 대표단, 파견 위원단
irritability ⓝ 화를 잘 냄, 성급함, 과민성
confrontation ⓝ 직면, 대면
courtesy ⓝ 공손함, 정중함, 공손한 말[행동]
quaint ⓐ 기이한, 이상한
notification ⓝ 통지, 통고
cabby ⓝ 택시 기사
apprehension ⓝ 염려, 우려, 걱정
reputation ⓝ 평판, 세평
hysteria ⓝ 병적 흥분, 과민반응
provoke ⓥ 유발하다, 화나게 하다
gratifying ⓐ 흐뭇한, 기쁜
heave ⓥ 들어올리다, 던지다
authorities ⓝ 당국, 관계자, 정부당국
bellicose ⓐ 호전적인, 싸움을 잘하는
pervasive ⓐ 널리 퍼지는

전문해석

토론토가 대륙에서 가장 고상한 도시 중 하나가 되고 있다는 소식을 듣고, 우리는 조사하기 위해 뉴욕에서 토론토로 갔다. 그들 도시의 평판을 지키려고 하고 그것의 위상에 대한 도전에 대해 걱정하는 뉴욕 시민들은 사실 걱정할 필요가 거의 없다. 3일간 체류한 후, 우리 대표단은 거의 참을 수 없는 과민반응의 부족에 주목하고 정상적인 짜증 상태를 유지하기 위해 많은 양의 블랙커피를 마셨다. 우리가 불쾌한 대립을 유발하기를 바라며 불평했던 지역 주민들은 Ⓐ 호전적이 되기를 거부했다. 그들은 만족스러운 대도시 히스테리를 즐기고 싶어 하지만 낯선 사람들 앞에서는 무례하게 보일 것이라고 믿었다고 그들은 말했다. 광범위한 현장 연구—4주간 지속—는 이 실패(토론토 사람들의 과민반응을 유발할 수 없었던 것)가 토론토의 "예의"라는 오랜 사회적 행동 패턴의 유지를 반영한다는 것을 납득시켰다. "예의"는 뉴요커에게 Ⓑ 익숙하지 않은 많은 진기한 형태로 나타난다. 그러므로, 예를 들어, 뉴욕 양키즈의 팬들은 토론토 야구장에서 운동장에 있는 선수들에게 화장지와 맥주 캔을 던지는 것이 나쁜 행동으로 간주된다는 것을 알면 놀랄지도 모른다. 토론토 택시 내부의 공식 문서에는 승객들이 당국에 불만 사항뿐만 아니라 택시 기사의 행동에 대한 Ⓒ 칭찬을 우편으로 보낼 수 있는 적절한 주소에 대한 통지가 포함되어 있다.

40 윗글의 빈칸 Ⓐ, Ⓑ, Ⓒ에 들어가기에 가장 적합한 것은? 빈칸 추론

① 소름 끼치는 – 호전적인 – 칭찬
② 서로 다른 – 순응하는 – 우려
③ 순응하는 – 널리 퍼지는 – 불안
✓ ④ 호전적인 – 익숙하지 않은 – 칭찬

| 분석 | 빈칸 Ⓐ가 포함된 문장의 직후 내용을 확인해 보면 토론토 사람들은 낯선 사람들에게 무례하게 보이고 싶어 하지 않음을 알 수 있으므로 토론토 사람들은 빈칸 Ⓐ에서 '호전적' 이기를 거부할 것이다. 다음으로 빈칸 Ⓑ의 경우, 직후의 뉴욕 양키즈 팬들의 예시를 확인해 보면 뉴요커들의 입장에서는 토론토 사람들의 예의가 '익숙하지 않은' 형태였을 것이며, 빈칸 Ⓒ는 예의를 중시하는 토론토 택시 내부라면 택시 기사의 행동에 대한 '칭찬'을 우편으로 보낼 수 있다는 예시가 와야 글의 흐름상 자연스러울 것이다. 따라서 보기 ④가 정답으로 적절하다.

---

41 윗글을 통해 추론할 수 있는 것으로 가장 적합한 것은? 내용 추론

✓① 뉴욕 사람들은 토론토 사람들로부터 많은 것들을 배울 수 있다.
② 뉴욕은 많은 예의 바른 사람들을 찾기에 좋은 장소이다. '뉴욕'을 '토론토'로 수정해야 함
③ 토론토 사람들은 그들의 스트레스를 완화시키기 위해 많은 양의 커피를 마신다. '토론토 사람들'을 '뉴욕 사람들'로 수정해야 함
④ 토론토 사람들은 화장지와 캔맥주를 경기장에 가져올 수 없다. 소지가 제한되는 것은 알 수 없음

| 분석 | 본문은 토론토 사람들의 "예의"를 확인한 뉴욕 시민들의 경험담을 바탕으로 한다. 따라서 보기 ①이 추론 가능한 진술이다.

[42–43] 2021 이화여대

| 정답 | 42 ⑤   43 ②

| 어휘 |
herald ⓥ 예고하다, 알리다
drawback ⓝ 결점, 문제점
proclivity ⓝ (흔히 좋지 못한) 성향
secondary @ 이차적인, 부차적인
enthusiasm ⓝ 열정, 열의
dozen ⓝ 12개짜리 한 묶음, 십여 명[개]로 된 무리
pitfall ⓝ (눈에 잘 안 띄는) 위험, 곤란
skim ⓥ (필요한 부분을 찾거나 요점을 알기 위해) 훑어보다
factitious @ 꾸며 낸, 인위적인
chatter ⓝ 수다, 재잘거림
homogeneity ⓝ 동종[동질]성, 균질성
blur ⓥ 흐릿해지다, 흐릿하게 만들다, 모호해지다

전문해석

오늘날, 많은 사람들은 디지털 책과 점점 더 스크린을 기반으로 하는 우리의 문화가 진지한 독서의 종말을 예고한다고 걱정하고 있다. 이건 말도 안 되는 소리다. 모든 새로운 기술에는 결과와 때로는 단점이 있지만, 인간은 이야기와 시 없이는 살 수 없다. 젊은 연인들은 항상 사포, 도네, 키츠를 읽을 것이다. '보바리 부인'과 '위대한 개츠비'는 낭만적 환상에 대한 우리의 성향에 대해 대체할 수 없는 논평으로 남을 것이다. 그들의 삶이 끝나기 전에 삶의 작은 의미를 만들기를 바라는 나이 든 사람들은 역사와 철학을 계속 공부할 것이다. 사람들이 페이지를 넘기거나 화면에서 픽셀을 보는지 여부는 부차적이다.

하지만 이것을 생각해 보자: 소셜 미디어를 통해 실비아 플래스(Sylvia Plath, 미국의 작가)를 발견한 오늘날의 젊은 여성은 전 세계의 친구들과 빠르게 자신의 흥분을 나눌 수 있다. 그녀는 Ariel이나 The Bell Jar에 대해 굿리드에 댓글을 남길 수도 있고, 온라인 토론 그룹에 참여할 수도 있고, 시인의 작품과 기억에 전념하는 사이트에 링크를 게시할 수도 있다. 그녀의 열정은 십여 명 또는 천 명의 사람들을 플래스로 더 이끌지도 모른다.

그것은 우리의 스크린 기반 문화의 한 가지 장점일 뿐이다. 오래되고 잊힌 책들은 이제 프로젝트 구텐베르크를 통해 쉽게 구할 수 있다. 도서관 전체를 주머니에 넣고 다닐 수 있다. 디지털화된 텍스트는 쉽고 빠르게 검색할 수 있으며, 노화된 눈을 위해 글꼴 크기를 확대할 수 있다.

Ⓐ 그럼에도 불구하고, 이러한 실질적인 이익은 동시에 다양한 함정을 만든다. 컴퓨터는 집중적인 관심과 책의 단어와 아이디어에 대한 고독한 참여 대신 대충 훑어보기를 장려한다. 윙윙거리는 인터넷은 의미 있는 대화뿐만 아니라 의미 없는 수다를 조장한다. 화면 자체가 실질적인 동질성을 부여한다: 제임스 본드는 제인 오스틴과 닮았고 스마트폰은 마인츠의 거대한 성경과 작은 미니어처 책 사이의 크기 차이를 흐리게 한다.

42 Ⓐ에 들어가기에 가장 적절한 것은? 연결사

① 사실
② 놀랄 정도로
③ 결과적으로
④ 게다가
✓ ⑤ 그럼에도 불구하고

| 분석 | 빈칸을 기준으로 직전 단락에서는 스크린 기반 문화의 장점이 나열되었고, 빈칸 이후로는 장점과 동시에 존재하는 다양한 단점들이 언급되었다. 따라서 빈칸의 앞뒤 내용이 역접되었으므로 빈칸에는 보기 ⑤가 정답으로 가장 적절하다.

43 윗글에서 추론할 수 없는 것은 무엇인가? 내용 비추론

① 독서 습관의 빠른 변화에도 불구하고, 사람들은 독서를 멈추지 않을 것이다.
✓ ② 디지털화된 텍스트들은 인쇄된 책들을 대체할 것이다.
③ 스크린에서 읽는 것은 우리가 인쇄된 책들이 가지고 있는 색다른 자료와 일반적인 특징들을 알지 못하게 한다.
④ 스크린 기반의 문화는 독자들의 책에 대한 적극적인 참여를 확대시킬 수 있다.
⑤ 온라인 북클럽의 모든 댓글들과 대화들이 의미 있는 것은 아니다.

| 분석 | 지문의 첫 단락에서 저자는 스크린을 기반으로 하는 문화가 독서의 종말을 예고하지 않을 것이라고 강조했다. 따라서 보기 ②는 지문을 바탕으로 추론할 수 없는 진술이다.

[44-46] 2012 이화여대

| 정답 | 44 ④   45 ②   46 ⑤

| 어휘 |
privacy ⓝ 사적 자유, 사생활
proximity ⓝ 근접, 가까움
minimal ⓐ 최소의, 극미한
communal ⓐ 공동의, 공용의
devise ⓥ 궁리하다, 발명하다
abode ⓝ 주소
dissimulation ⓝ 시치미 뗌, (감정의) 위장, 위선
hypocrisy ⓝ 위선
unobserved ⓐ 관찰[주의]되지 않은
Tuareg ⓝ 투아레그족[어]
robe ⓝ (길고 품이 넓은) 겉옷, 의상
indigo ⓝ 남색, 쪽빛
grant ⓥ 주다, 수여하다
in-laws ⓝ 인척
reserve ⓝ 비축, 예비, 보호구역
anonymity ⓝ 익명성
bestow ⓥ 주다, 수여하다
facelessness ⓝ 익명임
idiom ⓝ 관용구, 숙어
aloof ⓐ 멀리 떨어진, 무관심한
peril ⓝ 위험
aggregating ⓐ 종합의
incontrovertible ⓐ 이론[반박]의 여지가 없는
appreciable ⓐ 평가할 수 있는, 분명한, 상당한 정도의
appetizing ⓐ 식욕을 돋우는, 맛있어 보이는
ingenious ⓐ 독창적인
arresting ⓐ 흥미로운
apprehensive ⓐ 염려[우려]하는, 걱정하는
benevolent ⓐ 자비심 많은, 호의적인
skeptical ⓐ 회의적인, 의심이 많은
exert ⓥ (힘을) 발휘하다, 노력하다
antagonistic ⓐ 적대적인
undermine ⓥ ~의 근본을 침식하다, 훼손하다, 몰래 손상시키다
mind-boggling ⓐ 아주 놀라운, 믿어지지 않는
abdicate ⓥ (권리 등을) 버리다, 포기하다
subterfuge ⓝ 구실, 핑계, 속임수
futile ⓐ 쓸데없는, 무익한
withdrawal ⓝ 철수, 취소, 취하

전문해석

심지어 타인과의 물리적 근접성이 거의 일정한 조건에서도, 인간들은 그들의 사생활을 보호할 수 있는 가장 ⓐ 독창적인 방법을 찾는다. 많은 문화에서, 심지어 물리적 접근에 대한 최소한의 통제조차도 공동체적이고 가족적인 생활 중에는 얻기 어려울 수 있다. 어떤 마을들은 벽이 너무 얇아서 소리가 쉽게 들릴 수 있는 오두막을 가지고 있다. 다른 마을들은 부부나 가족들 사이를 분리시키는 벽이 전혀 없다. 그 후 사생활을 보호하기 위해 많은 방법이 고안되었다. 마을 사람들은 그들이 혼자 있고 싶거나 한두 명의 다른 사람들과 함께 있고 싶을 때, 며칠 또는 심지어 몇 달 동안 그들이 가는 마을 외곽에 개인적인 거처를 마련할 수 있을 것이다. 많은 문화들은 특정한 사적인 문제들이 알려지지 않은 채로 남아 있거나 관찰되지 않는 것을 허용하는 숨김과 위선의 수단과 함께 엄격한 에티켓 규칙을 발전시켰다. 이러한 방식으로 ⓑ 공동생활이나 군중 속에서도 타인에 대한 개방성에 대해 어느 정도 통제력을 행사하는 것이 가능하다.

이러한 통제가 어떻게 유지될 수 있는지에 대한 ⓒ 눈길을 끄는 예는 남색 면으로 된 긴 가운과 파란색 베일을 착용한 묵아프리카의 투아레그 사람들에 의해 제공되는데, 그들의 손, 발, 그리고 눈 주변을 제외하고는 거의 보이지 않는다. 그 베일은 집뿐만 아니라 밖에서도 입고, 심지어 먹거나 담배를 피울 때도 입는다. 어떤 사람들은 심지어 잠잘 때도 그것을 착용한다. 그 베일은 예를 들어 시댁이나 처가 등 특별한 존경을 받는 가족들이 있는 곳에서 얼굴을 가장 완벽하게 가린다. 한 관찰자는 베일이 의식적인 제한을 보호하고 ⓓ "위협적인 상황에서 상징적인 철수"를 허용한다고 언급했다. 베일은 고립이나 익명성을 제공하지는 않지만, 착용자의 얼굴을 가려 주며 사생활의 관용을 제공하고, 그가 여전히 사회의 일원이지만, 사회적 상호 작용의 위험으로부터 다소 초연할 수 있도록 해 준다.

44 빈칸 ⓐ와 ⓒ에 들어갈 말로 가장 적절한 것은? [빈칸 추론]

① 인상적인 – 응집시키는
② 논란의 여지가 있는 – 상당한
③ 즉각적인 – 식욕을 돋우는
✓④ 독창적인 – 눈길을 끄는
⑤ 상상력이 풍부한 – 걱정스러운

| 분석 | 빈칸 ⓐ의 뒤로 이어지는 내용 중 사람들이 마을 외곽에 개인적인 거처를 마련하거나 에티켓 규칙을 발전시켜 사생활을 보호하려고 했던 예시가 소개되므로 빈칸 ⓐ에는 공동체 생활 중에서 어렵지만 '독특한, 독창적인' 방법으로 사생활을 보호해 왔다는 것을 알 수 있다. 빈칸 ⓒ는 투아레그족의 베일이나 의복의 소개를 참고하여 해결하는데 그들의 의복은 손, 발, 눈 주변을 제외하고 착용자를 보이지 않게 하고 비록 옷일 뿐이지만 착용자의 신체 대부분을 가림으로써 그의 사생활을 보호해 주는 수단이므로 '눈길을 끄는, 관심이 가는'이라는 표현이 적절하다. 따라서 정답은 보기 ④이다.

45 어느 진술이 ⓑ를 가장 잘 완성하는가? [빈칸 추론]

① 다른 사회 계층, 학력, 그리고 국가 출신의 사람들과의 상호 작용의 수준을 조절하는 것은 자비로운 일이다
✓② 공동생활이나 군중 속에서도 타인에 대한 개방성에 대해 어느 정도 통제력을 행사하는 것이 가능하다
③ 공동생활에 적대적인 감정을 갖지 않을 수 있는 다른 사람들에게도 자신의 통제력을 행사하는 것은 회의적이다
④ 집단적 관계에서 타인에 대한 통제의 정도를 약화시키는 것이 바람직하다
⑤ 개인의 권리를 포기하지 않고 가족생활에 상당한 통제력을 행사하는 것은 놀라운 일이다

| 분석 | 빈칸 ⓑ는 첫 단락 마지막 문장에 해당하므로 다음 단락이 어떤 내용으로 시작되는지를 참고하여 정답을 결정하도록 한다. 다음 단락에서는 베일을 통해 자신의 신체 대부분을 가림으로써 사생활을 보호하는 방법을 앞 단락의 예시로 소개하고 있으므로 보기 ② '공동생활 또는 많은 사람들 속에서도 자신이 남들에게 공개되는 것을 어느 정도 통제할 수 있는 것이 가능하다'가 정답으로 적절하다.

46 빈칸 ⓓ의 인용문에 가장 적합한 것은 무엇인가? 빈칸 추론

① 교묘한 속임수 없이 빈번한 상호 작용
② 잠재적 지지자들에 대한 보호 장치
③ 예상치 못한 사건으로 인한 의심스러운 보안
④ 잠재적으로 불쾌하고 치명적인 만남으로부터의 헛된 후퇴
✓ 위협적인 상황에서 상징적인 철수

| 분석 | 이어지는 문장에서 베일은 사람들 사이의 상호 작용에서 오는 위험에서 한발 물러나 있을 수 있게 해 준다고 했으므로 이를 요약한 '상징적인 철수'라는 낱말이 포함된 ⑤가 가장 적합하다.

[47-50] 2012 항공대

| 정답 | 47 ①　48 ②　49 ③　50 ①

| 어휘 | **baby boomer** ⓝ (특히 제2차 세계 대전 후의) 베이비 붐 세대인 사람　　**cherish** ⓥ 소중히 여기다, 아끼다
tremendous ⓐ 엄청난, 광장한　　**appeal** ⓝ 매력　　**portable** ⓐ 휴대[이동]가 쉬운
child-rearing ⓝ 자녀 양육　　**nurture** ⓥ 양육하다, 육성하다　　**postwar** ⓐ 전쟁 후의, 제2차 세계 대전 후의
astute ⓐ 영리한　　**customize** ⓥ 주인이 원하는 대로 만들다, 주문 제작하다
latchkey child[kid] (열쇠를 가지고 다니는) 맞벌이 부부의 아이

전문해석

1946년과 1964년 사이에 태어난 사람들은 미국에서 베이비 붐 세대라고 불린다. 많은 베이비 붐 세대들이 이제 50세가 넘었지만, 그들은 여전히 젊음에 집착한다. 대부분은 계속해서 매우 활동적인 삶을 살고 있다. 이 그룹은 편리함을 소중히 여기는데, 이로 인해 대형 가전제품, 가구, 식료품, 기타 품목들의 가정 배달에 대한 수요가 증가하고 있다. 게다가, 편의성 문화의 확산은 조리된 테이크아웃 음식, 휴대 전화, 그리고 인터넷의 엄청난 매력을 설명한다.
베이비 붐 세대의 부모들은 그들의 아이들이 혼자서 스스로 생각하도록 키웠다. 자녀 양육 관행에 대한 연구는 1950년대와 1960년대의 부모들이 일관되게 "혼자 힘으로 생각하는 것"을 그들의 자녀들에게 육성해 주고 싶은 가장 큰 특징으로 꼽았다는 것을 보여 준다. 전후의 풍요로움은 또한 부모들이 그들의 아이들을 이전 어느 때보다 만족시켜 주도록 했다. 그들은 아이들을 대학에 보냄으로써 그들의 능력에 투자했다. 그들은 자녀들이 협동 정신보다 경쟁적 추진력, 팀워크보다 개인의 기술에 더 많은 보상을 주는 취업 시장에서 성공하도록 격려했다.
결과적으로, 그 세대의 규모는 기업들이 베이비 붐 세대의 떠오르는 개성에 맞추도록 격려했다. 최고령 베이비 붐 세대가 20여 년 전에 생계를 꾸리기 시작하기 이전에도, 영리한 사업가들은 수백만 명의 젊은이들에게 그들이 원하는 것을 제공함으로써 얻을 수 있는 이익을 기대했다. 기업들은 개인주의적 베이비 붐 세대에게 점점 증가하는 일련의 맞춤형 제품들과 서비스들을 제공했다.

---

47 다음 중 "베이비 붐 세대"의 특징을 제대로 나타내는 것은 무엇인가? 세부 내용 일치

✓ 미국의 대량 판매 시장
② 지옥의 묵시록
③ 박학다식한 사람
④ 불가능한 임무

| 분석 | 지문의 첫 단락에서 베이비 붐 세대의 등장으로 이들을 만족시키기 위한 시장의 규모가 커졌음을 언급했다. 따라서 보기 ①이 정답으로 가장 적절하다.

48	윗글은 주로 무엇에 관한 글인가? 주제

① 경제 원리
② 인구통계학적 경향 ✓
③ 상식
④ 경쟁과 협력

| 분석 | 지문의 소재는 '베이비 붐 세대'로 지문에서는 그들의 새로운 특성과 이로 인한 기업과 시장의 변화를 설명한다. 보기 ②의 demographic은 '특정 집단의 특성들'이라는 의미이므로 베이비 붐 세대의 특성이라 볼 수 있다. 따라서 보기 ②가 이 글의 주제이다.

49	다음 중 사실인 것은? 내용 일치

① 베이비 붐 세대는 방과 후 혼자 시간을 보내는 아이들 세대의 결과이다. 인과관계 언급 안 함
② 베이비 붐 세대는 경쟁과 개인의 능력의 가치를 과대평가한다. 과대평가에 대해서는 언급 안 함
③ 몇몇 사업가들은 미래의 주요 고객들을 예측할 만큼 현명했다. ✓
④ 그들의 아이들을 키우기 위해 베이비 붐 세대들은 협동적인 팀워크에 의존했다. 팀워크보다 개인의 기술에 더 많은 보상을 더 격려함

| 분석 | 지문의 마지막 단락에서 '영리한 사업가들은 수백만 명의 젊은이들에게 그들이 원하는 것을 제공함으로써 얻을 수 있는 이익을 기대했다.'고 했으므로 보기 ③이 정답으로 가장 적절하다.

50	다음 중 마지막 문장 뒤에 나올 것 같은 문장은 무엇인가? 내용 추론

① 그것은 집, 자동차, 가구, 전자제품, 그리고 심지어 신념이다. ✓
② 한 지역에 신규 인력이 대거 유입되면서 모든 유형의 기업에 많은 새로운 기회가 창출된다.
③ 하지만, 오늘날의 성숙한 소비자들은 이전 세대의 소비자들보다 더 부유하고, 더 건강하고, 더 나은 교육을 받는다.
④ 그들은 전통적인 요구와 관심사를 충족시키는 제품과 서비스를 선택한다.

| 분석 | 지문의 마지막 문장에서는 '기업들은 개인주의적 베이비 붐 세대에게 점점 증가하는 일련의 맞춤형 제품들과 서비스들을 제공했다.'고 했으므로 그다음에 이어질 문장으로 가장 적절한 것은 관련 제품과 서비스에 관한 구체적 사례일 것이다. 따라서 보기 ①이 정답으로 적절하다.

| 배경지식 | 베이비 붐(Baby boom): 출생률의 급상승기로 전후에 많이 일어나는 현상이며 대한민국에서는 한국 전쟁 이후, 유럽이나 미국에서는 제2차 세계 대전 이후 태어난 세대에 해당

4강 언어 / 문학 / 예술

01	③	02	③	03	④	04	④	05	⑤	06	③	07	③	08	①	09	②	10	③
11	②	12	①	13	④	14	③	15	②	16	①	17	②	18	④	19	②	20	①
21	③	22	③	23	④	24	①	25	⑤	26	⑤	27	③	28	①	29	④	30	④
31	③	32	④	33	④	34	③	35	②	36	③	37	②	38	①	39	②	40	④
41	④	42	③	43	①	44	④	45	②	46	①	47	②	48	①	49	③	50	④
51	③	52	③	53	④	54	②												

[01–02] 2013 중앙대

| 정답 | 01 ③ 02 ③

| 어휘 |
- labored ⓐ 힘든, 공들인
- absorption ⓝ 몰입
- variation ⓝ 변주곡
- gift ⓝ 재능
- exposition ⓝ 제시부
- movement ⓝ 악장
- gestation ⓝ 창안
- transcend ⓥ 초월하다, 넘어서다
- WoO 작품번호 없는 작품들
- improvisation ⓝ 즉흥 연주
- development ⓝ 전개부
- virtuosity ⓝ 기교
- vocal ⓝ 성악
- phenomenal ⓐ 엄청난
- recapitulation ⓝ 재현부
- culmination ⓝ 절정

전문해석

베토벤의 작곡과의 싸움은 힘들게 진행되었다. 어떤 작품은 몇 년에 걸친 힘든 창작 끝에 이루어졌다. 하지만 일단 완벽한 형태를 가지게 되자, 그의 대부분의 작품들은 즉각적인 성공을 거두게 되었다. 점차 늘어나던 중산층은 그의 작품들의 즉흥성, 힘, 극적인 기교를 즐겼고, 반면 문화 엘리트들은 그가 18세기의 음악 스타일을 철저하게 흡수하고, 이를 넘어서는 것에 감명을 받았다. 보통 베토벤의 작품들을 세 시기로 나누지만, 그가 비엔나에 도착하기 전의 네 번째 시기 역시 고려되어야 한다. 왜냐하면 그때 이미 그는 많은 성악 및 실내악은 물론, 대단히 훌륭한 피아노 변주곡도 작곡했기 때문이다. 이러한 초기 작품들은 (작품번호 없는 작품들이라는 의미의) 'WoO' 번호로 정리되어 있다. 그의 초기의 명성은 건반을 가지고 즉흥 연주를 하는 엄청난 재능에서 비롯되었다. 몇몇 사람들은 모차르트보다도 뛰어나다고 하였다. 따라서 그의 초기 작곡들이 대부분 피아노를 위한 곡인 것은 당연해 보인다. 베토벤의 이른바 '초기' 시기는 1792년 그가 22세의 나이에 비엔나에 도착한 이후 시작된다. 여기에서 그는 소나타 이론을 받아들이고, 그다음 균형 잡히고, 활과 같은 구조에서 좀 더 역동적이고 급박한 형태로 변형시키기 시작하였다. 새로운 형태에서는 제시부와 전개부 다음에 오는 세 번째 부분인 재현부는 반복이 아니라 절정을 이루었다. 처음에는 최초의 음악적 이념을 탐구하고 다듬어 가면서, 그리고 관례적인 세 개의 악장이 아니라 네 개의 악장을 선호하면서, 베토벤의 소나타 작품들은 대단한 성공을 거두었다. 하지만, 그의 성공이 점점 커져 가면서, 그의 작곡들은 더욱 표현적이면서 집중적인 것이 되었다. 프랑스어로는 '열정' 혹은 '감정'이라는 의미의 비창 소나타(베토벤 자신이 이름 붙인 것이다)는 그의 최고의 걸작으로 간주되고 있다.

01 윗글의 제목으로 가장 적절한 것은? 제목

① 베토벤의 음악적 즉흥성 너무 지엽적
② 베토벤의 피아노 작품에서 특수함 너무 지엽적
③ 작곡가로서 베토벤의 초기 삶 ✓
④ 베토벤의 열정적인 소나타 걸작 너무 지엽적

| 분석 | 첫 단락에서 베토벤의 시기를 세 시기로 나누지만, 그 이전의 한 시기를 덧붙여야 한다고 했다. 그리고 두 번째 단락은 일반적인 세 시기 중 첫 번째 시기에 대해 설명하고 있으므로, 전반적으로 베토벤의 초기에 대한 설명의 글이라고 볼 수 있다.

---

02 윗글의 내용과 일치하는 것은? 〔내용 일치〕

① 베토벤의 몇몇 작품들은 즉흥 연주에 수년이 걸렸다.
② 베토벤은 작품 *Pathétique*을 자신의 걸작에 대한 잘못된 이름으로 여겼다.
✓ 사실, 베토벤의 음악적 업적은 네 시기로 나눌 수 있다.
④ 베토벤의 초기 명성은 그의 균형 잡힌 활과 같은 음악 구조에 기초하고 있다.

| 분석 | 첫 문단에서 '보통 베토벤의 작품들을 세 시기로 나누지만, 그가 비엔나에 도착하기 전의 네 번째 시기 역시 고려되어야 한다.'라고 했다. 즉흥 연주는 그 자리에서 만드는 것이므로 즉흥 연주에 수년이 걸렸다는 ①은 지문과 불일치이다.

[03-04] 2019 한양대

| 정답 | 03 ④   04 ④

| 어휘 | **pidgin** ⓝ 피진어(어떤 언어, 특히 영어·포르투갈어·네덜란드어의 제한된 어휘들이 토착 언어 어휘들과 결합되어 만들어진 단순한 형태의 혼성어. 서로 다른 언어를 쓰는 사람들의 의사소통 필요에 의해서 형성됨)
creole ⓝ 크리올어(유럽의 언어와 특히 서인도 제도의 노예들이 사용하던 아프리카어의 혼성어로 모국어로 사용되는 언어)
marginal ⓐ 주변부의   **syntactic** ⓐ 구문론의   **lexicon** ⓝ 어휘 목록

〔전문해석〕

피진어와 크리올어는 한 언어를 공유하지 않는 사람들이 의사소통하기 위한 필요의 결과물이다. 하지만, 피진어는 이러한 목적을 위해 기존에 존재하는 언어나 방언에서 시작한 것이 아니라 오히려 두 언어의 특정한 결합이라는 점에서 민족 언어 혹은 국제어와 다르다. 로레토 토드(Loreto Todd)에 따르면, 피진어는 특정한 제한적 의사소통의 필요성을 충족시키기 위해 공용어를 갖지 않은 사람들 간에서 발생하는 <u>주변부의</u> 언어이다. 접촉의 초기 단계에서 피진어의 사용은 세부적인 개념들의 교환이 요구되지 않고, 거의 한쪽 언어에서 들여온 적은 어휘만으로 충분한 거래로 한정된다. 또한, 피진어의 구문론적 구조는 접촉하는 (기존의) 언어들의 구조보다 훨씬 단순한데, 피진어의 많은 특징들이 접촉하는 언어들의 용법들을 명백히 반영하지만, 다른 특징들은 피진어에만 고유하다. 크리올어는 피진어가 한 언어 공동체의 모국어가 될 때 발생한다. 피진어의 특징인 단순한 구조는 크리올어 안으로 넘어오 03④ 지만, 크리올어는 하나의 모국어로서 인간 경험의 전 범위를 표현할 수 있어야만 하므로, 어휘가 확장되고 종종 훨씬 더 정교한 구문론적 체계가 발전하게 된다.

---

03 윗글의 내용과 가장 가까운 것은? 〔내용 일치〕

① 크리올어는 피진어보다 더 단순한 구조를 가진다.
② 피진어의 어휘는 주로 접촉하는 두 언어로부터 유래한다.
③ 피진어는 접촉하는 기존 언어들 가운데 하나로 간주될 수 있다.
✓ 피진어는 접촉하는 언어들의 용법을 반영하는 특징들 외에도 그 자체의 고유한 특징들을 가지고 있다.
⑤ 피진어는 공용어를 사용했던 집단들 간의 의사소통을 촉진하기 위한 수단으로 개발된다.

| 분석 | 이 글은 두 언어가 특정하게 결합하여 만들어진 피진어와 크리올어의 특징을 기술하고 있는 글이다. 피진어만의 특징들도 글 속에서 기술하고 있으므로 ④의 진술은 지문과 일치하는 내용이다.

04 윗글의 빈칸에 들어갈 말로 가장 적절한 것은? 빈칸 추론

① 시적인
② 토착적인
③ 복잡한
✓ ④ 주변부의
⑤ 수사적인

| 분석 | 피진어의 특징은 제한적 의사소통만 하고, 세부적인 개념 교환은 어려우며, 약간의 어휘만으로 한정된다고 했으므로 피진어는 주요한(main, center) 언어라기보다는 그와 반대되는 주변적인(marginal) 언어라는 것을 알 수 있다.

| 배경지식 | 크리올 언어(Creole languag): 피진어가 사람들 사이에서 전해져 그 사회에 모국어가 된 것을 크리올 언어라고 한다. 피진은 주로 상인들 사이에서 생겨났으며 문법과 어휘가 간략한 것이 특징이다. 크리올은 시제, 진행형 등이 비교적 체계적으로 정해져 있으며, 조어법도 형성되어 있는 등 일반적인 언어의 체계를 확인할 수 있다.

[05-07] 2014 성균관대

| 정답 | 05 ⑤   06 ③   07 ③

| 어휘 |
picaresque ⓐ 악한을 소재로 한
superfluous ⓐ 남는, 과잉의, 불필요한
doggedly ⓐd 완강하게, 집요하게, 끈질기게
lyrical ⓐ 서정시 조의, 서정적인, 아름답게 표현된, 감상적인
swap ⓥ (물물)교환하다, 맞바꾸다
revolutionary ⓐ 혁명의, 혁명적인, 대개혁을 일으키는 ⓝ 혁명가
coherent ⓐ 분명한, 시종일관된, 통일성 있는
conjure ⓥ (악마 등을) 주술로 불러내다, 생각해 내다, 마법을 쓰다
galore ⓐ (명사 뒤에 쓰여) 풍부한, 성대한
bathe ⓥ 목욕시키다, 흠뻑 적시다, 헤엄치다, 둘러싸이다
supernatural ⓐ 초자연의, 이상한
sumptuousness ⓝ 사치, 호화, 화려
episodic ⓐ 에피소드적인, 삽화로 이루어진, 일시적인
weighty ⓐ 무거운, 중요한, 영향력 있는
laboured ⓐ 힘든, 곤란한, 애쓴
overly ⓐd 과도하게, 지나치게
faithful ⓐ (원본에) 충실한, 성실한, 정확한
bewildering ⓐ 어리둥절하게 만드는, 당황하게 하는

전문해석

살만 루슈디(Salman Rushdie) 경이 1981년 많은 상을 수상한 "자정의 아이들"의 초고를 제출했을 때 거기에는 추가적인 설명자의 목소리가 포함되어 있었다. 다행히도 센스가 있는 그의 출판인은, 현대 인도의 탄생을 그리는 이 악한소설(惡漢小說)이 이미 충분히 복잡하다는 생각을 가졌고 따라서 이 쓸데없는 인물은 삭제되었다. 영화로 만들기 위해 자기 작품을 각색하는 데 4년을 보낸 살만 경은 그의 영화 대본을 위해서도 똑같은 단순함을 적용했어야만 했다. 이 영화는 너무나도 끈질기게 원작에 충실한 바람에, 영화에는 플롯이 넘쳐 나고 이 이야기의 서사적 아름다움도 다 사라져 버렸다. 인도가 독립하는 바로 그 순간에 태어난 Saleem과 Shiva는 한 혁명가에게 잘 보이려고 하는 한 간호사에 의해 출생 시에 바꿔치기 된다. 여기에서의 표현은 그 주제만큼이나 야심적이고, 그리고 우선 영화의 앞 절반은 더 통일성이 있는데 이 부분은 감탄할 만하다. 인도계 캐나다인인 디파 메타(Deepa Mehta) 감독은, 실크와 사리, 그리고 넘치는 노래들로 영화를 엄청난 잔치거리로 만들어 냈다. 모든 것이 초자연적인 빛을 흠뻑 받고 있다. 그러나 이러한 종류의 화려함은 이야기가 스크린에서 전개되어 가는 에피소드의 구현 방법에 모자라는 점을 보상해 줄 수 없다. 영화 관람객이 좋아하게 되는 등장인물들은 문장 하나로 죽어 버린다. 심지어는 제법 중량감이 있는 연기들, 특히 성장한 Saleem의 역을 맡은 사티아 바바(Satya Bhabha)의 연기조차도, 너무 억지 같고 모호하다는 느낌으로부터 영화를 구조해 주지 못한다.

정답과 해설_ 77

05 윗글의 제목은 아마도 _____ 이다. 제목

① 두 갈래의 생각(망설이는): 살만 루슈디의 전기
② 훌륭한 각본을 만드는 것은 무엇인가
③ 위대한 작가의 정체성 위기
④ 영화화의 쇠퇴
✓ 저급한 영화를 만든 좋은 책

| 분석 | 이 글의 전체적 내용은 Rushdie 경의 작품이 소설은 훌륭하지만 영화로는 실패작이라는 것이다. 따라서 가장 제목으로 적합한 것은 ⑤ '저급한 영화를 만든 좋은 책'이다.

06 윗글에 따르면 다음 중 옳은 것은 무엇인가? 내용 일치

① 그 책의 출판사는 그 소설이 영화로 만들어지기에는 너무 복잡하다고 주장했다.
② 영화감독은 이 영화가 원작 소설의 서정적인 아름다움을 표현할 수 없다고 생각했다.
✓ 그 영화는 지나치게 복잡한 줄거리 때문에 끔찍하게 고통받는다.
④ 영화가 소설에 충실하지 않기 때문에 살만 루슈디의 메시지는 성공적으로 전달되지 못했다.
⑤ 살만 루슈디는 이 영화를 위해 몇 명의 캐릭터를 제거했다.

| 분석 | 지문에서 '이 영화는 너무나도 끈질기게 원작에 충실한 바람에, 영화에는 플롯이 넘쳐 나고 이 이야기의 서사적 아름다움도 다 사라져 버렸다.'고 언급했다. 따라서 ③은 지문과 일치한다.

07 윗글의 어조는 어떤가? 글의 어조

① 찬양하는
② 모순적인, 반어적인
✓ 비판적인
④ 당황케 하는
⑤ 시적인

| 분석 | 이 글은 살만 루슈디의 소설은 성공적이지만, 영화로 각색한 대본에서는 부족한 부분이 많다고 비판하는 글이다. 반어적으로 비꼬지는 않았기 때문에 ironic은 정답이 될 수 없다. 따라서 이 글의 어조는 critical이다.

[08-11] 2013 경희대

| 정답 | 08 ① 09 ② 10 ③ 11 ②

| 어휘 |
manifesto ⓝ 성명
call for 요구하다
rhetoric ⓝ 수사학, 말
intersect ⓥ 교차하다, 횡단하다
agitated ⓐ 선동적인

coin ⓥ 만들어 내다
sweeping ⓐ 광범위한, 압도적인
bombastic ⓐ 과장된
simultaneous ⓐ 동시의
swirl ⓥ 소용돌이치다

exalt ⓥ 칭찬하다
repudiation ⓝ 거절, 거부
Cubist ⓝ 입체파
vibrant ⓐ 진동하는, 생생한
crescendo ⓝ 점점 세어지기, 점층법

전문해석

미래파는 프랑스 파리의 신문 르 피가로가 이탈리아 시인이자 편집자인 필리포 토마소 마리네티(Filippo Tommaso Marinetti)의 성명문을 발표했던 1909년 2월 20일에 처음 소개되었다. 마리네티는 문화와 사회 내에서 과거의 예술을 ⓐ 버리고 변화, 독창성, 혁신 등을 ⓑ 찬양하고자 하는 자신의 목표를 반영하기 위해 미래파라는 단어를 만들어 냈다. 마리네티의 성명서는 자동차의 신기술과 그것의 속도와 힘, 움직임의 아름다움을 찬양했다. 폭력과 갈등을 칭송했던 그는 전통적인 가치관에 대한 철저한 거부와 미술관과 도서관 같은 전통적인 기관들의 파괴를 요구했다. 그 성명서의 수사법은 과도하게 과장된 것이었다. 그 공격적인 어조는 의도적으로 대중의 분노를 유발하고 논쟁을 일으키도록 의도된 것이다. 마리네티의 성명서는 밀라노에 있는 젊은 예술가들로 하여금 미래주의적 사상을 시각 예술에 적용하도록 고무시켰다. 마리네티처럼 그들은 독창성을 추앙했으며 전해 내려오는 예술적 전통에 대한 그들의 ⓒ 경멸을 표현했다. 그들은 움직임, 속도, 변화의 감각을 가시적으로 묘사하고자 했다. 이것을 이루기 위해 미래파 화가들은 한 물체의 여러 면을 동시에 보여 주기 위해 조각난 교차 면들과 선을 사용하는 입체파 기법을 채택했다. 미래파 그림들은 입체파 작품보다 더 밝고 생생한 색감을 가지고 있고, 리듬감 있게 소용돌이치는 형태들의 격렬한 움직임이 ⓓ 점점 강해지는 역동적이고 선동적인 구성을 보여 주었다.

---

08 윗글의 빈칸 ⓐ와 ⓑ에 들어갈 말로 가장 적절한 것은? 빈칸 추론

① 버리다 – 찬양하다 ✓
② 정당화하다 – 변호하다
③ 동화되다 – 수정하다
④ 입증하다 – 승인하다

| 분석 | 빈칸이 포함된 문장 뒤에서 자동차의 신기술을 찬양했고, 전통적 가치관을 거부했다고 언급되어 있으므로, 그와 같은 말을 만들어 줘야 한다. 빈칸 ⓐ 뒤는 '과거의 예술'이므로 '버리다'가 적절하고, 빈칸 ⓑ 뒤는 '변화, 독창성, 혁신'이므로 '찬양했다'가 적절하다.

---

09 윗글에 나타난 Futurism에 관한 설명 중 사실인 것은? 내용 일치

① 미래파 예술가는 전통적 예술을 거부하는 데 있어서 온건했다.
② 미래파 예술가는 자신들의 그림에서 조각난 물체들을 보여 주었다. ✓
③ 미래파 예술가는 현실에 대한 새로운 인식을 반대했다.
④ 미래파 예술가에게, 대중의 감정을 자극하는 것은 금기이다.

| 분석 | 지문의 마지막 부분에서 '미래파 화가들은 한 물체의 여러 면을 동시에 보여 주기 위해 조각난 교차 면들과 선을 사용하는 입체파 기법을 채택했다.'고 언급했다. 따라서 ②는 지문과 일치한다.

---

10 윗글의 빈칸 ⓒ에 들어갈 말로 가장 적절한 것은? 빈칸 추론

① 애정
② 존경
③ 경멸 ✓
④ 감탄

| 분석 | 미래파의 성격은 앞에서도 언급했듯이 과거의 것을 버리는 혁신적인 성격이다. 따라서 예술적 전통을 '경멸'하는 것이 적절하다.

11. 윗글의 밑줄 친 ⓐcrescendos의 의미에 가장 가까운 것은? 동의어

① 동요
② 강화 ✓
③ 보급
④ 공표

| 분석 | crescendo는 '점점 강해짐, 점증'의 의미를 갖는데, intensification은 '강화'의 의미이므로 동의어로 적절하다.

[12-14] 2013 고려대

| 정답 | 12 ① 13 ④ 14 ③

| 어휘 |
encompass ⓥ 포함하다   stringed instrument 현악기   incorporate ⓥ 합치다
eclectic ⓐ 절충적인, 폭넓은   amalgamation ⓝ 합병, 융합   evoke ⓥ 환기시키다
bluegrass ⓝ 블루그래스(기타와 밴조로 연주하는 미국의 전통적인 컨트리 음악)

전문해석

'올드타임(혹은 올드타이미)'는 가장 오래된 형태의 녹음된 컨트리 음악을 가리킨다. 20년대 초반에 처음으로 녹음된 그 스타일과 사운드는 1800년대 내내 일관성을 유지했다. 이 음악이 다양한 영향을 포함하고는 있지만, 이 음악은 예를 들어 바이올린과 같은 현악기로 연주되었던 영국의 포크 음악에 그 기원을 두고 있다. 1800년대 후반에 들어, 미국의 시골에서는 포크송을 스패니시 기타는 물론 아프리카의 밴조를 가지고 연주하기 시작했고, 여기에 도브로, 베이스, 워시보드와 같은 다른 악기들도 더했다. 1900년대에 걸쳐 이 컨트리 포크 음악은 동시대의 영향들을 통합하였는데, 특히 블루스와 보드빌 코미디가 합쳐졌다. 이렇게 시골에서 벌어진 절충적인 조합이 20년대 컨트리 음악의 사운드였고, 이 사운드가 '올드타임' 컨트리로 영구적으로 동일시되게 되는데, 왜냐하면 이 음악이야말로 컨트리의 뿌리를 환기시키기 때문이다. 지미 로저스(Jimmie Rodgers)가 컨트리를 산업화 시대로 가져오면서 컨트리 음악이 30년대 들어 발전하기 시작하지만, 20세기 말까지도 올드타임의 전통을 털끝만큼도 바꾸지 않으면서 올드타임을 연주하는 그룹들이 있었다. 올드타임 안의 한 중요한 전통으로는 블루그래스가 있는데, 이는 40년대 후반 컨트리 음악이 점점 현대화되는 것에 대한 반발로 등장한 것이었다.

13 ④

---

12. 다음 중 "올드타임" 컨트리 음악에 대해 추론할 수 없는 것은? 내용 추론

① 그것은 1900년대 후반까지 순수하게 남아 있었다. ✓
② 지미 로저스는 진보적인 올드타임 컨트리 가수였다.
③ 그것은 영국 민요에서 유래되었다.
④ 미국인들이 그것의 악기 연주 범위를 넓혔다.

| 분석 | 마지막 부분에서 지미 로저스가 컨트리 음악을 발전시켰다는 말은 더 이상 컨트리가 순수하지 않을 수 있다는 말이다. 블루그래스는 그 순수함을 지키겠다는 것이다. 따라서 컨트리 음악은 약간의 순수하지 않고 변화가 있었다는 것을 알 수 있다.

---

13. 윗글에 따르면, "블루그래스"에 대한 설명으로 옳은 것은? 내용 일치

① 그것은 민속 음악을 원래의 형태로 보존했다.
② 그것은 오래된 컨트리 음악과 팝 음악의 혼합을 통합하려고 노력했다.
③ 그것은 블루스의 현대적인 영향으로부터 발전했다.
④ 그것은 올드타임 컨트리 음악의 변화하는 면에 대한 반발이었다. ✓

| 분석 | 마지막 문장에서 'One major style within old-time was bluegrass, which developed in the late '40s as a reaction

to the increasing modernization of country music'이라고 언급했는데 블루그래스는 컨트리 음악이 점점 현대화되는 것에 대한 반발이라고 할 수 있다. 따라서 ④가 지문과 일치한다.

14 밑줄 친 "eclectic amalgamation"과 가장 가까운 의미를 고르시오. 동의어
① 절대적인 소외
② 고전적 고색
✓ ③ 선택적 혼종
④ 지역적 이주

| 분석 | eclectic은 '취사선택하는(selecting)'의 의미이며, amalgamation은 '합동, 합병'이라는 의미이다.

[15-16] 2015 한양대

| 정답 | 15 ② 16 ①

| 어휘 | **pidgin** ⓝ 피진어(어떤 언어, 특히 영어·포르투갈어·네덜란드어의 제한된 어휘들이 토착 언어 어휘들과 결합되어 만들어진 단순한 형태의 혼성어. 서로 다른 언어를 쓰는 사람들의 의사소통 필요에 의해서 형성됨)
creole ⓝ 크리올어(유럽의 언어와 특히 서인도 제도의 노예들이 사용하던 아프리카어의 혼성어로 모국어로 사용되는 언어); 크리올 사람 (특히 서인도 제도에 사는, 유럽인과 흑인의 혼혈인)   **transaction** ⓝ 거래, 매매; 처리 과정
syntactic ⓐ 구문론[통사론]의   **usage** ⓝ (단어의) 용법[어법/사용]
Gaul ⓝ 골, 갈리아 (고대 켈트 사람의 땅; 지금의 북이탈리아·프랑스·벨기에 등을 포함함)

전문해석

피진어와 크리올어는 의사소통할 수 있는 언어를 공유하지 못한 사람들의 필요성의 산물이다. 그것들은 국가 언어 및 국제 언어들과 다른데, 피진어는 이러한 목적에 부합하기 위해 선택된 기존에 이미 존재하는 언어나 방언으로서 시작되지 않았다는 점이다. 피진어는 오히려 두 언어의 특별한 결합이었다. 로레토 토드(Loreto Todd)는 피진어와 크리올어에 대해서 다음과 같이 말한다.
피진어는 공통의 언어를 가지고 있지 않은 사람들 사이의 어떤 제한된 의사소통을 성취하기 위해 발생한 주변적인 언어이다. 접촉의 초기 단계에 의사소통은 생각의 세부적인 교환이 요구되지 않으며, 한 언어로부터 거의 독단적으로 이끌어 낸, 몇 안 되는 수의 단어들이면 충분하다. 피진어의 구문적인 구조는 접촉하고 있는 언어의 구조보다 덜 복잡하고 덜 유연하다. 그리고 비록 많은 피진어의 특징들이, 접촉하고 있는 언어의 특징을 명백히 반영함에도 불구하고, 다른 특징들은 피진어에만 독특한 것이다.
크리올어는 피진어가 언어 공동체의 모국어가 되었을 때 발생한다. 피진어를 특징짓는 단순한 언어적 구조는 크리올어에 의해서 전승된다. 그러나 모국어로서 크리올어는 인간 경험의 모든 범위를 표현할 수 있어야 하기 때문에, 어휘들은 확장되고 흔히 보다 정교한 구문 체계로 진화한다. 크리올어는 흔히 진정한 언어로 여겨지지 않고, 그 결과로서 열등하다고 취급되기 때문에, 예를 들어, 영어와 프랑스어가 피진어의 결과일지도 모른다는 사실에 주목하는 것은 가치 있는 일이다. 프랑스어의 경우는 원주민인 갈리아인들과 정복자인 로마인들 간의 접촉을 통해서 성립했고, 영어의 경우는 원주민인 앵글로색슨족과 영국의 동쪽 해안지대에 정착한 덴마크인들과의 접촉을 통해서 성립했다.

15 윗글의 내용과 일치하지 않는 것은? 내용 일치
① 피진어는 보통 두 개의 다른 언어에서 발전한다.
✓ ② 피진어의 어휘는 일반적으로 접촉한 두 언어에서 가져온다.
③ 크리올어는 보통 피진어보다 더 넓은 범위의 인간 경험을 표현할 수 있다.
④ 접촉한 언어의 구조는 피진어의 구조보다 일반적으로 더 융통성이 있다.

| 분석 | 두 번째 단락에서 '접촉의 초기 단계에 의사소통은 생각의 세부적인 교환이 요구되지 않으며, 한 언어로부터 거의 독단적으로 이끌어 낸 몇 안 되는 수의 단어들이면 충분하다.'라고 언급되었다. 따라서 피진어의 어휘는 일반적으로 접촉한 두 언어에서 가져온다는 것은 지문과 일치하지 않는다.

16 윗글의 내용으로 추론할 수 있는 것은? 내용 추론

☑ ① 프랑스어는 아마도 크리올어일 것이다.
② 영어는 아마도 피진어일 것이다.
③ 피진어들은 철학적 사상의 교환을 촉진하기 위해 발전한다.
④ 크리올어는 언어 공동체가 그것을 모국어로 받아들이면 피진어가 된다.

| 분석 | 마지막 단락에서 영어와 프랑스어가 피진어의 결과라고 하였는데, 크리올어는 피진어가 모국어일 때 발생한다고 하였다. 피진어의 결과물이라는 것은 다시 말하면 크리올어를 말하는 것이므로, 영어와 프랑스어는 크리올어라고 할 수 있다. 따라서 ①은 맞는 진술이지만, ②는 지문과 일치하지 않는 진술이다.

[17-18] 2017 서강대

| 정답 | 17 ② 18 ④

| 어휘 | **consonant** ⓝ 자음　　**vowel** ⓝ 모음　　**segmental** ⓐ 분절의
stress ⓝ (발음의) 강세　　**rhythm** ⓝ 규칙적인 반복, 율동, 리듬　　**intonation** ⓝ 억양, 음조
suprasegmental ⓐ 초분절적인　　**prosody** ⓝ 운율 체계
building-block ⓝ 집짓기 블록, 기본 구성물　　**syllable** ⓝ 음절
phrase ⓝ 구, 구절　　**discourse** ⓝ 담론, 담화　　**make sense** 이치에 맞다
break down 고장 나다, 실패하다, 무너지다, 좌절되다　　**string** ⓥ 꿰다, 길게 이어지다
address ⓥ 다루다, 처리하다　　**stream** ⓝ 흐름, 연속, 줄기　　**provided** ⓒⓞⓝⓙ 만약 ~라면
disparate ⓐ 서로 전혀 다른, 이질적인

전문해석

언어의 음성 체계는 두 가지 범주, 즉 자음과 모음(분절적 특징이라고 알려진) 및 강세, 리듬, 억양과 같은 좀 더 보편적 측면들(초분절적 특징 또는 운율 체계라고 알려진)로 분류된다. 전통적으로 음성 체계는 음성 〉 음절 〉 단어 〉 구절 〉 문장 〉 확장된 담화라는 식의 구성적 형태로 기술되고 가르쳐져 왔다. 분석적 관점에서 보면 이치에 맞지만, 이것은 언어 학습자들이 일반적으로 언어를 경험하는 방식이 아니다. 의사소통이 무너지지 않고는 화자로써 우리가 말하는 것에 대해 음성 단위로 혹은 심지어 음절 단위로 일반적으로 생각하는 것은 아니다. 그러므로 한 번에 한 가지 음성을 습득하여 결국 음성들을 하나로 잇게 된다는 상향식 접근은 버리고, 일련의 언어적 흐름 속에서 음성 체계를 다루는 좀 더 하향식 접근으로 대체하기에 이르렀다.

17 빈칸에 가장 적절한 단어나 구를 고르시오. 연결사

① ~하지 않도록　　☑ ② ~하지 않는 한
③ (만약) ~라면　　④ ~하는 한에서는

| 분석 | 우리가 말을 하면서 자음 하나하나, 한 음절 한 음절 생각하면서 말을 해야 한다면 대화가 되지 않을 것이다. 따라서 '의사소통이 무너지지 않고는 그런 식으로 생각할 수 없다'는 말이 되어야 한다. 따라서 unless가 가장 적절하다. 또한 lest는 '~하지 않기 위하여'의 의미를 갖는 접속사인데 lest절은 반드시 (should R)이 와야만 한다. lest가 빈칸에 들어간다면, 빈칸 뒤 동사가 breaks down이 아니라 break down이 와야 한다.

18 윗글의 내용과 일치하지 <u>않는</u> 진술을 고르시오. `내용 일치`

① 운율 체계(prosody)는 자연적인 담화에서 분절적 특징(segmental features)보다 더 중요한 것으로 간주된다.
② 자음과 모음은 음성의 분석적 관점에서 볼 때 구성요소에 해당한다.
③ 언어 기술과 언어 학습은 상당히 상이하다.
✔ 의사소통의 붕괴는 언어의 분석적 성질을 잘 보여 준다.

| 분석 | 빈칸 연결사에 unless를 넣었다면 이 글은 의사소통이 무너지지 않고서는 우리가 분석적으로 생각하면서 말하는 것은 아니라는 것이다. 따라서 의사소통의 붕괴가 보여 주는 것은 언어의 분석적인 성질이 아니라 언어는 하나의 흐름으로 다루어진다는 것이다. 따라서 ④는 글의 내용과 일치하지 않는 진술이다.

[19-20] 2014 한양대

| 정답 | 19 ② 20 ①

| 어휘 |
conventional ⓐ 전통적인, 관습적인
phase ⓥ (단계적으로) 실행하다, 예정하다 ⓝ 단계, 국면
diffuse ⓐ 흩어진, 널리 퍼진, 산만한
prominent ⓐ 현저한, 두드러진, 저명한
shrouded ⓐ 수의를 입힌, 가린
cram ⓥ (억지로) 채워 넣다, 잔뜩 먹다, 주입식으로 하다
digressive ⓐ 본론을 떠난, 지엽적인
overstuffed ⓐ 지나치게 채워 넣은
permanence ⓝ 영구, 영속, 불변
underscore ⓥ 강조하다, 뒷받침하다

explicit ⓐ 명백한, 분명한, 노골적인, 터놓고 말하는
discriminate ⓥ 구별하다, 차별 대우하다
piecemeal ⓐ 조금씩의, 단편적인 ⓐⓓ 점차로, 따로따로
antecedent ⓝ 선례, 경력, 이전의 일, 이전 상황 ⓐ 앞서는, 우선하는
supernumerary ⓐ 정원 이상의, 여분의 ⓝ 정원 외의 사람, 임시 고용인
exhaustive ⓐ 철저한, 남김 없는, 소모적인
exploration ⓝ 탐험, 탐사, 개발, 탐구
juxtapose ⓥ 나란히 놓다, 병렬하다

deliberate ⓐ 계획적인, 신중한, 침착한
inference ⓝ 추리, 추측, 추정
adventitious ⓐ 우연의, 외래의, 우발적인
climactic ⓐ 점층법의, 절정의
chance discovery 우연한 발견
recount ⓥ 상술하다, 이야기하다, 열거하다

전문해석

제임스(James)의 초기 소설들은 전통적인 서술기법을 사용하였다: 명백한 인물의 특색화, 분명하게 단계적 순서를 거쳐 일어나는 사건들을 서로 연결 짓는 행동, 확실하게 윤곽이 정해지고 특수하게 기술된 배경. 그러나 이러한 그의 기법은, 전체적인 중요성을 독자가 끈질기게 집중하고 예민하게 추론을 해야만 깨달을 수 있는 세밀하게 차별된 상세 설명을 모아 놓은, 차츰 더 미묘하고 더 신중하고 더 분산적인 스타일로 바뀌게 되었다. 그의 후기 소설들은, 급작스럽고 돌발적인 행동들을 <u>줄이고</u> 날카로운 충격을 연이어 제시하기보다는 천천히 차츰차츰 생각을 추가한다. 감춰져 있던 것에서 갑자기 커튼을 젖히지 않고 천천히 열어 나간다. 그러한 기법은 제임스의 근본적인 주제, 즉 인간 행동 자체가 아닌, 인간의 행동이나 상호 작용을 만들어 내고 그것들을 통해 만들어지는 심리 상태들을 다루는 데에 더 적합하다. 제임스는 등장인물들이 무엇을 하느냐보다는 도덕적 심리적 내력, 지각, 그리고 그들의 행동에 수반하는 결과들에 더 관심이 있었다. 이것이 그가 흔히 행위보다는 "경우"를 더 많이 이야기한 이유이다. 따라서 그의 이야기들은 점점 더 길어지는 반면, 이야기가 설명하는 행동들은 점점 더 단순해지고 눈에 덜 보이게 되었다. 그것은, 과도하게 많은 것을 담고 있는 액션 소설들이 그렇듯이, 그 이야기들이 우연하고 이차적인 사건들, 산만한 휴지, 또는 잉여적 등장인물들로 가득 차 있어서가 아니라, 그가 그의 상황의 모든 뉘앙스를 하나도 빠짐없이 상세하게 제시하고 있기 때문이다. <u>일반적으로 소설의 흥미는, 클라이맥스 사건으로 점점 발전하다가, 마침내 등장인물의 외적인 운명을 이야기책에서 나오는 영원함에 대한 약속으로 결말지어 주는, 눈에 보이는 행동의 다양성과 흥분에 있다.</u> 그러나 제임스의 소설은 그 특별한 흥미로움이, 등장인물들이 천천히 독자들에게 공개됨에 따라 독자들이 탐구와 우연한 발견을 통해 등장인물들의 개인적 상황의 현실로의 정신적 적응에 대한 풍부한 분석을 하도록 유도해 가는 데에 있다.

19	윗글의 빈칸에 들어갈 말로 가장 적절한 것은? 빈칸 추론
	① 의존하다　　　　　　　　　✓ ② 줄이다
	③ 강조하다　　　　　　　　　④ 나란히 놓다

| 분석 | 제임스의 초기와 후기 소설을 대조하는 것으로 빈칸에는 전통적인 기법으로부터 새로운 기법으로의 변화를 나타내야 하므로 전통적인 방법은 '사용을 줄인다'는 것이 가장 적합하다.

20	윗글의 내용과 일치하지 <u>않는</u> 것은? 내용 일치
	✓ ① 제임스의 후기 소설은 액션이 클라이맥스로 가면서 점점 더 발전하는 특징이 있다.
	② 제임스의 후기 소설은 도덕적, 심리적 복잡성 수준이 그의 초기 소설과 다르다.
	③ 제임스의 후기 소설은 그가 자신의 상황의 모든 뉘앙스를 철저히 세부적으로 제공했기 때문에 장황해졌다.
	④ 제임스의 첫 소설은 단계적인 순서를 강조하는 전통적인 서술 기법을 사용한다.

| 분석 | 지문의 마지막 부분에서 James의 후기 소설은 등장인물들의 행동이 클라이맥스에 도달하면서 점진적으로 발달하는 방식(기존의 전통적인 소설 방식)을 따르지 않았다고 했다. 따라서 ①은 지문과 일치하지 않는다.

[21] 2013 중앙대

| 정답 | ③

| 어휘 | geometric ⓐ 기하학적인　　　plane ⓝ 평면, 면　　　anatomy ⓝ 해부학
totality ⓝ 총체성　　　halt ⓥ 멈추다　　　germinate ⓥ (감정이나 생각이) 생기다
at the same time 동시에　　　patch ⓝ 조각, 파편　　　charcoal ⓝ 숯, 목탄
skeleton ⓝ 뼈대, 윤곽　　　all at once 갑자기, 단번에　　　intuitive ⓐ 직관적인
wall up in 가두다　　　vibration ⓝ 진동, 반응, 느낌　　　cradle ⓝ 요람

전문해석

세잔의 회화는 과학도 전통도 부정하지 않는다. 파리에 있는 동안 그는 매일같이 루브르에 갔다. 그는 그림 그리는 법은 배워야만 하며, 평면과 형태에 대한 기하학적 연구가 이 배움의 과정에서 반드시 필요한 부분이라고 믿었다. 그는 풍경의 지질학적 구조에 대해서도 연구했다. 하지만 가시적 세계에서 표현되는 이 추상적인 관계가 그림 그리는 행위에 영향을 미쳐야 한다고 확신했다. 해부학과 디자인의 규칙들은 그의 붓질마다 나타나는데, 이는 마치 테니스 시합에서 각각의 스트로크가 테니스 경기 규칙들을 전제로 하고 있는 것과 마찬가지이다.

하지만 화가의 행동을 유발하는 것이 절대로 원근법, 기하학, 색채를 지배하는 법칙, 혹은 어떤 특정한 지식 하나에 국한된 것이 되어서는 안 된다. 어떤 그림을 서서히 나타나게 만드는, 화가의 행동을 자극하는 것으로는 단지 하나의 것만이 존재할 수 있다. 그것은 총체적이고, 절대적 충만 속의 풍경으로, 세잔이 바로 '모티프'라고 불렀던 것이다. 그는 풍경의 지질학적 기반을 발견하는 것으로 시작하곤 했다. 그리고는, 세잔에 따르면, 그는 거기서 멈추고 커다랗게 된 눈으로, 풍경에서 '생겨나는' 모든 것을 보았다. 그런 다음 그는 한 번에 그림의 모든 부분들을 그리기 시작한다. 색의 조각들을 이용해서 원래의 지질학적 뼈대에 대한 목탄 스케치를 에워싸며 그림을 그린다. 이 그림은 충만성과 밀도를 가진다. 이 그림은 구조와 균형 속에서 자라나서, 한꺼번에 확 성숙에 도달한다. "내 안에서 풍경은 스스로를 생각한다." 세잔은 말했다. "나는 그 풍경의 의식이다." <u>이 '직관적 과학'보다 자연주의에서 더 먼 것은 세상에 없다.</u> 세잔은 그가 없다면 각각의 의식의 분리된 삶에 갇혀 있었을 것들을 재포착하여 눈에 보이는 대상으로 바꾸어 놓았다. 그것은 외형의 진동으로, 바로 그것이 사물들의 요람이다.

21 ③

다음 글의 내용과 일치하지 않는 것은? 내용 일치

① 세잔에게, 기하학이나 색을 지배하는 법칙에 대한 지식은 화가의 행동에 동기를 부여하는 유일한 요소는 아니었다.
② 세잔은 어떤 풍경의 지질학적 구조에 대한 연구가 그림을 그리는 방법을 배우는 데 필요한 부분이라고 믿었다.
✓ ③ 세잔의 "모티프"는 그림에서 눈에 보이는 세계의 역할을 강조한 현대 자연주의 관점을 가장 잘 반영한다.
④ 세잔의 기여가 없었다면, 외형의 진동은 각각의 의식의 분리된 삶 위에 드러나지 않았을 것이다.

| 분석 | 글의 마지막 부분에서 세잔의 '직관적 과학'은 자연주의와 거리가 멀다(Nothing could be farther from naturalism than this "intuitive science.")고 하였다. 따라서 세잔의 "모티프"는 자연주의 관점을 잘 반영한다는 ③의 진술은 지문과 일치하지 않는다.

[22-23] 2019 한양대

| 정답 | 22 ③   23 ④

| 어휘 |
sensuous ⓐ 감각적인
harmonic ⓐ 화성의
amplify ⓥ 확장하다
underline ⓥ 강조하다
delicacy ⓝ 섬세함
chromatic ⓐ 반음계의
exemplify ⓥ 구현하다
affectation ⓝ 가식, 꾸밈
aversion ⓝ 반감
orgiastic ⓐ 흥분시키는, 진탕 마시고 노는
milieu ⓝ 환경
profundity ⓝ 심오함

전문해석

현대의 음악 청취자들에게 드뷔시(Debussy)는 실질적으로 프랑스 음악을 규정하는데, 내가 의미하는 바는 (그의 감각적 섬세함뿐 아니라 바그너(Wagner)와 슈트라우스(Strauss)에서처럼 끊임없이 분주하게 흥분을 고조시키며 클라이맥스로 치닫는 고밀도의 반음계적 전개를 특징으로 하는 19세기 후반 독일 음악의 화성적 양식들에 대한 그의 반감도 포함한) 그의 음악의 본질적 특성들이 이제 본질적으로 "프랑스적" 특징으로 간주되기에 이르렀다는 것이다. 그러나 월시(Walsh)는 드뷔시가 자신의 음악적 환경을 단순히 확장하고 구현하는 것이 아니라 의식적이고 완고하게 시대의 흐름을 거슬렀음을, 특히 독일 음악이 프랑스 작곡가들에게 미친 심대한 영향과 관련하여 그렇게 했음을 분명히 한다. 바그너(Wagner)는 19세기 후반 파리에서 피해 갈 수 없는 존재였지만, 드뷔시는 독일 음악 영향에 대한 비난을 더 먼 과거로 거슬러 올라가 글루크(Gluck)에게로 던졌다. 드뷔시는 그가 독일적인 "심오한 척 하는 가식이나 모든 것을 곱절로 강조하려는 욕구"로 인식되는 것보다도 라모(Rameau)의 "섬세하고 매혹적인 유연함"을 더 선호한 점에서 묵묵히 급진적이었다.

22 윗글의 제목으로 가장 적절한 것은? 제목

① 더 멀리 글루크로까지 거슬러 올라감: 드뷔시 음악의 뿌리 너무 지엽적
② 불가사의한 재능: 프랑스적이면서 동시에 독일적인 지문 내용과 불일치
✓ ③ 무엇이 드뷔시 음악을 근본적으로 프랑스적이게 만드는가
④ 음악사에 묻힌 무명의 영웅을 재발견함 지문 내용과 불일치
⑤ 드뷔시의 연금술: 지구적 갈등을 소재로 하여 음악이라는 텍스트 만들기 언급 안 함

| 분석 | 이 글의 작가는 드뷔시의 음악 특징이 본질적으로 프랑스적 특징이라고 말하고, 그 이유를 설명하고 있다. 따라서 ③이 제목으로 가장 적절하다.

23 밑줄 친 "swam against the current"의 의미로 가장 적절한 것은? 밑줄 의미 추론

① 독일 청중들의 취향에 영합하지 않다
② 프랑스 음악에 대한 개인적 선호를 통제하다
③ 세상으로부터 철수하여 자신의 예술의 내면세계로 침잠하다
✓ ④ 독일 음악의 형식 논리와 고밀도의 질감을 모방하지 않다
⑤ 섬세함과 매력으로 규정되는 당시의 음악적 경향성을 억제하다

| 분석 | 이 글의 내용은 드뷔시는 독일 음악의 영향을 거부하고 프랑스적인 특성을 찾으려고 했다는 것이다. 지문에 언급된 기존 독일 음악의 특징은 '고밀도의 반음계적 전개', '심오한 척하는 가식', '모든 것을 과다하게 강조하려는 경향'인데, 밑줄 친 당대의 그 흐름을 거슬렀다는 것은 결국 이러한 독일의 특징을 따라 하지 않았다는 의미이다. 따라서 ④가 가장 적절하다.

[24-26] 2012 성균관대

| 정답 | 24 ① 25 ⑤ 26 ⑤

| 어휘 | graphic ⓐ 문자의, 그림의, 도표의　　symbolism ⓝ 상징주의, 상징　　graphology ⓝ 필적학, 필적 감정
forensic science 법의학　　critical ⓐ 중요한, 중대한　　consistence ⓝ 일관성
stroke ⓝ 붓질, 필체　　scribble ⓥ 휘갈겨 쓰다　　biased ⓐ 편향된, 치우친
infamous ⓐ 악명 높은　　control ⓝ 시험의 대조군

전문해석

문자 상징체계의 흥미로운 측면 하나는 글자 구조 내의 다양한 글자체들을 얼마만큼 신뢰성 있게 해석할 수 있는가의 정도이다. 필체의 심리 연구를 지칭하는 필적 감정은 백 년이 넘는 세월 동안 행해져 왔다. 필적학을 최초로 본격 학문 분야로서 정립한 사람은 프랑스의 수도원장 장 이폴리트 미숑(Jean Hippolyte Michon)이었다. 필적 감정가들의 주장에 의하면 한 개인의 필적을 주의 깊고 면밀하게 분석하면 그의 인성에 대해 중요한 정보를 밝힐 수 있다. 예컨대 필적을 분석하면 특정 직업에 그 사람이 어울리는지 여부를 알 수 있다는 것이다. 최근 몇 년간 필적 감정가들은 필적 관련 신원과 모방을 중요하게 취급하는 여러 전문 분야와 과학수사에 고용되어 일해 왔다. 필적 감정은 분명히 과학으로서 발전할 수 있는 여지가 있다. 필적의 크기, 모양, 각도, 선의 방향, 필적의 농도 같은 변수들을 원칙상 과학적으로 엄밀하게 기술할 수 있기 때문이다. 그러나 필적 감정은 의심을 받아 왔는데, 이는 휘갈겨 쓴 서명 따위에 근거하여 성격을 말해 주고 운명을 예측하는 필적 감정이 시골 농산물 품평회나 해변의 휴양지에서 누린 인기 때문이었다. 필적 감정은 또한 평판이 좋거나 나쁜 사람들 위주로만 이루어져 왔다. 즉, 성공의 기초를 필적 하나에서 식별은 하지만, 이 26⑤에 대한 객관적 대조군은 없다.

24 윗글의 가장 좋은 제목은 _____ 일 것이다. 제목

✓ ① 필적 분석의 역사
② 최근 구직자들 사이에서 필적학의 인기 언급 안 함
③ 문자 상징체계의 신화적 기원 언급 안 함
④ 필기 대체로서 디지털 서명 언급 안 함
⑤ 범죄 수사에 있어서 필적학의 활용 너무 지엽적

| 분석 | 이 글은 필적학의 전반적인 부분에 대한 기원과 발전의 과정을 기술하는 글이다. 따라서 글 전체를 포괄하는 제목은 ① '필적 분석의 역사'가 가장 적합하다.

| **25** | 빈칸에 들어갈 말로 가장 적절한 것은? 연결사
① 더욱이
② 그러므로
③ 분명히
④ 공식적으로
✓ ⑤ 그러나

| 분석 | 빈칸 앞은 필적학이 과학으로서의 가치를 가지고 있다는 내용이고 빈칸 뒤는 시골 농산물 품평회나 해변의 휴양지에서의 인기 때문에 미신이었다는 내용이므로 역접의 연결어가 들어가야 한다.

| **26** | 윗글에 따르면 다음 중 사실인 것은? 내용 일치
① 정부는 일반 대중을 오도하는 경우가 많았기 때문에 필기 관행을 통제했다.
② 미송은 새로운 분야에 대한 연구 보조금을 받은 첫 번째 사람이었다.
③ 유명한 사람과 악명 높은 사람의 차이를 확인하는 것은 필적학자들에게 가장 중요한 과제이다.
④ 필적학은 시골 사람들의 미신적인 생각을 바꾸는 데 기여했다.
✓ ⑤ 필적학은 종종 단순한 점재 기술로 여겨졌다.

| 분석 | 지문에서 "필적 감정은 의심을 받아 왔는데, 이는 휘갈겨 쓴 서명 따위에 근거하여 성격을 말해 주고 운명을 예측하는 필적 감정이 시골 농산물 품평회나 해변의 휴양지에서 누린 인기 때문이었다"라고 하였으므로 정답은 ⑤ '필적학은 종종 단순한 점재 기술로 여겨졌다.'이다. ②의 경우 미송이 필적학을 학문 분야로 정립한 최초의 사람인 것은 맞지만 보조금과는 관련이 없으므로 지문과 일치하지 않는다.

[27-29] 2016 이화여대

| 정답 | 27 ③   28 ①   29 ④

| 어휘 | **divergent** ⓐ 분기하는, 갈라지는; (관습 등에서) 일탈한   **impel** ⓥ 재촉하다; 억지로 하다
farce ⓝ 소극(笑劇), 광대극; 익살   **schematically** ⓐⓓ 개략적으로, 도식적으로   **occult** ⓐ 비술적인, 초자연적인
exact ⓥ 요구하다, 강제하다, (세금 따위를) 강제로 거두어 들이다   **verbose** ⓐ 장황한

전문해석

자신의 소설에 몰두했던 작가로서 토머스 하디(Thomas Hardy)의 충동들은 갈라지는 다양한 것들이었다. 그러나 그 충동들이 항상 조화롭게 작동하는 것은 아니었다. 하디는 호기심보다는 공감에 의해서 자극받았다고 할지라도, 어느 정도까지는 그의 소설 속에 등장하는 인물들의 심리를 탐구하는 데 흥미로워했다. 때때로 그는 소극에 대한 충동은 물론이고 희극에 대한 충동(그의 모든 무심한 냉정함도 불구하고)도 느꼈다. 그러나 그는 더 자주 비극 쪽으로 기울어졌고 그 비극을 기록했다. 그는 또한 그 문구의 몇몇 의미에서 문학적인 사실주의에도 관심을 가졌다. 그는 평범한 사람들을 묘사하고 싶어 했다. 그는 그들이 처한 딜레마에 대해서 사색하기를 원했다(그것도 불행하게, 심지어 개략적으로). 그리고 그는 물질적인 세상을 정확하게 기록하기를 원했다. 결국 그는 사실주의자 이상이 되고 싶어 했다. 그는 단지 사건들을 정확하게 기록하는 진부함을 넘어서고자 했고, 더 나아가 초자연적인 것과 낯선 것에 대한 그의 인식도 표현하고자 했다. 그의 소설들 속에서, 이 다양한 충동들은 자주 불가피하게 서로서로 희생당했는데, 그 이유는 불가피하게도 하디가 플로베르나 제임스 같은 소설가들이 신경 쓰는 방식으로 신경 쓰지 않았고, 가장 적은 저항의 길을 택했기 때문이다. 따라서 하나의 충동은 종종 더 새로운 충동에 굴복했고, 불행하게도 타협을 이끌어 내는 대신에 단순하게 사라졌다. 현실을 향해 전례 없는 빛을 던지고 싶은 욕망은, 꽃의 구조와 질감을 정확하고 구체적으로 기록하는 소설가-과학자로서의 욕망에 갑작스럽게 자리를 내주었다. 이런 경우 29 ④

에, 새로운 충동은 최소한 에너지 넘치는 것이었고, 그러한 충동에 대한 탐닉은 편안한 문체라는 결과를 초래하지 않았다. 그러나 다른 경우에, 하디는 추상적으로 분류하고 도식화하고자 하는 그의 치명적으로 편안한 (문체적) 충동을 선호해서 위험하고 에너지가 넘치는 (문체적) 충동을 포기했다. 편안한 충동에 빠져들었을 때, 그의 문체―작가의 문학적 가치에 대한 확실한 지표인―는 확실히 장황해졌다. 하디의 약점은 이들 분기하는 충동들이 오고 가는 것을 통제하지 못한 그의 무능력과, 에너지 넘치고 모험적인 충동들을 만들어 내고 Ⓐ 지속하는 것을 꺼리는 것으로부터 비롯되었다.

27 윗글의 제목으로 가장 적절한 것은? 제목
① 분기적 충동: 소설 속의 통일성 문제 지문 내용과 불일치
② 현실과 낯선 것들: 하디의 두 가지 관심 분야 너무 지엽적
✓③ 하디의 소설적 충동: 통제의 문제
④ 하디의 소설에서 평범한 사람들의 역할 너무 지엽적
⑤ 장황함: 하디의 치명적 약점 너무 지엽적

| 분석 | 이 글은 소설가 토머스 하디와 그가 가졌던 다양한 충동들에 대하여 기술하고 하디의 약점으로 그러한 충동들을 통제하지 못한다고 기술했으므로 글 전체를 담을 수 있는 포괄적인 ③이 제목으로 가장 적절하다. 나머지 보기는 너무 지엽적이라고 할 수 있다.

28 빈칸 Ⓐ에 가장 적절한 것은? 빈칸 추론
✓① 지속시키다
② 종속시키다
③ 억제하다
④ 보충하다
⑤ 보조금을 주다

| 분석 | 빈칸 앞에 and로 연결되어 있으므로, 흐름상 cultivate와 같은 맥락의 단어가 필요하다. 따라서 ① '지속시키다'가 문맥상 가장 적절하다.

29 윗글을 통해 추론할 수 없는 진술은? 내용 추론
① "문학적 사실주의"라는 용어는 하나 이상의 정의에 취약하다.
② 작가의 문체는 작가의 문학적 가치를 측정할 수 있는 믿을 만한 수단으로 간주된다.
③ 편안한 (문체적) 충동에 대한 탐닉은 하디를 장황한 스타일로 이끌었다.
✓④ 플로베르와 제임스는 그들의 소설에서 하디가 하디 소설에서 탐닉하는 충동보다 더 많은 충동을 탐닉했다.
⑤ 희극적 요소는 비극보다 하디의 소설에 덜 자주 등장한다.

| 분석 | 두 번째 단락에서 '하디의 소설들 속에서, 이 다양한 충동들은 자주 불가피하게 서로서로 희생당했는데, 그 이유는 불가피하게도 하디가 플로베르나 제임스 같은 소설가들이 신경 쓰는 방식으로 신경 쓰지 않았다.'라고 언급했다. 그 뒤에서도 하디는 그들과 달라서 다양한 충동을 겪었다고 했으므로 하디가 플로베르와 제임스보다 더 많은 충동을 탐닉했다고 할 수 있다. 따라서 ④는 지문과 일치하지 않는다.

[30-32] 2016 홍익대

| 정답 | 30 ④ 31 ③ 32 ④

| 어휘 |
various ⓐ 가지각색의
autobiography ⓝ 자서전
encompass ⓥ 둘러싸다, 포위하다; 포함하다
funeral ⓝ 장례식
get someone far 성공하게 하다, 성과를 거두게 하다
distinction ⓝ 구별, 차별; 대조, 대비
factual ⓐ 사실의, 사실에 입각한
theological ⓐ 신학의

reflection ⓝ 반사; 반영; 반성, 숙고
at a pinch 꼭 필요하면

treatise ⓝ 논문, 보고서

opposition ⓝ 반대, 방해, 적대
discrimination ⓝ 구별, 식별; 차별
meditation ⓝ 명상, 묵상

sermon ⓝ 설교

maxim n. 격언, 금언

not least 특히
saga ⓝ 전설, 무용담
Genesis ⓝ 창세기

전문해석

문학이 무엇인지를 정의 내리고자 하는 시도는 지금까지 다양하게 있어 왔다. 예컨대 당신은 문학을 픽션이라는 의미에서 '상상의' 글—문자 그대로 사실이 아닌—로 여길 수도 있을 것이다. 그러나 심지어 사람들이 흔히 문학이라는 표제하에 포함시키는 것들을 잠시 살펴보는 것을 통해서도 이러한 정의가 충분치 않다는 사실을 알 수 있다. 17세기 영문학은 셰익스피어, 웹스터, 마벌, 밀턴 등이 포함된다. 그러나 프랜시스 베이컨의 수필, 존 던의 설교, 버니언의 영적인 자서전, 그리고 토머스 브라운 경이 쓴 모든 글도 포함된다. 경우에 따라서는 홉스의 '리바이어던'이나 클라렌든의 '혁명의 역사'도 포함되는 것으로 볼 수 있을 것이다. 17세기 프랑스 문학은 코르네유와 라신의 글과 더불어 라로슈푸코의 격언집, 보쉬에의 장례식 연설, 부알로의 시에 대한 논문, 세비녜 부인이 딸에게 쓴 편지들, 그리고 데카르트와 파스칼의 철학서도 포함된다. 19세기 영문학에는 대개 램(벤담은 아니고), 매컬리(마르크스는 아니고), 밀(다윈이나 허버트 스펜서는 아니고)이 포함된다.

결국, '사실'과 '허구' 사이의 구별은 그다지 성공적이지 못한 것처럼 보이는데, 그 이유는 특히 그러한 구별 자체가 종종 의심스럽기 때문이다. 예컨대, '역사적' 진실과 '예술적' 진실의 대립에 대한 우리의 반대는 초기 아이슬란드의 영웅전설에는 전혀 적용될 수 없다는 주장이 있어 왔다. 16세기 말과 17세기 초 영국에서, '소설'이라는 단어는 실제 일어난 사건과 허구의 사건에 두루 쓰였던 것으로 보이며, 심지어 뉴스 기사조차 사실적이라고 거의 여겨지지 않았다. 소설과 뉴스 기사는 명백하게 사실적인 것도 아니었고 명백하게 허구적인 것도 아니었다. 따라서 지금 우리가 하는 것처럼 이 두 범주를 명확히 구별하는 것은 당시에는 적용되지 않았다. 기번은 의심할 나위 없이 자신이 역사적 진실을 쓰고 있다고 생각했을 것이다. 그리고 아마도 '창세기'의 저자 또한 그랬을 것이다. 그러나 그들이 쓴 글을 일부 사람들은 '사실'로 읽고, 다른 사람들은 '허구'로 읽는다. 뉴먼은 분명히 자신의 신학적 묵상이 사실이라고 생각했지만, 많은 독자들에게 지금 그의 글은 '문학'이다. 더 나아가, 만일 '문학'이 많은 '사실인' 글을 포함하고 있다면, 문학은 또한 꽤 많은 허구를 배제하기도 한다. 만화 '슈퍼맨'과 Mills and Boon 출판사의 소설들은 허구임에도 불구하고 일반적으로 문학, 더 나아가 위대한 문학으로 여겨지지 않는다는 것은 분명하다. 만일 문학이 '창조적이고' 혹은 '상상력이 넘치는' 글이라면, 이는 곧 역사, 철학, 자연과학 등이 창조적이지 않고 상상력도 넘치지 않는다는 것을 의미하는 것일까? 당연히 그렇지 않을 것이다.

---

30 윗글은 다음과 같은 주제를 가진 에세이의 일부일 가능성이 가장 높다: 주제

① '소설'이라는 단어의 다양한 용법 키워드 없음
② '역사적'과 '예술적'의 대립 키워드 없음
③ 사실과 허구의 구별 키워드 없음
✓ 문학의 의미와 정의

| 분석 | 이 글의 키워드는 문학이며 첫 번째와 두 번째 단락 모두 문학의 정의, 의미, 역사에 관하여 기술하고 있다. 따라서 글 전체를 담는 주제로는 '문학의 의미와 정의'가 가장 적절하다.

31 윗글에서 추론할 수 있는 가능성이 가장 높은 것은 다음 중 어느 것인가? 내용 추론

① 문학은 허구적인 글, 즉 문자 그대로 사실이 아닌 글이라고 생각할 수 있다.
② 역사, 철학, 자연과학은 사실에 근거하기 때문에 독창적일 수 없다.
✓③ 사실적인 글과 허구적인 글이 명확하게 구분되지 않았던 시기가 있었다.
④ '사실'과 '소설'을 구분하는 것은 문학이 무엇인지 확인하려고 할 때 매우 유용하다.

| 분석 | 두 번째 단락에서 '6세기 말과 17세기 초 영국에서, '소설'이라는 단어는 실제 일어난 사건과 허구의 사건에 두루 쓰였던 것으로 보이며, 심지어 뉴스 기사조차도 사실적이라고 거의 여겨지지 않았다.'라고 언급했다. 따라서 ③은 지문을 통해 알 수 있다.

32 윗글에 따르면, 문학은 '허구적인' 글쓰기에만 제한될 수 없는데 그 이유는 _____. 세부 내용 파악

① 문학에 대한 전문가가 아닌 사람들은 보통 허구적인 글들만 문학에 포함된다고 생각한다
② 역사, 철학, 자연과학 분야에 있는 글들처럼 사실적인 글들은 창의적이지도 않고 독창적이지도 않다
③ 17세기 영국 문학은 셰익스피어, 웹스터, 마벌 그리고 밀턴을 포함한다
✓④ 사실적인 글들은 종종 문학으로 간주되며, 허구적인 글들이 언제나 문학에 포함되는 것은 아니다

| 분석 | 두 번째 단락에서 많은 사실적인 글들이 문학에 속하며, 허구적인 글들이 배제되기도 한다고 했다.

[33-36] 2018 단국대

| 정답 | 33 ④ 34 ② 35 ② 36 ③

| 어휘 |
denotation ⓝ (언어의 문자 그대로의) 뜻, 외연적 의미, 명사적 의미
connotation ⓝ 언외의 의미, 함축적 의미
unprovokedly ⓐⓓ 정당한 이유 없이
offensive ⓐ 모욕적인, 공격적인
amicable ⓐ 우호적인
vigorously ⓐⓓ 정력적으로, 힘차게
boldly ⓐⓓ 대담하게, 분명히
assertive ⓐ 단언하는, 단정적인
deadly ⓐ 치명적인, 생명에 관계되는
not necessarily 반드시 ~인 것은 아니다
evoke ⓥ (감정을) 유발하다
depending on ~에 따라
context ⓝ 문맥, 전후 관계; 상황
assumption ⓝ 추측, 짐작
inference ⓝ 추론
instructor ⓝ 강사, 교사
impressionist ⓝ 인상파 화가
departure ⓝ 이탈
serene ⓐ 고요한, 차분한
be diagnosed with ~라고 진단받다

전문해석

[A] 단어는 종종 외연과 함축적 의미라는 두 가지 형태의 의미를 지닌다. 외연은 감정적 반응을 덧붙이지 않은 단어의 실제 사전적 정의를 가리킨다. 예를 들어, 만일 당신이 'aggressive'라는 단어를 찾아본다면, 당신은 그것이 ⓐ 정당한 이유 없이 공격적인, ⓑ 아주 우호적인, ⓒ 대단히 정력적인, 그리고 ⓓ 명백히 단언적인을 의미함을 알게 될 것이다. 만일 일종의 치명적인 질병의 치료법을 묘사하기 위해 사용된다면, 'aggressive'는 긍정적인 감정적 반응을 갖는다. 반대로, 만일 영업사원이 공격적이라고 당신의 친구가 불평한다면, 당신이 그 영업사원에 대해 생각하는 그림은 반드시 긍정적인 것은 아니다. (33 ④) 따라서 'aggressive'라는 단어는 그 단어가 쓰이는 상황에 따라서 긍정적인 감정과 부정적인 감정을 모두 야기한다. 단어들에 대해 당신이 느끼는 함축적 의미는 당신의 가정들 중 일부가 되어, 당신의 추론에 영향을 미친다.

[B] 작가들과 연설가들은 함축적인 언어를 의도적으로 사용하여 당신의 추론을 형성한다. 그들은 보편적 함축적 의미를 지닌 단어를 사용함으로써 이 일을 해낸다. 따라서 그들은 그 선택된 단어에 당신이 특정한 방식으로 감정적 반응을 보일 것으로 기대한다. 예를 들어, 미술사 수업을 당신이 듣고 있다고 생각해 보자. 이 미술사 수업에서 강사는 인상파 화가인 클로드 모네(Claude Monet)의 후기 작품들 중 일부에 대해 토론하고 있다. 학생들이 그림을 형태와 양식으로 평가하는 법을 습득하기를 강사가 원하기 때문에, 모네에 관한 의견을 포함시키는 것을 신중하게 피한다. Ⓐ 그러나 모네의 후기 그림에 대해 논평할 때, 그는 "명백하게도 무작위로 선택한 빨간색과 주황색은 모네가 똑같은 풍경을 그린 초기 그림에서 사용한 보다 차분한 파란색과 초록색에서 멀어진 것

입니다."라고 말한다. 화가의 색상 선택을 가리키기 위해 사용된 'random'이라는 단어는 보다 부정적인 함축적 의미를 갖는다. 반면, 'serene'이라는 단어는 보다 긍정적인 함축적 의미를 갖는다. 강사의 'random'과 'serene'이라는 단어 사용은 ⑧ 그(강사)가 모네의 후기 그림들에서는 초기 그림들에서 받았던 만큼의 인상을 받지 못하고 있음을 당신이 추론하도록 도와준다.

---

33 단락 [A]에 따르면 'aggressive'의 긍정적인 의미를 갖는 것은? <mark>문맥상 의미 파악</mark>

① 공격적인 행동은 감정적 고통의 신호이다.
② 사람들은 오늘날의 경쟁 시장에서 영업사원들이 대개 공격적이라고 불평한다.
③ 나의 친구는 공격적인 형태의 암 진단을 받았다.
✓④ 그 의사는 감염을 치료하기 위해 공격적인 접근을 했다.

| 분석 | 첫 번째 단락에서 질병 치료법에 사용한 'aggressive'는 긍정적인 의미라고 했기 때문에 ④ '그 의사는 감염을 치료하기 위해 공격적인 접근을 했다.'는 진술에서 '공격적인'은 긍정적인 의미임을 알 수 있다. 반면 ①, ②, ③은 모두 'aggressive'가 부정적인 의미로 사용되었다.

---

34 단락 [A]에서 밑줄 친 부분 중 다시 써야 할 부분을 고르시오. <mark>어휘</mark>

① ⓐ 정당한 이유 없이 공격적인
✓② ⓑ 상당히 우호적인
③ ⓒ 대단히 정력적인
④ ⓓ 명백히 단언적인

| 분석 | 'aggressive'가 '공격적인, 적극적인, 단언적인'이라는 뜻을 갖고 있는데 이와 반대되는 '우호적인'이라는 뜻을 가질 수는 없으므로 ⓑ는 '우호적인'과 반대의 의미로 고쳐야 문맥상 적절하다.

---

35 단락 [B]의 빈칸 Ⓐ에 들어갈 말로 가장 적절한 것은? <mark>연결사</mark>

① 따라서   ✓② 그러나
③ 그렇지 않으면   ④ 게다가

| 분석 | 빈칸 Ⓐ 앞에서는 강사가 모네에 관한 자신의 주관적 의견을 학생들에게 심어 주는 행동을 피하고 있다고 했는데, 빈칸 Ⓐ 뒤에서는 강사가 함축적 언어를 이용하여 자신의 의견을 암시적으로 말하고 있으므로 역접의 연결어가 필요하다. Otherwise와 However 둘 다 역접이지만 내용상 반대의 대조를 나타낼 수 있는 However가 정답이다.

---

36 단락 [B]에서 빈칸 Ⓑ에 들어갈 말로 가장 적절한 것은? <mark>빈칸 추론</mark>

① 그가 모네의 초기 그림들보다 후기 그림들을 보다 선호했다.
② 그가 모네의 후기와 초기 그림들 모두에서 감동받는다.
✓③ 그가 모네의 후기 그림들에서는 초기 그림들에서 받았던 만큼의 인상을 받지 못한다.
④ 그가 모네의 초기와 후기 그림들 모두에게 감동받지 못한다.

| 분석 | 단락 [B]에서 강사가 모네의 초기 작품에 대해서는 'serene'이라는 긍정적인 의미의 단어를 사용했고, 후기 작품에 대해서는 'random'이라는 부정적인 의미의 단어를 사용했으므로 강사는 모네의 초기 그림을 후기 그림보다 선호한다는 것을 알 수 있다. 따라서 빈칸에는 ③이 적절하다.

[37-39] 2018 성균관대

| 정답 | 37 ②   38 ①   39 ②

| 어휘 |
- **flourish** ⓥ 번창하다, 번성하다
- **albeit** ⓒⓞⓝⓙ 비록 ~이기는 하나
- **recession** ⓝ 경기 후퇴
- **tempting** ⓐ 유혹하는, 부추기는
- **paperback** ⓝ 페이퍼백(종이 한 장으로 표지를 장정한, 싸고 간편한 책)
- **shrink** ⓥ 줄어들다, 움츠러들다
- **pitch** ⓥ 광고하다, 사라고 설득하다
- **be in a person's skin** 남의 입장에서 생각하다
- **take a hit** 타격을 입다
- **patchy** ⓐ 긁어 모은, 조화가 안 된
- **in particular** 특히, 특별히
- **alternative** ⓝ 대안
- **content** ⓐ 만족한
- **glib** ⓐ 입심 좋은, 말을 잘하는, 경박한
- **knock** ⓥ 부딪치다, 충돌하다
- **fragile** ⓐ 부서지기 쉬운, 취약한
- **dominate** ⓥ 지배하다, 우위를 차지하다
- **flat** ⓐ 활기 없는, 부진한, 불경기의
- **artform** ⓝ 예술 형식, 장르
- **unleash** ⓥ 풀어놓다; 촉발시키다

전문해석

당신은 문학 소설이 매우 건강한 상태에 있다고 아마도 생각할 수도 있을 것이다. 스코틀랜드의 에든버러에서부터 영국의 배스에 이르는 많은 곳에서 도서 축제들이 번영하는 중이다.

하지만 사실을 살펴본다면, 조금 더 걱정스러운 그림이 드러난다. 전 세계적인 금융 위기 이후 영국에서 예술을 위한 자금 지원이 크게 타격을 입었던 것은 잘 알려져 있다. 문화 기관을 위한 공적 자금 지원이 타격을 입었고 미술 시장이 심각하게 타격을 입었다. 그 후 10년 동안 부분적이고 미약하나마 회복의 조짐을 보여 왔다. 그러나 문학 소설 판매의 경우는 그렇지 않아서 경기 침체에서 회복되지 않고 있다. 문제의 악영향이 특히 문학 소설에 미치고 있다. 장르 소설은 디지털 판매를 선점하고 있어서 (문학 소설에 비해) 사정이 더 낫다. 스마트폰의 등장은 기차에서 가도 오도 못하거나 버스를 기다리는 경우 페이퍼백에 대한 대안으로 게임이나 최신 기사를 제공함으로써 영향을 가했다. 다른 한편, 문학 소설의 가격은 여전히 낮아서 전체 시장의 가치는 축소되었다.

이것은 작가들뿐 아니라 독자들에게도 중요하다. 아마도 누군가는 문학 소설을 (과거의) 19세기와 20세기의 예술 형식으로 간주하고 만족해야 하며, 그리고 만일 (그 당시 위대한 소설가) 디킨스(Dickens)가 지금도 활동한다면, 넷플릭스에 작품을 사라고 광고했을 가능성을 인정하는 것으로 만족해야 할 것이다. 그러나 이것은 그럴듯한 소리일 뿐이다. 당연히 소설은 여전히 중요하다. 소설은 특정하고 특별한 것에 관한 관심을 통해 보편적인 진리를 풀어놓는다. 소설은 독자들을 다른 장소, 다른 시대, 다른 사람의 입장에 자리하게 한다.

---

37 윗글에 따르면, 스마트폰의 대중화가 특히 _____의 매출에 심각한 타격을 가했다. [세부 내용 파악]

① 장르 소설   ✓ 페이퍼백
③ 역사소설   ④ 디지털 소설
⑤ 두꺼운 표지의 책

| 분석 | 두 번째 단락에서 '스마트폰의 등장은 기차에서 가도 오도 못하거나 버스를 기다리는 경우 페이퍼백에 대한 대안으로 게임이나 최신 기사를 제공함으로써 영향을 가했다.'라고 언급했다. 따라서 스마트폰의 대중화는 페이퍼백에 매출에 타격을 가했음을 알 수 있다.

---

38 밑줄 친 "pitching to"의 의미는 _____이다. [표현, 문맥상 의미]

✓ 호소하다   ② 저주를 퍼붓다
③ ~에 맞서 자신만의 문학적 지위를 설립하다   ④ 엄청난 영향을 미치다
⑤ ~와 이익을 협상하다

| 분석 | pitch는 '던지다; 광고하다, 호소하다'의 의미이다. 밑줄 친 부분의 내용은 과거의 위대한 소설가인 디킨스조차도 현시대에

살았다면 넷플릭스와 같은 디지털에 뒤처질 수밖에 없다는 맥락이다. 따라서 pitching to는 '~에 광고하다, ~에 호소하다'의 의미이다.

39 윗글에 따르면 다음 중 옳은 것은? 내용 일치

① 지금까지 예술 시장에서 회복의 기미가 보이지 않았다.
✔ 장르 소설은 디지털 판매로 큰 이익을 얻었다.
③ 예술 시장은 세계적인 금융 위기의 큰 타격을 피해 왔다.
④ 문학 소설의 가격 책정은 경제 상황에 맞게 흔들렸다(변했다).
⑤ 소설 형태의 중요성이 영화의 중요성으로 현재 대체되는 중이다.

| 분석 | 두 번째 단락에서 '장르 소설은 디지털 판매를 선점하고 있어서 (문학보다) 사정이 더 낫다.'라고 언급했다. 따라서 ②는 지문과 일치하는 내용이다. 또한 두 번째 단락 마지막에서 '금융 위기 이후 회복의 조짐을 보이고 있는 예술 시장에서 문학 소설의 가격은 여전히 낮았다'고 했으므로 ④는 지문과 일치하지 않는다.

[40-41] 2020 서강대

| 정답 | 40 ④   41 ④

| 어휘 |
recall ⓥ 생각해 내다, 상기하다
manuscript ⓝ 원고, 사본, 필사본
edition ⓝ (초판·재판의) 판, 간행
exemplary ⓐ 모범적인, 본보기의; 전형적인
fairy tale 동화
undergo ⓥ (영향·변화 따위를) 받다, (시련 등을) 경험하다, 당하다
psychological ⓐ 심리학의; 정신적인
socialization ⓝ 사회화
come to terms with (좋지 않은 일을) 받아들이는 법을 배우다
ambivalence ⓝ (애증 따위의) 반대 감정 병존, (상반되는) 감정의 교차; 양면 가치
disregard ⓥ 무시하다; 경시하다
textual ⓐ 본문의; 원문의
overlook ⓥ 못 보고 넘어가다, 간과하다; (잘못된 것을) 못 본 체하다
abandonment ⓝ 포기, 유기; 방종
patriarchy ⓝ 가부장제
minimize ⓥ 최소로 하다; 경시하다
victimizer ⓝ 가해자, 희생시키는 사람
depict ⓥ 묘사하다, 서술하다
stepmother ⓝ 계모, 의붓어머니
align ⓥ 정렬시키다; 제휴하게 하다
witch ⓝ 마녀
devour ⓥ 게걸스럽게 먹다, 먹어 치우다
motif ⓝ 주제, 테마; 동기, 자극
incident ⓝ 사건
definitive ⓐ 결정적인; 명확한; 완성된
authentic ⓐ 믿을 만한, 진정한, 진짜의
translate ⓥ 번역하다; 쉬운 말로 다시 표현하다
perspective ⓝ 시각, 전망, 견지
revise ⓥ 개정하다, 수정하다, 교정하다
non-recognition ⓝ 인지[인식]하지 않음
vital ⓐ 절대로, 필요한, 지극히 중요한
folk tale 설화, 전설
overcome ⓥ 극복하다
uncanny ⓐ 무시무시해서 기분 나쁜; 기묘한; 초자연적인
homey ⓐ 가정의; 마음 편한, 아늑한
transform ⓥ 변형시키다
threaten ⓥ 협박하다, 위협하다

전문해석

그림(Grimm) 형제가 1808년과 1810년 사이 어느 때인가에 도르첸 빌트(Dortchen Wild)가 들려준 "헨젤과 그레텔"의 이야기를 처음 듣고서 1810년 웰렌베르크 원고에 "Das Brüderchen und das Schwesterchen"(어린 남매)이라는 제목으로 그 이야기를 썼다는 사실을 떠올려 보자. 그것은 1812년 Children and Household Tales 초판에 그들이 발표했던 글에 비해 매우 짧고 매우 달랐다. 최근 연구에서 게르하르트 노이만(Gerhard Neumann)은 "헨젤과 그레텔"을 동화 장르의 전형으로 생각하고 헨젤과 그레텔이 자신들의 집을 떠나고 그 결과 정신적인 사회화를 겪는다고 주장한다. 이러한 정신적인 사회화 과정을 통해 헨젤과 그레텔은 엄마와 집이 사랑스럽기도 하고 잔인하기도 하다는 사실을 깨달아야 하고 생존을 위해 이러한 양면성을 받아들이는 방법을 배워야 한다는 것이다. 그러나 노이만의 연구는 그 이야기의 텍스트 안에서 그리고 텍스트와 텍스트 사이에서 발전된 내용을 무시했고, 가난, 유기, 가부장제와 같은 중요한 이슈들을 무시했다. 비판적 책 읽기는 가해자로서의 아빠의 역할을 최소화하고 아이들을 잡아먹고 싶어 하는 마녀와 "계모"를 동일선상에서 묘사하기 위해 그림 형제가 만든 텍스트의 변화에 초점을 맞춰야만 한다. 47년 동안

그림 형제는 그 이야기를 계속해서 고쳐 나갔고, 몇 가지 중요한 테마와 사건을 추가했다. 오늘날, 1857년 버전인 *Kinder- und Hausmarchen*(아이들과 가정의 이야기)이 가장 최종적인 "진본"으로 여겨지고 있다. 그러나 도르첸 빌트(Dortchen Wild)가 처음으로 들려줘서 그 내용을 받아 적어 그림 형제의 관점에서 옮겨지고 그런 다음 수없이 편집하고 수정한 텍스트가 어떻게 "진짜"나 "원본"으로 간주될 수 있는 것일까? 이 질문은 중요한 문제점, 즉 번역에 대한 우리의 인식 부족을 나타낸다. 번역은 구전 설화의 역사에 있어서 대단히 중요하다. 어떤 면에서, 번역이란 프로이트(Freud)가 "das Unheimliche", 즉 인생에서 겪는 괴기한 것이라 부르는 것을 극복함으로써, 낯선 것이 익숙해지게 되고 우리가 그것에 대해 편안함을 느끼도록 하는 것이다. 번역가는 "um-heimlich", 즉 편하게 느껴지지 않는 것을 택해서 그것을 "heimlich", 즉 편하게 느껴지는 무엇인가로 변형시키고, 그 결과 우리는 만약 그렇지 않으면(번역에 의한 변형이 없으면) 우리가 이해할 수 없는 것들로부터 위협을 받지 않게 된다.

40 작가는 _____을 증명하기 위해 인생에서 경험하는 괴기한 것이라는 프로이트의 개념을 중점적으로 다루고 있다. 내용 파악
① "헨젤과 그레텔"은 아이들의 정신적 사회화 과정을 보여 주는 전형적인 동화라는 것
② 그림 형제는 "헨젤과 그레텔"을 번역하는 과정에서 가해자로서의 엄마의 역할을 최소화한다는 것
③ 번역은 다른 누군가의 말을 본래 의도에 따라 가능한 한 충실하게 해석하는 것이라는 것
✓ 번역은 어떤 텍스트를 검토하고 자신의 언어로 되풀이해 옮겨서 낯선 이야기가 친숙해지게 하는 것을 수반한다는 것

| 분석 | 프로이트가 언급된 마지막 부분에서 "번역은 인생에서 겪는 괴기한 것이라 부르는 것을 극복함으로써, 낯선 것이 익숙해지게 되고 우리가 그것에 대해 편안함을 느끼도록 하는 것이다."라고 언급했다. 따라서 작가가 프로이트의 개념을 중점적으로 다룬 이유는 ④ '번역은 어떤 텍스트를 검토하고 자신의 언어로 되풀이해 옮겨서 낯선 이야기가 친숙해지게 하는 것을 수반한다는 것'을 증명하기 위함이라 할 수 있다.

41 윗글로부터 가장 추론 가능한 진술을 고르시오. 내용 추론
① 웰렌베르크 원고는 "헨젤과 그레텔"의 최초 버전을 포함하고 있는데, 이것은 가장 원본 텍스트로 여겨지고 있다.
② 도르첸 빌트는 빌헬름 그림에게 어머니가 의붓자식들을 잡아먹으려 하는 이야기를 들려주었다.
③ 게르하르트 노이만의 연구는 19세기 독일 중산층의 가난과 기근에 대한 태도를 살펴본다.
✓ "헨젤과 그레텔"의 이야기는 19세기 전반기에 많은 개정판이 있었다.

| 분석 | 지문에서 헨젤과 그레텔 이야기에 대해 다양한 연도의 버전이 있다고 언급했으며, 또한 "그림 형제는 그 이야기를 계속해서 고쳐 나갔고, 몇 가지 중요한 테마와 사건을 추가했다"고 했으므로, '19세기 전반기(1800년대) 동안 이 이야기는 많은 개정판들이 있었다'는 것은 지문을 통해 추론 가능하다.

[42-44] 2012 숭실대

| 정답 | 42 ③ 43 ① 44 ④

| 어휘 | underpin ⓥ 받쳐 주다, 떠받치다
tyrant ⓝ 전제군주
keep track of ~을 추적하다
supersede ⓥ 대신하다
subtlety ⓝ 미묘함
scribe ⓝ 인쇄술 발명 이전의 필경사
slip ⓥ 미끄러지다; 전달하다
vicissitude ⓝ 흥망성쇠, 변화
clay ⓝ 점토
impression ⓝ 새긴 것, 각인한 것
dole out 분배하다
thou ⓝ you의 고어
whim ⓝ 변덕
prosaic ⓐ 단조로운, 무미건조한
token ⓝ 쇳조각, 토큰
swell ⓥ 부풀다, 늘다
chronicler ⓝ 연대기 작가, 역사가
literacy ⓝ 글자를 읽고 쓰는 것

전문해석

가장 위대한 발명품은 확실히 문자임에 틀림없다. 문자는 단지 문명의 토대 중 하나에 불과한 것이 아니다. 문자는 꾸준히 축적된 지적 성취를 떠받치고 있다. ⓐ <u>물리적 형태</u>로 아이디어를 포착함으로써 문자는 이 생각들이 왜곡되지 않고 시공간을 가로지르게 하고, 전제군주의 변덕과 역사의 흥망성쇠는 물론 응집된 인간의 기억과 구전 전통을 전승하게 해 준다.

<u>문자의 기원은 단조롭다. 기원전 4,000년 농경사회가 농산물을 추적하는 계산 체계의 도구인 문자를 발명한 것은 시인이 아니라 회계원이었다.</u> 처음에는 점토로 된 봉투에 밀이나 소나 직물을 나타내는 무늬 점토 조각들을 저장함으로써 거래를 기록했다. 하지만 젖은 점토판에 눌러서 표시를 하면 되는데 점토 조각을 왜 쓰겠는가? 이 누른 자국들은 다시 날카로운 바늘로 점토에 긁거나 찔러 넣은 ⓑ <u>문자들</u>로 대체되었다. 점토 조각들이 문자에 자리를 내주었던 것이다.

인간의 정착지가 마을에서 최초의 도시로 확장되면서 문자는 행정상의 이유로도 필요해졌다. 그러나 문자는 빠르게 더 유연해지고 풍부한 표현력을 지니게 되어 분배한 배급물이나 오래전에 죽은 왕들의 목록뿐만 아니라 인간 사상의 ⓒ <u>미묘함</u>을 포착할 수 있게 되었다. 그리고 이를 통해 철학자들과 시인과 역사가들은 이전 사상가들의 사상과의 관계 속에서 자신의 사상을 위치시키고 주장을 펼치고 정교화하게 되었다. 각 세대는 조상들의 사상 위에 사상을 구축하게 되었고 철학과 상업과 과학과 문학의 광범위한 진보가 가능해졌다.

초기 문자 체계가 대단히 복잡했다는 것을 고려해 볼 때 문자의 놀라운 점은 사람들이 이걸 배웠다는 점이다. 그들이 이를 배운 이유는 고대 이집트의 필사 훈련 ⓓ <u>교과서</u>에 나타나 있다. 이 필기 교과서는 다른 직업보다 필경사가 되는 것이 Ⓐ <u>우수한 점</u>을 강조하고 있다. 이를 다룬 제목으로는 "군인이나 사제나 제빵사가 되지 말라", "농사꾼이 되지 말라", "전사가 되지 말라" 등이 있다. 이 마지막 글은 다음과 같이 시작된다. "필경사가 되는 데 마음을 두어라. 그러면 전 세계를 지배하리니." 초창기의 필경사들은 글을 읽고 쓴다는 것이 힘이라는 것을 알고 있었던 것이다. 지금 이 힘은 인류 대부분에게 미치고 있고 다른 어떤 발명품보다 인간의 진보에 더 많은 일을 해 놓았다.

---

42 다음 중 나머지와 다른 하나는 무엇인가? `지시어`

① ⓐ 물리적 형태
② ⓑ 부호
✓③ ⓒ 미묘함
④ ⓓ 책

| 분석 | 이 글의 핵심어는 문자인데 physical form, symbol, texts는 모두 문맥상 문자와 관련이 있지만 subtleties는 생각의 미묘함이라 했으므로 물리적인 문자가 아닌 추상적 개념이다.

---

43 빈칸 Ⓐ에 가장 적절한 것은 무엇인가? `빈칸 추론`

✓① 우수함
② 유연함
③ 외설적임
④ 단순함

| 분석 | 빈칸 Ⓐ 뒤를 보면 다른 직업보다 필경사가 되라고 언급하고 있으며, 필경사가 되면 전 세계를 지배한다고 했으므로, 필경사가 다른 어떤 직업보다 위대하다고 할 수 있다. 따라서 빈칸에 적절한 것은 ① '우수함'이다.

---

44 윗글에 따르면 다음 중 사실인 것은? `내용 일치`

① 사람들은 행정적인 문제 때문에 마을에서 도시로 이동했다.
② 글쓰기의 역사에서 초기 체계는 누구나 쉽게 배울 수 있었다.
③ 요즘 세상의 대부분의 사람들은 글을 읽고 쓰지 못한다.
✓④ 글은 기록을 보관하기 위한 목적으로 발명되었다.

| 분석 | 두 번째 단락에서 "기원전 4,000년 농경사회가 농산물을 추적하는 계산 체계의 도구인 문자를 발명한 것은 시인이 아니라 회계원이었다."고 언급했으므로 문자의 발명은 농산물 추적과 보관을 위한 목적이라고 할 수 있다. 또한 ①의 경우 행정 문제 때문에 이주한 것이 아니라 인간의 이주 때문에 행정상의 이유로 문자가 필요해졌다는 것이므로 지문과 일치하지 않는다.

[45-47] 2015 한국외대

| 정답 | 45 ② 46 ① 47 ②

| 어휘 |
- decency ⓝ 체면, 품위; 예절
- ambiguous ⓐ 애매모호한
- tolerance ⓝ 관용
- dogma ⓝ 독단적인 신조
- work for ~을 지지하다
- communality ⓝ 공동체의 상태[특징]; 공동체적인 일치[조화], 연대감, 단결성
- seize ⓥ 장악하다, 점령하다
- relinquish ⓥ 포기하다
- renounce ⓥ 포기하다, 단념하다
- loathe ⓥ 혐오하다
- dystopia ⓝ 반이상향, 암울한 미래
- progression ⓝ 진행, 진전, 연속, 연쇄
- craftsmanship ⓝ 장인정신

전문해석

아일랜드 출신의 작가 조지 오웰(George Orwell)의 삶과 문학은 단 한 가지에 대한 믿음으로 요약될 수 있다. 그 단 한 가지 믿음은 인간의 품위이다. 비록 그 정의가 애매한 점이 없지는 않으나, 인간의 품위라는 그 정의는 근본적인 위엄과, 무엇보다도 정직과 관용을 담고 있다. 오웰은 독단적인 신조, 이데올로기적이고 정치적인 교의, 계획된 사회 개혁, 그리고 종교적 절대주의에 반대했다. 그 대신 그는 개인들의 표현의 권리, 특히 소수인종의 권리와 언론의 자유를 지지하는 것을 선호했다.

인간의 품위에 대한 오웰의 감각은 해방과 표현의 개념에 기반하고 있다. 인간의 품위는 수동적으로 누리게 되는 것이 아니라, (능동적으로) 지지를 표명하고 추구해야 하는 것이다. "자유의 비밀은 용기다"라는 구절은, 자신들의 의견을 표현하는 일과 타인의 의견에 대해 관용을 발휘하는 일을 용감하게 행하는 의무가 사람들에게 부여되어 있다는 것을 의미한다. 오웰에게 있어서 품위란 무엇보다도 먼저 공동체적인 연대, 상식, 그리고 평범한 사람들에 대한 존중을 의미했다. 그는 자유가 평등에 의해서 부정되도록 지시하는 마르크스주의에 열정적으로 반대했다. 그는 진정한 사회주의가 권력을 Ⓐ 움켜쥐는 것에 의해서가 아니라 공정하고 열린 토론을 Ⓑ 보장하는 것에 의해서 가능하게 될 것이라고 믿었다.

오웰은 이데올로기를 필수로 하는 공산주의와 같은 추상적인 이론을 혐오했다. 이것은 그의 반전체주의적인 작품인 '동물 농장'과 디스토피아를 다룬 고전인 '1984'에서 볼 수 있는데, 오웰은 이 두 작품을 통해서 반독재적이고, 반계급적이며, 반차별적인 사회를 추구했다. 오웰은, 단지 사회를 위해서가 아니라 사회의 진전을 위해서 이러한 비인간적인 체제들과 맞서 싸우는 것이 인간된 의무라고 믿었다.

---

45 윗글은 다음 중 무엇에 관한 글인가? 주제
① 오웰의 문학적 기법과 장인정신 언급 안 함
✓② 오웰 문학의 철학적 관점
③ 오웰의 성격에 대한 비판적 검토 언급 안 함
④ 오웰의 문학적 경력의 발전 언급 안 함

| 분석 | 이 글은 모든 단락에서 오웰의 문학작품에 흐르고 있는 철학적 관점에 대해서 다루고 있으므로 ②가 이 글의 주제로 가장 적절하다.

---

46 다음 중 오웰에 의해 반대될 가능성이 가장 적은 것은 무엇인가? 내용 파악
✓① 정부의 권한을 제한할 필요성
② 자유보다 평등의 선택
③ 정치적 이념 고수
④ 의심 없는 종교에 대한 믿음

| 분석 | 오웰이 소수인종들과 개인을 옹호하고 그것을 억압하는 모든 종류의 권력에 대해서 비판적인 태도를 취했다는 것은 정부의 권한을 제한하자는 것이다. 따라서 ①은 오웰이 반대하는 것이 아니라 지지하는 것이다.

47 문맥상 다음 중 빈칸 ⓐ와 ⓑ에 가장 적절한 단어로 짝지어진 것은? 빈칸 추론

① 포기하다 – 격려하다
✓② 포획하다 – 보장하다
③ 사로잡다 – 제한하다
④ 포기하다 – 억제하다

| 분석 | 빈칸 앞에서 오웰은 '자유가 평등에 의해서 부정되도록 지시하는 마르크스주의에 열정적으로 반대했다.'고 했으므로 오웰은 기존의 마르크스 사상을 부정했다는 것을 알 수 있다. 따라서 오웰이 생각하는 진정한 사회주의는 권력을 '움켜쥐는' 것이 아니라, 공정하고 열린 토론을 '보장하는' 것에 의하여 가능하게 될 것이라고 해야 한다.

[48-51] 2016 가톨릭대

| 정답 | 48 ① 49 ③ 50 ④ 51 ③

| 어휘 | think of A as B A를 B로 생각하다
less A than B A라기보다는 오히려 B(= more B than A)
inherent ⓐ 고유한, 타고난, 내재적인
display ⓥ 나타내다; 전시하다; 드러내다
relate A to B A를 B와 관련시키다
isolate ⓥ 분리[격리/고립]시키다
constant ⓐ 일정한, 끊임없는
identify ⓥ 밝히다, 확인하다; 동일시하다
whatsoever ⓐ 조금의 ~도 (없는)(= whatever)
pore over 주시하다, 자세히 보다; 숙고하다
for some reason or another 이러저러한 이유로[이유 때문에]
value ⓥ 소중히 여기다
functional ⓐ 기능적인
ontological ⓐ 존재론(상)의, 존재론적인
empty ⓐ 공허한; 빈
far from 결코 ~아니다(= never)
discriminate ⓥ 구별하다; 차별하다
cease to do ~하는 것을 멈추다[그만두다]

전문해석

문학은 특정한 종류의 글에 의해서 드러나는 어떤 고유한 특성이나 일련의 특성이라기보다는 사람들이 자신과 글을 관련짓는 수많은 방식이다. 문학이라고 다양하게 불려 온 모든 것들로부터 어떤 일련의 지속적이고 본질적인 특징을 분리하기는 쉽지 않다. 실제로, 모든 게임들에 공통된 단 하나의 구분 짓는 특징을 찾아내고자 시도하는 일은 아마 불가능하다. 문학의 본질 따위는 존재하지 않는다. 만일 그것이 문학으로써 글을 읽는 것을 의미하는 것이라면, 어떤 글이든 비실용적으로 읽을 수 있는데, 그것은 어떤 글이든 시적으로 읽을 수 있는 것과 같다. 만약 내가 철도 연결 편을 알아보기 위해서가 아니라 현대적인 존재로서의 삶의 속도와 복잡함에 관한 일반적인 성찰을 나 자신 속에서 자극하기 위해 기차 시간표를 바라본다면, 나는 그것을 문학적으로 읽는 것이라고 말할 수 있을 것이다. 문학이란 말은 '잡초'라는 말과 유사하게 작용한다. 잡초는 특정한 종류의 식물이 아니라, 이런저런 이유 때문에 정원사가 주변에 있는 것을 원하지 않는 식물이다. 아마도 문학은 이것과는 정반대의 것을 의미할 것이다. 문학은 이런저런 이유로 해서 누군가가 그 가치를 높이 평가하는 어떠한 종류의 글이다. 철학자들이 말하듯, 문학과 잡초는 존재론적인 용어라기보다는 기능적인 용어이다: 그 용어들은 사물의 고정된 존재에 대해서가 아니라 우리가 무엇을 행하는가에 대해서 말하고 있는 것이다. 이런 의미에서 '문학'은 순수하게 형식적이고 텅 빈 유형의 정의이다. 어떤 경우에도, 우리 자신을 언어와 관련짓는 실용적인 방식과 비실용적인 방식 사이에 뚜렷한 경계선을 그을 수 있을지 여부는 불분명하다. 즐거움을 얻기 위해 소설을 읽는 것은 정보를 얻기 위해 도로 표시판을 읽는 것과는 분명히 다르다. 그러나 마음의 수양을 위해서 생물 교과서를 읽는 것은 어떤가? 이러한 읽기는 언어를 실용적으로 다루는 것인가 혹은 그렇지 않은 것인가? 많은 사회에서 문학은 종교적 역할과 같은 고도로 실용적인 기능을 수행해 왔다. 실용적인 것과 비실용적인 것을 날카롭게 구별하는 일은 문학이 더 이상 실용적인 기능을 할 수 없는 우리 사회와 같은 곳에만 가능할지 모른다.

48
윗글의 제목으로 가장 적절한 것은? 제목

✓ ① 문학이란 무엇인가?
② 문학을 읽는 방법 너무 지엽적
③ 문학의 이용과 오용 언급 안 함
④ 문학의 중요성 언급 안 함

| 분석 | 이 글은 문학이 가진 독특한 특징과, 문학이라 불리는 글들이 무엇인지, 문학이 아닌 글들은 무엇인지에 관하여 기술하고 있다. 따라서 이 글 전체를 담는 포괄적인 ① '문학이란 무엇인가?'가 제목으로 적절하다.

49
빈칸에 가장 적절한 단어를 고르시오. 빈칸 추론

① 언어적 관점에서 그것들을 비교하는 것은 불가능하다
② 그것들은 사람들이 삶의 의미를 측정하는 지표로 작동한다
✓ ③ 그것들은 사물의 고정된 존재에 대해서가 아니라 우리가 무엇을 행하는가에 대해서 말하고 있는 것이다
④ 우리는 그것들의 유용성과 상관없이 그것들의 존재에 직접적인 접근을 할 수 없다

| 분석 | 빈칸 앞의 콜론(:)은 재진술을 나타내므로 콜론 앞 문장과 같은 말을 만들어야 한다. 존재론(ontology)은 고정된 존재(fixed being)로 나타낼 수 있고, 기능적인(functional)은 무엇을 행하는가(what we do)로 나타낼 수 있으므로 ③이 빈칸에 가장 적절하다.

50
작가에 따르면, 과학책도 _____ 한 경우에 문학으로 읽힐 수 있다. 내용 파악

① 그것들이 인간의 삶에 실용적인 수단을 제공한다
② 그것들은 우리에게 세상에 대한 가치 있는 지식을 준다
③ 그것들이 유창한 언어로 쓰였다
✓ ④ 우리가 그것을 경외감을 지니고 대한다

| 분석 | 지문의 중간쯤에서 작가는 문학을 "이런저런 이유로 해서 누군가가 그 가치를 높이 평가하는 어떠한 종류의 글이다."라고 정의했다. 따라서 그 어떤 책이라도 그 책을 읽는 사람이 그 책의 가치를 높이 평가했다면(존중, 경외감) 문학이라고 할 수 있다.

51
윗글에 따르면, 다음 중 사실이 아닌 것은? 내용 일치

① 일부 여행자들에게는 철도 시간표가 문학으로 읽힐 수 있다.
② 어떤 종류의 글도 실용적일 뿐만 아니라 비실용적으로 읽힐 수 있다.
✓ ③ 적절한 노력을 하면 독서 과정에서 문학의 본질을 쉽게 이끌어 낼 수 있다.
④ 문학은 사회마다 다르게 기능해 왔다.

| 분석 | 지문의 처음 부분에서 작가는 "문학의 본질 따위는 존재하지 않는다."라고 언급했다. 따라서 ③ '문학의 본질을 쉽게 이끌어 낼 수 있다'는 지문과 일치하지 않는다.

[52-54] 2012 숭실대

| 정답 | 52 ③ 53 ④ 54 ②

| 어휘 | pidgin ⓝ 피진어(서로 다른 언어 사용자들 간의 교역에 쓰이는 인공어)
creole ⓝ 크리올어(두 언어 간의 접촉에서 유래된 모국어)   interchangeable ⓐ 상호 교환 가능한
on a regular basis 정기적으로, 규칙적으로   mother tongue 모국어
cobble together 조잡하게 끼어 맞추다   missing ⓐ 빠진, 없어진   echelon ⓝ 계층
work against ⓥ ~에 불리하게 작용하다   full-fledged ⓐ 완전한, 자격이 충분한

전문해석

'피진어'와 '크리올어'는 일반 대중이 흔히 서로 바꾸어 쓰는 표현이지만 언어학에서는 각각 구체적 의미와 차이가 있다. '피진어'는 한 주민 집단이 여러 개 다른 언어를 사용하고 규칙적으로 소통하지만, 그 주민의 어떤 한 언어도 다른 언어보다 우위를 차지하지 않는 상황을 포함한다. 이러한 상황은 다양한 사회가 교역하거나 다양한 지역의 노예들이 한 지역으로 옮겨지는 곳에서 종종 발견된다. 이러한 언어를 사용하는 이들은 화자의 모국어에서 온 단어를 이용하여 상호 언어를 만들고 극도로 유연하고 단순화된 문법을 사용한다. 대부분의 언어학자들은 피진어를 Ⓐ <u>완전한</u> 언어가 아니라 상황 때문에 조잡하게 짜 맞추어져 필요 없을 때는 버려지는 언어라고 생각한다.

크리올어는 그것이 대다수 사용자들의 모국어라는 사실 때문에 피진어와 다르다. 어휘는 다른 언어에서 광범위하게 빌려 왔지만 문법은 어휘를 제공한 언어와 공통점이 거의 없다. 문법과 구문은 다른 오래전에 정립된 언어만큼 Ⓑ <u>완벽히 발달되어</u> 있다.

피진어를 만든 상황이 지속되면 아이들의 첫 세대는 피진어를 자신의 모국어로 배울 것이다. 이것이 피진어를 크리올어로 곧바로 발달시키는가, 그렇게 하는 데 한 세대 이상이 걸리는가에 관해서는 논란이 있다. 신경언어학자들은 모든 인간이 태어날 때부터 언어를 습득하는 방식의 공통점을 지적하고 크리올어 사용자들의 첫 세대가 피진어에 없는 언어의 측면을 창출한다고 말한다. 역사가들은 첫 20~30년간 발견되는 어휘와 구문과 발음의 빈번한 변화를 지적하며 이것이 안정화되는 데 한 세대 이상이 걸린다는 것을 보여 준다.

피진어와 크리올어 둘 다 사회의 낮은 계층에 의해 쓰이기 때문에 이 언어들은 부모 언어의 퇴화된 형태라고 경멸받는다. 크리올 언어는 사용자들이 부모 언어를 사용하는 사람들과 동떨어져서 자신의 문화적 사회적 정체성을 유지하는 곳에서 살아남는다. 크리올어는 정부와 경제적 힘이 이들에게 불리하게 작용해도 종종 살아남는다.

52 다음 중 빈칸 Ⓐ와 Ⓑ에 가장 적절한 것은 무엇인가? 빈칸 추론

① 완전히 발달된 – 기본적인
② 기본적인 – 지속되는
③ 완전한 – 완전히 발달된 ✓
④ 임시의 – 완전히 이해된

| 분석 | 빈칸 Ⓐ의 경우에는 not A but B 구조이므로 A와 B는 서로 반대의 표현이 와야 한다. 따라서 '조잡하게 만들어진 것'이 아니라 '완전하게 갖추어졌다'는 의미가 와야 한다. 빈칸 Ⓑ의 경우에는 다른 모든 오래전부터 언어라고 인정받고 있는 언어와 비교되고 있으므로, 크리올 언어의 문법은 다른 언어만큼 잘 발달되었다는 표현이 들어가야 한다.

53 윗글에 따르면, 다음 중 사실이 아닌 것은? 내용 일치

① 피진어는 둘 이상 언어 간 접촉의 결과이다.
② 신경언어학자들과 역사학자들은 피진어가 어떻게 크리올어로 발달하는지에 대한 의견이 다르다.
③ 사람들은 피진어와 크리올어에 대해 부정적인 태도를 갖는 경향이 있다.
④ 크리올 언어의 사용은 부모 언어를 저하시킬 것이다. ✓

| 분석 | 지문의 마지막 단락에서 "이 언어들은 부모 언어의 퇴화된 형태라고 경멸받는다."라고 언급했다. 이는 크리올어, 피진어가 부

모 언어의 퇴화된 형태라는 것이지 부모 언어를 퇴화시키는 것은 아니다. 따라서 ④ '크리올 언어의 사용은 부모 언어를 저하시킬 것이다.'는 진술은 지문과 일치하지 않는다.

54 윗글에 따르면, 다음 중 피진어에 대해 사실이 아닌 것은? 내용 일치

① 피진 언어들은 일반 언어보다 문법이 단순하다.
② 피진 언어는 그 언어를 사용하는 사람의 절반 이상에게 모국어이다. ✓
③ 피진어를 말하는 사람은 일반적으로 열등한 사회 계층에 속한다.
④ 피진 언어는 피진 언어에 기여한 언어에서 어휘를 가져온다.

| 분석 | 피진어를 모국어로 쓰는 사람이 얼마나 되는가에 대한 내용은 지문에서 언급한 적이 없다. 따라서 ② '피진 언어는 그 언어를 사용하는 사람의 절반 이상에게 모국어이다.'는 지문을 통해 알 수 없다.

5강 역사 / 지리

01	③	02	②	03	③	04	①	05	④	06	②	07	③	08	①	09	①	10	③
11	①	12	②	13	⑤	14	④	15	②	16	①	17	②	18	⑤	19	①	20	②
21	②	22	②	23	③	24	③	25	①	26	②	27	④	28	③	29	④	30	③
31	③	32	④	33	③	34	①	35	④	36	②	37	④	38	③	39	④	40	①
41	②	42	④	43	⑤	44	②	45	③	46	⑤	47	①	48	②	49	⑤	50	⑤
51	③	52	①	53	④														

[01-02] 2012 홍익대

| 정답 | 01 ③ 02 ②

| 어휘 | periphery ⓝ (어떤 범위의) 주변, (덜 중요한) 주변부 resident ⓝ (특정 지역) 거주자
missionary ⓝ (외국에 파견되는) 선교사   civilian ⓝ 민간인   stockman ⓝ 목축업자, 축산업자
the bulk of ~의 대부분   static ⓐ (변화·움직임 없이) 고정된   hypnotize ⓥ 최면을 걸다, 혼을 빼놓다
stagnant ⓐ 고여 있는, 침체된   backwater ⓝ (발전이나 변화 등의 영향을 덜 받는) 후미진 곳, 벽지

전문해석

1694년에 다시 정복된 뉴멕시코는 스페인 제국의 주변부에 자리 잡았다. 역사가 오아카 L. 존스(Oakah L. Jones)가 보여 준 뉴스페인의 북쪽 국경의 정착민들은 유럽에서 가져온 기본적인 제도들과 함께 독특한 문화를 발전시켰지만, 다른 환경 조건들의 도전에 맞게 수정했다. 주민의 대다수는 군인도 선교사도 아닌 민간인 정착민—농부, 일용직 노동자, 목축업자, 장인이었다. 뉴멕시코는 정착민들을 끌어들일 수 있는 농업과 목장 운영을 제외하고 (다른 것은) 거의 없었고, 외딴섬의 전초기지와 유사한 동떨어지고, 노출되어 있고, 외딴 국경지대로 남아 있었다. 그럼에도 불구하고, 대부분의 인구가 열심히 일하고, 개인적으로 소규모 농부와 장인을 고용하고, 증가하는 인구, 인종의 혼합과 계층 차이의 모호함으로, 뉴멕시코는 정적인 것이 아니었다. 뉴멕시코는 영국계 미국인들이 나중에 상상했던 최면에 걸린, 정체된, 지루한 벽지(후미진 곳)는 아니었다.

01 다음 중 역사학자 오아카 L. 존스가 고치려고 시도하는 편향된 견해가 아닌 것은? 세부 내용 불일치

① 뉴멕시코는 외지고 고립된 지역이었기 때문에 정적이었다.
② 스페인 제국의 국경에 거주하는 대다수의 주민들은 군인들과 선교사들이었다.
✓③ 뉴스페인 북쪽 국경의 정착민들은 유럽의 기관들을 그 지역의 환경 조건에 적응시키기 위해 혼합 문화를 발전시켰다.
④ 영국계 미국인들은 뉴멕시코 지역을 텅 빈, 정체된 공간으로 생각했다.

| 분석 | 본문 두 번째 문장에서는 오아카 L. 존스의 견해를 서술하고 있다. 따라서 보기 ③은 반박하려는 견해가 아니므로 정답이다.

02 다음 중 "정착민들을 끌어들일 수 있는 농업과 목장 운영을 제외하고"로 언급될 가능성이 가장 높은 것은 무엇인가? 밑줄 추론

① 원예학   ✓② 금
③ 서비스   ④ 인구

| 분석 | 농업과 목축업을 제외하고 정착민들을 끌어들일 만한 요인을 보기 중에서 추론해야 한다. 보기 ②의 경우 일반적으로 금전적 이익 때문에 많은 사람들을 끌어들일 수 있는 원인이므로 정답에 가장 적절하다.

[03-04] 2013 한양대

| 정답 | 03 ③ 04 ①

| 어휘 |
responsibility ⓝ 책임
fashion ⓝ 유행
fiction ⓝ 소설, 허구
unambiguously ⓐⓓ 분명[명료]하게
in so far as ~하는[인] 한에 있어서
fudge ⓥ 얼버무리다, 날조하다
abuse ⓝ 남용
anthropology ⓝ 인류학
distinguish ⓥ 구분하다
on the basis of ~을 기반으로, ~에 근거하여
come up with ~을 생각하다, ~을 제시하다
intellectual ⓐ 지적인, 지능의
in short 요컨대
fundamental ⓐ 필수적인, 근본적인

전문해석

우리 역사학자들은 일반적으로 역사적 사실에 대해, 그리고 특히 역사의 남용에 대해 비판할 책임이 있다. 나는 이러한 책임 중 첫 번째 책임에 대해서는 거의 할 말이 없다. 두 가지 양상을 제외하고는 아무 말도 할 필요가 없을 것이다. 하나는 현재의 유행으로 소설가들이 그들의 줄거리를 만들기보다는 줄거리를 기록된 현실에 근거하는 것이다. 따라서 역사적 사실과 허구 사이의 경계를 혼동하는 것이다. 다른 하나는 대학, 특히 문학과 인류학과에서 "포스트모더니즘"이라는 지적 유행의 부상인데, 이는 객관적인 존재를 주장하는 모든 "사실"이 단순히 지적 구조일 뿐이라는 것을 암시한다. 즉, 사실과 허구 사이에 명확한 차이가 없다는 것이다. 하지만 차이가 있다. 그리고 역사학자로서, 그 둘을 구별하는 능력은 절대적으로 중요하다. 우리는 우리의 사실을 발명할 수 없다. 엘비스 프레슬리(Elvis Presley)가 죽었거나 아니거나 둘 중 하나이다. 신뢰할 수 있는 증거가 있는 한, 그 질문은 증거에 근거하여 명확하게 대답될 수 있다.

03 윗글의 빈칸에 들어갈 말로 가장 적절한 것은? 빈칸 추론
① "역사 소설"이라는 새로운 용어를 생각해 내는 것
② 역사와 문학 사이의 간극을 메우는 것
✓③ 역사적 사실과 허구 사이의 경계를 혼동하는 것
④ 문학적 상상력이 역사적 사실보다 낫다는 것을 증명하는 것

| 분석 | 빈칸 앞에는 '결과'를 서술하는 순접표현 'thus'가 있으므로 연결표현 직전의 서술과 인과관계가 되는 내용으로 빈칸을 추론해 본다. 본문 네 번째 문장에서는 '현재의 유행으로 소설가들이 그들의 줄거리를 만들기보다는 줄거리를 기록된 현실에 근거하는 것이다.'라고 서술했다. 따라서 그 결과 역사적 사실과 허구 사이의 경계가 섞이거나 혼동되었을 것이다. 보기 ③이 정답으로 적절하다. 참고로 본문에서 작가는 역사의 남용에 대해 소설가들을 비판하기 때문에 보기 ②의 경우 부정적 뉘앙스를 포함하지 않아 정답으로 보기 어렵다.

04 윗글의 내용으로부터 유추할 수 없는 것은? 내용 비추론
✓① 저자는 소설을 읽는 것을 좋아하지 않는다.
② 저자는 포스트모더니즘에 호의적이지 않다.
③ 저자는 엘비스 프레슬리가 죽었다고 확신한다.
④ 저자는 역사적 사실이 결코 지적 구조가 될 수 없다고 믿는다.

| 분석 | 본문에서 저자가 역사의 남용에 대해 소설가들을 비판했다고 해서 작가가 소설을 읽는 것을 좋아하지 않는다는 것을 유추하기 어렵다. 따라서 보기 ①이 유추할 수 없는 진술이다.

[05-07] 2021 한국외대

| 정답 | 05 ④ 06 ② 07 ③

| 어휘 |
affluence ⓝ 부유, 풍부, 유입   embassy ⓝ 대사관, 대사관저   pique ⓥ 불쾌하게 하다
consolidate ⓥ 굳히다, 강화하다, 통합하다   speckle ⓥ ~에 반점이 생기게 하다, 얼룩덜룩하게 하다, 산재하게 하다
griffin ⓝ 그리핀(사자 몸통에 독수리의 머리와 날개를 지닌 신화적 존재)
delegation ⓝ (조직, 국가 등의 의사를 대표하는) 대표단   vertically ⓐⓓ 수직으로, 수직적으로

전문해석

430년 전 르네상스 시대에 그려진 희귀한 60페이지의 세계 지도가 마침내 전시되었다. 역사가들은 이탈리아 밀라노에 살았던 우르바노 몬테(Urbano Monte)(1544~1613)라는 Ⓐ 지도 제작자에 대해 몇 가지 기본적인 세부 사항을 알고 있다. 그의 가족의 부유함 때문에, 몬테는 일할 필요가 없었다. 오히려, 그는 도서관을 위해 책을 모으고 지도를 만드는 것을 포함한 학문적인 관심사를 추구하면서 시간을 보냈다. 유럽에 있는 첫 번째 일본 대사관을 방문한 것은 지리학에 대한 그의 관심을 불러일으켰다. 그래서, 그는 지리적 지식을 통합하기 위해 지도를 만드는 프로젝트에 착수했다. 현대 자료에 의존하여, 그는 독특한 북극 관점을 사용하는 지도를 그렸다. 이 예측은 매우 특이하지만 그 당시로는 상당히 정확했다. 가장 왜곡된 것으로 보이는 곳 중 하나는 남극인데, 당신이 위에서 본다면 ⓐ 바닥이 굉장히 클 것이기 때문이다. 세계의 대륙과 섬들에 대해 알고 있는 것을 그리는 것 외에도, 몬테는 유니콘, 인어, 그리핀, 그리고 심지어 코끼리를 운반하는 거대한 새를 포함한 환상적인 동물들의 삽화로 지도를 산재하게 했다. 그는 또한 스페인의 펠리페 2세와 그의 스페인 함대에서 태평양과 대서양을 점찍은 여러 척의 배들을 포함한 정치 지도자들과 그들의 군대를 끌어들였다. 이상하게도, 몬테는 일본 대표단을 만났음에도 불구하고, 그는 일본 섬들을 수직이 아닌 수평으로 그렸다. 하지만, 그는 일본을 꽤 크게 만들었고, 떠오르는 태양의 나라(일본)에 대한 그의 지식을 보여 주면서 일본의 지리를 채웠다.

05 다음 중 Ⓐ에 가장 적절한 것은 무엇인가? 빈칸 추론
① 인류학자
② 지질학자
③ 해양학자
✓ ④ 지도 제작자

| 분석 | 본문 네 번째 문장에서 우르바노 몬테는 '도서관을 위해 책을 모으고 지도를 만드는 것을 포함한 학문적인 관심사를 추구'했다고 서술했다. 따라서 그는 '지도 제작자'일 것이므로 보기 ④가 정답이다.

06 다음 중 ⓐ가 지시하는 것과 가장 가까운 것은 무엇인가? 밑줄 추론
① 북극
✓ ② 남극
③ 떠오르는 태양의 나라
④ 태평양과 대서양

| 분석 | 본문 아홉 번째 문장에서는 '남극'에 대해 서술하고 있으므로 밑줄 친 ⓐ는 '남극'을 지시하는 것이다.

07 다음 중 몬테의 지도에 대한 설명으로 맞는 것은? 세부 내용 일치

① 그것은 세계를 여행할 사람들의 편의를 위해 고안되었다.
② 그것은 현장 학습을 기반으로 하며 오늘날의 기준에서 매우 정확하다.
✓③ 그것은 저명한 인물들뿐만 아니라 신화적인 생명체들이 사는 세상을 묘사한다.
④ 그것은 당시로서는 남극 중심의 독특한 세계관을 보여 준다.

| 분석 | 본문의 10번째 문장에서 '몬테는 유니콘, 인어, 그리핀, 그리고 심지어 코끼리를 운반하는 거대한 새를 포함한 환상적인 동물들의 삽화로 지도를 산재하게 했다'고 서술했다. 유니콘이나 인어 등을 신화적인 생명체로 볼 수 있으므로 보기 ③은 몬테의 지도에 관한 설명과 일치한다.

[08-09] 2012 중앙대

| 정답 | 08 ① 09 ①

| 어휘 |
monarchy ⓝ 군주제, 군주국
the nobility ⓝ 귀족
pension ⓝ 연금
extravagant ⓐ (사람이) 낭비하는, 사치하는
constraint ⓝ 강제, 속박, 구속
sovereign ⓝ 군주
accommodation ⓝ 적응, 순응, 수용[숙박] 시설
hold ⓝ 영향, 지배(력), 억제
intricacy ⓝ 복잡한 사항[내용]

Versailles ⓝ 베르사유(궁전)
dispense ⓥ 나누어 주다, (서비스를) 제공하다
emulation ⓝ 경쟁, 겨룸, 대항
residence ⓝ 거처, 주소, 주택
pointless ⓐ 힘없는, 적절하지 못한, 무의미한
chateau ⓝ (프랑스의) 성, 대저택
subject ⓝ (군주국의) 국민, 신하

intermediary ⓝ 중재자, 중개인
compulsory ⓐ 강제적인, 필수의
courtier ⓝ (왕을 모시는) 신하
chapel ⓝ 교회당
layout ⓝ 구획, 설계
vicinity ⓝ 부근, 가까움, 근접

전문해석

절대 군주제에서는, 모든 권력이 왕에게서 나온다. 베르사유 궁전에서, 루이 14세는 그에게 모든 것을 빚진 중재자들(중간 관리자들)을 통해 통치하는 왕국의 주인이었던 것처럼, 자신의 집(궁전)의 주인이었다. 정부 업무에서 제외된 귀족들은 더 이상 실질적인 권력을 갖지 못했지만, 그럼에도 불구하고 그들은 궁정에 출두해야 할 필요성을 느꼈다. 그곳에서 왕은 공직, 토지, 직함, 연금 등의 호의를 베풀었다. 명성과 외모에 기반을 둔 이 사회에서, 경쟁은 끊임없고, 사치는 필수적이며, 삶은 사치스러웠다. 이런 식으로 루이 14세는 ⒶⒶⒶ 그의 신하들에 대한 지배력을 가지고 있었다. 모든 면에서 지배해야 하는 사람은 바로 그 사람이었다. 그의 눈에는 힘의 행사와 겉으로 드러나는 표시가 하나였고 같은 것이었다. 그의 거주지는 가장 크고 아름다워야 했고 그의 영광을 상징하는 장식으로 가득 차 있어야 했다. 고귀한 의미에서, 왕의 집에 모인 하인들의 수는 가장 많아야 했고, 그의 궁은 날에 따라 가장 많은 사람들, 3,000명에서 10,000명 사이의 신하들이 참석해야만 했다. 이 거대한 군중들은 엄격하게 규제되어야 했다. 예절과 그 제약들—왕에게 접근할 수 있는 사람, 왕 앞에 앉을 권리가 있는 사람, 누구보다 지위가 높은 사람 등—은 오늘날 우리에게 무의미하게 보일 수 있다. Ⓑ 하지만, 예절은 계급, 즉 왕의 우위를 확인하는 역할, 즉 궁정 내의 위계질서를 확인해 주는 역할을 했기 때문에 필수적이었다. 그것은 주권자의 가장 사적인 순간들—아침에 일어나고, 밤에 잠자리에 들고, 식사를 하고, 산책을 하러 가는 것—에 적용되었고 이것은 국가의 행위가 왕의 개인적인 행위로 보일 때, 이런 개인적인 행위 또한 국가의 행위로 인식되었다. 베르사유의 또 다른 특별한 특징, 그리고 자연스럽게 외국인들을 놀라게 한 것은 정원과 대저택 내부가 모두 대중에게 크게 개방되어 있다는 것이었다. 그들이 궁정의 일원이든 아니든 간에, 누구나 예배당에 가기 위해 그의 대저택을 가로질러 가는 왕을 볼 수 있었다. 대표성, 정부, 숙박, 서비스 등 모든 기능이 장소의 배치를 설명한다. 하지만 그것은 하루 만에 이루어진 것이 아니다.

08 윗글의 빈칸 Ⓐ와 Ⓑ에 들어가기에 가장 적절한 것은? 빈칸 추론

✓① 그의 신하들에 대한 지배력을 가지고 있었다 – 하지만
② 법원에 대한 그의 권한을 행사했다 – 그러므로
③ 그의 신하들이 확고한 통제하에 있었다 – 게다가
④ 빈곤층을 위한 주거를 제공했다 – 그럼에도 불구하고

| 분석 | 본문의 첫 번째 그리고 세 번째 문장에서는 '모든 권력이 왕에게 나온다'거나 '귀족들은 더 이상 실질적인 권력을 갖지 못했다'고 서술했다. 빈칸 Ⓐ가 포함된 문장의 직후 문장에서도 '모든 면에서 지배해야 하는 사람'이 왕이라고 했다. 따라서 빈칸 Ⓐ의 경우 보기 ①, ②, ③ 모두 정답으로 가능하다. 빈칸 Ⓑ의 경우 직전 문장에서는 '예절과 제약의 무의미함'을 서술하였으나 빈칸 Ⓑ 뒤로는 내용이 역접되어 '예절은 필수적'이라 했다. 따라서 빈칸 Ⓑ에 역접표현이 포함된 보기 ①이 정답으로 가장 적절하다.

09 윗글의 제목으로 가장 적절한 것은? 제목

✓① 모든 권력의 거주지
② 현대식 귀족의 탄생
③ 왕의 대정원과 그 주변
④ 법정에서의 예절의 복잡성과 그 제약

| 분석 | 본문은 절대 군주제 시대의 베르사유 궁전이 왕의 권력의 상징으로서 가지고 있는 의미를 서술하고 있다. 주요 소재인 '베르사유 궁전'을 포함하는 보기가 글의 제목으로 가장 적절하다. 보기 ①의 '모든 권력의 장소'가 '베르사유 궁전'을 지시할 수 있으므로 정답이다.

| 배경 지식 | 절대 군주제(Absolute monarchy): 군주가 어떠한 법률이나 국가 기관에도 구속을 받지 않고 절대적 권한을 가지는 정치 체제이다.

[10-12] 2021 단국대

| 정답 | 10 ③ 11 ① 12 ②

| 어휘 | amalgamation ⓝ 결합체, 융합체   romance ⓝ 전기[공상/모험] 소설, 중세 기사 이야기
partition ⓝ 분할, 분배   severalty ⓝ 각자, 개별(성), 단독 보유   eminence ⓝ (특히 전문 분야에서의) 명성
allegory ⓝ 우화, 풍자   peculiarity ⓝ 기이한 특징, 특이한 점, 특성

전문해석

역사는, 적어도 이상적인 완벽 상태에서, 시와 철학의 혼합물이다. 그것은 특정 인물과 사건을 생생하게 묘사함으로써 일반적인 진실을 마음에 각인시킨다. 하지만, 사실, 그것을 구성하는 두 개의 적대적 요소가 완벽한 결합을 형성하는 것으로 알려진 적은 없었다. 그리고 마침내, 우리 시대에, 그들은 완전히 그리고 공언적으로 분리되었다. 좋은 역사는, 적절한 의미에서, 우리가 가지지 않았다. 하지만 우리는 좋은 역사소설과 좋은 역사수필을 가지고 있다. 상상력과 이성은 문학의 영역을 분할했고 이제는 전체를 공통적으로 유지하는 대신 각각의 부분들을 유지한다.

과거를 현재로 만들고, 먼 곳을 가까이 오게 하고, 우리를 위대한 사람의 사회나 강력한 전투의 장이 내려다보이는 명성에 배치하고, 우화 속에서 의인화된 자질로 간주하고 싶은 인간의 살과 피가 있는 현실에 투자하고, 그들의 언어, 예절, 복장의 모든 특이성으로 우리 앞에 조상들을 불러내고, 그들의 집 위에서 우리에게 보여 주기 위해, 역사가에게 적절하게 속하는 이 의무들의 부분들은 역사 소설가에 의해 전용되었다. 다른 한편으로, 역사 철학을 추출하고, 사건과 사람에 대한 판단을 지시하고, 원인과 결과의 연관성을 추적하고, 도덕적, 정치적 지혜에 대한 이전 시대의 일반적인 교훈의 발생에서 끌어내는 것은 별개의 작가들의 일이 되었다.

10	윗글의 주요 구성 형식은 무엇인가? 글의 구성
① 역사적 서술	② 과정 분석
✓③ 비교와 대조	④ 원인과 결과

| 분석 | 본문에서는 시와 철학, 상상력과 이성, 역사와 역사소설과 수필, 그리고 역사가와 역사 소설가가 하는 일을 차이점을 바탕으로 서술하고 있다. 따라서 보기 ③의 '비교와 대조'가 본문의 주요 구성 형식이다.

11	첫 번째 단락에서, 적대적인 두 쌍으로 설명되지 않은 것은? 세부 내용 불일치
✓① 개별과 역사	② 상상과 이성
③ 소설과 수필	④ 시와 철학

| 분석 | 보기 ①의 두 쌍은 언급되지 않았으므로 정답이다.

12	두 번째 단락의 목적은 무엇인가? 글의 목적
① 역사 소설의 우월성과 그들이 제공할 수 있는 것을 주장하기 위해
✓② 각각의 역사소설과 역사수필이 무엇을 제공하는지 설명하기 위해
③ "과거를 현재"로 만들고 "먼 곳을 가깝게" 가져오는 과정을 설명하기 위해
④ 어떤 유형의 역사가 우수한지 평가하고, 독자에게 답을 남기기 위해서

| 분석 | 본문 두 번째 단락의 주요 소재는 '역사소설과 역사수필'이다. 보기 ②만 주요 소재를 포함하고 있으므로 정답이다.

[13-14] 2016 성균관대

| 정답 | 13 ⑤ 14 ④

| 어휘 | nestle ⓥ (아늑한 곳에) 자리잡다	nomadic @ 유목 생활을 하는	orthodox Christianity 정통 기독교
run ⓝ 운영, 연속	de jure 합법적인, 법률상의	philatelist ⓝ 우표 수집가
protectorate ⓝ (강대국의 지배를 받는) 보호국		trance ⓝ 무아지경
drone ⓝ 낮게 웅웅거리는 소리	channel ⓥ 보내다
hark back to ~을 기억하다[회고하다], ~을 들먹이다

전문해석

몽골의 북쪽 국경을 따라 자리 잡은 투바는 놓치기 쉽다. 모스크바에서 (투바까지) 직항편은 없다. (투바까지 가는) 유일한 방법은 근처 시베리아 도시에서 터보프롭 비행기(낡은 구형 비행기)를 타거나 주변 산을 통과하는 장거리 운전이다. 이 지역의 308,000명의 사람들 대부분은 투바족 원주민들로, 그들 중 일부는 여전히 전통적인 유목 생활 방식을 실천하고 있다. [A] (이 지역에서) 샤머니즘과 불교는 러시아의 지배적인 종교인 러시아 정교보다 더 널리 퍼져 있다. [B] 투바 국립 관현악단의 예술 감독인 옥사나 툴류쉬(Oksana Tyulyush)는 "신은 위에 있고 모스크바는 멀리 있다."라고 빈정거린다. [C] 러시아인들은 역사 대부분을 몽골이나 중국의 통치하에 살았던 이 지역에 대해 거의 알지 못한다. [D] 1921년과 1944년 사이에 투바인들은 타누 투바 또는 투바 인민 공화국으로서 잠시 동안 "법적인" 독립을 즐겼고 일련의 기이한 모양의 우표들을 발행함으로써 우표 수집가들을 기쁘게 했다. [E] 제2차 세계 대전이 끝난 후, 소련이 개입하여 현지 당국의 요청에 따라 투바를 공식적인 보호국으로 만들었다. [F] 대부분의 외부인에게, 투바는 음악으로 가장 잘 알려져 있다: 한 가수가 동시에 여러 개의 (건반의) 음을 칠 때 만들어지는 무아지경을 유발하는 윙윙대는 소리인 흐미, 즉 목구멍 노래로 가장 유명하다. 흐미는 공연자들이 주변의 물, 바람, 짐승들을 인도하기 위해 노력하면서 자연에서 영감을 받았다. 투바에서 전통을 기억하는 것은 소련 붕괴 후 남겨진 공백을 메우는 데 도움이 되었다.

13 다음 중 '투바'에 대해 사실이 아닌 것은? 세부 내용 불일치

① 산으로 둘러싸여 있다.
② 중국과 몽골에 의해 통치되곤 했다.
③ 한때는 독립국이었다.
④ 전통적인 목구멍 노래로 유명하다.
☑ ⑤ 제2차 세계대전 후에 러시아의 침략을 받았다.

| 분석 | 본문 아홉 번째 문장에서 따르면, 투바는 제2차 대전 이후 투바당국의 요청에 따라 소련의 공식적인 보호국이 되었다고 했으므로 러시아의 침략을 받았다고 볼 수 없다. 따라서 보기 ⑤가 정답이다.

14 윗글을 세 단락으로 나눌 때, 가장 적절한 경계는 무엇인가? 단락 나누기

① [A] and [C]   ② [B] and [E]
③ [C] and [E]   ☑ ④ [C] and [F]
⑤ [D] and [F]

| 분석 | 본문 시작부터 [C] 직전까지는 투바의 지리적, 인구적 특징을 서술하며 [C]에서 [F] 직전까지는 투바의 역사에 대해 다루고 있다. 마지막으로 [F]부터는 투바의 전통 음악인 '흐미'에 대한 서술이 이어진다. 따라서 본문은 [C]와 [F]를 경계로 세 단락으로 나눌 수 있다.

| 배경지식 | 흐미(Khoomei): 한 명의 가창자가 저음과 고음을 동시에 부르는 몽골족 특유의 가창 기법으로, 2009년 유네스코 인류무형문화유산 대표목록에 등재되었다.

[15–16] 2018 가톨릭대

| 정답 | 15 ②   16 ①

| 어휘 |
distinct ⓐ 별개의, 다른
absurd ⓐ 불합리한, 부조리한
prig ⓝ 까다로운 사람, 잔소리꾼
overinflated ⓐ 지나치게 팽창한
smother ⓥ 숨 막히게 하다, 질식시키다
crop up 불쑥 나타나다, 발생하다
old-fashioned ⓐ 구식[고풍]의, 시대에 뒤떨어진
designation ⓝ 지시, 지정, 명칭

critic ⓝ 비평가, 평론가, 감정사
stuffily ⓐⓓ 숨막혀서, 답답하게
puncture ⓥ 찌르다, (찔러서) 구멍을 내다, 망쳐 놓다
distinguishing ⓐ 특징적인, 특색을 이루는
profusion ⓝ 대량, 풍부, 사치
pejorative ⓐ 경멸적인, 비난투의
uniformly ⓐⓓ 획일적으로

predecessor ⓝ 전임자, 선조, 선배
complacent ⓐ 만족한, 자기만족의
distaste ⓝ (음식물에 대한) 싫음, 혐오
aftereffect ⓝ 여파, 잔존효과
prudish ⓐ 고상한 체하는, 점잔 빼는
multi-faceted ⓐ 많은 측면을 가진
applicable ⓐ 적절한, 적용[응용]할 수 있는

전문해석

1901년 빅토리아 여왕이 사망했을 때, 이전 세기의 많은 업적들에 대한 반발이 발생했다. 이것은 빅토리아 시대가 다른 시대와 별개의 시기라는 인식을 강화했다. 20세기의 초기 수십 년 동안 작가들은 빅토리아 시대의 작가들로부터 자신들을 분리하기 위해 노력했다. 그때 대부분의 문학비평가들은 빅토리아 시대의 선배 작가들을 다소 터무니없는 인간들, 그들의 삶의 방식과는 거의 공통점이 없는 자만심에 찬 잔소리꾼들로 여기는 것이 유행이었다. 조지아 시대 (1911년~36년)의 작가들은 리튼 스트레이치(Lytton Strachey)가 Eminent Victorians에서 했던 것처럼 과도하게 부풀려진 빅토리아 시대의 풍선에 구멍을 내는 것을 매우 즐겼다. 그들의 재치 있는 묘사는 빅토리아 시대의 삶과 문학의 구별되는 특징을 식별할 뿐만 아니라, 그 시대의 숨 막히는 풍부함에 대한 작가들의 혐오감을 드러낸다.

빅토리아 시대의 작가들에 대한 조지아인들(작가들)의 반응은 이제 취향의 역사의 문제일 뿐이지만, 빅토리아 시대라는 용어가 신중하거나 구식인 것처럼 독점적인 경멸적 의미로 사용될 때 그 후유증은 여전히 발생한다. 현대의 역사학자들과 비평가들은 이제 빅토리아 시대가 우리가 모더니즘과 동일시하는 쟁점들 그리고 문제들과 싸우고 있는 풍부한 다면적인 사회의 예라고 생각한다. 그래서, 그 시대에 빅토리아 시대라는 단일 명칭을 붙이는 것은 <u>복잡성을 감소시킨다</u>. 거의 70년의 기간 동안, 우리는 일반화가 균일하게 적용될 것이라고 기대하기 어렵다.

---

15 빈칸에 들어갈 말로 가장 적절한 것은? [빈칸 추론]

① 문제들을 무시한다
✓ ② 복잡성을 감소시킨다
③ 동정적 반응들을 불러일으킨다
④ 역사의식을 말살한다

| 분석 | 빈칸이 포함된 문장을 기준으로 앞뒤 내용을 살펴보고 빈칸을 추론해 본다. 빈칸이 포함된 문장이 결과를 나타내는 So로 시작되므로 직전 문장은 '원인'이 제시되었을 것이다. 직전 문장에서 빅토리아 시대를 '풍부한 다면적인 사회의 예'라고 했으므로 그 결과 빅토리아 시대에 단일 명칭을 붙이는 것은 다면성을 줄어들게 할 것이다. 따라서 보기 ②가 빈칸에 가장 적절하다.

---

16 다음 중 위 지문에 따른 사실이 아닌 것은? [내용 불일치]

✓ ① 빅토리아 시대 사람들은 가혹한 비판을 받을 만한 사람들이었다.
② 빅토리아 시대 사람들은 그들만의 독특한 태도와 행동을 가지고 있었다.
③ 빅토리아 시대의 용어는 조지아 시대의 많은 작가들에게 경멸적인 뉘앙스를 가지고 있었다.
④ 20세기 초의 대부분의 비평가들은 빅토리아 시대의 전임자들과 거리를 두었다.

| 분석 | 본문의 첫 번째 단락에서는 작가들과 문학비평가들이 빅토리아 시대의 작가들과 자신들을 차별화하고 비판하는 내용이 서술되었다. 하지만 보기 ①에서처럼 빅토리아 시대 사람들이 비판을 받을 만하다는 언급은 없다. 따라서 정답은 ①이다.

[17-18] 2016 성균관대

| 정답 | 17 ②   18 ⑤

| 어휘 |
duel ⓝ 결투
anachronistic ⓐ 시대착오의, 시대에 뒤진
outlaw ⓥ 불법화하다, 금하다
archaism ⓝ 고풍, 고풍의 습관, 고어
be peppered with ~ 세례를 받다
swashbuckling ⓐ 허세를 부리는, (영화가) 모험에 찬
hot-headed ⓐ 성미 급한, 격하기 쉬운
rail against ~을 욕하다
hark back to ~을 기억하다[회고하다], ~을 들먹이다
glamorous ⓐ 화려한, 매력이 넘치는
burgeoning ⓐ 급증하는

전문해석

수 세기 동안 두 남자가 결투에서 맞붙는다는 생각은 시대착오적인 것처럼 보였다. 19세기 작가인 기 드 모파상(Guy de Maupassant)은 그것이 "우리의 불합리한 관습의 마지막"이라고 선언했다. 그 2세기 전에, 프랑스의 왕 루이 14세는 결투를 봉건적인 고풍으로 불법화하려고 했다. 그러나 그럼에도 불구하고, 19세기와 심지어 20세기 초의 문학은 모험에 찬 사람들에 대한 이야기로 가득 차 있다. 왜일까? 18세기 초에 많은 작가들은 결투를 벌이는 사람들을 성급한 사람으로 묘사했다. 19세기까지, 비록 그것이 여전히 더 오래된 중세 시대에서 시작된 것처럼 보였지만, 결투는 꽤 매력적으로 여겨졌다. 윌리엄 메이크피스 새커레이(William Makepeace Thackeray)의 "신사 배리 린든의 회고록"(1844)에서 주인공은 "비겁한 권총들"을 욕하고 "명예롭고 남성적인 남성들의 무기"를 기억한다. <u>그리고 20세기 초에 급증한 폭력과 비교해 볼 때 결투는 또한 눈에 띄게 신중하게 보일 수 있다.</u> 1908년의 G.K. 체스터튼(G.K. Chesterton) 소설의 한 인물은 무정부주의자로 의심되는 사람이 그에게 결투를 신청함으로써 그가 폭탄을 터뜨리는 것을

막는다. 하지만, 두 번의 세계 대전 이후, 그 매력은 사라지기 시작했다. 에블린 워(Evelyn Waugh)의 "장교들과 신사들"(1955)에서 한 캐릭터는 만약 그가 결투에 도전받는다면 웃을 것이라고 인정한다.

---

17 윗글의 가장 좋은 제목은 _____ 이다. 제목

① 현대적인 결투 　　　　　　　✓ ② 문학에서의 결투
③ 결투의 기원 　　　　　　　　④ 구식의 어리석은 행위로서의 결투
⑤ 폭력의 역사

| 분석 | 본문에서는 문학작품에서 '결투'에 대해 어떻게 묘사하고 있는지를 서술하고 있다. 따라서 주요 소재인 '문학'과 '결투'가 포함된 보기 ②가 정답으로 적절하다.

---

18 밑줄 친 표현은 결투가 _____ 라는 것을 암시한다. 밑줄 추론

① 합법화되었다 　　　　　　　② 거의 사라졌다
③ 무정부주의의 무작위적인 행동이다 　④ 공격성의 낮은 형태이다
✓ ⑤ 질서가 잡힌 폭력의 한 형태이다

| 분석 | 밑줄 친 문장에서 '20세기 초에 급증한 폭력'이란 본문 마지막 문장의 '두 번의 세계 대전'을 의미한다. 그렇다면 문학작품 속에서의 결투가 두 번의 세계 대전과 비교하여 '신중하게 보일 수 있다는 것'은 무차별적이고 무질서하지 않다는 의미이다. 따라서 보기 ⑤가 정답으로 가장 적절하다.

[19-21] 2016 한국외대

| 정답 | 19 ① 　20 ② 　21 ②

| 어휘 |
traumatic ⓐ 정신적 외상의, 대단히 충격적인　　　　**stunning** ⓐ 기절할 만큼의, 놀라게 하는
welcoming ⓐ (방문객에게) 따뜻한, 따뜻이 맞이하는　　**draw** ⓝ (사람을) 끌어들이는 것, 추첨
fringe ⓥ 둘레[가장자리]를 형성하다　　**gorgeous** ⓐ 호화로운, 아주 멋진, 찬란한　　**gilded** ⓐ 금박을 입힌, 금빛의
cobblestone ⓝ (철도·도로용의) 자갈, 조약돌　　**rejuvenate** ⓥ 도로 젊어지게 하다
shroud ⓥ 뒤덮다, ~에 수의를 입히다; 숨기다　　**dot** ⓥ 여기저기 흩어 놓다, 산재하다
ascent ⓝ 상승, 등정, 등반　　**spell** ⓥ (어떤 단어의) 철자를 쓰다[말하다]　　**humpback whale** 혹등고래
reef ⓝ 암초

전문해석

충격적이지만 풍부한 역사, 놀라운 풍경, 그리고 이 대륙에서 가장 환영받는 사람들의 고향인 콜롬비아는 ⓐ 남미 여행자들에게 자연의 관광지다. 40년 동안 지속된 내전에도 불구하고, 향상된 보안 상황들은 관광의 급격한 증가로 이어졌다. 외국인들과 콜롬비아인들은 모두 이제 구름 숲이 우거진 산, 야자수로 둘러싸인 해변, 그리고 멋진 식민지 도시들의 이 멋진 낙원을 훨씬 더 많이 탐험할 수 있다. 남아메리카에서 유일하게 태평양과 카리브해를 국경으로 접하는 콜롬비아는 아마존 열대 우림에서 눈 덮인 산, 열대 섬에 이르기까지 광범위한 생태계를 제공한다. 금박을 입힌 카리브해 해안과 자갈로 뒤덮인 식민지의 매력에서부터 커피 농장의 무리에 이르기까지 콜롬비아는 라틴 아메리카를 한 나라 안에 보호하고 있다. 가브리엘 가르시아 마르케스(Gabriel Garcia Marquez)의 마법의 카르타헤나(스페인의 황금도시), 부흥한 대도시를 놓쳐서는 안 된다. 더욱 신비에 싸인 것은 500개 이상의 실물 크기의 고대 조각상들이 주변 시골에 흩어져 있는 산 아구스틴이다. 콜롬비아의 다양한 지형은 야외 탐험가들이 다이빙, 등산, 뗏목 타기, 트레킹을 하기에 비옥한 땅이다. 남미의 가장 상징적인 트레킹(코스)가 여기 있다. 시우다드 페르디다는 타이로나 문명의 고대 유적

지로 가는 정글 산책로이며, 국립공원 내의 수많은 오르막길은 두려움 없는 도보 여행자들을 안데스산맥의 가장 높은 곳에 이르게 한다. 프로비덴시아의 세계적인 암초는 스쿠버 다이버들에게 수생 천국을 의미하며, 태평양 연안의 고래 관찰자들은 야생의 장엄한 혹등고래를 볼 수 있다.

19 다음 중 ⓐ의 예가 아닌 것은? 밑줄 추론

✓ ① 40년에 걸친 내전
② 한 무리의 커피 농장
③ 아마존 열대 우림
④ 고대 유적지로서의 정글 산책

| 분석 | 보기 ①의 '40년에 걸친 내전'은 밑줄 친 ⓐ의 '자연 관광지'의 예가 아니다.

20 다음 중 윗글의 주요 내용은 무엇인가? 주제

① 콜롬비아의 자연사
✓ ② 콜롬비아에서 가볼 만한 곳들
③ 콜롬비아 국가 안보
④ 콜롬비아의 스포츠 기회

| 분석 | 본문은 콜롬비아의 다양한 관광지와 그 특징들을 소개하고 있다. 따라서 보기 ②가 정답으로 적절하다.

21 다음 중 윗글에 명시되거나 암시되지 <u>않은</u> 것은? 내용 불일치 / 내용 비추론

① 콜롬비아는 여행하기에 안전하지 않은 곳이었다.
✓ ② 콜롬비아는 이웃 국가들과 공통점이 거의 없다.
③ 당신은 안데스산맥의 정상까지 하이킹할 수 있다.
④ 콜롬비아는 카리브해와 태평양의 나라이다.

| 분석 | 본문 다섯 번째 문장에서 '콜롬비아는 라틴 아메리카를 한 나라 안에 보호하고 있다.'고 했으므로 라틴 아메리카 내의 인접한 나라들과 공통점이 있을 것이다. 따라서 보기 ②가 정답으로 적절하다.

[22-24] 2013 성균관대

| 정답 | 22 ② 23 ③ 24 ③

| 어휘 | fall victim to ~의 희생자가 되다
depredation ⓝ 약탈, 침식
black market ⓝ 암시장
gold fever 금광열, 황금열
unleash ⓥ (강력한 반응이나 감정 등을) 촉발시키다, 불러일으키다
to date 지금까지
looter ⓝ 약탈자, 도둑

pillaging ⓝ (특히 전시에) 약탈, 강탈
warlord ⓝ (반군 등 비정규군의) 군 지도자, 군벌
antiquities ⓝ 유물, 골동품
annual ⓐ 연간의, 매년의
land mine 지뢰

on par with ~와 대등한, 동등한 수준인
ignite ⓥ ~에 불을 지피다, 흥분시키다
spirit ⓥ 재빨리 채어 가다
rape ⓝ 강탈, 약탈
bear fruit 결실을 보다

전문해석

아프가니스탄을 20년이 넘는 전쟁 후에 다시 일어서게 하기 위해 2001년부터 7년간 계속된 전투에서, 이 나라의 역사적인 유적지들은 무시되어 왔다. 그것의 고대 유산은 1220년에 발흐를 폐허로 만든 칭기즈 칸 군대의 약탈과 동등하게 약탈의 전염병의 희생자가 되었다. 조직범죄 규모의 무단 발굴은 유물의 국제 암시장과 관련성을 지닌 지역 군벌들과 심지어 정부 관리들의 지원을 받는 전문 갱단들에 의해 수행된다. 이 불법 거래에 대한 추정치는 매우 다양하지만, 정부 당국은 이를 국가의 마약 거래와 거의 동등한 40억 달러에 달하는 것으로 추산하고 있다. 이것은 중앙아시아 문명의 발전에 있어 그 나라의 중요한 역할을 막 이해하기 시작한 역사가들과 고고학자들에게 상처를 준다. 20세기 중반 아프가니스탄에서 고고학 연구의 꽃이 피면서 상상할 수 없는 가치를 지닌 보물들이 발견되었다. 이러한 발견들은 또한 그 나라의 금 열풍에 불을 붙였고, 수백 명의 프리랜서 "고고학자"들이 농부의 연간 수입을 훨씬 초과하는 암시장에서 가치를 지닌 자신들의 보물을 발굴하도록 영감을 주었다. 그 후 1979년부터 전쟁은 취약한 정부의 보호마저 없앴고, 수천 점의 귀중한 유물들이 나라 밖으로 유출되었다. 하지만 2001년 12월 탈레반의 몰락과 그에 따른 권력 공백이 지금까지 아프가니스탄의 유산에 대한 가장 파괴적인 약탈을 촉발시켰다. <mark>역설적이게도</mark> 빈곤과 전쟁이 이 장소들을 안전하게 지켜 준 것이다. 분쟁의 시기에, 민간인들은 집을 떠나는 것을 두려워했고, 지뢰에 대한 두려움은 많은 사람들이 땅을 파지 못하게 했다. <mark>지뢰 제거를 위한 전국적인 캠페인이 결실을 맺고 있기 때문에, 약탈자들은 수년 동안 손대지 않았던 유적지로 돌아오고 있으며, 심지어 새로운 장소들을 발견하고 있다.</mark>

24 ③

---

22 윗글의 가장 좋은 제목은 _____ 일 것이다. `제목`

① 아프가니스탄의 불법 거래 감소 ✓② 아프가니스탄의 보물찾기 역사
③ 아프가니스탄의 지뢰 반대 전국 캠페인 ④ 역사학자들과 아프가니스탄의 문화유산
⑤ 진행 중인 아프가니스탄의 군사력과의 전쟁

|분석| 본문에서는 약탈의 희생자가 된 아프가니스탄의 유적지와 유산에 대해 서술하고 있다. 따라서 주요 소재인 '아프가니스탄'과 '유산의 약탈'이 제목에 포함되어야 할 것이다. 보기 ②의 '보물찾기'는 약탈자들의 입장에서 '유산의 약탈'과 유사한 의미로 볼 수 있으므로 정답은 보기 ②가 가장 적절하다.

---

23 다음 중 빈칸에 들어갈 말로 가장 적절한 것은? `빈칸 추론`

① 결과적으로 ② 여전히
✓③ 역설적이게도 ④ 대조적으로
⑤ 예상대로

|분석| 빈칸 앞 문장에서는 전쟁이 '아프가니스탄의 파괴적인 약탈을 촉진시켰다'고 했으나 빈칸 이후로는 전쟁으로 '민간인들은 집을 떠나는 것을 두려워했고, 지뢰에 대한 두려움은 많은 사람들이 땅을 파지 못하게 했다.'고 서술했다. 약탈을 촉진시킬 것 같던 환경이 오히려 약탈을 감소시켰다는 내용과 연결되려면 역접의 표현이 필요할 것이다. 따라서 보기 ③이 정답으로 가장 적절하다.

---

24 윗글에 따르면 다음 중 옳은 것은? `내용 일치`

① 농부들은 전문 약탈자들로부터 가장 큰 피해를 입었다. `농부들의 피해는 언급 없음`
② 탈레반 세력의 쇠퇴는 역사적 유물을 보존하려는 국가적 노력에 긍정적인 영향을 미쳤다. `탈레반의 몰락은 가장 파괴적인 약탈을 촉발시킴`
✓③ 지뢰를 제거하기 위한 성공적인 작전은 약탈자들이 다시 공격하도록 고무시켰다.
④ 아마추어 고고학자들과는 달리, 전문 약탈자들은 국내 마약 거래의 지원을 받았다. `마약 거래의 지원을 받은 내용은 언급 없음`
⑤ 정부 관계자들은 무단 발굴을 막기 위해 최선을 다했다. `전쟁은 정부의 보호를 없애고 유물을 나라 밖으로 유출시킴`

| 분석 | 본문의 마지막 문장에서 '지뢰 제거를 위한 전국적인 캠페인이 결실을 맺고 있기 때문에, 약탈자들은 수년 동안 손대지 않았던 유적지로 돌아오고 있으며, 심지어 새로운 장소들을 발견하고 있다.'고 했으므로 ③이 정답이다.

[25-26] 2013 한국외대

| 정답 | 25 ①   26 ②

| 어휘 |
Nazism ⓝ 독일 국가 사회주의, 나치즘   anti-Semitism ⓝ 반유대주의, 유대인 배척   by a long shot 결코, 절대로, 확실히
persecution ⓝ (특히 종교상의) 박해   perpetuate ⓥ 영구화하다, 영속시키다
manifest ⓥ (특히 감정이나 태도를) 나타내다   sweeping ⓐ 광범위한, 포괄적인
propaganda ⓝ (정치 지도자 등에 대한 허위) 선전   launch ⓥ 시작하다, 출시하다
take over ~로부터 인계받다, (정권이나 정당 등을) 탈취하다   outrageous ⓐ 지나친, 터무니없는
ritual ⓐ 관습의, 의례적인   unleavened ⓐ 누룩[이스트]을 넣지 않은
Passover ⓝ (유대교의) 유월절, (p-) 유월절에 제물로 바치는 어린 양   scapegoat ⓝ 희생양
crony ⓝ 친구, 옛벗   orchestrate ⓥ (복잡한 계획을 은밀히) 조직하다
gut ⓝ 소화관, 내장; 배짱, 용기   colossal ⓐ 거대한

전문해석

1930년대 독일에서 나치즘이 발생했을 때, 반유대주의는 새로운 것이 아니었다—결코 아니었다. 유대인들은 편견과 박해의 긴 역사를 겪었다. 비록 나치가 수 세기 동안의 거짓말을 영구화했지만, 이번에는 그 거짓말들이 가장 파괴적인 영향을 미칠 것이다. 이전과는 달리, 반유대주의는 "최종 해결책"으로 알려진 광범위한 국가 정책에서 나타났는데, 이 정책은 지구상에서 유대인을 제거하려고 했던 것이다.

이를 달성하기 위해, 아돌프 히틀러(Adolf Hitler)와 그의 선전부 장관 요제프 괴벨스(Joseph Goebbels)는 독일 국민들에게 유대인들이 그들의 적이라는 것을 확신시키기 위해 대대적인 캠페인을 시작했다. 언론을 장악한 후, 그들은 제1차 세계 대전 패전 등 독일의 모든 문제에 대해 유대인을 비난하는 거짓말을 퍼뜨렸다. 그중 하나는 유대인들이 기독교 어린이들의 의식적인 살해에 관여하고 유월절에 먹는 누룩을 넣지 않은 빵에 피를 사용했다고 주장하는 중세 시대의 터무니없는 거짓말이었다.

유대인들을 희생양으로 삼아, 히틀러와 그의 친구들은 그들이 "큰 거짓말"이라고 부르는 것을 만들어 냈다. 이 이론은 거짓말이 아무리 커도(더 정확히는 너무 커서) 충분히 반복하면 사람들이 믿을 것이라고 말한다. 히틀러는 모든 사람이 작은 거짓말을 하지만, 거대한 거짓말을 할 용기가 있는 사람은 거의 없다고 추론했다. 다시 말해서, 큰 거짓말은 가능성이 매우 낮기 때문에, 사람들은 그것을 받아들이게 될 것이다.

25 다음 중 윗글의 제목으로 가장 적절한 것은? 제목

① 나치의 큰 거짓말 ✓
② 유대인과 제1차 세계 대전
③ 나치즘의 출현
④ 인종 차별의 역사

| 분석 | 본문에서는 '나치의 반유대주의'에 대해 서술하고 있다. 히틀러는 유대인에 대해 거짓말을 지어내 그들이 적이라는 인상을 주려고 했으며 특히 마지막 단락에서는 "큰 거짓말"이라고 불리는 캠페인을 소개했다. 따라서 제목에는 유대인에 대한 박해나 꾸며진 거짓말과 같은 소재가 포함되어야 하므로 정답은 보기 ①이 가장 적절하다.

26 다음 중 히틀러와 나치에 대해 언급되지 않은 것은? 내용 불일치

① 그들은 거짓말이 클수록 더 많이 받아들여질 것이라고 믿었다.
✓ ② 그들은 유대인들에 대한 증오를 강화하기 위해 많은 새로운 거짓말을 지어냈다.
③ 그들은 수 세기 동안 널리 유포되었던 거짓을 재활용했다.
④ 그들은 유대인들이 기독교 어린이들을 죽이고 그들의 피를 빵에 섞었다고 주장했다.

| 분석 | 본문 첫 문장에서 '반유대주의'는 새로운 것이 아니었으며 유대인에 대한 오해와 편견은 긴 역사를 가지고 있다고 서술했다. 또한 본문 두 번째 단락에서 나치가 유대인들을 비난하기 위해 퍼뜨린 거짓말은 '중세 시대의 터무니없는 거짓말'로 설명되어 있다. 그러므로 보기 ②와 같이 히틀러와 나치가 '많은 새로운 거짓말을 지어냈다'고 보기는 어렵다. 정답은 ②이다.

배경지식 반유대주의(Anti-semitism): 인종적, 종교적, 경제적인 이유로 유대인을 배척하거나 절멸하려는 사상

[27-28] 2018 숭실대

| 정답 | 27 ④ 28 ③

| 어휘 |
obscure ⓐ 불명료한, 애매한; 어두운
embodiment ⓝ 구체화, 구상화
kingship ⓝ 왕의 신분, 왕위, 왕권
grant ⓥ 승인하다, 인정하다, 수여하다
rise from the dead 부활하다, 소생하다
date back to (시기가) ~까지 거슬러 올라가다
mummy ⓝ 미라
ostrich ⓝ 타조

personification ⓝ 의인화, 인격화
resurrect ⓥ (사상·관례 등을) 부활시키다
consort ⓝ (통치자의) 배우자
sprout ⓥ 싹이 나다, 자라기 시작하다
cult ⓝ (종교상의) 예배, 제사
crook ⓝ 사기꾼, 굽은 것, 지팡이

fertility ⓝ 비옥함, 다산, 풍부
divine ⓐ 신의, 신성의
adversary ⓝ (언쟁·전투에서) 상대, 적수
resurrection ⓝ 소생, 부활, 부흥
archaize ⓥ 고풍으로 하다, 구식을 본뜨다
flail ⓝ (곡물을 떠는) 도리깨

전문해석

우시르라고도 불리는, 오시리스는 고대 이집트의 가장 중요한 신들 중 하나이다. 오시리스의 기원은 불분명한데, 그는 하(下)이집트 내의 부시리스의 지역 신이었고, 지하 세계의 비옥함의 화신이었을지도 모른다. 그러나, 기원전 2400년경, 오시리스는 분명히 두 가지 역할을 했다. 그는 비옥함의 신이었고, 죽은 자와 부활한 왕의 화신이었다. 이 두 가지 역할은 차례로 이집트의 신적인 왕권의 개념과 결합되었다. 죽을 때의 왕은 지하 세계의 신 오시리스가 되었고, 죽은 왕의 아들인 살아 있는 왕은 하늘의 신 호루스와 동일시되었다. 오시리스와 호루스는 그러므로 아버지와 아들이었다. 여신 이시스는 왕의 어머니였고 그러므로 호루스의 어머니였고 오시리스의 배우자였다. 세스 신은 오시리스의 살인자이자 호루스의 적수로 여겨졌다.

오시리스는 죽은 자들의 통치자였을 뿐만 아니라, 싹이 트는 초목부터 나일강의 매년 홍수에 이르기까지 저승에서부터 모든 생명을 부여하는 힘이었다. 기원전 2000년경부터 사망한 왕들뿐만 아니라 모든 사람들이 죽을 때 오시리스와 연관된다고 믿어졌다. 그러나 오시리스와의 이러한 동일성은 부활을 의미하지는 않는데 왜냐하면 오시리스조차도 죽은 자들로부터 살아나지 못했기 때문이다. 대신, 그것은 저승과 현세의 자손들을 통한 삶의 부활을 의미했다. 이러한 보편화된 형태로, 오시리스의 숭배는 이집트 전역으로 퍼져 나갔고, 종종 지역의 비옥함과 저승의 신들에 대한 숭배와 결합했다. 28 ③

오시리스에 대한 가장 오래된 묘사는 기원전 2300년으로 거슬러 올라가지만, 신왕국(기원전 1539~1075) 이전에 그에 대한 묘사는 드문데, 그가 가슴에 팔짱을 끼고, 한 손은 지팡이를 잡고, 다른 한 손은 도리깨를 들고 있는 미라의 고풍스러운 형태로 보여졌다. 그의 머리에는 상(上)이집트의 흰 왕관과 두 개의 타조 깃털로 구성된 왕관이 있었다.

27 다음 중 제목으로 가장 적절한 것은? 제목

① 오시리스의 가문
② 오시리스의 죽음
③ 오시리스의 미라화
✓ ④ 고대 이집트의 오시리스 문화

| 분석 | 본문에서는 고대 이집트의 신 오시리스에 대해 설명하고 있다. 고대 이집트에서 오시리스는 생명을 부여하는 힘과 죽은 자들을 통치하는 두 가지 역할을 했고 본문은 이에 대해 상세히 서술하고 있다. 따라서 제목으로는 주요 소재인 '고대 이집트'와 '오시리스'가 언급된 보기 ④가 가장 적절하다.

28 다음 중 사실이 아닌 것은? 내용 불일치

① 오시리스는 하이집트에서 지역 신들 중 하나로 처음 등장했다.
② 세스는 오시리스를 죽였고, 오시리스는 호루스의 뒤를 이었다.
✓ ③ 부활의 상징으로, 오시리스는 죽은 자들로부터 다시 살아났다.
④ 오시리스의 표현의 한 형태는 신왕국의 미라의 표현이었다.

| 분석 | 본문의 두 번째 단락 세 번째 문장에서 '오시리스조차도 죽은 자들로부터 살아나지 못했기 때문이다.'라고 했으므로 보기 ③은 본문의 내용과 일치하지 않는다.

[29-30] 2018 이화여대

| 정답 | 29 ④   30 ③

| 어휘 |

startling ⓐ 깜짝 놀랄, 놀랍도록 선명한
wage ⓥ (전쟁·토론 등을) 벌이다
communally ⓐⓓ 공동의, 집단들이 관련된
proximity ⓝ (거리·시간상으로) 가까움
emulate ⓥ 모방하다, ~와 우열을 다투다
civilized ⓐ 문명화된, 개화된
apparent ⓐ 눈에 보이는, 뚜렷한
liberate ⓥ 해방하다, 자유롭게 하다

howling ⓐ 울부짖는, 휘몰아치는, 엄청난
ongoing ⓐ 계속 진행 중인
mobile ⓐ 움직이기 쉬운, 이동성이 있는
stark ⓐ 굳어진, 냉혹한, 극명한
occasion ⓝ (특정한) 경우, 기회
tribal ⓐ 부족의, 종족의
habituate ⓥ 습관들게[익숙하게] 하다
prevail ⓥ 우세하다, 이기다

raid ⓝ 습격, (경찰의) 현장 급습
campaign ⓝ (일련의) 군사행동, 선거운동
encampment ⓝ (집단적인) 야영지
wind up (어떤 장소·상황에) 처하게 되다
emigration ⓝ (타국으로의) 이주
flummox ⓥ 당황하게[혼란스럽게] 하다
captive ⓝ 포로, 노예, 사로잡힌 사람
disgusted ⓐ 정떨어진, 싫증난, 분개한

전문해석

아마도 미국에 관해 가장 놀라운 사실 하나는, 세계 강대국이 된 현대 국가들 중 유일하게 석기시대 부족들이 살고 있는 3천 마일에 걸친 쓸쓸한 황야에 맞서서 그렇게 되었다는 사실일 것이다. 1600년대 필립 왕의 전쟁에서부터 1924년 히우그란지를 가로지르는 마지막 아파치 소 떼 습격까지, 미국은 기술적으로 15,000년 동안 기술적으로 거의 변하지 않은 원주민들을 상대로 계속되는 군사 행동을 벌였다. 300년을 거치면서, 인디언들이 이동식 또는 반영구적인 야영지에서 공동생활을 하는 동안, 미국은 호황을 누리고 있는 산업사회가 되었다.

여러 세대에 걸쳐 이 두 문화가 근접한 것은 양쪽 모두에게 어떻게 살아야 할지에 대한 냉혹한 선택권을 주었다. 놀라운 수의 미국인들이—대부분 남성들이—자신들의 사회에 머물기보다는 결국 인디언 사회에 합류하게 되었다는 것은 인간 본성에 대해 어떤 것을 말해 줄지도 모른다. 그들은 인디언들을 모방했고, 그들과 결혼했고, 그들에게 입양되었으며, 어떤 경우에는 심지어 그들과 함께 싸웠다. 29④ 그리고 그 반대는 거의 일어나지 않았다. 인디언들은 백인 사회에 합류하기 위해 도망가지 않았다. 이민은 항상 문명화된 사회에서 부족사회로 가는 것처럼 보였고, 그것은 서양 사상가들로 하여금 그들의 사회에 대한 그러한 명백한 거부를 어떻게 설명해야 할지에 대해 당황하게 만들었다.

"인디언 아이가 우리 사이에서 자랐고, 우리의 언어를 배우고 우리의 관습에 익숙해졌을 때" 벤저민 프랭클린(Benjamin Franklin)은 1753년에 한 친구에게 "[그러나] 그가 그의 친척들을 보러 가서 한 인디언이 그들과 함께 이야기하게 한다면, 그가 돌아오도록 설득할 수 없다"라고 썼다. 반면에, 프랭클린은 인디언들로부터 해방된 백인 포로들이 Ⓐ <u>자신의 집에 있게 하는 것은 거의 불가능했다</u>고 계속 썼다. "비록 그들의 친구들에 의해 몸값이 지불되고, 그들과 함께 영국들 사이에 머물도록 하기 위해 상상할 수 있는 모든 친절로 대했지만, 짧은 시간에 그들은 우리의 삶의 방식에 혐오감을 느끼게 되었다…그리고 숲으로 다시 탈출하는 첫 번째 좋은 기회를 잡는다."

29 윗글의 주요 내용은 무엇인가? `주제`
① 미국인들은 적대적인 인디언들이 점령한 황무지에 위대한 문명을 건설하는 데 성공했다.
② 인디언들은 백인 미국인들을 큰 호의와 친절로 대했다.
③ 인디언들 사이에서 우연히 생활하게 된 미국인들은 그들의 미개한 관습에 거부감을 느꼈다.
✓ 많은 미국인들이 인디언들 사이에서 살기 위해 문명을 떠나는 선택을 했다.
⑤ 문명 생활에 대한 거부는 미국의 문화 엘리트들 사이에서 우려의 원인이었다.

| 분석 | 두 번째 단락에서는 많은 미국인들이 발달된 산업사회가 아닌 인디언 사회에 합류했으며 그것이 서양 사상가들을 당혹스럽게 했다는 내용을 다루고 있다. 이후 마지막 단락에서는 벤저민 프랭클린의 글을 통한 예시를 통해 주제를 부연하고 있다. 따라서 주제로는 보기 ④가 적절하다.

30 다음 중 Ⓐ에 들어가기에 가장 적절한 표현은? `빈칸 추론`
① 이상한 공격적인 경향을 보였다
② 돌아와서 기뻐했다
✓ 자신의 집에 있게 하는 것은 거의 불가능했다
④ 그들의 회복된 삶을 천천히 받아들였다
⑤ 만족시키기 어려웠다

| 분석 | 빈칸 뒤의 콜론(:) 표시를 통해 앞 진술에 대한 부연설명이 이어짐을 추론할 수 있다. 콜론 뒤에서 인디언으로부터 해방된 백인 포로들은 친절하게 대해주더라도 다시 인디언들에게로 돌아가려고 숲에서 탈출할 기회를 잡는다는 내용이 이어지므로 이와 연관된 내용의 보기 ③이 정답으로 가장 적절하다.

[31-33] 2015 성균관대

| 정답 | 31 ③ 32 ④ 33 ③

| 어휘 | **backlash** ⓝ (정치·사회적) 반발, 저항
libidinous ⓐ 호색의, 정욕을 느끼는
nonconformity ⓝ 불일치, 부적합, 따르지 않음; 비국교도
Anglican ⓝ 영국 성공회교도
fondle ⓥ 귀여워하다
louche ⓐ 수상쩍은, 평판이 나쁜
shenanigan ⓝ 허튼소리, 사기, 속임수

speak for ~ 대신 말하다
chap ⓝ 놈, 녀석
going ⓝ 떠나기, 속도, (힘든) 일
Tory ⓝ (영국 보수당원) 토리당원, 보수주의자
opine ⓥ ~라고 생각하다, 의견을 밝히다
virtuous ⓐ 덕이 높은, 고결한

전문해석

언제 그리고 왜 상황이 바뀌기 시작했을까? 17세기 후반은 특히 극단적인 청교도주의에 대한 반발이 시작되는데 그것은 특히 성욕이 왕성한 찰스 2세에 의해 궁정에서 벌어지는 소동을 목격한 상류층들 사이에서 일어났다. 그러나 첫 번째 성 혁명의 이유들은 복잡하고 다양했다. 사람들의 대도시로의 이주는 전통적인 도덕에 대한 구속을 더 어렵게 만들었고 한편 대량 인쇄된 매체의 폭발은 생각을 퍼뜨리고 성적인 허튼소리들에 대한 풍부한 관심을 이용했다. 여행자들이 매우 다른 성 문화에 대한 이야기를 가지고 돌아옴에 따라 탐험 또한 (성 혁명에) 영향을 미쳤다. 그러나 핵심적인 원인은 비국교도의 확산이었고, 이것은 교회의 권위를 잠식했다. 고위 토리 성공회 신자인 사무엘 존슨(Samuel Johnson)이 1750년 "모든 사람은 자신의 양심에 따라 자신의 행동을 규제해야 한다"라고 의견을 냈을 때 많은 사람들을 대변했다. 1732년에 설립된 스코틀랜드의 Begger's Benison club의 중상류층 구성원들은 분명히 그들이 술을 마시고, 노래를 부르고, 나체의 여성들을 어루만질 수 있는 모임을 주선하는 것을 아무렇지 않게 생각했다. 그러나 성에 대한 18세기 후반의 태도를 우리가 가진 성에 대한 태도의 원형으로써 보는 것은 잘못된 것이다. 성 해방은 주로 부유한 계급에 국한되어 있었다. 일반적으로 남성이 성적 기회를 추구하는 것이 "자연스러운" 반면, 여성은 본능적으로 더 도덕적이라고 생각했다.

---

31 윗글의 가장 좋은 제목은 _____일 것이다. 제목

① 근대 초기 영국의 성범죄
② 18세기 영국의 성과 형벌
✓③ 18세기 영국에서 도덕이 어떻게 개인적이 되었는가
④ 18세기 영국의 여성의 성적 자유
⑤ 18세기 영국에서 성을 단속하는 방법

| 분석 | 본문에서는 최초의 성 혁명이 어떻게 나타나게 되었는지 다양한 이유들을 나열하며 서술했다. 그런데 최초 성 혁명의 원인이나 기원에 대한 보기는 없으므로 본문의 내용이 반영되어 있는 보기를 고르도록 한다. 보기 ③이 정답으로 가장 적절하다.

---

32 윗글에 따르면 다음 중 최초의 성 혁명에 기여한 요인이 아닌 것은? 세부 내용 불일치

① 도시화
② 종교적 관용
③ 사상의 유통
✓④ 여성의 타락
⑤ 청교도의 쇠퇴

| 분석 | 본문에서는 최초의 성 혁명의 원인으로 '여성의 타락'은 언급하지 않았다. 본문의 마지막 문장에서 '일반적으로 남성이 성적 기회를 추구하는 것은 자연스러웠고 여성은 본능적으로 더 도덕적이라고 생각했다.'고 했으므로 보기 ④가 정답으로 가장 적절하다.

---

33 18세기 후반의 성적 해방은 _____로 제한되었다. 세부 내용 일치

① 노동자 계층
② 도시 사람들
✓③ 부유한 사람들
④ 교육받은 사람들
⑤ 정치가들

| 분석 | 본문의 열 번째 문장에서는 '성 해방은 주로 부유한 계급에 국한되어 있었다.'고 했다. 따라서 보기 ③이 정답으로 가장 적절하다.

| 배경 지식 | 청교도주의(Puritanism): 칼뱅주의를 이어받고 성경에 나타나는 신과의 계약에 기초를 두는 새로운 사회의 실현을 지향하는 사상이나 생활 태도 |

[34-36] 2018 한국외대

| 정답 | 34 ①   35 ④   36 ② |

| 어휘 |
span ⓥ (얼마의 기간에) 걸치다, 이어지다
archaeological ⓐ 고고학의
makeup ⓝ 화장, 조립, 성질
formula ⓝ 식, 공식
whiten ⓥ 희게 하다, 표백하다
lady of the night 매춘부
fashionable ⓐ 유행의, 유행하는, 유행을 따른
ingredient ⓝ 원료, 재료, 성분
divert ⓥ (딴 데로) 돌리다
postwar ⓐ 전후의, (특히) 제2차 세계 대전 후의
second-class ⓐ 이류의, 열등한
concealer ⓝ 컨실러(피부 흠을 감추어 주는 화장품)

전문해석

화장품의 역사는 적어도 6천 년에 걸쳐 있으며, 지구상의 거의 모든 사회에 존재한다. 화장품의 고고학적 증거는 고대 이집트와 그리스에서 유래한다. 고대 로마의 일부 여성들이 피부를 하얗게 만들기 위해 화장품 제조법을 발명했다고 알려져 있다. 1900년대 동안, 화장품은 여전히 '매춘부'에 의해 주로 사용되었기 때문에 인기가 없었다. 1910년경, 화장품은 발레와 연극 스타들의 영향으로 미국과 유럽에서 유행하게 되었다. 제2차 세계 대전 동안, 화장품은 기본적인 성분이 전쟁 물자에 사용되었기 때문에 공급이 부족했다. Ⓐ 역설적이게도, 화장품이 제한된 이 시기에 립스틱, 파우더, 그리고 페이스크림이 (사람들이) 가장 원하는 것이었고, 대부분의 (화장품) 실험이 전후 시기 동안 수행되었다. 이것은 화장품 개발자들이 전쟁이 그 이후에 굉장한 호황을 일으킬 것이라고 정확히 예측했기 때문이다. 1960년대와 1970년대 동안, 페미니즘에 의해 영향을 받은 많은 여성들이 여성의 2등 지위에서 그들을 단순히 성적 대상으로 만든 화장품의 역할에 Ⓑ 반대했다. 비록 현대의 화장품이 주로 여성들에 의해 사용되었지만, 점점 더 많은 남성들이 그들 얼굴의 특징을 향상시키기 위해 화장품을 사용하고 있다. 화장품 브랜드들은 남성을 위해 특별히 제작된 컨실러과 같은 제품들을 출시하고 있다. 그러나 많은 사람들이 화장을 하는 남성들이 전통적인 성 역할을 무시한다고 느끼기 때문에 이에 대해 약간의 논란이 있다. 그러나 다른 사람들은 Ⓒ 여자들이 화장품을 사용한다면 남자들도 화장품을 사용할 권리가 있다고 느끼기 때문에 이것을 지속적인 성 평등의 표시로 본다.

34 다음 중 빈칸 Ⓐ와 Ⓑ에 가장 적절한 단어로 짝지어진 것은? [빈칸 추론]

✓① 역설적이게도 – 반대했다
② 실제로 – 고수했다
③ 슬프게도 – 양보했다
④ 자연스럽게 – 대응했다

| 분석 | 빈칸 Ⓐ의 경우에는 빈칸 직전 문장에서 '제2차 세계 대전 동안, 화장품은 기본적인 성분이 전쟁 물자에 사용되었기 때문에 공급이 부족했다.'고 했는데 빈칸 다음으로는 공급이 부족한 상황에서 사람들의 욕구는 증가했으므로 빈칸에는 역접표현이 적절하다. 한편, 빈칸 Ⓑ는 페미니즘의 영향을 받은 여성들은 화장품이 여성을 성적 대상으로 만들었기 때문에 화장품의 역할에 '반대'했을것으로 추론할 수 있다. 따라서 보기 ①이 정답으로 가장 적절하다.

35 다음 중 빈칸 ⓒ에 가장 적절한 것은? 빈칸 추론
① 남자들은 여자들을 위한 화장품을 구입해야 한다
② 남자들은 남성적이기만 하면 화장품을 자유롭게 살 수 있다
③ 남자들은 오랫동안 그들의 화장품을 구입해 왔다
✓④ 여자들이 화장품을 사용한다면 남자들도 화장품을 사용할 권리가 있다

| 분석 | 빈칸 ⓒ가 포함된 본문의 마지막 문장을 참고하면 빈칸에는 '성평등의 표시'와 관련된 표현이 적절하다. 보기 ④에만 여성과 같이 남성도 화장을 할 권리가 있다는 성평등에 관한 언급이 있으므로 정답으로 가장 적절하다.

36 윗글에 따르면 다음 중 사실이 아닌 것은? 내용 불일치
① 배우들은 1910년대에 화장의 인기에 기여했다.
✓② 피부를 하얗게 만드는 제조법은 그리스에서 처음 등장했다.
③ 남성 전용 컨실러가 있다.
④ 제2차 세계 대전 후 화장품의 열풍이 일어났다.

| 분석 | 본문의 세 번째 문장에서 '고대 로마의 일부 여성들이 피부를 하얗게 만들기 위해 화장품 제조법을 발명했다고 알려져 있다.'고 했다. 피부를 하얗게 만드는 제조법은 그리스가 아닌 로마에서 발명했으므로 보기 ②가 정답으로 가장 적절하다.

| 배경지식 | 페미니즘(Feminism): 성별로 인해 발생하는 정치, 경제, 사회 문화적인 차별을 없애야 하는 견해

[37-39] 2013 성균관대

| 정답 | 37 ④ 38 ③ 39 ④

| 어휘 |
ragged ⓐ 누더기가 된, 다 해진
aquatic ⓐ 수생의, 물의
toil away 피땀 흘려 일하다
rowdy ⓐ 난폭한, 떠들썩한
web-footed ⓐ 물갈퀴발의, 물갈퀴이 있는
woodsman ⓝ 숲에 사는 사람, 나무꾼
weather-beaten 비바람에 거칠어진, 햇볕에 탄, 세파에 시달린
partaker ⓝ 분담자, 관여자
log ⓝ 통나무, 원목

baleen whale 수염 고래
deign ⓥ ~한다는 듯이 굴다
backwoods ⓝ 산간벽지, 오지
reception ⓝ 응접, 접대, 접수처
frenzied ⓐ 열광한, 격노한, 제멋대로인
ring ⓥ 둘러싸다
wearying ⓐ (몹시) 지친, 피곤한

gorge ⓥ 잔뜩 먹다, 배불리 먹다
decidedly ⓐⓓ 확실히, 분명히, 단호히
monopoly ⓝ 독점, 전매
excursion ⓝ 회유, 소풍, 여행
coarse ⓐ 조잡한, 열등한, 거친
thorny ⓐ 가시가 많은, 곤란한
fir ⓝ (서양) 전나무

전문해석

퀘벡주 북쪽에 위치한 타두삭(Tadoussac) 마을은 산과 복잡한 해안선 사이에 있으며, 이곳에서 사기네이 피오르(Saguenay Fjord)의 신선한 강물이 세인트로렌스강의 따뜻하고 염분이 높은 물속으로 흘러 들어간다. 매년 5월부터 10월까지, 그것은 교차로에서 번창하는 크릴새우를 먹기 위해 모인 수염고래들을 보기 바라는 관광객들로 넘쳐 난다.

하지만 내륙으로 떠돌기로 작정한 사람들은—친밀하고, 저렴하고, 확실히 캐나다적인—다른 종류의 야생 동물 관찰 경험을 하게 될 것이다. 5센트 동전 앞면에 있는 작은 비버 한 마리가 타두삭의 잊힌 산간벽지에서 고생하고 있기 때문이다. 비버가 없다면, 모피 독점 때문에 1600년에 설립된, 이전 프랑스 무역소의 역사는 거의 (지금과) 같을 수 없을 것이다.

37 ④
39 ④

이 마을의 유일한 유스호스텔인 시끄러운 붉은 지붕의 메종 메저리크도 마찬가지였다. 무료 비버 관람 투어는 매일 오후 5시에 이 호텔 리셉션에서 출발하는데, 이때 물갈퀴가 있는 설치류들이 밤새 일을 하기 위해 깨어난다. 21년 동안, 이 여행은 같은 나무꾼이 이끌었다. 그의 얼굴은 지저분하게 자란 흰 머리가 덮고 있고 덥수룩한 턱수염으로 이어진다. 코코(Coco)는 그가 잘 아는 습지만큼이나 거칠고 날씨에 시달린다. "나는 바다보다 숲이 더 좋다."라고 그는 퉁명스러운 프랑스어로 말한다. (요청하면 그는 훨씬 더 퉁명스러운 영어로 번역할 것이다.) 참가자들은 빽빽한 전나무와 다섯 그루의 통나무로 쌓아 놓은 비버의 집들로 둘러싸인 호수인 랑세-아-로에서 (관광을) 시작한다. 호수 주변을 걷는 피곤한 관광은 쉬면서 가면 약 두 시간이 걸린다. 코코는 혼자 45분 만에 등산로를 올라간다.

37 윗글의 주요 소재는 무엇인가? 주제
① 캐나다의 외진 곳
② 수염 고래의 화려함
③ 삼림 vs. 해안선
④ ✓ 비버 관찰
⑤ 야생 생활을 즐기는 방법

| 분석 | 본문의 시작은 수염 고래를 보기 위해 모여든 관광객들을 언급했으나 본문 두 번째 단락에서 역접되어 세 번째 단락까지 야생 동물 관찰 경험 중 비버 관찰에 관한 서술로만 이루어져 있다. 따라서 본문의 주요 소재는 보기 ④이다.

38 다음 중 윗글에 대한 설명으로 옳지 않은 것은? 내용 불일치
① 많은 관광객들이 수염 고래를 보기 위해 모인다.
② 이 마을에는 호스텔이 하나밖에 없다.
③ ✓ 비버는 고래보다 더 인기가 있다.
④ 비버의 사진은 캐나다의 5센트 동전에 있다.
⑤ 코코는 이중언어 가이드다.

| 분석 | 본문에 따르면 비버와 고래의 인기를 비교하는 내용은 없다. 따라서 정답은 ③이 가장 적절하다.

39 밑줄 친 부분은 무엇을 의미하는가? 밑줄 추론
① 메종 메저리크 호스텔은 그렇게 오래되지 않았다.
② 이 호스텔은 프랑스 모피 상인들을 위해 지어지지도 않았다.
③ 유스호스텔 건물도 볼거리다.
④ ✓ 비버가 없었다면, 호스텔 손님들이 많지 않았을 것이다.
⑤ 그 장소는 호스텔 손님들에게도 잊히지 않았다.

| 분석 | 밑줄 친 부분 바로 전 문장, 즉 두 번째 단락 마지막 문장에서 '비버가 없다면, 모피 독점 때문에 1600년에 설립된, 이전 프랑스 무역소의 역사는 거의 (지금과) 같을 수 없을 것이다.'라고 했다. 따라서 마을의 유일한 유스호스텔 또한 비버가 없었다면 비버 관찰을 하러 온 관광객들이 투숙하지 않았을 것이므로 보기 ④가 정답으로 적절하다.

[40-42] 2022 숭실대

| 정답 | 40 ①   41 ②   42 ④

| 어휘 | refrain from ~을 하지 않다   exquisite ⓐ 절묘한, 정교한   bandage ⓝ 붕대

computed tomography 컴퓨터 단층 촬영(CT)
protrude ⓥ 불쑥 나오다
mummification ⓝ 미라화, 미라로 만드는 것
post-mortem ⓐ 사후의
inflict ⓥ 주다, 입히다, 가하다
wrap ⓥ 감싸다, 포장하다
infection ⓝ 전염, 감염
forearm ⓝ 팔뚝
grave robber ⓝ (골동품이나 보물을 훔치기 위한) 도굴꾼

전문해석

고대 이집트 파라오의 미라 시신이 Ⓐ <u>디지털 방식으로</u> "벗겨진" 후 수천 년 만에 처음으로 연구되었다. 기원전 1525년부터 1504년까지 통치했던 아멘호테프 1세의 미라는 140년 전 데이르 엘 바하리의 한 유적지에서 발견되었다. 하지만 고고학자들은 그 정교한 안면 마스크와 붕대를 보존하기 위해 그것(미라)을 여는 것을 자제해 왔다. 컴퓨터 단층 촬영(CT) 스캔은 이제 파라오와 그의 매장에 대해 이전에 알려지지 않은 정보를 드러냈다. "우리는 3,000년 이상 싸여 있었던 왕의 얼굴을 보게 되었다"라고 카이로 대학 영상의학과 교수인 사하라 살렘(Sahar Saleem) 박사가 BBC에 말했다. 그녀는 그녀가 충격을 받은 첫 번째는 아멘호테프 1세가 좁은 턱과 작고 좁은 코, 곱슬곱슬한 머리, 그리고 약간 튀어나온 윗니를 가진 고대 이집트의 첫 번째 파라오인 그의 아버지 아흐모세 1세의 얼굴과 얼마나 닮았는지였다고 말했다.

연구원들은 또한 아멘호테프 1세가 대략 169센티미터의 키였고, 그가 죽었을 때 그의 나이는 약 35세였다는 것을 확인했다. 살렘 박사는 (미라의) 스캔 영상이 보여 준 것처럼 그가 사망할 당시에 매우 좋은 신체 상태와 건강 상태였으며, 질병으로 인한 상처나 부상의 흔적은 없었다고 말했다. 그것은 그가 감염이나 바이러스의 결과로 사망했다는 것을 암시했다.

연구원들은 아멘호테프 1세의 미라화와 매장에 대한 통찰을 얻을 수 있었는데, 그는 두 팔을 가슴에 포개어 접은 최초의 파라오였고, 특이하게도 그의 뇌는 제거되지 않았다. 그들은 또한 그의 미라가 이 죽음 이후 약 4세기를 통치했던 제21왕조의 사제들에 의해 "애정을 기울여 수리되었다"고 결론 내렸다. 그 스캔 영상은 미라가 무덤 도굴꾼들에 의해 가해졌을 가능성이 있는 다수의 사후 손상을 겪었다는 것을 보여 준다.

---

40 다음 중 Ⓐ에 들어가기에 가장 적절한 것은? 〔빈칸 추론〕

✓① 디지털 방식으로
② 완력으로
③ 예상대로
④ 예술적으로

| 분석 | 본문 첫 단락의 세 번째와 네 번째 문장에 따르면 고고학자들은 미라를 여는 것을 자제해 왔으며 컴퓨터 단층촬영(CT) 스캔으로 이전에 알려지지 않은 정보를 발견했다. 따라서 미라의 시신은 디지털 방식인 컴퓨터 단층촬영(CT) 스캔을 활용하여 그 비밀이 '벗겨진' 것 이므로 보기 ①이 정답으로 적절하다.

---

41 다음 중 올바른 것은 무엇인가? 〔내용 일치〕

① 아멘호테프 1세의 미라는 4백 년 전에 처음 발견되었다. 140년 전에 처음 발견됨
✓② 연구원들은 발견 직후 미라가 된 시신을 열지 않았다.
③ 아멘호테프 1세의 뇌는 제거되었고 잘 보존되었다. 세 번째 단락에서 뇌는 제거되지 않았다고 언급함
④ 아멘호테프 1세는 심각한 건강 문제로 고통받고 있었다. 두 번째 단락에서 사망할 당시 건강 상태가 좋았다고 언급함

| 분석 | 본문의 세 번째 문장에서 아멘호테프 1세의 미라는 여는 것을 자제해 오다가 최근에서야 CT 스캔으로 정보를 확인했으므로 보기 ②가 정답이다.

42 다음 중 제목으로 가장 적절한 것은? 제목

① 알려지지 않은 이집트 미라 목록
② 미라화된 아멘호테프 1세의 발견
③ 파라오 매장지의 역사
✓④ 아멘호테프 1세에 대해 드러난 정보

| 분석 | 본문에서는 CT 스캔으로 밝혀진 이집트의 파라오 아멘호테프 1세에 대한 새로운 정보들을 다루고 있다. 따라서 보기 ④가 제목으로 적절하다.

[43-46] 2018 아주대

| 정답 | 43 ⑤ 44 ② 45 ③ 46 ⑤

| 어휘 | **paternalistic** ⓐ 가부장적인   **integrity** ⓝ 성실, 정직   **sobriety** ⓝ 절주, 절제, 침착
puritanism ⓝ 청교도주의, (도덕·종교상의) 엄격주의   **potent** ⓐ 세력 있는, 유력한, 강력한
proletariat ⓝ 무산 계급

전문해석

[A] 빅토리아 여왕의 64년 통치 기간(1837~1901) 동안, 위대한 정치가들에 의해 이끌리고 위대한 산업 확장의 지원을 받은 대영 제국은 매우 거대한 규모로 성장해서 "그곳에는 태양이 지지 않는다."라고 불렸다. 빅토리아의 긴 통치 기간 동안 영국의 제도들과 "삶의 방식"은 많은 변화를 겪었다. 귀족의 오락과 삶에 대한 그녀(여왕)의 거부는 일반 사람들이 이 평범한 아내이며 과부인 여왕과 자신들을 동일시할 수 있도록 했고, 이것은 군주제에 대한 대중적 지지의 부활로 이어졌다. 무엇보다도, 그녀의 본질적으로 중산층인 관점과 삶의 방식은 중산층 계급의 상승과 결합하여 가치관—가정의 가부장적 성실과 훈육, 공공 생활의 절제와 철저한 금욕주의—에 대한 확신을 이끌었는데 이것은 이후 1980년에 대처(Thatcher) 정부가 회귀하고 싶어 했던 "빅토리아 시대의 가치"로 알려졌다. 43⑤

[B] 중산층이 빅토리아 시대 영국에서 확장되는 것과 동시에 노동자 계급도 확장되었다. 산업 혁명은 이제 두 번째 단계에 접어들었다. 새로운 산업들이 발달되고, 새로운 공장들이 지어지고, 영국의 제품들이 전 세계로 수출되었으며 영국은 "세계의 공장"으로 알려지게 되었다.

[C] 새로운 공장과 마을에서의 삶은 끔찍한 고난 중 하나였다. 남자, 여자, 그리고 아이들은 낮은 임금을 위해 위험하고 건강하지 않은 환경에서 하루에 15시간 또는 16시간을 일했고 소설 *Bleak House*에서 찰스 디킨스(Charles Dickens)에 의해 생생하게 묘사된 더럽고 음울한 빈민가에서 살았다. 45③

[D] 그동안에 노동자 계급은 조직화되고 있었다. 카를 마르크스(Karl Marx)의 사상이 영국 노동자들 사이에서 결코 많은 지지를 얻지 못했지만(비록 마르크스 자신이 런던에 사는 동안 그의 작품의 대부분을 연구하고 썼음에도 불구하고), 사회주의 사상은 그럼에도 불구하고 후기 빅토리아 시대 영국에서 강력한 힘이었다. 19세기의 마지막 25년 동안 노동조합 조직의 엄청난 증가가 있었고 1893년 키어 하디(Keir Hardie)가 이끄는 노동당의 설립은 46⑤ 의회에서 무산계급에게 더 큰 발언권을 주었다.

---

43 [A] 단락에 따르면, 다음 중 1980년 대처 정부가 돌아가기를 원했던 가치로 추측할 수 있는 것은? 세부 내용 추론

① 성적 해방   ② 인권의 존엄성
③ 정치적 해방   ④ 남녀평등
✓⑤ 공공 생활의 절제

| 분석 | 본문 [A] 단락에서는 두 번째 문장부터 영국의 제도와 삶의 방식에 변화를 준 빅토리아 시대의 가치가 서술되었다. 또한 '빅토리아 시대의 가치'를 '가정의 가부장적 성실과 훈육, 공공 생활의 절제와 철저한 금욕주의'라고 했다. 이후 대처 정부가 그때의 가치관으로 회귀하고자 했으므로 보기 ⑤가 정답으로 적절하다.

44 다음 중 [C] 단락에서 dreary라는 밑줄 친 단어를 가장 잘 대체할 수 있는 것은 무엇인가? 밑줄 추론

① 건조한 ✓② 음울한
③ 감소한 ④ 불투명한
⑤ 당황한

| 분석 | 본문에서 dreary는 '음울한, 쓸쓸한'이라는 의미로 사용되었으므로, 유사한 의미의 보기 ② gloomy(음침한)가 정답으로 적절하다.

45 [C] 단락에 따르면, 찰스 디킨스의 소설 *Bleak House*는 _____ 때문에 언급된다. 세부 내용 일치

① 그것은 중산층이 카를 마르크스의 사상에 기초하여 지배적인 자본주의 계급에 의해 그들에 대해 실행되는 부당함과 잘못에 대항하여 싸우도록 촉발했다
② 그것은 후기 빅토리아 시대의 영국에서 그 수가 크게 줄어든 노동자 계급의 끔찍한 고난을 생생하게 묘사했다
✓③ 그것은 빅토리아 시대 영국의 노동자 계급의 끔찍한 노동과 생활 환경을 훌륭하게 폭로했다
④ 그것은 산업 혁명의 초기에 중산층과 노동자 계층 사이의 협력적인 관계를 묘사했다
⑤ 그것은 세계의 작업장으로서의 영국인의 자부심을 나타내는 한편 후기 빅토리아 시대 영국의 노동자 계층의 끔찍한 노동 조건에 초점을 맞추고 있다

| 분석 | 본문 [C] 단락에서 '남자, 여자, 그리고 아이들은 낮은 임금을 위해 위험하고 건강하지 않은 환경에서 하루에 15시간 또는 16시간을 일했다'고 했으며 이것이 찰스 디킨슨의 소설에서 생생하게 묘사되었다는 내용이 이어졌다. 따라서 보기 ③이 정답으로 적절하다.

46 윗글에 따르면 다음 중 옳은 것은? 내용 일치

① 카를 마르크스는 런던에서 공부하고 산 적은 없지만 영국 경제의 통찰력 있는 연구자였다. 네 번째 단락에서 카를 마르크스는 런던에서 작품 대부분을 연구하고 집필했음을 언급함
② 카를 마르크스의 아이디어는 19세기 영국 노동자들에 의해 열광적으로 받아들여졌다. 네 번째 단락에서 카를 마르크스의 사상은 노동자들에게 지지를 얻지 못했음을 언급함
③ 빅토리아 여왕은 귀족적인 삶의 방식을 실천하는 동시에 자신을 중산층과 동일시함으로써 그녀의 왕권을 강화하려고 시도했다. 첫 단락에서 빅토리아 여왕은 중산층의 삶의 방식을 실천했음을 언급함
④ 산업 혁명은 후기 빅토리아 시대 영국에서 시작되었다. 산업 혁명의 두 번째 단계가 시작됨
✓⑤ 사회주의의 사상은 후기 빅토리아 시대 영국에서 매우 영향력이 있었다.

| 분석 | 본문 [D] 단락의 두 번째 문장에서 '사회주의 사상은 그럼에도 불구하고 후기 빅토리아 시대 영국에서 강력한 힘이었다'고 했다. 따라서 보기 ⑤는 본문의 내용과 일치한다.

| 배경 지식 | 빅토리아 시대(Victorian Age): 1837~1901년까지 영국의 빅토리아 여왕이 통치한 시대로 영국 역사상 가장 번영하여 강력한 경제력과 군사력으로 세계를 지배

[47-50] 2020 아주대

| 정답 | 47 ① 48 ② 49 ⑤ 50 ⑤

| 어휘 | accumulate ⓥ 모으다, (재산 따위를) 축적하다
not so much A as B A라기보다는 차라리 B다
no other than ~ 이외의 아무도 아닌, 바로 ~인 chronology ⓝ 연대학, 연대기
epoch ⓝ (중요한 사건·변화가 일어난) 시대, 신기원 catalyst ⓝ 촉매(제), (변화의) 기폭제
remarkable ⓐ 주목할 만한, 현저한 discard ⓥ (불필요한 것을) 버리다

전문해석

[A] 인류의 기억이 오직 구전 전통에 의해서만 전해지는 한 지식의 진보는 고통스러울 정도로 더뎠다. 예를 들어, 어떤 원시인 남자나 여자는 오래전에 위대한 적인 불을 복종시키고 삶을 더 좋게 만들게 할 수 있다는 것을 발견했다. 어떤 체계적인 의사소통 수단이 없었다면, 이 새로운 지식이 보편화되기까지 여러 세대가 걸렸을 수도 있다. 문자의 발명으로 특히 모든 인간들이 이용할 수 있는 지식의 축적 과정이 가속화되었다. 오늘날 컴퓨터와 같이 인류의 축적된 지식을 저장하고 재생하는 장치들은 그 자체로 그것을 개선하기 위한 진보적인 노력의 대상이 된다.

[B] 그렇기 때문에, 인류의 역사는 인류 지식의 진보와 발전의 역사다. 개인이나 심지어 국가들의 행위들을 다룬다기보다는 인류 전체의 업적과 실패를 ⓐ 다루는 보편적 역사는 적어도 다름 아닌 인류의 지식이 오랜 시간 동안 어떻게 성장하고 변화해 왔는지에 대한 설명이다.

[C] 따라서 지식의 역사로 생각되는 보편적 역사는 지금까지 만들어진 모든 발견과 발명의 연대기가 아니다. 그중 많은 것들이 궁극적으로 ⓑ 거의 가치가 없는 것들이다. 대신에, 그것은 인류가 다양한 시대에 습득하고 성장하는 (지식) 저장고에 추가하는 중요한 새로운 지식에 대한 가장 광범위하고 일반적인 용어로 말해지는 이야기여야 한다. 그것은 또한 어떻게 지식이 증가했는지보다 더 많이 변화했는지에 대한 이야기이며, 이것들이 ⓒ 다음 시대와 무관해 보였기 때문에 지식의 주요 요소들이 어떻게 포기되거나 완전히 상실되었는지에 대한 이야기이다.

[D] 예를 들어, 로마 제국의 몰락은 거의 보편적인 Ⓐ 대재앙이면서, 유럽 세계 어디에서나 비참함과 고통을 초래했다. 그럼에도 불구하고, 혹은 아마도 그것 때문에, 다음 여러 세기에 새로운 종류의 지식이 등장했다. 그 새로운 지식의 대부분은 ⓓ 견디지 못했지만, 우리가 폐기했지만 언젠가 다시 회귀할 수도 ⓔ 있을 주목할 만한 삶의 방식의 예시로 남아 있다.

47 다음 중 윗글의 제목으로 가장 적절한 것은? 제목

✓① 보편적 역사의 정의
② 로마 제국의 중요성
③ 지식의 끊임없는 진보
④ 지식 전달의 장애물들
⑤ 문자언어의 중요성

| 분석 | 본문의 주요 소재는 '보편적 역사'다. 보기 ①에만 유일하게 소재가 언급되었으므로 글의 제목으로 적절하다.

48 다음 중 [D] 단락의 빈칸 Ⓐ에 들어갈 말로 가장 적절한 것은? 빈칸 추론

① 자본주의 ✓② 대재앙
③ 역사주의 ④ 구원
⑤ 촉매

| 분석 | 빈칸 ⓐ 뒤에 이어지는 내용에서 로마 제국의 멸망이 '유럽 세계 어디에서나 비참함과 고통을 초래했다.'고 했다. 따라서 빈칸에는 비참함과 고통을 초래할 만한 보편적인 '대재앙'으로 보는 것이 바람직하다. 보기 ②가 정답이다.

49 올바른 문장이 되기 위해 바꿔야 할 밑줄 친 단어나 어구를 고르시오. 무관한 단어
① ⓐ ~와 마찬가지로
② ⓑ 거의 가치가 없는
③ ⓒ 다음 시대
④ ⓓ 견디는
✓⑤ ⓔ 어느 쪽의

| 분석 | ⓔ의 which절 이후에는 완전한 절이 올 수 없으므로 ⓔ에 문법적 오류를 해결하기 위해 관계대명사 which 앞에 전치사 to를 넣어야 한다.

50 윗글에 따르면 다음 중 옳은 것은? 내용 일치
① 보편적인 역사는 문자 언어의 발명 이후 모든 형태의 지식을 축적해 왔다. 문자 언어의 발명이후로 한정 할 수 없음
② 비록 그것들이 때때로 겹치기는 하지만, 보편적인 역사는 국가마다 다르다. 보편적 역사는 인류 전체의 업적과 실패를 다룸
③ 유럽 사람들은 로마 제국의 몰락 이후 그들만의 독특한 보편적인 역사를 구축했다. 보편적 역사를 독특한 것으로 볼 수 없음
④ 문자의 발명은 지식의 전달을 가속화했고, 이것은 서양이 지배하는 것을 돕는다. 서양이 지배하는 것을 돕는다는 내용은 없음
✓⑤ 비록 어떤 종류의 지식은 세상에 대한 힘을 잃었지만, 나중에 그 힘을 되찾는 것이 가능하다.

| 분석 | 단락 [D]의 마지막 문장에서는 새로운 지식의 대부분이 '우리가 폐기했지만 언젠가 다시 회귀할 수도 있을 주목할 만한 삶의 방식의 예시로 남아 있다.'고 했다. 따라서 보기 ⑤는 내용과 일치하는 진술이다.

[51-53] 2012 숭실대

| 정답 | 51 ③ 52 ① 53 ④

| 어휘 |
mountain range 산맥, 산악지방
depict ⓥ 그리다, 묘사하다, 기술하다
shrivel ⓥ 주름지다, 시들다, 줄어들다
primate ⓝ 영장류 (동물)
towering ⓐ 높이 솟은, 거대한
monastery ⓝ (주로 남자) 수도원
treacherous ⓐ 배반하는, 불확실한
monk ⓝ 수도자, 수도승
skeleton ⓝ 골격, 해골
have it that ~에 따르면 …이다
ceremonial ⓐ 의식의, 의례상의
fanciful ⓐ 공상에 잠긴, 공상의, 변덕스러운
revere ⓥ 숭배하다
yeti ⓝ (히말라야산맥의) 설인

전문해석

외딴 히말라야산맥에 높은 곳에 팡보체 불교 수도원이 서 있다. 폭설 동안, 그곳은 수도원의 의식용 뿔피리 소리를 듣는 여행객들에 의해서만 발견될 수 있다. 벽은 수도원으로 가는 불확실한 길을 묘사하는 네팔 전통 그림들로 줄지어 있다.

그리고 그중에는 우리가 예티라고 부르는 전설적인 유인원 같은 생명체의 그림도 있다. 이것은 수년 동안, 수도원에서 (길고 뚱뚱한 손가락과 굽은 손톱을 가진 성인 인간의 것 크기 정도의) 주름진 손도 전시되어 있었고 그것이 그들을 불운으로부터 보호한다고 믿었던 수도승들에 의해 숭배되었던 것을 알 때까지는 상상으로 보일 수 있다.

3년 전 런던에 있는 왕립 외과 대학에서 인간과 영장류의 해골들 사이를 돌아다니다가 최근에서야 이 대학의 헌터리안 박물관 금고에서 발견된 주름진 손가락을 우연히 발견했다는 사실이 없었다면, 나는 이 이야기에 대해 아무것도 알지 못했을 것이다. 이 손가락에는 "팡보체 손에서 온 예티의 손가락"이라는 표시가 붙어 있었다. 나는 이 손가락 뒤에 어떤 이야기가 있었는지 그리고 어떻게 런던에 오게 되었는지 궁금했다. "팡보체 손"의 나머지 부분은 어디에 있을까? 그리고 이 손가락이 고대 전설의 예티 손가락에 속한다고 주장하는 표시 뒤에는 어떤 진실이 숨어 있을까? 이 신화에는 예티, 즉 혐오스러운 설인이 네팔과 티베트의 히말라야 지역에 서식하는 거대한 생명체ⓐ라는 것이 이곳에서는 예티에 대한 이야기로 대대로 전해 내려오고 있다.

그곳에서 발견된 홍적세(2,500,000년 전에서 11,700년 전)의 화석 유적은 300,000년 전에 멸종된 거대한 유인원인 기간토피테쿠스라고 불리는 생명체의 해골을 보여 준다. 이 ⓐ 거대한 영장류들은 키가 약 10피트에 달했고 몸무게는 0.5톤이었다. 그들은 지금의 중국, 인도, 베트남에서 우리 인류의 조상들과 함께 살았을 가능성이 있다. 그러나 과학계는 일반적으로 이 종을 단순히 크고 멸종된 유인원으로 간주하고—예티는 전설에 불과하다.

53 ④

---

51 다음 중 Ⓐ에 들어가기에 가장 적절한 것은? 빈칸 추론

① this   ② that
✓ it   ④ them

| 분석 | 빈칸 앞 'The myth has'와 'that' 사이에 알맞은 표현을 넣어 관용표현을 완성하는 빈칸 문제이다. 'have it that'은 '~에 따르면 …이다'라는 의미로 이를 완성하기 위해 보기 ③이 들어가는 것이 알맞다.

---

52 다음 중 ⓐtowering과 의미가 가장 가까운 것은? 밑줄 추론

✓ 큰   ② 털이 많은
③ 묵직한   ④ 튼튼한

| 분석 | 밑줄 친 towering은 '우뚝 솟은, 큰'이라는 의미이다. 따라서 보기 ①과 그 의미가 가장 가깝다.

---

53 윗글에 따르면 다음 중 사실이 아닌 것은? 내용 불일치

① 궂은 날씨에 팡보체는 도달하기 어렵다.
② 예티의 손가락 중 하나가 런던에 전시되어 있다.
③ 예티족은 거의 틀림없이 인간과 먼 친척이다.
✓ 이 화석은 예티의 현재 존재를 증명하는 것으로 남아 있다.

| 분석 | 본문의 마지막 문장에서 과학계에서는 예티를 멸종된 유인원으로 간주하나 이것은 전설에 불과하다는 내용이 서술되었다. 따라서 보기 ④에서처럼 화석이 예티의 현재 존재를 증명하는 것으로 보기 어렵다.

6강 철학 / 종교

01	④	02	②	03	⑤	04	⑤	05	②	06	①	07	①	08	②	09	②	10	③
11	③	12	②	13	④	14	②	15	①	16	④	17	⑤	18	⑤	19	④	20	②
21	①	22	④	23	③	24	②	25	④	26	①	27	①	28	④	29	③	30	①
31	④	32	②	33	③	34	④	35	②	36	③	37	④	38	⑤	39	①	40	②
41	②	42	③	43	④	44	②	45	③	46	⑤	47	②	48	③	49	④	50	④
51	②	52	①																

[01-02] 2014 서강대

| 정답 | 01 ④ 02 ②

| 어휘 |
protagonist ⓝ 주역, 주인공, 주창자, 수령
crusade ⓥ 십자군에 참가하다, 개혁 운동에 참가하다
migrant ⓐ 이동하는
win out 이기다, 성공하다, 헤쳐 나가다
conversion ⓝ 개종, 변환, 전환, 전향, 환산
reproduction ⓝ 재생, 재생산, 복제, 생식
level off 평평하게 하다, 안정상태가 되다, 수평이 되다
approximate ⓐ 근사한, 대체의, 대략의
degeneration ⓝ 퇴보, 악화, 타락, 퇴화
surpass ⓥ 능가하다, ~보다 낫다

전문해석

빠르게 현대화되어 가는 사회들에서 만일 전통적인 종교가 현대화의 필요에 적응할 수 없다면, 서양의 기독교와 이슬람 종교가 확산될 가능성이 있다. 이러한 사회에서는 서양 문화의 가장 성공적인 주인공은 신고전주의 경제학자들이나, 개혁을 추진하는 민주주의자들이나 다국적 기업의 경영진들이 아니다. 그 주인공은 기독교 선교사들이며 앞으로도 계속 그럴 것이다. 또한 애덤 스미스(Adam Smith)나 토머스 제퍼슨(Thomas Jefferson)이 도시 이주민들과 중등교육을 처음으로 받은 세대들의 심리적인, 정서적인, 도덕적인, 사회적인 요구를 충족시켜 줄 수 없다. 예수 그리스도 또한 그들의 요구를 충족시키지는 못하겠지만 앞의 사람들보다는 가능성이 조금 더 높다. 하지만, 장기적으로 볼 때 무함마드가 완전히 성공할 것이다. 기독교는 주로 개종에 의해 확산되며 이슬람은 대화와 번식(출생)에 의해 확산된다. 세계 기독교인 비율은 1980년대에 30퍼센트로 정점을 찍었으며, 정체 상태에 있다가 지금은 하락하는 추세에 있으며, 아마도 2025년까지는 세계 인구의 약 25퍼센트 정도에 이르게 될 것이다. 무슬림들은 이들의 극도로 높은 인구 증가율로 인해 그 비율이 획기적으로 늘어나서 세기(20세기에서 21세기로)의 전환점쯤에는 20퍼센트에 도달할 것이며, 몇 년 후에는 기독교인의 비율을 앞질러서, 2025년쯤이 되면 아마도 세계 인구의 30퍼센트에 이르게 될 것이다.

01 빈칸에 들어갈 말로 가장 적절한 것을 고르시오. 빈칸 추론

① 현대화
② 타락
③ 교육
✓④ 번식

| 분석 | 빈칸 뒤를 보면 이슬람교도들은 극도로 높은 인구 증가율로 인해 이슬람교의 비중이 증가할 것이라고 했으므로 이슬람교가 확산되는 가장 큰 요소는 인구 증가라고 할 수 있다. 따라서 인구 증가를 나타내는 ④ '번식'이 정답으로 가장 적절하다.

02 윗글에 따르면 다음 중 추론할 수 없는 것은? 내용 추론

① 기독교와 이슬람교는 사회를 빠르게 현대화하는 데 중요한 역할을 할 것 같다.
✓ ② 도시 이주자들의 사회적 요구는 아마도 다국적 기업 임원들에 의해 충족될 것이다.
③ 세계에서 기독교인의 비율은 1980년대가 2000년대보다 더 높았다.
④ 2025년까지, 세계의 이슬람교도의 수는 기독교인의 수를 넘어설 것이다.

| 분석 | 본문의 초반부에 '이러한 사회들에서는 서양 문화의 가장 성공적인 주역은 신고전주의 경제학자들이나, 개혁을 추진하는 민주주의자들이나 다국적 기업의 경영자들이 아니다.'라고 언급하였는데, 보기 ②의 도시 이주자들을 충족시켜 줄 인물들이 다국적 기업 임원들이라는 것은 서로 상반된 진술이라고 할 수 있다. 따라서 ②는 지문을 통해 추론할 수 없다.

[03-04] 2019 광운대

| 정답 | 03 ⑤ 04 ⑤

| 어휘 |
observe ⓥ (법률·규칙 등을) 지키다, 준수하다; (의식 등을) 거행하다
fasting ⓝ 단식, 절식
pillar ⓝ 기둥; 받침, 지주(支柱)
biographical ⓐ 전기의, 전기체의
hadith ⓝ 하디스(무함마드의 언행록)
breastfeeding ⓝ 모유수유
phenomenon ⓝ 현상
polar night 극야(極夜)
be instructed to do ~하도록 지시받다
cursing ⓝ 저주
revelation ⓝ (신의) 계시
last ⓥ 지속하다
account ⓝ 설명, 이야기
scorching heat 찌는 듯한 무더위, 폭염
diabetic ⓐ 당뇨병의, 당뇨병 환자의
midnight sun (극지에서 한여름에 볼 수 있는) 백야(白夜)
timetable ⓝ 시간표, 일정표
negate ⓥ 무효로 하다, 부정[부인]하다
self-defense ⓝ 자기방어, 정당방위
Muslim ⓝ 이슬람교도
Quran ⓝ 코란, 이슬람교의 경전
crescent moon 초승달
compile ⓥ 편집하다; 편찬하다
pregnant ⓐ 임신한
menstruate ⓥ 생리하다
engage in ~에 관여[참여]하다
insulting ⓝ 모욕적인 언동

전문해석

라마단은 이슬람력의 9월이며, 무함마드가 (알라신으로부터) 코란을 처음으로 계시받은 것을 Ⓐ 기념하기 위해 단식하는 달로, 전 세계 이슬람교도들이 이슬람 신앙에 따라 준수하고 있다. 이 연례 의식은 '이슬람의 다섯 기둥' 가운데 하나로 여겨진다. 하디스(무함마드의 언행록)로 편찬된 수많은 전기적(傳記的) 이야기들을 따라, 라마단이 있는 달은 육안으로 본 초승달에 근거해 29일 내지 30일 동안 지속된다. 라마단이라는 단어는 찌는 듯한 무더위나 메마른 상태를 의미한다. (라마단 기간 동안의) 단식은 성인 이슬람교도들에게 의무사항인데, 질병을 앓고 있거나, 여행 중이거나, 연세가 많거나, 임신, 모유수유, 당뇨병, 만성질병, 생리 중인 사람들은 예외로 인정된다. 백야(白夜)나 극야(極夜) 같은 자연 현상이 나타나는 지역에 사는 이슬람교도들은 메카(Mecca)의 시간을 따라야 하지만, 보다 일반적으로 알려진 지침은 해당지역(백야나 극야가 나타나는 지역)에 사는 이슬람교도들은 자신이 거주하는 곳과 가장 가까이 있는, 낮과 밤이 구분되는 국가의 시간을 따를 것을 권고한다. 새벽부터 일몰까지 단식하는 동안, 이슬람교도들은 음식 및 음료 섭취, 흡연, 그리고 성관계를 피해야 한다. 이슬람교도들은 모욕적인 말, 저주, 거짓말 등 옳지 않은 말과 싸움(정당방위는 예외)과 같이 단식에 대한 보상을 물거품으로 만들어 버릴 수 있는 나쁜 행동을 또한 Ⓑ 삼가야 한다.

03 윗글의 빈칸 Ⓐ, Ⓑ에 들어갈 말로 가장 적절한 것은? 빈칸 추론

① 지키다 – 숙고하다
② 간과하다 – 그만두다
③ 기념하다 – 상징하다
④ 무시하다 – 해결하다
✓ ⑤ 기념하다 – 삼가다

| 분석 | 라마단은 이슬람교도들이 단식하는 달로 지켜진다고 했으므로, 이렇게 지켜지는 것은 이슬람교의 창시자인 무함마드가 신으로부터 코란을 계시받은 것을 '기념하기' 위해서일 것이다. 따라서 빈칸 Ⓐ에는 celebrate나 commemorate가 적절하다. 빈칸 Ⓑ는 앞 문장에서 라마단 단식 기간 동안에 피해야 할 것을 진술하고 있으므로 같은 맥락의 의미를 만들어야 한다. 따라서 leave off나 refrain from이 가능하다.

04 윗글의 내용과 일치하지 않는 것은? 내용 일치

① 라마단과 초승달이 육안으로 보이는 것은 관련이 있다.
② 라마단 기간 동안 금식은 특정 상황에서는 선택 가능하다.
③ 메카의 시간은 다른 국가에 사는 이슬람교도들에 의해 준수된다.
④ 라마단 기간 동안 저주와 싸움은 금지되지만, 일부의 경우에는 허용된다.
✓⑤ 이슬람교도들은 라마단 기간 동안 일몰 이후 음식이나 음료 섭취를 해서는 안 된다.

| 분석 | 본문의 마지막 부분에서 단식하는 시간은 새벽부터 일몰까지라고 언급하였으므로 ⑤가 본문과 일치하지 않는다.

| 배경지식 | 라마단(Ramadan): 이슬람력 9월에 지켜지는 이슬람의 종교의식이다. 어원은 '강렬한 더위' 또는 '타오르는 메마름'을 의미하는 아라비아어에서 비롯되었다.

[05-06] 2011 고려대

| 정답 | 05 ② 06 ①

| 어휘 |
rationalism ⓝ 합리주의, 이성론　　empiricism ⓝ 경험주의　　epistemology ⓝ 인식론
warranted ⓐ 확실한, 보장된　　correspond to ~에 상응하다, 일치하다　　outstrip ⓥ ~보다 뛰어나다, 앞지르다
complementary ⓐ 보충하는, 보족(補足)의　　　　　　　　　　　　insofar as ~하는[인] 한에 있어서
surpass ⓥ ~보다 낫다, 능가하다　　garner ⓥ 모으다(collect), 축적하다
ascertain ⓥ 확인하다, 조사(調査)하다, 알아내다　　　　　　　categorization ⓝ 분류, 범주화

전문해석

지식의 특성, 근원들과 한계를 연구하는 데 헌신하는 철학 분야인 인식론에는 합리주의와 경험주의 사이의 논쟁이 발생한다. 우리는 운 좋게 추정해 봄으로써 진정한 믿음을 형성할 수 있다. 확실한 믿음을 얻는 방법은 모호하다. 더욱이, 세상을 알기 위해, 우리는 세상에 대해 생각을 해야 하며, 그리고 사상에서 우리가 활용하는 개념을 얻는 방법이나 우리의 개념을 이용해서 세상을 구분하는 방식이 설령 있다 하더라도 실제로 존재하는 세상의 구분과 일치하는지에 대해 어떤 확신을 가지고 있는지는 불확실하다.
합리주의자들은 우리의 개념과 지식이 감각적 경험과 별개로 얻어질 수 있는 중요한 방법이 있음을 주장한다. 경험주의자들은 감각적 경험이 모든 개념과 지식의 궁극적인 원천임을 주장한다. 합리주의자들은 우리의 지식의 내용물이 감각 경험이 제공할 수 있는 정보를 능가하는 경우가 있음을 주장한다. 경험주의자들은 보완적인 사고방식이라는 것을 제시한다. 그들(경험주의자들)은 우선 우리가 경험을 통한 지식을 가지고 있는 한에 있어서는, 경험이 합리주의자들이 말하는 지식을 어떻게 제공해 주는지에 대한 이야기를 밝히고 있다.

05 밑줄 친 부분과 의미상 가장 가까운 것을 고르시오. 밑줄 의미 파악

① 경험은 반드시 지식을 왜곡하는 정보를 생산하기 마련이다.
☑ ② 우리는 경험으로부터 얻은 데이터를 능가하는 지식을 얻을 수 있다.
③ 경험만으로도 지식을 양산하기에 충분하다.
④ 원시 경험으로부터 지식을 얻는 것은 불가능해진다.

| 분석 | outstrip은 '뛰어넘다, 능가하다'의 의미이고 따라서 밑줄 친 부분의 내용은 우리의 지식은 감각 경험이 만들어 내는 정보를 뛰어넘는다는 것을 말하고 있다. 따라서 ②가 정답이다.

06 윗글에 따르면, 다음 중 인식론에서 묻는 것 질문이 아닌 것은? 세부 내용 파악

☑ ① 어떤 종류의 지식이 가치가 있는가?
② 우리가 어떻게 어떤 믿음의 진실을 확인할 수 있는가?
③ 세계에 대한 우리의 분류가 얼마나 타당한가?
④ 어디에서 우리의 개념적 도구들이 오는가?

| 분석 | 인식론을 통해서 우리가 그 답을 얻을 수 있는 질문이 아닌 것을 고르는 문제이다. 지문에 따르면 인식론을 통하여 우리가 개별적 지식의 가치를 알 수 있는지는 언급이 없다. 따라서 정답은 ①이다.

[07-08] 2016 가톨릭대

| 정답 | 07 ① 08 ②

| 어휘 | being ⓝ 존재   becoming ⓝ 생성   assume ⓥ 가정하다
manifest ⓐ 명백한   building block ⓝ 구성요소
intrinsically ⓐⓓ 천성적으로, 자연스럽게, 본질적으로   void ⓝ 공간; 허공; 무(無)
dualism ⓝ 이원론

전문해석

B.C. 5세기경, 그리스의 철학자들은 파르메니데스(Parmenides)의 견해와 헤라클레이토스(Heraclitus)의 견해 사이에 날카롭게 존재하는 철학적 견해차를 극복하기 위해 노력했다. 파르메니데스의 불변하는 존재라는 사상과 헤라클레이토스의 영원한 생성이라는 사상을 화해시키기 위해서, 그리스 철학자들은 이 세계에는 어떤 불변하는 물질이 분명히 존재하며, 그 물질이 뒤섞이고 분리되는 가운데 이 세계의 변화가 야기된다고 가정했다. 이러한 가정을 통해서 눈에 보이지 않는 최소 물질단위인 원자라는 개념이 탄생했고, 이 원자라는 개념은 데모크리토스(Democritus)의 철학에서 가장 명확하게 표현되었다. 그리스의 원자론자들은 정신과 물질 사이에 명확한 선을 그렸고, 물질은 몇 가지의 기본적인 구성요소로 이루어져 있다고 상상했다. 이런 구성요소들은 텅 빈 공간에서 이동하는 순수하게 수동적이고 본질적으로는 죽은 물질이었다. 이 구성요소들이 움직이게 되는 원리는 설명되지 않았다. 하지만 그 원인은 종종 외부 힘과 연결되었고, 이 외부 힘들은 물질과는 근본적으로 다른 정신에서 기원하는 것으로 가정되었다. 그 뒤를 이은 세기들 동안, 이 이미지는 서양 사상의 본질적인 요소가 되었는데, 그것이 곧 정신과 물질, 그리고 육체와 영혼이라는 이원론이다.

07 윗글은 주로 무엇과 관련된 글인가? 주제

☑ ① 서양 이원론의 기원
② 서양사상의 주요 문제점 언급 안 함
③ 정신과 물질 사이의 관계 너무 포괄적
④ 그리스 철학자들의 신비로운 세상 언급 안 함

| 분석 | 이 글은 서양의 이원론이 정립되게 된 배경을 구체적으로 기술하고 있다. 따라서 이원론의 기원이 이 글의 주요 내용으로 적절하다.

> **08** 윗글에 따르면 다음 중 사실이 <u>아닌</u> 것은? 내용 일치
>
> ① 파르메니데스와 헤라클레이토스는 그리스 사상의 대립되는 두 가지의 극이었다.
> ✓ 파르메니데스와 헤라클레이토스는 한때 그들의 생각을 조화시키기 위해 함께 일했다.
> ③ 그리스 원자론자들은 정신과 물질의 두 다른 세계를 믿었다.
> ④ 서양사상의 전통은 주로 이원론적 세계관에 담겨 있다.

| 분석 | 파르메니데스와 헤라클레이토스가 그들의 사상을 화해시키기 위해 함께 일을 했다는 진술은 지문에서 언급하지 않은 내용이므로 지문을 통해 알 수 없다.

| 배경 지식 | 이원론(Dualism): 한 체계 안에 본질적인 두 상태 혹은 두 부분이 있고, 이 요소들은 서로 독립적이기에 다른 것으로 환원되지 않는다고 주장하는 철학적 입장을 말한다.

[09-10] 2011 서강대

| 정답 | 09 ② 10 ③

| 어휘 |
messenger ⓝ 예고, 전조, 전령
humanity ⓝ 인류
firmament ⓝ 하늘, 창공
rugged ⓐ 울퉁불퉁한
demotion ⓝ 좌천, 격하, 강등
laity ⓝ (성직자가 아닌) 평신도, 평민 계층
Aristotelian ⓐ (철학자) 아리스토텔레스의, 아리스토텔레스학파의
accretion ⓝ 증가, 융합

gravely ⓐⓓ 중대하게, 심하게
blindfold ⓐ 눈이 가려진, 눈가리개를 한
be crowded with ~로 가득 차 있다
ludicrous ⓐ 우스꽝스러운
egotism ⓝ 이기주의, 자기중심주의
rule ⓥ 통치하다
rudiment ⓝ 기본, 기초

downgrade ⓥ 격하시키다, 강등시키다
doctrine ⓝ 교의, 신조, 학설, 주의
naked eye 육안
unique ⓐ 고유한, 독특한
witty ⓐ 재치 넘치는, 기지 넘치는

diversion ⓝ 전환, 기분전환

전문해석

갈릴레오가 *Sidereus Nuncius*, 즉 별에 대한 전언, 혹은 천문학적 메시지를 출간한 지 400년이 되었다. 이 책은 우주 내에서의 인간의 위치를 심하게 격하시키는 동시에 인류에게 맹목적 종교 교리에 가려져 있었던 우주의 신비를 드러내 주었다. 그 작은 책에서 갈릴레오는 하늘에는 육안으로는 보이지 않는 별들이 무수하다는 것, 달의 표면이 매끄럽고 우스꽝스러울 정도로 완전한 성직자들의 천체가 아니라 울퉁불퉁하다는 것, 그리고 지구가 위성(달)을 가진 유일한 행성이 아니므로 우주 내에서 차지했던 중심적 위치에서 <u>강등</u>될 대상이라는 점을 보여 주었다. 그 폭발적인 책은 <mark>갈릴레오가 라틴어로 쓴 유일한 책이었다</mark>. 다른 모든 책은 토스카나어 (이탈리아 표준어)로 되어 있었다. *Galileo: Watcher of the Skies*라는 재치 넘치는 책에서 데이비드 우튼(David Wootton)은 갈릴레오가(혹은 갈릴레오 자신이 말하기로 자신이) 피렌체 동포들이 자신에 대해 생각하는 바에 주로 관심이 있었다고 주장한다. 그리고 유럽의 다른 곳에서 라틴어로 읽히고 있는지 여부와 상관없이 자신의 작품이 금지되었을 때, 갈릴레오는 그 작품들이 이탈리아에서 잊힐까 두려워했다. 토스카나어는 이탈리아 북부 전역에서 교양 있는 평민 계급이 읽을 수 있는 언어였다. <mark>반면 라틴어는 아리스토텔레스의 사상이 지배하던 대학의 언어였다.</mark>
10 ③

09
다음 중 윗글의 밑줄 친 단어를 가장 잘 대체할 수 있는 것은 무엇인가? 동의어

① 전환　　　　　　　　　　　☑ 좌천
③ 증대　　　　　　　　　　　④ 기본

| 분석 | demotion은 '좌천, 강등, 격하'의 의미이므로 relegation(좌천, 격하)이 동의어로 적절하다.

10
윗글에서 추론할 수 <u>없는</u> 것은? 내용 추론

① Sidereus Nuncius가 우주에서의 인간의 우월함에 대한 생각이 틀렸음을 보여 주었다.
② 갈릴레오는 동시대의 피렌체인들에게 무시당하는 것을 두려워했다.
☑ Sidereus Nuncius의 출판은 아리스토텔레스의 우주 개념이 다시 활기를 띠게 했다.
④ 라틴어는 갈릴레오 시대의 학문적 연구와 글쓰기의 주요 매체였다.

| 분석 | 지문에서 갈릴레오의 저서 Sidereus Nuncius는 갈릴레오가 라틴어로 쓴 유일한 책이라고 언급했는데 그 당시 라틴어는 아리스토텔레스 사상이 지배하던 대학의 언어라고 했다. 하지만 그렇다 해서 갈릴레오가 아리스토텔레스의 책이 아리스토텔레스의 사상과 관련되어 있다고 추론하는 것은 불가능하므로 ③은 지문을 통해 알 수 없는 내용이다. 한편 ④의 '라틴어는 갈릴레오 시대의 학문적 연구와 글쓰기의 주요 매체였다.'는 지문 맨 마지막에서 토스카나어는 평민 계급의 언어였고 라틴어는 대학의 언어라고 하였으므로 지문과 일치한다.

[11-12] 2016 국민대

| 정답 | 11 ③　12 ②

| 어휘 | **filial piety** 효도　　　　　　　**Confucianism** ⓝ 유교　　　　　　**delve** ⓥ 뒤지다, 탐구하다, 조사하다
　　　　hierarchy ⓝ 위계, 계층, 계급, 지배층　**protocol** ⓝ 외교 원본, 문서의 원본　**indicator** ⓥ 지표, 척도
　　　　register ⓝ 기록, 등록부

전문해석

유교가 종교인가라는 질문을 받았을 때 "그렇다"라고 대답하는 한국인들은 그다지 많지 않다. 그러나 만일 질문을 약간 바꾸어서, 유교의 가장 핵심적인 부분인 효도를 행할 용의가 있느냐고 묻는다면 대부분의 한국인들은 주저하지 않고 "그렇다"라고 답할 것이다. 한국인들에게 유교는 그들의 일상적인 활동에서 분리된 특정한 가르침이라기보다는 그들의 삶 그 자체다. 이것은 심지어 젊은 세대의 경우에도 통용되는 사실이다. 그들은 유교를 강하게 싫어하고 유교가 전근대적이라고 믿는다. 그들의 머릿속에서 유교는 현대를 살아가는 세대들에게 맞는 적합성을 ⓐ 품고 있지 않은 과거 왕조시대의 이데올로기에 지나지 않는다. 그러나 그들의 삶을 조금 더 깊이 들여다보면, 우리는 그들이 여전히 유교의 가치체계 속에 깊이 빠져 살고 있다는 것을 발견할 수 있게 된다. 예를 들어, 한국에서는 거의 모든 사람들이 나이를 기준으로 위계질서를 유지하는 관례를 따른다. 어떤 사람을 처음 만날 때, 누가 서열이 더 높고 낮은지를 결정하기 위해 나이를 비교한다. 학교에서는 나이를 비교할 필요가 없는데, 그 이유는 학년이 이미 나이의 ⓑ 지표이기 때문이다. 이와 같이 저학년 학생들은 고학년 학생들을 형 혹은 언니 같은 가족 용어로 부르고, 그들에게 말을 건넬 때 존경심이 담긴 명칭을 사용한다.

11
빈칸 ⓐ와 ⓑ에 가장 알맞은 것은 무엇인가? 빈칸 추론

① 보여 주다 – 기부자　　　　　② 숨기다 – 지휘자
☑ 품다 – 지표　　　　　　　　　④ 포함하다 – 중재자

| 분석 | 빈칸 Ⓐ는 과거 왕조시대의 이데올로기는 현대 세대들과는 맞지 않을 것이므로 현대 세대와 관련성을 보여 주지 못하거나 관련성을 품지 못한다는 것이 적절하다. 따라서 show와 bear가 가능하다. 빈칸 Ⓑ는 학교에서의 학년은 나이의 지표라고 할 수 있으므로 indicator만이 적합하다.

---

12 윗글의 제목으로 가장 적절한 것은? 제목

① 사회적 관계에서 연령의 중요성 너무 지엽적
✓ ② 한국적 가치체계 속의 뿌리 깊은 유교
③ 한국 사회에 가하는 유교의 지속적인 영향력의 감소 지문 내용과 불일치
④ 한국에서 젊은 세대의 유교에 대한 반감 언급 안 함

| 분석 | 이 글은 한국 사회를 지배하고 있는 유교에 관한 내용이라 할 수 있다. 따라서 제목으로 가장 적합한 것은 ②라고 할 수 있다.

[13-15] 2015 경기대

| 정답 | 13 ④ 14 ② 15 ①

| 어휘 |
Judaism ⓝ 유대교 animism ⓝ 정령신앙
Russian Orthodox Church 러시아 정교회 atheism ⓝ 무신론
agnosticism ⓝ 불가지론 Orthodoxy ⓝ 동방 정교회 tenacity ⓝ 끈기, 집요함
staying power 지구력 patriarch ⓝ 가장, 족장, 정교의 총대주교 pilgrimage ⓝ 순례여행
governance ⓝ 통치, 지배 exalt ⓥ 높이다, 승진시키다, 칭찬[찬양]하다 deify ⓥ 신격화하다
ecclesiastical ⓐ 교회의 secular ⓐ 세속적인

전문해석

러시아에서는 기독교, 유대교, 이슬람교, 정령신앙 등을 포괄하는 다양한 종교들이 공존하고 있다. 가장 흔한 종교는 기독교이고 기독교들 가운데 대다수는 러시아 정교회 신도들이다. 러시아 정교회는 1,000년 이상 존재해 왔고 심지어는 소비에트 연방 통치 시절의 공식적인 무신론과 그 당시보다 두드러졌던 불가지론 속에서도 살아남았다.
공산주의 시절 동안 러시아 정교회를 믿는 사람들은 경력과 교육 기회를 희생했다. 러시아 정교회의 끈질긴 강인함은 종교를 가지고 있지 않은 러시아인들이 스스로를 러시아 정교회 신자라고 기꺼이 부르는 이유를 설명해 줄지도 모른다. 이와 같은 지속적인 힘이 모스크바의 알렉세이 2세가 운영하는 러시아 정교회를 이끈다. 알렉세이 미하일로비치 리디거(Aleksey Mikhailovich Ridiger)라는 이름으로 태어난 미래의 러시아 정교회 총대주교는 매우 신앙심이 깊은 집안 출신이다. 소년이었을 때 알렉세이는 종종 부모의 손에 이끌려 매년 열리는 순례여행에 참여하곤 했는데, 확실히 그는 이 순례여행을 통해서 자신이 선택하게 될 종교적인 삶의 길에 대해서 깊이 숙고하기 시작했다. 총대주교로서 알렉세이는 그의 통치 방식으로 찬양받고 있다. 그러나 그가 신격화된 것은 아니다. 그는 교회 언론과 세속 언론을 통해 교회사와 평화 구축에 관한 글을 발표하였고 이를 통해 러시아와 해외에서 러시아 정교회의 이미지를 신장시켜 왔다.

---

13 다음 중 윗글의 필수 정보를 가장 잘 표현한 것은? 내용 파악

① 러시아 정교회는 소련의 통제하에 금지되었다.
② 신을 믿는 러시아인은 거의 없다.
③ 알렉세이 2세는 교회의 신도를 확대했다.
✓ ④ 러시아 정교회는 러시아 내에서 강력한 멤버십의 오랜 역사를 가지고 있다.

| 분석 | 이 글은 러시아에서 다양한 종교들 중에서 가장 많은 종교는 기독교이고, 그중에서 대다수는 러시아 정교회 신도들이며, 그것

이 사회에 깊이 뿌리내리고 있다는 것을 주로 다루고 있다. 따라서 ④가 지문의 필수 정보라고 할 수 있다.

14 윗글에 따르면 모스크바의 알렉세이 2세는 _____이다. _{내용 파악}
① 역사학자　　　　　　　　　　　② 교회의 고위 관리 ✓
③ 세속적인 지도자　　　　　　　　④ 무신론자

| 분석 | 러시아 정교회를 통치하고 있다는 진술로부터 알렉세이 2세가 러시아 정교회의 고위성직자임을 추론할 수 있다.

15 다음 중 빈칸에 들어갈 말로 가장 알맞은 것은? _{빈칸 추론}
① 신앙심이 깊은 ✓　　　　　　　② 부유한
③ 비뚤어진　　　　　　　　　　　④ 섬뜩한

| 분석 | 빈칸 뒤에서 '알렉세이는 종종 부모의 손에 이끌려 매년 열리는 순례여행에 참여하곤 했는데, 확실히 그는 이 순례여행을 통해서 자신이 선택하게 될 종교적인 삶의 길에 대해서 깊이 숙고하기 시작했다.'고 언급했으므로 알렉세이의 집안은 신앙심이 깊은 집안일 것이다.

| 배경 지식 | 기독교(Christianity): 예수 그리스도를 구주로 고백하는 신앙 공동체를 크게 3가지로 구분하며 정교회(Orthodoxy)와 가톨릭교회(Catholic), 개신교회(Protestantism)로 나눌 수 있다. 한국은 기독교에서 개신교와 가톨릭이 주를 이루는 반면 러시아는 기독교 중 정교회가 지배하는 국가이다.

[16-18] 2014 성균관대

| 정답 | 16 ④　17 ⑤　18 ⑤

| 어휘 |
cardinal ⓝ 추기경
showdown ⓝ 발표, 공개, 최종단계, 대결
compromise ⓥ 타협하다, 화해하다
predecessor ⓝ 전임자, 선배
testimony ⓝ 증언, 증거, 십계
upbraid ⓥ 신랄하게 비판하다, 비난하다
have no truck with ~와 거래[관계]하지 않다
truck ⓝ 잡품, 잡화
abortion ⓝ 유산, 낙태
clash ⓥ 충돌하다, 부딪치다

conclave ⓝ 비밀회의, 가톨릭교회에서 교황을 선출하는 추기경단의 선거회
faction ⓝ 당파, 파벌
transitional ⓐ 변화하는
evangelization ⓝ 복음 선교, 복음 전도
controversial ⓐ 논쟁의
liberal ⓐ 자유주의의, 진보적인

liberation theology 해방신학
euthanasia ⓝ 안락사
dogmatic ⓐ 독단주의의, 교리의

the Curia 쿠리아, 로마 교황청
vigorous ⓐ 정력 왕성한, 원기 왕성한
recall ⓥ 생각해 내다, 상기하다, 상기시키다
hallmark ⓝ 특징, 특질, 증명

stem ⓥ (흐름을) 막다[저지하다]
staunchly ⓐⓓ 철두철미하게, 완고하게
adoption ⓝ 채택, 입양
assassination ⓝ 암살, 손상

전문해석

호르헤 마리오 베르고글리오(Jorge Mario Bergoglio) 추기경이 세계 12억 가톨릭 세례교인의 40%에 이르는 교인이 있는 대륙인 라틴 아메리카 출신의 첫 교황이 되었다. 교황을 선출하는 115명의 회의인 콘클라베는 바티칸 내부인물들에 의해 주도된 당파와, 쿠리아라 부르는 로마 교황청에 대한 철저한 개혁을 요구하는 주로 영어와 독일어를 쓰는 추기경들의 그룹, 양자 사이에 대결을 할 준비가 되어 있는 것으로 보였었다. 콘클라베의 구성원들은 결국 그들이 이미 잘 알고 있는 타협적 후보를 선택함으로써 이 문제를 해결하였다. 76세인 프란시스 교황은 또 다른 과도기적 지도자로 간주될 수 있을 만큼 충분히 나이가 들었으나, 세계에서 가장 큰 기독교회에 변하지 않는 흔적을 남길 만큼 충분히 원기 왕성하다. 전임 교황 베네딕트 16세와 마찬가지로 신임 교황은 복음 전파를 가장 중요하게 생각하며, 그가 선택한 이름, 즉 영감을 주는 Assisi 성 프란시스와 첫 예수회 선교사인 성 프란시스 사비에

르를 연상시키는, 그의 이름이 그것을 보여 준다. 그는 작년 아르헨티나의 사제들에게 "나가서 당신들의 간증을 다른 사람들에게 전하라"고 말하였다. 그가 아르헨티나에서 일하던 시기의, 좀 논쟁거리가 되기도 하지만, 더 긍정적인 그의 특징은 가난한 자들의 이익에 관한 강조였다. 2009년 그는 당시 아르헨티나 대통령이었던 네스토르 키르치네르(Nestor Kirchner)의 정부를 가난의 확산을 막지 못했다는 이유에서 신랄하게 비판하면서, 인권은 테러에 의해서만이 아니라 <u>불공정한 경제 구조</u>에 의해서도 유린이 되었다고 주장했다. 그럼에도 불구하고 프란시스 교황은 진보주의자는 아니다. 그는, 비록 대다수의 지지자들은 예수회 회원들이기는 했지만 교회의 업무를 급진적인 사회개혁과 연결 짓는 라틴 아메리카의 인기 있는 운동인, 해방신학 얘기를 늘어놓지 않는다. <u>프란시스 교황은 전혀 아니다</u>. 그는 낙태, 안락사, 동성애 부부에 의한 입양 등에 대해 교회의 가르침을 철저하게 방어해 왔다. 그는 동성결혼을 승인한 일을 "신의 계획을 파괴하려는 시도"라고 부르면서 아르헨티나의 크리스티나 페르난데스(Cristina Fernandez) 대통령과 충돌하였다.

16 다음 중 빈칸에 들어갈 말로 가장 적절한 것은? 빈칸 추론

① 납치와 고문
② 독단적인 종교의 가르침
③ 정치적 암살
✓ ④ 불공정한 경제 구조
⑤ 종교적 믿음의 결여

| 분석 | 빈칸 앞 문장에서 가난의 확산을 막지 못했다고 했으며, 그 앞 문장에서 그의 긍정적인 특징은 가난한 사람들의 이익에 관한 강조였다고 했으므로 빈칸에는 가난과 관련된 단어가 들어가야 적절하다. 따라서 정답은 ④이다.

17 밑줄 친 표현 "Not Francis"는 Francis가 _____ 을 의미한다. 밑줄 의미 파악

① 그 당시에는 인기가 없었다
② 예수회의 지지자가 아니었다
③ 정치에 관여하지 않았다
④ 사회적 문제를 무시하고 싶지 않았다
✓ ⑤ 해방신학과 연관되기를 거부했다

| 분석 | 앞 문장을 받아서 다시 재진술한 강조라고 볼 수 있는데, 앞 문장이 He had no truck with liberation theology(그는 해방신학과 관계를 맺지 않았다.)를 그대로 받아서 Francis는 전혀 그러지 않았다는 의미이다.

18 윗글에 따르면 다음 중 사실인 것은? 내용 일치

① 프란치스코는 대중에게 완전히 알려지지 않았기 때문에 새로운 교황으로 선출되었다.
② 프란시스는 임시 지도자로서의 한계를 깨달았다.
③ 프란시스는 그의 이름이 전임자들과 구별될 수 있기 때문에 그의 이름을 선택했다.
④ 교황은 교회의 행정 기관인 큐리아에서 선출된다.
✓ ⑤ 교황의 스타일과 기원은 새롭지만 그의 생각은 보수적이다.

| 분석 | 지문의 마지막에서 '프란시스 교황은 진보주의자는 아니다. 그는, 비록 대다수의 지지자들은 예수회 회원들이기는 했지만 교회의 업무를 급진적인 사회개혁과 연결 짓는 라틴 아메리카의 인기 있는 운동인, 해방신학 얘기를 늘어놓지 않는다.'라고 언급했으므로 그는 보수적이라는 것을 알 수 있다. 그가 선출될 때 그는 잘 알려진 인물이었으며, 그는 전임 교황과 동일한 기조(복음 강조)를 갖고 있으며, 그가 선출된 곳은 교황청이 아니라 콘클라베이다.

[19-20] 2014 한양대

| 정답 | 19 ④ 20 ②

| 어휘 | pros and cons 찬반
posit ⓥ 놓다, 앉히다
utilitarian ⓐ 공리적인, 실리적인, 실용적인, 실용성을 중히 여기는
irrelevant ⓐ 부적절한, 관련 없는
misery ⓝ 불행, 고통

전문해석

만일 당신이 결정을 내리기 위해서 장단점의 목록을 만들어 본 적이 있다면 당신은 도덕적 추론에서 공리주의적 방법을 사용한 것이다. 주요한 윤리 이론 중 하나인 공리주의는 어떤 행위를 도덕적으로 옳고 그른 것으로 결정하는 데에 핵심은 그 행위의 결과라고 주장한다. 우리의 의도가 좋았는지 나빴는지는 무관하다. 중요한 것은 우리의 행위의 결과가 좋으냐, 나쁘냐이다. 공리주의자들에게는 행복이 인간의 최상의 목표이며 가장 큰 도덕적 선이다. 따라서 어떤 행위 때문에 가장 큰 불행이 있으면 그 행위는 도덕적으로 그릇된 것이다. 그 반대로 만일 한 행동 때문에 커다란 행복이 있다면 그 행위는 도덕적으로 옳다고 할 수 있다. 공리주의자들은 우리가 어떤 행위를 하기 전에 그 행위의 잠재적인 결과를 조심스럽게 계산해야 한다고 믿고 있다. 이 행위가 우리 또는 다른 사람을 행복하게 만들 것인가? 이 행위가 우리 또는 다른 사람을 불행하게 할 것인가? 공리주의자들에 따르면, 우리는 가장 많은 사람에게 가장 많은 선(행복)을 만들어 주는 일을 선택해야 한다. 그러나 이것은 결정하기가 어려울 수 있다. 왜냐하면, 때로는 한 행위가 단기적으로는 행복을 가져오지만 장기적으로는 불행을 가져올 수도 있기 때문이다. 공리주의의 또 다른 문제점은 공리주의에 따르면 한 사람을 목표의 수단으로 사용하고 한 사람, 또는 소수의 행복을 다수의 행복을 위해 희생하는 것이 용인될 뿐 아니라 때로는 필요하다고 생각한다는 것이다.

19 윗글의 공리주의 정의에 따르면, 배고픈 아이들을 먹이기 위해 빵을 훔친 행동은 아마도 _____. 내용 파악

① 절도는 불법이기 때문에 도덕적으로 틀리다
② 좋은 의도를 가졌기 때문에 도덕적으로 옳다
③ 그것은 다른 사람의 권리를 위반했기 때문에 도덕적으로 틀리다
✔ ④ 그것은 긍정적인 결과를 가졌기 때문에 도덕적으로 옳다

| 분석 | 공리주의는 의도와 과정보다는 결과에 초점을 두기 때문에 배고픈 아이를 위해 빵을 훔치는 일은, 결과가 긍정적이기 때문에 도덕적으로 올바른 행동일 것이다.

20 윗글의 내용과 가장 어울리는 견해는? 내용 일치

① 큰 선한 행동이 종종 어떤 큰 대가를 가져온다.
✔ ② 도덕적 의사결정을 위해 공리주의를 사용하는 것이 항상 쉬운 것은 아니다.
③ 장기적인 결과가 단기적인 결과보다 도덕적으로 더 중요하다.
④ 장단점의 목록은 중요한 의사결정을 내리는 가장 효율적인 기술이다.

| 분석 | 지문의 마지막 부분에서 'This can be difficult to determine(이것은 결정하기 어려울 수 있다)'라고 언급했다. 따라서 지문과 일치하는 것은 ②이다.

| 배경지식 | 공리주의(Utilitarianism): 19세기 이래 영국을 중심으로 발달한 윤리적 사상이다. 인간 행위의 윤리적 기초를 개인의 이익과 쾌락의 추구에 두고, 무엇이 이익인가를 결정하는 것은 개인의 행복이라고 하며, '도덕은 최대 다수의 최대 행복을 목적으로 한다.'고 주장한다. 이를 최대 행복의 원리(Greatest Happiness Principle)라고 부른다.

[21-24] 2014 홍익대

| 정답 | 21 ① 22 ④ 23 ③ 24 ②

| 어휘 |
Philosophy ⓝ 철학
conviction ⓝ 신념, 확신
mineralogist ⓝ 광물학자
candid ⓐ 정직한, 솔직한, 공평한
cease ⓥ 그만두다, 멈추다
apparent ⓐ 뚜렷한, 명백한
insincere ⓐ 불성실한

primarily ⓐⓓ 최초로, 처음에는
prejudices ⓝ 편견, 침해
ascertain ⓥ 확인하다, 조사하다
confess ⓥ 고백하다, 인정하다
astronomy ⓝ 천문학
residue ⓝ 나머지, 찌꺼기
discontented ⓐ 불만족스러운

result from ~이 원인이다
definite ⓐ 뚜렷한, 명확한
as long as ~하는 한은
account for ~을 설명하다, ~을 차지하다
uncertainty ⓝ 불확실성
investigation ⓝ 조사, 연구
forthright ⓐⓓ 솔직한, 똑바른, 솔직하게

전문해석

다른 모든 학문과 마찬가지로 철학은 일차적으로 지식을 목표로 한다. 그것이 목표하는 지식은 여러 과학의 덩어리에 통일성과 체계를 주는 그러한 종류의 지식이며, 우리의 신념과 편견과 믿음의 근거의 비판적 고찰로부터 만들어지는 종류의 지식이다. 그러나 철학이 갖고 있는 질문들에 대해 확실한 답을 제공하려는 의도에 있어서 엄청나게 큰 성공을 거두었다고 주장하기는 어렵다. 만일 당신이 수학자나 광물학자, 역사학자나 어떤 학자에게 그의 과학에 의해 어떠한 확정적인 지식들이 확인되었냐고 묻는다면, 그의 대답은 아마도 당신이 들을 마음이 있는 한 계속해서 설명을 할 것이다. 그러나 만일 당신이 동일한 질문을 철학자에게 했다면, 그는, 만일 그가 ⓐ 솔직하다면, 그의 학문이 다른 과학에서 성취된 것과 같은 긍정적인 결과들을 이룩해 내지 못했다고 고백해야만 할 것이다. ⓑ 이것은 어떤 주제에 대해 단정적인 지식이 가능해진다면 이 주제는 더 이상 철학이라고 부를 수가 없고 다른 과학 영역이 되기 때문이라는 사실에 의해 부분적으로는 설명된다는 것이 사실이다. 하늘에 대한 모든 연구는, 지금은 천문학에 속하는데, 한때 철학의 영역에 포함되어 있었으며, 뉴턴의 위대한 연구는 '자연 철학의 수학적 원리'라고 불렸었다. Ⓐ 이와 유사하게 인간의 마음에 관한 연구도, 한때는 철학의 일부였지만, 지금은 철학과는 분리되어 심리학이 되었다. 따라서 크게 말해, 철학의 불확실성은 실제보다 더 분명해 보인다. 그처럼 확정적인 답이 이미 있는 그 질문들은 과학으로 넘겨져 있고, 현재로서는 확정적인 답을 줄 수 없는 그 문제들만 철학이라고 부르는 잔여물의 형태로 남아 있게 된 것이기 때문이다.

21
윗글의 주요 주제는 _____이다. 주제
✓ ① 철학의 목표와 목적을 규정하는 어려움
② 천문학, 심리학 및 철학 사이의 관계 너무 지엽적
③ 철학에서 지식을 탐구하는 기쁨과 행복 언급 안 함
④ 철학에서 성공적인 연구의 척도 너무 지엽적

| 분석 | 이 글은 전반적으로 철학의 목표와 연구 대상을 정의하는 데 있어서의 어려움을 다루고 있으므로 글의 주제로 가장 적합한 것은 ①이다.

22
다음 중 ⓐ 대신 사용 가능한 것은? 동의어
① 대단한
② 불성실한
③ 불만이 있는
✓ ④ 솔직 담백한

| 분석 | candid는 '솔직한'이란 의미로 '단도직입적인', '솔직 담백한'의 의미를 갖는 forthright(= frank)가 정답이다.

23 ⓑthis는 무엇을 의미하는가? 지시어

① 철학에 의해 만들어진 우리의 편견, 확신, 신념의 근거에 대한 비판적인 조사
② 철학을 포함한 다양한 유형의 과학에 의해 확인된 명백한 진실들
✓ ③ 지식 철학이 지향하는 것에 대한 명백한 답의 부족
④ 구체적인 답을 가진 과목이 천문학, 심리학과 같은 별개의 과학이 된다는 사실

| 분석 | 지시어 this는 문맥상 그 앞의 내용인 '철학자의 학문이 다른 과학에서 성취된 것과 같은 긍정적인 결과들을 이룩해 내지 못했다고 고백해야만 할 것이다.'를 가리키므로 정답으로 적절한 것은 ③이다.

24 다음 중 Ⓐ에 들어갈 말로 가장 적절한 것은? 연결사

① 대조로　　　　　　　　　　　　✓ ② 유사하게
③ 따라서　　　　　　　　　　　　④ 그럼에도 불구하고

| 분석 | 주어진 빈칸의 앞에는 뉴턴의 천체학 연구도 답이 나오기 전에는 철학에 속하였다는 것이며, 빈칸의 뒤에는 인간의 마음에 대한 연구도 처음에는 철학에 속하였다가 나중에 심리학이 되었다는 것이므로, 이 둘을 이어 주는 접속사는 '이와 유사하게'가 가장 적합하다.

[25-26] 2011 중앙대

| 정답 | 25 ④　26 ①

| 어휘 |
dub ⓥ ~라고 칭하다, ~라는 별명으로 부르다　　　subsequent ⓐ 차후의, 다음의
crux ⓝ 중요점, 핵심　　Cartesian ⓐ 데카르트의, 데카르트 철학의　　skeptic ⓝ 회의론자
modish ⓐ 유행의, 최신 모드의　　for the sake of ~을 위하여　　sagacious ⓐ 총명한
coercion ⓝ 강제, 위압, 강요　　rational ⓐ 이성적인, 합리적인　　deduction ⓝ 연역(법), 공제
staunch ⓐ 신조에 철두철미한, 완고한, 충실한

전문해석

르네 데카르트(René Descartes)는 프랑스 철학자, 수학자, 물리학자, 그리고 작가였다. 그는 '현대 철학의 아버지'라 불렸으며, 많은 후대의 서구 철학은 오늘날까지도 면밀히 연구되고 있는 그의 글에 대한 하나의 반응이다. 특히, '제1의 철학에 관한 고찰(Meditations on First Philosophy)'은 계속해서 대부분의 대학 철학과의 기본서이다. 게다가, '방법 서설(Discourse on the Method)'은 모든 철학서를 통틀어 가장 영향력 있는 책 중의 하나가 되었고 여전히 그러하다. 그 철학서 4장에서, 데카르트는 그 유명한 철학 명언인 "Cogito ergo sum", 즉 '나는 생각한다, 고로 존재한다'라는 말을 남겼다. 다른 명언으로 자주 데카르트가 사용한 "de omnibus dubitandum(우리는 모든 것을 의심해야 한다)"은 데카르트 학파의 핵심을 잘 표현하고 있다. 이 말은 신앙인들에게는 이상하게도 Ⓐ 냉소적인 충고로 보일지 모른다. 그리고 정말로, 그 말로 인해 그는 그 시대의 성직자에게 평판이 좋지는 않았다. 그러나 데카르트가 회의적 방법을 이용할 때, 그는 역설적으로 어느 정도 종교의 입장에 이르렀다. 그 방법을 이용할 때 그의 목적은 항상 분명했다. 데카르트가 반발해서 글을 쓰게 만들었던 미셸 몽테뉴(Michel de Montaigne)와 다른 회의론자들과는 다르게, 데카르트는 회의를 위한 회의를 하는 당대의 사고방식에는 일말의 관심이 없었다. 그의 목적은 회의를 통해서 Ⓑ 확실하게 가시적인 것에 도달하는 것이었다. 이것이 본질적으로 17세기 물리학의 과학적 절차였고, 그러한 과학적 절차 속에서 회의는 지속적인 역할을 했다. 즉, 의심할 여지 없이, 가능한 한 확고해지기까지는 '어떤 것도 사실로 받아들이지 않는다는 것'이다.

25 윗글의 빈칸 Ⓐ, Ⓑ에 들어갈 말로 가장 적절한 것은? 빈칸 추론

① 현명한 – 불신
② 회의적인 – 강제성
③ 합리적인 – 공제
✓ ④ 냉소적인 – 확신

| 분석 | 빈칸 Ⓐ는 바로 뒤 문장에 그 당시 종교인들로부터 환영받지 못했음이 표현되어 있다. 따라서 'cynical'이 들어가야 하고, 빈칸 Ⓑ의 경우는 '확고해지기(established)까지는 아무것도 받아들이지 않는다'는 마지막 문장에서도 알 수 있듯이 확실성(certainty)이라는 말이 가장 적합하다.

26 윗글의 내용과 일치하는 것은? 내용 일치

✓ ① 데카르트와 몽테뉴는 의심의 방법에 대한 태도가 달랐다.
② 데카르트의 철학적 진술은 때때로 역설적인 메시지를 전달한다.
③ 데카르트는 종교인들 사이에서 충실한 지지자들이 많았다.
④ 데카르트는 물리학보다 수학 분야에서 훨씬 더 큰 기여를 했다.

| 분석 | 글의 후반부에서 데카르트는 당대의 사고방식에는 관심이 없었고 몽테뉴는 그와는 입장이 달랐음을 알 수 있다. 따라서 ①이 정답이다. ②의 경우에는 데카르트의 철학적 견해가 역설적인 메시지를 전달한다고 했으나, 그가 전달하고자 하는 내용 자체가 역설적이라는 것이 아니라 종교와의 관계에 있어 그의 입장이 결국에는 어느 정도 종교의 입장과 태도를 같이한다는 것이다.

[27–28] 2011 서강대

| 정답 | 27 ① 28 ④

| 어휘 |
be obsessed with ~에 사로잡히다
medieval ⓐ 중세의
benchmark ⓝ 기준, 척도
unquestioned ⓐ 의심받지 않는, 확실한
at the expense of ~을 희생시켜, ~을 대가로
iconography ⓝ 도상(학)
stir ⓥ 흔들다
enforce ⓥ 집행하다
demotion ⓝ 파면
haberdasher ⓝ 신사용 양품 장수(셔츠·모자·넥타이 등을 팖); (주로 영국) 방물장수(바늘·실·단추 등을 팖)
heretic ⓝ 이교도, 이단자
miracle ⓝ 기적
Christendom ⓝ 기독교 세계, 기독교 국가들, 기독교계
credibility ⓝ 신뢰성
other-worldly ⓐ 내세의
figure ⓝ 인물
insistent ⓐ 뚜렷한, 끈질긴
police ⓥ 단속하다, 감시하다
go hand-in-hand 손잡고 함께 가다
seamstress ⓝ 침모, 여자 재봉사
antique ⓐ 고대의, 골동품인
credulity ⓝ 신앙
consistency ⓝ 일관성
salt A with B A를 B로 흥미롭게 만들다
supernaturalism ⓝ 초자연주의
denial ⓝ 부인
chronicler ⓝ 연대기 기록자

전문해석

고대 후기와 중세의 기독교 국가들보다 기적에 사로잡혀 있었던 문명은 없었다고 해도 과언이 아니다. 천 년 이상의 세월 동안 프로테스탄트 개혁 때까지 기독교 세계에서 기적은 종교적 신빙성과 신앙의 확실한 기준이었다. 세속적인 것을 대가로 내세를 고양시키는 익숙한 관행은 놀라울 정도의 일관성을 가지고 표현되었는데, 여기에는 비잔틴 제국 도상의 영원한 순수성에서 베네러블 베데(Venerable Bede)와 같은 인물들의 글까지 포함된다(베네러블 베데는 자신의 18세기 영국사 거의 페이지마다 흥미진진한 기적을 끼워 넣어 흥미를 더했을 뿐만 아니라, 영어로 시를 쓴 최초의 시인이었던 캐드몬(Caedmon)을 '많은 사람들의 마음을 움직여 이 승을 혐오하고 천국의 것들을 열망하게 한 작가'라고 칭송했다). 간단히 말해서 이는 중세 비평가들이 제공할 수 있었던 가장 높은 칭송이었다. 중세 사회의 끈질긴 초자연주의, 즉 끊임없이 철학자들의 사상을 검열하고 이단자들을 망설이지 않고 화형에 처했던

강력한 교회가 집행했던 초자연주의는 결국 자연의 규칙성을 완전히 부정하기에 이르렀다. 중세의 초자연주의는 자연 그 자체를 파괴시켰던 것이다.

27 다음 중 빈칸에 들어갈 말로 가장 적절한 것은? 빈칸 추론
① 이단자들 ✓
② 바느질 도구 판매상
③ (여자) 재봉사들
④ 연대기 작가

| 분석 | 철학자들의 사상을 끊임없이 검열하고 화형(처벌)한다고 했으므로 여기에 알맞은 어휘는 이교도, 이단자를 나타내는 'heretics'가 적절하다.

28 윗글에 가장 적합한 제목은 무엇인가? 제목
① 역사와 도상
② 개신교 혁명의 여파
③ 종교와 문명
④ 기적과 기독교 ✓

| 분석 | 지문은 전반적으로 중세 기독교 국가들의 미신을 그리는 글이므로 제목으로 가장 적합한 것은 ④ '기적과 기독교'이다.

[29-31] 2015 항공대

| 정답 | 29 ③   30 ①   31 ④

| 어휘 | inquisition ⓝ 심문, 종교 재판소   deviant ⓐ 정상에서 벗어난   ban ⓥ 금하다
         intolerance n 불관용, 편협함   Crusade ⓝ 십자군 운동   fundamentalist ⓝ 근본주의자
         witch ⓝ 마녀   denounce ⓥ 비난하다, 탄핵하다   tribunal ⓝ 재판소

전문해석

수 세기 동안 로마 가톨릭교회는 ⓐ 종교 재판소를 유지했다. 종교 재판소는 교리에서 벗어난 생각을 가진 많은 사람을 죽음으로 내몰았고 책들을 금지하거나 불태웠는데, 오늘날까지도 일부 책들은 로마 가톨릭교회에 의해 금지된 상태다. 이란에서는 (이란의 최고 지도자이던) A. R. 호메이니(A. R. Khomeini)가 1989년 사망하기 직전에 살만 루슈디(Salman Rushdie)가 쓴 '사탄의 시'를 금지했고 모든 신자들에게 그 책의 저자와 발행자를 죽이도록 부추겼다. 기독교 국가의 많은 사람들이 이러한 행위로 인해서 큰 충격을 받은 것은, 자신들의 나라에서 (과거에) 보여 준 종교적 불관용의 역사에 비추어 보면 어느 정도 놀라운 일이다. 호메이니의 행동을 비롯한 일부 예외적인 경우가 있긴 하지만 이슬람교는 역사적으로 다른 종교에 대해 로마 가톨릭 기독교보다 더 관용적이었다. 수십만 명의 목숨을 앗아 간 중세의 십자군은 이슬람교가 아니라 기독교가 보여 준 종교적 불관용의 결과물이었다. 이슬람 터키 제국에서는 유대인들을 관대하게 대했으며 그들은 특별세를 내기만 하면 자신들의 종교 생활을 영위할 수 있었다. 반면에 (서구에서는) 일반적으로 보다 관대하다고 여겨지고 있는 개신교도들조차도 종교적 불관용이 유발한 희생자들을 만들어 왔다. 지난 수 세기에 걸쳐 개신교 국가들 또한 마녀로 추정되는 사람들 불태워 죽였다. 21세기 초에도 근본주의의 기독교 설교자들은 해리포터 시리즈를 악마가 쓴 작품이라고 비난했다.

29 빈칸에 들어갈 말로 가장 적절한 것을 고르시오. `빈칸 추론`
① 더 번영한
② 다른 종교에 덜 관용적인
✓ ③ 다른 종교에 더 관용적인
④ 덜 번영한

| 분석 | 빈칸 뒤에서 수십만 명의 목숨을 앗아 간 중세의 십자군 운동은 이슬람이 아니라 기독교가 보여 준 것이라고 하였다. 따라서 로마 가톨릭이 이슬람보다 역사 속에서 더 잔인했다는 것이다. 빈칸의 주어는 이슬람교이므로 이슬람교가 로마 가톨릭보다 더 관용적이었다가 맞는 표현이다.

30 ⓐ "Inquisition"은 _____ 을 의미한다는 것을 이 지문에서 유추할 수 있다. `문맥상 의미 파악`
✓ ① 이단을 발견하고 탄압하기 위해 만들어진 로마 가톨릭교회의 종교 재판소
② 많은 공상적인 사상과 생각을 불러일으킨 로마 가톨릭교회의 불법적 유산
③ 극심한 정신적 심문의 총칭
④ 개인의 권리나 사생활을 침해하는 상황

| 분석 | inquisition은 '종교 재판소'의 의미이며 바로 뒤 문장에서 '교리에서 벗어난 생각을 가진 많은 사람을 죽이고 책을 금지하거나 불태우는 곳'이라고 언급했는데 이를 통해서도 의미의 유추가 가능하다.

31 윗글에 따르면, 다음 중 사실이 아닌 것은? `내용 일치`
① 살만 루슈디의 책은 이란에서 읽는 것이 금지되었다.
② 개신교도들은 로마 가톨릭 신자들이 그랬던 것처럼 불관용의 희생자들을 만들어 냈다.
③ 해리포터 시리즈는 일부 기독교인들에 의해 부정적인 평가를 받았다.
✓ ④ '사탄의 시'는 허영심과 편협성 때문에 금지되었다.

| 분석 | '사탄의 시'는 종교적 편협성 때문에 금지된 것이지 그 책의 내용이 허영심과 편협한 것은 아니다. 따라서 ④는 지문과 일치하지 않는다.

[32-34] 2016 서강대

| 정답 | 32 ② 33 ③ 34 ④

| 어휘 | engaging ⓐ 남의 마음을 끄는, 매력 있는   incorporeal ⓐ 형체[육체]가 없는, 무형의; 영적인(= spiritual)
naturalist ⓝ 자연주의자; 박물학자   immortal ⓐ 불멸의   substance ⓝ 물질; 실체, 본질, 요지, 의미
disparate ⓐ 다른, 이종의, 공통점이 없는   implication ⓝ 함축; 함축된 것, 암시; 연루, 말려들기
extrapolate ⓥ 외삽법에 의해 추정하다, 외삽법을 행하다   immaculate ⓐ 오점[결점] 없는, 완전한
absolute monarch 절대 군주   diaspora ⓝ 집단 이주; (특히 유대인의) 이산
bulwark ⓝ 성채, 보루; 방파제; 방호물   gamut ⓝ 전 범위, 전반

전문해석

마카리(Makari)의 매력적인 이야기는 르네 데카르트(René Descartes)와 더불어 시작된다. 그리스 철학이 기독교와 하나로 섞인 이래로, 영혼은 "자연, 인간, 그리고 신을 통합시켜 주는 연결 고리라고 여겨져 왔다."라고 마카리는 쓰고 있다. 그러나 17세기에 기독교는 위기에 처했고, 많은 사람들은 형체가 없는 영혼이라는 개념을 물질로 이루어진 것으로 점점 더 이해되고 있던 기계적인 세계와의 조화가 어렵다는 사실을 발견했다. 데카르트는 영혼의 개념을 신체로부터 분리된 "생각하는 존재"라고 좁힘으로써 회의적인 자연철학자들의 요구를 만족시키고자 했다. 이와 같이 프랑스의 철학자인 데카르트는 불멸의 영혼에 대한 기독교적인 믿음에 새로운 생명을 불어넣어 주었다. (하지만) 그 ⓐ 범위의 정반대 극단에는 토머스 홉스(Thomas Hobbes)가 서 있었는데, 그는 비물질적인 존재 같은 것은 없다고 생각했다. 그의 견해에 따르면, 영혼은, 이성적인 존재 그리고 신과 같은 존재라기보다는, 질병과 오류에 걸리기 쉬운 경향을 가지고 있는 물질이었다. ⓑ 생각하는 존재의 본성에 관한 이와 같은 상반된 견해들은 기념비적인 의미를 가지고 있다. 그리고 이러한 상반된 견해들은 마카리가 제기한 담론이 단지 하나의 지적 운동이 아닌 그 이상의 것으로서의 중요성을 가지고 있음을 증명해 보여 주었다. 인간이 필연적으로 갈등을 만들어 내고야 마는 동물적 감정에 의해 지배받는 존재라고 결론을 내리고 난 후, 홉스가 제시한 결론은 권력을 절대 군주에게 넘겨주는 것이었다.

32 윗글과 가장 일치하는 진술을 고르시오. [내용 일치]

① 유럽 철학은 17세기에 점점 종교적으로 변했다.
✓ ② 마카리는 현대 세속 철학의 성장을 기록했다.
③ 홉스는 "질병과 오류"에 대한 인간의 성향을 근거로 현대적인 형태의 민중 선동을 지지했다.
④ 데카르트는 기계 세계의 중요성을 강조했다.

| 분석 | 이 글은 마카리가 기술한 철학의 역사를 데카르트에서 홉스까지에 걸쳐서 기술하고 있다. 데카르트의 영혼의 정의가 아직 종교적 성향을 버리지 못했다면, 홉스의 영혼의 정의는 종교적 성향을 버린 완전한 세속적인 정의라 할 수 있다. 이 모든 것을 마카리가 기술하고 있으므로, ② '마카리는 현대 세속 철학의 성장을 기록했다.'는 지문과 일치한다. 한편 ③에서 demagoguery (민중 선동)는 absolute monarch(절대 군주)로 나와야 지문과 일치한다.

33 윗글의 빈칸 ⓑ에 가장 적절한 문장을 고르시오. [빈칸 추론]

① 홉스의 견해는 데카르트의 견해와 일치하지만 한 단계 더 나아가 추정했다.
② 홉스는 데카르트의 완벽한 영혼에 대한 개념을 물질적인 용어로 번역함으로써 그의 생각을 강화했다.
✓ ③ "생각하는 것"의 본질에 대한 상반된 관점은 기념비적인 의미를 가지고 있었다.
④ 홉스는 "나는 생각한다, 그러므로 나는 존재한다."가 아니라 "나는 생각한다, 그러므로 나는 존재한다. 그러나 나는 존재한다, 그러므로 나는 또한 생각한다."라는 유명한 주장을 했다.

| 분석 | 앞뒤 내용을 보았을 때 데카르트는 홉스와 영혼의 개념에 관하여 상반된 생각을 갖고 있음을 알 수 있다. 보기 ①, ②는 데카르트와 홉스의 생각이 같다는 의미이므로 들어갈 수 없다. ③의 생각하는 존재는 영혼을 지칭하며 데카르트와 홉스가 그것에 관하여 상반된 생각을 갖고 있다는 보기이므로 정답으로 옳다. ④도 데카르트와 홉스가 생각이 다르다는 보기이나, 데카르트의 이성주의와 홉스의 경험주의의 차이를 기술하고 있으므로 정답이 될 수 없다.

34 윗글의 빈칸 ⓐ에 알맞은 것을 고르시오. [빈칸 추론]

① 디아스포라(고국을 떠나는 사람·집단의 이동) ② 방어물
③ 무명   ✓ ④ 범위, 영역

| 분석 | 문맥상 데카르트와 홉스가 서로 상반된 생각을 갖고 있는데 그렇다면 홉스는 데카르트와 그 '범위'에 있어서 정반대에 서 있다고 해야 자연스럽다. 따라서 정답은 ④가 적절하다.

[35-37] 2017 한국외대

| 정답 | 35 ② 36 ③ 37 ④

| 어휘 |
puzzle ⓥ 애먹이다, 괴롭히다
morality ⓝ 도덕성
stray ⓥ 탈선하다, (주제 등에서) 벗어나다
inverse ⓝ 반대, 역
usurp ⓥ (권력·지위 등을) 빼앗다
racist joke 인종 차별주의적 농담
downgrade ⓥ 품질[지위]을 떨어뜨리다; 좌천시키다
conventional ⓐ 인습적인
arrogant ⓐ 거만한, 오만한

postulate ⓥ 가정하다
vindicate ⓥ ~의 정당성을 입증하다, 옹호하다, 지키다
school of thought 학파
immorally ⓐⓓ 부도덕하게
coup ⓝ 쿠데타
deferential ⓐ 경의를 표하는, 공손한
self-interested ⓐ 자기 본위의, 이기적인
untoward ⓐ 운이 나쁜; 귀찮은, 성가신

exploit ⓥ 이용하다
hypothesize ⓥ 가설을 세우다, 가정하다
embezzle ⓥ 유용하다, 횡령하다
disparage ⓥ 헐뜯다, 비방하다
servility ⓝ 노예근성, 비굴, 굴종
commitment ⓝ 헌신, 전념; 위임
mirror image 거울상(좌우 반대의 모습)

전문해석

무엇이 사람들로 하여금 잘못된 행동을 하게 만드는 것일까? 이 질문은 플라톤(Plato) 이후의 여러 철학자들을 당혹스럽게 만들었는데, 플라톤은 다음과 같은 유명한 질문을 던진 바 있다. 만약 당신이 마법의 반지를 하나 발견했는데, 이 반지가 은행을 터는 것이든, 세상을 손에 넣는 것이든, 적을 노예로 만드는 것이든 무엇이든 당신이 원하는 일을 하게 해 준다고 한다면, 당신은 그렇게 할 것인가? 플라톤은 이 반지를 이용해 나쁜 짓을 저지르는 데 따르는 희생이 보상에 비해 크다면, 도덕성이 지켜질(부도덕한 짓을 하지 않을) 것이라고 가정했다. 플라톤은 사람들이 개인적인 이득의 유혹 때문에 ⓐ 곧게 뻗은 좁은 길에서 벗어난다고 가정했다. 그러나 이와 반대되는 가설을 세운 또 다른 학파가 있다. 그 가설에서는 사람들은 사회에 순응하기를 원하기 때문에 자신의 핵심적인 가치와 반대될 때조차도 부도덕하게 행동하는 것으로 본다. 다시 말하면, 사람들은 ⓐ 다른 사람들이 자신을 어떻게 보는가에 너무 신경을 쓴다는 것이다. 대부분의 사람들의 경우, 나쁜 짓이라는 것이 수백만 달러를 횡령한다거나 쿠데타를 통해 권력을 빼앗는다거나 하는 것이 아니라, 어떤 사람을 헐뜯는 일에 동참한다거나 인종 차별적인 농담에 웃음을 터뜨린다거나 하는 정도이다. 우리가 이런 행동을 하는 이유는 어떤 문제도 일으키길 원치 않기 때문이다. 임마누엘 칸트(Immanuel Kant)는 이와 같은 종류의 지나치게 공손한 태도를 '노예근성'이라고 부른다. 노예근성은 다른 사람들의 가치와 헌신을 떨어뜨리는 것이라기보다는 다른 사람들의 가치와 헌신에 비해 상대적으로 당신 자신의 가치와 헌신을 떨어뜨리는 것이다. 따라서 노예근성이 있는 사람은 플라톤의 설명에서 발견되는 인습적이고 이기적인 부도덕한 사람의 거울상(반대 모습)이다. 칸트에게 있어, 노예근성을 가진 사람들은 도덕적 평등과 존경을 자신에게는 다른 사람들에게만큼 허용하지 않는 사람들이다. 그들은 오만하거나, 성가시거나, 무례하게 보이지 않기 위해서 이렇게 행동하며, 이렇게 함으로써 사회화되어 사회에 순응하고 잘못된 행동을 하게 되는 것이다.

35 윗글에 따르면, ⓐ가 의미하는 것과 가장 가까운 것은 무엇인가? 문맥상 의미

① 굽지 않은 길
✓② 정직하고 윤리적으로 행동하는 것
③ 학업적인 목표를 위해 노력하는 것
④ 당신의 목적지로 가기 위한 가장 빠른 지름길

| 분석 | '개인적인 이득의 유혹 때문에 곧게 뻗은 좁은 길에서 벗어난다'는 것은 옳지 않은 길로 빠지는 것이므로, 곧게 뻗은 좁은 길이 의미하는 것은 '정직하고 윤리적으로 행동하는 것'이라고 볼 수 있다.

36 다음 중 빈칸 Ⓐ에 가장 적절한 것은? 빈칸 추론

① 다른 사람들을 따르는 것이 잘못된 행동이라고 생각한다
② 사회를 거부하고 그들의 가치를 증진시키는 데 너무 노력한다
✓③ 다른 사람들이 그들을 바라보는 것에 너무 신경을 쓴다
④ 올바른 행동을 하는 데 너무 집착한다

| 분석 | 빈칸 앞에서 "사람들은 사회에 순응하기를 원하기 때문에 자신의 핵심적인 가치와 반대될 때조차도 부도덕하게 행동한다."라고 했는데, '사회에 순응한다는 것은 다른 사람들의 행동에 맞춘다는 것이고, 이것은 다른 사람들의 시선이나 생각을 의식한다는 것을 의미한다. 따라서 ③이 빈칸에 적절하다.

37 윗글에 따르면, 다음 중 사실이 아닌 것은? 내용 일치

① 플라톤은 사람들이 개인적인 이익을 위해 잘못된 행동을 한다고 생각했다.
② 칸트는 노예근성의 사람들이 (사회에) 순응하기를 원하기 때문에 부도덕한 행동을 한다고 생각했다.
③ 플라톤은 부도덕한 행동의 비용(희생)이 너무 많으면 도덕성이 지켜질 것이라고 생각했다.
✓④ 칸트는 노예근성의 사람들이 종종 권력을 찬탈한다고 생각했다.

| 분석 | 칸트는 노예근성을 가진 사람들이 "수백만 달러를 횡령한다거나 쿠데타를 통해 권력을 빼앗는다거나 하는 것이 아니라, 어떤 사람을 헐뜯는 일에 동참한다거나 인종 차별적인 농담에 웃음을 터뜨린다거나 하는 정도이다."라고 했다. 칸트가 생각한 노예근성의 사람들이 권력을 빼앗는 사람들인 것은 아니므로 ④가 정답이다.

[38-40] 2016 성균관대

| 정답 | 38 ⑤ 39 ① 40 ②

| 어휘 | **advance an argument** 주장을 제기하다   **paraphrase** ⓥ 바꿔 말하다   **point** ⓝ 주장
undergraduate ⓝ 대학생, 대학[학부] 재학생   **peculiar** ⓐ 독특한, 고유의

전문해석

종교를 촉진하기 위해 종종 제기되는 주장은, 예수님의 말씀을 전하는 마태복음을 알기 쉽게 풀어 말하는 것을 통해서 종교가 사람들로 하여금 그들의 이웃을 그들 자신처럼 사랑하도록 이끈다는 것이다. 만일 이것이 진실이라면 이것은 매우 강력한 주장이다. 그러나 과연 그럴까? 이것은 시카고 대학의 발달 신경과학자인 장 데서티(Jean Decety)가 Current Biology라는 학술지에 실린 연구 논문에서 묻고 있는 질문이다.

Dr. Decety가 종교와 이타주의 사이의 관련성에 대해서 과학적인 방법으로 의문을 제기한 첫 번째 인물은 아니다. 그럼에도 불구하고 그는 심리학자들에 의해서 사랑받는, 표준화되어 있으면서도 특별한 실험용 동물인 대학생에 의존하지 않고 이 일을 수행한 최초의 인물들 중 한 사람이다. 그 대신, 그는 5세부터 12세 사이에 있는 아이들과 아이들의 가족들을 관찰하기 위해서 미국인 동료들뿐만 아니라 캐나다, 중국, 요르단, 남아프리카 공화국 그리고 터키에 있는 연구자들과 함께 공동 작업을 수행했다.

38 'it'이 의미하는 것은 무엇인가? 지시어

① 대부분의 사람들은 종교적이다.　　② 신앙의 대상은 중요하지 않다.
③ 예수가 사람들의 사랑을 강조했다.　④ 과학과 종교는 다르지 않다.
✓⑤ 종교는 다른 사람을 돕게 한다.

| 분석 | 'it'이 가리키는 내용은 앞 문장의 'it leads people to love their neighbors as themselves'이다. 따라서 종교가 다른 사람을 돕게 한다는 말이 사실인지를 묻고 있다. 'were it true'는 가정법 과거형 문장의 조건절에 해당되는 부분으로, 원래 문장은 'if it were true'이다.

39 빈칸에 가장 적합한 하나를 고르시오. 빈칸 추론
☑ ① 이타주의 ② 개인주의
③ 이기주의 ④ 자본주의
⑤ 자기중심주의

| 분석 | 빈칸에는 이웃을 자신과 같이 사랑하라는 앞 단락의 중심 내용을 그대로 포괄하는 단어가 들어가야 한다. 따라서 이타주의 "altruism"이 정답으로 적절하다.

40 지문에 따르면 심리학자가 가장 선호하는 실험의 대상은 _____이다. 내용 파악
① 아이들 ☑ ② 대학생들
③ 미국인들 ④ 동물들
⑤ 연구자들

| 분석 | 지문의 후반부 laboratory animal (beloved by psychologists), the undergraduate student 문장에서 실험실의 동물과 콤마 뒤의 대학생이 동격의 명사로 쓰인 것이다. 따라서 '심리학자가 사랑하는 실험실의 동물'은 '대학생'이므로 '대학생'이 정답으로 적절하다.

[41-42] 2020 서울여대

| 정답 | 41 ② 42 ③

| 어휘 |
division ⓝ (사회·단체 내의) 분열
commission ⓝ 수수료
province ⓝ 지방, 지역
overlord ⓝ 대군주; 지배자, 권력자
comparable ⓐ 비교되는, 필적하는
hard-working ⓐ 근면한, 열심히 일하는
pomp ⓝ 화려, 장관; 겉치레, 허식
hold sway in ~을 지배하다
grandeur ⓝ 장엄함, 웅장

Protestant ⓝ (개)신교도, 프로테스탄트
canvas ⓝ 유화, 그림
rise against ~에 대해 반란[모반]을 일으키다
Spaniard ⓝ 스페인 사람
outlook ⓝ 사고방식, 견해, 견지
parsimonious ⓐ 지극히 검소한, 인색한
mellow ⓥ 부드러워지다, 원숙해지다
sober ⓐ 진지한, 엄숙한; 수수한, 점잖은
sparing ⓐ 아끼며 사용하는, 절약하는, ~에 인색한

innumerable ⓐ 셀 수 없이 많은, 무수한
glorification ⓝ 영광을 찬양함, 찬미, 찬양
adhere ⓥ 신봉하다, 지지하다
devout ⓐ 독실한, 경건한
exuberant ⓐ 넘치는; 열광적인
burgher ⓝ (특정 소도시의) 시민[주민]
restraint ⓝ 규제, 통제, 자제

전문해석
유럽이 가톨릭과 개신교 진영으로 분열된 것은 네덜란드와 같은 작은 나라들의 예술에도 영향을 미쳤다. 오늘날 벨기에로 불리는 남부 네덜란드는 가톨릭 진영에 남았고, 우리는 앤트워프(Antwerp: 벨기에 북부의 주)에서 활동하던 루벤스(Rubens)가 어떻게 교회와 왕자, 그리고 왕들로부터 엄청나게 많은 수수료를 받고 그들의 권력을 찬양하기 위한 그림을 큰 화폭에 그렸는지 알게 되었다. 그러나 네덜란드의 북부 지방들은 그들의 가톨릭계 지배자들인 스페인인들에 대항하여 봉기했고, 그들의 부유한 상업도시에 살던 대부분의 주민들은 개신교 신앙을 고수했다. 네덜란드의 이러한 개신교 상인들의 취향은 경계 건너 남부에 팽배해 있던 취향과 매우 달랐다. 이 사람들(북부 개신교 상인들)은 그들의 사고방식에 있어 영국의 청교도들에 다소 견줄만 했는데, 독실하고, 근면하며, 검소한 사람들로, 대부분은 남부식의 넘치는 화려함을 매우 싫어했다. 그들의 안전이 강화되고 부가 증가하자 그들의 사고방식

이 누그러졌지만, 17세기 네덜란드의 이 (북부) 주민들은 가톨릭 유럽을 휩쓸고 있던 완전한 바로크 양식을 받아들이지 않았다. 건축에서도 그들은 어느 정도 진지한 자제를 선호했다. 17세기 중반 네덜란드 성공의 절정기에 암스테르담의 시민들이 그들의 신생국가의 자부심과 업적을 반영하기 위한 거대한 시청 건물을 건립하기로 결정했을 때, 그들은 그 시청의 웅장함에도 불구하고 건물의 외관이 단순하고 장식이 많이 들어가지 않은 모델을 선택했다.

42 ③

41 루벤스는 _____ 화가였다. 내용 이해

① 네덜란드의 부유한 개신교 상인들에 의해 지원을 받은
✓ 교회와 궁전을 장식할 거대한 그림을 좋아한
③ 활기 넘치는 남부 네덜란드 양식의 경향이 없었던
④ 17세기 북부 네덜란드 그림에 커다란 영향을 준

| 분석 | 앤트워프에서 활동하던 루벤스는 수수료를 받고 교회와 왕자, 그리고 왕들의 권력을 찬양하는 그림을 그렸다고 했으므로 ②가 정답이다.

42 윗글에 따르면 다음 중 옳은 것은 무엇인가? 내용 일치

① 암스테르담의 거대한 시청은 완전한 바로크 양식으로 지어졌다.
② 개신교의 승리는 남부 네덜란드 그림에 뚜렷하게 나타났다.
✓ 네덜란드의 개신교 상인들은 국가에 대한 자긍심을 보여 주기를 원했다.
④ 개신교 네덜란드 화가들은 스페인 후원자들을 위해 수많은 그림을 그렸다.

| 분석 | 개신교를 믿었던 암스테르담 시민들이 신생 국가의 자부심과 업적을 반영하기 위한 거대한 시청 건물을 세우기로 결정했다고 했으므로 ③이 글의 내용과 일치한다. ① 가톨릭 유럽을 휩쓸고 있던 완전한 바로크 양식을 받아들이지 않았다고 했다. ② 권력자들을 찬양하기 위한 그림이 남부 네덜란드 그림에서 뚜렷하게 나타난다. ④ 남부 화가(가톨릭)들이 스페인 후원자들의 후원을 받아 그림을 그렸다.

[43-46] 2011 성균관대

| 정답 | 43 ④   44 ②   45 ③   46 ⑤

| 어휘 |
promulgate ⓥ 발표하다
embody ⓥ 구체화하다, 체현하다
specimen ⓝ 견본
alert ⓥ ~에게 경고하다, 경종을 울리다
patient ⓐ 인내심 있는
long to do ~하고 싶은 생각이 간절하다
empathy ⓝ 감정이입, 공감
hostility ⓝ 적대감, 반감
revenge ⓥ 보복하다

noble ⓐ 고귀한, 숭고한
natural state 자연 상태
scavenge for ~을 찾아다니다
in person 몸소, 직접
tutor ⓝ 가정교사
clamber 기어 올라가다
primitive ⓐ 원시적인
cruelty ⓝ 잔인성
immoral ⓐ 부도덕한

savage ⓝ 야만인
innately ⓐⓓ 본디, 내재적으로
awareness ⓝ 자각, 인식
optimism ⓝ 낙관주의
defeat ⓝ 패배, 실패
moral rule 도덕률
innocent ⓐ 순수한, 때 묻지 않은
malice ⓝ 악의
pre-moral ⓐ 도덕 이전의, 도덕 이전 상태의

전문해석

프랑스 철학자 루소(Rousseau)가 자연 상태의 인간은 본디부터 선하다는 자신의 믿음을 구체화한 '고결한 미개인' 개념을 발표한 지 몇 년 지나지 않아, 바라건대 이 사상을 증명할 실제 표본이 정말로 숲에서 걸어 나왔다. 1800년 1월 9일 프랑스 남부의 생 세르냉 마을에서 일어났던 일이었다. 숲에서 나온 이 기이한 동물은 식량을 찾다가 잡혔고 겉모습은 야생 동물 같았지만 분명히 직립 보행을 하고 있었다. 이 동물을 붙잡은 사람들이 그것이 인간임을, 즉 12세가량의 남자아이임을 알아채자마자 이들은 아이를 돌보려고 했다. '아베롱의 야생아'로 알려진 아이는 말도 못 했고 자신이 인간이라는 자각도 보여 주지 않았다. 하얀 빵을 주자 그는 즉시 뱉어 버렸고 지나치게 가까이 다가오는 사람은 누구나 물어뜯었다. 과학자들에게 경종을 울릴 시간이었다. 여기 고귀한 미개인이 몸소 나타난 것이다.

그 후 수개월 동안 이 소년을 인간으로 되돌리려는 시도들이 행해졌다. 낙관론을 견지한 채로 사람들은 그에게 빅터라는 이름을 지어 주었고 인내심 강한 가정교사와 그를 어머니 같은 헌신으로 사랑하게 된 여성을 제공하는 혜택도 주었다. 그러나 이 가여운 인간에 대한 실험들은 실패를 되풀이했고 그는 자신이 살던 숲의 자유를 되찾고 싶어 했다. 저녁 초대를 받은 소년은 쥘 수 있을 만큼 작은 것들을 죄다 훔쳐서 나무 위로 기어 올라갔고 이에 깜짝 놀란 손님들은 루소가 살아서 자신의 이론이 틀렸다는 것을 보지 못한다는 사실에 분개했다. 그러나 정말 루소의 이론은 반박된 것일까? 절도는 특정 도덕률을 위반한 것이긴 하지만 도둑에게 규칙이 아무런 의미가 없을 경우 그 자체로 악을 의미하지는 않는다. 더 설득력 있는 사실은 빅터가 자신이 아닌 타인의 눈으로 세상을 볼 수 없었다는 점, 그리고 감정이입하는 능력이 없었다는 점이다. 그는 사람들이 어떻게 (자신을) 해칠 수 있는지는 습득했지만 타인이 자신의 욕구를 충족시켜 주는 사람 아닌 다른 방식으로 존재한다는 것을 인식하도록 학습하지는 못했던 것이다. 이 소년은 원시적 자연 상태가 본질적 선이라는 것을 증명하지는 못했지만, 그렇다고 원시 상태가 이기적이라는 것을 증명한 것도 아니었다. 이는 원시 상태가 순수하지 않다는 뜻 역시 아니다. 소년은 악이나 잔인성을 드러낸 것이 아니었고 보복하고자 하지도 않았으며 다른 개인들을 향해 직접적인 적대감을 발산하지도 않았다. 소년은 Ⓐ 부도덕하다기보다는 Ⓑ 도덕 이전의 상태 속에 존재했던 것이다.

43 윗글의 가장 좋은 제목은 _____ 이다. 〔제목〕

① 옳고 그름을 구별하는 방법
② 인간 교육의 중요성
③ 적자생존
④ ✓ 원시 상태의 도덕률
⑤ 인간의 공감 능력의 원인

| 분석 | 이 글은 아베롱의 소년을 예로 들어 원시 사회의 인간과 도덕법칙의 관계를 논하고 있다. 따라서 ④가 글의 제목으로 적절하다.

44 윗글에 따르면 다음 중 사실인 것은? 〔내용 일치〕

① 소년이 처음 발견되었을 때, 그는 프랑스 귀족의 잃어버린 아들로 오해받았다.
② ✓ 빅터는 적절한 교육과 모성애를 제공받았다.
③ 그 소년을 잡은 사람들은 그의 폭력적인 성격 때문에 그를 경찰에 넘겼다.
④ 과학자들을 가장 놀라게 한 것은 이 소년이 다른 사람들을 이해하는 능력이 뛰어나다는 것이다.
⑤ 과학자들은 그 소년이 구조대원들에 의해 학대를 당했다는 것을 발견했다.

| 분석 | 두 번째 단락에서 '인내심 강한 가정교사와 그를 어머니 같은 헌신으로 사랑하게 된 여성을 제공하는 혜택도 주었다.'고 언급하였다. 따라서 ②는 지문과 일치한다.

45 다음 중 빈칸 Ⓐ와 Ⓑ에 가장 적절한 것은? 빈칸 추론

① 인간적인 – 비인간적인
② 비인간적인 – 인간적인
✓③ 부도덕한 – 도덕 이전의
④ 도덕 이전의 – 부도덕한
⑤ 도덕과 관계없는 – 부도덕한

| 분석 | 야생 소년의 행위가 인간 사회의 도덕률로 판단할 수 없다는 것이 이 글의 요지인데, 따라서 그 소년은 부도덕하다기보다는 도덕 이전의 상태에 있다고 보아야 한다. not so much A as B가 'A라기보다는 오히려 B'의 뜻이므로 정답은 ③이다.

46 윗글에 따르면, 빅터의 이야기는 결국 인간이 선천적으로 _____는 것을 시사한다. 내용 파악

① 난폭한
② 불성실한
③ 좋은
④ 악의
✓⑤ 자기중심적인

| 분석 | 이 글의 내용으로 보았을 때 야생 소년은 악하거나 선하다는 기준으로 판단할 수 없는 존재이고 타인에게 감정이입을 하지 못한 채 자신의 욕구에만 충실했으므로 보기에서 가장 적합한 것은 ⑤ '자기중심적인'이다. 문맥상 폭력, 부정직, 선악은 인간 존재의 내재적 특성에 어울리지 않는다.

[47-49] 2020 홍익대

| 정답 | 47 ② 48 ③ 49 ④

| 어휘 |
cleavage ⓝ 분열; (의견 등의) 불일치
foreshadow ⓥ ~의 전조가 되다, 예시하다
in the same vein 같은 맥락에서
notion ⓝ 관념, 개념
conceive of A as B A를 B로 생각하다
subject ⓝ 주어
formulation ⓝ 형식화, 공식화
appeal ⓥ 호소하다; 간청하다, 빌다
intent ⓝ 의향, 의도
by virtue of ~의 힘으로, ~ 덕택으로
presuppose ⓥ 미리 가정[예상]하다, 전제로 하다

analytic ⓐ 분석적인
distinction ⓝ 구별, 차별; 차이
self-contradictory ⓐ 자기모순적인
clarification ⓝ 명시, 해명, 설명
attribute ⓥ (~의) 탓으로 하다, (성질 따위가) 있다고 생각하다(to)
conceptually ⓐⓓ 개념적으로
shortcoming ⓝ 결점, 단점
containment ⓝ 포함, 포괄; 봉쇄
evident ⓐ 분명한, 명백한, 뚜렷한
pursue ⓥ 추적하다, 추구하다

synthetic ⓐ 종합적인
picturesqueness ⓝ 생생함
explanatory ⓐ 설명적인, 해석의
dubious ⓐ 의심스러운, 수상한
contain ⓥ 포함하다
predicate ⓝ 술부, 술어
metaphorical ⓐ 은유적인
restate ⓥ 새로[고쳐] 진술하다

전문해석

칸트(Kant)가 제기한 분석적 진리와 종합적 진리의 차이는 흄(Hume)이 제시한 관념들의 관계와 사실들의 문제 간의 구분과 라이프니츠(Leibniz)가 제시한 이성적 진리와 사실적 진리와의 구분에서 이미 예고되었다. 라이프니츠는 이성적 진리를 모든 가능한 세계에서 참인 것이라고 말했다. 세세한 것들을 제쳐두고 보면, 이것은 이성적 진리란 거짓일 수 있는 가능성이 전혀 없는 진리라고 말하고 있는 것이다. 같은 맥락에서 우리는 분석적 진술이 그것을 부정하면 자기모순이 되는 진술로 정의됨을 듣는다. 그러나 이러한 정의는 설명적 가치가 거의 없다. 왜냐하면, 이런 분석성의 정의에 필요한 매우 넓은 뜻에서 보면 자기모순이라는 개념도 분석성의 개념 자체와 마찬가지로 명료화될 필요가 있기 때문이다. 그 두 개념은 의심스러운 한 동전의 양면인 것이다.

칸트는 분석적 진술을 주어에 이미 개념적으로 포함된 것 이외의 아무것도 그 주어에 속성으로 부가하지 않는 진술로 생각했다. 분석성에 대한 이러한 공식화는 두 가지 결점이 있다. 즉 그것은 주어-술어 형식의 진술에만 한정되며, 또한 은유적 차원에 머물고 있는 포함이라는 개념에 호소한다는 점이다. 그러나 칸트의 의도는 분석성 개념에 대한 그의 정의에서보다 그가 그 개념을 사용하는

용도에서 더욱 분명하게 나타나며, 이것은 다음과 같이 고쳐 말해질 수 있다. 즉, 어떤 진술이 사실을 고려함이 없이 의미에 의해 참일 때, 그 진술은 분석적이다. 이러한 방향에 따라 미리 전제된 의미의 개념을 검토해 보자.

47 다음 중 윗글의 주제로 가장 적절한 것은? 주제
① 이성적 진리와 사실적 진리에 대한 흄의 구분 너무 지엽적
✓ 라이프니츠의 이성적 진리와 칸트의 분석적 진술
③ 라이프니츠의 철학에서 가능한 세계와 사실의 진실 사이의 관계 너무 지엽적
④ 칸트 철학에 있어서 주어-술어 형식의 진술이 갖는 중요성 너무 지엽적

| 분석 | 첫 번째 단락의 주요 내용은 '라이프니츠가 생각하는 이성적 진리'에 대해 이야기하고 있고, 두 번째 단락에서는 칸트의 분석적 진술에 대해 논하고 있다. 그러므로 이 둘을 포괄하는 ②가 정답으로 적절하다.

48 윗글에 따르면, 다음 중 추론할 수 <u>없는</u> 것은? 내용 추론
① 라이프니츠의 이성적 진리에 대한 개념은 칸트의 분석적 진리와 비교될 수 있다.
② 칸트는 분석적 진술은 그것이 가진 의미 자체로 인해 항상 참이라고 생각했다.
✓ 분석적 진리와 종합적 진리에 대한 칸트의 구분은 흄과 라이프니츠의 철학보다 앞선다.
④ 라이프니츠는 이성에 의해 참인 진술은 가능한 모든 세계에서 참이어야 한다고 생각했다.

| 분석 | 첫 문장에서 "칸트가 제기한 분석적 진리와 종합적 진리의 차이가 흄과 라이프니츠의 철학에서 이미 예고되었다."고 했으므로, ③은 선후 관계가 뒤바뀐 진술이다. foreshadow는 '예고하다, 전조가 되다'라는 의미인데 지문에서는 수동태로 사용하였음을 주의해야 한다.

49 다음 중 윗글 다음에 올 것으로 가장 적절한 것은? 내용 추론
① 포함의 개념에 대한 설명
② 분석의 정의에 대한 비판
③ 진리의 개념에 대한 설명
✓ 의미의 개념에 대한 논의

| 분석 | 지문의 마지막 문장에서 이러한 방향에 따라 미리 전제된 의미의 개념을 검토해 보자고 했으므로 이어질 내용은 '의미의 개념에 대한 논의'가 적절하다.

[50-52] 2018 홍익대

| 정답 | 50 ④ 51 ② 52 ①

| 어휘 | formulate ⓥ 만들어 내다
in keeping with ~와 조화[일치]하여
discursive ⓐ 종잡을 수 없는; 논증적인
emblem ⓝ 상징
teleological ⓐ 목적론적인
integral ⓐ 필수의, 불가결한
Vitruvian Man 비트루비우스적 인간(인체비례도)
dictum ⓝ 격언, 속담
uphold ⓥ (원칙 등을) 지지하다
Humanism ⓝ 인본주의
ordain ⓥ (운명을 미리) 정하다
creed ⓝ 교리; 주의
double up ~로도 또한 사용되다
boundless ⓐ 무한한
doctrine ⓝ 교리; 주의, 견해
intrinsically ⓐⓓ 본질적으로

predicate ⓥ (사실 등에) ~의 근거를 두다(on), ~에 걸려 있다
classical Antiquity 고전고대(서양의 고전 문화를 꽃피운 고대 그리스·로마 시대의 총칭으로, 호메로스가 읊은 미케네 문명 시대로부터 로마 제국 쇠퇴기까지의 약 2,000년)　coincide with ~와 부합하다[일치하다]
hegemonic ⓐ 패권주의적인, 패권을 장악한, 헤게모니의
self-aggrandizing ⓐ 자기 과시하는　geo-political ⓐ 지정학적인
espouse ⓥ 지지하다, 옹호하다　celebrated ⓐ 유명한
fascism ⓝ 파시즘(절대 권력을 쥔 독재자가 이끄는 정치 체제)

rendition ⓝ 번역; 표현
mutation ⓝ 변화; 돌연변이
canonize ⓥ 찬양하다
attribute ⓝ 특성, 속성
self-reflexivity ⓝ 자기 반영성, 자기 성찰성

전문해석

그 모든 것의 시작에는 그가 있는데, 그는 맨 처음 프로타고라스(Protagoras)에 의해 '만물의 척도'라고 공식화되었고, 나중에 이탈리아 르네상스에서 보편적인 모델로 갱신되고, 레오나르도 다빈치(Leonardo da Vinci)의 비트루비우스적 인간(인체비례도)에서 표현된 '인간'에 대한 고전적 이상(고전적으로 이상적인 모습의 인간)이다. 그것은 신체적 완벽함의 이상인데, mens sana in corpore sano(건강한 신체에 건전한 정신을)라는 고전 속담과 조화를 이루어, 일련의 지적, 논증적, 정신적인 가치들의 집합으로도 통한다. 그들은 인간에게 있는 '인간적인' 것이 무엇인가에 대한 특정 견해를 다 함께 지지한다. 게다가, 그들은 인간이 그들의 개인적, 집단적 완전성을 추구할 수 있는 거의 무한한 능력을 흔들림 없이 확실하게 주장한다. 그 성스러운 상(이상적 인간의 상)은 인간 능력들의 생물학적, 논증적, 도덕적 확장을 결합하여 목적론적으로 정해진, 합리적인 진보 사상으로 만들어 내는 하나의 주의(교리)로서의 인본주의의 상징이다. 인간의 이성이 가진 특유하고 자율적이며, 본질적으로 도덕적인 능력에 대한 믿음은 고도로 인본주의적인 이 교리(신조)의 핵심적인 한 부분을 형성하며, 이 교리는 본질적으로 고전적 고대와 이탈리아 르네상스의 이상을 18세기와 19세기에 와서 번역한 것에 바탕을 두고 있다.

이 모델은 개인들뿐 아니라 그들의 문화에 대해서도 기준을 정해 준다. 인본주의는 역사적으로 하나의 문명적 모델로 발전했으며, 이 문명적 모델은 유럽을 자기 성찰적 이성의 보편화 능력과 부합하는 것으로 보는 특정한 유럽 개념을 형성했다. 인본주의적 이상이 하나의 패권주의적 문화 모델로 바뀌는 변화는 헤겔(Hegel)의 역사철학에 의해 찬양받았다. 이 자기확장적 시각에서는 유럽은 하나의 지정학적 위치일 뿐 아니라, 그것의 특성을 적절한 그 어느 대상에도 줄 수 있는 인간 지성의 보편적인 속성이기도 하다고 가정한다. 이것은 에드문트 후설(Edmund Husserl)이 자신의 유명한 에세이 '유럽과학의 위기(The Crisis of European Sciences)'에서 지지한 견해로, 이 수필은 1930년대 유럽 파시즘의 커져 가는 위협으로 상징되는 지적, 도덕적 쇠락에 대항하여 이성의 보편적 능력을 열정적으로 옹호한 글이다. 후설의 견해에 의하면, 유럽은 스스로를 비판적 이성과 자기성찰성의 발생지로 선언하는데, 이 두 특성은 모두 인본주의적 기준(규범)에 기초해 있다.

---

50 다음 중 인간에 대한 다른 세 가지 견해와 관련이 없는 것은? 내용 파악

① 무한한 인간의 능력을 주장하는 주의
② 비트루비우스적 인간(인체비례도)
③ 만물의 척도
✓ ④ 파시즘의 위협으로 상징되는 도덕적 쇠락

| 분석 | ①, ②, ③은 모두 인간에 대한 인본주의적 견해임에 반해, ④는 반인본주의적 견해이다. 따라서 ④가 정답이다.

---

51 윗글에서 저자는 왜 에드문트 후설의 에세이를 언급하는가? 내용 파악

① 그가 유럽의 인본주의의 마지막 계승자라는 것을 주장하기 위해
✓ ② 고전적인 이상이 근현대적 기준에 미친 영향을 설명하기 위해
③ 비판적 이성과 자기성찰성이라는 특성들의 예를 제시하기 위해
④ 인본주의의 상징적인 이미지를 설명하기 위해

| 분석 | 둘째 단락 첫 문장인 '이 모델'은 첫 단락에서 언급한 인간에 대한 고전적 이상과 생각(인본주의)을 말한다. 이 인본주의적 인간 개념이 (근현대) 유럽 문화에 기준으로 적용되어, 유럽이 자기성찰적 이성의 보편화 능력과 부합하며, 유럽이 마치 인간 지성의 보편적인 속성인 것으로 생각되며, 유럽에서 탄생했다고 하는 '비판적 이성'과 '자기성찰성'이라는 두 특성도 인본주의적 기준(규범)에 기초해 있는 것이 되는데, 이러한 생각을 지지하는 것이 후설이다. 따라서 작가는 ② '인간에 대한 고전적 이상이 근현대 유럽 문화의 기준에 미친 영향을 설명하기 위해' 후설의 에세이를 언급하고 있다고 할 수 있다. ③ 후설의 에세이가 비판적 이성과 자기성찰성이라는 특성들의 예를 들고 있는 것은 아니다.

52 윗글에 의하면, 다음 중 옳은 것은? 내용 일치

✓ 레오나르도 다빈치는 '인간'에 대한 보편적인 모델을 고전적 고대로부터 물려받았다.
② 이탈리아 르네상스의 사상들은 고전적 고대와 상반된다.
③ 헤겔은 인본주의 이상이 패권주의 모델로 바뀌는 변화와 관련이 없다.
④ 인본주의는 보편적인 기준들과는 아무런 관련이 없다.

| 분석 | 첫 문장에서 '인간'에 대한 고전적 이상은 맨 처음 프로타고라스에 의해 '만물의 척도'라고 공식화되고, 나중에 레오나르도 다빈치의 비트루비우스적 인간(인체비례도)에서 표현되었다고 했으므로 이것은 레오나르도 다빈치의 '인간'에 대한 모델은 고전 고대로부터 물려 받았다고 할 수 있다. 따라서 ①이 지문과 일치하는 내용이다. ② 고전적인 이상은 이탈리아의 르네상스로 갱신된 것이다. ③ "인본주의적 이상이 패권주의적 문화 모델로 바뀌는 변화는 헤겔의 역사철학에 의해 찬양받았다."고 했다. ④ 인간에 대한 고전적인 이상은 이탈리아의 르네상스에서 보편적인 모델로 갱신되었다고 했고 이런 고전적으로 이상적인 인간의 성스러운 상은 인본주의의 상징이라고 했다.

| 배경지식 | 인본주의(Humanism): 흔히 다음과 같이 세 가지로 나누어 생각하는 경향이 많다. 1. 인간의 고통을 극소화하고 복지를 증진시키려는 모든 도덕적·사회적 운동을 통칭하는 것으로 이해되는 경우가 많다. 2. 신이나 자연이 숭배의 대상이 아니라, 오직 인간성(humanity)만이 존귀하다고 믿는 실증주의적 인간성 숭배의 사상을 일컫는 경우도 있다. 3. 예수 그리스도의 신성(神性)을 부인하고 그 인격성(人格性)만을 주장하는 신학사상을 일컫는 말로도 사용된다.

7강 교육 / 심리

01	①	02	④	03	④	04	④	05	③	06	①	07	①	08	②	09	③	10	④
11	④	12	②	13	④	14	②	15	③	16	③	17	①	18	④	19	④	20	④
21	⑤	22	⑤	23	③	24	④	25	①	26	①	27	③	28	②	29	④	30	①
31	②	32	③	33	④	34	③	35	③	36	④	37	①	38	④	39	③	40	②
41	④	42	③	43	③	44	④	45	①	46	④	47	②	48	①	49	③	50	④
51	④																		

[01-03] 2021 세종대

| 정답 | 01 ①   02 ④   03 ④

| 어휘 |
people-pleasing 사람들 비위 맞추기
depletion ⓝ 수분 감소, 고갈, 소모
egocentric ⓐ 자기중심의, 이기적인
brake ⓝ 제동(을 거는 것), 제동장치
there is a fine line between A and B A와 B는 종이 한 장 차이다
people pleaser ⓝ 남의 비위를 맞추는 사람
validation ⓝ 확인, 비준
a slew of 많은

전문해석

사회적 존재로서, 다른 사람들과 잘 지내는 것은 우리의 본성이다; 우리의 생존과 성공은 그것에 달려 있다. 그러나 건강한 사회적 행동과 만성적인 비위 맞추기로 인한 정서적 고갈의 경험은 종이 한 장 차이다. 만성적인 비위 맞추기의 일반적인 징후와 그것을 극복하는 몇 가지 방법이 있다. [A]

사회 심리학자인 수잔 뉴먼(Susan Newman)에 따르면, 사람들은 주변의 모든 사람들이 행복하기를 원하고, 그들은 그것을 유지하기 위해 그들에게 요구되는 모든 것을 할 것이라고 한다.

남의 비위를 맞추는 사람들은 누군가가 그들에게 도움을 요청할 때 종종 ⓐ 예라고 말해야 한다고 느낀다. 이것은 그들이 중요하게 느끼고 다른 사람의 삶에 기여하는 것처럼 느끼게 만든다. 그들은 ⓑ 아니요라고 말할 때 다른 사람들이 그들을 어떻게 볼 것인지 걱정한다. 사람들은 게으르고, 이기적이거나, 완전히 자기중심적으로 보이고 싶지 않다. 그들은 친구든, 가족이든, 동료든, 자신이 미움을 받고 그 집단으로부터 단절될 것을 두려워한다. [B]

남의 비위를 맞추는 사람들은 외부의 검증을 갈망한다. 사람들의 개인적인 안정감과 자신감은 다른 사람들의 승인을 얻는 것에 기반한다고 임상 심리학자 린다 틸먼(Linda Tillman)은 말했다. 결과적으로, 남의 비위를 맞추는 사람들은 핵심적으로 자신감이 부족하다고 그녀는 말했다. [C]

남의 비위를 맞추는 많은 사람들은 사람들의 비위를 맞추는 것이 심각한 위험을 가질 수 있다는 것을 깨닫지 못하고 있다. 그것은 그들에게 많은 압박과 스트레스를 줄 뿐만 아니라 근본적으로 그들은 너무 많이 남의 비위를 맞춰서 스스로를 아프게 할 수 있다.
03 ④
[D] [여기 당신이 남의 비위를 맞추는 사람이 되는 것을 그만두는 것을 돕기 위한 많은 전략들이 있다. 누군가 당신에게 부탁을 할 때마다 당신은 항상 거절할 수 있는 선택권이 있다는 것을 기억하라. 당신의 우선순위를 설정하라. 당신의 우선순위와 가치를 아는 것은 남의 비위를 맞추는 것에 제동을 걸도록 도와준다.]

01 빈칸 Ⓐ와 Ⓑ에 가장 적절한 단어로 짝지어진 것은? 빈칸 추론

✓① 예 : 아니요
② 예 : 네
③ 아니요 : 아니요
④ 아니요 : 예

| 분석 | 본문 세 번째 단락의 내용으로 미루어 보아 빈칸 Ⓐ의 경우 남의 비위를 맞추는 사람들은 누군가 도움을 요청했을 때 승낙해야만 다른 사람의 삶에 기여하는 것처럼 느끼게 만들 것이므로 '네'가 적절하다. 빈칸 Ⓑ는 뒤 내용에서 사람들이 이기적으로 보이고 싶어 하지 않는다고 했으므로 그들이 '아니요'라고 말했을 때 다른 사람들이 그들을 어떻게 생각할지를 걱정할 것임을 유추할 수 있다. 따라서 보기 ①이 정답으로 가장 적절하다.

02 주어진 단락이 들어가기에 가장 적절한 곳은? 문장 삽입

> 여기 당신이 남의 비위를 맞추는 사람이 되는 것을 그만두는 것을 돕기 위한 많은 전략들이 있다. 누군가 당신에게 부탁을 할 때마다 당신은 항상 거절할 수 있는 선택권이 있다는 것을 기억하라. 당신의 우선순위를 설정하라. 당신의 우선순위와 가치를 아는 것은 남의 비위를 맞추는 것에 제동을 걸도록 도와준다.

① [A] ② [B]
③ [C] ✓④ [D]

| 분석 | 본문 마지막 단락 첫 문장에서 '남의 비위를 맞추는 많은 사람들은 사람들의 비위를 맞추는 것이 심각한 위험을 가질 수 있다는 것을 깨닫지 못하고 있다.'고 했다. 글의 흐름상 일반적으로 작가의 문제 제기 후 해결 방안을 모색하는 내용이 오는 것이 자연스럽기 때문에 본문 가장 마지막 문장에 해당 내용을 삽입하는 것이 바람직하다. 따라서 정답은 보기 ④다.

03 다음 중 윗글에서 유추할 수 있는 것은? 내용 추론

① 남의 비위를 맞추는 것은 사회적 존재로서 인간의 건강한 사회적 행동 중 하나다. — 본문에서는 남의 비위를 맞추는 것을 극복해야 하는 것으로 설명함
② 수잔 뉴먼은 사람들을 행복하게 하는 몇 가지 팁을 제공했다. — 행복하기 위한 팁은 본문에 언급되지 않음
③ 린다 틸먼에 따르면, 낮은 자신감이 만성적으로 남의 비위를 맞추는 것의 유일한 이유라고 한다. — 네 번째 단락에서 낮은 자신감 뿐만 아니라 외부의 검증에 대한 갈망도 이유가 됨을 언급함
✓④ 남의 비위를 맞추는 사람들은 자신에게 많은 압박과 스트레스를 주는 경향이 있다.

| 분석 | 본문 마지막 두 단락의 내용을 참고하면 남의 비위를 맞추는 사람들은 스스로에게 압박과 스트레스를 더 주는 경향이 있으므로 보기 ④가 정답으로 가장 적절하다.

[04-05] 2012 숙명여대

| 정답 | 04 ④ 05 ③

| 어휘 | **bully** ⓝ (약자를) 괴롭히는 사람 **bullying** ⓝ 집단 따돌림, 학교폭력, 왕따 **school district** 학군(구)
heed ⓥ ~에 조심하다 **gauge** ⓥ (특수 기구를 써서) 측정하다, (남의 기분이나 태도를) 판단하다
quantify ⓥ 양을 표시하다 **avert** ⓥ 방지하다, 피하다 **discipline** ⓝ 규율, 훈육
referral ⓝ (사람을 전문적인 도움을 받을 곳으로) 보내기, 소개 **in that** ~라는 점에서
commitment ⓝ 약속, 전념, 헌신 **deal with** ~을 처리하다, ~을 다루다
write something up (흔히 이미 해 놓은 메모를 바탕으로) ~을 완전히 기록하다

| 전문해석 |

뉴욕주는 학교들이 집단 따돌림에 대해 강경하게 대처할 것을 요구하고 있으며, 지역 학군들로부터 판단할 때 이러한 요구에 주의를 기울이고 있다. 사실, 많은 집단 따돌림 방지 노력들은 수년간 시행되어 왔다. 하지만 관리자들과 교육자들은 그것들의 효과를 측정하는 것이 불가능하지는 않지만 어렵다고 말한다. "이러한 프로그램들로 인해 방지된 사례들을 추적하는 것은 어렵기 때문에, 이것을 <u>수량화하기</u>는 어렵습니다."라고 톰 필립스(Tom Phillips)는 말했다. "우리가 말할 수 있는 것은 더 적은 비율의 학생들이 공식적인 훈육 절차를 통해 다뤄지고 있기 때문에 훈육 의뢰 데이터의 사용을 통해 학교의 분위기가 훨씬 더 긍정적이었다는 것입니다. 이것은 또한 단순히 학생에 대해 평가하여 학교 행정부에 회부하는 것보다 문제가 발생했을 때 그 학생을 다루는 교직원들의 헌신을 말해 줍니다. 교사의 개입과 관여의 영향은 아무리 강조해도 지나치지 않습니다."라고 그는 이메일에서 말했다.

04 윗글의 제목으로 가장 적절한 것은? 제목
① 규율과 처벌
② 학교폭력 가해자, 학교폭력 피해자 그리고 방관자
③ 학교를 바꾸는 왕따, 한 번에 한 명의 아이
④ ✓ 학교폭력 방지 노력을 성공시키는 방법
⑤ 학생들의 글쓰기 보고서 작성의 필요성

| 분석 | 본문에서는 학교폭력 방지 노력들과 정확한 수량화는 어렵지만 그 노력에 성과가 있음을 서술하고 있다. 따라서 보기 ④가 정답으로 가장 적절하다.

05 빈칸에 들어갈 말로 가장 적절한 것은? 빈칸 추론
① 수정하다　　　　　　　② 진행하다
③ ✓ 수량화하다　　　　　④ 포기하다
⑤ 나타내다

| 분석 | 빈칸이 포함된 문장의 직전 문장에서 '그것들의 효과를 측정하는 것이 불가능하지는 않지만 어렵다'고 했다. 따라서 빈칸에도 '측정'과 연관된 표현을 삽입해야 할 것이다. 보기 ③이 정답으로 적절하다.

[06-08] 2017 국민대

| 정답 | 06 ① 　07 ① 　08 ②

| 어휘 | relatively ⓐ 비교적, 상대적으로　　permanent ⓐ 영구적인, 영속적인　　interact ⓥ 상호 작용을 하다
infer ⓥ 추리하다, 추측하다　　demonstrate ⓥ 증거를 들어가며 보여 주다, 입증하다
motor skill 운동 기능[숙달]　　fatigued ⓐ 피로한, 지친　　consistent ⓐ 일관된, 일치하는, 조화되는

| 전문해석 |

학습은 일반적으로 경험과 훈련, 생물학적 과정과의 상호 작용으로 인해 발생하는 행동의 비교적 영구적인 변화라고 여겨진다. <u>학습 과정을 지도하고 학습을 평가하는 데 있어 교사가 가지고 있는 문제 중 하나는 학습을 직접 관찰할 수 없다는 것이다.</u> 학습은 사람의 행동이나 수행으로부터만 추론될 수 있을 것이다. 수행은 관찰 가능한 반면 학습은 관찰 가능하지 않다. 이것은 교사들에게 어려움을 초래하는데, 때로는 학생들이 학습했는데도 학습한 것에 따라 수행하지 않고, 때로는 학습하지 않았지만 마치 학습한 것처럼 수행하기 때문이다. 예를 들어, 학생은 당신이 그 혹은 그녀를 관찰할 때 운동 기술을 수행할 수 있지만 다시 일관된 방식으로 그 기술을 제시할 수 없을 수 있다. ⓐ <u>마찬가지로</u> 학생은 기술을 학습했지만 피곤할 수 있고 운동 기술을 보여 주지 못할 수 있다.

그것이 학습이 이루어졌는지 여부를 결정하는 데 있어서 일관된 관찰 가능한 수행이라는 개념이 중요한 이유이다. 만약 학생들이 능력을 일관되게 시연할 수 없다면, 그들은 아마도 학습하지 못했을 것이다.

07 ①

06 빈칸 ⓐ에 들어가기에 가장 적절한 것은? 빈칸 추론
① 마찬가지로 ✓
② 결과적으로
③ 놀랍게도
④ 그럼에도 불구하고

| 분석 | 본문 다섯 번째 문장에서 학습과 수행이 꼭 일치하지 않는다는 내용을 서술한 후 이어지는 내용은 그 예시가 소개되었다. 빈칸 직전과 빈칸 이후 문장은 모두 예시에 해당되며 유사한 내용이므로 역접표현이나 인과관계로는 볼 수 없다. 따라서 보기 ①이 정답으로 적절하다.

07 윗글은 주로 무엇과 관련된 글인가? 소재
① 학습 평가 방법 ✓
② 운동 기술을 정의하는 방법
③ 인간 성과의 일관성
④ 운동 기술 학습의 특징

| 분석 | 본문에서 작가는 학습을 평가하는 방법에 대해 문제를 제기한 후 그 해결방안으로 '일관된 관찰 가능한 수행'이라는 개념을 제시했다. 따라서 소재로는 '학습의 평가'에 대해 언급한 보기 ①이 적절하다.

08 다음 중 윗글에 언급되지 않은 것은? 내용 불일치
① 우리는 학습을 직접 관찰할 수 없다.
② 교사들은 학생들의 수행을 측정하는 데 일관성이 없다. ✓
③ 학습은 경험, 훈련 및 생물학적 과정과의 상호 작용에서 비롯된다.
④ 학생들은 때때로 그들이 성공적으로 배운 운동 기술을 수행하지 못한다.

| 분석 | 본문에서는 '교사들의 일관성 부족'에 대해서는 다루지 않았다. 따라서 보기 ②가 정답으로 적절하다.

[09-10] 2014 서강대

| 정답 | 09 ③　10 ④

| 어휘 | **inasmuch as** ~이므로, ~인 한, ~인 점을 고려하면
disciplinary ⓐ 훈련상의, 규율의, 학문 분야의　　　　　　　　　　**constitute** ⓥ 구성하다, 조직하다
construe ⓥ 해석하다, 추론하다　　**explicit** ⓐ 명백한, 분명한　　**couch** ⓝ 침상, 소파, 잠자리
vague ⓐ 어렴풋한, 막연한, 애매한　　**admonition** ⓝ 훈계, 권고, 충고　　**perpetuate** ⓥ 영속시키다, 불멸하게 하다

전문해석

학교 교육은 주로 언어적 과정이며, 언어는 종종 학생들을 평가하고 차별화하는 무의식적인 수단으로 작용한다. [A] 내용과 학문적인 지식이 언어를 통해 구성되고 제시되므로, 학문적인 주제의 학습은 특정한 의사소통적인 목적을 달성하기 위해 언어적으로 조직된 텍스트를 읽고 쓰는 것을 의미한다. [B] 학교에서, 학생들은 그들이 배운 것과 그들이 생각하는 것을 공유하고 평가하고 더 나아가 도전받거나 지원받을 수 있는 방식으로 보여 주기 위해 언어를 사용할 것으로 기대된다. [C] 〈하지만 언어적 패턴 그 자체가 학생들과 교사들의 관심의 초점이 되는 경우는 드물다.〉 그들의 관심은 전형적으로 그들이 읽고 반응하는 텍스트의 내용에 집중되며 언어가 그 내용을 구성하는 방식에는 집중되지 않는다. 게다가, 언어 사용에 대한 교사들의 기대는 거의 분명하지 않으며, 학교 과제에서 언어 사용과 관련하여 기대되는 많은 것은 "너만의 생각을 말하라"거나 "분명히 하라"는 교사의 모호한 권고들에 여전히 자리 잡고 있다. 글쓰기 과제는 특정한 텍스트 유형이 전형적으로 어떻게 구조화되고 조직화되는지에 대해 학생들에게 명확한 지침 없이 할당된다. [D] 이러한 이유들로 크리스티(1985)는 언어를 학교 교육의 "숨은 교육 과정"이라고 불렀다. 학생들의 능력에 대한 판단은 종종 그들이 그들의 지식을 어떻게 언어로 표현하는지에 기초한다. 이러한 판단을 형성하는 평가, 상담, 그리고 교실에서의 상호 작용은 자주 분명하게 제시되지 않은 가치를 영구화하고 유지시킨다. 이것은 학습의 언어적인 도전에 대한 세심한 분석이 학생들이 직면하는 어려움과 그들이 공부한 주제에 대해 말하고 쓸 때 보여 주는 한계들을 이해하기 위해 중요하다는 것을 암시한다.

09 주어진 문장이 들어가기에 가장 적절한 곳을 고르시오. 문장 삽입

하지만 언어적 패턴 그 자체가 학생들과 교사들의 관심의 초점이 되는 경우는 드물다.

① [A] ② [B]
✓ [C] ④ [D]

| 분석 | 주어진 문장을 삽입해야 할 경우에는 본문에 표시된 각 보기의 앞뒤 내용의 응집성이 부족한 부분을 찾아보고 정답을 결정하도록 한다. 보기 ③인 [C] 뒤에 'their attention'은 앞 문장에 지시사와 호응하는 표현이 필요하지만 본문의 경우에는 누락되어 있다. 따라서 주어진 문장의 '학생들과 교사의 관심'이 'their attention'과 호응하도록 [C]에 주어진 문장을 삽입한다.

10 윗글의 제목으로 가장 적합하지 <u>않은</u> 것은? 제목

① 학교 교육의 언어
② 학교 교육의 숨은 교과 과정
③ 학습의 언어적 과제
✓ 학교 교육에 대한 교과적 지식

| 분석 | 보기 ①, ②, ③의 경우 본문에서 다룬 소재에 해당되지만 ④ '학교 교육에 대한 교과적 지식'은 본문에 서술된 내용이 아니므로 보기 ④가 적합하지 않은 제목이다.

[11-13] 2015 서강대

| 정답 | 11 ④ 12 ② 13 ④

| 어휘 | archaic ⓐ 고풍의, 낡은, 구식의 irreproachable ⓐ 흠잡을 데 없는, 비난할 수 없는, 결점이 없는
accentuate ⓥ 강조하다, 두드러지다, 한층 악화시키다 chimerical ⓐ 공상의, 비현실의, 망상의
coherence ⓝ 부착성, 응집성, 일관성 fixation ⓝ 고착, 고정, 집착 pathology ⓝ 병리학, 병리, 병상

전문해석

18세기가 아이를 구성하는 것, 즉 아이들의 발달에 뒤따랐던 교육 규칙들, 즉 아이에게 적합한 세계에 관심을 가졌을 때, 아이들 주변에 어른의 세계와 아무런 관련이 없는 비현실적이고 추상적이고 고풍의 환경을 형성하는 것이 가능해졌다. 어른의 갈등으로부터 아이를 보호하려는 반박할 수 없는 목표를 가진 현대 교육의 전체적인 발전은 한 사람에게 아이로서의 그의 삶과 어른으로서의 그의 삶을 분리시키는 거리를 강조한다. 다시 말해, 아이들에게 갈등을 피하게 함으로써, 그것은 그를 주요한 갈등, 즉 어린 시절과 그의 실제 삶 사이의 모순에 노출시킨다. 만약 누군가가 교육 제도들에서, 어떤 문화가 그것의 모든 갈등과 모순을 가지고 그것의 현실을 직접적으로 투영하는 것이 아니라, 그것을 변명하고 정당화하고 그것을 Ⓐ 현실과 동떨어진 일관성으로 이상화하는 신화를 통해 현실을 간접적으로 반영한다고 덧붙인다면, 만약 누군가가 그것의 교육에서 어떤 사회가 그것의 황금기를 꿈꾼다고 덧붙인다면, 집착과 병적인 되보는 단지 주어진 문화에서만 가능하며, 그것들이 과거 경험의 현재 내용으로의 동화를 허용하지 않는 범위 내에서 급격하게 증가한다는 것을 이해하게 된다.

---

11 빈칸 Ⓐ에 가장 적절한 단어를 고르시오. `빈칸 추론`

① 진짜의
② 일치하는
③ 현존하는
✓ ④ 현실과 동떨어진

| 분석 | 빈칸 앞 동사의 병렬구조를 감안하여 빈칸을 추론해 본다. 현실을 변명하고, 정당화하고 이상화하는 것은 일관성이 현실과 거리감이 있다는 것을 반영한다. 따라서 보기 ④가 정답으로 가장 적절하다.

---

12 윗글에 따르면, 왜 어린 시절은 주요한 갈등을 일으키는가? `세부 내용 일치`

① 아이들은 그들이 가장하는 것만큼 순수하지 않다.
✓ ② 어린 시절은 과거와 현재 사이에 갈라진 틈을 만든다.
③ 어린 시절은 성인기와 다르지 않다.
④ 아이들은 병적인 퇴행으로 가득 차 있다.

| 분석 | 본문 두 번째와 세 번째 문장에서 현대 교육의 발전은 어린 시절과 성인기의 현실을 분리시킨다고 서술했다. 따라서 보기 ②가 정답으로 적절하다.

---

13 다음 중 윗글의 내용과 일치하지 않는 것은? `내용 불일치`

① 18세기 교육 기관들은 유년기와 성인기를 분리했다.
② 어린 시절은 고대 황금기와 관련이 있다.
③ 성인기는 어린 시절보다 더 실제적인 것으로 추정된다.
✓ ④ 어린 시절은 본질적으로 갈등이 부족하다.

| 분석 | 본문 세 번째 문장에 따르면 아이들에게 갈등을 피하게 할 수는 있지만 어린 시절에 본질적으로 갈등이 부족하다는 것은 언급되지 않았다. 따라서 보기 ④가 일치하지 않는 진술이다.

[14-15] 2020 항공대

| 정답 | 14 ② 15 ②

| 어휘 | extensive ⓐ 광범위한, 폭넓은   bisociation ⓝ 이연 연상(무관해 보이는 두 개념을 연결해서 생각하는 것)

coincidence ⓝ 우연의 일치, 부합	**self-consistent** ⓐ 사리에 맞는, 자기모순이 없는	
incompatible ⓐ 양립할 수 없는, 모순되는	**frame of reference** (행동이나 판단을 지배하는) 준거 기준	
intersect ⓥ 가로지르다, 교차하다	**vibrate** ⓥ 진동하다, 흔들리다	**associative** ⓐ 연합하는
novelty ⓝ 신기함, 새로움	**induce** ⓥ 설득하다, 야기하다, 유발하다	**cognitive** ⓐ 인식[인지]의
exceptional ⓐ 예외적인, 이례적인 뛰어난	**discharge** ⓝ 방사, 방출, 해방	**far-reaching** ⓐ 멀리까지 미치는, 광범위한
disparate ⓐ 다른, 공통점이 없는	**expansive** ⓐ 포괄적인	**traverse** ⓥ 가로지르다, 횡단하다
exhilaration ⓝ 들뜬 기분, 유쾌, 흥분		

전문해석

*The Act of Creation*에서, 심리학자 아서 쾨슬러(Arthur Koestler)는 불연속적 아이디어들의 우연적 일치를 전달하기 위해 이연 연상이라는 용어를 도입함으로써 인간의 창조적 과정에 대한 그의 광범위한 연구를 요약했다. 그는 창조적 행위를 어떤 상황이나 아이디어, 즉 L을, 자기 일관적이지만 습관적으로 양립할 수 없는 두 가지 준거의 틀에서 인식하는 것으로 설명했다. 두 준거의 틀이 교차하는 사건 L은, 원래 그랬듯이, 두 가지 다른 파장에서 동시에 진동하도록 만들어진다. 이 상황이 지속되는 동안, L은 단지 하나의 연상 맥락에만 연결되는 것이 아니라, 두 가지 맥락과 이중 연상된다. 창조적 아이디어에서 우리가 가치를 두는 것은 단지 그것들의 겉보기의 새로움이 아니다. 새로움 그 자체는 그것이 인지적 매체에 새로운 연결 경로, 즉 장을 여는 효과를 가지고 있고 이것이 예외적인 에너지의 방출을 요구할 수도 있기 때문에 흥분을 유발한다. 그러나 이러한 경험을 하고 나면 흥분은 수명이 짧아질 수도 있다—일단 개방된 경로들은 같은 방식으로 다시 열 수 없다. 더 풍부한 창조적 행위는 이질적인 개념들을 연결하는 복잡하고 광범위한 새로운 경로를 여는 것에 있는데, 경로의 수가 더 많을수록 흥분의 수준도 더 커진다. 쾨슬러의 용어로는, 여러 이연 연상들을 증식시킨다. 만약 우리의 존재감이 적어도 부분적으로, 활발한 정신 상태의 존재에 의존한다면, 더 활발한 정신 상태가 더 광범위한 인식 또는 존재감을 만들어 내는 것이라는 결론이 따른다. 그리고 정신 상태가 언제든지 더 다양하고 복잡할수록, 그것들을 횡단하기 위해 더 많은 상응하는 에너지가 요구되므로, 그러므로 육체적인 흥분이 더 커질 것이다.

14 다음 중 윗글의 제목으로 가장 적절한 것은? 제목

① 이중 연상된 흥분의 부정적인 영향
☑ ② 새로움과 흥분의 탄생
③ 인지적 매개체와 연상 맥락
④ 에너지의 복잡한 물리적 특징

| 분석 | 본문에서는 창조적 과정에 대한 아서 쾨슬러의 연구를 소개했다. 그에 따르면, '새로움'이 인지적 매체에 새로운 경로들을 만들어 내고 '흥분'을 유발한다고 했다. 따라서 본문의 소재는 '새로움'과 '흥분'이 모두 언급되어야 하고 보기 ②가 정답으로 적절하다.

15 다음 중 윗글에서 추론할 수 있는 것은? 내용 추론

① 불연속적인 아이디어들을 연결하는 인간의 능력에는 한계가 있다. 인간은 창조적 행위를 통해 불연속적 아이디어들을 연결할 수 있음
☑ ② 창의성은 완전히 새로운 어떤 것을 생산하는 데 반드시 포함되지 않는다.
③ 파괴는 창조의 반대 극단이다. 관련된 언급 없음
④ 과학적으로 측정되지 않는 한, 창의적 사고 그 자체는 거의 쓸모가 없다. 창의적 사고를 통해 광범위한 인식이나 존재감을 만들어 낼 수 있다고 언급했고 과학적 측정 여부와 가치와의 관련성은 언급하지 않음

| 분석 | 본문 다섯 번째 문장에서 '창조적 아이디어에서 우리가 가치를 두는 것은 단지 그것들의 겉보기의 새로움이 아니다'라고 했고 여덟 번째 문장에서는 '더 풍부한 창조적 행위는 이질적인 개념들을 연결하는 복잡하고 광범위한 새로운 경로를 여는 것'에 있다고 했다. 따라서 창의성이란 새로운 것의 생산에만 국한되지는 않는 것으로 보기 ②가 윗글에서 추론할 수 있는 진술이다.

[16-17] 2016 국민대

| 정답 | 16 ③　17 ①

| 어휘 | **nervous disorder** 신경쇠약, 신경질환　　**engagement** ⓝ 약속, 맹세, 약혼
embark ⓥ (배에) 승선하다, 착수하다, 시작하다

전문해석

지그문트 프로이트(Sigmund Freud)는 결코 심리학자로 출발하지 않았다. 더구나 그는 말년까지 자신을 사회 심리학 분야에 기여한 것으로 여기지 않았다. 그는 단순히 ⓐ 신경 장애의 치료를 전문으로 하는 비엔나의 내과의사였다. ⓑ 이 활동이 그를 ⓒ 사회적 행동을 이해하는 근본적으로 새로운 방식으로 이끌 것이라는 것은 그가 ⓓ 이 작업을 하고 있을 때 프로이트가 상상하지 못했던 것이었다.

사실, 프로이트는 그가 그의 개업하기 전에 이미 서른 살이었다. 그리고 개업한 이유는 원래 과학적이라기보다는 재정적이었다. 4년의 약혼 기간 이후, 프로이트는 1886년 가을에 마사 버네이스(Martha Bernays)와 결혼했다. 그는 그와 그의 아내가 시작하게 될 새로운 가족뿐만 아니라 그의 부모님을 위한 지원을 제공할 필요가 있었다. 개선된 재정적인 안정성을 찾기 위해, 지그문트 프로이트가 개인 의사로서의 그의 경력을 시작한 것은 바로 이 시기였다.

16 다른 것들과 의미가 같지 않은 것은? 무관한 단어

① ⓐ
② ⓑ
✓③ ⓒ
④ ⓓ

| 분석 | 보기 ①, ②, ④는 프로이트의 신경 장애 치료를 가리키며 ③만 다른 의미이다.

17 윗글에 따르면 다음 중 옳은 것은? 내용 일치

✓① 어떤 면에서 그의 재정적인 상황은 프로이트가 개인 의사가 되도록 강요했다.
② 프로이트는 자신을 사회 심리학 분야의 기여자로 보지 않았다. 말년까지는 사실이나 그 이후에 관한 언급은 없음
③ 처음부터 프로이트는 인간의 정신을 이해하는 선구자가 되기로 결심했다. 본문 첫 문장에서 프로이트는 심리학자로 경력을 시작하지 않았음을 언급함
④ 불행하게도 프로이트의 결혼은 그가 중요한 심리학 연구를 포기하도록 만들었다. 결혼 때문에 심리학 연구를 포기한 것은 언급되지 않았음

| 분석 | 본문 두 번째 단락 첫 문장에서 프로이트가 '개업한 이유는 원래 과학적이라기보다는 재정적이었다.'고 했다. 따라서 보기 ① 이 정답으로 적절하다.

| 배경지식 | 지그문트 프로이트(Sigmund Freud): 오스트리아의 생리학자, 정신병리학자, 정신분석의 창시자로 무의식과 억압의 방어기제에 대한 이론, 환자와 정신분석자의 대화를 통해 정신적 병리를 치료하는 정신분석학적 임상 치료 방식을 창안한 것으로 유명함

[18-19] 2018 한양대

| 정답 | 18 ④　19 ④

| 어휘 | **persistence** ⓝ (결과의) 지속, 영속, 고집　　**tolerate** ⓥ 용인하다, (불쾌한 일 등을) 참다
intriguing ⓐ 아주 흥미로운, 흥미[호기심]를 돋우는　　**twist** ⓝ 비틀기, 꾸불꾸불함, (사실의) 왜곡
competence ⓝ 적성, 자격, 능력　　**transactional** ⓐ 업무의, 거래의

전문해석

많은 면에서 장기간의 지속은 우리를 다시 원점으로 되돌려 조정하도록 한다. 장난감이 너무 예측 가능하게 되면, 더 이상 재미가 없다. 만약 유아가 소리를 낼 때마다 부모가 온다면, 부모를 부르는 것에는 노력이 필요하지 않을 것이다. 학습자들을 가장 크게 사로잡는 것은 해결이 가능하지만 쉽지는 않은 도전이다. 그러한 도전을 꿰뚫어 해결책을 찾기 위해서, 젖먹이 혹은 걸음마를 배우는 유아는 어느 정도의 좌절감을 견딜 수 있어야 한다. 성인 파트너(부모)는 아이가 멈춰서 더 많은 정보를 수집할 수 있을 뿐 아니라 집중력과 흥분을 유지할 수 있도록 돕는다. 흥미로운 반전으로, 연구원들은 아이의 역량이 아이를 지원하는데 있어서 어머니의 투자와 만족도에 영향을 미치는지 궁금했다. 그들은 약간의 좌절감을 통해 신체적이고 사회적인 과제를 완수할 수 있는 능력을 측정하기 위해서 6개월과 18개월 된 아이들을 살펴봤다. 그들은 또한 엄마의 만족감과 부모로서의 역량을 측정했다. 유능한 유아들은 자신감 있는 엄마들을 가지고 있었다. 덜 유능한 유아들은 덜 만족하는 엄마들을 가졌다. 이것은 엄마들이 너무 높은 기대치를 가졌거나 혹은 아이들의 노력을 지원해 주기 위한 더 적은 기술을 가지고 있었기 때문이다. 어느 쪽이든, 그것은 학습에 대한 이러한 접근 방식에 <u>거래적인</u> 특성이 있을 수 있음을 암시한다.

18 윗글의 빈칸에 들어갈 말로 가장 적절한 것은? 빈칸 추론

① 생물학적
② 인본주의적인
③ 불가역의
✓ ④ 거래적인

| 분석 | 본문 마지막 두 문장의 내용을 참고하여 빈칸을 유추한다. 학습에 있어서 아이의 유능성과 엄마의 만족감 사이에는 관련이 있으므로 빈칸에는 '두 대상이 서로 영향을 주고받는다'는 의미가 포함된 표현을 선택하도록 한다. 보기 ④의 경우 '거래적'이란 '두 대상이 교류하는 것'을 의미하므로 빈칸에 가장 적절하다.

19 윗글의 내용과 일치하지 <u>않는</u> 것은? 내용 불일치

① 장난감이 더 기대될수록, 아이는 덜 즐겁다.
② 아이들의 능력은 엄마들의 만족도와 관련이 있다.
③ 학습자가 해결이 가능하지만 쉽지는 않은 해결책을 찾기 위해서는 좌절감을 참는 것이 필요하다.
✓ ④ 성인 파트너는 유아가 당면한 과제에 대한 답을 찾을 수 있도록 즉시 지원해야 한다.

| 분석 | 본문 3~6번째 문장을 참고하여 일치하지 않는 진술을 찾아본다. 본문 세 번째 문장에서 '유아가 소리를 낼 때마다 부모가 온다면, 부모를 부르는 것에는 노력이 필요하지 않을 것이다.'라고 서술했고 여섯 번째 문장에서는 '성인 파트너(부모)는 아이가 멈춰서 더 많은 정보를 수집할 수 있을 뿐 아니라 집중력과 흥분을 유지할 수 있도록 도와주는 것이다.'라고 했다. 따라서 본문의 내용상 부모의 즉각적인 개입이나 지원은 부적절한 것이며 보기 ④는 일치하지 않는 진술이다.

[20-21] 2015 성균관대

| 정답 | 20 ④   21 ⑤

| 어휘 | intrigued ⓐ 아주 흥미로워하는, 궁금해하는   gratification ⓝ 만족감   confection ⓝ 당과 제품, 정교한 것
fret ⓥ 조마조마하다, 조바심치다   attainment ⓝ 성과, 성취, 달성

전문해석

연구자들은 만족감을 피하거나 미루는 능력이 삶의 결과와 관련이 있는지에 대해 오랫동안 관심을 가져 왔다. 가장 잘 알려진 실험은 "마시멜로" 실험인데, 이 실험에서 15분 동안 과자를 먹는 것을 자제할 수 있었던 아이들에게만 두 번째 과자가 주어졌다. 기다릴 수 없었던 아이들은 성인이 되면서 낮은 수입과 좋지 않은 건강 상태를 가지는 경향이 있었다. 스톡홀름 대학의 데이비드 린달(David Lindahl) 박사는 스웨덴의 한 조사에서 나온 자료를 사용했는데, 조사에서는 13,000명의 13세 아이들에게 지금 140달러를 받고 싶은지 아니면 5년 후에 1,400달러를 받고 싶은지를 물어보았다. 그들 중 약 5분의 4가 기다릴 준비가 되었다고 말했다. 이전의 연구자들과는 달리, 린달 박사는 모든 아이들을 추적할 수 있었고, 아이들 부모의 배경과 인지 능력을 확인할 수 있었다. 그는 더 적은 액수의 돈을 즉시 원하는 13세 아이들이 더 큰 보상을 기다리겠다고 한 아이들보다 향후 18년 동안 범죄로 유죄 판결을 받을 가능성이 32% 더 높다는 것을 발견했다. 그는 성급한 사람들은 즉각적인 혜택을 선호하기 때문에 잠재적인 처벌에 의해 단념될 가능성이 낮다고 믿는다. 하지만 한 사람의 범죄 경로가 이미 청소년기에 설정되어 있다고 조바심을 가지는 사람들은 절망해서는 안 된다. 린달 박사는 해결책을 제시한다. 응답자들의 교육이 분석에 포함되었을 때, 그는 더 높은 교육적 성취가 지연된 만족에 대한 선호와 연결되어 있다는 것을 발견했다. "따라서 저는 학교 교육이 사람들로 하여금 미래에 더 가치를 두도록 만듦으로써 범죄를 저지르는 것을 막을 수 있다고 생각합니다"라고 린달 박사는 설명한다.

---

20 윗글의 최상의 제목은 _____ 일 것이다. 【제목】

① 유혹과 처벌
② 인간의 행동과 법적 허점
③ 참을성 없는 아이들을 교육하는 방법
✓ ④ 시간 선호와 범죄 행위
⑤ 고등교육의 한계

| 분석 | 본문은 즉각적인 만족과 지연된 만족 중에서 어디에 더 많은 가치를 추구하느냐에 따라 미래의 범죄 경력이 연관될 수 있음을 시사하고 있다. 보기 ④의 '시간 선호'란 '미래보다 현재의 만족을 더 선호하는 것'이다. 따라서 보기 ④가 정답으로 적절하다.

---

21 윗글에 따르면, 린달 박사의 연구는 _____ 주장한다. 【세부 내용 일치】

① 학력과 인내심은 관련이 없다고
② "마시멜로" 실험은 더 이상 어린이의 자기 통제를 효과적으로 측정하는 역할을 하지 않는다고
③ 보상을 미루는 아이들은 나중에 범죄자가 될 가능성이 더 높다고
④ 인내가 항상 미덕은 아닌 것을
✓ ⑤ 학교 교육은 사람들이 보상을 연기할 가능성을 더 많이 만들 수 있는 것이라고

| 분석 | 본문 마지막 두 문장에서 린달 박사의 최종적 주장이 서술되었다. 그 내용은 '학교 교육이 사람들로 하여금 미래에 더 가치를 두도록 만듦으로써 범죄를 저지르는 것을 막을 수 있다'는 것이다. 따라서 보기 ⑤가 정답으로 적절하다.

| 배경 지식 | 시간 선호(Time preference): 미래의 이익과 비교된 현재의 이익을 더 선호하는 것으로 지연된 혜택보다 현재의 이익을 선호하는 개인의 기본적인 심리학적 특징

[22-24] 2014 이화여대

| 정답 | 22 ⑤   23 ③   24 ④

| 어휘 |
phenomenologist ⓝ 현상학자
vantage ⓝ 우월, 유리한 지위, 이익
vantage point ⓝ 유리한 지위[위치], (과거를 생각해 보는) 시점
conducive ⓐ 도움이 되는, 이바지하는
facilitate ⓥ (손)쉽게 하다, 촉진하다
therapeutic ⓐ 치료의, 치료법의
incriminate ⓥ ~에게 죄를 씌우다
articulate ⓐ (말이) 분명히 발음된, (생각이) 명확히 표현된
inhibition ⓝ 금지, 규제, 억제
foster ⓥ 조성하다, 발전시키다
empathy ⓝ 감정이입, 공감

전문해석

대부분의 현대 현상학자들은 자기 보고가 행동에 관한 중요한 모든 것을 드러내지 않을 수도 있고 성격에 관한 완벽한 모습을 보여 주지 않을 수도 있다는 것을 알고 있었다. 사람들은 자신의 행동에 대한 이유를 의식할 수 있지만, 예를 들어, 자신의 감정, 인식, 행동의 측면에 대해 불편하거나 부끄럽다면 보고할 수 없거나 보고하기를 원하지 않을 수도 있다. 혹은 그들은 그들의 경험 전부를 의식하지 않을 수도 있는데, 이 경우에는 그들이 아무리 노력해도 의사소통을 할 수 없다. 로저스(Rogers)와 같은 현상학자들은 그것을 한계로 간주하기보다는 그 또는 그녀를 이해하기 위한 중요한 시점으로서 그 사람의 기준 프레임에 주목한다.

심리학자의 임무는 성장에 ⓐ <u>도움을 주며</u> 치료적 맥락에서 감정과 자신에 대한 자유로운 탐색을 용이하게 하는 조건들을 제공하는 것이다. 이것은 사람들이 자신의 진술이 자신에게 죄를 짓게 하거나 자신의 미래에 대한 부정적인 결정으로 이어질 수 있다고 두려워할 때 자신에 대해 정직하기를 기대할 수 없기 때문이다. 사적인 감정을 더 많이 인식하고 분명히 표현하기 위해서는, 불안과 억제를 감소시키고 자기 공개를 ⓑ <u>촉진시킬 수 있는</u> 위협적이지 않은 분위기가 필요하다. 그래서 현상학적으로 지향적인 심리학자들은 개인이 개방적인 자기 탐색을 위해 더 편안함을 느낄 수 있는 수용, 따뜻함, 공감의 조건을 만들기 위해 노력한다. 이러한 수용 조건은 "환자 중심" 치료에서 생생하게 보여진다. 로저학파 학자들은 환자가 제공하는 데이터의 타당성과는 ⓒ <u>관계없이</u>, 개인이 자신과 자신의 경험을 어떻게 해석하는지 관찰하기 위해 (환자와의) 인터뷰를 활용한다.

22 ⑤

22 윗글에서 유추할 수 있는 진술을 고르시오. 〔내용 추론〕

① 자기 보고는 성격 특성에 대한 중요한 모든 것을 보여 준다. 본문의 첫 문장에서 자기 보고는 성격에 대한 완벽한 모습을 보여 주지 않을 수 있음을 언급함
② 사람들은 그들의 모든 경험을 의식한다. 사람들이 그들의 경험 전부를 의식하지 않을 수도 있음을 언급함
③ 명상은 자기 인식을 향상시키는 방법이다. 본문에 언급 없음
④ 건강한 성격은 개인의 진정성을 숨김으로써 달성된다. 두 번째 단락에서 감정을 더 많이 인식하고 표현하기 위해 자기 공개가 필요함을 언급함
✓ 심리학자들은 그 사람의 자아 개념을 탐구하기 위해 인터뷰를 사용한다.

| 분석 | 본문의 마지막 문장에서 심리학자들은 '개인이 자신과 자신의 경험을 어떻게 해석하는지 관찰하기 위해 (환자와의) 인터뷰를 활용한다.'고 했다. 따라서 보기 ⑤는 유추할 수 있는 진술이다.

23 빈칸 ⓐ와 ⓑ에 들어갈 말이 알맞게 짝지어진 것은? 〔빈칸 추론〕

① 구체적인 – 격려하다
② 전도성의 – 낙담시키다
✓ 도움이 되는 – 촉진하다
④ 도움이 되는 – 제외하다
⑤ 형태상의 – 주춤하게 하다

| 분석 | 본문의 내용에 따르면 빈칸 ⓐ에서 심리학자는 내담자의 성장에 '도움'을 주어야 할 것이며, 그러려면 상담자의 불안이나 억제를 감소시켜서 자기 공개를 '촉진해야' 할 것이다. 따라서 보기 ③이 정답이다.

24 빈칸 ⓒ에 들어갈 말로 가장 적절한 것은? 빈칸 추론

① ~에 의하면
② ~을 희생하여
③ ~에도 불구하고
④ ~에 관계없이 ✓
⑤ ~에 관하여

| 분석 | 빈칸의 앞 내용은 내담자가 제공하는 데이터에 관해 언급했고 빈칸의 뒤 내용은 심리학자의 관찰에 관해 언급했다. 본문의 내용에 따르면 심리학자들은 개인이 자신과 자신의 경험을 어떻게 해석하는지에 더 큰 관심을 갖고 있으므로 내담자 개인이 제공하는 데이터와 심리학자의 판단은 서로 관련이 없을 것이다. 따라서 보기 ④가 정답으로 적절하다.

| 배경지식 | 현상학(Phenomenology): 하이데거(Heidegger), 베커(Becker) 등의 현상학파 학자들의 철학운동을 지칭하는 개념으로, 인간의 의식과 삶의 과정에서 발생하는 다양한 현상을 포착하여 그 본질을 직관적으로 파악하고 기술하려는 움직임을 뜻함

[25-26] 2014 중앙대

| 정답 | 25 ① 26 ①

| 어휘 | **radiograph** ⓝ 방사선 (투과) 사진 **inattentional** ⓐ 부주의한, 무심한 **deliberately** ⓐⓓ 신중히, 일부러
imprudent ⓐ 경솔한, 무분별한, 조심하지 않는 **laypeople** ⓝ 보통사람, 일반인, 평신도
expertise ⓝ 전문가의 의견, 전문적 지식 **anomaly** ⓝ 변칙, 이례, 이상

전문해석

사람들은 종종 예상될 때 쉽게 주목되는 것과 예상되지 않을 때 주목되어야 하는 것을 혼동한다. 병원에서 방사선 사진을 검토할 때 자주 사용되는 절차는 주의 집중의 환상에 영향을 받는다. 의사들이 다른 것을 찾을 때조차도 그들 자신은 또한 이미지에서 예상치 못한 문제를 발견할 것이라고 가정한다. 부주의로 인한 실명의 영향을 줄이기 위해, 눈은 예상치 못한 것을 향한 채로 의도적으로 같은 이미지를 다시 검토할 수 있다. 연구 참가자들이 예기치 않은 일이 일어날 수 있다는 것을 알 때, 그들은 지속적으로 고릴라(실험에서 예상치 못한 물체)를 본다—즉 예상하지 못한 것이 집중된 주의의 목표물이 된 것이다. 그러나 예상치 못한 일에 주의를 기울이는 것이 만병의 치료법은 아니다. 우리는 주의를 집중할 수 있는 자원이 제한되어 있고, 예상치 못한 사건들에 약간의 주의를 기울이는 것은 우리의 주요 작업에 사용할 수 있는 주의가 적다는 것을 의미한다. 방사선과 의사에게 엑스레이에서 예상된 문제를 감지하는 것으로부터 시간과 자원을 빼앗아 그곳에 있을 것 같지 않은 것에 대신 집중하도록 요청하는 것은 경솔한 것이다. 더 효과적인 전략은 이 환자의 사례와 잠정적인 진단에 대해 잘 모르는 두 번째 방사선 의사가 이미지를 검사하고 첫 번째(검사)에서 발견하지 못했을 수 있는 이차적 문제를 찾는 것이다.

그래서 그들의 의학 전문 분야에서 10년간의 훈련을 받은 전문가들조차 그들의 전문 분야에서 예상치 못한 대상을 놓칠 수 있다는 것이 드러났다. 비록 방사선과 의사들이 일반인들보다 방사선 사진의 특이한 측면을 더 잘 감지할 수 있지만, 그들은 다른 사람들과 마찬가지로 주의 집중의 제한을 겪는다. 그들의 전문 지식은 더 큰 집중에 있는 것이 아니라, 영상의 중요한 특징들을 감지하는 데 있어 그들의 경험과 훈련에 의해 형성된 더 정확한 예측에 있다. 경험은 그들이 드문 이상 징후가 아닌 일반적인 문제들을 찾도록 안내하고, 대부분의 경우, 그 전략은 현명하다.

25 윗글의 빈칸에 들어갈 말로 가장 적절한 것은? 빈칸 추론

✓ ① 드문 이상 징후가 아닌 일반적인 문제를 찾다
② 동일한 이미지를 새로운 눈으로 재검토하다
③ 예상된 그리고 예상치 못한 문제들을 모두 감지하다
④ 다른 방사선 전문의의 진단을 듣다

| 분석 | 빈칸 직전의 두 문장에서 방사선과 의사들도 '주의 집중의 제한'을 겪지만 그들의 '경험과 훈련'에 의해 형성된 예측을 한다고 서술했다. 따라서 빈칸은 방사선과 의사들의 전략을 설명하는 내용이 삽입되어야 하고 그들은 특별하지는 않지만 일반인보다는 빈번한 경험을 통해 판단할 것이므로 보기 ①이 정답으로 적절하다.

26 윗글을 통해 추론할 수 있는 것으로 가장 적절한 것은? 내용 추론

✓ ① 우리는 익숙한 작업에 참여할 때 예상치 못한 것을 발견할 가능성이 적다.
② 익숙함은 우리의 주의력 자원을 주요 업무에서 해방시킬 수 있다. 예상치 못한 사건에 주의를 기울일 때 주요 업무에서 주의력이 적어짐을 언급함
③ 숙련된 방사선 전문의 한 명이면 정확한 진단을 받을 수 있다. 방사선 전문의들도 주의 집중의 제한을 겪기 때문에 한 명 이상의 방사선 전문의의 진단의 정확도가 높을 수 있음
④ 집중적인 훈련을 통해 우리의 주의력 자원을 확장할 수 있다. 훈련을 통해 향상되는 것은 예측력임

| 분석 | 본문의 내용에 따르면 일반인이나 의사 모두 주의 집중의 제한을 겪기 때문에 보기 ①이 정답으로 적절하다.

[27 – 28] 2019 숭실대

| 정답 | 27 ③   28 ②

| 어휘 | comprehensive ⓐ 포괄적인, 종합적인   utility ⓝ (수도·전기·가스 같은) 공익사업, 유용성
amass ⓥ 긁어 모으다, (재산을) 축적하다   get in the way of 방해되다, 방해하다   hamper ⓥ 방해하다
reread ⓥ 다시 읽다, 재독하다   summarize ⓥ 요약하여 말하다   write down 적어 놓다, 기록하다
spread out 몸을 뻗다, 더 널리 퍼지다   cram ⓥ 밀어 넣다, 벼락치기 공부를 하다   get through ~을 빠져 나가다[통과하다]
at intervals (시간적·공간적) 간격을 두고   retrieval ⓝ 만회, 복구, 회복

전문해석

최근 심리과학협회가 발표한 종합 보고서에서, 저자들은 10가지 학습 전략을 면밀히 조사하고 자신들이 축적한 증거를 바탕으로 효용이 높은 것부터 낮은 것까지 각각 등급을 매긴다. 여기 보고서의 결론에 대한 간단한 안내가 있다.
중요한 부분을 강조하고 밑줄을 치는 것은 저자들의 비효율적인 학습 전략 목록을 이끌었다. 비록 그것들이 일반적인 관행이지만, 연구들은 그것들이 단순히 본문을 읽는 것 이상의 어떤 이점도 제공하지 않는다는 것을 보여 준다. 일부 연구는 중요 부분을 강조하는 것이 학습을 방해할 수 있다고 심지어 지적한다. 그것이 개별적인 사실에 주의를 끌도록 하기 때문에, 연결성을 만들고 추론을 끌어내는 과정을 방해할 수 있다. 거의 마찬가지로, 다시 읽는 관행, 즉 당신이 사용할 수 있는 더 나은 일부 기술보다 훨씬 덜 효과적인 일반적인 연습도 좋지 않다. 마지막으로, 본문에 포함된 요점을 요약하거나 적는 것은 그것에 숙련된 사람들에게 도움이 될 수 있지만, 다시 말하지만, 당신의 공부 시간을 보내는 훨씬 더 나은 방법들이 있다. 강조하기, 밑줄 치기, 다시 읽기 그리고 요약하기는 모두 저자들에 의해 "낮은 효용"으로 평가되었다.
강조하기, 다시 읽기와 같은 익숙한 관행들Ⓐ 과는 대조적으로 그것들을 뒷받침할 가장 많은 증거가 있는 학습 전략들은 심리학 실험실 밖에는 잘 알려져 있지 않다. 예를 들어, 분산 학습을 살펴보라. 이 전략은 한 번의 마라톤(장시간 학습)에 참여하는 것보다 당신의 학습 시간을 여러 차례로 넓히는 것을 포함한다. 28② 마지막 순간의 벼락치기한 정보는 당신이 그 시험이나 회의를 통과하도록 해 줄 수 있지만, 그 (학습)자료는 기억에서 빠르게 사라질 것이다. 시간이 지남에 따라 간격을 두고 그 자료를 공부하는 것이 훨씬 더 효과적이다. 그리고 2주든 2년이든, 당신이 그 정보를 더 오래 기억하고 싶을수록, 그 간격은 더 길어야 한다.

보고서의 저자들이 강력히 추천하는 두 번째 학습 전략은 연습 시험이다. 그렇다, 더 많은 시험들—그러나 이것들은 성적을 위한 것은 아니다. 연구는 정보를 마음에 새기는 행위만으로도 지식이 강화되고 미래에 (그 정보를) 기억하는 데 도움이 된다는 것을 보여 준다. 분산 학습, 혹은 분산 연습 그리고 연습 시험 모두 저자들에 의해 "높은 유용성"을 가진 것으로 평가되었다.

27 다음 중 Ⓐ에 들어가기에 가장 적절한 것은? 빈칸 추론
① ~을 대신해서
② ~에 더하여
✓ ~와는 대조적으로
④ ~을 대신하여

| 분석 | 빈칸 Ⓐ 뒤에는 효율이 낮은 익숙한 관행이 소개되나, 주절에서는 실험실 밖에서 잘 알려져 있지 않은 학습전략으로 '분산 학습'이나 '연습 시험'에 대해 서술하고 있으므로 서로 대조를 이룬다. 따라서 빈칸은 보기 ③이 적절하다.

28 다음 중 사실이 아닌 것은? 내용 불일치
① 저자들의 비효율적인 학습 전략 목록에는 사람들 사이에서 가장 인기 있는 학습 전략이 포함되어 있다.
✓ 가장 효과적인 학습 전략은 일반 대중에게 잘 알려져 있다.
③ 연습 시험은 향후 정보 검색에 도움이 된다.
④ 단기의 집중적인 노력은 장기의 광범위한 노력보다 지식을 유지하는 데는 덜 효율적이다.

| 분석 | 본문 세 번째 단락의 첫 문장에서 '강조하기, 다시 읽기와 같은 익숙한 관행들과는 대조적으로 그것들을 뒷받침할 가장 많은 증거가 있는 학습 전략들은 심리학 실험실 밖에는 잘 알려져 있지 않다.'고 했다. 따라서 보기 ②는 사실이 아니다.

[29-30] 2016 명지대

| 정답 | 29 ④ 30 ①

| 어휘 |
devour ⓥ 걸신들린 듯 먹다, 집어삼키다, 파괴하다
drain ⓥ (액체를) 배출시키다, 빼내다
fridge ⓝ 냉장고
temptation ⓝ 유혹, 유혹함
persevere ⓥ 인내하며 계속하다
geometry ⓝ 기하학
ubiquitous ⓐ (동시에) 도처에 있는
craving ⓝ 갈망, 열망
superficial ⓐ 깊이 없는, 얄팍한, 피상적인
stiff drink 독한 술
intriguing ⓐ 흥미를 자아내는
depletion ⓝ 고갈, 소모
insoluble ⓐ 해결할 수 없는, 녹지 않는, 불용성의
reserve ⓝ 비축, 저장; 예비
lubricant ⓝ 미끄럽게 하는 것, 윤활유
get even with ~에 앙갚음하다, 원수를 갚다
tub ⓝ 통, 대야
raid ⓥ 불시에 들이닥치다
succumb ⓥ 굴복하다, 압도되다
radish ⓝ 무
subsequent ⓐ 뒤의, 차후의
culprit ⓝ 죄인, 범죄자

전문해석
스트레스가 많은 시험이나 면접을 끝내고 나와서 아이스크림 한 통을 다 먹을 수 있다고 생각해 본 적이 있는가? 혹은 아마도 당신을 (감정적으로) 지치게 한 감상적인 영화를 보고 난 후일 것이다. 왜 스트레스가 많은 경험을 견디는 많은 사람들은 독한 술을 원하거나 혹은 지방과 당분이 많은 음식을 찾아 냉장고를 급습하기를 원할까? 한 가지 흥미로운 생각은 우리가 이러한 유혹에 굴복했을 때, 자아 고갈을 경험하고 있다는 것이다.
자아 고갈은 미국의 심리학자 로이 바우마이스터(Roy Baumeister)로부터 비롯되었는데, 그는 스트레스를 주는 것을 견디는 것은 의지력을 소진시켜 오히려 그렇지 않다면 피했을 유혹에 굴복하게 한다고 믿었다. 그의 연구 중 하나에서, 그는 배고픈 학생들이 맛있는 초콜릿 쿠키보다 쓴 무를 먹도록 했다. 심지어 샐러드에 무를 조금 넣는 것을 좋아하는 사람들도 그 일을 어렵게 느낄 것이다.

하지만, 바우마이스터는 식습관에 관심이 없었다. 그는 학생들이 해결할 수 없는 기하학 과제에 얼마나 오래 매달릴지에 정말 관심이 많았다. 기하학 과제에서 약 20분 동안 쿠키를 먹도록 허용된 학생들은 평균 20분 정도 기하학 과제에 매달린 반면, 무를 먹도록 강요된 학생들은 단 8분 만에 포기했다. 그들은 무를 먹는 것에 그들의 모든 의지력을 소진해서 어려운 문제를 완성하는 또 다른 상황에 대처할 수 있는 여분의 의지력을 덜 갖게 되었다.

그러므로 노력이 필요한 한 가지 일에 대한 수행은 노력이 필요하다는 것을 제외하고는 전혀 관련이 없는 후속 상황에 대해 예측하지 못한 결과를 초래할 수 있다. 이것이 바우마이스터가 의지력을 고갈될 수 있는 정신 근육으로 간주하는 이유이다.

29 빈칸에 들어갈 말로 가장 적절한 것을 고르시오. 빈칸 추론
① 인간관계에서 어디에나 있는 윤활유
② 스트레스를 피하는 데 필수적인 요소
③ 건강한 식단 조리법의 유일한 재료
✓ ④ 고갈될 수 있는 정신 근육

| 분석 | 빈칸이 포함된 본문의 마지막 단락은 실험의 최종 결론에 해당되며 이는 첫 문장의 'therefore'라는 표현을 통해서 짐작이 가능하다. 빈칸은 직전 단락의 마지막 내용과 연결되어야 하는데 두 번째 단락 마지막 문장에서 학생들은 한 가지 일에 모든 의지력을 소진해서 또 다른 상황에 대처할 의지력이 감소했다. 따라서 의지력은 '소진될 수 있는' 것으로 간주되어야 한다. 따라서 보기 ④가 정답으로 적절하다.

30 윗글의 제목으로 가장 적절한 것을 고르시오. 제목
✓ ① 스트레스가 많은 날 음식을 갈망하는 원인으로서의 자아 고갈
② 현재 진행 중인 감정적 고통 대 육체적 굶주림
③ 균형 잡힌 식사 습관을 통해 내부의 무에 되갚음하라
④ 과제 난이도: 체중 증가에 대한 피상적인 변명

| 분석 | 본문의 주요 소재는 '자아 고갈'이다. 따라서 소재가 언급된 선택지 ①이 정답으로 적절하다.

[31-34] 2015 동덕여대

| 정답 | 31 ② 32 ③ 33 ④ 34 ③

| 어휘 | markedly ⓐ 뚜렷하게   adequacy ⓝ 적절성, 적합성
halo effect 후광 효과(하나의 탁월한 특질 때문에 그 인물 전체의 가치를 과대평가하는 일)
horn effect 뿔 효과(하나의 요소를 부정적으로 평가한 후 전체를 부정적으로 생각하는 편향)
primacy effect 초두 효과(먼저 제시된 정보가 나중에 들어온 정보보다 전반적인 인상 현상에 더욱 강력한 영향을 미치는 것)
skew ⓥ 비스듬히 움직이다   predictor ⓝ 예언자, 예보자

전문해석

실험들은 구직자를 선정하는 데 있어서, 면접은 기껏해야 방해물이고 심지어 해를 끼칠 수도 있다는 것을 보여 주었다. 이 연구들은 면접관들의 판단들이 현저하게 다르고 구직자들의 적절성과 관련이 거의 없거나 전혀 없다고 밝혔다. 이것이 사실이어야만 하는 많은 이유들 중에서, 특히 세 가지가 두드러진다. 첫 번째 이유는 후광 효과로 알려진 판단의 오류와 관련이 있다. 만약 한 사람이 한 가지 눈에 띄는 좋은 특성을 가지고 있다면, 그들의 다른 특성들은 실제보다 더 좋은 것으로 판단될 것이다. 그러므로, 말쑥하게 옷을 입고 자신감을 보이는 사람은 그 또는 그녀의 실제 능력과 상관없이 일을 잘할 수 있다고 판단될 가능성이 있다. 뿔 효과는 ⓐ 본질적으로 같은 오류지만, 한 가지 특정한 나쁜 특성에 초점을 두는 것이다. 여기서 그 사람은 (한 가지 나쁜 특성 때문에) 일을 잘할 수 없다고 판단될 것이다.

면접관들은 또한 초두 효과라고 불리는 효과에 의해 편견을 갖게 된다. 이 오류는 나중의 정보에 대한 해석이 이전에 연결된 정보에 의해 왜곡될 때 발생한다. 따라서, 면접 상황에서, 면접관은 대부분의 면접 시간을 처음 몇 순간에 지원자가 준 인상을 확인하려고 노력한다. 연구들은 그러한 인상이 지원자의 적성과 무관하다는 것을 반복적으로 증명했다.

대조 효과라고 알려진 현상 또한 면접관들의 판단을 왜곡시킨다. 적합한 후보자는 유난히 똑똑하게 보이는 이전의 후보자와 대비되기 때문에 과소평가될 수 있다. 마찬가지로, 약한 인상을 보여 준 지원자 다음(순서)의 평균적인 지원자는 그 혹은 그녀의 실제보다 더 적합하다고 판단될 수 있다.

인사 선발의 한 형태로서 면접이 부적절한 것으로 보여 왔기 때문에, 더 정확하게 후보 적합성을 예측하는 다른 선발 절차가 고안되어 왔다. 고안된 다양한 테스트들 중에서 이를 가장 성공적으로 수행하는 것으로 보이는 예측 변수는 다양한 언어 및 공간 테스트로 측정된 인지 능력이다.

33 ④
34 ③

31 "ⓐ본질적으로 같은 오류"라는 말에 의해 저자가 의미한 것은 무엇인가? 밑줄 추론

① 오류의 효과는 동일하다.
✓② 그 오류는 같은 종류의 오판에 근거한다.
③ 그 효과는 부정적인 특성에만 초점을 맞춘다.
④ 개인은 그 일을 할 능력이 떨어지는 것으로 간주된다.

| 분석 | 밑줄 친 ⓐ의 주어는 '뿔 효과'로 이것이 직전에 소개된 '후광 효과'와 '본질적으로 같은 오류'라는 것은 잘못된 판단을 이끄는 효과라는 뜻을 나타낸다. 따라서 보기 ②가 정답으로 가장 적절하다.

32 다음 중 전형적인 면접 오류가 발생하는 면접을 기준으로 채용할 수 있는 지원자는? 세부 내용 일치

① 매우 지적으로 보이는 사람을 따라다니는 옷차림이 단정하고 자신감 있는 사람
② 옷차림이 단정하고 자신감 있는 사람을 따르는 자신감 없고 옷차림이 단정한 사람
✓③ 겉보기에 결함이 있는 사람을 따라다니며 옷을 잘 입고 자신감 있는 사람
④ 옷을 잘 입고 자신감 있는 사람을 따르는 자신감 있는 사람

| 분석 | 본문 세 번째 단락에서는 '대조 효과'에 대해 설명했는데 보기 ③이 바로 대조 효과에 해당되는 예시이므로 정답이다.

33 다음 중 가장 적합한 구직자를 찾는 면접관의 행동에 대해 저자가 동의할 가능성이 높은 진술은? 세부 내용 일치

① 면접관은 첫인상을 확인하기 위해 시간을 보내야 한다.
② 면접관은 자신감 있고 옷을 잘 입어야 한다.
③ 면접관은 이 과정이 적합한 사람을 찾는 데 방해가 된다는 것을 알아야 한다.
✓④ 면접관은 최고의 지원자를 선택할 수 있는 다른 방법을 찾아야 한다.

| 분석 | 본문에서 저자는 면접 상황에서 면접관들이 경험하는 여러 가지 편견들을 나열했다. 보통 문제 제기 이후에는 저자의 해결 방안이 나오는데 본문 마지막 단락에서 언어 및 공간 테스트가 긍정적으로 소개되었다. 따라서 보기 ④에 저자가 동의할 가능성이 높다.

34 다음 중 다음 단락에서 논의할 가능성이 가장 높은 것은 무엇인가? 뒤 내용 추론

① 그 밖에 지원자에 대한 판단 착오
② 판정 효과의 종류에 대한 자세한 정보
✓ ③ 인지 능력을 측정하는 테스트에 대한 더 많은 정보
④ 면접에 포함된 기타 선발 절차

| 분석 | 본문 마지막 문장에서 소개된 '언어 및 공간 테스트'에 관한 정보가 이어지는 것이 가장 자연스럽다. 따라서 보기 ③을 정답으로 한다.

[35-36] 2016 성균관대

| 정답 | 35 ③ 36 ④

| 어휘 |
eco- [pref] 생태, 환경의 뜻
crisp ⓝ (감자를 얇고 동그랗게 잘라 튀긴) 감자칩
perverse ⓐ (사고방식·태도가) 비뚤어진
estimate ⓝ 추정치, 견적서
control ⓝ 지배(권), (실험에서) 통제(집단)
hitch ⓝ (뜻밖의) 장애, 지장; 매듭, 연결부
designer jeans 유명 디자이너의 청바지, 고가의 청바지

전문해석

하버드 경영대학원의 Uma Karmarkar 교수와 듀크 푸콰 경영대학원의 Bryan Bollinger 교수의 최근 논문은 식료품을 살 때 자신의 장바구니를 가져오는 쇼핑객들이 그것에 대해 스스로에게 보상하고 싶어 한다는 것을 발견했다. 2년 동안 저자들은 미국의 슈퍼마켓의 거래를 추적했다. 아마도 놀랄 것도 없이, 자신의 장바구니를 가져온 쇼핑객들이 상점의 장바구니를 사용한 사람들보다 더 많은 친환경 제품을 구입했다. 하지만 친환경 쇼핑객들은 또한 단것, 아이스크림, 그리고 감자칩을 사는 경향이 더 높았다. 심리학자들은 이런 종류의 행동을 "도덕적 허가"라고 부른다. 비록 이런 예는 무해해 보일 수 있지만, 결과는 비뚤어질 수 있다. 2011년 매사추세츠주의 물 절약에 관한 연구는 그것(비뚤어진 결과)을 보여 준다. 실험에서, 약 150채의 아파트는 두 개의 그룹으로 나뉘었다. 절반은 물 절약 팁과 일주일에 한 번 사용량 추정치를 받았고, 나머지 절반은 대조군의 역할을 했다. 물을 적게 사용하도록 권고받은 가구들은 그렇게 했다: 그들의 소비는 대조군에 비해 평균 6% 감소했다. 문제는 그들의 전기 소비가 5.6% 증가했다는 것이다. 다시 말해서, 도덕적 허가는 매우 강해서 원래의 미덕 행동을 다소 능가했다.

도덕적 허가는 미덕 행동이 의무가 아닐 때 발생하는 것으로 보인다. 한 연구에서, 참가자들은 사회봉사를 하는 자신을 상상했다. 그리고 나서 그들은 두 가지 보상 중 하나를 선택하도록 요청받았다: 관대한 것(디자이너 청바지 한 벌)과 실용적인 것(청소기)이다. 만일 그들이 교통법규 위반으로 사회봉사를 선고받았다고 상상하라고 들었다면, 그들은 그 청바지를 선택할 가능성이 만약 그들이 스스로를 자원봉사자라고 생각했을 때보다 훨씬 낮았다.

35 "도덕적 허가"라는 밑줄 친 표현은 _____의 경향을 의미한다. 밑줄 추론

① 다른 사람들 앞에서 도덕적으로 행동하는 것
② 다른 사람들보다 도덕적으로 우월하다고 느끼는 것
✓ ③ 좋은 일을 한 것에 대해 마음껏 즐기는 것
④ 자신에게 도덕적인 일을 할 수 있도록 허락하는 것
⑤ 나쁜 짓을 한 것에 대해 벌을 주는 것

| 분석 | 밑줄 친 "도덕적 허가"는 이런 종류의 행동이라고 지시되었으므로 앞 단락의 내용을 참고하여 정답을 고른다. 본문 첫 단락에서 사람들은 상점에 장바구니를 가져왔다는 이유로 스스로에게 더 많이 보상하는 구매 행위를 했다. 따라서 밑줄 친 표현은 보기 ③의 경향을 의미한다.

36 다음 중 빈칸에 들어갈 말로 가장 적절한 것은? 빈칸 추론

① 사람들은 다른 사람들에 대해 나쁘게 생각한다
② 사람들은 법을 위반한다
③ 사람들은 희생을 마다하지 않는다
✓ ④ 미덕 행동은 의무가 아니다
⑤ 소비 패턴이 변화하다

| 분석 | 빈칸 뒤에 이어지는 연구의 내용에 따르면, 개인의 책임이나 의무로서가 아니라 자기 결정에 의해 미덕 행위를 한 경우에 도덕적 허가가 발생했다. 따라서 도덕적 허가는 보기 ④처럼 미덕 행동이 의무가 아닐 때 발생한다.

[37-39] 2015 한국외대

| 정답 | 37 ① 38 ④ 39 ③

| 어휘 | extraversion ⓝ 외향성 gravitate ⓥ (사람 등이) ~에 자연스럽게 끌리다
celebrity ⓝ 유명 인사, 명성 draining ⓐ 물을 빼내는, 배수하는 neuroticism ⓝ 신경증적 성질, 신경질

전문해석

대체로, 외향성의 척도에서 높은 점수를 받은 개인들은 자극을 추구하는 경향이 있는 반면, 낮은 점수를 받은 사람들은 그것을 회피하는 경향이 있다. 전형적인 외향성을 묘사하도록 요청받았을 때, 대부분의 사람들은 외향성을 사회적 상호 작용에 대한 선호와 동일시하며, 활기찬 "파티광"을 생각하는 경향이 있다. 그러나 외향성에서 높은 점수를 받은 사람들은 단지 사회적인 자극 이상을 추구한다. 그들은 또한 활동적인 여가, 여행, 심지어 유명인을 포함하여, 다른 자극적인 상황으로 끌리는 경향이 있다.

반면에, 내향적인 사람들은 일반적으로 자극에 대해 더 낮은 친화력을 가진다. 그들은 거의 모든 자극에 ⓑ 활력적이기보다는 ⓐ 기진맥진해진다. 일반적인 믿음과 달리, 그들이 사회적 불안과 신경증에 높은 점수를 얻지 않는 한, 내성적인 사람들은 반드시 사회적 상황에 대해 부끄러워하거나 두려워하지 않는다. 37 ①

이에 근거하여, 어떤 사람은 외향적인 사람들이 자극적인 상황에 대한 그들의 욕구를 충족시킬 수 있는 극단적인 환경들에 끌릴 것이라고 추측할 수 있지만, 내향적인 사람들은 그것들(극단적인 환경들)이 매력적이지 않다고 여길 것이다. 그러나, 극단적인 환경들은 또한 사람들을 단조로움과 고독─외향적인 사람들은 혐오적이라고 여길 것이지만, 반면 균형 잡힌 내향적인 사람들은 인내하고 심지어 즐기는 경험─에 노출시킬 수 있다. 39 ③

37 저자에 따르면 외향적인 사람들은 _____ 경우 극단적인 활동을 즐길 가능성이 가장 높다. 세부 내용 추론

✓ ① 충분히 자극적일
② 사람들 사이에서 매우 인기가 있을
③ 리더십을 기르는 데 도움이 되는
④ 많은 유명 인사들을 끌어들이는

| 분석 | 본문 첫 번째 단락의 내용을 참고하면 외향적인 사람들은 자극적인 상황에 끌리는 경향이 있다. 따라서 보기 ①이 정답으로 적절하다.

38
다음 중 빈칸 Ⓐ와 Ⓑ에 들어갈 말이 알맞게 짝지어진 것은? 빈칸 추론

① 신나는 – 지루한
② 위협적인 – 제한하는
③ 유익한 – 유해한
④ ✓ 기진맥진한 – 활력적인

| 분석 | 빈칸이 포함된 문장의 직전 내용에서 '내향적인 사람들은 자극에 더 낮은 친화력을 가진다'고 했다. 그러므로 내향적인 사람들은 자극에 대해 활력적이기보다는 기진맥진해질 것이다. 보기 ④가 정답으로 가장 적절하다.

39
다음 중 윗글에서 내성적인 사람에 대해 언급한 것은? 세부 내용 일치

① 그들은 지적 자극을 간절히 원한다.
② 그들은 신경증에 취약하다.
③ ✓ 그들은 일반적으로 수줍음이 많은 것으로 여겨진다.
④ 그들은 고독한 활동을 두려워한다.

| 분석 | 본문에 따르면 내향적인 사람들은 외향적 사람들과 달리 사회적 상호 작용에 대한 선호도가 낮고 단조로움과 고독을 즐긴다. 따라서 보기 ③이 정답으로 적절하다.

[40 – 42] 2019 국민대

| 정답 | 40 ② 41 ④ 42 ③

| 어휘 | **operant conditioning** 조작적 조건형성　**classical conditioning** 고전적 조건형성　**association** ⓝ 협회, 연계, 연상
reinforcement ⓝ (특히 감정이나 생각들의) 강화　　　　　　　　　　　**positive reinforcer** 정적 강화물
presentation ⓝ 제출, 제시, 수여　　**negative reinforcer** 부정 강화물　**aversive stimulus** 혐오 자극

전문해석

현대 심리학의 지형을 바꾼 B. F. 스키너(B. F. Skinner)는 학습의 습득을 설명하기 위해 조작적 조건화라는 용어를 Ⓐ 새로 만들었다. 조작적 조건화는 유기체가 바람직한 결과를 산출하는 방식으로 행동하는 방법을 배우는 과정이다. 그것이 그 환경에서 작동하도록 설계되었기 때문에 그 행동은 "조작자"라고 불린다. 즉, 수동적인 반응을 초래하는 자극 사이의 연관성의 학습을 포함하는 고전적 조건화와는 대조적으로 조작적 조건화는 자발적으로 방출되는 행동과 그 결과 사이의 연관학습을 포함한다.
스키너는 또한 '보상'이나 '만족' 대신 강화라는 용어를 사용했다. 객관적으로 정의된 강화는 사전 반응의 가능성을 Ⓐ 증가시키는 자극이다. 강화에는 두 가지 유형이 있다: 긍정적 강화인자와 부정적 강화인자이다. '긍정적인 강화인자'는 긍정적인 자극의 제시를 통해 사전 반응을 강화한다. 대조적으로, '부정적인 강화인자'는 회피적인 자극의 제거를 통해 반응을 강화한다.
42 ③
스키너는 처벌이 부정적 강화의 한 형태가 아니라는 것을 재빨리 지적했다. 비록 이 둘(긍정적 강화와 부정적 강화)은 종종 혼동되지만, 처벌은 역효과를 갖는다: 그것은 사전 반응의 가능성을 Ⓑ 감소시킨다. 처벌에는 두 가지 유형이 있다. '긍정적인 처벌인자'는 특정 행동을 약화시키기 위해 혐오적인 자극의 제시를 통해 반응을 약화시킨다. 이와 대조적으로, '부정적인 처벌인자'는 전형적으로 긍정적인 것으로 특징지어지는 자극의 제거를 통해 행동을 약화시킨다.

40
밑줄 친 ⓐcoined와 가장 의미가 가까운 것은? 밑줄 추론

① 유도했다
② ✓ 발명했다
③ 지시했다
④ 반복했다

| 분석 | 밑줄 친 동사 'coined'는 '(새로운 표현을) 만들어 내다'라는 뜻으로 쓰였으므로, 의미가 가장 가까운 것은 보기 ②의 'invented'이다.

---

41 빈칸 ⓐ와 ⓑ에 들어갈 말이 바르게 짝지어진 것은? 빈칸 추론

① 진정하다 – 폐지하다
② 부인하다 – 승인하다
③ 거절하다 – 받다
✓ 증가하다 – 감소하다

| 분석 | 빈칸 ⓐ에 이어지는 내용에 따르면 두 가지 유형의 강화가 모두 사전 반응을 '증가'시켰다. 빈칸 ⓑ의 경우 처벌은 강화와 혼동되지만 역효과를 일으키므로 사전 반응의 가능성을 '감소'시킬 것이다.

---

42 윗글에 따르면, 다음 중 사실인 것은? 내용 일치

① 긍정적인 처벌인자는 행동을 장려하는 자극이다. 긍정적 처벌인자는 행동을 약화시킴
② 부정적 강화인자는 행동을 감소시키는 자극이다. 부정적 강화인자는 행동을 강화시킴
✓ 긍정적 강화는 행동의 확률을 향상시킨다.
④ 부정적 처벌은 부정적 강화와 같다. 부정적 처벌인자는 행동을 약화시키며 부정적 강화인자는 행동을 강화시킴

| 분석 | 본문의 두 번째 단락에서 긍정적 강화인자는 이전에 있었던 반응을 '강화시킨다'고 했으므로 보기 ③은 사실이다.

| 배경 지식 | 조작적 조건화(Operant conditioning): 행동주의 심리학 이론으로 어떤 반응에 대해 선택적으로 보상함으로써 그 반응이 일어날 확률을 증가 혹은 감소시키는 방법

[43–44] 2021 성균관대

| 정답 | 43 ③   44 ④

| 어휘 | uplift ⓥ 희망[행복감]을 주다, (사회적) 지위를 높이다, (정신을) 고양하다
dignify ⓥ 위엄있어 보이게 하다, 중요한 것처럼 보이게 만들다
aspiration ⓝ 열망
expiry date ⓝ (계약서 등의) 만기 날짜
integrate ⓥ 통합하다, 융합하다
fulfil ⓥ 충족시키다, 이행하다, 실현하다
contribute to ~에 기여하다
inequality ⓝ 불평등, 불균형
parliament ⓝ 의회, 국회

전문해석

교육은 희망을 주는 힘이기도 하고 통합적인 힘이기도 하다. 교육은 사람들이 존엄한 삶을 영위할 수 있는 기술과 지식을 습득함에 따라 그들의 열망을 충족시키고 사회에 기여함에 따라 희망을 준다. 교육을 통해 삶을 개선함에 따라 우리가 불평등의 격차를 줄일 수 있는 더 나은 기회를 가지기 때문에 그것은 또한 통합적인 힘이다. 희망을 주는 힘과 통합하는 힘은 서로를 강화한다. 두 가지 목적은 오늘날 ⓐ <u>도전받고 있다</u>. 급속한 기술 발전은 학교와 고등교육에서 습득한 기술과 지식의 만료일을 단축시켰고, 세계화는 사회적 불평등을 확대시켰다. 최근 나는 의회에서 교육의 통합적 측면을 강화하기 위해 우리가 무엇을 했고 앞으로 할 것인지에 대해 광범위하게 이야기했다. 오늘 나는 불평등에 대해 이야기하지 않을 것이다. <u>오늘 나는 교육이 삶을 계속해서 행복하게 하고 우리의 젊은이들을 미래에 대비시키기 위해 우리가 해야 할 변화에 대해 이야기할 것이다. 이것은 세계의 모든 교육자들이 묻고 있는 가장 핵심적인 질문이다—우리의 젊은이들을 미래를 위해 어떻게 준비시킬 것인가?</u>
43 ③

43 연설의 대상인 독자는 ＿＿＿＿＿＿＿다. 세부 내용 일치

① 의원들
② 신문기자
③ ✓ 교육자들
④ 외교관들
⑤ 부모들

| 분석 | 본문의 마지막 두 문장을 토대로 연설의 대상을 유추할 수 있다. 저자는 '교육이 삶을 계속해서 행복하게 하고 우리의 젊은이들을 미래에 대비시키기 위해 우리가 해야 할 변화에 대해 이야기할 것이다.'라고 했으며 이것이 '세계의 모든 교육자들이 묻고 있는 가장 핵심적인 질문'이라고 했다. 따라서 독자는 보기 ③의 '교육자들'일 것이다.

44 빈칸 ⓐ에 들어갈 말로 가장 적절한 것은? 빈칸 추론

① 유지된
② 달성된
③ 추구된
④ ✓ 도전받는
⑤ 승진한

| 분석 | 빈칸 ⓐ 뒤로 이어지는 문장에서 '급속한 기술 발전'과 '세계화'는 교육의 목적에 부정적 영향을 주기 때문에 부정적 뉘앙스의 표현을 빈칸에 삽입하도록 한다. 보기 ④가 정답으로 적절하다.

[45-47] 2019 한국외대

| 정답 | 45 ① 46 ④ 47 ②

| 어휘 | **ubiquitous** ⓐ (동시에) 도처에 있는   **ubricant** ⓐ 윤활유   **unmask** ⓥ 가면을 벗기다, 정체를 드러내다
differentiate ⓥ 구별 짓다   **take on** 떠맡다, 고용하다, 태우다   **spontaneous** ⓐ 자발적인, 즉흥적인
crow's feet 눈개[눈꼬리]의 잔주름   **droop** ⓥ (특히 지치거나 약해져서) 아래로 처지다, 늘어지다
trace ⓝ 자취, 흔적, 조금   **furrowing** ⓝ 미간을 찡그리는 것
tell-tale ⓐ 감추려 해도 드러나는, 비밀을 폭로하는   **feign** ⓥ (감정 등을) 가장하다, ~인 척하다

전문해석

어디에서나 볼 수 있는 사회적 윤활유인 거짓 미소는, 불쾌함을 가리는 것과 진정한 기쁨을 반영하는 미소 속의 특정한 근육 패턴을 구별하는 새로운 연구에 의해 밝혀졌다. 심리학자 에크만(Ekman) 박사와 그의 동료들은 사람이 표정을 바꿀 때 얼굴의 100개 이상의 근육 패턴을 분석하는 기술을 개발했다.⁴⁵ ① 그들의 방법으로, 그들은 얼굴이 주어진 감정적인 표정을 취할 때 어떤 근육이 작용하는지 정확하게 알아낼 수 있었다.⁴⁷ ②

거짓말에 관한 연구에서, 진짜 미소는 두 가지 점에서 불행한 감정을 감추는 미소와 달랐다. 자연스러운 미소에서, 볼이 위로 움직이고 눈 주변의 근육이 조여서 눈꼬리의 잔주름을 만들고 눈썹 주변의 피부가 눈 쪽으로 약간 처지게 했다. 그러나 거짓 미소에서, 그 얼굴은 기쁨의 표현으로 추정될 수 없는 미소 뒤에 불행한 감정의 흔적을 보여 준다. 예를 들어, 눈썹 사이의 근육(미간)이 약간 찡그려지는 것과 같다. 특별히 환한 미소를 짓지 않으면, 눈은 잔주름을 만들지 않을 것이다. 그리고 심지어 그때에도, 꾸며내기 어려운 눈썹 주변의 피부의 처짐이 나타나지 않을 것이다. 이 연구는 때때로 사람이 미소라는 가면 뒤에 신체적인 고통, 감정적인 고뇌, 또는 사악한 의도를 숨기려고 할 때를 알기 위해 미묘한 신호에 의존할 필요가 있는 사람들에게 특히 중요할 수 있다.

45

다음 중 윗글의 제목으로 가장 적절한 것은? 제목

✓ ① 진짜와 거짓 미소의 분석
② 얼굴 표정과 근육 움직임
③ 얼굴에 나타난 감정의 표정 읽기
④ 누군가가 거짓말을 하고 있는지 확인하는 방법

| 분석 | 본문은 얼굴의 근육 패턴을 통해 진짜 미소와 거짓 미소의 차이를 분석한 연구에 대해 서술하고 있다. 'Anatomy'는 '해부학' 외에 '면밀한 분석'이라는 의미도 있으므로 보기 ①이 글의 제목으로 가장 적절하다.

46

윗글에 따르면, 다음 중 진짜 미소를 나타내는 것은? 세부 내용 일치

① 주름진 눈꺼풀
② 찡그려진 눈썹
③ 늘어진 눈썹 선
✓ ④ 아래로 처진 눈썹

| 분석 | 본문의 다섯 번째 문장에서 '자연스러운 미소에서, 볼이 위로 움직이고 눈 주변의 근육이 조여져서 눈꼬리의 잔주름을 만들고 눈썹 주변의 피부가 눈 쪽으로 약간 처지게 했다.'고 했다. 따라서 ④가 진짜 미소를 나타낸다.

47

다음 중 윗글에 명시되거나 암시되지 <u>않은</u> 것은 무엇인가? 내용 불일치 / 내용 비추론

① 진짜 미소를 지을 때 볼이 위로 올라간다.
✓ ② 얼굴 근육은 100개가 넘는다.
③ 이 연구는 범죄 수사에 활용될 수 있다.
④ 거짓으로 미소 짓는 것은 흔한 일이다.

| 분석 | 본문 두 번째 문장에 따르면 에크만 박사와 그의 동료들은 '얼굴의 100개 이상의 근육 패턴을 분석하는 기술'을 개발했다. 보기 ②는 얼굴 근육이 아닌 '근육 패턴'으로 수정되어야 한다.

[48-51] 2022 아주대

| 정답 | 48 ① 49 ③ 50 ④ 51 ④

| 어휘 | interchangeable ⓐ 교환[교체]할 수 있는　refer to ~에 돌리다, 언급하다, 적용되다　go hand in hand 관련되다, 함께 가다
inflict ⓥ (괴로움 등을) 가하다　merger ⓝ 합병, 합동　narcissistic ⓐ 자애적인, 자기도취증에 빠진
profound ⓐ (영향·느낌 등이) 엄청난, 심오한　authentic ⓐ 진본인, 진짜인
empathy ⓝ 감정이입, 공감　intuit ⓥ 직감하다, 직관하다　pervasive ⓐ 만연하는, (구석구석) 스며드는
preclude ⓥ 방해하다, 가로막다, 불가능하게 하다　crowd out 밀어내다
come into play 작동하기 시작하다　idealization ⓝ 이상화(된 것)　crave ⓥ 갈망하다, 열망하다

전문해석

[A] 비록 많은 사람들이 "죄책감"과 "수치심"이라는 두 단어를 교환하여 사용하지만, 심리학적 관점에서 그 둘은 사실 다른 경험을 나타낸다. 죄책감과 수치심은 때때로 관련된다. 하나의 행동이 수치심과 죄책감을 모두 유발할 수 있는데, 전자는 우리가 우리 자신에 대해 어떻게 느끼는지를 반영하고, 후자는 우리의 행동이 다른 사람에게 해를 끼쳤다는 인식과 관련이 있다. 다른 말로 하자면,

48 ①

수치심은 자기 자신과 관련이 있고, 죄책감은 다른 사람들과 관련이 있다.

[B] Dictionary.com에 따르면 죄책감은 잘못된 일을 했다는 인식과 관련이 있다. 그것은 우리의 행동에서 생겨난다(비록 그것이 환상 속에서 발생하는 것이라 할지라도). 수치심은 죄책감을 인식하는 데에서 비롯될 수 있지만 분명히 죄책감과 같은 것은 아니다. 그것은 우리가 다른 사람들에게(그리고 우리 자신에게) 어떻게 보이는지에 대한 고통스러운 감정으로서, 반드시 우리가 과거에 한 어떤 행동에 의존하는 것은 아니다. 나는 한번은 디너 파티에서 누군가에게 상처를 주는 말을 한 적이 있는데, 어느 정도는 그 말에 상처를 주려는 의도를 갖고 있었다. 나중에 내가 친구에게 상처를 줬다고 생각했기 때문에 죄책감을 느꼈다. 더 고통스럽게도, 나는 내가 그런 식으로 행동하는 부류의 사람이라는 사실에 대해 수치심 또한 느꼈다. 다른 누군가에게 고통을 가한 결과로써 죄책감이 들었고, 나 자신과 관련해서는 수치심을 느꼈다.

[C] 당신이 다른 사람에게 끼쳤을지도 모르는 해악에 대해 죄책감을 느끼기 위해서는, 당신은 먼저 그 혹은 그녀를 별개의 개인으로 인정해야만 한다. 따라서, 분리와 통합 문제로 힘들어하고 있는 사람이 자신의 감정을 표현하기 위해 죄책감이라는 단어를 사용하더라도, 그 사람은 진짜 죄책감을 느끼지 않을 수 있다. 자기애적 행동을 보이는 많은 사람들은 종종 깊은 수치심을 겪지만 다른 사람들에 대한 진정한 관심은 거의 없다. 그들은 진정으로 죄책감을 느끼지 않는 경향이 있다. 죄책감은 다른 누군가가 느낄 수 있는 감정을 직감하는 능력에 의존하므로, 자기애적 성격 장애에서 발견되는 공감의 결핍은 진짜 죄책감을 가능하지 않게 만든다.

[D] 수치심이 특히 만연할 때, 그것은 진정한 염려와 죄책감이라는 감정의 발달을 막을 수 있다. 자신이 손상되는 것에 대한 의식이 너무나 강력하고 고통스러워서 그것이 다른 사람에 대한 감정을 밀어낸다. 그러한 경우에, 이상화가 종종 작동한다. 즉 다른 사람들이 우리가 갈망하는 이상적인 수치심 없는 삶을 살아가는 완벽하고, 운 좋은 사람들로 여겨지는 것이다. 강력한 질투는 아마도 (무의식적인) 결과다. 그런 경우에, 우리가 질투하는 대상에게 상처를 줄 때 우리는 그것에 죄책감을 느끼기보다는 그것을 즐기게 될 것이다.

---

48 윗글에 따르면 다음 중 죄책감에 대한 사실이 아닌 것은? `세부 내용 불일치`

① ✓ 죄책감은 타인과의 지향적인 연결을 방해한다.
② 죄책감은 특정 행동에 대한 비난을 포함한다.
③ 죄책감 성향은 공감과 정적으로 연관되어 있다.
④ 죄책감은 수치심보다 더 정교한 인지 능력을 필요로 한다.
⑤ 죄책감을 느끼는 능력은 다른 사람들을 별개로 보는 심리적 성장에 달려 있다.

| 분석 | 본문 [A] 단락에서 '죄책감은 다른 사람들과 관련'이 있고 '우리의 행동이 다른 사람에게 해를 끼쳤다는 인식과 관련'이 있다고 했다. 따라서 타인과의 연결을 방해하는 감정이 아니므로 보기 ①은 죄의식에 대한 사실이 아니다.

---

49 다음 중 [C] 단락의 제목으로 가장 적절한 것은 무엇인가? `제목`

① 수치심과 죄책감 속의 자아
② 수치심, 죄책감 그리고 정신분석
③ ✓ 진정한 수치심과 죄책감
④ 도덕적 감정으로서의 수치심과 죄책감
⑤ 수치심과 대인관계 감수성의 연관성

| 분석 | 본문 [C] 단락에서 저자는 진정한 죄책감이 무엇인지에 대해 설명했다. '다른 사람에 대한 인정과 관심'이 진정한 죄책감의 원천이며, 자기애적 성격장애자의 사례를 통해 '다른 사람에 대한 관심과 그들의 고통에 대한 공감이 결핍된 수치심'은 병적인 자기애일 뿐, 진정한 수치심은 아니라고 말했다. 따라서 보기 ③이 정답으로 적절하다.

| **50** | 다음 중 [D] 단락을 가장 잘 요약한 것은 무엇인가? 요지
① 수치심이 없는 상태는 질투의 원인이다.
② 수치심은 다른 사람들의 이상화로 이어질 수 있다.
③ 수치심의 성향은 종종 질투에 의해 야기된다.
✓④ 수치심에 대한 자기 집중은 다른 사람들에 대한 민감성을 방해할 수 있다.
⑤ 수치심의 감정은 피해를 입었다는 느낌에 의해 유도된다.

| 분석 | 본문 [D] 단락의 첫 문장에서 '수치심이 만연할 때, 그것은 진정한 염려와 죄책감이라는 감정의 발달을 막을 수 있으며 다른 사람에 대한 감정을 밀어낸다'고 했다. 따라서 보기 ④가 단락을 가장 잘 요약한 진술이다.

| **51** | 윗글에서 저자의 주장을 가장 잘 요약한 것은? 주제
① 수치심과 죄책감은 다른 감정을 유발한다.
② 수치심과 죄책감은 대인관계의 공감과 관련이 있다.
③ 수치심의 자기 집중은 죄책감의 발달을 방해할 수 있다.
✓④ 수치심과 죄책감의 차이는 자아의 역할에서 살펴볼 수 있다.
⑤ 수치심은 자신에 대한 부정적인 평가를 포함하는 반면, 죄책감은 자신에 대한 긍정적인 평가를 포함한다.

| 분석 | 본문에서는 죄책감과 수치심을 구별하고 있다. 요약하자면 수치심은 자기 자신에 대한 관심과, 죄책감은 타인에 대한 관심과 관련된 것이다. 특히 [D] 단락에서는 '수치심이 특히 만연할 때, 그것은 진정한 염려와 죄책감이라는 감정의 발달을 막을 수 있다. 자신이 손상되는 것에 대한 의식이 너무나 강력하고 고통스러워서 그것이 다른 사람에 대한 감정을 밀어낸다.'고 했으므로 '수치심과 죄책감이 자아의 역할에 있어서 차이가 있다'고 볼 수 있다. 정답은 보기 ④가 적절하다.

PART 2 자연과학

8강 과학 / 기술

01 ②	02 ②	03 ④	04 ①	05 ③	06 ②	07 ③	08 ②	09 ④	10 ①
11 ②	12 ③	13 ②	14 ②	15 ①	16 ②	17 ④	18 ④	19 ③	20 ③
21 ①	22 ②	23 ②	24 ③	25 ④	26 ②	27 ④	28 ②	29 ②	30 ⑤
31 ②	32 ④	33 ②	34 ②	35 ③	36 ①	37 ②	38 ②	39 ①	40 ④
41 ①	42 ②	43 ④	44 ②	45 ②	46 ④	47 ④	48 ②	49 ①	

[01-02] 2012 성균관대

| 정답 | 01 ② 02 ②

| 어휘 |
significant ⓐ 중요한
gene ⓝ 유전자
product ⓝ 산물
in response 이에 대한 대응으로
wearily ⓐd 지루하게, 지쳐서; 싫증이 나서
consequently ⓐd 그 결과, 결과적으로
determinism ⓝ 결정론(이 세상의 모든 일은 일정한 인과 관계의 법칙에 따라 결정된다는 이론)
cloning ⓝ 복제
essentialism ⓝ 본질론(사물의 본질이 원래부터 존재한다는 믿음)
stock A with B A에게 B를 제공하다[보급하다]
theologian ⓝ 신학자
undeniably ⓐd 부인할 수 없도록
outstanding ⓐ 뛰어난
assumption ⓝ 추정, 가정
reiterate ⓥ 반복하다
uterine ⓐ 자궁의
what's more 게다가, 그뿐만 아니라

전문해석

복제에 관한 미디어 과장의 가장 중요한 문제는 인간이 단지 유전자의 산물이라는 쉬운 가정, 즉 대개 '유전자 본질론'이라 불리는 관점이다. 텔레비전 사회자들과 라디오에 나오는 명사들은 마이클 조던(Michael Jordan)을 복제한 유전자를 가진 구성원으로만 이루어진 농구팀을 만드는 게 가능한지 묻는다. 철학자, 신학자들과 기타 전문가들이 이 질문 때문에 녹초가 되어 내놓는 대답은 비록 인간의 행동이 부인할 수 없을 정도로 유전적 인자를 갖고 있지만 자궁 내 환경, 가정 환경, 사회 환경, 식사, 다른 개인의 이력 등 여러 가지 다른 요인들이 개인의 발달에 중요한 역할을 한다는 것이다. 따라서 뛰어난 운동선수의 DNA에서 추출한 복제인간이라 해도 스포츠에 관심이 없을 수도 있다. 게다가 복제 이슈는 대중 매체가 과학의 '진보'를 멈출 수 없다고 암시하면서 결국 기술 결정론, 과학 결정론의 태도를 키우고 있는 방식을 보여 준다. 물론 많은 과학자들도 이러한 태도를 공유하고 있으며, 인간의 고통을 유발할 수 있는 연구 참여에 대한 윤리적 책임을 받아들이지 않으려 하는 경우가 지나치게 많다.

---

01 윗글의 가장 적절한 제목은 _____ 일 것이다. 제목

① 과학 발전의 이로움들 중심 키워드 없음   ✓② 매체와 복제의 윤리
③ 복제 방지 캠페인에 대한 미디어의 기여 지문 내용과 불일치   ④ 스포츠와 과학적 결정론 중심 키워드 없음
⑤ 법을 통한 복제 규제 언급 안 함

| 분석 | 이 글은 복제와 관련하여 언론매체가 과장하는 방식의 문제점을 지적하는 글이라고 볼 수 있다. 따라서 제목으로는 ② '매체와 복제의 윤리'가 적절하다.

| 02 | 윗글에 따르면 다음 중 사실인 것은? 내용 일치 |

① 과학자들은 도덕적 논쟁에 대해 객관적인 태도를 취할 자격이 있다.
☑ 언론은 DNA가 운명이라는 생각에 사로잡혀 있는 것 같다.
③ 대부분의 과학자들은 복제 연구가 제한될 필요가 있다는 것을 인정한다.
④ 대부분의 신학자들은 과학에 대한 지식이 거의 없다.
⑤ 인간 복제에 대한 언론의 부정적인 관심이 너무 많았다.

| 분석 | 이 글의 주요 내용은 언론 매체가 복제를 본질론, 결정론적으로 과장하여 다루고 있는 것에 대한 비판을 다루고 있는 글이다. 따라서 ② '언론은 DNA가 운명이라는 생각에 사로잡혀 있는 것 같다'는 것은 이 글이 주제와 일치하는 말이다.

[03-04] 2016 중앙대

| 정답 | 03 ④ 04 ①

| 어휘 | unique ⓐ 유일한, 독특한, 견줄 수 없는   inspiration ⓝ 자극, 격려, 고무, 동기; 영감   objectivity ⓝ 객관성, 객관적 타당성
appeal ⓝ 애원, 호소; 항소   ruthlessly ⓐⓓ 무자비하게, 잔인하게   valid ⓐ 근거가 확실한; 유효한
adverse ⓐ 적의를 품은; 역의; 반대의   trial ⓝ 실험; 시도; 재판   fervent ⓐ 뜨거운, 열렬한
dispassionate ⓐ 감정적이 아닌, 냉정한(calm); 공평한   exercise ⓝ 실험의 과정

전문해석

과학자들만의 창의성은 어떤 독특한 고유한 특징을 가지고 있다. 우선 과학자들은 문제를 충분히 잘 알고 있기 때문에, 그가 선택한 문제에 관해서라면 그 문제에 Ⓐ 답이 없는 질문들(아직 해결되지 않은 부분들)이 있다는 것을 제외하고 그 문제에 대해서 그 누구보다도 잘 알고 있다. 과학자는 통찰력과 영감을 통해서 문제 중 하나에 대한 가능한 답을 제안한다. 예를 들어 원자의 가능한 구조가 무엇인가? 무엇이 원자들을 결합시켜서 분자를 형성하게 하는가? 어떤 수단을 통해서 살아 있는 세포는 분출되는 화학에너지를 세포의 벽 속에 저장시키는 것일까? 이런 질문에 대한 제안된 해답이 형성될 때, 비로소 창의적인 순간이 도래한다. 자연스레 과학자는 자신이 옳다는 것을 증명하고 싶어 한다. 따라서 그것을 확인하는 실험의 수행은 일반적으로 널리 알려진 것처럼 Ⓑ 냉정한(이성적인) 과정은 절대로 아니다. 실험이란 사실상 온갖 감정들의 경연장이다. 객관성은 과학자의 빼어난 구상이 틀렸음을 보여 주는 증거를 아무리 싫더라도 기꺼이 받아들이는 데 있다. 일단 자연이 판결을 내리고 나면, (과학계에서) 항소란 존재할 수 없다. 판결이 나는 즉시, 과학자는 그의 창조의 산물이 타당한지 여부를 무자비하게 통보받는다.
 04 ①

| 03 | 윗글에서 내용의 흐름상, 빈칸 Ⓐ와 Ⓑ에 들어가기에 가장 적절한 것은? 빈칸 추론 |

① 무한한 명령 – 불리한 재판
② 가정된 가설 – 열렬한 경험
③ 창의적 가능성 – 지원적 과제
☑ 답이 없는 질문들 – 냉정한 과정

| 분석 | 빈칸 Ⓐ 다음 문장에 나오는 그 질문들(the questions)이라는 표현을 보면 앞 문장에 questions가 언급되어야 한다는 것을 알 수 있다. 따라서 빈칸 Ⓐ는 '답이 없는 질문들'이 적합하다. 빈칸 Ⓑ의 경우, 다음 문장에서 실험은 온갖 감정을 수반한다(Experiment carries all the emotion)고 했으므로, 그 앞에는 실험이 일반적으로 생각하듯이 감정에 좌우되지 않고 실행되는 것은 아니라고 표현하는 것이 타당하다. 따라서 빈칸 Ⓑ에는 dispassionate exercise가 적합하다.

04 **윗글을 통해 추론할 수 있는 것으로 가장 적절한 것은?** 내용 추론

☑ ① 객관성은 과학자가 가능한 답을 제시할 때 가장 중요한 자질이다.
② 과학계는 실험 가능한 현상에 대한 연구로 제한될 필요가 있다.
③ 과학자들은 과학적인 문제를 탐구하는 과정에서 창의력을 발휘한다.
④ 영감을 주는 개념은 실험 결과를 해석하는 데 중요한 역할을 한다.

| 분석 | 글의 전반부는 과학자의 독창성에 관한 내용이 주를 이루고 있지만 독창성이 이 글의 주요한 내용은 아니다. 글의 중반에서 답이없는 의문점 중 어느 하나에 대해 가능성 있는 답을 형성할 때 독창성이 발휘된다(The creative moment occurs when the suggested answer is being formed.)고 말한 이후에는 과학자의 올바른 자세에 관해 이야기하고 있다. 즉 과학자는 자신이 그렇게 독창적으로 제시한 답이 옳다고 입증되길 원하겠지만, 그래서 실험에는 온갖 감정이 수반되겠지만, 자신의 구상이 틀렸다는 증거도 기꺼이 받아들일 수 있어야 한다는 저자의 주장이 드러나고 있다. 따라서 이러한 요지를 담고 있는 ①이 지문의 내용을 통해 추론 가능하다고 볼 수 있다.

[05-07] 2013 고려대

| 정답 | 05 ③   06 ②   07 ③

| 어휘 |
simultaneous ⓐ 동시의
sheer ⓐ 대단한
be in the air 퍼져 있다, 분위기가 감돌고 있다
climate ⓝ 분위기, 환경
calculus ⓝ 미적분
milieu ⓝ 환경
set off 일으키다, 유발하다
be reluctant to ~을 꺼리다
prior knowledge 사전 지식

전문해석

과학 역사가들이 '다발성'이라고 부르는 동시 발견 현상은 지극히 흔한 것으로 판명되고 있다. 과학과 철학에서 아주 중요한 에너지 보존의 법칙은 1847년 줄(Joule), 톰슨(Thomson), 콜딩(Colding), 헴홀츠(Helmholz)에 의해 네 번이나 독립적으로 만들어졌다. 1842년 로버트 메이어(Robert Mayer)는 이들보다 먼저 예견하기도 했다. 다발성이 이렇게 많은 이유는 단지 하나이다. 어떤 의미에서 보자면 과학의 발견은 불가피한 것이다. 그 발견들은 특정한 시간과 공간의 지적 분위기의 산물로서 여기저기 만연하고 있다. 그래서 두 명의 사람들에 의해 역사의 똑같은 시간에 미적분이 발명된 것에 놀라서는 안 된다. 라이프니츠(Leibniz)와 뉴턴(Newton)은 사실 한 번도 같이 앉아서 그들의 연구를 상세하게 공유했던 적이 없다. 하지만 이들은 공통의 지적 환경 속에 살고 있었다. 06 ②

물론 뉴턴은 이런 방식으로 보지 않았다. 그는 1660년대 중반에 미적분 연구를 했는데, 이를 발표하지 않았다. 라이프니츠가 자신의 미적분을 1680년대에 들고나왔을 때, 뉴턴 진영에 있던 사람들은 라이프니츠가 뉴턴의 연구를 훔쳤다고 비난하며 17세기 엄청난 과학 스캔들 중 하나를 일으켰다. 이는 불가피한 인간적 반응이다. 우리는 위대한 발견들이 만연하고 있다는 것을 믿으려 들지 않는다. 우리는 위대한 발견들은 우리 머릿속에 있다고 믿고 싶어 한다.

05 **빈칸에 들어갈 말로 가장 적절한 것을 고르시오.** 빈칸 추론

① 상대적으로 시기가 맞는
② 당황스러울 정도로 신비로운
☑ ③ 지극히 흔한
④ 완전히 새로운

| 분석 | 빈칸 뒤의 내용을 보면 에너지 보존 법칙은 네 명이나 되는 사람이 동시에 만들었다는 예시가 나와 있는데, 이것은 '과학에서 동시다발적으로 발명을 하는 일이 흔하다'는 것을 보여 주는 예시이다. 따라서 빈칸에 알맞은 말은 ③ '지극히 흔한'이다.

06 다음 중 "다발성"에 대해 추론할 수 있는 것은? 내용 추론

① 그것들은 시간과 장소를 초월하지 않는다.
✓② 그것들은 서로에 대한 사전 지식 없이 일어난다.
③ 그것들은 발견자의 평판을 향상시킨다.
④ 그것들은 정보는 이미 발견된 정보에 중요성을 더한다.

| 분석 | 지문에서 언급된 뉴턴과 라이프니츠의 예를 통해 알 수 있듯이 둘은 서로의 연구에 대해서 전혀 모르는 상태라고 했다. 따라서 시간과 장소를 초월해서 발생하는 것이 "다발성"이다. 따라서 ①은 틀렸고 ②는 지문과 일치한다.

07 윗글의 요지는 무엇인가? 글의 요지

① 아이디어 표절은 경쟁자들 사이에 만연해 있다.
② 동일한 발견에 대해 여러 과학자에게 공을 돌려야 한다.
✓③ "다발성"은 과학적 발견이 예정되어 있다는 증거이다.
④ 과학 역사학자들은 객관적으로 "다발성"을 기록해야만 한다.

| 분석 | 첫 번째 단락에서 다발성이 흔하다고 진술하고 그 이유는 단지 하나이며, '그러한 과학의 발견은 불가피했다는 것이다.'라고 언급했는데 이 문장을 이 글의 요지로 볼 수 있다.

[08-09] 2015 항공대

| 정답 | 08 ②   09 ④

| 어휘 |
sensing ⓝ 감지
pupil ⓝ 동공, 눈동자
intuition ⓝ 직관(력), 직감
proceed ⓥ 진행하다, 시작하다
humbly ⓐⓓ 겸손하게
conceit ⓝ 자만심
disentangle ⓥ (얽힌 것을) 풀다
conjecture ⓝ 추측
reflect ⓥ (상을) 비추다
stand in the way 방해하다
anomaly ⓝ 변칙, 예외적인 것
tedious ⓐ 지루한, 따분한

전문해석

감지 유형의 가장 훌륭한 과학적 사례가 아이작 뉴턴(Isaac Newton) 경이었다. 그는 3백 년간 과학계에 우선 사실을 먼저 보고 그런 다음 신중한 추론을 하도록 설득했다. 실제 세계는 우리가 원하는 대로 존재하는 것이 아니었으며, 또한 우리의 바람에 아무런 영향을 받지 않았다. 우리는 신이 준 현실을 우리의 눈으로 겸손하게 반영해야 하며 우리의 믿음이나 자만심이 방해하게 해서는 안 된다. 우리가 모든 사실을 확신한 후에만 우리는 추론을 시작해야 한다. 그러나 과학은 계속 발전하며, 이론물리학은 또 하나의 도전이고, 혼란스러운 예외적인 일들을 풀기 위해 직관이 필요하다. 알베르트 아인슈타인(Albert Einstein)은 직관력으로 유명했으며, 흥미로운 직감이 떠오르면 면도를 하다가 베이기도 했다. 그러나 이것이 그가 이용할 수 있는 사실들을 무시했다는 것을 의미하는 것은 아니다. 직감을 얻은 후에, 그는 그것에 대해 실험을 진행했다—이것이 하나의 유형이 또 다른 유형이 추측한 것을 증명하는 데 어떻게 도움을 주는가에 대한 사례이다.

08 윗글의 가장 적절한 제목은 무엇인가? 제목

① 과학 분석의 지루한 발달 과정 지문 내용과 불일치
✓② 감지 대 직관
③ 빅 데이터의 신중한 발전 중심 키워드 없음
④ 변칙과 불확실성의 줄어드는 경향 중심 키워드 없음

| 분석 | 이 지문은 중간에 있는 접속사 Yet을 기준으로 해서 두 가지의 개념을 대조로 설명한 글이다. 전반부는 사실을 중시하는 '감지(sensing) 유형'의 사례로 뉴턴에 대해 서술하고 있으며, 후반부는 이론물리학에서 변칙적인 것들을 해결하기 위해 '직관(intuition)'도 필요하며, 아인슈타인의 경우를 예로 들고 있다. 따라서 제목으로 적합한 것은 ② '감지 대 직관'이다.

09 윗글에 따르면 다음 중 사실인 것은? 내용 일치

① 뉴턴은 상황을 분석했고 열심히 사실을 살펴보았다. 이것들은 자명한 것이므로, 일반적인 이론화가 필요하지 않다.
② 아인슈타인은 문제의 의미를 이해하는 깊은 통찰력을 얻었다. 이것들은 자명한 것이므로, 사실의 뒷받침이 필요하지 않다.
③ 아인슈타인은 문제의 의미를 이해하는 깊은 통찰력을 얻었다. 사실은 맥락에 따라 좌우된다. 일단 그는 맥락을 파악하면, 사실 그 자체에 대해서는 생각할 필요가 없었다.
✓ ④ 뉴턴은 상황을 분석했고 열심히 사실을 살펴보았지만, 그런 다음 그는 이 문제의 의미가 명확해질 때까지 추론하기 시작했다.

| 분석 | 지문에서 뉴턴에 대해서는 '우선 사실을 관찰하고 나서 신중한 추론을 하였다'고 언급하고, 아인슈타인에 대해서는 '직감을 얻은 후 그것에 대해 실험하였다'고 언급했다. 따라서 이 유형에 맞는 것은 ④이다.

[10-11] 2017 한국외대

| 정답 | 10 ① 11 ②

| 어휘 | **blockchain** ⓝ 블록체인(중앙관리 서버가 아닌 참여자들의 개인 장비에 분산 저장시켜 공동으로 관리하는 네트워크)
approximate ⓐ (기준에) 가까운, 근접하는   **permanent** ⓐ 영속하는, 영구적인   **hack** ⓥ 자르다; 컴퓨터에 불법 침입하다
approval ⓝ 승인; 찬성   **delete** ⓥ 삭제하다

전문해석

블록체인(blockchain)은 모든 인터넷 접속자가 살펴볼 수 있는 거대한 개방형 디지털 기록이다. 이 기록은 한 개인이나 기관이 아니라, 분산네트워크상의 대략 9,000여 대의 컴퓨터에 의해 관리되고 있다. 컴퓨터 소유주가 자원해서 자신의 컴퓨터를 네트워크에 포함시키는 이유는 컴퓨터의 사용 대가로 종종 금전적 보상을 받기 때문이다. 기록된 모든 정보는 영구적이다. 정보를 변경할 수 없는 이유는 컴퓨터마다 기록을 복사하여 보관하기 때문이다. 당신이 이 시스템을 해킹하고자 한다면, 네트워크상의 모든 컴퓨터를 해킹해야 한다. 이런 시도가 여러 번 있었지만, 해킹은 불가능한 것으로 입증되었다. 여러 컴퓨터의 전체 능력은 세계 최고의 슈퍼컴퓨터 500대를 합친 것보다 더 크다. 그리고 2~3분에 한 번씩 새로운 정보를 기록에 추가할 수 있지만, 이것은 모든 컴퓨터가 승인할 때에, 즉 모든 컴퓨터에서 새로운 정보가 정확하고 만족스럽다고 판단할 때에만 그러하다. 모든 사람이 블록체인의 작동 방식을 알고는 있지만, ⓐ <u>완전히 자동화되어</u> 있기 때문에 그 방식을 변경할 수는 없다.

10 윗글에 의하면, 다음 중 블록체인과 일치하는 것은? 내용 일치

✓ ① 블록체인은 정보가 안전하다.
② 블록체인은 500개의 슈퍼컴퓨터로 구성되어 있다.
③ 소유주들은 블록체인의 정보를 삭제할 수 있다.
④ 블록체인의 일원이 되기 위해서 사람은 비용을 지불한다.

| 분석 | 지문에서 블록체인은 분산형 네트워크로 구성되어 있어서 해킹이 불가능하다고 했으며, 정보의 보관이 영구적이라고 언급하였으므로, ①이 지문과 일치하는 내용이다.

11 문맥으로 보아, Ⓐ에 가장 적절한 것은? 빈칸 추론

① 통제받지 않는
✓ ② 완전히 자동화된
③ 정기적으로 업데이트되는
④ 자유롭게 접근할 수 있는

| 분석 | 지문에서 블록체인이 정보를 변경할 수 없는 이유는 컴퓨터가 알아서 기록을 복사하여 보관하기 때문이라고 하였고, 정보를 추가할 경우에도 모든 컴퓨터가 승인할 때만 가능하다고 했다. 이것은 모든 것을 인간이 아닌 컴퓨터에 의하여 철저하게 통제받는다고 할 수 있는데, 컴퓨터가 모든 것을 알아서 처리하는 것을 우리는 '자동화'라고 부를 수 있다. 따라서 ②가 정답으로 적절하다. 블록체인은 컴퓨터에 의하여 철저한 통제를 받으므로 ① '통제받지 않는'은 정답이 될 수 없다.

[12-13] 2015 고려대

| 정답 | 12 ③ 13 ②

| 어휘 |
glamorous ⓐ 화려한, 매력 넘치는
ill-conceived ⓐ 잘못 고안된
fatal ⓐ 치명적인, 돌이킬 수 없는
consequence ⓝ 결과
literally ⓐⓓ 말[문자] 그대로
metaphorical ⓐ 은유[비유]의, 은유를 쓴
perseverance ⓝ 인내(심)
expeditious ⓐ 신속한, 효율적인
obduracy ⓝ 고집, 완고, 냉혹
vulnerability ⓝ 상처받기 쉬움, 취약성

전문해석

전반적으로 과학은 화려하고 멋진 일이 아니다. 하나의 과학적 데이터를 얻기 위해서 과학자들은 일상적으로 실험실에서 몇 달을 보내거나 현장에서 몇 년을 보낸다. 심지어 가장 생산성 있는 연구원들도 지속적으로 곤경에 처하며, 자신의 길을 헤쳐 나가야 한다. 그러는 동안에, 대부분 연구원의 노력은 결과적으로 잘못 고안된 계획이나, 단지 운이 좋지 않았던 가설들로 인해 낭비되거나 사라진다. 하지만 그들은 계속해서 일을 하며, 종종 치명적인 결과를 얻기도 한다. 과학에 있어 작업(연구)의 어려움은 필연적이다. 누군가는 과학의 진정한 주제가 현실의 냉혹함이라고 주장할 수 있을 것이다.
그리고 과학에 쓰이는 것은 또한 과학적인 논문에, 적어도 최고의 과학 논문에 쓰인다. 그것은 해답에 관한 것이라기보다 오히려 질문에 관한 것이다: 왜 시간은 오직 한 방향으로 흐르는 것인가? 생명은 어떻게 시작되었는가? 네안데르탈인들에게 무슨 일이 일어났는가? 이런 이야기들은 흥미롭기도 하지만 힘에 벅차기도 하다. 이러한 질문들은—어떤 의미에서는 말 그대로, 또 어떤 의미에서는 비유적으로—도달하기 어려운 곳으로 우리를 이끈다. 그것들은 우리에게 새로운 방식으로 세상을 바라볼 것을 청한다.

12 윗글로부터 추론할 수 없는 것은 무엇인가? 내용 추론

① 의미 있는 결과물을 얻기 위해 과학자들은 종종 원래 계획했던 것보다 더 많은 시간과 에너지를 소모한다.
② 과학적 연구의 결실은 인내를 통해 얻을 수 있다.
✓ ③ 연구의 성공은 신속한 실험에 기인한다.
④ 최고의 과학 논문조차도 반드시 명료한 설명을 제공하는 것은 아니다.

| 분석 | 과학적 연구의 어려움을 설명하고 있는 지문으로, 과학적인 작업에는 오랜 시간과 노력이 필요하며, 그 결과 또한 해답을 얻기보다 오히려 해결하기 힘든 새로운 의문을 제기하는 경우가 더 많다는 것이 글의 중심 요지인데 ③은 이 글 전체 요지에서 벗어난다.

13 빈칸에 가장 적절한 것을 고르시오. 빈칸 추론

① 놀라운 인간의 지능　　　　　　　　② 현실의 냉혹함 ✓
③ 우주의 기원　　　　　　　　　　　④ 우리의 고통에 취약함

| 분석 | 첫 번째 단락은 과학적인 작업의 어려움에 관하여 설명하고 있다. 세미콜론 앞에서도 '과학에 있어 작업(연구)의 어려움은 필연적이다'라고 언급했다. 이와 같은 맥락의 정답을 골라야 한다. 노력을 아무리 한다 해도 좀처럼 답을 허락하지 않는 것이 과학이므로 빈칸에는 '현실의 냉혹함'이 적절하다.

[14-15] 2013 한양대

| 정답 | 14 ② 15 ①

| 어휘 |
routine ⓐ 일상적인　　　　　　breakthrough ⓝ 획기적인 발전　　　come to terms with 익숙해지다
compelling ⓐ 압도적인, 흥미로운　pose a threat 위협을 제기하다　　　untold ⓐ 무수한, 막대한
outright ⓐ 무조건의, 철저한　　 address ⓥ 문제를 다루다, 치료하다　sequence ⓝ 연쇄
concomitantly ⓐⓓ 부수적으로　 spawn ⓥ 낳다, 대량 생산하다　　abuse ⓝ 남용, 오용
within the reach of ~이 이용할 수 있는 범위 내에 있는　　　　　　　raw material 원자재
weapons of mass destruction 대량 살상 무기　　　　　　　　　　　self-replication 자기 복제
cusp ⓝ 뾰족한 끝　　　　　　be on the cusp of ~하기 직전에 있다　bequeath ⓥ 남기다, 전하다, 물려주다

전문해석

거의 일상적으로 일어나는 과학의 획기적 발전 속에 사는 데 익숙해졌지만, 우리는 압도적인 21세기 기술이 이전에 왔던 기술과는 다른 위협을 제기하고 있다는 사실에 대해 아직도 잘 알지 못하고 있다. 이 모든 기술 하나하나는 무수히 많은 가능성을 제공하고 있다. 커즈와일(Kurzweil)이 자신의 로봇 꿈에서 보았던 거의 불사의 전망이 우리를 앞으로 나아가게 하고 있고, 유전 공학은 대부분의 질병을 완전히 치료하지는 못하겠지만, 어느 정도의 치료를 곧 제공해 줄 수 있다. 나노테크놀로지와 나노의학은 더 많은 질병을 치료할 수 있다. 이들이 합쳐져서, 우리의 평균 수명을 상당히 연장시켜 줄 수 있다.

Ⓐ 하지만, 이러한 기술 각각과 더불어, 연속적인 소규모의 개별적으로 현명한 발전들은 엄청난 힘과 함께 큰 위험성을 야기한다. 유전학, 나노공학, 로봇공학과 같은 21세기의 기술은 너무나 강력하여 완전히 새로운 종류의 사고와 기술 남용을 대량 생산할 수 있다. 가장 두려운 것은, 처음으로 이러한 사고와 기술 남용들이 개인이나 소집단이 널리 이용할 수 있는 범위 안에 들어가게 되었다는 점이다. 이들은 대규모 설비나 아주 희귀한 원자재도 필요로 하지 않는다. 지식 하나만으로도 그것들의 사용이 가능해질 것이다. Ⓑ 따라서 우리는 대량 살상 무기의 가능성을 가지게 된 것에 그치는 것이 아니라, 지식으로 가능한 대량 살상의 가능성도 가지게 되었다. 그리고 이 파괴 가능성은 자기 복제 능력에 의해 엄청나게 확대되고 있다. 내 생각에는 우리가 극단적인 악을 더 완성하기 직전에 있다고 해도 지나친 말이 아니다. 이 악의 가능성은 민족국가에 주어진 대량 살상 무기의 가능성을 넘어 놀랍고 끔찍할 정도로 극단적인 개인들에게까지 퍼져 나가고 있다.

14 윗글의 빈칸 Ⓐ, Ⓑ에 들어갈 말로 가장 적절한 것은? 연결사

① 그러나 - 그러나　　　　　　　　② 그러나 - 따라서 ✓
③ 따라서 - 그럼에도 불구하고　　　④ 따라서 - 마찬가지로

| 분석 | 첫 번째 단락은 기술의 장점에 대하여 기술하고 있는데, 두 번째 단락은 기술의 부정적인 측면을 기술하므로 빈칸 Ⓐ에는 역접의 연결사가 적절하므로 But, Yet이 가능하다. 빈칸 Ⓑ는 앞뒤 모두 지식이 가능케 한 대량 살상에 관하여 기술하므로 순접의 연결사가 와야 한다.

15 윗글에 드러난 필자의 어조로 가장 적절한 것은? 글의 어조

✓ ① 비판적인 ② 풍자적인
③ 일구이언하는 ④ 서술적인

| 분석 | 이 글의 전체 요지는 두 번째 단락이라 할 수 있는데, 기술의 발전으로 인해 이제 우리는 개인들이 대량 살상 무기를 쉽게 이용 가능한 극단적인 악의 상태에 있다고 비판하는 글이라고 볼 수 있다.

[16-18] 2012 한국외대

| 정답 | 16 ② 17 ④ 18 ④

| 어휘 |
preview ⓝ 시연, 미리보기
section ⓝ 섹션, 부분
display ⓝ 진열
action figure 영웅 캐릭터 인형
launch ⓥ 착수하다
plaything ⓝ 장난감
spark ⓥ 촉발시키다
offset ⓥ 상쇄시키다
promote ⓥ 촉진시키다
apartheid ⓝ 차별

ignite ⓥ 불을 붙이다
in favor of ~을 선호하여
replace ⓥ 대체하다
merchandise ⓝ 제품, 상품
feature ⓥ 특징으로 갖다
meet someone halfway 타협하다
reveal ⓥ 드러내다
negatively ⓐⓓ 부정적으로
beneficial ⓐ 유익한, 도움이 되는
be on to something 무언가를 꾸미다, 무언가를 알아보다

discard ⓥ 버리다
neutral ⓐ 중립적인
dedicated ⓐ 전용인, 오직 특정 목적을 위한
soft toy 봉제완구
systematically ⓐⓓ 체계적으로
in an attempt to do ~할 목적으로
insist ⓥ 주장하다
potential ⓝ 잠재력
rebellion ⓝ 반발

전문해석

2012년 크리스마스 장난감에 대한 미리보기가 선천성, 후천성, 장난감 그리고 성별에 대한 새로운 논쟁에 불을 붙였다. 251년 된 런던의 장난감 가게인 햄리스(Hamleys)는 최근에 성 중립적인 진열을 선호하여 분홍색의 '여아용' 그리고 파란색의 '남아용'으로 표시된 섹션들을 버렸다. 바비 인형 전용층과 영웅 캐릭터 인형 전용층이 없어졌기 때문에, 상품은 이제 종류(예를 들어 봉제완구)와 관심사(예를 들어 옥외용 장난감)에 따라 분류되게 되었다. 하지만 장난감 제조업체 레고는 '프렌즈'라는 제품을 선보였는데, 이는 여자아이들이 파스텔 색깔의 벽돌을 이용하여 카페나 미용실을 지을 수 있게 하는 장난감이다.

도대체 누가 옳은 것인가? 장난감에서 성별이 체계적으로 제거되어야 하는가? ⓐ 아니면 공학에 대한 여자아이들의 관심을 키우기 위해 여자아이들과 타협하는 레고가 현실적인 걸까? 레고는 신제품 프렌즈가 성별은 서로 다른 역할을 하고, 미취학 여아는 예쁘고 이야기를 할 수 있게 해 주는 장난감을 좋아한다는 것을 밝혀낸 연구를 기반으로 하였다고 말한다. ⓑ 레고는 성이 공정하기 위해서는 성별에 특화되어야 한다고 주장한다.

이러한 연구 결과는 아이들이 놀이하는 환경이 새로운 태도를 조장한다는 미취학 아동에 대한 새로운 연구에 의해 상쇄된다. 성별에 따라 나뉜 역할을 장려하는 것은 아이들의 잠재력에 부정적인 영향을 미치는 반면, 다양한 역할을 조장하는 것은 유익할 수 있다. 성차별에 대한 반발은 이미 시작되었고, 햄리스는 이에 대해 아마도 무언가를 알아채고 있는 것 같다.

16 밑줄 친 ⓐ에서 필자는 독자들이 성이 장난감에서 _____ 되어야 할지 말지에 대해 생각해 보기를 요구한다. 내용 파악

① 명백히 보존
✓ ② 부분적으로 수용
③ 완전히 제거
④ 강력하게 강화

| 분석 | 'meet someone the halfway'는 '타협하다'라는 의미이다. 여자아이들이 '공학'에 관심을 갖게 하고자 여자용 장난감을 만들었다는 말이다. ①, ④는 성을 보존했다는 의미이므로 정답이 될 수 없고 타협한다는 의미와 같은 말은 극단적 의미인 ③ '완전한 제거'가 아니라 ② '부분적인 수용'이 적절하다.

17 밑줄 친 부분 ⓑ에 대한 가장 좋은 해석은 무엇인가? 밑줄 의미 추론

① 사회적으로 책임감을 가지기 위해, 장난감 회사들은 여자아이들의 선호에 맞는 더 많은 장난감을 제공해야 한다.
② 장난감 회사는 성별 선호도를 통합하는 제품을 개발해야 한다.
③ 남자아이와 여자아이는 이성을 위해 고안된 장난감을 가지고 놀도록 권장되어야 한다.
✓ 장난감 회사들은 남자아이들을 위한 것인지 여자아이들을 위한 것인지를 나타내는 그들의 상품에 명확한 라벨을 붙여야 한다.

| 분석 | 레고의 주장은 성적으로 공정한 것은 오히려 성적으로 구분해야 한다는 것이다. 다시 말해 특정 성별의 특성을 장난감이 반영해야 한다는 것이 레고의 주장이므로, 이에 알맞은 것은 ④ '장난감 회사들은 남자아이들을 위한 것인지 여자아이들을 위한 것인지를 나타내는 그들의 상품에 명확한 라벨을 붙여야 한다.'이다.

18 윗글의 가장 좋은 제목은 무엇인가? 제목

① 어린아이들이 가장 좋아하는 장난감 언급 안 함
② 2012년 크리스마스 세일을 준비하는 장난감 가게들 언급 안 함
③ 남자아이와 여자아이가 잘 어울릴 수 있는가? 언급 안 함
✓ 장난감의 세계는 성별이 없어야 하는가?

| 분석 | 이 글의 핵심 키워드는 장난감, 성별이며 그것이 있어야 할지 말아야 할지를 논쟁의 형태로 다루는 글이다. 따라서 적절한 제목은 ④이다.

[19~20] 2014 서강대

| 정답 | 19 ③   20 ③

| 어휘 | **introvert** ⓝ 내향적인 사람, 내성적인 사람   **extrovert** ⓝ 사교적인 사람, 외향적인 사람   **prospect** ⓝ 전망, 경치; 예상, 기대
limbic system ⓝ 대뇌변연계   **mammal** ⓝ 포유동물   **instinctive** ⓐ 본능적인, 직감적인
amygdala ⓝ 편도체   **nucleus accumbens** 대뇌측좌핵   **gusto** ⓝ 취미, 기쁨, 활기
spur ⓥ 박차를 가하다   **neocortex** ⓝ 신피질   **faculty** ⓝ 능력, 수완, 재력; 학부, 교수단
rationality ⓝ 합리성, 순리성, 도리를 앎   **efficient** ⓐ 능률적인, 효과적인, 유효한   **conflict** ⓝ 갈등, 싸움, 전투
equilibrium ⓝ 평형상태, 균형   **turmoil** ⓝ 소란, 소동   **distinctive** ⓐ 독특한, 특이한

전문해석

왜 내향적인 사람과 외향적인 사람이 보상의 기대에 대해 서로 다르게 반응하는지에 대해서 이해를 하려면 뇌의 구조에 대해 좀 알아야 한다. 우리의 대뇌변연계는 대부분의 원시 포유류와 공유하고 있고 Dorn이 "과거 뇌"라고 부르는 것인데 감정적이고 본능적이다. 이것은 편도체를 포함하는 다양한 구조로 이루어져 있으며, 흔히 뇌의 "쾌락 센터"라고 부르는 대뇌측좌핵과 매우 밀접하게 연결되어 있다. Dorn에 따르면 이 과거 뇌는 우리에게 끊임없이, "그래, 그래, 그래! 더 먹어. 더 마셔. 위험을 감수해. 얻을 수 있는 모든 기쁨을 누려. 그리고 무엇보다도 절대로 생각하지 마"라고 말하고 있다. 이 과거 뇌의 보상을 추구하고 쾌락을 좋아하는 뇌가 사람들로 하여금 평생의 저축을 카지노에서의 칩으로 간주하도록 촉진하였다고 생각한다. 우리는 신피질이라고 부르는 "새로운 뇌"도 갖고 있는데 이것은 대뇌변연계가 나온 이후 수천 년이 지난 후에 생겨났다. 이 새 뇌는 사고, 계획, 언어, 결정 등과 같이

우리 인간을 인간답게 만드는 바로 그 능력들을 담당하고 있다. 비록 새로운 뇌가 우리의 감정적인 생활에도 중요한 역할을 하고 있지만 그것은 합리성이 자리 잡는 곳이다. Dorn에 따르면 이곳이 하는 역할은 우리에게 "안 돼, 안 돼, 안 돼! 그거 하지 마. 그건 위험하고, 말도 안 되고, 네게 아니면 네 가족에게 아니면 네 지역 사회에 도움이 안 되니까."라고 말해 주는 것을 포함한다. 과거 뇌와 새로운 뇌는 서로 같이 협동하지만 항상 효율적인 것은 아니다. 때로는 실제로 이 두 뇌가 갈등을 일으키는데 이때 우리의 결정은 두 뇌 중에 어떤 뇌가 더 강력한 신호를 보내느냐에 따라 이루어진다.

19 빈칸에 가장 적절한 것을 고르시오. 빈칸 추론

① 평형
② 균형
✓ ③ 갈등
④ 소란

| 분석 | 빈칸 뒤에서 둘 중의 어느 하나가 더 강력한 신호를 보낸다고 언급했고, 빈칸 앞에서는 두 뇌가 서로 효율적으로 협동하지 못한다는 말이 있다. 따라서 효율적으로 협동하지 못하는 것은 '갈등과 충돌'이라 할 수 있으므로 빈칸에 가장 적합한 것은 ③ '갈등'이다.

20 윗글에 따르면, 다음 중 추론할 수 없는 것은? 내용 추론

① 새로운 뇌는 우리의 감정적인 삶에서 중요한 역할을 한다.
② 과거 뇌는 보상과 즐거움을 추구하는데, 이것은 종종 사람들을 무모하게 만든다.
✓ ③ 우리는 과거 뇌와 새로운 뇌를 원시 포유류와 공유한다.
④ 유전학적으로, 새로운 뇌는 인간을 다른 동물들과 확실히 다르게 만드는 것이다.

| 분석 | 지문의 중반에서 '우리는 신피질이라고 부르는 "새로운 뇌"도 갖고 있는데 이것은 대뇌변연계가 나온 이후 수천 년이 지난 후에 생겨났다.'고 언급했다. 따라서 우리의 과거 뇌는 다른 포유동물과 공유하고 있지만, 새로운 뇌를 공유하는 것은 아니라는 것을 알 수 있으므로 ③은 지문과 일치하지 않는다.

[21-23] 2016 항공대

| 정답 | 21 ① 22 ② 23 ④

| 어휘 |
object v 반대하다
plead guilty 죄를 인정하다
sophistication ⓝ 궤변; 세련, 정교
ingenuity ⓝ 창의력, 발명의 재주, 정교
dispensation ⓝ 특별 허가, 특별 면제
inquisitive ⓐ 탐구적인, 캐묻기 좋아하는

exaggerate ⓥ 과장하다
overstatement ⓝ 과장
presumably ⓐⓓ 아마
A is no more B than C is D A가 B가 아닌 것은 C가 D가 아닌 것과 같다
pejorative ⓐ 경멸적인, 비방적인, 가치를 떨어뜨리는, 악화시키는
ridiculous ⓐ 웃기는, 우스꽝스러운, 터무니없는

artificiality ⓝ 인공, 인공물
astronaut ⓝ 우주 비행사
equate ⓥ 동일시하다

전문해석

사람들은 내가 우리 세계의 인위성을 과장하고 있다고 반대할지도 모른다. 돌이 중력의 법칙을 따르는 것처럼 인간도 중력의 법칙을 따라야 한다. 그리고 살아 있는 생명체로서 인간은 양식을 위해 그리고 그 이외의 다른 많은 방식으로 생물학적 현상의 세계에 의존해야만 한다. 내가 좀 과장을 하고 있기는 하지만, 나는 동시에 그 과장이 사소한 것이라고 주장하고자 한다. 우주 비행사는 물론이고 심지어 비행기 조종사도, 중력의 법칙을 따르고 있다고 말하는 것이 완벽하게 자연스러운 현상이긴 하지만, 그 말의 진실을 알기 위해 우리는 자연법칙을 따른다는 것의 의미를 보다 세밀하게 살펴보아야 한다. 아리스토텔레스(Aristotle)는 무거운 것이 상승하고 가벼운 것이 하강한다는 것을 자연스럽다고 생각하지 않았다. 그러나 우리 현대인은 아마도 아리스토텔레스가 이해했던 것

보다 더 깊게 자연스러운 것에 대해 이해하고 있을 것이다. 따라서 우리는 생물학적인 것을 자연스러운 것과 동일시하는 일에 대해 신중해야 한다. 숲은 자연의 현상이다. 하지만 농업은 분명 자연의 현상이 아니다. 우리가 우리의 양식을 의존하고 있는 바로 그 생물의 종들은—우리의 옥수수와 우리의 소—우리의 창의성의 산물(인공물)이다. 경작해 놓은 밭은 아스팔트 도로가 자연의 일부가 아닌 것처럼 자연의 일부가 아닌 동시에 자연의 일부이기도 하다. 이러한 예들은 우리가 가지고 있는 문제의 조건을 결정짓는데, 그 이유는 우리가 인공물이라고 부르는 것들이 자연으로부터 괴리되어 있지 않기 때문이다. 인공물들도 <u>자연법칙을 무시하거나 위반하도록 면제받지 않는다</u>. 동시에 인공물은 인간의 목적과 목표에 부합되게 만들어진다. 인공물은 하늘을 날고 잘 먹고 싶은 우리의 욕망을 충족시키기 위해서 현재와 같은 모습이 된 것이다.

---

21 빈칸에 들어갈 말로 가장 적절한 것은? `빈칸 추론`

① ✔ 자연법칙을 무시하거나 위반하도록 면제받지 않다
② 자연법칙을 무시하거나 위반하도록 면제받다
③ 인위적인 법칙을 무시하거나 위반하도록 면제받지 않다
④ 인위적인 법칙을 무시하거나 위반하도록 면제받다

| 분석 | 인공물도 자연과 동떨어져 있는 것이 아니라는 내용이 앞 문장에 언급되고 있으므로, 빈칸에는 인공물도 '자연법칙의 지배를 받는다'는 표현이 들어가는 것이 옳다.

---

22 윗글의 적절한 제목을 고르시오. `제목`

① 자연법칙의 복잡한 성격 `중심 키워드 없음`
② ✔ 인공물의 복잡한 성격
③ 자연과학의 경멸적인 성격 `중심 키워드 없음`
④ 인위성의 경멸적인 성격 `지문 내용과 불일치`

| 분석 | 자연과 관련된 인공물의 특징들이 열거되고 있는 지문으로, 인공물이 자연과 인공을 넘나드는 복잡한 성격을 소유한다는 것이다. 따라서 제목으로 ② '인공물의 복잡한 성격'이 적절하다.

---

23 인공적인 것에 대한 저자의 태도를 어떻게 설명할 수 있는가? `작가의 태도`

① 깜짝 놀라는   ② 우스꽝스러운
③ 즐거운   ④ ✔ 탐구적인

| 분석 | 저자는 인공물에 대한 호기심을 드러내며, 인공물의 성격에 관해 논하고 있는 글이므로 ④ '탐구적인(inquisitive)' 글이라 볼 수 있다.

[24–26] 2021 단국대

| 정답 | 24 ③　25 ④　26 ②

| 어휘 | at one's disposal of ~의 마음대로 쓸 수 있는
dictator ⓝ 독재자
contemporary ⓐ 현대의, 동시대의
Big Brother ⓝ 독재자
enlarge ⓥ 확대하다
propagandist ⓝ 선전자, 선교사
omnipresent ⓐ 편재하는
would-be ⓐ (장차) ~이 되려고 하는
rotary ⓐ 회전하는
spool ⓝ 필름 감개, (녹음테이프의) 빈 릴
neurology ⓝ 신경학

empiricist ⓝ 경험주의자　　　practitioner ⓝ 실천하는 사람　　　insight ⓝ 통찰, 간파
nightmare ⓝ 악몽

> **전문해석**
>
> 히틀러 시절부터 독재자가 되려는 자의 손에 맡길 수 있는 기술적 장치의 병기고는 상당히 확대되었다. 라디오, 시끄러운 스피커, 움직이는 사진 카메라, 회전식 프레스뿐만 아니라, 현대의 선전가는 텔레비전으로 고객의 목소리뿐만 아니라 이미지를 방송할 수 있고, 자기 테이프의 릴에 이미지와 목소리 모두를 녹음할 수 있다. 기술의 진보 덕분에 독재자는 이제 거의 신만큼 어디에나 존재할 수 있다. 또한 독재자가 될 지망자의 손이 강화된 것은 기술적인 측면에서만이 아니다. 히틀러 시대 이후 많은 연구가 전파자, 세뇌자, 뇌 해독자의 특별한 영역인 응용심리학과 신경학 분야에서 수행되어 왔다. 과거에 사람들의 마음을 바꾸는 기술에 있어서 이 전문가들은 경험주의자였다. 시행착오를 통해 그들은 많은 기술과 절차를 고안해 냈다. 그러나 왜 그것들이 효과적인지 정확히 알지 못한 채 매우 효과적으로 사용했다. 오늘날 마인드 컨트롤 기술은 과학이 되어 가는 과정에 있다. 이 과학의 실천가들은 자신들이 무엇을 하고 있고 왜 하고 있는지 알고 있다. 그들은 실험 증거의 거대한 토대 위에 확고히 확립된 이론과 가설에 의해 그들의 연구에 인도된다. 새로운 통찰력과 이러한 통찰력에 의해 가능해진 새로운 기술 덕분에, "히틀러의 전체주의 체제에서 거의 실현된" 악몽이 곧 완전히 실현될지도 모른다.

---

24 빈칸에 들어갈 말로 가장 적절한 것은? **빈칸 추론**

① 꿈　　　　　　② 환상
✓ 과학　　　　　④ 미스터리

| 분석 | 빈칸 뒤에서 과학에 종사하는 사람들과, 연구에 대해 이야기하고 있으므로 빈칸에는 '과학'이 적절하다.

---

25 윗글에 따르면, 어떤 것이 사실인가? **내용 일치**

① 히틀러의 전체주의와 같은 것은 기술의 시대에서는 불가능한 것이다.
② 사람들은 선전 기법에 의해 쉽게 조작되지 않는다.
③ 히틀러는 TV를 포함하여 모든 종류의 선전 기법을 사용했다.
✓ 세뇌 기술(마인드 컨트롤 기술)은 과학의 수준까지 발전해 왔다.

| 분석 | 빈칸의 정답을 맞혔다면 내용은 "오늘날 마인드 컨트롤 기술은 과학이 되는 과정에 있다."가 되고, 이것은 ④와 일치하게 된다.

---

26 윗글의 적절한 주제는 무엇인가? **글의 주제**

① 히틀러와 선전 너무 지엽적
✓ 독재와 대중조작
③ 기술과 경험주의 중심 키워드 없음
④ 히틀러와 새로운 신경학 기술 너무 지엽적

| 분석 | 전반적으로 이 글은 독재와 대중조작에 관하여 기술하며 그것이 과학이 되어 가고 있다고 말하는 글이다.

[27-29] 2014 성균관대

| 정답 | 27 ④　28 ②　29 ②

| 어휘 | miniaturization ⓝ 소형화　　　tracking ⓝ 위치 추적　　　gizmo ⓝ 장치, 기계

privacy ⓝ 사적 자유
roam ⓥ 거닐다, 방랑하다, 배회하다
grave ⓐ 엄한, 근엄한
domestic violence 가정폭력
dehumanize ⓥ 비인간화하다
enamor ⓥ 반하게 하다, 매혹하다
annoying ⓐ 성가신, 귀찮은, 지겨운
assault ⓝ 강습, 습격
surveillance ⓝ 감시, 감독
prone ⓐ 쉬운, 경향성이
enthusiast ⓝ 열광자, 팬
savvy ⓐ 정통한, 요령 있는
snoop ⓥ 배회하다, 엿보다
deter ⓥ 제지하다, 만류하다, 단념시키다

전문해석

연장된 배터리 수명과 소형화는 위치 추적을 더 값싸고 더 실용적으로 만들어 주고 있다. 가장 쉬운 방법은 스마트폰을 사용하는 것이다. 많은 모바일 운영업체들은 별도의 돈을 내면 아이들을 추적할 수 있는 서비스를 제공하고 있지만, 무료로 위치 추적을 할 수 있는 애플리케이션의 숫자가 급속히 증가하고 있다. 이러한 서비스와 장치들은 아이들의 위치 정보를 알려 주거나 아이들의 행동에 대해 경고를 보내 주기도 한다. 일본과 미국의 부모들은 이런 장비에 대해 무척 관심이 많다. 아이들의 안전에 대해서 덜 걱정하고 있는 것으로 보이며 또한 더 복잡한 프라이버시 법이 있는 유럽인들은 이 장치에 별로 매력을 느끼지 못한다. 적극적인 지지자들은 위치 추적은 더 적은 자유가 아닌 더 많은 자유를 준다고 말한다. 자신의 아이들을 쉽게 찾을 수 있다는 것을 알고 있는 부모들은 더욱 기꺼이 아이들이 더 돌아다니도록 놔둘 수 있다. 십 대들은 성가신 전화를 안 받아도 된다. 비판하는 사람들은 위치 추적이 아이들을 정말로 보호해 주지 못한다고 말한다. 원가를 아는 유괴범들은 전화기나 경보 추적 장치를 (빼앗아서) 버릴 것이다. 그리고 어쨌든 잘 모르는 사람들이 아이를 공격하는 일은 거의 없다. 아이들의 살해범은 부모일 가능성이 가장 높으며 공격보다는 사고가 훨씬 더 심각한 위험이다. 위치 추적은 아이들이 강으로 떨어지는 것을 방지해 주지 못한다. 그리고 같은 기술이 어른들이 다른 사람을 엿보게 할 수도 있다. 미국에서는 모바일 전화 가입자들은 가족 전화 플랜을 사용하는 모든 가족들이 위치 추적 서비스에 가입할 수가 있다. 가정폭력의 생존자들 중 위치 추적 때문에 도망치는 일이 더 어렵다고 말하는 사람들이 있다. 부모들은 아이들을 돌봐 주는 사람들을 감시하기 위해 웹캠을 사용한다. 아이들이 출국을 하면 문자 메시지로 아버지에게 알려 주는 사우디 정부 기관은 남자들이 자신의 아내들을 추적하는 데에 도움을 주고 있다.

---

27 윗글의 가장 좋은 제목은 _____이다. 제목

① 새로운 가족?: 현대 관계의 변화 중심 키워드 없음
② 기술과 아이들에게 긍정적인 측면 지문 내용과 불일치
③ 국가 감시 윤리 언급 안 함
✔④ 아이들을 추적하는 것: 프라이버시가 아닌 부모에게 좋은 일
⑤ 기술: 신뢰할 수 없는 하인 언급 안 함

| 분석 | 이 글은 기술의 발전으로 인해 위치 추적을 할 수 있게 되었는데 그것의 장점보다는 단점의 내용을 주로 기술하고 있다. 그렇다 해서 기술이 신뢰할 수 없느냐의 문제는 아니므로 ⑤는 정답이 될 수 없고 소거를 통해 ④를 고를 수 있다.

---

28 다음 중 빈칸에 가장 적합한 것은 무엇인가? 빈칸 추론

① 추적 장치는 납치범들에 의해서도 사용될 수 있다
✔② 추적은 아이들을 실제로 보호하지 못한다
③ 추적 장치는 너무 비싸다
④ 십 대들은 추적 장치를 가지고 다니는 것을 좋아하지 않는다
⑤ 스마트폰은 추적 장치보다 더 효율적이다

| 분석 | 빈칸 뒤의 내용이 "원가를 아는 유괴범들은 전화기나 경보 추적 장치를 (빼앗아서) 버릴 것이다."라는 것은 위치 추적이 아이들을 안전하게 보호해 줄 수는 없다는 내용이므로 ② '위치 추적은 아이들을 실제로 보호하지 못한다'가 빈칸에 적절하다.

> **29** 윗글에 따르면 다음 중 사실인 것은? 내용 일치
>
> ① 높은 추적 비용으로 인해 추적 장치의 광범위한 사용이 제한된다.
> ✓ 추적 장치는 비인간화 경향을 촉진할 수 있다.
> ③ 유럽인들은 서로를 더 신뢰하기 때문에 추적 장치에 별로 관심이 없다.
> ④ 모바일 추적 서비스는 사우디아라비아에서 가정폭력을 예방하는 데 도움이 된다.
> ⑤ 아이들은 어른들보다 감시하기 쉽다.

| 분석 | 위치 추적의 반대 의견을 보면 프라이버시 침해, 가정폭력 조장, 어른들의 다른 사람 엿보기 등이라 할 수 있는데, 이것들은 '추적 장치'가 갖는 '비인간화 경향'이라 할 수 있다. 따라서 ②는 지문과 일치하는 내용이다.

[30-31] 2018 광운대

| 정답 | 30 ⑤ 31 ②

| 어휘 |
bust ⓝ 실패, 파산, 불황
currency ⓝ 통화, 화폐
massive ⓐ 부피가 큰; 육중한, 무거운; 대량의
surge ⓝ 큰 파도; (감정 따위의)격동
hallmark ⓝ 품질증명; 검증서, 증명; (현저한) 특징, 특질
in terms of ~에 관하여, ~의 관점에서
whimper ⓝ 흐느껴 우는 소리, 불평
lowdown ⓝ 실정, 진상, 내막
speculation ⓝ 사색, 숙고; 투기, 사행
import ⓥ 수입하다
novelty ⓝ 신기함; 새로운 것, 색다른 것
gauge ⓥ 재다, 측정하다, 평가[판단]하다
soar ⓥ (물가 따위가) 급등하다, 치솟다
collateral ⓝ 담보물
bulb ⓝ 구근; 전구
a flurry of 부산한, 갑작스레 몰아치는
miss out 좋은 기회를 놓치다, 실패하다
collapse ⓥ 붕괴하다, 무너지다; 폭락하다
ultimately ⓐⓓ 결국, 마침내
demand ⓝ 수요
fade ⓥ 흐릿해지다, 시들다; 자취를 감추다
scarce ⓐ 부족한, 결핍한; 드문, 희귀한
spectacular ⓐ 눈부신, 깜짝 놀라게 하는
speculative ⓐ 사색적인; 투기의

전문해석

비트코인 열풍이 역사상 가장 큰 실패 중의 하나가 될 것인가? 워렌 버핏(Warren Buffett)과 같은 사람들에 따르면, 올해 그 가상 화폐의 엄청난 가격상승—1,400%가 넘게 올랐다—은 거대한 ⓐ 투기성의 버블의 모든 특징들을 다 가지고 있다. 버블이 터지고 나면, 그 결과는 ⓑ 깜짝 놀랄 일이 될 것이다. "버블이 어떤 식으로 끝나는지에 관해서, 버블의 역사는 버블이란 서서히 꺼지지 않고 뻥 하고 터지는 법이라고 말해 줍니다. 저는 이번에도 다르지 않을 거라 생각합니다."라고 ANZ의 경제학자인 샤론 졸러(Sharon Zoller)는 말했다. 앞으로의 사태를 좀 더 잘 이해하기 위해, 역사적으로 유명한 금융 버블인 튤립 파동의 내막을 소개하고자 한다. 17세기 초에, 튤립 구근에 대한 투기는 네덜란드에서 튤립의 가치를 전대미문의 높은 가격으로 몰아갔다. 튤립은 터키에서 새로 수입됐던 것으로, 당시에는 매우 새로운 것이었다. 그 당시로부터 얻을 수 있는 하드 데이터는 ⓒ 부족하기 때문에, 가격이 얼마나 많이 치솟았는지를 정확하게 측정하기가 어렵다. 그러나 사람들은 자산들의 집을 담보로 잡히고 있었다. 여러 버블들과 마찬가지로, 인간의 탐욕과 좋은 기회를 놓칠 것만 같은 두려움에 의해 가격이 주도되었다. 투기꾼들은 훨씬 더 높은 가격으로 팔 수 있기를 바라면서 튤립 구근을 사고 있었다. 반면에, 그것은 지속되지 않았다. 서둘러 팔아치우려는 소동은 도미노 현상을 일으켰고, 가격은 폭락했다. ⟨외환중개업체 오안다(Oanda)의 아시아 지역 트레이딩 담당자인 스티븐 이네스(Stephen Innes)는 비트코인 버블도 같은 길을 가게 될 수 있다고 믿는다.⟩ "가격은 보통 사람들이 감당할 수 없는 수준이 될 것이고, 궁극적으로는 수요가 사라지게 됩니다."라고 그는 말했다.

30 다음 주어진 표현이 들어갈 위치로 가장 적절한 곳은? 문장 삽입

외환중개업체 오안다(Oanda)의 아시아 지역 트레이딩 담당자인 스티븐 이네스(Stephen Innes)는 비트코인 버블도 같은 길을 가게 될 수 있다고 믿는다.

① [A]　　② [B]
③ [C]　　④ [D]
✓ [E]

| 분석 | 주어진 문장은 '비트코인 버블도 같은 길을 가게 될 것'이라는 전문가의 견해에 해당하는데, 다른 버블의 결과가 좋지 않다는 말 뒤에 위치해야 자연스럽다. 따라서 주어진 문장은 '네덜란드 튤립 파동의 결말'에 대해 언급한 부분 다음인 [E]에 들어가는 것이 적절하다.

31 윗글의 빈칸 Ⓐ, Ⓑ, Ⓒ에 들어갈 말로 가장 적절한 것은? 빈칸 추론

① 부족한 – 깜짝 놀라는 – 투기적인
✓ ② 투기적인 – 깜짝 놀라는 – 부족한
③ 부족한 – 투기적인 – 부족한
④ 투기적인 – 부족한 – 깜짝 놀라는
⑤ 깜짝 놀라는 – 부족한 – 투기적인

| 분석 | 빈칸 Ⓐ는 가격이 엄청나게 올랐다는 것은 투기적인 일이므로 '투기적인'이라는 의미의 'speculative'가 적절하다. 빈칸 Ⓑ의 경우, 뒤에서 버블은 서서히 꺼지기보다 일시에 터지게 될 것이라 했으므로 '장관의, 깜짝 놀라게 하는'의 의미인 'spectacular'가 적절하다. 마지막 빈칸 Ⓒ는 so 이하의 문장과 인과관계를 이루고 있는데, 가격이 얼마나 많이 올랐는지를 정확하게 측정하기가 어려운 것은 자료가 부족하기 때문일 것이다. 따라서 '부족한'의 의미인 scarce가 적절하다.

[32-33] 2020 한양대

| 정답 | 32 ④　33 ②

| 어휘 | innate ⓐ 선천적인, 타고난
hedonic ⓐ 쾌락의
predetermined ⓐ 미리 결정된
umami ⓝ 감칠맛
glutamate ⓝ 글루타민산염
affinity ⓝ 친밀감, 친연성
account for ~을 설명하다
toxicity ⓝ (유)독성
unpalatable ⓐ 불쾌한 구미에 맞지 않는
pungency ⓝ 얼얼함
chili ⓝ 고추
modify ⓥ 수정하다
makeup ⓝ 체질, 기질
predisposed ⓐ ~의 성향이 있는

전문해석

기본적인 맛에 대한 선천적인 쾌락적 반응의 증거에도 불구하고 대부분의 특정한 음식을 좋아하고 싫어하는 것이 ⓐ 미리 결정된 것이 아니다—예를 들어, 아무도 날 때부터 블루 치즈를 좋아하는 사람은 없다. 이것은 기본적인 감각적 자질이 ⓑ 중요하지 않다는 것을 말하는 것은 아니다. 그와는 반대로 단맛, 짠맛, 쓴맛, 감칠맛(글루타민산염 맛), 그리고 거의 확실히 지방까지 포함해 맛에 대한 비교적 고정적인 쾌락적 반응은 출생 당시 혹은 출생 직후에 존재하며, 음식 선호에 지속적으로 영향을 미친다. 아이들이 매우 단 음식에 대해 보여 주는 강렬한 친밀감, 그리고 소금 맛과 짠 음식에 대한 선호가 초기에 발달해 평생 지속되는 것은 ⓒ 보편적인 것 같다. 서양의 대부분의 사람들은 지방 함량이 높은 식단을 선택한다. 그러나 유아기를 넘어 발전하는 음식에 대한 호불호의 광범위한 범위를 선천적 반응이 설명하지는 못한다. 예를 들어, 인간과 많은 다른 포유류들은 아주 낮은 수준의 쓴맛도 감지할 수 있는데, 그것은 쓴맛이 독성의 잠재적인 신호이기 때문에 그 맛을 ⓓ 맛있게 생각하는 것이다. 그러나 커피와 맥주는 일반적으로 처음 먹었을 때는 거부되는 반면 궁극적으로 세계적 음료 중에서 가장 강력한 경쟁자가 된다. 매운 음식의 얼얼함 또한 처음에는 거부된다. 그러나 전 세계적으로 고추는 음식의 양념으로서 소금에 버금간다. 그러므로 음식 선택에 있어서 선천적인 영향은 명백히 중요하지만, 이런 영향은 우리가 음식을 경험하면서 ⓔ <u>고쳐지게 된다</u>(생리적인 체질과 문화 모두 경험의 작동 허용 범위를 부분적으로 결정한다 할지라도). 그렇다면 우리의 선천적인 선호보다 더 중요한 것은 <u>우리가 음식을 좋아하거나 싫어하기를 학습하는 경향이 있다</u>는 사실이다.

---

32 윗글의 밑줄 친 ⓐ~ⓔ 중 문맥상 낱말의 쓰임이 적절하지 않은 것은? 글의 흐름 파악

① ⓐ　　　　　　　　　　② ⓑ
③ ⓒ　　　　　　　　　　✓ ⓓ
⑤ ⓔ

| 분석 | '쓴맛이 독성의 잠재적인 신호'를 보여 준다고 했기 때문에, 우리는 스스로 보호하기 위해 쓴맛이 나는 음식을 '맛없는' 것으로 인식해야 할 것이다. 따라서 ⓓ를 unpalatable로 고쳐야 자연스럽다.

---

33 윗글의 빈칸에 들어갈 말로 가장 적절한 것은? 빈칸 추론

① 식품은 다양한 이유로 거부될 수 있다
✓ 우리는 음식을 좋아하거나 싫어하기를 학습하는 경향이 있다
③ 우리는 다양한 잠재적 영양소에 접근할 수 있다
④ 음식의 쾌락적 가치는 문호에 따라 크게 다를 수 있다
⑤ 음식 선호도는 문화적 맥락에 의해 강하게 영향을 받는다

| 분석 | 빈칸 앞에서 '음식을 경험하면서 음식에 대한 선천적인 영향이 고쳐진다고 했기 때문에 결국 음식의 호불호는 후천적으로 학습한다고 할 수 있다. 한편, 후천적인 것에는 교육, 문화, 환경 등으로 나눌 수 있는데 ⑤의 문화는 그중에 하나라고 할 수 있으며 ②에 포함되므로 더 포괄적인 ②를 골라야 한다.

[34-35] 2017 단국대

| 정답 | **34** ④　　**35** ③

| 어휘 | **term** ⓝ 기간, 조건; 용어　　　　　　**architecture** ⓝ 건축학 구조; 구성, 설계　　　**artificial intelligence** 인공지능
structure ⓥ (복잡한 것을) 구축[조직]하다　　**cartoon** ⓝ 만화, 풍자화; 밑그림　　　　**comprise** ⓥ 함유하다; 의미하다, 구성하다
node ⓝ 마디, 결절; (컴퓨터의) 교점(네트워크의 분기점이나 단말 장치의 접속점)　　**dumb** ⓐ 말을 못 하는; 우둔한, 어리석은
extremely ⓐⓓ 극단적으로, 대단히, 몹시　　**tackle** ⓥ 다루다, 처리하다　　　　　　**layer** ⓝ 층, 단층
magnification ⓝ 확대, 과장; 배율, 확대도　　**grid** ⓝ 격자, 모눈, 그리드　　　　　　**process** ⓝ 진행, 경과, 과정, 처리
complicated ⓐ 복잡한, 까다로운　　　　**constituent** ⓐ 구성하는, 조직하는; ~의 성분을 이루는

전문해석

'신경망', '기계학습', '딥 러닝'은 실제로 무엇을 의미하는가? 이 세 가지 용어를 당신은 아마도 최근에 들어 봤을 가능성이 높다. 신경망은 인공 지능의 바탕이 되는 일종의 컴퓨터 아키텍처이다. 이러한 신경망은 뇌의 밑그림처럼 보이도록 컴퓨터를 구조화하는 방법인데, 이 밑그림은 웹상에서 서로 연결되어 있는 뉴런(신경세포) 같은 노드들로 이루어져 있다. 이 노드들의 경우, 개별적으로는 우둔해서 매우 단순한 질문에만 대답하지만, 집합적으로는 어려운 문제들도 다룰 수 있다. 보다 더 중요한 점은, 적절한 알고리즘을 사용하는 경우에는 학습도 가능하다는 것이다. 기계학습은 신경망에 실행시킬 수 있는 프로그램으로, 여러 데이터 가운데서 특정한 답을 찾을 수 있도록 컴퓨터를 교육시킨다. 딥 러닝은 널리 보급된 것이 10년에 불과한 특정 종류의 기계학습으로, 이것이 널리 보급된 것은 두 가지 새로운 자원, 즉 비용이 적게 드는 처리 능력과 (다르게는 인터넷으로도 알려져 있는) 풍부한 자료 덕분이었다.

딥 러닝 시스템이 사진을 보고 있는 경우, 각각의 층은 본질적으로 서로 다른 배율로 사진을 다룬다. 맨 아래층은 (사진에서) 5x5 화소의 격자를 보고, 그 격자 안에 무엇이 나타나는지를 단순히 '예', '아니요'로만 대답할 것이다. 만약 '예'라고 대답을 했다면, 그 위에 있는 층이 이 격자가 더 큰 모양 속으로 어떻게 맞춰지는지 살펴본다. 예를 들어, 이것이 어떤 선이나 모서리의 시작점인지를 알아보는 것이다. <u>이러한 과정</u>이 점차 쌓여서, 가장 복잡한 자료조차도 그것을 구성 요소로 나눔으로써 소프트웨어가 이해할 수 있게 해 준다.

---

34 윗글에 의하면 다음 중 옳은 것은? `내용 일치`

① 딥 러닝 시스템에서는, 가장 복잡한 자료를 맨 아래층에서 이해할 수 있다.
② 딥 러닝은 기계학습을 가능하게 하는 컴퓨터 아키텍처의 일종이다.
③ 비용이 적게 드는 처리 능력과 풍부한 자료가 신경망 시스템이 개발을 가능하게 했다.
✓ ④ 신경망 시스템에서는 개별적인 노드들이 어려운 문제를 집합적으로 다룬다.

| 분석 | 지문에서 "신경망의 노드들이 개별적으로는 우둔해서 매우 단순한 질문에만 답하지만, 집합적으로는 어려운 문제들도 다룰 수 있다."고 언급했다. 따라서 ④가 지문과 일치하는 진술이다.

---

35 다음 중 밑줄 친 부분이 가리키는 것은? `지시어`

① 맨 아래층에서 복잡한 정보를 처리하는 것
② 어려운 문제를 집합적으로 다루는 것
✓ ③ 낮은 층에서 단순한 질문에 대답하는 것
④ 복잡한 자료를 구성 요소로 쪼개는 것

| 분석 | 이러한 과정이 점차 누적되어 복잡한 자료를 처리한다고 했으므로 단순하고 쉬운 과정이 누적되어 복잡한 것을 처리해야 문맥상 맞다. 따라서 이러한 과정은 앞에서 언급한 '예', '아니요'와 같은 단순한 처리를 가리킨다.

| 배경 지식 | 딥 러닝(Deep learning): 딥 러닝은 머신 러닝의 하위 분야로, 기본적으로 3개 이상의 계층으로 된 신경망이다. 이러한 신경망은 인간의 뇌의 능력에 한참 못 미치지만 인간의 뇌의 행동을 흉내 내어 대량의 데이터로부터 '학습'을 수행한다. 딥 러닝은 자동화를 제공하는 많은 인공 지능(AI) 애플리케이션과 서비스의 기반이 되며, 인간의 개입 없이 분석적 작업과 물리적 작업을 수행한다. 딥 러닝은 자율주행 자동차와 같은 새로운 기술뿐만 아니라 디지털 비서, 음성 지원 TV 리모컨, 신용카드 사기 탐지와 같은 일상적 제품과 서비스를 뒷받침한다.

[36-37] 2020 서강대

| 정답 | 36 ① 37 ②

| 어휘 | observation ⓝ 관찰, 관측
consciousness ⓝ 의식, 자각
grasp ⓥ 이해하다, 파악하다
experiment ⓝ 실험
subjective ⓐ 주관적인
investigation ⓝ 조사, 연구, 수사

feature ⓝ 특징, 특색, 두드러진 점
demanding ⓐ 힘든, 벅찬
conceive of A as B A를 B로 이해하다
physics ⓝ 물리학
accessible ⓐ 접근하기 쉬운, 입장 가능한

cognitive ⓐ 인식의; 인식력이 있는
interaction ⓝ 상호 작용, 대화
self ⓝ 자기, 자신, 자아
preference ⓝ 더 좋아함, 편애
objective ⓐ 객관적인

전문해석

이러한 간단한 관찰은 인공 지능 의식 테스트로 이어지는데, 이 테스트는 현상적 의식(PC)을 갖춘 인공 지능들을 단순히 작업 기억과 주의력 같은 인지 의식의 특징만을 갖는 인공 지능들로부터 Ⓐ 선별하는 것이다. 이 테스트는 일련의 점점 더 어려워지는 자연 언어 대화들을 인공 지능에 던져 주고 인공 지능이 우리가 의식과 연관시키는 내적 경험에 기초한 개념을 얼마나 쉽게 파악하고 이용할 수 있는지를 알아보려고 한다. 단지 인지 능력은 갖고 있지만 좀비인 생명체는, 적어도 우리가 그 생명체의 데이터베이스 안에 의식에 대한 Ⓑ 사전의 지식이 없게 해 놓기만 하면, 이러한 개념을 갖지 못할 것이다. 가장 기초적인 수준에서는, 우리는 단지 기계에 그 기계가 스스로를 물리적인 자신 이외의 어떤 것으로 이해하고 있는지를 물어볼 수 있을 것이다. 우리는 또한 일련의 실험을 실시하여 인공 지능이 미래에는 과거와 다른 특정 종류의 사건이 일어나는 것을 선호하는 경향이 있는지를 알아볼 수도 있을 것이다. 물리학에서 시간은 Ⓒ 대칭적이며, 적어도 효과적으로 박싱-인(boxing-in)된다면, 의식 없는 인공 지능은 그 어떤 것도 선호하지 않을 것이다. 이와 대조적으로 의식 있는 존재는 경험되는 현재에 초점을 맞추며, 우리의 주관적인 감각은 미래로 향한다. "인공 지능 의식 테스트" 또는 줄여서 "ACT 테스트"는 기계의 의식을 객관적으로 조사할 수 있게 만드는 쪽으로의 첫 단계 역할을 할 것이다.

* 현상적 의식(PC): 누군가의 내적 경험의 질적 느낌—당신을 내면에서부터 어떻게 느끼는가
** 박싱-인: 인공 지능이 세상에 관한 정보를 얻거나 정해진 영역 밖에서 행동하거나 할 수 있게 하는 것(인공 지능 자체 안에서 입력된 명령만 수행하게 하는 것)

---

36 다음 중 윗글로부터 추론할 수 없는 진술은? **내용 추론**

✓① ACT 테스트는 인공 지능의 인지 의식을 식별하기 위해 고안되었다.
② 현상적 의식이 있는 생물체는 사후 세계를 상상할 수 있다.
③ 인공 지능 좀비는 인지 의식을 가지고 있으며 현상적 의식이 있는 시스템처럼 행동하지 않을 수도 있다.
④ 작업 기억과 주의력은 인지 의식의 두 가지 구조적 특징이다.

| 분석 | 기존에 있던 인공 지능은 작업 기억, 인지 능력만을 갖고 있는 인공 지능이라면 새로운 인공 지능은 현상적 의식(PC)을 갖는 것인데 ACT 테스트가 그 둘을 구분 지어 준다는 것이다. 따라서 ①에서 ACT 테스트는 인지적 의식을 식별(기존)하는 것이 아니라 PC(새로운 것)를 식별하기 위한 것이라고 해야 하므로 ①은 지문과 일치하지 않는 진술이다. 또한 현상적 의식(PC)이 있는 것은 자신에 대한 의식이 있으며 과거와 현재, 미래에 대한 선호도 존재할 것이다. 따라서 ②는 지문과 일치하는 진술이다.

---

37 빈칸 Ⓐ, Ⓑ, Ⓒ에 들어갈 알맞은 단어를 고르시오. **빈칸 추론**

① 구별 짓다 – 예상에 의한 – 체계적인
✓② 선별하다 – 사전에 – 대칭적인
③ 고립시키다 – 보조적인 – 원심력의
④ 구별하다 – 체력 회복의 – 구심력의

| 분석 | 빈칸 Ⓐ는 ACT는 PC를 가진 인공 지능과 단지 인지적 의식을 갖고 있는 인공 지능을 현상적 의식이 있는 인공 지능을 '구별하고', '선별하는' 테스트라고 해야 자연스럽다. 따라서 빈칸 Ⓐ는 'differentiate', 'single out', 'separate'가 가능하다. 빈칸 Ⓑ는 인공 지능이 어떤 개념을 갖고 있으려면 '사전에' 정보를 입력해 주어야 하므로 'antecedent'가 가능하다. 마지막으로 빈칸 Ⓒ는 시간이라는 것을 물리학에서 어떻게 바라보는가인데 의식이 있는 인간이라면 과거, 현재, 미래를 다 동등하게 중요도를 부여하지 않을 것이다. 따라서 인간이라면 과거, 현재, 미래의 시간을 대칭으로 생각하지 않을 테지만 기존 물리학은 인간이 아니므로 과거, 현재, 미래의 시간을 '대칭적'으로 생각할 것이다.

[38-39] 2015 성균관대

| 정답 | 38 ② 39 ①

| 어휘 |
on the face of it (겉으로) 보기에는, 표면적으로는
stern ⓐ 엄격한, 단호한, 근엄한
crowning ⓐ 최고의, 더없는
equation ⓝ 방정식
pagan a. 이교도의
rationality ⓝ 합리성, 순리성
dazzling ⓐ 눈부신, 현혹적인
clockwork ⓝ 시계[태엽] 장치
deity ⓝ 신, 신성
fortitude ⓝ 인내, 용기, 불굴의 정신
stranglehold ⓝ 목조르기; 속박, 자유를 억누르는 힘
paid-up ⓐ 열렬한, ~을 강력히 지지하는; (회비 등을) 다 납부한
arcane ⓐ 비밀의, 불가해한
deft ⓐ 솜씨가 좋은, 능란한, 능숙한
orbit ⓝ 궤도
inscrutable ⓐ 불가사의한, 측량할 수 없는
unpromising ⓐ 가망이 없는, 유망하지 않은
diagram ⓝ 도형, 도표
numerological ⓐ 수비학의, 숫자점의
geometer ⓝ 기하학자
sorcerer ⓝ 마법사, 마술사

전문해석

겉보기에, 분명 1600년대는 "천재의 시대"라는 설명에 적합한 후보는 아니었다. 모두가 신을 경외하는 시대였으며, 홍수부터 소행성까지, 모든 것들이 시기심 많고 엄중한 신성의 불가해한 의지로 여겨졌다. 하지만 현대적이고 과학적인 세계관이 꽃을 피운 것은 이러한 가망성 없는 토대로부터였다. 이 시대 최고의 업적—아이작 뉴턴(Isaac Newton)의 "자연 철학의 수학적 원리"—은 지금까지 쓰인 가장 영향력 있는 책들 중 하나에 속한다. 그리고 수학적인 끈기를 소유한 매우 난해한 이 책의 도표를 이해하려는 사람들은 감탄에 말문이 막혀 버리게 된다. 기괴한 천재로부터 유래된 방정식들은 아직까지도 차를 디자인하고, 교량을 건설하고, 우주로 우주선을 날리는 데 사용되고 있다.

[B] 하지만 이 시대의 유산은 일련의 유용한 이론들 그 이상이다. 일상생활의 분명한 혼란 이면에, 우주가 몇몇 단순한 방정식으로 묘사될 수 있는 규칙적이고 질서정연한 기계와 같다는 뉴턴과 요하네스 케플러(Johannes Kepler)와 같은 사람의 직관은 놀랍게도 옳은 것으로 입증되었다. 과학적 혁명의 진정한 유산이 되는 것은 이런 보편적인 사고이다.

[D] 표준적인 설명은 서구 사상에 교회와 교회의 지지를 받은 일부 이교도적인 사상가들이 수 세기 동안 공들여 왔던 자유를 억압하는 속박을 새로운 과학이 깨 버렸다고 우리에게 알려 주고 있다. 이것은 대체로 사실이지만, 현실은 이보다 훨씬 더 복잡하다. 최초의 과학자들은 현대 물질주의와 합리성에 대한 열렬한 신봉자로 갑자기 등장한 것은 아니었다. 뉴턴은 자신의 생애를 오늘날 우리가 알고 있는 과학을 추구했던 시기와 연금술과 성경의 수비학 암호를 강박적으로 연구하던 때와 같은, 더 오래되고 불가해한 학문을 추구하던 시기로 나누었다. 뉴턴은 세상에 대한 그의 위대한 사상 체계가 현란한 기술을 지닌 기하학자인 신에게 바치는 찬사가 되길 바랬다. 다른 사람들이 그의 사상 체계를 받아들여 일단 우주적인 시계태엽이 감기고 나면, 행성이 궤도를 움직이는 데 더 이상 신적인 개입이 필요 없을 것이라 추정하게 되었을 때, 그는 실망했다. 어떤 의미에서, <u>그는 최초의 과학자가 아니라 마지막 마법사였다</u>.

38 윗글을 3개의 단락으로 나눌 수 있을 때 어느 것이 적절한 경계인가? 단락 나누기

① [A]와 [C]   ✓② [B]와 [D]
③ [B]와 [F]   ④ [C]와 [E]
⑤ [D]와 [F]

| 분석 | 단락을 3개로 나누는 문제이다. 단락이 3개라면 각 단락에 맞는 주제가 있다는 것을 생각하면서 접근해야 한다. 첫 번째 단락의 주제는 17세기가 과학이 꽃필 시기는 아니었지만, 그 속에서 현대적이고 과학적인 세계관이 도래한 시기였다는 것이다. 그리고 뉴턴을 그 예로 들어서 설명하고 있다. 두 번째 단락은 17세기 유산이 이러한 유용한 이론이라고 할 수 없으며 진정한 유산은 이런 사상에 내재된 보편성이라는 것이다. 그리고 마지막 세 번째 단락은 '이러한 오늘날 최초의 과학자들이라고 부르는 사람들은 종교적인 성향을 함께 갖고 있었다'를 뉴턴을 예시로 들어 설명하고 있다. 따라서 적절한 단락 나누기는 [B]와 [D]라고 볼 수 있다. [F]에서 뉴턴은 앞 문장의 예시로 언급되었으므로 단락을 나누면 안 되는 것에 주의해야 한다.

39	밑줄 친 표현은 ＿＿＿＿＿＿의 의미를 함축하고 있다. 밑줄 의미 추론

✓ ① 우주가 질서 정연한 장소라는 그의 확신은 그의 종교적인 믿음에서 비롯되었다
② 그는 우주가 인간이 이해할 수 있는 어떤 것이라고 생각했다
③ 그의 과학적인 업적은 연금술에 관한 그의 믿음으로 인해 약화되었다
④ 그는 과학자도 주술사도 아니었다
⑤ 그의 과학적인 업적이 주술사로서의 본 모습을 숨겨 주었다

| 분석 | 세 번째 단락의 주제가 최초의 과학자들은 종교적 성향을 소유했다는 것이고, 그 예로 뉴턴을 소개하고 있다. 뉴턴은 과학적인 업적과 종교적인 성향을 동시에 갖고 있었으므로 마지막 문장인 "그는 최초의 과학자가 아니라 마지막 마법사였다."는 것도 문맥상 그는 종교적이면서 과학적이었다는 말이 된다. 따라서 정답은 ① '우주가 질서 정연한 장소라는 그의 확신은 그의 종교적인 믿음에서 비롯되었다'이다.

[40-42] 2011 경희대

| 정답 | 40 ④ 41 ① 42 ②

| 어휘 | jiggling ⓝ 움직임, 변동   analogy ⓝ 유추, 유사, 비슷함   downpour ⓝ 억수, 호우
damp ⓐ 축축한, 습기 찬   come off 떼어낼[제거할] 수 있다   fluctuate ⓥ 오르내리다, 변동하다

전문해석

에너지 보존이란 세상에 존재하는 전체 에너지가 똑같은 상태로 유지되는 것을 의미한다. 그러나 고르지 못한 상황에서도 에너지가 상당히 균일하게 퍼질 수가 있어 어떤 상황에서는, 그 에너지가 한쪽에서 다른 쪽으로 이동할 수 없게 되는 경우가 있는데, 즉 에너지를 더 이상 제어할 수 있는 방법이 없게 된다. 이런 식으로 나는 하나의 유추를 통해서 다소 어려운 개념을 제시해 볼 수 있다고 생각한다. 당신이 몇 장의 수건을 가지고 해변에 앉아 있는데 갑자기 엄청난 폭우가 쏟아진다고 상상해 보라. 될 수 있는 한 재빨리 그 수건을 집어 들고 탈의장으로 달려간다. 그때 당신은 당신의 몸을 말리기 시작하고, 그리고 당신은 수건이 약간 젖어 있지만 그러나 당신보다 더 말라 있음을 발견한다. 당신은 수건이 상당히 젖을 때까지 수건으로 계속 말리는데 결국에는 그것이 당신을 말려 주는 것만큼이나 당신을 젖게 한다. 그때 다른 수건으로 말려 보려고 하게 되고 곧 당신은 끔찍한 것을 발견한다. 즉, 모든 수건이 축축해지면 당신 또한 그렇게 된다는 것이다. 비록 당신이 많은 수건을 갖고 있다 하더라도 더 이상 말릴 방법은 없는 것이다. 왜냐하면 ⓐ 수건이 젖어 있는 것이나 당신이 젖어 있는 것에는 차이가 없기 때문이다. 나는 소위 '어느 정도면 물을 쉽게 제거할 수 있다'라고 말할 수 있는 일정의 양을 가늠할 수 있게 된다. 수건도 마찬가지로 당신과 같이 쉽게 물을 제거할 수 있는 정도가 있고, 그래서 당신이 수건으로 당신의 몸을 닦을 때, 당신의 몸에 있던 물기가 수건으로 옮기는 만큼이나 수건에 있던 물기가 당신에게 묻게 되는 것이다. 그러나 그것은 당신에게 있는 양의 물기만큼 수건에 있는 물기의 양이 똑같다는 것을 의미하는 것은 아니다. 즉, 큰 수건은 작은 수건보다 더 많은 물기를 가지게 될 것이다. 그러나 그것들의 눅눅함은 다를 것이 없다. 그래서 물건들이 똑같이 축축함을 가지고 있으면 더 이상 당신이 할 수 있는 것은 아무것도 없다.

40	윗글의 제목으로 가장 적절한 것을 고르시오. 제목

① 에너지와 물의 연관성 인식 지문 내용과 불일치
② 에너지 절약 필요성 분석을 위한 물의 이용 지문 내용과 불일치
③ 물을 아끼는 것이 에너지를 지킨다 지문 내용과 불일치
✓ ④ 에너지 재활용 방식의 이해

| 분석 | 본문에서 설명하는 물은 에너지이고 젖은 몸을 마른 수건으로 닦는 것이 에너지가 이동하는 모습이다. 그러나 이러한 에너지

의 이동이 더 이상 불가능해지는 경우가 생기는데 그것이 바로 수건들이 모두 젖어서 물이 더 이상 닦이지 않는 것이고, 이러한 에너지의 불규칙한 이동을 통해 에너지의 분포가 균일해진다. 여기서 에너지의 불규칙한 이동이 에너지의 재활용 과정을 의미하므로 적절한 제목은 ④의 '에너지 재활용 방식의 이해'이다.

---

41 Ⓐ에 적합한 말을 고르시오. 빈칸 추론

☑ ① 수건이 젖는 것과 당신 스스로가 젖는 것 사이에 차이 없음
② 젖은 수건과 마른 수건으로 몸을 말리는 것의 큰 차이
③ 당신이 밖으로 다시 돌아갈 때 젖을 것이기 때문에 차이 없음
④ 젖은 수건과 마른 수건의 큰 차이

| 분석 | 빈칸 Ⓐ에는 젖어 있는(비에 맞은) 수건을 아무리 가지고 있더라도 말릴 수가 없는 이유로 몸에 있던 물이 수건에 그리고 수건에 있던 물이 다시 몸에 묻기 때문으로 결국에는 '수건의 물과 몸의 물에는 차이가 없기 때문'이라고 한 ①이 정답이다.

---

42 윗글에 나온 비유의 목적은 다음과 같다: 내용 파악

① 똑같이 나누어진 에너지는 물과 비슷한 기능을 할 수 있다.
☑ ② 에너지는 그것의 분포가 변동하고 그것의 양이 그대로 유지된다는 점에서 물과 같다.
③ 수건은, 물에 젖으면, 같은 양의 물을 몸의 표면에 나누어 준다.
④ 계속해서 당신 스스로를 말림으로써, 건조된 물은 다른 수건에 재사용될 수 있다.

| 분석 | 수건과 물에 대한 비유를 통해서 이야기하고자 하는 목적을 묻는 문제로 본문은 에너지의 분배는 변동의 등락을 거듭하며 그리고 그 양은 똑같은 상태를 유지한다는 점에서 에너지는 물과 같다는 것을 보여 주는 글이다. 따라서 ②가 적절한 정답이다.

[43-46] 2012 항공대

| 정답 | 43 ④   44 ②   45 ②   46 ④

| 어휘 |
emit ⓥ 방출하다
interference behavior 간섭 거동
photoelectric effect 광전 효과
discontinuous ⓐ 불연속적인
frequency ⓝ 진동수, 주파수
refraction ⓝ 굴절
destructive interference 상쇄 간섭
be composed of ~로 구성되다
photon ⓝ 광자, 광양자
interference ⓝ 간섭, 상쇄
quantum ⓝ 양자
corpuscle ⓝ 미립자
electron ⓝ 전자

전문해석

19세기의 시작까지도 빛은 한 원천에서 방출되어 눈에 들어오며 시각을 자극하는 입자들의 흐름으로 이해되었다. 이러한 빛의 입자 이론을 만든 주요 창시자는 뉴턴(Newton)이었다. 대부분의 과학자들은 뉴턴의 빛의 입자 이론을 받아들였다. 하지만, 뉴턴의 살아생전에 또 하나의 이론이 제시되었다. 1678년 네덜란드의 물리학자이자 천문학자인 크리스티안 하위헌스(Christiaan Huygens)는 빛의 파동 이론이 반사와 굴절의 법칙들을 설명할 수 있음을 보여 주었다.

하지만 파동 이론은 몇 가지 이유 때문에 Ⓐ 즉각적으로 수용되지는 않았다. 첫째, 당시에 알려져 있던 모든 파동들은 일종의 매개체를 통해 움직였는데, 태양에서부터 오는 빛은 텅 빈 우주 공간을 가로질러 지구로 올 수 있었다. 또, 만일 빛이 일종의 파동이라면 장애물 주변에서 구부러질 것이고, 따라서 우리는 구석구석까지 잘 볼 수 있어야 할 것이다.

빛의 파동적 성격을 처음으로 분명히 증명한 것은 1801년 토머스 영(Thomas Young)이었는데, 그는 적절한 조건에서 빛은 간섭 거동을 한다는 것을 보여 주었다. 하나의 원천에서 방출되어, 두 개의 상이한 경로를 따라 움직이는 빛의 파동이 어떤 지점에 이르러 결합하며, Ⓑ 파괴적 간섭에 의해 서로를 상쇄시켜 버렸다. 과학자들은 어떻게 두 개 이상의 입자들이 모여서 서로 상쇄될 수 있

는지 상상할 수 없었기 때문에 그러한 행동은 입자 모델에 의해 설명될 수 없었다.
1905년 아인슈타인(Einstein)은 논문 한 편을 발표하는데, 이 논문은 빛의 양자 이론을 만들고, 광전 효과에 대해 설명했다. 그는 빛이 미립자, 다시 말해 에너지의 불연속적인 양자로 구성되어 있다는 결론에 도달했다. 이러한 미립자 혹은 양자가 지금은 그 입자적 성격을 강조하기 위해 광자라고 불리고 있다. 전자는 마치 전자가 입자에 의해 부딪치는 것처럼 빛의 한 광자와 상호 작용을 한다. 하지만 광자는 파동과 같은 특성도 가지고 있는데, 광자를 정의하기 위해 주파수를 이용한다는 사실만 보아도 알 수 있다.

46 ④

---

43 다음 중 빈칸 Ⓐ에 가장 적합한 것은 무엇인가? 빈칸 추론

① 빛의 본질적인 측면을 결코 굴절시키지 않았다
② 즉시 수용을 얻었다
③ 빛의 본질적인 측면을 설명했다
✓ ④ 즉시 수용을 얻지 못했다

| 분석 | 첫 번째 빈칸 뒤의 내용에 단서가 있다. 뒤의 내용이 기존에 파동은 매개체가 있어야 하지만 빛은 매개체가 없이 가로지른다고 언급하였다. 따라서 빛이 파동이라는 이론은 그 당시 생각과 어긋난 것이므로 즉시 수용을 얻어 내지는 못했을 것이다.

---

44 윗글의 주제는 _____ 일 것이다. 주제

① 에너지의 질 중심 키워드 없음
✓ ② 빛의 성질
③ 빛의 측정 너무 지엽적
④ 내부 전반사 중심 키워드 없음

| 분석 | 이 글은 빛의 성질에 관한 설명의 역사를 기술하고 있다.

---

45 빈칸 Ⓑ에 적절한 단어를 채우시오. 빈칸 추론

① 건설적인 지도
✓ ② 파괴적인 간섭
③ 부적절한 조작
④ 적절한 조작

| 분석 | 빈칸 앞에서 빛의 파동이 서로 결합하여 cancel each other(서로를 상쇄시킨다)고 하였으므로 서로가 서로에게 간섭하여 파괴한다는 것을 알 수 있다. 따라서 ② '파괴적인 간섭'이 정답으로 적절하다.

---

46 우리는 윗글에서 아마도 _____ 을 추론할 수 있다. 내용 추론

① 고전적인 전자파 이론은 간섭의 영향을 무시한다.
② 빛의 주요 측면은 파동 모델을 통해 가장 잘 이해된다.
③ 빛의 최종 분석에서, 뉴턴의 관점이 옳다.
✓ ④ 빛은 많은 물리적 특성을 가지고 있다. 어떤 것은 파동과 연관되어 있고 다른 것은 입자와 연관되어 있다.

| 분석 | 이 글은 빛이 입자인지, 파동인지에 관하여 기술하고, 마지막 단락에서는 결국 빛은 파동성과 입자성을 동시에 갖고 있다는 결론을 맺고 있다. 따라서 ④가 지문을 통해 추론 가능한 진술이다.

| 배경 지식 | 빛의 속성: 빛은 입자성과 파동성을 동시에 지니고 있다. 빛이 입자인가 파동인가 하는 논쟁은 역사적으로 오랜 시간 계속되어 왔다. 17세기 빛의 입자설과 파동설이 대립하였으나, 18세기 뉴턴을 거치면서 입자론이 굳어졌다. 그러다가 19세기에 들어온 1801년 토머스 영의 이중 슬릿 실험을 통해 다시 파동설이 우세하였으며, 프레넬의 '빛의 파동 이론' 등에 의해 파동설이 자리 잡게 되었다. 여기에 맥스웰은 1873년 전자기파 가설을 내세우며 빛과 전자기파는 본질적으로 같은 것이라고 주장하였다. 하지만 20세기에 들어서 막스 플랑크의 양자 가설, 아인슈타인의 광전 효과 실험, 콤푸턴의 X선 산란 실험 등을 통해 빛의 입자성이 증명되었다. 이후 빛의 파동과 입자라는 이중성은 양자역학을 통해 이해될 수 있었으며, 이에 따라 현대 물리학에서는 빛의 성질을 입자성과 파동성을 동시에 지녔다고 정의한다. |

[47-49] 2016 홍익대

| 정답 | 47 ④ 48 ② 49 ① |

| 어휘 | electromagnetic ⓐ 전자기의; 전자석의   magnetism ⓝ 자기, 자기성, 자력
Van de Graaff generator 밴더그래프 발전기   mountaintop ⓝ 산꼭대기
visceral ⓐ 내장의, 내장을 침범하는   clump ⓝ 수풀, 덤불, ~의 덩어리   epitome ⓝ 개략, 요약, 축도, 전형
retina ⓝ (눈의) 망막   peripatetic ⓐ 걸어 돌아다니는, 순회하는 |

전문해석

십여 년간 아인슈타인을 괴롭혀 온 역설은 다음과 같다. 1800년대 중반에 영국 물리학자인 마이클 패러데이(Michael Faraday)의 실험적 작업에 관한 정밀한 연구 이후, 스코틀랜드 물리학자인 제임스 클러크 맥스웰(James Clerk Maxwell)은 자기장의 틀 속에서 전기와 자력을 결합시키는 데 성공했다. 심한 폭풍우가 치기 직전에 산꼭대기에 있거나, 밴더그래프 발전기(Van de Graaf generator) 가까이에 서 있게 된다면, 당신은 자기장이 무엇인지 몸소 느끼게 될 것이다. 왜냐하면 직접 느꼈기 때문이다. 당신이 느끼지 못했다면, 자기장은 전자기선이 통과하게 되는 공간 지역으로 스며드는 전자기력선의 흐름과 같은 것이다. 예를 들어 자석 주위에 철 가루를 뿌리면, 철 가루가 형성한 질서정연한 패턴이 눈에 보이지 않는 자력선의 일부를 찾아낸다. 특히 건조한 날에 털 스웨터를 벗다가 바스락거리는 소리를 듣거나, 순간적인 자극을 한두 번 느끼게 된다면, 당신은 스웨터 속 섬유로 쓸려나간 전하에 의해 발생된 전기력의 증거를 목격하고 있는 것이다. 이것과 모든 다른 전자기적 현상을 하나의 수학적 체계 속에 통합하는 것을 넘어서 맥스웰의 이론은—예상치 않게—전자기적 교란이 일정하게 결코 변하지 않는 속도로 움직이며, 이 속도는 빛의 속도와 맞먹는다는 것을 보여 줬다. 이것으로부터 맥스웰은 가시광선 자체도 특정 유형의 전자기적 파장에 불과한 것이며, 이 파장은 이제는 망막 속 화학 물질과 상호 작용을 하여 시력을 발생시키는 것으로 이해되는 파장이라는 것을 깨닫게 되었다. 더군다나(이것이 더 중요한데) 맥스웰의 이론은 또한 모든 전자기적 파장이—그중에는 가시광선도 있는데—순회하는 여행자의 축도라는 것을 보여 주었다. 이 파장은 결코 멈추지 않으며, 결코 속도를 늦추지도 않는다. 빛은 항상 빛의 속도로 여행한다.

우리가 빛의 속도로 빛을 추적하게 되면 무슨 일이 일어날까?라는 질문을 할 때까지는 모든 것이 다 괜찮고 좋았다. 뉴턴의 운동 법칙에 근거한 직관적인 사고는 우리가 빛의 파장을 따라잡게 될 것이며 따라서 그 파장은 정지한 것처럼 보이게 될 것을 알려 준다. 빛은 움직이지 않고 서 있게 될 것이다. 하지만 맥스웰의 이론과 모든 믿을 만한 관찰에 따르면, 정지한 빛과 같은 그런 것은 없다. 아무도 자신의 손바닥에 움직이지 않는 빛의 덩어리를 쥐어 보지 못했다. 따라서 문제. 다행스럽게도, 아인슈타인은 다수의 주도적인 물리학자들이 이 문제로 고민하고 있다는 (그리고 많은 엉뚱한 길로 가고 있다는) 사실을 모르고 있었으며, 맥스웰과 뉴턴의 역설을 순전히 자기 사고의 개인적인 영역에서 숙고했다.

49 ①

47 윗글에 따르면 다음 중 전자기장을 체험한 경우가 아닌 것은? 내용 파악

① 심한 폭풍우가 일어나기 직전, 산 정상에서 가지게 되는 느낌
② 자석 근처에 뿌리면 철 가루가 보여 주게 되는 패턴
③ 건조한 날 털 스웨터를 벗을 때 듣게 되는 바스락거리는 소리
✓④ 빛이 지속적이고 변하지 않는 속도로 여행한다는 사실에 대한 인식

| 분석 | 지문의 내용을 보았을 때 ④는 전자기적 교란이 빛과 동일한 성질을 지니고 있다는 점을 설명하면서 언급되는 내용이므로 우리가 자기장을 경험하는 경우가 아니다.

48 윗글에 따르면, 아인슈타인이 직면한 문제는 다음 중 어느 것인가? 내용 파악

① 자석 주변에서의 철 가루 패턴이 털 스웨터에서 찾아볼 수 있는 패턴과 다르다.
✓② 심지어 우리가 빛의 속도로 광선을 쫓아가더라도, 빛은 결코 정지된 상태일 수 없다.
③ 빛은 일종의 전자기적 파장일 뿐이며 망막 속 화학 물질과 상호 작용을 할 수 있다.
④ 빛은 전자력선의 흐름으로 공간의 영역을 침투할 수 있다.

| 분석 | 첫 문장에서 아인슈타인을 괴롭혀 온 역설은 다음과 같다고 설명하고 맥스웰의 실험을 언급하고 그 결과는 첫 번째 단락의 마지막에 언급되며 "(빛의) 파장은 결코 멈추지 않으며, 결코 속도를 늦추지도 않는다. 빛은 항상 빛의 속도로 여행한다."라고 하였다. 그런데 뉴턴의 운동의 법칙은 빛의 파장을 따라잡으면 그 파장은 정지한 것처럼 보인다는 것이다. 빛을 따라잡는다면 정지한 것처럼 보여야 하지만 맥스웰의 실험에서는 정지되지 않았으므로 ② '심지어 우리가 빛의 속도로 광선을 쫓아가더라도, 빛은 결코 정지된 상태일 수 없다.'는 맥스웰의 결과값이 아인슈타인이 직면한 문제로 적절하다.

49 다음 중 윗글에서 추론될 가능성이 가장 낮은 것은? 내용 추론

✓① 맥스웰과 뉴턴 둘 다 운동 법칙과 빛의 속도 사이의 역설을 인식했다.
② 맥스웰은 패러데이의 실험에 관한 철저한 조사를 통해 전기와 자력을 통합시킬 수 있었다.
③ 맥스웰의 이론에 따르면, 뉴턴의 운동 법칙에 근거한 빛의 속도에 대한 예측은 입증되지 않는다.
④ 자석 근처에서의 철 가루의 패턴과 털 스웨터의 소리는 모두 자기장에 의해 설명될 수 있다.

| 분석 | 지문에서 뉴턴의 운동 법칙과 맥스웰의 이론 사이의 역설에 직면하게 된 것은 아인슈타인이다. 따라서 ①은 지문에서 추론할 수 없다.

9강 우주 / 지구

01	②	02	①	03	⑤	04	③	05	①	06	④	07	⑤	08	①	09	④	10	①
11	③	12	④	13	①	14	③	15	①	16	①	17	②	18	④	19	①	20	①
21	②	22	②	23	③	24	①	25	②	26	④	27	①	28	③	29	②	30	①
31	③	32	⑤	33	④	34	④	35	②	36	①	37	①	38	④	39	②	40	⑤
41	①	42	②	43	②	44	②	45	①	46	④	47	③								

[01] 2015 서강대

| 정답 | ②

| 어휘 |
- iteration ⓝ (컴퓨터 소프트웨어의) 신판(新版); 되풀이, 반복
- suspend ⓥ (매)달다, 걸다, (공식적으로) 중단하다, 연기하다
- neutrino ⓝ 중성 미자(중성자가 양성자와 전자로 붕괴될 때에 생기는 소립자), 뉴트리노
- sprinkle ⓥ 흩뿌리다
- atomic nucleus 원자핵
- float ⓥ 뜨다, 떠다니다
- radio wave 전파
- proton ⓝ 양성자
- smattering ⓝ 소수, 조금; 수박 겉핥기의 지식
- acronym ⓝ 두문자어(몇 개 단어의 머리글자로 된 말)

전문해석

ANITA를 만나 보라. 엄밀하게, **ANITA III는 Antarctic Impulse Transient Antenna의 세 번째 버전이기 때문이다**. 그것이 앞으로 며칠 안에 발사될 때, 그 안테나의 일은 남극 얼음판이 방출하는 전파를 기록하기 위해 거대한 풍선에 매달려 남극의 얼음 위를 떠다니는 것이다. 이 전파들은 얼음을 통과하는 중성 미자에 의해 생성되며, 남극을 세계에서 가장 큰 중성 미자 검출 실험실로 만든다. **ANITA가 찾는 특정한 중성 미자들은 극도로 높은 에너지를 가지고 있다.** 그것들이 어디에서 왔는지 아무도 알지 못하며, 엄밀히 말하자면, 더 작은 장치였던 ANITA I과 II가 중성 미자를 발견하는 데 실패했기 때문에 중성 미자가 존재한다는 것은 사실로 알려져 있지 않다. 하지만 이론에 따르면, 어떤 거대한 폭발이 또한 우주 광선을 만들어 내는 한 중성 미자는 그곳에 있어야 한다. 우주광선은 속도가 빠른 양성자로 약간의 더 무거운 원자핵들과 함께 흩뿌려진 후, 지구 대기와 같은 어떤 것과 부딪칠 때까지 공간을 날아다니다 (부딪치면) 다른 입자들 무리로 분해된다. 그것들은 한 세기 동안 알려져 왔지만, 전기적으로 충전되어 있을 때 그들의 경로가 은하의 자기장에 의해 구부러지기 때문에 그들의 기원은 여전히 미궁 속이다. 그것은 그들이 오는 방향이 그들을 생성한 무엇을 가리키지 않는다는 것을 의미한다. 그러나 중성 미자들은 그 이름이 암시하듯이, 전기적으로 중성이다. 따라서 그들의 경로는 그들의 기원을 향해야 한다.

다음 글과 가장 일치하는 문장을 선택하시오. 내용 일치

① ANIT I 및 II는 ANITA III보다 작은 장치였기 때문에 실패했다. 장치의 크기와 발견의 실패는 관련이 없음
✓② ANITA는 중성 미자를 연구하는 데 사용되는 장치의 이름의 머리글자다.
③ 중성 미자는 전기적으로 중성이기 때문에 감지되지 않았다. 중성 미자의 발견과 전기적으로 중성인 특징은 관련이 없음
④ 우주광선은 저속 양성자다. 우주광선은 속도가 빠른 양성자임

| 분석 | 본문의 두 번째 문장에서 ANITA가 Antarctic Impulse Transient Antenna의 머리글자라는 것을 알 수 있으므로 보기 ②가 정답이다.

[02-03] 2019 숙명여대

| 정답 | 02 ① 03 ⑤

| 어휘 | earthquake ⓝ 지진 epicenter ⓝ (지진의) 진앙, 진원지 displacement ⓝ 이동, 변위
periodic ⓐ 주기적인, 정기의 accompany ⓥ 동반하다 vibration ⓝ 진동
subsequent ⓐ 다음의, 차후의 unconsolidated ⓐ 굳지 않은, 통합되지 않은
amplitude ⓝ 넓이, 진폭 deposit ⓝ 퇴적물 bedrock ⓝ (지질) 기반암
withstand ⓥ 잘 견뎌 내다, 버티다

전문해석

지진의 영향은 진원지를 둘러싸고 있는 넓은 지역에서 가장 강력하다. 지표면의 균열은 수 야드의 수평 및 수직적인 방향 이동과 함께 종종 발생한다. 그런 움직임은 일반적으로 큰 지진 동안에는 발생하지 않는다. '단층 크리프'라고 불리는 약간의 주기적인 움직임이 너무 작아서 느낄 수 없는 미세 지진을 동반할 수 있다. 지진 진동의 정도와 그에 따른 지역의 피해는 부분적으로 지면의 특성에 의존한다. 예를 들어, 지진 진동은 빈약하게 채워진 흙이나 강의 침전물Ⓐ과 같이 비고형 표면 물질에서 더 오래 지속되고 더 큰 파동 진폭을 갖는다; 암반 지역은 더 적은 영향을 받는다. 최악의 피해는 극심한 진동을 견디도록 구조물이 건설되지 않은 인구가 Ⓑ밀집한 도시 지역에서 발생한다.

02 다음 중 윗글에 대해 사실이 아닌 것은? 내용 불일치

① ✓ 대규모의 지진이 일어나는 동안, 보통 수평 지진과 수직 지진이 발생한다.
② 지면의 특성은 부분적으로 지진 진동의 정도에 영향을 미친다.
③ 인구가 밀집된 도시 지역은 최악의 피해를 입을 수 있다.
④ 수평 및 수직 지진은 일반적으로 대규모의 지진이 발생하는 동안에는 발생하지 않는다.
⑤ 지진의 진동은 굳지 않은 표면 물질보다 굳은 표면 물질에서 더 짧게 지속될 수 있다.

| 분석 | 본문 세 번째 문장에서 큰 지진 동안에는 지면의 수평적이고 수직적인 방향의 움직임이 발생하지 않는다고 했으므로, 보기 ①은 사실이 아니다.

03 빈칸 Ⓐ와 Ⓑ에 들어갈 말로 알맞게 짝지어진 것은? 빈칸 추론

① ~와 같은 - 분명히
② ~와 같은 - 좀처럼 ~하지 않는
③ ~에 대해서 말하자면 - 거의 ~ 않다
④ 예를 들면 - 거의 ~ 않다
⑤ ✓ ~와 같은 - 조밀하게

| 분석 | 빈칸 Ⓐ 다음에 언급한 '빈약하게 채워진 흙이나 강의 침전물'은 빈칸 Ⓐ 앞의 '비고형 표면 물질'의 예시이기 때문에, Ⓐ에는 '~와 같은'이 적절하다. 다음으로 빈칸 Ⓑ가 포함된 문장에서 '최악의 피해'가 발생하려면 진동을 견디지 못하는 구조물이 인구가 '밀집한' 도시 지역에 있어야 할 것이다. 따라서 Ⓑ에는 '조밀하게'가 적절하다. 따라서 정답은 보기 ⑤이다.

[04-06] 2016 항공대

| 정답 | 04 ③ 05 ① 06 ④

| 어휘 | encouragement ⓝ 격려, 자극 emit ⓥ 방출하다, 방사하다 pulse ⓝ 맥박, 파동

radio wave 전파	neutron ⓝ 중성자	magnetic field 자기장
radius ⓝ (원이나 구의) 반지름	critical ⓐ 결정적인, 비판적인, (분량·상태 등이) 임계의	
detect ⓥ 발견하다, 탐지하다	pioneering ⓐ 개척적인, 선구적인	exert ⓥ (힘·지력을) 발휘하다, 쓰다
gravitational force 중력	latent ⓐ 숨어 있는, 잠재적인	coal cellar (주택의) 지하 석탄 저장고
inflated ⓐ 부푼, 팽창한	concave lens 오목렌즈	

> **전문해석**

블랙홀의 존재에 대한 연구는 1967년 케임브리지의 조슬린 벨-버넬(Jocelyn Bell-Burnell)이라는 연구생에 의해 전파의 규칙적인 파동을 방출하는 하늘에 있는 물체들의 발견과 함께 더욱 자극되었다. 처음에 벨과 그녀의 지도교수인 안토니 휴이시(Antony Hewish)는 그들이 은하계의 외계 문명과 접촉했을지도 모른다고 생각했다. 그러나 결국 그들은 펄서라는 이름의 물체들이 사실은 자기장과 주변 물질 사이의 복잡한 상호 작용 때문에 전파의 파동을 방출하며 회전하는 중성자별이라는 덜 낭만적인 결론에 이르렀다. 이것은 우주 서부극의 작가들에게는 나쁜 소식이었지만, 그 당시 블랙홀을 믿었던 우리 같은 소수들에게는 매우 희망적이었다: 그것은 중성자별이 존재한다는 최초의 긍정적인 증거였다. 중성자별의 반지름은 약 10마일인데, 이는 별이 블랙홀이 되는 임계 반지름의 몇 배에 불과하다. 만약 별이 그렇게 작은 크기로 붕괴될 수 있을지라도, 다른 별들이 훨씬 더 작은 크기로 붕괴되어 블랙홀이 될 수 있다고 기대하는 것은 타당하지 않다. 블랙홀은 어떤 빛도 방출하지 않는다는 의미를 가졌는데, 어떻게 우리가 블랙홀을 발견하기를 바랄 수 있을까? 그것은 마치 석탄 저장고에서 검은 고양이를 찾는 것처럼 보일 수도 있다. 다행스럽게도, 방법이 하나 있다. 존 미첼(John Michell)이 1783년 그의 선구적인 논문에서 지적했듯이, 블랙홀은 여전히 근처의 물체들에 중력을 작용시킨다.

04 ③   06 ④

04 윗글은 주로 _____ 에 관한 것이다. 소재
① 블랙홀의 유산   ② 블랙홀의 기능
✓ 블랙홀의 발견   ④ 블랙홀의 잠재력

| 분석 | 본문은 블랙홀의 존재와 그 발견에 관한 연구에 대해 서술하고 있다. 따라서 정답은 보기 ③이 적절하다.

05 빈칸에 들어갈 말로 가장 적절한 것을 고르시오. 빈칸 추론
✓ 석탄 저장고에서
② 부풀려진 풍선 모형으로
③ 삼각형 모양의 유리 조각을 통해
④ 오목렌즈 망원경으로

| 분석 | 빈칸을 포함한 문장의 직전 문장에서 블랙홀을 발견하기 어려운 이유는 블랙홀이 빛을 방출하지 않아 어둠 속에 있기 때문이라고 했다. 따라서 빈칸에서 검은 고양이를 찾기 힘든 장소로는 검은색이 눈에 잘 띄지 않는 공간을 골라야 할 것이므로 보기 ①이 정답으로 적절하다.

06 다음 중 올바른 것은? 내용 일치
① 벨과 휴이시는 은하계의 외계 문명과 접촉했다. 외계 문명과 접촉했다는 그들의 예측만 언급되고 사실은 아님
② 별은 거대한 크기로 커지고 블랙홀이 될 수 있다. 별이 작은 크기로 붕괴되어 블랙홀이 될 수 있음
③ 블랙홀의 존재는 1967년에 완전히 알려졌다. 규칙적 파동을 방출하는 물체들의 발견이 블랙홀의 완전한 발견을 의미하지는 않음
✓ 블랙홀은 근처의 물질에 중력을 행사할 수 있다.

| 분석 | 본문의 마지막 문장에서 '블랙홀은 여전히 근처의 물체들에 중력을 작용시킨다'고 했으므로 보기 ④는 올바른 진술이다.

| 배경 지식 | 블랙홀(Black hole): 초고밀도에 의하여 생기는 중력장의 구멍으로 항성이 진화의 최종 단계에서 한없이 수축하여 중심부의 밀도가 빛을 빨아들일 만큼 매우 높아지면서 생김 |

[07-08] 2019 성균관대

| 정답 | 07 ⑤ 08 ①

| 어휘 | exoplanet ⓝ 태양계 밖의 행성, 외계 행성   promising ⓐ 가망 있는, 유망한
rule of thumb 경험 법칙(경험에 바탕을 둔 방법), 어림 감정

전문해석

"우리가 '잠재적으로 거주 가능한' 외계 행성들이라는 말을 할 때, 그것은 거주할 만한 조건에 필요한 행성의 측정 가능한 특성들을 가리키는 용어입니다."라고 아레시보의 푸에르토리코 대학의 아벨 멘데스(Abell Mendez) 교수는 말한다.
그러면, 이런 외계 행성들은 아무것도 보장할 수는 없는 유망한 목표물인 것이다. 그러나 행성의 거주 가능성에 관한 대중적인 논의를 지배하는 두 개의 범주가 있다. 첫째로, 그것이 지구의 일반적 크기 범위에 들어가는가(그러므로 암석 상태일 가능성이 있는가) 이며, 둘째로, 거주가 가능한 구역으로 알려져 있는 영역 안에 있는가이다. 07 ②
이것은 호스트 항성 근처에서 액체 상태로 행성 표면의 물을 유지시키기에 충분한 별빛이 있는 거리 범위이다. 그 항성과 너무 가까우면 열기가 물을 끓여 증발시켜 버리고, 너무 멀리 떨어져 있으면 모든 물이 얼고 말 것이다. 07 ①④③
이것들은 유용한 경험 법칙들이지만, 많은 요인들이 행성이 얼마나 거주 가능한지에 영향을 미친다. 그리고 일부 요인들은 기술적 한계 때문에 논의에서 제외된다.

---

07 _____은 거주 가능한 외계 행성을 위한 필요조건에 포함되지 않는다. 세부 내용 불일치

① 물
② 크기
③ 거리
④ 별빛
✓⑤ 태양

| 분석 | 본문의 두 번째 단락에서 거주 가능한 외계 행성의 필요조건들을 언급했다. 필요조건 중 '태양과의 적절한 거리'가 있었으나 '태양' 자체는 언급되지 않았으므로 필요조건에 포함되지 않는다. 따라서 정답은 보기 ⑤이다.

---

08 밑줄 친 "rules of thumb"은 _____을 의미한다. 밑줄 추론

✓① 실제 경험에 기초한 기준들
② 이론적 추론에 의해 도출된 절차들
③ 과학적 관찰에서 유도된 최고의 규칙들
④ 지출에 기초한 주요 기준들
⑤ 정교한 계산으로 만들어진 쉬운 절차들

| 분석 | 밑줄 친 'rules of thumb'은 '경험에 바탕을 둔 방법'이나 '경험 법칙' 혹은 '어림짐작'이라는 의미를 가진다. 보기 ①이 의미로 가장 적절하다.

[09-10] 2019 한양대

| 정답 | 09 ④ 10 ①

| 어휘 |
fresh ⓐ 맑은, 소금기 없는
staggering ⓐ 어마어마한, 경이적인
glacier ⓝ 빙하
roughly ⓐd 대충
scarcity ⓝ 부족, 결핍, 기근
sustain ⓥ 유지하다, 계속하다
exacerbate ⓥ (고통·병 따위를) 악화시키다
agriculture ⓝ 농업
account for 설명하다, 처리하다
livestock ⓝ 가축
consumption ⓝ 소비
forecast ⓥ 예상[예측]하다, 예고하다
precipitation ⓝ 낙하, 강수[강우]량
variability ⓝ 변하기 쉬움, 변이성
flooding ⓝ 홍수
drought ⓝ 가뭄
blight ⓥ 마르게 하다, 손상시키다, (초목 따위를) 황폐시키다
ensure ⓥ 보장하다, 보증하다
consistent ⓐ 일관된

전문해석

물은 지구 표면의 약 75%를 덮고 있지만, 오직 3%만이 마실 수 있고, 나머지는 소금물이다. 적은 양의 담수 중 어마어마한 99%는 세계의 빙하 아래 깊숙이 묻혀 있기 때문에 접근할 수 없다. 쿠무(Kummu) 등(2010)에 따르면, 세계 인구의 약 3분의 1이 물 부족으로 위험에 처해 있으며, 인구 증가는 단지 문제를 악화시킬 뿐이다. 인간은 생존하기 위해 물이 필요할 뿐만 아니라, 또한 농작물에 물을 주고 가축을 유지하기 위해 물에 크게 의존한다. 사람들은 일반적으로 하루에 약 5리터의 물을 마시는 반면, 농업은 세계 담수 소비의 대부분을 차지한다. 세계 일부 지역에서는 물 부족이 식량 생산 능력을 심각하게 제한한다. 코우머(Cummou)와 람스토르프(Rahmstorf) (2012)는 또한 기후 변화가 강수 변동성(즉, 비의 <u>변동성</u>)을 증가시켜 식량 생산을 방해하는 홍수와 가뭄의 위험을 높일 것이라고 예측했다. 그렇다면, 지속적이고 안정적인 담수 공급을 보장하기 위해 어떤 해결책이 있을까?

09 윗글의 빈칸에 들어갈 말로 가장 적절한 것은? 빈칸 추론
① 부피
② 부족
③ 과잉
✓ ④ 변동

| 분석 | 빈칸 앞 'i.e.'는 '즉'이라는 뜻으로 괄호 앞 '강수 변동성'과 그 의미가 같은 표현을 빈칸에 넣어야 할 것이다. 따라서 보기 ④가 정답으로 가장 적절하다.

10 윗글의 내용과 일치하지 않는 것은? 내용 불일치
✓ ① 지구에 있는 물의 99%는 우리가 마실 수 없다.
② 인구 증가는 물 부족을 악화시킨다.
③ 농사는 사람이 소비하는 것보다 더 많은 물을 필요로 한다.
④ 강수량 부족은 미래에 농업을 악화시킬 것이다.

| 분석 | 본문의 첫 번째 문장에서 '물은 지구 표면의 약 75%를 덮고 있지만, 오직 3%만이 마실 수 있고'라고 했다. 따라서 보기 ①은 내용과 맞지 않는 진술이다. 마실 수 있는 3%의 담수 중 99%가 빙하 아래에 있어 접근할 수 없다는 본문 두 번째 문장을 잘못 이해하지 않도록 유의한다.

[11-12] 2020 항공대

| 정답 | 11 ③ 12 ④

| 어휘 |
at stake 중대한, 성패가 달려 있는
arbitrarily ⓐd 임의적인, 제멋대로의
disjointed ⓐ 연결이 안 되는, 일관성이 없는

정답과 해설 _ 203

elegant ⓐ 우아한, 명쾌한, 정밀한
outstanding ⓐ 눈에 띄는, 미해결의
state of affairs 상황, 현상
disjoint ⓥ (낱낱으로) 해체하다, 토막으로 만들다
paradox ⓝ 역설, 역설적인 사람[상황]
press for ~을 강요하다, ~을 요구하다
grossly ⓐⓓ 지독히, 극도로

전문해석

중대한 문제를 고려할 때 궁극적 지식 혹은 궁극적 설명이라는 개념은 계속 다루어 그것에 대한 논리적 결론에 이를 만한 것이다. 냉엄하게 표현하자면, 우주의 궁극적인 본질을 아는 것(또는 만약 당신이 원한다면 '모든 것의 이론' 또는 '최종 이론')은 실제로 우주에 대한 모든 것, 일어난 모든 것, 일어날 모든 것을 알고 있다는 것을 사실상 의미할 것이다. 비록 모든 알려진 힘들의 작용에 대한 경이적일 정도로 정밀한 통합적 공식을 만들어 내게 된다 해도, 모든 것에 대한 이론을 임의로 분리된 연구 분야, 예를 들어 물리학으로 제한할 수는 없다. [A] 이것 외에도 예를 들어, 우리가 힘에 대해 알고 있는 것을 어떻게 알고 있는지에 대한 중요한 질문에 주의를 기울여야 할 것이다. [B] 다른 말로 하자면, 우리는 어떻게 우주를 의식하고 있을까? 그러한 통합된 힘의 이론이 어떻게 우리가 전쟁의 본질이나 세계적 빈곤, 또는 농담을 이해하는 데 도움이 될까? 단지 한 가지가 알려지지 않은 채로 남아 있는 한, 우리가 우주에 대해 알고 있는 것이 부분적이고, 불완전하며, 따라서 궁극적으로 설명되지 않는 한, 단지 어떤 것들에 대한 이론일 뿐인 모든 것에 대한 이론을 제안할 수는 없다. [C] 더 나아가 하나의 역설을 가리키는데, 과학 자체는 세상에는 알아야 할 것이 더 많고, 사실 우리는 자연 현상의 많은 측면에 대해 몹시 무지하다는 바로 그 가정에서 나아가는 것이고 실제로, 과학자들이 연구 자금을 요청할 때 과학자들이 자주 강조하는 것은 바로 이 문제의 상태이다. [D] 〈따라서 우리가 모르는 것이 없다는 것을 말해 줄 수 있다는 것은 모든 것에 대한 어떤 이론의 요구사항처럼 보인다.〉 그러나 우리가 무엇을 모르는지 우리는 어떻게 알 수 있을까?

---

11 다음 중 윗글의 제목으로 가장 적절한 것은? 제목

① 질서의 가장자리에서 출현한 과학
② 지식의 출현
✓③ 궁극적 지식의 허위
④ 과학에서 인과관계의 환상

| 분석 | 본문은 '궁극적 지식'에 대해 다루고 있는데 저자는 7번째 문장에서 '모든 것에 대한 이론을 제안할 수는 없다'고 주장했다. 이어서 마지막 문장에 이르기까지 이와 관련된 역설을 소개하고 마지막 문장을 의문문을 종결하면서 '궁극적 지식'에 대해 강한 의구심을 제기하고 있다. 따라서 보기 ③이 제목으로 가장 적절하다.

---

12 다음 글이 들어갈 가장 적합한 위치를 찾으시오. 문장 삽입

> 따라서 우리가 모르는 것이 없다는 것을 말해 줄 수 있다는 것은 모든 것에 대한 어떤 이론의 요구사항처럼 보인다.

① [A]　　　② [B]
③ [C]　　　✓④ [D]

| 분석 | 주어진 문장의 'So'의 기능은 '결과'이므로 앞 내용과의 '인과관계'를 고려하여 문장을 삽입하도록 한다. 본문에서 저자는 모든 것을 설명할 수 있는 '궁극적 지식'에 대해 일관되게 회의적 태도를 유지했다. [D] 앞 문장에서는 과학계의 역설에 대해 언급하며 이어지는 내용도 '역설적 상황'에 해당할 것이다. 본문 마지막 문장에서 'But'이 앞 내용과 역접이 되려면 직전에 '우리가 모르는 것'에 대한 언급이 삽입되어야 할 것이다. 따라서 주어진 문장을 [D]에 삽입하면 '우리가 모르는 것이 없다'와 '무엇을 모르는지는 알 수 없다'가 서로 역설적인 상황이 된다. 정답은 ④이다.

[13-15] 2011 단국대

| 정답 | 13 ①　14 ③　15 ①

| 어휘 |

manned landings 유인 착륙
favor ⓥ 찬성하다, 선호하다
projectile ⓝ 투사물, 발사체
crush ⓥ 눌러서 뭉개다, 짓밟다
orbit ⓝ 궤도
appeal ⓝ 매력
boil away 증발하다

consensus ⓝ 합의, 여론
be discounted by ~에 의해 무시되다
mass ⓝ 덩어리, 질량, 다량
vaporize ⓥ 증발시키다, 기화시키다
combination ⓝ 결합, 연합
volatile ⓐ 휘발성의, 폭발하기 쉬운

astronomer ⓝ 천문학자
planetary ⓐ 행성의, 행성의 작용에 의한
collide with ~와 충돌하다
high-velocity ⓐ 고속의
bulk ⓝ 크기, 부피, 덩어리
precisely ⓐⓓ 엄밀히, 정확하게

전문해석

1960년대 아폴로 프로젝트의 유인 착륙에 의해 해결되지 않은 채 남아 있는 한 가지 큰 의문은 달의 기원이었다. 이제 천문학자들 사이에서 "거대 충돌" 이론을 선호하는 여론이 증가하고 있는데, 이 생각은 1975년에 처음 제기되었을 때 대부분의 사람들은 무시했던 것이었다. 달은 45억 년 전, 이 이론에 따르면, 지구 질량의 약 7분의 1에 해당하는 행성 발사체가 지구와 충돌했을 때 시작되었을 수도 있다. 충돌의 에너지는 두 천체의 주요 부분을 짓누르고 기화시켜서, 화씨 12,000도에 달하는 고온으로 고속의 물질을 분출했다. 불과 몇 시간 내에, 그 물질 중 일부는 지구에서 충분히 멀리 떨어져 다시 합쳐져서 궤도에 남아 있을 수 있었다. 지구 자체는 오래된 행성과 발사체의 덩어리의 결합체로 다시 형성되었다. 거대한 충격 시나리오가 매력적인 한 가지 이유는 그것이 아폴로에서 발견된 모든 화학적 발견을 설명하는 것처럼 보이기 때문이다. 예를 들어, 달 암석에는 물, 나트륨 및 기타 휘발성 물질이 부족한데, 정확히는 충돌 후 빠른 속도로 증발할 물질들이다.

---

13 다음 중 빈칸에 들어갈 말로 가장 적합한 것은? 빈칸 추론

✓① 증발
② 응축
③ 침전
④ 변형

| 분석 | 빈칸 앞 대시(—)는 앞 내용의 동격이거나 보충 설명에 해당된다. '휘발성 물질' 뒤에서 이 구두점을 사용했으므로 '휘발성 물질'에 대한 보충 설명으로 이해하여 충돌 후 '기화'나 '증발'될 물질로 빈칸을 완성해야 한다. 따라서 보기 ①이 정답이다.

---

14 "거대 충돌" 이론에 따르면, 다음 중 달을 가장 잘 묘사하는 것은? 세부 내용 일치

① 지구로부터 분리된 지구의 일부다.
② 지구와 충돌한 행성 발사체다.
✓③ 지구의 한 부분과 그것과 충돌하는 행성 발사체다.
④ 지구에 가까이 와서 궤도에 남아 있는 행성 발사체다.

| 분석 | 본문 3~5번째 문장에서 지구와 충돌한 행성 발사체가 충돌 후 고속의 물질들을 분출했고 이것이 지구에서 멀리 떨어져 궤도에 남아서 달이 되었다고 서술했다. 따라서 보기 ②가 정답이다.

---

15 다음 중 아폴로 프로젝트에 관한 사실에 해당하는 것은? 세부 내용 일치

✓① 그것은 달의 기원에 대한 질문에 대답하지 않았다.
② 그것은 "거대 충돌" 이론의 틀을 확립했다. 아폴로 프로젝트가 아니라 1975년 연구에 의해 설득력을 가지게 된 것
③ 그것은 처음으로 달을 궤도에 올리는 데 성공했다. 달을 궤도에 올리는 것은 "거대 충돌" 이론과 관련됨
④ 그것은 "거대 충돌" 이론만큼 주목을 끌지 못했다. 본문에 언급 없음

| 분석 | 본문 첫 번째 문장에서 '아폴로 프로젝트의 유인 착륙에 의해 해결되지 않은 채 남아 있는 한 가지 큰 의문은 달의 기원이었

다'고 했다. 따라서 정답은 보기 ①이다.

> **배경 지식** 거대 충돌 이론(Giant impact hypothesis): 달의 생성을 설명해 주는 과학적 가설들 중 하나로 원시 지구가 부서져 생긴 파편 등이 모여 달이 되었다는 가설

[16-17] 2016 한양대

| 정답 | 16 ① 17 ②

| 어휘 | light wave ⓝ 광파, 빛의 파장　　impinge ⓥ 치다, 부딪치다, 충돌하다　　retina ⓝ 망막
　　　　interim ⓝ 사이, 동안　　　　　　absurd ⓐ 어리석은　　　　　　　　　optic nerve 시신경
　　　　inference ⓝ 추론　　　　　　　　physiology ⓝ 생리학

전문해석

내가 어두운 밤에 별, 말하자면 시리우스를 보고 있다고 가정하자. 만약 물리학이 믿을 수 있는 것이면, 수년 전 시리우스에서 이동하기 시작한 빛의 파장이 (천문학자들이 계산하는 특정 시간 후) 지구에 도달하고, 내 망막에 충돌하여 내가 시리우스를 보고 있다고 말하게 한 것이다. 이제 빛의 파장이 나에게 정보를 전달하는 시리우스는 그 파장이 출발했을 때 존재했던 시리우스이다. 그러나 이 시리우스는 더 이상 존재하지 않을 수 있다. 그 사이에 사라졌을 수도 있다. 더 이상 존재하지 않는 것을 볼 수 있다고 말하는 것은 터무니없는 일이다. 지금 내가 보고 있는 것은 무엇이든, 그것이 시리우스가 아니라는 결론이다. 실제로 내가 보는 것은 특정 크기, 모양, 강도의 노란색 조각이다. 나는 이 노란색 조각이 수년 전에 수백만 마일 떨어진 곳에 (물리적 사건의 연속적인 사슬에 의해 연결된) 기원을 가지고 있었다고 추론한다. 그러나 이 추론은 잘못되었을 수도 있다. 내가 별이라고 부르는 노란색 조각의 기원은 코에 가해진 타격일 수도 있고, 배의 돛대에 매달려 있는 램프일 수도 있다.
이것만이 연관된 유일한 추론은 아니다. 내가 노란색 조각을 보고 있다고 생각하는 것은 사실이지만, 내가 정말로 이 믿음을 유지하는 것이 정당한가? 물리학과 생리학에 관한 한, 우리가 말할 자격이 있는 모든 것은 시신경이 특정 방식으로 자극되고 있으며, 그 결과 뇌에서 특정 사건이 일어나고 있다는 것이다. 우리가 정말로 이것보다 더 이상 말하는 것이 정당한가? 직접적으로 우리는 "시신경이 이런저런 방식으로 자극받고 있다"라는 단순한 진술을 넘어 이 사실로부터 "따라서 나는 이런저런 특징의 대상을 보고 있다"라고 결론짓는다. 우리는 추론을 이끌어 내고 그 추론은 오류에 빠지기 쉽다.

> **16** 윗글의 빈칸에 들어갈 말로 가장 적절한 것은? **빈칸 추론**
> ✓① 오류에 빠지기 쉽다
> ② 실제로 존재하는 세계로 인도된다
> ③ 그것의 기원을 실제로 보고 그것을 확인하는 것이다
> ④ 세상이 오직 우리의 뇌 밖에만 존재한다는 것을 인식하는 것이다

| 분석 | 빈칸이 단락의 마지막 문장에 있다면 그 직전 문장과 해당 단락의 첫 문장을 확인하도록 한다. 글이 양괄식 구성이거나 단락이 시작부터 순접으로 진행된다면 첫 문장을 확인하는 것이 마지막 문장에 넣을 표현을 추론하는 데 도움이 된다. 일단 빈칸이 포함된 문장의 직전에 '직접적으로 우리는 "시신경이 이런저런 방식으로 자극받고 있다"라는 단순한 진술을 넘어 이 사실로부터 "따라서 나는 이런저런 특징의 대상을 보고 있다"라고 결론짓는다.'라고 했다. 이것은 단순한 진술을 바탕으로 우리가 추론을 이끌어 낸다는 마지막 문장과 자연스럽게 연결된다. 또한 단락의 첫 문장에서 '이것이 유일한 추론이 아니다'라고 한 것은 첫 단락의 마지막 문장에서 추론이 오류가 있을 수 있음을 언급한 것과 관련된다. 두 번째 단락 역시 오류가 있는 추론임을 설명하기 위해 유일한 추론이 아니다라고 단락을 시작했을 것이므로 빈칸에는 ①이 가장 적절하다.

17 윗글의 내용과 가장 거리가 먼 것은? 내용 불일치

① 시리우스는 더 이상 우주에 존재하지 않을 수도 있다.
✓ ② 바깥세상은 우리가 인식하는 것과 같다.
③ 우리가 보는 것은 우리의 뇌에서 일어나는 특정한 사건에 의해 발생한다.
④ 외부 세계의 존재 자체는 알려진 것이 아니라 추론된 것일 뿐이다.

| 분석 | 본문에 따르면 우리가 인식하는 것은 오류가 있는 추론일 뿐이므로 실제 세상은 우리의 인식과는 다를 것이다. 보기 ②가 본문과 거리가 먼 진술이다.

[18-19] 2011 중앙대

| 정답 | 18 ④ 19 ①

| 어휘 |
gravity-free ⓐ 무중력
compression ⓝ 압축, 압착, 요약
spinal disc 척추 디스크
plump ⓐ 부푼, 부드럽고 풍만한
backache ⓝ 요통
counterpull ⓝ 역압, 미는 힘

weightless ⓐ 무게가 없는 듯한, 무중력의
spine ⓝ 척추, 등뼈
lengthen ⓥ 길게 하다, 늘이다
concurrent ⓐ 동시(발생)의, 동반하는, 같은 의견의
nerve irritation 신경 자극
combat ⓥ ~와 싸우다, 분투하다

weight-bearing ⓐ 무게를 견디는
squeeze ⓥ 꽉 쥐다, 짜내다, 압착하다
gravitational pull 중력
musculature ⓝ 근육 조직
rigorous ⓐ 엄격한, 가혹한

전문해석

NASA의 한 연구는 우주에서 무중력 상태의 12주 동안, 우주비행사들은 평균 2인치씩 자란다고 밝혔다. 왜 무중력 환경에서 빠른 성장이 일어나는가? 그 질문에 대답하는 한 가지 방법은 중력이 척추에 미치는 영향을 관찰하는 것이다. 아침과 밤 사이에, 앉거나 서 있거나 걷는 것과 같은 중력에 의해 가능한 매일의 체중을 견디는 활동은 척추에 압박을 야기한다. 이 압박은 척추 디스크에서 나오는 액체를 근처의 연조직으로 짜낸다. 하루가 끝날 때쯤, 디스크에서 사라진 액체는 사람을 0.5인치에서 4분의 3인치 정도 더 작아지게 한다. 몸이 스스로 무게를 견디지 않아도 되는 수면 동안, 그 액체는 다시 척추 디스크에 스며들면서, 몸을 이전의 키까지 늘린다. 우주에서, 지구에서처럼, 혈류로부터 수분이 척추의 디스크에 모이지만, 중력이 없기 때문에, 어떤 압축도 발생하지 않는다. 수분은 디스크에서 빠져나가지 않는다. 그것은 남아 있어서, 디스크를 더 잘 부풀리고 결과적으로 사람을 더 키가 크게 만든다. 대부분의 사람들은 높은 선반에 있는 것들에 더 쉽게 닿을 수 있도록 1~2인치 더 큰 것을 신경 쓰지 않을 것이다. 그러나, 무중력 환경에서 발생하는 키 증가와 척추 당김은 자주 요통과 신경 자극과 같은 부정적인 영향을 동시에 수반한다. 게다가, 중력의 역압에 맞서 몸을 똑바로 유지하기 위해 지구에서 인간의 골격과 근육 조직은 강하게 유지되어야 한다. 무중력 환경에서, 근육과 뼈는 사용되지 않기 때문에 약해지는 경향이 있다. 우주비행사들은 우주에 있는 동안 엄격한 운동 루틴을 유지함으로써 이것과 싸운다.

18 윗글의 빈칸에 들어갈 말로 가장 적절한 것은? 빈칸 추론

① 척추 디스크를 둘러싼 연조직이 체중을 견디도록 발달시키는 방법
② 일상 활동과 체중 사이의 관계
③ 근육 조직이 중력에 대항하기 위해 어떻게 작용하는지
✓ ④ 중력이 척추에 미치는 영향

| 분석 | 빈칸 뒤로 이어지는 설명을 참고하여 빈칸을 추론한다. 체중을 견뎌야 하는 아침에는 척추의 액체가 줄어들어 키가 작아지고 중력의 영향을 받지 않는 수면 동안에는 다시 그 액체가 척추로 스며들게 되므로, 우주의 무중력 상태에서 키가 커지는 이유는 척추에 가해지는 중력과 관련이 있다. 따라서 정답은 보기 ④이다.

19 윗글의 내용과 일치하지 않는 것은? `내용 불일치`

✓ ① 우주에서, 우주비행사들은 잠을 자고 난 후 예전의 키로 돌아온다.
② 우주비행사들은 척추 디스크가 수분을 유지하기 때문에 우주에서 키가 자란다.
③ 사람은 지구에서 저녁보다 아침에 더 키가 크다.
④ 무중력 환경은 종종 인체에 부정적인 영향을 미친다.

| 분석 | 본문의 7번째 문장에서 '수면 동안, 그 액체는 다시 척추 디스크에 스며들면서, 몸을 이전의 키까지 늘린다'고 했다. 이것은 우주가 아닌 지구에서 발생하는 상황이므로 보기 ①은 본문의 내용과 일치하지 않는다.

[20-21] 2022 덕성여대

| 정답 | 20 ① 21 ②

| 어휘 |
gravitational force 중력
nebula 성운(가스와 먼지 등으로 이루어진 성간 물질)
clump ⓝ 덩어리
dense ⓐ 밀집한, 밀도가 높은
give birth to (일이) ~을 일으키다, ~의 원인이 되다
orbit ⓥ (천체의 둘레를) 궤도를 그리며 돌다
planetesimal theory 미행성설(태양계의 행성이나 위성은 무수한 미소천체가 모여 생긴 것이라는 설)
inner planet 지구형 행성(수성, 금성, 지구, 화성)
Mars ⓝ 화성
Venus ⓝ 금성
Mercury ⓝ 수성
Jovian Planet 목성형 행성(4개의 큰 외행성: 목성, 토성, 천왕성, 해왕성)
Jupiter ⓝ 목성
Saturn ⓝ 토성
Uranus ⓝ 천왕성
Neptune ⓝ 해왕성
differentiation ⓝ 구분, 차별화
water vapour 수증기
condense ⓥ 응축하다, 압축하다
silicate rock 석회 규산연암
astronomical ⓐ 천문학의
volatile ⓐ 휘발성의, 폭발하기 쉬운

`전문해석`

우주의 중력은 지구의 형성에 중요한 역할을 했다. 태양 성운의 가스와 먼지는 중력의 끌어당김에 의해 형성되었다. 이 힘은 가스와 먼지가 점점 더 커질 때까지 계속해서 한데 끌어당겼고, 그러고 나서 성운은 그 자체로 줄어들기 시작했다. 구름의 중심은 매우 조밀하고 뜨거워졌다. 구름의 중심부에서 핵반응이 곧 별을 탄생시켰다. 태양은 이런 식으로 형성되었고, 태양이 가지고 있는 에너지는 행성이 형성될 수 있도록 했다.

대부분의 과학자들은 다른 별이 태양에 가깝게 지나가서 태양으로부터 물질이 떨어지도록 했을지도 모른다고 믿는다. 물질이 충분히 커서 그 조각들이 식고 고체가 되었을 때, 그들이 태양 주위를 돌면서 서로 가까워지기 시작했다. 이것은 미행성설이라고 불리고 그 덩어리들은 미행성체라고 불린다. 미행성체들은 서로를 흡수했고 뒤이어 행성들을 형성했다. [A] 이 이론은 지구, 화성, 금성, 수성 등 지구형 행성들의 구성은 암석인 반면, 외부 행성들의 구성은 대부분 가스이기 때문에 매우 가능성이 높다. [B] 〈규산염 암석으로 구성된 이 천체들은 너무 뜨거워서 휘발성 기체로 응축되지 못하고 행성으로 형성되었다.〉 하지만, 태양에서 멀리 떨어진 곳에서는 목성, 토성, 천왕성, 해왕성 등 목성형 행성들이 축적되고 형성될 수 있을 정도로 온도가 충분히 차가웠다. [C]

행성이 되기 전에 미행성체의 지구는 긴 발전 단계를 거쳤다. 더 무거운 물질은 중심으로 가라앉았고, 더 가벼운 물질은 표면으로 올라갔다 [D] 우리는 이러한 움직임을 층별 분화라고 부른다. 그 결과, 지구는 중심부, 맨틀 그리고 지각으로 층별로 형성되었다. 게다가, 화산 활동은 많은 양의 수증기를 방출했고, 이것은 바다로 응축되었다.

20 저자는 지구의 기원에 대해 무엇을 암시하고 있는가? 세부 내용 일치

① 미행성설은 타당하다. ✓
② 과학자들은 지구가 어떻게 형성되었는지 추측할 수 있을 뿐이다. 미행성설로 지구의 형성을 설명했으므로 추측이 아님
③ 천문학자들은 지구의 기원에 대해 의견이 다르다. 본문에 언급 없음
④ 그것은 태양의 기원보다 덜 중요하다. 지구와 태양의 기원에 대한 중요도를 비교하지 않음

| 분석 | 본문에서는 '미행성설'로 지구의 기원에 대해 자세하게 설명하고 있는데 이 이론의 타당성에 의구심을 제기하는 내용은 없다. 또한 나머지 보기에는 모두 오류가 있으므로 보기 ①이 정답으로 가장 적절하다.

21 다음 문장은 어디에 추가될 수 있는가? 문장 삽입

규산염 암석으로 구성된 이 천체들은 너무 뜨거워서 휘발성 기체로 응축되지 못하고 행성으로 형성되었다.

① [A]
② [B] ✓
③ [C]
④ [D]

| 분석 | 주어진 문장은 '규산염 암석으로 구성된 이 천체'들에 대해 언급하므로 직전 문장에 천체들이 나열되고 행성의 구성을 설명하는 부분에 문장을 삽입해야 한다. 두 번째 단락의 마지막 문장은 역접표현인 'However'로 시작하는데 목성, 토성, 천왕성, 해왕성은 목성형 행성들로 온도가 차가웠다고 서술했으므로 직전 내용은 고온의 다른 행성들에 대해 언급해야 자연스럽다. 주어진 문장을 [B]에 삽입하는 것이 흐름상 자연스럽다.

| 배경지식 | 미행성설(Planetesimal hypothesis): 태양 부근을 지나는 항성의 인력에 의하여 태양에서 떨어져 나온 물질들이 응집하여 태양계의 행성들이 만들어졌다는 이론으로 오늘날에는 학설로 믿지 않음

[22-23] 2018 항공대

| 정답 | 22 ② 23 ③

| 어휘 |
extrapolate ⓥ (~을 기반으로) 추론하다
be on top of each other 서로서로 엉겨 붙어 있다, 쌓여 있다
equation ⓝ 방정식
all but 거의, ~ 외에 모두
quantum theory ⓝ 양자론
spontaneously ⓐ 자발적으로, 자연스럽게
cosmic microwave background 우주 마이크로파 배경
imprint ⓝ 자국, 흔적, 인상
patent ⓥ 특허를 얻다, 특허를 주다
royalty ⓝ 특허권 사용료

전문해석

1920년대까지, 모든 사람들은 우주가 본질적으로 정적이고 시간이 지나도 변하지 않는다고 생각했다. 그러고 나서 우주가 확장하고 있다는 것이 발견되었다. 먼 은하들은 우리로부터 멀어지고 있었다. 이것은 그들이 과거에는 틀림없이 서로 더 가까웠다는 것을 의미했다. 만약 우리가 추론해 본다면, 우리는 우리 모두 약 150억 년 전에 서로 한데 엉겨 붙어 있었음을 알 수 있다. 이것은 우주의 시작인 빅뱅이었다. 하지만 빅뱅 이전에는 어떤 것이 있었을까? 만약 없었다면, 무엇이 우주를 창조했을까? 왜 우주는 그런 방식으로 빅뱅으로부터 생겨났을까? 우리는 우주 이론이 두 부분으로 나눠질 수 있다고 생각하곤 했다. 첫째, 한번에 모든 공간을 차지한 우주의 상태를 고려했을 때, 맥스웰 방정식이나 일반 상대성 이론과 같은 우주의 진화를 결정짓는 이론들이 있었다. 둘째, 우주의 초기 상태에 대한 질문은 없었다. 우리는 첫 번째 부분에서 좋은 진전을 이루었고, 이제 가장 극단적인 상황을 제외한 모든 상

황에서의 진화의 법칙에 대한 지식을 가지고 있다. 그러나 최근까지, 우리는 우주의 초기 조건에 대해 거의 알지 못했다. 하지만, 진화의 법칙과 초기 조건으로의 이러한 구분은 시간과 공간이 분리되고 구별되는 것에 달려 있다. 극단적인 상황에서, 일반 상대성 이론과 양자 이론은 시간이 다른 공간 차원처럼 행동하도록 허용한다. 이것은 시간과 공간 사이의 구분을 제거하고, 진화의 법칙이 초기 상태를 결정할 수 있다는 것을 의미한다. 우주는 무에서 자발적으로 스스로를 창조할 수 있다. 게다가, 우리는 우주가 다른 상태에서 생성되었을 확률을 계산할 수 있다. 이러한 예측은 매우 초기 우주의 흔적인 우주 극초단파 배경의 더블유맵 위성에 의한 관측과 매우 잘 일치한다. 우리는 우리가 창조의 신비를 해결했다고 생각한다. 아마도 우리는 우주에 대해 특허를 받아 모든 사람에게 그들의 존재에 대한 사용료를 부과해야 할지도 모른다.

22 빈칸을 가장 잘 채우는 문장을 고르시오. 빈칸 추론

① 우주로 뻗어 나갈 가능성
② 창조의 신비 ✓
③ 인류의 미래
④ 관측을 통한 우주의 문제

| 분석 | 빈칸 뒤의 본문 마지막 문장에서 '우리는 우주에 대해 특허를 받아 모든 사람에게 그들의 존재에 대한 사용료를 부과해야 할지도 모른다.'고 가정한 부분을 참고하여 빈칸을 추론해 본다. 보통 '특허'란 '새로운 발명이나 발견'을 인정받는 것이므로 우리가 우주에 대해 특허를 받고 존재하는 모두에게 사용료를 부과할 수 있는 권리를 얻으려면 '우주의 창조'나 '우주의 시작'에 대해 알아냈어야 할 것이다. 따라서 보기 ②가 빈칸에 가장 적절하다.

23 다음 중 올바른 것은 무엇인가? 내용 일치

① 은하계가 우리에게 더 가까이 이동하고 있다는 것은 부인할 수 없다. 우주는 확장하고 있음
② 진화 법칙은 우주의 초기 상태에 적용될 수 없다. 16번째 문장에서 진화의 법칙은 우주의 초기 상태를 결정할 수 있음을 언급함
③ 시간과 공간의 차이는 극단적인 상태에서 사라질 수 있다. ✓
④ 우주의 나이를 계산하는 것은 어떤 경험적인 관찰에 의해서도 뒷받침되지 않는다. 더블유맵 위성의 관찰 결과가 경험적 관찰에 해당됨

| 분석 | 본문 15~16번째 문장에서 '극단적인 상황에서는 시간이 다른 공간 차원처럼 행동하도록 허용'하고 '시간과 공간 사이의 구분을 제거'한다고 했다. 따라서 보기 ③은 올바른 진술이다.

[24-25] 2021 숭실대

| 정답 | 24 ① 25 ②

| 어휘 | slip ⓥ 미끄러지다, 빠져나가다   hypocenter ⓝ (지진의) 진원지
epicenter ⓝ (지진의) 진원지, 진앙, (문제의) 핵심   foreshock ⓝ 지진의 초기미동, 전진
mainshock ⓝ 주진, 본진   aftershock ⓝ 여진, 여파   the inner core ⓝ 내핵
outer core ⓝ 외핵   mantle ⓝ (지구의) 맨틀, 덮개, 막   crust ⓝ 지각, 굳어진 표면
tectonic plate ⓝ 판상을 이루어 움직이는 지각의 표층   plate boundary 판 경계
unstick ⓥ (붙어 있는 것을) 잡아떼다

전문해석

지진은 지구의 두 블록이 갑자기 서로를 미끄러져 지나갈 때 발생하는 것이다. 그들이 미끄러지는 표면을 단층 또는 단층 평면이라고 한다. 지진이 시작되는 지표 아래의 위치를 저심층이라고 하고, 지표면 바로 위의 위치를 진앙이라고 한다.

때때로 지진에는 초기 미동이 있다. 이것들은 다음에 발생하는 더 큰 지진과 같은 장소에서 발생하는 더 작은 지진이다. 과학자들은 더 큰 지진이 발생할 때까지 지진이 초기 미동이라고 말할 수 없다. 가장 큰, 주요 지진은 본진이라고 불린다. 본진은 항상 여진이 뒤따른다. 이것들은 본진과 같은 장소에서 나중에 발생하는 더 작은 지진이다. ==본진의 크기에 따라, 여진은 본진 이후에 몇 주, 몇 달, 심지어 몇 년 동안 계속될 수 있다.== 25 ②

그렇다면, 무엇이 지진을 일으키고 그것들은 어디에서 발생할까? 지구는 네 개의 주요 층을 가지고 있다: 내부 중심부, 외부 중심부, 맨틀 그리고 맨틀의 표면. 지각과 맨틀의 꼭대기는 우리 행성의 표면에서 얇은 피부를 구성한다. 그러나 이 피부가 모두 한 조각으로 있는 것은 아니다. 그것은 지구의 표면을 덮고 있는 퍼즐처럼 많은 조각들로 이루어져 있다. 그것뿐만 아니라, 이 퍼즐 조각들은 서로를 지나 미끄러지고 서로 부딪히며, 계속 천천히 움직인다. 우리는 이 퍼즐 조각들을 지각판이라고 부르고, 그 판의 가장자리는 판 경계라고 부른다. ==판 경계는 많은 단층으로 구성되어 있고, 세계의 대부분의 지진은 이 단층에서 발생한다.== 판의 가장자리가 거칠기 때문에, 그들은 판의 나머지 부분이 계속 움직이는 동안 막힌다. 마지막으로, 판이 충분히 멀리 이동했을 때, 가장자리가 그 단층 중 하나에 붙지 않고 지진이 발생한다. 24 ①

---

24 다음 중 사실인 것은? 내용 일치

☑ 대부분의 지진은 판 경계의 단층에서 발생한다.
② 지진의 진원지는 출발점 바로 아래에 위치해 있다. 언급 없음
③ 여진이 발생하기 전에 본진이 발생하지만 여진이 발생하지 않을 수도 있다. 본진은 항상 여진이 뒤따름
④ 지진은 지구가 한 조각에 여러 개의 층을 가지고 있기 때문에 발생한다. 여러 조각의 지각판의 경계는 단층으로 구성되고 지진은 이 단층에서 발생

| 분석 | 본문 두 번째 단락 8번째 문장에서 '판 경계는 많은 단층으로 구성되어 있고, 세계의 대부분의 지진은 이 단층에서 발생한다.'고 했다. 따라서 보기 ①은 사실이다.

---

25 다음 중 지진의 지속 시간을 결정하는 것은? 세부 내용 일치

① 지진의 발생 시간
☑ 본진의 크기
③ 전진의 횟수
④ 단층의 크기

| 분석 | 본문 두 번째 단락 마지막 문장에서 '본진의 크기에 따라, 여진은 본진 이후에 몇 주, 몇 달, 심지어 몇 년 동안 계속될 수 있다.'고 했다. 따라서 보기 ② '본진의 크기'가 지진의 지속 시간을 결정한다.

[26-29] 2022 세종대

| 정답 | 26 ④ 27 ① 28 ③ 29 ②

| 어휘 |
- **grim** ⓐ 엄숙한, 암울한
- **panacea** ⓝ 만병통치약
- **sovereignty** ⓝ 주권, 통치권
- **collision** ⓝ 충돌
- **extensive** ⓐ 광대한, 다방면에 미치는
- **fraught** ⓐ (좋지 않은 것들) 투성이의
- **bolthole** ⓝ 피난 장소, 도피처
- **martian** ⓐ 화성의
- **magnify** ⓥ 확대하다
- **array** ⓝ 배열
- **optimism** ⓝ 낙천주의, 낙관론
- **province** ⓝ 지방, 지역
- **liable** ⓐ 책임을 져야 할
- **unparalleled** ⓐ 비할 데 없는, 전대미문의
- **protocol** ⓝ 의정서, 규약

engagement ⓝ 약속, 계약
frontier ⓝ 국경, 국경 지방
terrestrial ⓐ 지구의, 지상의
romanticize ⓥ 낭만적으로 묘사하다
fetter ⓝ 족쇄, 속박, 구속
soybean ⓝ 콩
anarchic ⓐ 무정부(주의)의
governance ⓝ 통치, 관리, 지배

전문해석

지구가 기후 변화, 느린 성장 그리고 걱정스러운 정치에 대한 암울한 뉴스를 직면하고 있는 때에, 우주는 낙관론에 대한 놀라운 이유를 제공하는 것처럼 보일지도 모른다. 그러나 그것은 만병통치약도 아니고 도피처도 아니다. [A] 〈그리고 그 약속을 실현하기 위해서는 큰 문제가 해결되고 위험을 피해야 한다.〉 큰 문제는 법을 발전시키는 것이다. 1967년의 우주조약은 우주를 "모든 인류의 영역"으로 선언하고 주권에 대한 주장을 금지하고 있다. 이것은 해석의 여지를 많이 남긴다. 누가 생명 유지를 위해 달의 극에 있는 얼음을 사용할 가장 좋은 권리를 가지고 있을까? 화성의 정착민들이 환경에 대해 그들이 좋아하는 것을 하도록 허용해야 할까? 누구에게 위성 충돌에 대한 책임이 있나? [B] 그러한 불확실성은 우주에서의 무력 사용이라는 위험을 확대시킨다. 미국이 지구상에서 무력을 투사할 수 있는 전대미문의 능력을 갖고 있는 것은 광범위한 인공위성의 배치에 의존한다. 다른 나라들은, 이것을 알고, 반위성 무기들을 만들었다. 그리고 우주에서의 군사 활동은 잘 검증된 협약이나 교전 규칙이 없다. [C]
우주를 낭만화된 '개척시대의 서부', 인류가 족쇄를 벗어 던지고 자신의 운명을 재발견할 수 있는 무정부주의적 변경 지역으로 홍보하는 것은 실수다. 우주가 약속을 이행하기 위해서는 통치가 필요하다. [D] 세계가 철근과 콩의 지상 무역에 관한 규칙에 동의할 수 없는 상황에서, 그것은 큰 요청처럼 보일지도 모른다. 하지만 통제가 없다면, 지구 너머에 있는 모든 잠재력은 기껏해야 또 다른 50년을 기다려야 이행될 수 있을 것이다. 최악의 우주는 지구의 문제를 가중시킬 수 있다.

---

26 저자가 윗글을 쓴 주된 목적은 무엇인가? 〔글의 목적〕

① 1967년의 우주조약의 역할을 설명하기 위해
② 우주에서의 군사협정의 필요성에 대해 논하기 위해
③ 우주 자원의 밝은 미래를 기술하기 위해
✓ ④ 우주 개발과 관련된 잠재적인 문제들을 알리기 위해

| 분석 | 본문에서 저자는 우주 개발에 대한 낙관론을 경계하며 이와 관련된 법규를 발전시킬 것을 주장하고 있다. 따라서 글을 쓴 목적으로는 보기 ④가 적절하다.

---

27 아래 문장의 가장 적합한 위치는 어디인가? 〔문장 삽입〕

> 그리고 그 약속을 실현하기 위해서는 큰 문제가 해결되고 위험을 피해야 한다.

✓ ① [A]   ② [B]
③ [C]   ④ [D]

| 분석 | 주어진 문장에서 '그 기대'는 앞 문장에 언급되어야 하며 주어진 문장 뒤로는 해결방안이 제시되어야 할 것이다. 본문 첫 번째 문장에서 언급한 (우주에 대한) 낙관론이 '그 기대'이며 [A] 뒤로 나열되는 내용들이 해결되어야 할 문제들이다. 따라서 주어진 문장은 [A]에 삽입되어야 한다.

---

28 우주 개발에 관한 윗글의 어조로 가장 적절한 것은? 〔어조〕

① 의심스러운   ② 희망적인
✓ ③ 우려하는   ④ 혐오스러운

| 분석 | 본문 마지막 두 문장에서 저자는 '통제가 없다면, 지구 너머에 있는 모든 잠재력은 기껏해야 또 다른 50년을 기다려야 이행' 될 수 있고 '최악의 우주는 지구의 문제를 가중시킬 수 있다.'고 했다. 따라서 우주 개발에 대한 어조로는 보기 ③이 가장 적절하다.

29 윗글에 따르면 다음 중 사실인 것은? 내용 일치

① 달의 얼음은 우주군을 지탱하기 위해 적절하게 사용될 수 있다. 생명 유지를 위한 달의 얼음 사용의 권리에 대한 의구심 제기함
✓ 1967년의 우주조약은 우주 문제를 다루기에 충분하지 않을 것이다.
③ 위성 충돌은 화성인들의 평화로운 정착을 방해할 것이다. 위성 충돌과 화성인 정착의 관련성은 언급되지 않음
④ 만약 세계가 지상 무역에 동의한다면 우주는 지구의 문제가 될 것이다. 지상 무역에 동의하지 않는다는 가정만 소개됨

| 분석 | 본문의 5번째 문장부터 저자는 1967년의 우주조약이 다른 해석의 여지를 남긴다고 주장한 뒤 그 세부 사항들을 나열했다. 나열된 사항들은 모두 저자의 의구심을 유발하므로 저자는 이 조약이 우주 문제를 다루기에는 충분하지 않다고 볼 것이다. 따라서 보기 ②가 정답이다.

[30-32] 2011 성균관대

| 정답 | 30 ① 31 ③ 32 ⑤

| 어휘 |
neighboring ⓐ 이웃의, 가까운
to date 지금까지
exoplanet ⓝ 태양계 외 행성
orbit ⓥ ~ 주위를 돌다
queer ⓐ 이상한, 기묘한
Icarus ⓝ (그리스 신화) 이카루스(밀랍으로 붙인 날개로 날다가 아버지 다이달로스(Daedalus)의 경고를 무시하고 태양에 너무 접근해 밀랍이 녹아 바다에 떨어졌다는 인물)
remark ⓝ 주의, 소견, 말
last ⓥ 계속되다, 지속되다
light-year ⓝ 광년(빛이 1년간에 나아가는 거리)
benighted ⓐ 밤이 된, 어리석은, 미개한
gigantic ⓐ 거대한
comet ⓝ 혜성
nucleus ⓝ 핵, 핵심
spin ⓥ 돌리다, 회전하다
untold ⓐ 말하지 않은, 밝혀지지 않은
evidently ⓐⓓ 분명하게, 명백히
shrink ⓥ 줄다, 움츠리다
exotica ⓝ 이국적인[진기한] 것[곳]
glare ⓝ 번쩍이는 빛, 눈부신 빛, 섬광
amid prep ~의 한가운데[사이]에
cricket ⓝ 귀뚜라미
firefly ⓝ 반딧불이, 개똥벌레
firework ⓝ 불꽃놀이, 번득임
interrogate ⓥ 질문하다, 심문하다
transparent ⓐ 투명한
transient ⓐ 일시적인, 순간적인

전문해석

인간이 우리의 행성을 탐험하는 데 수천 년이 걸렸고, 우리의 이웃 행성들을 이해하는 데 수 세기가 걸렸지만, 요즘은 매주 새로운 세계들이 발견되고 있다. 지금까지, 천문학자들은 태양이 아닌 다른 항성들의 궤도를 도는 세계인 370개 이상의 "외계 행성"을 발견했다. 많은 행성들이 생물학자 J. B. S. 할데인(J. B. S. Haldane)이 "우주는 우리가 생각하는 것보다 더 기묘할 뿐만 아니라, 앞으로 우리가 생각할 수 있는 것보다 더 기묘하다"고 한 유명한 말을 확인할 정도로 매우 이상하다. 지구로부터 260광년 떨어져 있는 이카루스 같은 "뜨거운 토성"이 있는데, 이것은 매우 빠르게 그것의 부모 항성 주위를 돌고 있어서 그곳에서 1년은 3일도 채 안 된다. 150광년 밖에 있는 또 다른 항성 주위를 돌고 있는 것은 그을린 "뜨거운 목성"인데, 이것의 상부 대기가 거대한 혜성 같은 꼬리를 형성하기 위해 발사되고 있다. 한때 강력했던 별의 잔해가 도시 크기의 회전하는 원자핵으로 수축된 펄서 주위를 도는 세 개의 흉측한 행성들이 발견되었고 한편 무수한 세계들이 분명히 그들의 항성 속으로 떨어졌거나 그들의 태양계 밖으로 던져져 영원한 어둠 속에서 떠도는 "떠돌이"가 되었다.

그러한 이국적인 세계 속에서, 과학자들은 우리가 알고 있는 것처럼 생명체가 살 수 있는 적당한 거리(너무 뜨겁지도 너무 차갑지도 않은)로 항성 주위를 돌고 있는 지구와 비슷한 행성들에 대한 힌트를 얻기를 간절히 바라고 있다. 우리의 행성과 비슷한 행성은 아직 발견되지 않았는데, 아마도 그것들이 눈에 잘 띄지 않기 때문일 것이다. 별의 눈부신 빛 속에서 우리처럼 작고 어두운 행성을 보는 것은 불꽃놀이에서 반딧불이를 보려고 하는 것과 같고, 별에 대한 중력의 영향을 감지하는 것은 토네이도 속에서 귀뚜라미 소리

를 듣는 것과 같다. 하지만 기술을 한계까지 다다르게 함으로써, 천문학자들은 다른 지구를 발견하고 생명체의 징후를 캐물을 수 있는 날을 향해 빠르게 접근하고 있다.

30 문맥에 따르면, 지구의 부모 항성은 _____ 일 것이다. 세부 내용 일치
① 태양 ✓
② 토성
③ 달
④ 행성
⑤ 혜성

| 분석 | 본문에 따르면 부모 항성이란 행성이 그 주변을 도는 항성이므로 문맥상 태양일 것이다. 따라서 정답은 보기 ①이다.

31 빈칸에 가장 적합한 표현은 _____ 일 것이다. 빈칸 추론
① 너무 큰
② 떠돌아다니는
③ 눈에 잘 안 띄는 ✓
④ 투명한
⑤ 일시적인

| 분석 | 빈칸이 포함된 문장의 뒤로 소개되는 예시들을 참고하여 빈칸을 추론한다. 다음 문장에서 예를 든 것처럼 '불꽃놀이에서 반딧불이를 보려고 하는 것'이나 '토네이도 속에서 귀뚜라미 소리를 듣는 것'과 같이 행성들은 '발견하기 어려운' 특성을 가졌을 것이다. 보기 ③ '눈에 잘 안 띄는'이 정답으로 가장 적절하다.

32 윗글의 가장 좋은 제목은 _____ 일 것이다. 제목
① 우리만의 행성: 지구
② 이카루스 같은 "뜨거운 토성"
③ 이상한 우주
④ 떠돌이(행성)들
⑤ 새로운 지구 찾기 ✓

| 분석 | 본문에서는 '우주에 존재하는 지구와 비슷한 행성의 발견'에 대해 서술하고 있다. 따라서 보기 ⑤가 정답으로 가장 적절하다.

[33-35] 2022 단국대

| 정답 | 33 ④ 34 ③ 35 ②

| 어휘 |
geology ⓝ 지질학
derive ⓥ 끌어내다, 획득하다
exclusively ⓐⓓ 배타적으로, 독점적으로
give rise to 낳다, 일으키다
clay ⓝ 점토, 찰흙
coal ⓝ 석탄
external ⓐ 외부의, 밖의
crust ⓝ 지각
mutation ⓝ 변화, 돌연변이

geologist ⓝ 지질학자
discourse ⓝ 강연, 담론, 의견의 교환
pursue ⓥ 추구하다, 수행하다, 계속하다
distinct ⓐ 별개의, 다른, 독특한
chalk ⓝ 백악, 분필
slate ⓝ 점판암
flourish ⓥ 번영[번성]하다
channel ⓝ 물길, 수로, 경로

inquiry ⓝ 연구, 탐구, 질문, 조사
mineral kingdom ⓝ 광물계
successive ⓐ 잇따른, 계속되는
consist of ~로 구성되다
limestone ⓝ 석회석[암]
granite ⓝ 화강암
remains ⓝ (죽은 사람이나 동물의) 유해
trajectory ⓝ 궤도, 궤적

> 전문해석

지구는 어떤 물질로 구성되어 있으며, 이 물질들은 어떤 방식으로 배열되어 있는가? 이것들은 지질학이 몰두되어 있는 첫 번째 질문이며, 지질학은 그리스어로 지구 'ge', 그리고 담론을 뜻하는 'logos'에서 이름이 유래한 과학이다. 경험하기 이전에 우리는 이런 종류의 조사가 광물계, 그리고 지구 표면 또는 그 아래의 다양한 깊이에서 발생하는 다양한 암석, 토양, 그리고 금속과 관련이 있을 것이라고 상상했을 수 있다. 하지만, 그러한 연구를 수행하면서 우리는 곧 지구의 표면과 내부의 이전 상태에서 일어난 연속적인 변화와 이러한 변화를 야기한 원인을 고려하게 되었다. 그리고 여전히 더 특이하고 예상치 못한 것은 우리는 곧 동물 창조의 역사 또는 과거의 다른 시기에 지구에 살았던 다양한 동물과 식물 종에 대한 연구에 참여하게 된다는 것이다.

지구의 고체 부분이 점토, 백악, 모래, 석회석, 석탄, 점판암, 화강암 등과 같은 뚜렷한 물질로 구성되어 있다는 것을 모두 알고 있지만, 관찰하기 전에는 일반적으로 이 모든 것들이 우리가 지금 보고 있는 상태에서 처음부터 남아 있었다고—현재의 형태와 현재의 위치에서 만들어졌다고—생각되었다. 지질학자는 지구의 외부 부분이 우리가 지금 보고 있는 상태에서 사물의 시작 단계나 순식간에 모두 생성된 것이 아니라는 증거를 발견하면서 곧 다른 결론에 도달한다. 그와는 반대로, 지질학자는 그것들이 매우 다양한 상황에서 그리고 연속적인 기간을 거쳐 점차적으로 실제 형태와 상태를 획득했다는 것을 보여 줄 수 있는데, 각 기간 동안 서로 다른 종족의 생명체가 땅과 물에서 번성했으며, 이 생물의 잔해는 여전히 지구의 지각에 묻혀 있다.

33 다음 중 첫 번째 단락에 포함되는 글쓰기 방식은 무엇인가? `글의 구성`

① 비평　　　　　　　　　② 내레이션(이야기 서술)
③ 분류　　　　　　　　　✔④ 정의

| 분석 | 본문은 지질학의 의미와 지질학자의 연구 방향에 대해 서술하고 있다. 따라서 보기 ④ '정의'가 정답으로 가장 적절하다.

34 밑줄 친 부분과 가장 의미가 가까운 것은 무엇인가? `밑줄 추론`

① 경로　　　　　　　　　② 궤도
③ 돌연변이　　　　　　　✔④ 형태

| 분석 | 'configuration'은 '형태'라는 의미이므로 보기 ④와 가장 의미가 가깝다.

35 윗글에 따르면, 어느 것이 사실인가? `내용 일치`

① 비록 지질학은 처음에 지구의 변화에 대한 연구라고 생각되었지만, 추가적인 연구는 동물과 식물의 역사가 그 주제의 일부라는 것을 보여 준다.
✔② 비록 지질학은 처음에 광물에 대한 연구로 생각되었지만, 추가적인 연구는 동물과 식물도 그 주제의 일부라는 것을 보여 준다.
③ 비록 지질학은 처음에 지구 표면에 대한 연구로 생각되었지만, 추가적인 연구는 지표면 아래의 깊은 곳 또한 주제의 일부라는 것을 보여 준다.
④ 비록 지질학은 처음에 창조의 역사에 대한 연구라고 생각되었지만, 추가적인 연구는 동물과 식물도 그 주제의 일부라는 것을 보여 준다.

| 분석 | 본문 첫 단락의 3~4번째 문장에서 지질학은 처음에는 암석이나 금속과 같은 광물에 대한 연구로 생각되었지만, 연구를 수행하면서 동식물 창조의 역사, 즉 과거 동식물에 대한 연구에 참여하게 되었다고 했다. 따라서 보기 ②가 정답으로 적절하다.

[36-37] 2019 건국대

| 정답 | 36 ③ 37 ①

| 어휘 | **astronomer** ⓝ 천문학자 **spacecraft** ⓝ 우주선 **be scheduled to** ~할 예정이다
orbit ⓝ 궤도, 범위 **map** ⓥ 지도를 만들다[그리다] **lander** ⓝ 상륙자, (달 등에의) 착륙선
investigate ⓥ 조사하다, 연구하다 **Antarctica** ⓝ 남극 대륙 **valley** ⓝ 골짜기, 계곡
promising ⓐ 가망 있는, 유망한 **fossil** ⓝ 화석, 시대에 뒤진 사람

전문해석

1993년 8월이 다가옴에 따라 전 세계의 천문학자들은 흥분하여 기다리고 있었다. 미국의 우주선인 마스 옵서버는 화성 주위의 궤도로 이동하여 지구로 새로운 징보를 보내기 시작할 예정이었다. 화성을 (지도로) 그리는 것 외에도, 마스 옵서버는 화성의 대기와 표면을 연구할 예정이었다. ⓐ 불행하게도, 과학자들은 8월 24일에 마스 옵서버와의 연락이 끊겼다. 8억 4천5백만 달러의 비용이 든 마스 옵서버의 임무는 실패했다.

대조적으로, 미국의 ⓑ 이전 화성 탐사는 큰 성공을 거두었다. 1976년, 두 대의 미국 우주선이 생명체의 흔적을 찾기 위해 화성에 착륙했다. 바이킹 착륙선들이 수행한 실험들은 부정적인 결과를 낳았다. 하지만, 과학자들은 우주에 있는 우리의 가까운 이웃에 대해 여전히 의문을 갖고 있었다. 그들은 화성에 있는 생명체의 가능성에 대해 더 조사하고 싶었다. 이것이 마스 옵서버 임무의 목적이었다.

과학자들은 바이킹 임무에 ⓒ 만족했다. 우주선이 착륙한 두 장소는 안전한 착륙 장소를 제공했지만, 특별히 흥미로운 장소는 아니었다. 과학자들은 화성에 생명체가 사는 지구의 특정한 장소들과 비슷한 다른 지역들이 있다고 믿고 있다. 예를 들어, 남극의 얼음으로 덮여 있지 않은 지역, 남부 빅토리아랜드는 화성의 한 지역과 ⓓ 유사하다.

남부 빅토리아랜드의 건조한 계곡에서, 평균 기온이 영하이지만, 생물학자들은 바위와 얼어붙은 호수에서 단순한 생명체를 발견했다. 아마도 이것은 화성의 몇몇 지역들에서도 마찬가지일 것이다.

과학자들은 화성에 대한 또 다른 조사를 원한다. 그들은 그 행성의 표면을 지도화하고 더 유망한 위치에 우주선을 착륙시키기를 원한다. 그들은 고대 생명체의 잔해인 화석을 찾기를 원한다. 만약 화성에 생명체가 존재했다면, 과학자들은 미래의 임무가 모래 아래나 얼음에서 그것의 기록을 찾을 수도 있다고 믿는다. 그들은 마스 옵서버의 임무 실패에 매우 ⓔ 실망했고 새로운 임무를 시작하기를 원한다. ³⁷①

36 윗글의 밑줄 친 ⓐ~ⓔ 가운데, 문맥상 낱말의 쓰임이 적절하지 않은 것은? 무관한 어휘

① ⓐ ② ⓑ ✓ ⓒ ④ ⓓ ⑤ ⓔ

| 분석 | 본문 두 번째 단락 세 번째 문장에서 '바이킹 착륙선들이 수행한 실험들은 부정적 결과를 낳았다'고 했으므로 과학자들은 바이킹의 임무에 만족하지 않았을 것이다. 따라서 ⓒ는 부적절하며 반의어인 'dissatisfied'로 수정되어야 한다.

37 윗글의 제목으로 가장 적절한 것은? 제목

✓ ① 화성에서 생명체를 찾는 임무
② 마스 옵서버의 재앙
③ 화성에서의 천문학자들의 도전
④ 지구와 화성의 유사점
⑤ 우주여행을 위한 미래의 우주선

| 분석 | 본문에서는 화성에서 생명체의 흔적을 찾기 위해 바이킹 착륙선과 마스 옵서버를 활용했으나 결과적으로 둘 다 실패했다는 내용이 서술되었다. 그러나 본문의 마지막 문장에 따르면 마스 옵서버의 임무는 실패했지만 과학자들은 화성에 생명체가 존재하는지에 대한 새로운 연구를 원한다고 했다. 보기 ①이 글의 제목으로 가장 적절하다.

[38-40] 2021 성균관대

| 정답 | 38 ④ 39 ② 40 ⑤

| 어휘 |
solar system ⓝ 태양계, (천체의) 위성들
boost ⓥ 신장시키다, 북돋우다
odds ⓝ 가능성, 배당률
extraterrestrial ⓐ 지구 밖의, 외계의
house ⓥ 살 곳을 주다, 거처를 제공하다
unveil ⓥ 덮개를 벗기다, (새로운 계획이나 상품을) 발표하다
Milky Way galaxy 우리 은하(태양계가 포함된 은하)
Cancer ⓝ 게자리, 게자리인 사람 (pl. Cancri)
Jupiter ⓝ 목성
constellation ⓝ 별자리
astrobiologist ⓝ 우주생물학자
astrophysicist ⓝ 천체 물리학자

전문해석

유럽과 미국의 천문학자들은 목요일 우리와 유사한 궤도에 있는 행성들을 가진 두 개의 태양계의 발견을 발표했는데, 이 발견은 그것들(두 개의 태양계)이 외계 생명체를 수용할 가능성을 높여 준다. 모두 합쳐서, 천문학자들은 이전에 알려지지 않은 27개의 행성을 발견했다고 발표했고, 근처의 별들을 도는 알려진 행성의 수를 100개 이상으로 늘렸다.

캘리포니아 버클리 대학의 제프리 마시(Geoffrey Marcy)와 워싱턴 D.C. 카네기 연구소의 폴 버틀러(Paul Butler)가 이끄는 한 연구팀은 15개의 행성의 세부 사항을 발표했다. 제네바 대학의 스위스 천문학자 마이클 마요르(Michael Mayor)가 이끄는 유럽 연구팀은 과학 회의에서 계획된 발표를 며칠 앞두고 12개의 세부 사항을 추가로 공개했다.

"우리 은하계 안에 우리 은하계와 같은 수십억 개의 행성계가 있을 것입니다."라고 마시는 말한다. 그의 팀은 게자리 55별이 목성의 것과 매우 유사한 원형에 가까운 궤도를 차지하고 있는 목성 같은 행성을 가지고 있다는 것을 발견했다. 거대한 가스 덩어리인 그 행성은 게자리 별자리에서 41광년 떨어진 게자리55를 도는 데 약 14년이 걸린다. 38 ④ 39 ②

마시의 팀은 지구와 같은 행성이 그 별을 도는 행성들로부터의 방해 없이 게자리55의 궤도를 안전하게 돌 수 있다고 계산한다. 그 유럽 팀은 또한 크기와 그것의 원형궤도를 닮은 목성과 비슷한 행성을 가진 다른 태양계에 대해 보고한다.

우주생물학자들은 외부의 거대한 가스(행성)들이 원형에 가까운 궤도를 따르는 태양계가 생명체가 있는 행성들을 가질 가능성이 더 높다고 말한다. 이론적으로, 목성이 분명히 태양계의 역사에서 그랬던 것처럼, 목성 같은 물체들은 혜성의 충돌로부터 더 작고 지구 같은 행성들을 가려낼 것이다. 이에 더해서, 원형궤도를 가진 행성은 다른 행성들의 궤도 안정성을 방해할 가능성이 더 적다. 프린스턴 대학의 천체 물리학자 데이비드 스페겔(David Spergel)은 "이제 우리는 갑자기 태양계가 특별하지 않다는 첫 번째 보고를 받았습니다."라고 말한다. 38 ④

38 윗글의 소재는 무엇인가? 주제

① 미지의 행성의 원형궤도 계산
② 항성계의 행성 간 거리
③ 과학 회의의 발표
④ 발견된 우리와 유사한 항성계 ✓
⑤ 발견된 목성을 닮은 행성

| 분석 | 우리 은하계 내부에서 태양계와 유사한 것들을 다수 발견한 사실에 대해 각종 연구를 인용하여 진술하고 있다.

39 어느 것이 사실인가? 내용 일치

① 게자리55가 살고 있는 이 행성은 게자리55의 주위를 도는 데 약 41년이 걸린다. 14년이 걸림
✓ ② 유럽의 천문학자 팀이 발견한 또 다른 태양계는 목성과 비슷한 행성을 가지고 있다.
③ 천문학자들이 발견한 이전에 알려지지 않은 행성의 수는 100개 이상이다. 27개임
④ 이론적으로, 목성과 같은 물체들은 더 큰 행성들을 가려낸다고 여겨진다. 더 작고 지구 같은 행성들을 가려냄
⑤ 원형궤도를 가진 행성은 다른 행성의 궤도 안정성을 촉진할 가능성이 적다. 방해할 가능성이 적음

|분석| 본문 세 번째 단락 두 번째 문장에서 유럽 연구팀은 '게자리55가 목성의 것과 매우 유사한 원형에 가까운 궤도를 차지하고 있는 목성 같은 행성을 가지고 있다는 것을 발견'했다고 서술했다. 따라서 보기 ②가 글의 내용과 일치하는 진술이다.

40 빈칸에 들어갈 말로 가장 적절한 것은? 빈칸 추론

① 중요하지 않다
② 위험에 처해 있다
③ 목성과 매우 비슷하다
④ 게자리55와는 너무 멀리 떨어져 있다
✓ ⑤ 특별하지 않다

|분석| 본문에서는 지구와 유사한 궤도에 있는 두 개의 태양계를 소개했는데 관련 연구를 통해 우리의 태양계가 '유일'하거나 '특별' 하지 않음을 알 수 있다. 따라서 보기 ⑤가 정답으로 가장 적절하다.

[41-43] 2021 가톨릭대

|정답| 41 ① 42 ② 43 ②

|어휘| rotate ⓥ 회전하다, (일을) 교대로 하다　spin ⓥ (빙빙) 돌다, 회전하다　revolve ⓥ (축을 중심으로) 돌다
rotation ⓝ (지구·천체의) 자전, 회전　counterclockwise ⓐ 시계 반대 방향으로　stationary ⓐ 움직이지 않는, 정지된
spherical ⓐ 구 모양의, 구체의　bulge ⓥ ~로 가득 차다, 툭 튀어나오다　inertia ⓝ 무력, 타성, 〈물리〉 관성
heat distribution 열 분포　latitude ⓝ 위도　revolution ⓝ 공전

전문해석

지구의 운동은 두 가지 요소를 가지고 있다. 지구는, 지구가 회전하는 가상의 선인, 축을 중심으로 '자전하고', 궤도에서 태양을 중심으로 '공전한다'. 지구의 자전에 대해서는, 많은 증거와 주장이 있다. 지구가 자전하기 때문에 태양, 행성, 그리고 별들은 동쪽에서 떠서 서쪽으로 진다. 또한 북반구의 관찰자들은 북극성을 중심으로 한 원에서 반시계 방향으로 움직이는 것을 볼 수 있다. 그러나 이러한 관찰은 회전하는 지구뿐만 아니라 움직이는 하늘을 가진 정지해 있는 지구에 의해서도 설명될 수 있다. 그러므로, 우리는 다음과 같은 더 강한 주장이 필요하다.

첫째, 지구는 정확히 구형이 아니다. 적도에서 지구를 통과하는 거리는 12,756km인 반면, 한 극에서 다른 극까지의 거리는 12,713km이다. 그래서 지구는 불룩한 모양을 하고 있고, 과학자들은 물질이 같은 방향으로 계속 움직이는 관성의 개념을 사용하여 그것을 설명한다. 만약 그 행성을 구성하는 물질이 그 행성의 중력에 의해 제자리에 고정되지 않는다면, 그것은 회전하는 바퀴의 진흙처럼 회전하는 행성으로부터 날아갈 것이다. 지구의 표면은 중력의 안쪽 끌어당김에 대항하여 물질이 튀어나오는 적도에서 가장 빠르게 움직인다. 그러므로 적도에 볼록한 부분이 생겨난다.

또 다른 증거는 지구의 바람 패턴에서 나온다. 만약 지구가 회전하지 않지만 같은 대기 열 분포를 유지한다면, 바람 패턴은 훨씬 더 간단해질 것이다. 적도에 가열된 공기는 극지방 쪽으로 이동하고, 높은 위도의 찬 공기는 적도 쪽으로 다시 이동할 것이다. 그 움직임은 북쪽과 남쪽으로 일직선일 것이다. 그러나, 지구의 자전이 바람을 굴절시키기 때문에 우리는 실제로 곡선의 바람 패턴을 관찰한다.

마지막으로, 우리는 지구가 자전하고 있다는 것을 직접적인 관찰로 알고 있다: 달에 있는 우주비행사들은 하루 24시간 동안 지구의 전체 표면을 보았다. 달은 하루에 한 번 지구 주위를 돌지 않는다. 따라서 지구는 자전해야 한다.

---

41 빈칸을 가장 좋은 표현으로 채우시오. `빈칸 추론`

① ✓ 지구는 틀림없이 자전한다
② 다른 행성들도 틀림없이 공전하지 않는다
③ 지구는 자전할 뿐만 아니라 공전도 한다 빈칸이 포함된 단락에서는 지구의 자전에 관한 증거만을 언급했음
④ 우주비행사들의 보고서는 수정되어야 한다

| 분석 | 빈칸 앞에 'Therefore'는 결과를 제시하므로 앞 내용과의 관련성에 따라 빈칸을 추론한다. 본문 마지막 단락에서 우리는 지구의 자전을 직접적으로 관찰할 수 있고 이 증거로 달에 있는 우주비행사들이 하루 종일 지구의 표면을 본다는 사실을 제시했다. 따라서 마지막 문장의 결론도 '지구의 자전'과 관련된 내용으로 채워져야 한다. 따라서 보기 ①이 정답으로 가장 적절하다.

---

42 윗글의 제목으로 가장 적절한 것은? `제목`

① 자전과 공전의 차이
② ✓ 지구 자전의 증거
③ 천문 관측의 수단들
④ 지구에서 관성과 중력의 상호 작용

| 분석 | 본문은 첫 단락부터 지구의 자전에 대한 많은 증거가 있다고 밝힌 뒤 이후 단락에서 더 강력한 증거에 대해 서술하고 있다. 따라서 보기 ②가 정답으로 가장 적절하다.

---

43 다음 중 지구 자전에 대한 부인할 수 없는 주장은 무엇인가? `세부 내용 일치`

① 태양과 별들은 동쪽에서 떠서 서쪽으로 진다. 첫 단락에 소개된 내용이지만 강력한 증거는 아님
② ✓ 지구의 바람 패턴은 직선이 아니라 곡선이다.
③ 북극의 별들은 북극성을 중심으로 원을 그리며 반시계 방향으로 움직인다. 첫 단락에 소개된 내용이지만 강력한 증거는 아님
④ 한 극에서 다른 극까지의 거리는 적도에서 지구를 통과하는 거리와 같다

| 분석 | 이 문제에서는 지구의 자전에 대한 부인할 수 없는 주장, 즉 강력한 주장이 무엇인지를 묻고 있다. 따라서 본문의 세 번째 단락에서는 지구의 자전에 대한 강력한 증거 중 두 번째로 '곡선의 바람 패턴'을 제시했으므로 보기 ②가 부인할 수 없는 주장이다.

배경지식
자전(Rotation): 천체가 자기 자신을 중심으로 회전하는 운동
공전(Revolution): 한 천체가 다른 천체 주위를 원이나 타원을 그리며 도는 운동

[44-45] 2022 중앙대

| 정답 | 44 ② 45 ③

| 어휘 | astronomy ⓝ 천문학 subvert ⓥ (체제를) 전복시키다, (믿음을) 뒤엎으려 하다
cosmology ⓝ 우주론(우주의 기원과 발달을 연구하는 학문) trample on 짓밟다, 무시하다
natural philosophy ⓝ 자연철학(우주, 물질, 인과성, 확률, 원소, 무한, 움직임과 변화, 성질, 시간과 공간 등을 대상으로 자연에 대한 설명

을 제시하는 근대 과학의 전신)
substantively @ 사실상, 독립하여
permanence ⓝ 영구, 영속성
blemish ⓝ 흠, 오점
elude ⓥ (벌이나 책임을) 피하다
foreshorten ⓥ 축소하다, 원급법으로 그리다
property ⓝ 재산, 성질, 특성

take ~ into account ~을 고려하다, ~을 계산에 넣다
eternal @ 영구한, 영원한
cyclicity ⓝ 변동성, 주기성
akin to ~에 유사한
couch ⓥ 나타내다, 표현하다
doctrine ⓝ 교리, 신조

generation ⓝ 세대, 발생
sunspot ⓝ 태양의 흑점
orbit ⓥ (천체의 둘레를) 궤도를 그리며 돌다
noticeably @ 눈에 띄게, 뚜렷하게

전문해석

갈릴레오는 코페르니쿠스 천문학을 아리스토텔레스적 우주론을 뒤집는 수학적 수단으로 사용하려고 시도했다. 그는 그것들이 자연철학의 이론화의 내용에 직접적인 영향을 미쳤기 때문에—천문학자가 물리학자에게 설명이 필요한 현상이 무엇인지 말해 주었기 때문에—자연철학자가 수학적 천문학자의 발견을 고려해야 한다고 강조함으로써 물리학과 수학 사이의 일반적인 ⒶⒶ 구별을 무시했다. 그가 이탈리아어로 집필한 '태양흑점에 관한 편지'(1613)라는 작품에서, 갈릴레오는 태양 표면에 다양한 흠집들이 존재한다고 주장하면서 이 점을 강하게 주장했다.

아리스토텔레스적인 하늘은 완벽하고 실질적으로 변하지 않는 것으로 여겨졌다. 하늘이 한 모든 일은 새로운 것의 발생을 보여 주지 않으면서 영원히 빙빙 도는 것이었다. 갈릴레오와 다른 사람들이 1611년에 태양의 표면에서 처음 본 흠집들은 ⒷⒷ 천체의 영구성과 순환성의 특징을 보여 주지 않는 것으로 보였고, 갈릴레오는 사실 그것들이 태양의 표면에서 불규칙하게 나타났다가 바뀌었다가 사라진 어두운 얼룩들이라고 주장할 기회를 가졌다. 그 점들이 태양의 표면 그 자체에 정확히 위치해야 한다는 것은 아리스토텔레스적인 주장에 중요했다. 갈릴레오의 발견에 대한 공로의 주요 경쟁자였던 예수회 소속의 크리스토프 샤이너(Christoph Scheiner)는 처음에는 그 점들이 사실 달과 비슷한 작은 물체들로 구성되어 있고, 지금까지 적절한 질서로 변형하기에 너무 수가 많아 무리를 지어 태양 주위를 돌았다고 생각했다.

그것에 따라서, 갈릴레오는 주의 깊고 기하학적으로 나타낸 관찰 추론을 제시하여, 첫째로, 흑점들이 태양의 표면을 가로질러 주변부로 이동할 때 흑점들의 폭이 분명하게 줄어든다(그리고 그에 상응하여 주변부에서 나타나 중심에 가까워질 때는 그에 폭이 넓어짐)는 것과, 둘째로, 흑점들이 태양 원반의 가장자리 근처에서 관찰되었을 때 단축되는 것으로 해석되는 이 효과는 흑점들이 태양 자체의 표면에 위치하는 것과 일치했다는 것을 보여 줬다. 갈릴레오는 이러한 필수적으로 평평한 부분이 태양 위로 올라가면 정확한 모양이 눈에 띄게 다를 것이라고 주장했다.

갈릴레오의 주장은 다음과 같은 요지로 이어진다: 만약 아무것도 없는 곳에서 명백하게 나타나고 궁극적으로 사라지는 어두운 조각들에 의해 태양의 표면이 ⒸⒸ 손상된 것이 입증된다면, 아리스토텔레스적인 이론과 반대로 하늘에 생성과 몰락이 있다는 것은 부인할 수 없는 사실이 된다. 갈릴레오는 그에 따라 사물의 외부적인 특성(여기서 태양흑점의 겉보기 크기, 모양 및 움직임)에 대한 '수학적인' 설명에서 하늘의 문제에 대한 적절한 '물리학적인' 결론으로 이동했다.

44 윗글의 빈칸 Ⓐ, Ⓑ, Ⓒ에 들어가기에 가장 적절한 것은? 빈칸 추론

① 분류 – 빙하의 – 줄어든
✓② 구분 – 천체의 – 손상된
③ 분파 – 지상의 – 번진
④ 구별 – 하늘의 – 소멸된

| 분석 | 빈칸 Ⓐ가 포함된 문장에서 자연철학자는 수학자의 발견을 고려해야 한다고 했으므로 물리학과 수학 사이의 '구분'이나 '구별'을 무시했다고 추론할 수 있다. 빈칸 Ⓑ의 경우에는 그 앞 문장에서 '하늘'이 '영원히 빙빙 도는 것'이라고 했으므로 '천체'와 관련된 내용이 들어가야 한다. 마지막으로 빈칸 Ⓒ가 포함된 문장은 갈릴레오의 주장을 담고 있는데 본문 첫 단락에서부터 갈릴레오는 태양 표면에 다양한 흠집들이 있음을 주장했으므로 '흠집'과 관련되는 표현이 와야 한다. 따라서 보기 ②가 정답으로 가장 적절하다.

45 윗글을 통해 추론할 수 없는 것은? 내용 비추론

① 아리스토텔레스는 하늘이 새로운 것의 발생을 보여 주지 않으면서 영원히 빙빙 돌고 있다고 믿었다.
② 갈릴레오에게 코페르니쿠스 천문학은 아리스토텔레스적 우주론의 전통적인 생각을 바꾸는 유용한 수학적 수단이었다.
✓ 물리학과 수학을 사용하는 아리스토텔레스적인 방법을 따라, 갈릴레오는 하늘의 물질을 설명하기 위해 두 개의 자연과학을 사용했다.
④ 태양 표면에서 변화하는 어두운 점들의 주의 깊은 관찰은 갈릴레오가 아리스토텔레스의 우주론이 틀렸다고 주장하도록 이끌었다.

| 분석 | 본문의 첫 문장에서부터 '갈릴레오는 코페르니쿠스 천문학을 아리스토텔레스적 우주론을 뒤집는 수학적 수단으로 사용하려고 시도'했으며 이후에도 아리스토텔레스의 우주론을 반박하는 내용이 이어지므로 갈릴레오가 아리스토텔레스의 방식을 따른다고 한 보기 ③은 추론할 수 없다.

| 배경 지식 | 갈릴레오 갈릴레이(Galileo Galilei): 이탈리아의 철학자, 과학자, 물리학자, 천문학자이며 업적으로는 망원경을 개량하여 관찰한 것, 운동 법칙의 확립 등이 있으며, 코페르니쿠스의 이론을 옹호하여 태양계의 중심이 지구가 아니라 태양임을 믿음

[46-47] 2020 이화여대

| 정답 | 46 ④   47 ③

| 어휘 |
roughly @ 대략, 거의
galaxy ⑪ 은하, 은하수
spiral galaxy 나선은하
launch ⓥ 시작하다, 착수하다
left-handed @ 왼손잡이의, 왼쪽으로 도는
baffle ⓥ 좌절시키다, 실패로 끝나게 하다
incorporate ⓥ 통합하다
get in on (조직이나 활동에) 참여하다
classification ⑪ 분류(법)
rotate ⓥ 회전하다, 회전시키다
right-handed @ 오른손잡이의, 오른쪽으로 도는
counterclockwise @ 시계 반대 방향으로
end up -ing 결국 ~하게 되다
transform ⓥ (외형을) 변형시키다, 바꾸다
contribution ⑪ 기부, 기여, 공헌
participate in ~에 참여하다
clockwise @ 시계방향으로, 오른쪽으로
refute ⓥ 논박하다, 반박하다
interactive @ 상호 작용을 하는
insight ⑪ 통찰, 간파, 통찰력

전문해석

오늘날 대부분의 천문학 데이터는 세계의 약 10,000명의 전문 천문학자들이 일생 동안 평가할 수 있었던 것보다 훨씬 더 많은 정보를 수집하는 로봇 시스템을 통해 자동적으로 수집된다. 하지만, 이제 그 행동에 참여하고 진정한 기여를 할 수 있는 방법을 가진 최소한 백만 명의 아마추어 천문학자들이 있다. [A] 2007년, 한 천문학자 그룹이 갤럭시주(Galaxy Zoo)라고 불리는 웹 기반 응용 프로그램을 작성했는데, 이것은 Sloan Digital Sky Survey에 의해 수집된 천문학 정보의 데이터베이스를 위한 재기 넘치고 게임 같은 사용자 인터페이스를 만들었다. [B] 사람들은 컴퓨터가 아직 매우 잘하지 못하는 특정한 종류의 은하 분류를 시각적으로 할 수 있는 것으로 밝혀졌다. 그래서 그 프로젝트는 대중들이 그 분류에 참여하는 것을 즐기도록 했고 또한 천문학자들이 나선 은하가 시계 방향으로 회전하는 경향이 있다는 이론을 시험하는 것을 도왔다. [C] Galaxy Zoo는 로봇 망원경으로 이미지화된 백만 개의 은하로 구성된 데이터 세트로 시작되었다. 참가자들은 그 이미지들을 보고 그 은하들을 "오른손잡이"(시계 방향으로 회전하는 것을 의미하는) 또는 "왼손잡이"(반시계 방향으로 회전하는)로 분류했다. 매우 많은 은하가 있기 때문에, 그 팀은 그 사이트의 방문객들이 그것들을 모두 끝마치는 데에 적어도 2년이 걸릴 수 있다고 생각했다. 그러나 그것을 시작한 지 24시간 이내에, 그 사이트는 시간당 70,000개의 분류를 받았고, 첫해에 거의 15만 명의 사람들로부터 5,000만 개 이상의 분류가 접수되었다. 그 노력은 대부분의 나선 은하가 오른손잡이라는 생각을 반박했다. 그것들 중 단지 절반만이 오른손잡이였던 것으로 밝혀졌다. [D] 훨씬 더 놀라운 것은, 그 프로젝트에 참가하는 네덜란드의 교사가 천문학자들을 너무 당황하게 만든 이상한 은하를 발견했고 결국 허블 망원경의 주목을 받게 만들었다는 것이다. [E] 2008년에, 마이크로소프트는 WorldWide 망원경(WWT)을 소개했고 천문학자들과 일반 대중에게 하늘, 행성, 은하의 상호 작용적인 3차원 이미지에 대한 접근을 제공했다. 방문객들은 표준 브라우저를 통해 그 이미지들을 볼

수 있고, 천문학 전문가들이 사용하는 똑같은 데이터를 시각화할 수 있다. WWT는 Galaxy Zoo의 분류들과 그 이상의 분류들을 통합한다. WWT와 같은 시각화 도구는 실제로 때때로 일반 시민의 도움을 받아 데이터에서 통찰력을 얻는 과학자의 능력을 변화시킬 수 있다.

46 윗글을 단락으로 나누는 가장 좋은 지점은 어디인가? 단락 나누기

① [A], [B], 그리고 [D]
② [A], [C], 그리고 [D]
③ [B], [C], 그리고 [D]
✓ ④ [A], [C], 그리고 [E]
⑤ [B], [D], 그리고 [E]

| 분석 | 본문 첫 문장부터 [A]까지는 '천문학 데이터 수집에 참여할 수 있는 최소 백만 명의 천문학자들'을 소개했고, [A]부터 [C]까지는 갤럭시주 프로그램을 통해 일반대중이 은하 분류에 참여하는 내용을 다뤘다. 또한 [C]부터 [E]까지는 갤럭시 주 프로그램의 상세한 과정과 결과에 대해 구체적으로 다룬 후, [E]부터 본문 마지막 문장까지 마이크로소프트의 WWT 프로그램과 그 의미에 대해 서술했다. 따라서 보기 ④가 정답으로 적절하다.

47 다음 문장 중 본문에서 나온 개념을 잘못 옮기고 있는 것은 무엇인가? 내용 추론

① 갤럭시주 프로젝트의 결과로, 천문학자들은 은하수가 시계 방향 또는 반시계 방향으로 회전하는 특별한 경향이 없다는 것을 발견했다.
② 천문학자들이 분석할 수 있는 정보가 너무 많아서 모든 정보를 분석할 전문 천문학자들이 충분하지 않다.
✓ ③ 컴퓨터는 어떤 은하가 "오른손잡이"인지 ""왼손잡이"인지를 결정하는 것과 같은 종류의 천문학 과제에서는 사람들만큼 능숙하지 않다.
④ 천문학자들이 갤럭시주 프로그램을 만들었을 때, 그들은 그들이 실제로 얻은 것만큼 빨리 결과를 얻을 것이라고 기대하지 않았다.
⑤ 인터넷의 시각화 도구는 현대의 아마추어 천문학자들이 과거의 전문 천문학자들보다 연구를 더 잘할 수 있다는 것을 의미한다.

| 분석 | 본문의 네 번째 문장에서 컴퓨터가 '아직 시각적인 은하 분류에 능숙하지 않다'고 언급했지만 천문학 과제를 해결하는 능력에 대한 사람과의 비교는 언급되지 않았다. 따라서 보기 ③은 잘못된 진술이다.

10강 건강 / 의학

01	③	02	④	03	②	04	③	05	③	06	④	07	③	08	④	09	⑤	10	②
11	⑤	12	③	13	①	14	④	15	③	16	④	17	②	18	④	19	④	20	①
21	①	22	②	23	②	24	④	25	③	26	③	27	③	28	④	29	④	30	②
31	④	32	②	33	④	34	④	35	②	36	④	37	②	38	②	39	③	40	②
41	①	42	①	43	④	44	⑤	45	③	46	④	47	④	48	③	49	②	50	④
51	④																		

[01-02] 2011 국민대

| 정답 | 01 ③ 02 ④

| 어휘 | **chronic** ⓐ 만성적인, 장기간에 걸친　　**let go of** ~에서 손을 놓다　　**succumb** ⓥ 굴복하다, 복종하다
keep track of ~에 대해 계속 알고[파악하고] 있다, ~을 기록하다　　**impudent** ⓐ 뻔뻔스러운, 염치없는, 무례한
destitute ⓐ 빈곤한, 궁핍한　　**sedentary** ⓐ 앉아 있는, 앉아 지내는　　**courteous** ⓐ 예의 바른, 공손한

전문해석
여기 건강한 노화를 위한 몇 가지 팁들이 있는데, 당신은 노후에 일어날 수 있는 만성적인 질병의 위험을 감소시키기 위해 이 팁들이 아마도 필요할 것이다. 30대와 40대의 남성들은 흔히 접촉 스포츠를 하다가 잘못해서 다치게 되고, 반면 50대와 60대의 남성은 보통 너무 ⓐ 앉아만 있다. 건강하게 노화되는 한 가지 비밀은 당신 행동의 위험성을 평가하는 방법을 아는 것이다. 또 다른 하나는 젊은 신체에만 적합한 운동들을 기꺼이 손에서 놓는 것이다.
만약 당신이 심장마비나 암과 같은 중년에 찾아오는 일반적 질병 중의 하나로 쓰러진다면, 분명 당신은 건강하게 노화되는 일을 경험할 기회를 놓치게 될 것이다. 이러한 것들을 피하려면, 당신은 개인 건강의 위험 요소들에 대해 알아야 하며, 이것들을 계속 파악하는 가장 좋은 방법은 매년 정기 건강진단을 받는 것이다.

01 윗글의 빈칸 ⓐ에 들어갈 말로 가장 적절한 것은? 빈칸 추론
① 무례한　　② 궁핍한
✓ ③ 주로 앉아서 지내는　　④ 예의 바른

| 분석 | while로 앞 문장과 뒤 문장이 반대되는 내용을 말하고 있다. 30대와 40대가 활동적인 스포츠를 하고 있으므로 그와 반대되는 말이 와야 한다. '50대와 60대는 활동적이지 않다'의 개념이 와야 하므로 '주로 앉아서 지내는'의 의미인 ③ sedentary가 적절하다.

02 윗글의 제목으로 가장 적절한 것은? 제목
① 가장 위험한 만성 질환 언급 안 함　　② 흔한 질병을 피하는 방법 언급 안 함
③ 정기적인 건강검진의 중요성 너무 지엽적　　✓ ④ 건강한 노화를 위해 해야 할 일

| 분석 | 이 글의 서두에서 건강하게 노화되는 팁들이 있다고 하고, 그것에 관하여 마지막까지 진술하였다. 따라서 ④가 제목으로 가장 적절하다.

[03-04] 2015 한국외대

| 정답 | 03 ② 04 ③

| 어휘 | stand out ⓥ 두드러지다, 쉽게 눈에 띄다
variant ⓝ 변종, 이형; 변형
link ⓝ 연관성
interplay ⓝ 상호 작용
obesity ⓝ 비만
confirm ⓥ 확인하다
whatsoever ⓐⓓ (부정문에서) 전혀, 어떤 종류의 것도
ailment ⓝ 질병
pediatrics ⓝ 소아과
extra ⓐ 추가의

전문해석

DNA가 체중에 어떻게 영향을 미치는지를 연구하는 과학자들 사이에서, FTO라고 불리는 유전자가 돋보인다. "그것은 비만에 관한 유전학의 ⓐ 대표 유전자입니다."라고 펜실베이니아 약학대 대학의 소아과 부교수인 스트루안 F. 그랜트(Struan F. Grante)는 말했다. 2007년에, 연구자들은 FTO의 흔한 변종을 가진 사람들이 그렇지 않은 사람들보다 더 육중해지는 경향이 있다는 것을 발견했다. 그 이후로, 여러 연구가 반복적으로 그 연관성을 확인했다. 평균적으로, 그 위험한 변종 하나는 체중에 3.5 파운드를 더한다. 그 유전자 두 개는 7파운드를 증가시키며—비만이 될 위험성을 50% 커지게 한다. 하지만 그 유전자가 항상 문제가 되었던 것은 아닌 것 같다. 만약 과학자들이 수십 년 전에 FTO를 연구했다면, ⓐ 그들은 결코 체중과의 연관성을 발견하지 못했을 것이다. 새로운 연구는 FTO가 제2차 세계 대전 이후에 태어난 사람들에게만 위험 요소가 되었다는 것을 보여 준다. 그 연구는 비만을 훨씬 뛰어넘는 문제를 제기한다. 유전자는 분명히 여러 가지 면에서 우리의 건강에 영향을 주지만, 환경 또한 그러하다. 종종 우리가 비만이나 암 또는 다른 질병에 걸리는지 여부에 차이를 만드는 것은 그것들(유전자와 환경) 사이의 상호 작용이다.

03 빈칸 ⓐ에 알맞은 것은 무엇인가? 빈칸 추론

① 대조
✓ ② 대표하는 것(인물)
③ 다른 면
④ (아직 정식으로 서명되지 않은) 각서

| 분석 | 빈칸 앞 문장에서 '과학자들 사이에서 FTO라고 불리는 유전자가 돋보인다'고 언급하였다. 그렇다면 FTO는 비만과 관련된 유전자의 표본이 될 것이다. poster child는 '포스터에 등장하는 아이'라는 의미인데 관용적으로 '어떤 활동의 대표적 인물, 대표하는 것'으로 쓰인다.

04 ⓐ의 가장 그럴듯한 이유는 다음 중 어느 것인가? 내용 파악

① FTO는 제2차 세계 대전 이후에 발견되었다.
② 그 당시에는 과학 연구가 행해지지 않았다.
✓ ③ 그 당시에는 환경이 매우 달랐다.
④ 수십 년 전에는 FTO가 사람들에게 존재하지 않았다.

| 분석 | 밑줄 뒤에서 제2차 세계 대전 이후를 언급하고, 환경 또한 영향을 준다고 언급하였다. 따라서 수십 년 전에 FTO를 연구했을 경우 체중과 연관성을 발견하지 못할 이유는 '지금과 환경이 달랐던 수십 년 전에는 연구 결과가 달랐을 것'이라고 할 수 있다.

[05-06] 2011 성균관대

| 정답 | 05 ③ 06 ④

| 어휘 |
mild ⓐ 온화한, 경미한
viral ⓐ 바이러스의
affect ⓥ ~에 영향을 미치다
susceptible to ~에 취약한, 영향받기 쉬운
resistance ⓝ 저항, 면역
GP(general practitioner) ⓝ 일반의, 내과 의사
symptom ⓝ 증상
cough ⓝ 기침
unblock ⓥ (막힌 곳을) 뚫다, 청소하다

flu ⓝ 독감
infection ⓝ 감염, 전염
toddler ⓝ 아장아장 걷는 유아
complication ⓝ 합병증
medicine ⓝ 의학, 의술
prescribe ⓥ 처방하다
soothe ⓥ 완화하다
sniffle ⓝ 코 훌쩍임

contagious ⓐ 전염력 있는
respiratory tract 호흡기
expectant ⓐ 출산을 앞둔
domain ⓝ 영역, 영토
frontline ⓝ 전선
pharmacy ⓝ 약국
ache ⓝ 통증
inflammation ⓝ 염증
shorten ⓥ 단축시키다

전문해석

일반적으로 더 경미한 증상을 보이는 일반 감기와 구별하자면, 독감은 호흡기의 전염성 바이러스 감염으로서 유아부터 임산부와 나이 많은 성인까지 누구든 걸릴 수 있다. 기존의 건강 상태에 따라 다르겠지만, 이들은 죽음에 이르는 독감 관련 합병증에도 취약하다. [B] 전통적으로, 독감과의 전쟁은 대개 서구 의학의 영역 내에 머물러 왔다. 어디에나 있는 독감 백신접종은 여전히 독감 바이러스와 신체의 면역력 사이의 최전선에 남아 있다. 독감 백신주사는 본질적으로 소량의 독감 바이러스를 가지고 있는데 신체가 이 소량의 바이러스와 싸우는 항체를 키우는 것을 학습하게 된다.
[D] 증상이 발현하면 사람들은 내과 의사나 약국을 찾아 도움을 청한다. 내과 의사들은 일반적으로 증상을 완화시키는 일련의 약을 처방해 주는데 여기에는 (해열 진통제인) 파라세타몰, (기침을 진정시키는) 코데인, (목의 염증을 가라앉히는) 단젠, (막힌 코를 뚫어 주거나 코의 훌쩍임을 멈추어 주는) 항히스타민제가 포함된다. 동시에 타미플루나 렐렌자와 같은 항생제는 몸 안의 바이러스 확산을 막아 줌으로써 독감 증상을 겪는 시간을 단축시키는 데 도움이 된다.

05 윗글을 세 단락으로 나누었을 때, 어느 것이 가장 적합한 경계가 되는가? 단락 나누기
① [A]와 [C]
② [A]와 [D]
✓③ [B]와 [D]
④ [B]와 [E]
⑤ [C]와 [E]

| 분석 | [A]의 경우 this group이 나오고 있으므로 앞 문장을 이어서 쓰고 있으므로 나누는 경계선이 될 수 없다. [B]부터 독감 백신접종에 관한 내용이며 그것이 [C]까지 이어지고 있다. [D]부터는 독감에 걸린 이후 약 처방에 관한 내용이 글의 마지막까지 이어지고 있다. 따라서 적절한 경계는 [B]와 [D]라고 할 수 있다.

06 윗글에 관하여 사실이 아닌 것은? 내용 일치
① 독감은 감기와 다르다.
② 독감은 일부 환자들에게 매우 치명적일 수 있다.
③ 독감은 일종의 바이러스에 의해 전염된다.
✓④ 독감 백신은 독감 바이러스를 제거한다.
⑤ 독감에는 치료법이 없다.

| 분석 | 지문에서 '독감 백신주사는 본질적으로 소량의 독감 바이러스를 가지고 있는데 신체가 이 소량의 바이러스와 싸우는 항체를 키우는 것을 학습한다.'고 하였다. 독감 백신은 독감 바이러스를 이용하여 신체의 항체를 키우는 방식인 것이지 독감 바이러스를 제거하는 것은 아니므로 ④는 지문과 일치하지 않는다.

[07-08] 2022 한국외대

| 정답 | 07 ③ 08 ④

| 어휘 |
simultaneously ⓐ 동시에, 일제히
debunk ⓥ 틀렸음을 밝히다
assign ⓥ 할당하다, 배당하다
black-and-white ⓐ 흑백의; 단순 명쾌한
extrovert ⓝ 외향적인 사람
introvert ⓝ 내성적인 사람
shortcoming ⓝ 결함, 단점
neatly ⓐ 깔끔하게
dimension ⓝ 차원, 관점
tidy ⓐ 깔끔한, 잘 정돈된

전문해석

세상에는 두 종류의 사람들이 있는데, 마이어스 브릭스 유형 지표(MBTI) 성격 검사를 신뢰하는 사람들과 그렇지 않은 사람들이다. MBTI는 세계에서 가장 인기가 많은 성격 검사인 동시에 가장 자주 잘못되었다고 밝혀진 검사이다. 매년 약 150만 명이 검사를 치르며 수백여 개의 대학뿐만 아니라 포춘(Fortune)에서 선정한 500대 기업 중 88%가 넘는 기업들이 직원 채용 및 교육에 MBTI 검사를 활용하고 있다. 디즈니사의 공주들에서부터 다스 베이더에 이르기까지 허구의 등장인물들마저 MBTI 유형을 부여받았다. 그 검사의 인기에도 불구하고, 많은 심리학자들은 MBTI 성격 검사를 비판한다. MBTI는 일부 연구에 따르면 동일한 사람이 재검사를 받으면 다른 결과를 얻을 수 있기 때문에 신뢰할 수 없다고 말한다. 하지만 테스트의 한계점 중 일부는 MBTI의 흑백논리적인 범주와 같은 개념적 설계에 내재되어 있는데, 예를 들어 당신은 외향적인 사람(E) 또는 내성적인 사람(I), 판단하는 자(J) 또는 (감정을) 느끼는 사람(F)과 같이 분류된다. 바로 이것이 단점인데, 많은 사람들은 성격의 영역에서 두 가지로 깔끔하게 분류되지는 않기 때문이다. 그 대신 사람들은 많은 차원을 가지고 있다. 실제로 많은 사람들은 평균에 가깝고, 상대적으로 소수의 사람들만이 양극단에 있다. 사람들을 깔끔한 상자 속에 넣음으로써 우리는 실제로 서로 다른 점보다 비슷한 점이 더 많은 사람들을 분리하고 있는 것이다.

07 다음 중 윗글의 주제는 무엇인가? **주제**

① MBTI의 기업에서의 용도
② MBTI가 인기를 끄는 이유
✓③ MBTI를 둘러싼 논란
④ 다양한 MBTI 범주에 대한 설명

| 분석 | MBTI 성격 검사가 가진 문제점을 지적하는 문제 제기의 글이라고 볼 수 있다. 따라서 주제로 ③ 'MBTI를 둘러싼 논란'이 가장 적절하다.

08 윗글에 따르면, 다음 중 옳지 않은 것은? **내용 일치**

① 사람들마다 내향성의 정도가 다를 수 있다.
② MBTI는 사람들을 판단하는 자 또는 느끼는 자로 분류한다.
③ 많은 기업들은 MBTI를 활용하여 구직자를 평가한다.
✓④ 같은 사람은 검사에서 항상 같은 결과를 받을 것이다.

| 분석 | 지문의 중반부에서 "일부 연구에 따르면 MBTI는 동일한 사람이 재검사를 받으면 이전과 다른 결과를 얻을 수 있어서 신뢰할 수 없다"라고 언급하였다. 따라서 같은 사람이라고 해서 항상 같은 검사 결과를 받을 수는 없을 것이므로 ④는 지문 내용과 일치하지 않는다.

|배경 지식| MBTI: 마이어스-브릭스 유형 지표(Myers-Briggs Type Indicator, MBTI)는 작가 캐서린 쿡 브릭스(Katharine C. Briggs)와 그녀의 딸 이사벨 브릭스 마이어스(Isabel B. Myers)가 카를 융의 초기 분석심리학 모델을 바탕으로 1944년에 개발한 자기보고형 성격 유형 검사로, 사람의 성격을 16가지의 유형으로 나누어 설명한 유사과학이다.
MBTI에서는 두 개의 태도 지표(외향-내향, 판단-인식)와 두 개의 기능 지표(감각-직관, 사고-감정)에 대한 개인의 선호도를 밝혀서 4개의 선호 문자로 구성된 개인의 성격 유형을 알려 준다. 따라서 MBTI 검사 결과로 생길 수 있는 성격 유형은 모두 16가지가 된다.
MBTI에서 파생된 MBTI 관계론(일명 사회인격학/소시오닉스)은 이론적으로는 어느 정도는 맞는 편이나, 현실에서는 인간관계를 맺고 유지하면서 생기는 변수가 크므로 타당성이 떨어진다. 그리고 각 유형 간 아비투스 차이 등은 일절 고려되지 않았기에 이론적으로도 완벽하지 않다.

[09-10] 2013 성균관대

|정답| 09 ⑤ 10 ②

|어휘|
pore over 읽다, 연구하다 refute ⓥ 반박하다
make headline 신문에 크게 취급되다, 유명해지다 mammogram ⓝ 유방 엑스선 사진
colonoscopy ⓝ 결장 내시경술 PSA test 전립선 특이항원검사 prescribe ⓥ 처방하다
antidepressant ⓝ 항우울제 peer-reviewed 전문가에 의해 평가된, 동업자에 의해 평가된
angioplasty ⓝ 혈관 성형술 unclog ⓥ 청소하다 heart artery 심장 동맥

전문해석

의학 전문지를 읽다가 그는 모든 유형의 발견들이 나중의 발견들에 의해 반박되는 것을 보고 놀랐다. 물론 의학계의 "(반박되어도) 신경 쓰지 마" 식의 태도는 더 이상 비밀이 아니다. 그리고 이러한 태도는 때로 신문에 크게 취급되기도 한다. 예를 들어 최근 몇 년 동안 대규모 연구와 더불어 과학자들은 대체로 동의하게 되었는데, 유방 엑스선 사진이나 결장 내시경술이나 전립선 특이항원검사는 우리가 알고 있는 것보다 훨씬 암을 탐지하는 데 유용하지 못하다는 것이다. 프로작, 졸로푸트, 팍실과 같은 널리 처방되는 항우울제는 대부분의 우울증에 대해서 위약보다 더 효과적이지 않다는 것도 밝혀졌다. 완전히 해를 멀리하는 것은 사실은 암의 위험을 증가시킨다는 것도 알게 되었다. 격렬한 운동 중에 물을 많이 마시라는 충고는 치명적일 수도 있다고 알게 되었다. 그리고 지난 4월에 이제까지 알고 있었던 것처럼 피시 오일을 먹고, 운동을 하고, 수수께끼를 푼다고 해서 알츠하이머병을 예방하는 데 도움이 되지 않는다는 것도 알게 되었다. 전문가들에 의해 수행된 연구들은 핸드폰의 이용이 뇌암의 원인이 될 수 있느냐에 대해서 상반된 결론을 도출하고 있다. 하루에 8시간 이상 자는 게 건강한지 혹은 위험한지, 매일 아스피린을 먹는 것은 생명을 구하는지 혹은 단축하는지, 일상적으로 혈관 성형술을 시술하는 것이 심장 동맥을 청소하는 데 약보다 효과가 있는지 없는지 등의 문제에 대해서도 상반된 결론들이 나오고 있다.

09 밑줄 친 "never mind"는 _____을 나타낸다. 밑줄 의미 추론

① 환자의 상태를 고려하지 않는다
② 의학과 무관하다
③ 의학 연구가 아니다
④ 의사의 조언과 다르지 않다
 그들의 주장이 옳은지에 대해서는 관심이 없다

|분석| never mind는 "괜찮아", "신경 쓰지 마"의 의미로 자신들의 의학적 발견들이 옳지 않았다는 것에 의학계는 별 신경을 쓰지 않는다는 의미이므로 ⑤가 정답으로 적절하다.

| **10** | 윗글에 따르면 _____. 내용 일치
① 대부분의 의사들은 매일 아스피린을 먹는다
✓② 많은 의학적 발견들이 논란이 되고 있다
③ 프로작은 위약보다 더 효과적이다
④ 휴대폰의 사용은 뇌암을 일으키지 않는다
⑤ 대부분의 사람들은 인터넷으로부터 의학 정보를 얻는다

| 분석 | 본문은 서두에서부터 많은 의학적 발견들이 나중에 옳지 않은 것이라고 반박되고 있으며, 현재 병원에서 처방하는 약들도 그렇게 효과적이지 않다고 하고 있다. 따라서 ②는 지문 내용과도 일치하는 말이면서 글의 요지와도 같은 맥락이다.

| 배경 지식 | 위약효과(Placebo effect): 심리학·의학 용어로, 효과가 없는 약제를 진짜 약으로 가장하고 섭취하였을 때, 환자의 병세가 실제로도 호전되는 현상이다. 대표적인 예로 임상실험의 대조군에서 아무 효과도 없는 약(포도당 등)을 처방받아 먹었음에도 병세가 호전되는 사례를 들 수 있다. 이름의 유래는 '내가 기쁘게 해 주지'라는 뜻을 가진 라틴어이다.

[11-12] 2018 성균관대

| 정답 | 11 ⑤ 12 ③

| 어휘 | misdiagnose ⓥ (질병·문제를) 오진하다   autism ⓝ 〈병리〉 자폐증   shockingly ⓐⓓ 깜짝 놀랄 만큼
grim ⓐ 엄(격)한, 암울한; 형편없는   unnoticed ⓐ 눈에 띄지 않는, 간과되는
struggle to keep up with ~에 뒤지지 않으려고 애쓰다, 고심하다   elaborate ⓐ 공들인; 복잡한, 정교한
crib ⓥ 도용하다, 베끼다, 표절하다   blend in 조화를 이루다, (주위 환경에) 섞여 들다
adolescence ⓝ 청년기, 사춘기   intriguing ⓐ 아주 흥미로운   overlap ⓝ 공통부분, 겹침
eating disorder 섭식 장애   anorexia ⓝ 신경성 식욕 부진증, 거식증   estimate ⓥ 추산[추정]하다

전문해석

마야(Maya)와 같은 젊은 여성이 되풀이하여 오진을 받는 일은 흔하다. 자폐증이 여자아이들보다 남자아이들에게 적어도 세 배 이상 흔하기 때문에 과학자들은 일상적으로 남자아이들만 연구에 포함한다. 그 결과 우리는 자폐증이 여자아이들과 남자아이들에게 있어 서로 다른가 그리고 어떻게 다른가에 관하여 놀랍게도 모르고 있다. 우리가 알고 있는 것은 형편없는데, 평균적으로 말해, 경미한 자폐증을 앓고 있는 여자아이들은 남자아이들보다 2년 더 늦게 진단받는다. 왜 이렇게 되었는지에 관한 일부 논쟁이 있다. 처음부터 여아들의 제한된 관심사—열차 시간표보다는 어쩌면 인형이나 책과 같은 것들—는 사회적으로 좀 더 용인되는 것 같아서 주목받지 못한다. 그러나 진단 테스트가 자폐증이 있는 남자아이들을 관찰한 것에 기초한다는 사실은 거의 확실히 오류와 지연의 원인이 된다.

십 대가 되면, 소녀들은 복잡한 사회관계의 규칙을 따르려고 애를 쓴다. 무엇을 말하고 어떻게 말을 할지에 대한 이런저런 정보를 도용하면서 많은 소녀들은 (또래 집단에) 섞이려고 노력을 하지만 그러다가 내적 자아를 다치게 된다. 사춘기가 시작되면 그들은 높은 비율로 우울증과 불안 장애를 겪는다. 연구들이 너무 적어서 얼마나 많은 여성이 두 질병(자폐증과 섭식 장애)을 겪고 있는지 추산하기 어렵지만, 몇몇 연구들은 또한 자폐증과 거식증과 같은 섭식 장애 사이의 아주 흥미로운 중복을 발견했다.

11 여자아이들의 자폐증은 잘 알려지지 않았는데 그 이유는 _____이다. 내용 파악

① 자폐 소녀들은 많지 않았다
② 자폐 소녀들의 부모들은 자신의 아이들을 숨긴다
③ 그것(자폐증)이 소년들의 그것과 다르지 않다
④ 자폐 소녀들은 오직 집에만 머무른다
⑤ 여자아이들의 자폐증은 많은 관심을 받지 못했다 ✓

| 분석 | 자폐증이 남자아이들에게 일반적이어서 자폐증에 대한 연구가 남자아이들을 대상으로만 이루어지며, 자폐증의 진단 테스트 또한 남자아이들을 관찰한 것에 기초하며, 여자아이들이 자폐의 증상(제한된 것에만 관심을 둠)을 나타내도 여자라는 이유로 사회에서 주목을 받지 못했다고 언급한 것을 단서로 '여자아이들의 자폐증은 관심을 받지 못해서 잘 알려지지 않았음'을 알 수 있다. 그동안 관심을 못 받아서 알려지지 않은 것이지 실제로 자폐 소녀들이 많지 않은 것은 아니다. 따라서 ①은 정답이 될 수 없다.

12 십 대 소녀들에게 나타나는 자폐증의 증상이 아닌 것은? 내용 파악

① 우울증
② 걱정
③ 체중 증가 ✓
④ 마른 몸
⑤ 소식

| 분석 | 두 번째 단락에서는 십 대 소녀들의 자폐증 증상을 설명하고 있다. "사춘기가 시작되면 우울증, 불안 장애의 발생 비율이 높아지고 일부 연구에서 자폐증과 거식증과 같은 섭식 장애 사이에서의 중복을 발견했다"고 언급했으므로 마른 몸이나, 소식도 자폐증의 증상으로 볼 수 있지만 ③ '체중 증가'와 관련된 내용은 언급한 적이 없다.

[13-14] 2017 국민대

| 정답 | 13 ① 14 ④

| 어휘 |
antidepressant ⓝ 항우울제, 우울증 치료제
by chance 우연히
schizophrenia ⓝ 정신 분열증
tuberculosis ⓝ 결핵
oxidase ⓝ 산화효소
inhibitor ⓝ 억제제
case ⓝ 병증, 환자
side-effect ⓝ 부작용
anxiety ⓝ 불안
nausea ⓝ 구역질
appetite ⓝ 식욕
sleep disturbance 수면장애
placebo ⓝ 위약, 가짜 약
trial ⓝ 시험

전문해석

우울증 치료제는 우연히 발견되었다. 1950년대에 정신 분열증과 결핵을 치료하는 데 사용되고 있던 약물들이 모노아민(세로토닌을 포함한)이라 불리는 뇌 화학물질의 수치를 증가시킴으로써 우울증을 억제시키는 성질을 보여 주었다. 이것이 TCA(삼환계 우울증 치료제)와 MAOI(모노아민 산화효소억제제)와 같은 우울증 치료제가 세상에 처음 나오도록 했다.

상업적으로 이용할 수 있는 모든 우울증 치료제는 여전히 모노아민 수치를 증가시켜 주는 방식으로 약효를 낸다. 현재의 우울증 치료제는 이전의 우울증 치료제보다 안전하며, 많은 환자에게서 효과적이지만, 불안, 구역질, 식욕 저하, 수면장애와 같은 부작용이 존재한다. 또한, 최대 50%의 사람들은 치료에 반응을 보이지 않으며, 반응을 보이는 사람들의 경우에도 우울증 치료제로 치료했는지 수주가 지난 후에야 효과를 볼 수 있다. 우울증 치료제는 또한 일부 약물 실험에서는 위약과 비교했을 때 매우 작은 이점들만 나타났다.

14 ④
현재 표준이 되는 우울증 치료제가 존재하지 않는 것은 우울증을 규정하는 것이 어렵기 때문일지도 모른다. 과학자들은 심지어 에스트로겐이나 스트레스 호르몬과 같은 호르몬들이 우울증과 관련이 있는지도 검토하고 있다.

너무나도 자주, 우울증은 살면서 일어나는 여러 가지 사건에 대해 보이는 자연스러운 반응일 수 있다. 그러나 (우울증에는) 화학물질과 호르몬 이외의 복잡한 정서적, 심리적, 사회적 요인들이 존재하므로, 우울증 치료제는 완전한 치료제가 될 수 없을 가능성이 높다. 운동, 대화 요법, 식이 요법은 모두 우울증에 도움을 줄 수 있을 것이다.

13 다음 중 우울증 치료제의 부작용이 아닌 것은? 내용 파악
 ✓① 우울증 치료제에 대한 면역
 ② 숙면을 취할 수 없음
 ③ 불수의적 구토 충동
 ④ 불안 및 심리적 긴장

| 분석 | 두 번째 단락에서 우울증 치료제의 부작용으로 수면 장애, 구역질, 불안과 같은 부작용들이 존재한다고 언급하였는데, ① '우울증 치료제에 대한 면역'은 지문에서 언급한 적이 없다.

14 윗글에 따르면 다음 중 사실이 아닌 것은? 내용 일치
 ① 우울증 치료제가 효과를 보기 위해서는 시간이 걸린다.
 ② 우울증은 화학물질과 호르몬 문제로 설명하고 끝낼 수는 없다.
 ③ 현재의 우울증 치료제는 이전의 우울증 치료제들과 대략 같은 기능을 한다.
 ✓④ 위약은 우울증을 대처하는 데 있어서 일반적인 우울증 치료제들보다 효과적이다.

| 분석 | "우울증 치료제는 일부 약물 실험에서 위약들과 비교했을 때 매우 작은 이점들만이 나타났다."라고 언급하였다. 즉 치료제가 위약보다 약간은 나은 효과를 보이는 것이므로, 위약이 우울증 치료제보다 더 효과적이라고는 할 수 없다. 따라서 ④는 지문과 일치하지 않는다.

[15-17] 2014 고려대

| 정답 | 15 ③   16 ④   17 ②

| 어휘 |
surgical ⓐ 외과의, 수술의
affirm ⓥ 확언하다, 단언하다
simulate ⓥ 가장하다, 흉내 내다
mannequin ⓝ 마네킹, 모델 인형
apprenticeship ⓝ 도제제도, 견습공 신분
sardonic ⓐ 냉소적인, 빈정대는

residency ⓝ 전문의 실습 기간
scrub ⓥ 비비다, 문지르다
trauma ⓝ 외상, 정신적 외상
diversity ⓝ 다양성, 차이
pedantic ⓐ 아는 척하는, 현학적인
cutting-edge ⓐ 날카로운, 최첨단의

intensive ⓐ 강한, 격렬한
scramble ⓥ 기어오르다, 급히 움직이다
resuscitate ⓥ 소생시키다
pedagogical ⓐ 교육적인, 교수법의
laudatory ⓐ 찬미의, 찬양의
immune ⓐ 면역성의

전문해석
거의 한 세기 동안, 외과 전문의 실습 기간은 집중적인 경험과 점점 늘어나는 책임의 기간이었다. 최근의 연구에서는, 외과의의 수술의 기술, 수술의 횟수, 그리고 환자의 수술 결과 사이에 강력한 상관관계가 있음을 보여 줌으로써 그러한 방식의 적절성을 확인해 주었다. 지난 10년 동안 젊은 수련외과의가 병원에 있는 시간의 한도가 정해져 있어서 이들이 수술에 참여하게 되는 기회가 줄어들었다. 과거 세대의 수습 의사들은 하루에 최소한 한 번의 수술에 참여했는데, 최근의 수습 의사들은 한 주에 두 번 혹은 세 번 정도의 수술에 참여할 시간밖에 없다. 병원에 있는 시간을 줄여서 손실된 시간 수를 계산하여, 선도적인 외과의들은 장차 외과의가 될 젊은이들이 거의 1년의 경험에 해당하는 만큼의 시간을 잃어버리고 있다고 예측한다. 외과 의학 자체도 변화하고 있고 외과 의사가 이제 알아야 하는 기술의 숫자도 늘어나고 있다. 새로운 약물치료의 발견은 과거에 보편적이었던 수술들을 완전히 없어진 것은 아니지만 그 시행회수를 줄이게 하였으며, 따라서 외과의들은 비록 자주 시행하지 않는 수술들이라도 그 수술들 모두 어떻게 하는 것인지를 알아야만 한다.

외과 훈련 프로그램들은, 온라인 교육 도구들을 개발하고 수습 의사들에게 시뮬레이션을 통한 수술실에서의 경험이나 전자 마네킹을 이용한 트라우마 환자들의 소생시키기 등을 경험할 수 있도록 함으로써, 줄어든 시간을 보충하면서도 계속적으로 늘어나고 있는 지식들을 커버하기 위해 애쓰고 있다. 그러나 외과연보에 실린 연구에서 보여 주듯이, 아무리 잘 만들어진 시뮬레이션 실험실이라도 1년 동안의 잃어버린 경험을 대체할 수는 없다.

17 ②

---

15 윗글의 요지는 무엇인가? 글의 요지

① 수술 훈련에서는 교육학적 방법의 다양성이 필요하다.
② 비교과서적 지식은 수술 견습 기간을 통해 얻을 수 있다.
✓ 어떤 것도 수술 훈련에서의 직접적인 경험을 보상할 수는 없다.
④ 온라인 강의들이 수술 기술을 습득하는 효과적인 수단이 될 수 있다.

| 분석 | 이 글은 외과 의사의 실습을 그 어떤 것으로도 대체할 수 없음에도 과거에 비해 수술 참여 횟수나 시간이 줄어들고 있음을 지적하는 글이다.

---

16 윗글의 어조는 무엇인가? 글의 어조

① 현학적인   ② 칭찬하는
③ 냉소적인(비꼬는)   ✓ 비판적인

| 분석 | 지문에서 '과거 세대의 수습 의사들은 하루에 최소한 한 번의 수술에 참여했는데, 최근의 수습 의사들은 한 주에 두 번 혹은 세 번 정도의 수술에 참여할 시간밖에 없다.' 등을 언급한 것으로 보아 글쓴이는 현재의 의료 교육에 대하여 비판적인 태도를 보여 주고 있다.

---

17 윗글에 따르면, "수습 의사"에 대한 설명으로 옳은 것은? 내용 일치

① 최첨단 기술들은 그들이 실수에 면역을 갖도록 만들었다.
✓ 시뮬레이션 훈련을 통해 가상의 수술을 수행할 수 있다.
③ 강의에 할애되는 시간이 병원에서 보내는 시간을 줄였다.
④ 그들은 복잡한 수술을 필요로 하지 않는 전공을 선택하는 경향이 있다.

| 분석 | 지문의 마지막 부분에서 "외과 훈련 프로그램들은, 온라인 교육 도구들을 개발하고 수습 의사들에게 시뮬레이션을 통한 수술실에서의 경험이나 전자 마네킹을 이용한 트라우마 환자들의 소생시키기 등을 경험할 수 있도록 해 줄 수 있다"고 언급한 것을 보면 수습 의사들은 시뮬레이션 훈련으로 가상의 수술을 수행하는 것은 가능하다는 것을 알 수 있다.

[18-20] 2011 경희대

| 정답 | 18 ④ 19 ④ 20 ①

| 어휘 |
misadventure ⓝ 불행, 재난
initiative ⓝ 창의, 솔선수범
disparity ⓝ 불일치, 괴리
capacity ⓝ 능력, 수용력
interventions ⓝ (경영) 해결책

malfeasant ⓐ 부정을 행하는
representative ⓝ 대표자, 대리인
affordability ⓝ 적당한 가격으로 구입할 수 있는 것; 감당할 수 있는 비용
cling to ~에 집착하다, ~을 고수하다
implement ⓥ 이행하다; (조건 등을) 충족하다

inadequately ⓐⓓ 부적절하게, 불충분하게
cutting edge 최첨단, 활력소
one-off ⓐ 단 한 번의

bundle ⓝ 묶음　　　　　　sustainable ⓐ 유지할 수 있는

전문해석

1999년에 의학협회에서는 미국의 의료 서비스가 확실히 환자들에게 위험하다고 보고했다. 수백 명 중에 한 명꼴로 다치거나, 수천 명 중에 한 명꼴로 의료 사고사로 사망했다. 그 원인은 부정행위를 하는 사람들 때문이 아니고 부적절하게 계획되고 운영되는 의료 서비스 제공의 체계에 있다. 그때 이래로 의료 서비스 제공자들은 안전 개선을 위한 다양한 계획에 투자를 해 왔다. 그러나 '뉴잉글랜드 의학저널(The New England Journal of Medicine)'에서 최근 발표한 사실에 따르면 상황이 개선되지 않았다는 것이다. 연구자들은 최적의 방법을 시행하고 있어 질적인 면과 안전에 있어 이를 개선하고자 선두를 달리고 있는 조직들 중 대표 격이라 여겨지는 노스캐롤라이나의 병원에서 성과 변화를 지켜보았다. 그 결과는 환자의 안전을 위한 치료가 그다지 성과가 없었다는 것이다. 이러한 Ⓐ 노력과 결과가 차이 나는 합당한 설명은 의료 서비스의 책임자들이 안전, 적절한 비용, 그리고 수용 능력에 있어서 우수함을 달성하기 위해 적합한 운영상의 변화에 투자하지 않았다는 것이다. 불행하게도, 많은 의료 서비스 기관들이 단 한 번의 개입의 노력으로 개선이 이루어질 수 있다는 생각에 계속해서 집착하고 있다는 것이다. 그들의 생각은 이렇다. 그 문제를 없애기 위해 여기저기에 모범적인 실천들을 해 나가고 개선 프로젝트를 이끌어 갈 수 있는 충분한 외부 인사만 영입한다면, 상황은 꽤 좋아질 거라는 거다. 그러나 슬픈 현실은 이러한 접근 방법이 개선을 시켜 준다고는 하지만, 그것들이 의미 있고 지속적이지 않다는 것이다.

---

18 윗글의 제목으로 가장 적절한 것은? `제목`

① 어떻게 모범적 실천들이 의료 서비스를 개선시키는가 `지문 내용과 불일치`
② 현대 병원의 새로운 경향 `언급 안 함`
③ 미래의 지속 가능한 병원 프로젝트 `언급 안 함`
✓④ 왜 모범적 실천들이 의료 서비스를 개선하지 못하는가

| 분석 | 이 글은 병원이 최선의 의료 서비스(health care)의 노력을 하고 있지만, 그 방법상에 문제가 있어서 서비스를 완전하게 개선하지 못하고 있고 그 이유를 설명하고 있다. 따라서 ④가 제목으로 적절하다.

---

19 글의 흐름상 빈칸 Ⓐ에 들어갈 말로 가장 적절한 것은? `빈칸 추론`

① 수입과 결과　　　　　　② 비용과 서비스
③ 서비스와 보건　　　　　✓④ 노력과 결과

| 분석 | 빈칸 앞 문장에서 개선을 위해 최고로 올바른 방법으로 노력하고 있는 병원을 관찰했지만 결과는 성과가 없다고 언급하였다. 따라서 빈칸은 '노력과 결과'의 차이라고 해야 적절하다.

---

20 윗글에 따르면 병원은 개선을 위해 다음 중 무엇을 해야 하는가? `내용 파악`

✓① 보다 중요하고 지속 가능한 접근법을 찾기
② 일회성의 경영 해결책 구하기
③ 병원에서 모범적 실천들을 시행하기
④ 최첨단 의료 서비스를 제공할 전문가를 고용하기

| 분석 | 병원들이 해야 할 일은 마지막 문장에 언급되어 있다. 모범적인 실천들을 한다면 상황이 좋아지는 것은 맞지만 현실은 지속적이지 않다고 하였다. 따라서 ③이 아닌 ① '보다 중요하고 지속 가능한 접근법을 찾기'가 이 글에서 언급한 병원이 해야 할 일로 더 적절하다.

[21-23] 2022 한국외대

| 정답 | 21 ① 22 ② 23 ②

| 어휘 |
process ⓥ (자료를) 처리하다
snore ⓥ 코를 골다
victim ⓝ 희생자, 피해자
sonic ⓐ 소리의, 음파의
therapy ⓝ 치료, 치료법
wavelength ⓝ 〈물리〉 파장
steady ⓐ 한결같은
potentially ⓐⓓ 잠재적으로
associate ⓥ 연상하다, 관련시키다

sensory ⓐ 감각의, 지각의
bark ⓥ (개·여우 따위가) 짖다
restless ⓐ 침착하지 못한; 제대로 쉬지 못하는
promising ⓐ 유망한
hue ⓝ 색조; 색상
visible ⓐ (눈에) 보이는
soothing ⓐ 마음을 진정시키는, 달래는 듯한
roar ⓝ 으르렁거리는 소리, 고함 소리

stimulus ⓝ 자극; 격려 (pl. stimuli)
leaky ⓐ 새기 쉬운; 새는 구멍이 있는
concentration ⓝ 집중, 전념
frequency ⓝ 주파수
intensity ⓝ 강도; 농도
current ⓝ 흐름, 해류

전문해석

만약 여러분이 잠자는 데 어려움을 겪는 사람이면, 누군가 아마도 여러분에게 백색 소음을 이미 제안했을 것이다. 좋든 싫든, 우리의 뇌는 우리가 잘 때도 감각 자극을 계속해서 처리하는데, 이것은 배우자가 코를 고는 소리, 개가 짖는 소리, 심지어 물이 새는 싱크대도 필시 우리가 잠 못 이루는 밤의 희생자가 되게 할 수 있음을 의미한다. 우리가 밤에 소음으로 잠을 깨는 이유는 명백하게는 소음 그 자체 때문이 아니라 소음의 갑작스러운 변화 때문이다. 백색 소음은 이와 같은 소음의 변화를 감추고 우리의 뇌가 좀 더 일관된 소리 환경의 이점을 누리도록 함으로써 효과를 발휘한다. 밤에 숙면을 취할 수 있다는 이점 외에도, 백색 소음은 기억력과 집중력과 관련해서도 유망한 결과를 보여 주었다. 음향 치료에 대한 많은 연구들은 백색, 분홍색, 갈색과 같은 특정한 소리 색조에 초점을 맞춰 왔는데, 그렇다면 그것들의 정확한 차이는 무엇일까? 아마도 이것들 중 가장 친숙하다고 할 백색 소음은 사용하지 않는 주파수에 맞춰진 라디오와 같은 소리를 낸다. 백색광이 가시광선 스펙트럼의 모든 파장을 동일한 강도로 포함하고 있는 것과 유사하게, 백색 소음은 인간의 귀에 Ⓐ 들리는 모든 주파수에 걸쳐 동일한 강도를 가지고 있다. 분홍색 소음은 높은 주파수를 줄여 놓은 백색 소음이다. 분홍색 소음은 비나 바람이 꾸준하게 내리거나 부는 소리를 닮았고, 종종 백색 소음보다 진정 효과가 더 큰 것으로 여겨진다. 분홍색 소음에 대한 여러 연구들은 분홍색 소음을 들으면서 잠을 자면 다음 날 우리의 기억을 향상시킬 수 있고, 장기적으로 기억을 향상시킬 잠재력도 있다는 것을 보여 주었다. 갈색 소음은 높은 주파수를 한층 더 낮춘 것이다. 분홍색 소음보다는 약간 더 '거친' 느낌으로, 강물이나 강한 바람의 거센 소리를 닮았다. 갈색 소음과 관련된 일반적인 효과는 긴장 완화, 집중력 향상이며, 당연히 수면 개선 효과도 포함된다.

21 다음 중 윗글의 제목으로 가장 적절한 것은? 제목

✓ ① 백색, 분홍색, 갈색 소음 사이의 차이
② 왜 우리는 백색, 분홍색, 갈색 소음을 간과하는가 언급 안 함
③ 음향 치료의 장단점 언급 안 함
④ 밤에 더 숙면을 취하는 방법 지엽적

| 분석 | 이 글은 백색 소음, 분홍색 소음, 갈색 소음의 특징과 차이점에 대해 설명하는 글이다. 따라서 이 글의 제목은 ①이 가장 적절하다.

22 윗글에 의하면, 다음 중 사실인 것은? 내용 일치

① 우리의 뇌는 우리가 자는 동안 감각 자극의 처리를 중단한다.
✓ ② 소음 자체보다는 소음의 변화가 우리를 밤에 잠에서 깨도록 만든다.
③ 분홍색 소음은 높은 주파수를 증가시킨 백색 소음이다.
④ 갈색 소음은 집중력은 향상시킬 수 있지만 수면은 향상시키지 않는다.

| 분석 | 지문에서 "우리가 밤에 소음으로 잠을 깨는 이유는 명백하게는 소음 그 자체 때문이 아니라 소음의 갑작스러운 변화 때문이다."라고 언급하였다. 따라서 ② '소음 자체보다는 소음의 변화가 우리를 밤에 잠에서 깨도록 만든다.'는 진술은 지문과 일치한다.

23 다음 중 Ⓐ에 들어가기에 가장 적절한 것은? 빈칸 추론

① 무관한   ✓② 들리는
③ 적용된   ④ 보이지 않는

| 분석 | 빈칸은 빛에 비유하여 소리를 설명하는 부분이다. 빛이 '보일 수' 있다면, 소리는 '들을 수' 있을 것이므로, 빈칸은 ② 'audible'이 적절하다.

| 배경지식 | 백색 소음(White noise): 음폭이 넓어 공해에 해당하지 않는 소음이다. 백색 잡음, 화이트 노이즈 등으로 불리며 무작위의 패턴을 보여 주기 때문에 랜덤 노이즈라고도 한다. 그래프로 나타내면 주파수 대역이 전체에 걸쳐 나타나는 평탄한 잡음이다.

[24-26] 2022 한성대

| 정답 | 24 ④   25 ③   26 ③

| 어휘 |
scramble ⓥ 재빨리 움직이다   facility ⓝ 시설, 기관   vaccinate ⓥ 예방[백신] 주사를 맞히다
interoperable ⓐ 공동 이용이 가능한   verifier ⓥ 입증자, 증명자   raw data (처리되지 않은) 미가공 데이터
tick ⓝ 체크 표시   cross ⓝ X표시   surge ⓝ 급증, 급등
unified ⓐ 통일된

전문해석

코로나19 대유행 기간 동안, 국가들은 바이러스가 국경을 넘거나 식당이나 체육관과 같은 실내 시설에 들어가는 것을 Ⓐ 막기 위해 빠르게 백신 여권을 만들어 왔다. 사람들은 종종 예방 접종을 받았거나 최근에 음성 판정을 받았거나 이전에 코로나19에 걸렸다가 회복되었음을 증명해야 한다. 기술 회사와 산업 협회가 이에 참여함에 따라 정부만 관계된 일이 아니다.

백신 여권의 문제점은 여권이 상호 운용되지 않는 점이다. 대부분의 백신 여권이 스마트폰이나 종이에 있는 QR코드로 동일하게 보이지만 코드를 스캔하면 문제가 될 수 있다. 다양한 인증 앱은 다양한 여권을 읽는다. 일단 코드가 스캔되면, 국가 또는 지역 보건 시스템이나 개인 정보 보호에 대한 입장에 따라 다양한 정보가 노출된다. 미국에서 발행되는 커먼패스(CommonPass)와 같은 일부 백신 여권은 백신 접종 상태에 대한 미가공 데이터(원자료)를 공유한다. 영국의 국민보건서비스(NHS)에서 사용하는 것과 같은 다른 백신 여권들은 체크 표시, X표 또는 기호만 보여 준다. 또한 백신 여권에 대한 규칙이 정해져 있지 않다. 예를 들어 이스라엘에서 감염률이 급증하는 동안 정부는 아직 부스터샷을 접종하지 않은 약 2백만 명의 주민들로부터 "녹색 여권"을 박탈했다. 25 ③

더욱 어려운 것은 보건 당국의 디지털 서명을 확인하는 통일된 시스템이다. 신뢰할 수 있는 모든 서명으로 구성된 데이터베이스를 구축하는 것은 비용이 많이 들고 정치적으로 복잡한 작업이다. 영국과 같이 국민보건서비스가 있는 나라들은 발행하는 곳이 한 곳이지만, 미국에서는 병원, 약국, 주 정부 등을 포함하여 300여 곳에 이른다.

24 빈칸 Ⓐ에 들어갈 수 없는 것은? 빈칸 추론

① 중지하다   ② 막다
③ 예방하다   ✓④ 용이하게 하다

| 분석 | 백신 여권을 만드는 목적은 바이러스가 퍼지는 것을 막기 위함일 것이다. 따라서 '막다'의 의미를 가진 ①, ②, ③은 빈칸에 들

어갈 수 있다. 하지만 facilitate(용이하게 하다)는 반대의 의미이므로 빈칸에 들어갈 수 없다.

25 다음 중 옳은 것은? 내용 일치
① 커먼패스는 미국에서 발행되지 않는다.
② 미국에서 보건 서비스를 발행하는 곳은 단 한 곳이다.
✓ ③ 국민보건서비스가 발행하는 백신 여권은 기호를 보여 준다.
④ 백신 여권은 개인의 사생활을 보호할 수 있기 때문에 문제가 된다.

| 분석 | 두 번째 단락에서 "영국의 국민보건서비스에서 사용하는 것과 같은 다른 백신 여권들은 체크 표시나 X표 또는 기호만 보여 준다."고 언급했다. 따라서 ③이 지문과 일치한다.

26 다음 중 백신 여권의 문제가 <u>아닌</u> 것은? 내용 파악
① 여권이 상호 운용되지 않는다.
② 백신 여권의 규정은 변경될 수 있다.
✓ ③ 기술 기업이 백신 여권에 관여하고 있다.
④ 다양한 기관의 다양한 디지털 서명을 모두 관리하려면 많은 비용이 든다.

| 분석 | 지문의 두 번째, 세 번째 단락을 보면 '여권이 상호 운용되지 않음', '녹색 여권을 박탈하는 것과 같이 규정이 변경될 수 있음' 그리고 '신뢰할 수 있는 모든 서명으로 구성된 데이터베이스를 구축하는 것은 비용이 많이 들고 정치적으로 복잡한 작업임'은 문제점으로 언급되었지만, 기술 회사가 백신 여권에 관여하는 것이 문제점은 아니므로 ③이 정답이다.

[27-29] 2018 숭실대

| 정답 | 27 ③   28 ④   29 ④

| 어휘 |
stabilize ⓥ 안정되다, 안정시키다 측정치)
liberally ⓐⓓ 자유롭게
haunt ⓥ 뇌리에서 떠나지 않다; 계속 문제가 되다
treadmill ⓝ 다람쥐 쳇바퀴 같은 일[생활]
in plain sight 앞이 (가리는 것이 없이) 잘 보여
palliative care unit (말기 환자의) 고통 완화 의료 시설
proxy ⓝ 대리권, 대리인
envision ⓥ 마음속에 그리다[상상하다]

vital sign 바이탈 사인, 생명 징후(사람이 살아 있음을 보여 주는 호흡, 체온, 심장 박동 등의
spiral ⓥ 급등[급증]하다
intensive-care unit 중환자실(ICU), 집중 치료실
walk by ~을 지나치다

wield ⓥ (권력 등을) 행사하다, 휘두르다
face-to-face ⓐ 마주 보는, 대면하는
crippled ⓐ 절름발이의, 불구[폐인]의
cog ⓝ 톱니; 톱니바퀴
initiative ⓝ 발의; 계획; 결단성
lay out (계획·주장 등을 잘 정리하여) 제시하다

전문해석
현대 의학은 한 사람이 죽음이 임박했을 경우 걷잡을 수 없이 쇠약해져 가는 생명 징후들을 안정화시킨 다음, 숨을 쉬지 못하고 먹거나 마실 수 없음에도 그 사람을 계속 살아 있게 할 수 있는 신과 같은 능력을 소유하게 되었다. 현대 의학은 이런 능력을 자유롭게 발휘하고 있다. 중환자실의 간호사로서, 나는 집중 치료를 받아 안정되어 그 결과 치명적인 상해나 질병으로 목숨을 잃진 않았지만 의사소통을 못 하거나 진료밖에 받지 못하는 환자들에 대한 기억을 떨쳐버릴 수가 없다. 나는 이와 같은 환자—다시는 대화를 할 수 없고, 계속해서 치료받는 단조로운 반복되는 생활을 할 수밖에 없는 처지에 놓인 환자—를 마주할 때, 거리에서 추위 떠는 절름발이 노숙자의 옆을 지나칠 때와 같은 부끄러움을 느낀다. 분명히 뭔가 잘못됐다. 그의 팔에 주삿바늘을 찌를 때면, 내가 노숙자를 발로 차고 있는 듯한 느낌이 든다.

그것은 잘 보이는 곳에 숨어 있는 도덕적 위기이지만, 여기에 관련된 사람들은 자기들은 단지 기계의 톱니바퀴에 불과하다고 주장한다. 내가 중환자실 담당 의사에게 왜 가족들에게 모든 것이 가장 좋을 경우의 예상 결과를 들려주고 "시간이 지나 봐야 알지요(두고 봅시다)"라는 말을 하는 대신 예상 결과에 대한 데이터와 확실한 설명을 해 주지 않는지 물어봤을 때, 그는 "말기 환자 병동(PCU)에 있는 사람들은 그렇게 할 수 있습니다. 하지만 중환자실에서는 그럴 시간이 정말 없어요."라고 말했다. 또 다른 내과 의사는 "시스템의 Ⓐ 무기력함"에 관하여 말했다. 현대 의학의 과잉 치료를 개혁하는 데 있어 먼저 실행에 옮기는 것은 일반 대중, 즉 환자의 일이다.

당신은 사전 의료 지시서를 작성함으로써 당신의 운명을 결정할 수 있다. 이 지시서는 당신이 의사소통할 수 없는 경우에 어떤 조치를 취해야 하는지를 설명할 수 있는 법적 문서이다. 당신의 희망 사항을 의료진에게 전달해 줄 수 있는 건강관리 대리인을 지명하라. 그리고 인생의 마지막을 어떻게 마음속에 그리고 있는지 계획해 봐라. 당신이 생명 유지 장치로 생명을 유지하고 싶지 않다면, 당신은 사전 의료 지시서에 그와 같이 명시할 수 있다. 만약 당신이 무슨 일이 있더라도 가능한 수명을 오랫동안 연장하기를 원한다면, 당신은 이런 희망을 주장할 수 있다. 어느 쪽이든, 가족들과 의료진들은 알아야 한다. 그것이 우리의 의료 체계를 보다 더 인도적인 말기 환자 치료 방식 쪽으로 나아가도록 하는 데 도움을 줄 것이다.

27 저자의 직업은 무엇인가? <내용 파악>

① 내과의
② 외과의
✓ 간호사
④ 약사

| 분석 | 첫 번째 단락에서 저자는 "중환자실의 간호사로서, 나는 집중 치료를 받아 안정되어 ∼"라고 언급하였으므로 저자는 간호사라는 것을 알 수 있다.

28 다음 중 Ⓐ에 가장 적절한 것은 무엇인가? <빈칸 추론>

① 특권
② 장점
③ 융통성
✓ 무기력함, 타성

| 분석 | 두 번째 단락 첫 부분에서 도덕적 위기가 있지만 관련된 사람들은 자신들을 단지 기계의 '톱니바퀴'에 불과하다고 언급한 뒤 중환자실의 의사들이 실제로 하는 말을 진술하고 있으므로 시스템 자체가 잘못되었음을 말하고 있다. 또한, 글쓴이가 중환자실 담당 의사에게 왜 가족들에게 제대로 설명해 주지 않는지 물어봤을 때, 그 의사는 중환자실에서는 그럴 시간이 없다는 부정적인 답변을 했다. 그렇다면 또 다른 의사도 의료 체계에 관하여 부정적인 말을 해야 할 것이다. ①, ②, ③은 모두 긍정의 단어이지만 ④ 'inertia'는 '활발하지 못함, 굳어진 습성, 무기력함'을 의미하는 부정적인 단어이므로 정답으로 적절하다.

29 다음 중 옳은 것은? <내용 일치>

① 중환자실은 환자들을 위한 완벽한 장치이다.
② 노숙자 또한 환자이다.
③ 사전 지침은 의무 사항이다.
✓ 사람들은 말기 치료 결정을 (스스로) 해야만 한다.

| 분석 | 마지막 단락에서 이 글의 저자는 "당신은 사전 의료 지시서를 작성함으로써 당신의 운명을 결정할 수 있다."고 하였다. 환자 스스로가 사전 지시서를 작성하여 의사 표현이 어려운 나중에 치료를 어떻게 할지 미리 밝혀 주는 것이 말기 치료에 대한 더 인도적인 접근이라고 하였다. 따라서 말기 치료는 스스로 결정해야 한다는 것은 지문과 일치한다고 볼 수 있다.

[30-31] 2012 중앙대

| 정답 | 30 ② 31 ④

| 어휘 |
fundamental ⓐ 근본적인
therapeutic ⓐ 치료의, 치료법의
dry mouth 구강 건조증
intent ⓝ 목적, 의도
side effect 부작용
premarketing ⓐ 시장에 출하하기 전의
prior to ~에 앞서
thalidomide ⓝ 탈리도마이드(진정·수면제의 일종)

pharmacology ⓝ 약리학(藥理學), 약물학
adverse effect 부작용
gastrointestinal ⓐ 위장의
labeling ⓝ 표시
associated with ~와 관련된, 연상되는
duration ⓝ 기간, 내구성, 지속
deformation ⓝ 기형, 불구

multiple ⓐ 다수의
nausea ⓝ 메스꺼움, 욕지기
lethal ⓐ 치사의, 치명적인
prescribe ⓥ 처방하다, 규정하다
Food and Drug Administration 식약청
toxicology ⓝ 독물학

denouement ⓝ 해결, 대단원, 결말

전문해석

약리학의 근본 원리는 모든 약은 다양한 (약의) 작용을 가진다는 것이다. 질병 치료에 있어 바람직한 작용들은 건강에 도움이 되는 것으로 여겨지지만, 반면에, 바람직하지 못하거나 환자에게 위험을 초래하는 작용은 '효과'라 불린다. 약의 부작용은 예를 들어 메스꺼움 또는 구강 건조증과 같은 사소한 것에서부터 다량의 위출혈과 같은 심각한 것에 이르기까지 광범위하다. 어떤 약들은 치명적이기도 하다. 따라서 부작용을 발견하는 효과적인 시스템은 모든 선진국 <u>의료 서비스의 중요한 요소</u>이다. 신약에 대해 이루어지고 있는 많은 연구는 이로운 효과를 최대화하고 부작용의 위험을 최소화하는 약의 용도의 조건들을 확인하는 것에 중점을 두고 있다. 의약품 표시 기재의 의도는 정확하게 이러한 지식체계들을 반영해서 의사들이 적절하게 약을 처방할 수 있게 하려는 것이다. 또는 처방전 없이 팔리더라도 소비자들이 적절하게 약을 이용할 수 있게 하려는 것이다. 미국의 현재 약물 조사 시스템은 새로운 처방약과 관련된 일반적인 부작용을 확인할 때 유용하며 정확하다는 것을 입증했다. 신약을 미국 식약청이 승인할 때, 의사들을 위한 약제 사용 설명서에 그 부작용에 대해 잘 설명하도록 한다. 그러나 그 조사 과정이 모든 부작용을 알아낸다고 신뢰할 수만은 없는데, 왜냐하면 시장 출시 이전 연구에 관련된 환자의 수가 상대적으로 적고, 그 연구의 비교적 짧은 기간 때문이다. 물론 동물 독성학 연구가 유독성에 대한 잠재성을 확인하려는 시도로서 시장 출시보다 먼저 이루어지고 있지만, 탈리도마이드로 인한 선천적 기형과 같은 잘 알려진 예가 보여 주듯이, <u>(동물 독성 반응에서) 음성인 연구결과물들이 인간에 대한 약물의 안전성을 보장해 주지는 않는다</u>.

31 ④

30 윗글의 빈칸에 들어갈 말로 가장 적절한 것은? 빈칸 추론
① 공중 보건 교육의 해결책
✓② 의료 서비스 체계의 중요한 구성 요소
③ 불법 약물 처방에 대한 현실적인 해결책
④ 의료 서비스를 간과함으로써 초래되는 의무적인 결과들

| 분석 | 빈칸 앞에서 다양한 부작용과 그것의 건강에 가하는 위험성에 관하여 이야기하고 빈칸은 이러한 부작용을 발견하는 효과적인 시스템에 관하여 진술하는 부분이다. 약의 부작용은 건강에 해를 가하기 때문에 이러한 약의 부작용을 사전에 발견하고 예방하는 시스템은 선진국의 의료 서비스에서 반드시 필요한 요소가 될 것이다. 따라서 정답으로는 ②가 적절하다.

31 윗글을 통해 추론할 수 있는 것으로 가장 적절한 것은? 내용 추론
① 대부분의 의사들은 처방약에 부작용이 있다는 것을 알지 못한다.
② 치료 효과가 있는 약은 유통 허가를 받는 경우가 거의 없다.
③ 소비자들은 약물의 적절한 지침을 이해하기가 어렵다.
✓④ 일부 희귀한 약물 부작용은 제한된 테스트에서는 발견되지 않는다.

| 분석 | 지문의 마지막 부분에서 "모든 부작용을 알아낸다고 신뢰할 수만은 없다"고 하였고, 또한 마지막 문장에서도 "동물 독성 반응에서 음성인 연구 결과물들이 인간에 대한 약물의 안전성을 보장해 주지는 않는다"고 하였다. 따라서 ④ '일부 희귀한 약물의 부작용은 제한된 테스트에서는 발견되지 않는다'는 진술은 지문을 통해 추론할 수 있는 진술이다.

[32-34] 2021 숭실대

| 정답 | 32 ② 33 ④ 34 ④

| 어휘 |
gene therapy 유전자 치료
nucleic acid ⓝ 핵산
recessively ⓐⓓ 퇴행적으로, 열성으로
deleterious ⓐ 유해한, 해로운
dominant ⓐ 〈유전학〉 우성의
CRISPER ⓝ 크리스퍼(유전자의 특정 부위를 절단해 유전체 교정을 가능하게 하는 리보핵산 기반 인공 제한효소)
eradication ⓝ 근절, 박멸
reservoir ⓝ 보균자

gene transfer 유전자 전달
insertion ⓝ 삽입, 끼워 넣기
imitation ⓝ 돌연변이
retinal ⓐ 망막의
recessive ⓐ 〈유전학〉 열성의

latent ⓐ 잠재하는, 잠복해 있는
sickle ⓐ 낫 모양의

therapeutic ⓐ 치료상의, 치료법의
fix a problem 문제를 해결하다
dysfunctional ⓐ 기능장애의
novel ⓐ 새로운

immunodeficiency ⓝ 면역 결핍

전문해석

인간 유전자 전달이라고도 불리는 유전자 치료는 질병을 치료하는 약으로 환자의 세포에 핵산을 전달하는 치료의 활용에 초점을 맞춘 의학 분야이다. 인간의 DNA를 수정하려는 최초의 시도는 마틴 클라인(Martin Cline)에 의해 1980년에 수행되었지만, 미국 국립 보건원에 의해 승인된 최초의 인간 핵 유전자 전달은 1989년 5월에 수행되었다. 인간 DNA를 세포핵 유전체에 직접 삽입한 것뿐만 아니라 유전자 전달을 이용한 최초의 치료 목적의 사용은 1990년 9월에 시작된 실험에서 프렌치 앤더슨(French Anderson)에 의해 이루어졌다. 그 방법은 많은 유전적인 질병들을 지금 당장 치료할 수 있거나 아니면 시간이 지나면 그 질병들이 치료될 수 있다고 여겨지고 있다.

1989년과 2018년 사이에 2,900개 이상의 임상실험이 수행되었으며, 그중에 절반 이상이 제1상에서 임상실험이었다. 2017년 현재, 스파크 테라퓨틱스의 럭스터나(Luxturna)와 노바티스의 킴리아(Kymriah)는 시장에 진입하기 위해 FDA의 첫 번째 승인된 유전자 치료법이다. 그 이후로, 다른 회사들의 유전자 치료 약품들 외에도 노바티스의 졸겐스마(Zolgensma)와 앨나일람의 파티시란(Patisiran)과 같은 약품들 또한 FDA의 승인을 받았다.

유전자 치료의 개념은 Ⓐ 유전적 문제를 그 근원에서 해결하는 것이다. 예를 들어, (대개 열성인) 유전적 질병에서, 특정 유전자의 돌연변이가 기능을 제대로 하지 못하는 단백질을 생성하는 경우, 유전자 치료를 사용하여, 해로운 돌연변이를 포함하지 않는, 그래서 제 기능을 하는 단백질을 만들어 내는 유전자의 복사본을 전달할 수 있을 것이다. 이 전략은 유전자 대체 치료라고 불리며 유전된 망막 질환을 치료하기 위해 사용된다.

유전자 대체 요법의 개념이 열성인 유전병에 대부분 적합하지만, 우성 유전 형식의 질환을 치료할 수 있는 새로운 전략이 제시되었다.

크리스퍼(CRISPR) 유전자 편집의 도입은 유전자 치료에서 그것의 적용과 활용을 위한 새로운 장을 열었는데, 그것은 어떤 유전자의 단순한 대체가 아닌, 특정한 유전적 Ⓑ 결함을 수정할 수 있게 하기 때문이다. 잠복된 인간 면역 결핍 바이러스(HIV) 감염원의 근절과 낫형의 세포 질환을 일으키는 돌연변이의 수정과 같은 의학적인 난제에 대한 해결책은 향후 몇 년 안에 치료의 선택지로 사용될 수 있을지도 모른다.

---

32 빈칸 Ⓐ에 가장 적합한 것은 다음 중 어느 것인가? 빈칸 추론

① 환자에게서 유전적 정보를 추출하는 것
✓ 유전적 문제를 근원에서 해결하는 것
③ 기능성 단백질을 제거하는 메커니즘을 생성하는 것
④ 인간에게 공통된 유전적 패턴을 식별하는 것

| 분석 | 빈칸 뒤의 예시를 보면 특정 유전자의 돌연변이가 제대로 작동하지 않는 단백질의 생성을 초래하는 경우 해로운 돌연변이를 갖고 있지 않은 동일한 유전자의 복사본을 전달하여 치료한다고 하였다. 즉 유전자의 돌연변이가 정상적이지 않은 단백질을 만들어 냈으므로 근원이라고 할 수 있는 돌연변이를 정상적인 유전자로 대체하여 해결한다는 것이다. 따라서 ② '유전적 문제를 근원에서 해결하는 것'이 빈칸에 적절하다.

33 빈칸 ⓑ에 가장 적합한 것은 다음 중 어느 것인가? 빈칸 추론
① 해결책　　　　　② 진단
③ 장점　　　　　　✓ ④ 결함

| 분석 | correction은 '수정', '교정'이라는 의미이다. 유전자 치료에서 잘못된 유전자를 대체하는 것이 아니라 유전적으로 잘못된 유전자를 수정하고, 교정한다는 맥락이므로 유전적 '결함'이 빈칸에 가장 적절하다.

34 다음 중 사실이 아닌 것은? 내용 일치
① 마틴 클라인은 인간의 DNA를 변형하려는 최초의 과학자였다.
② 치료 목적의 첫 유전자 전달은 1990년에 행해졌다.
③ 1989~2018년 임상실험의 절반 이상이 제1상에서 행해졌다.
✓ ④ 노바티스의 졸겐스마(Zolgensma)와 앨나일람의 파티시란(Patisiran)은 2017년 이전에 FDA 승인을 받았다.

| 분석 | 2017년 스파크 테라퓨틱스의 럭스터나와 노바티스의 킴리아가 FDA가 처음으로 시판을 허용한 유전자 치료제이다. 그 이후로 노바티스의 졸겐스마와 앨나일람의 파티시란도 FDA의 승인을 받은 것이므로 ④에 쓰인 before 부분은 after가 되어야 지문과 일치한다.

[35-38] 2018 서강대
| 정답 | 35 ②　36 ④　37 ②　38 ②
| 어휘 | margin ⓝ 가장자리, 주변부　　biomedical ⓐ 생체의학의　　startup ⓝ 신생 기업
　　　　herald ⓥ 알리다, 예고하다　　self-proclaimed ⓐ 자기 혼자 주장하는, 자칭의
　　　　foster ⓥ 촉진하다, 조장하다　　ethos ⓝ 기풍, 정신　　legitimacy ⓝ 합법성, 적법성
　　　　tailored ⓐ 맞춤 제작된　　democratize ⓥ 민주화하다

[전문해석]
최근까지 ⓐ 민주화된 의료 혁신의 선구자들은 우리 생체의학계의 연구 기관 및 규제 당국의 주변에 머물러 있었다(감시받아 왔다). 그러나 지난 단 2달 동안, 허가받지 않은 유전자 치료를 하면서 자신의 몸에 주사를 놓은 두 사람이 동영상을 널리 공유했다. 자신의 몸을 대상으로 실험을 한 두 사람 중의 한 명은 조시아 자이너(Josiah Zayner)로, 그는 가정용 유전자 편집 키트를 판매하는 신생 기업 오딘(Odin)의 CEO이다. 유전자 편집 기술로 스스로의 몸에 실험하는 것을 "허가받지 않은" 혁신의 새로운 형태라고 알려야 하는 것일까? 아니면 자칭 바이오해커라고 하는 사람들이 규제 체계를 시험해 봄으로써, 생체의학 혁신에 기여하는 시민들의 새로운 생태계에 피해를 가하게 될 것인가? [B] 〈자가 유전자 치료 실험은 감염과 면역 반응(거부반응)의 잠재적 가능성에서부터, 관련된 위험에 대한 이해의 부재와 환자들의 비현실적인 기대에 이르기까지 곤혹스러운 안전 및 윤리 문제들을 제기한다.〉 ⓑ 그러나, 유전자 편집 키트의 판매를 금지하는 것은 허약하고 일시적인 해결책일 뿐이다. 우리에게 필요한 것은 전통적인 연구 기관들 외곽에 책임 있는 혁신의 기풍을 진작시키는 일이다. 합법성을 부여하고 새로운 형태의 의료 연구들에 대해 맞춤 제작된 규제적 지원을 제공해야 할 긴급한 필요성을 깨달아야 한다. 이제 나아가야 할 길은 급진적이고, 규제되지 않은 과학을 홍보하는 것이 아니라, 시민, 환자, 윤리학자 규제당국이 동참하여 다시 생각해 보고 적절한 감독 체계를 마련하기 위한 참여 채널을 발전시키는 것이다.

35 빈칸 ⓐ와 ⓑ에 들어갈 말로 가장 적절한 것을 고르시오. 빈칸 추론

① 다국적의 – 더욱이 ② 민주화된 – 그러나 ✓
③ 생태계의 – 예를 들어 ④ 최적의 – 그럼에도 불구하고

| 분석 | 기존 연구 기관의 규칙이나 국가의 규제를 벗어나 자유롭게 의료 혁신을 추구하는 것을 정치적 용어로는 '민주주의'라고 할 수 있을 것이다. 따라서 빈칸 ⓐ에는 'democratized'가 적절하다. 빈칸 ⓑ의 앞 문장은 '바이오해커들이 해를 끼칠 수 있다'는 내용인데 빈칸 다음 문장은 '이들이 유전자 편집 키트를 판매하는 것을 금지하는 것이 해결책은 아니다'라고 말하고 있다. 따라서 빈칸 ⓑ에는 역접의 Yet이나 Nevertheless가 적절하다.

36 저자의 설명 방식은 _____의 그것과 매우 유사하다. 내용 파악

① 학술적 분석을 제공하는 연구자
② 뉴스 기사를 보도하는 일간지 기자
③ 고무적인 강연을 하는 동기부여를 하는 강연자
④ 어떤 윤리적 딜레마에 관한 의견을 제시하는 대중적 지식인 ✓

| 분석 | 이 글의 저자는 유전자 편집 키트와 그것을 이용한 자가 시술을 혁신이라고 할지, 아니면 금지해야 할지의 딜레마에 관하여 자신의 견해를 진술하고 있다. 그러면서 저자는 기존 의료계 밖에서 벌어지는 혁신적 연구들에 대해 합법성을 부여하고, 그것에 대해 적절한 규제와 감독을 시행하기 위해 관련 당사자들의 협의 채널이 필요하다고 제안하고 있다. 따라서 이 글을 쓴 저자는 아마도 ④ '어떤 윤리적 딜레마에 관한 의견을 제시하는 대중적인 지식인'일 것이다.

37 다음 중 윗글로부터 추론할 수 없는 것은? 내용 추론

① 생명공학은 개인이 집에서 유전자 치료를 실험할 수 있는 수준까지 발전했다.
② 미국 정부는 최근 전통적인 연구 기관 밖에서 의사의 자가 실험을 승인했다. ✓
③ 최근 의료 연구의 발전은 기업가 정신과 관련 있다.
④ 기존 의료계에 속하지 않은 시민들이 주도적인 역할을 할 수 있는 잠재력이 있음에도 불구하고, 많은 윤리적 문제들이 해결되지 않은 채로 남아 있다.

| 분석 | 저자는 '자가 유전자 편집 치료법에 대해 합법성을 부여하고, 새로운 형태의 의료 연구들에 대해 맞춤 제작된 규제적 지원을 제공해야 할 긴급한 필요성을 깨달아야 한다.'고 언급하였는데 그렇다고 하여 이미 미국 정부가 그 치료법을 승인했다고는 할 수 없다. 따라서 ②는 지문을 통해 알 수 없는 내용이다. 또한 본문의 오딘이라는 신생 기업 부분이 ③을 나타내고 있으므로 ③은 옳은 진술이다.

38 다음 문장이 들어갈 최적의 위치는 어느 곳인가? 문장 삽입

자가 유전자 치료 실험은 감염과 면역 반응(거부반응)의 잠재적 가능성에서부터, 관련된 위험에 대한 이해의 부재와 환자들의 비현실적인 기대에 이르기까지 곤혹스러운 안전 및 윤리 문제들을 제기한다.

① [A] ② [B] ✓
③ [C] ④ [D]

| 분석 | 제시된 문장을 요약하면 '자가 유전자 치료 실험은 안전 및 윤리 문제들이 있다'는 내용이므로 자가 유전자 치료의 문제점을 진술하는 부분에 들어가야 한다. [A]에서 [B] 앞까지는 의문문을 or로 연결하여 '자가 유전자 치료 실험은 혁신인 걸까?' 아니면 '피해를 끼칠 것인가?'의 내용인데 두 번째 의문문이 자가 유전자 치료의 문제될 부분을 진술하고 있으므로 주어진 문장은 [B]에 들어가는 것이 가장 적절하다.

[39-41] 2019 국민대

| 정답 | 39 ③ 40 ② 41 ①

| 어휘 |
pro tip 유용한 팁
speculate ⓥ 추측하다, 억측하다; 투기하다
resistant ⓐ 저항하는; 견디는, 내성이 있는
risk factor 위험 요인
add up 계산이 맞다; 이해되다; 조금씩 보태어 많아지다
chore ⓝ 지루한 일; 잡일, 허드렛일
trigger ⓥ 일으키다, 유발하다
positive ⓐ 확신하는, 확실한; 긍정적인
beneficial ⓐ 유익한, 이익을 가져오는
fidget ⓥ 안절부절못하다; 꼼지락거리다
lower ⓥ 낮추다, 내리다, 낮게 하다
negative ⓐ 부정적인; 소극적인
expert ⓝ 전문가
fasting ⓝ 단식, 금식
intervention ⓝ 조정, 중재, 간섭, 개입
log ⓥ 일지에 기록하다; 항해[비행]하다
affect ⓥ 영향을 미치다, 악영향을 끼치다
hippocampus ⓝ 해마

전문해석

건강하게 오래 사는 데 도움이 될 만한 몇 가지 팁이 있다. 가장 먼저, 다이어트를 들 수 있다. 체중 감량은 아마도 혈압을 낮추고 혈당 수치가 좋아지는 것과 같은 많은 긍정적인 변화를 가져올 것이다. 그러나 일부 전문가들은 금식이 또한 우리 몸으로 하여금 스트레스에 내성을 많이 갖게 만들며, 이는 세포 수준에서 유익한 효과를 나타낼 수 있다고 추측한다. 한 전문가는 "다이어트가 노화와 노화로 인한 질병을 지연시키기 위한 가장 강력한 개입"이라고 말한다.

지난 2년 동안, 과학자들은 하루 종일 앉아 있는 것과 같이 Ⓐ 움직이지 않는 행동이 조기 사망의 위험 요인이라는 것을 보여 주었다. 그들은 앉아서 보내는 시간이 제2형 당뇨병과 비알코올성 지방간 질환의 위험 증가와 관련돼 있다는 사실을 발견했다. 너무 많이 앉아 있는 것이 끼치는 온갖 나쁜 영향들을 운동을 해서 모두 없앨 수는 없다. 그러나 좋은 소식은 가만히 앉아 있는 것을 제외하면 무엇을 하든—심지어 몸을 꼼지락대는 것도 가치가 있다—보탬이 될 수 있다는 것이다. 신체활동을 가장 적게 기록한 사람들은 향후 10년 안에 심장질환이 발생할 위험이 가장 높았는데, 이것은 충격적이지 않다. 그러나 과학자들에게 놀라웠던 사실은 낮 동안 조금만 더 움직여도—집 안 여기저기서 허드렛일을 하는 것과 같이—심장질환의 위험을 줄이기에 충분했다는 점이다.

이제는 우리의 감정이 우리 몸의 상태에 영향을 미친다는 것을 과학자들은 분명하게 받아들이고 있다. 연구 결과들은 분노와 스트레스가 아드레날린과 같은 스트레스 호르몬을 우리 혈액에 방출시킬 수 있다는 것을 오랫동안 보여 주었는데, 이렇게 되면 심장은 더 빠르고 강하게 뛰게 된다. 스트레스는 심지어 우리 뇌가 알츠하이머병에 얼마나 잘 대항하는지에도 영향을 미칠지 모른다. 과학자들은 젊었을 때 노화에 대해 더 부정적인 태도를 가진 사람들의 경우 해마의 크기가 더 작아져 있었다는 사실을 발견했는데, 해마는 뇌의 일부분으로, 이것의 크기가 작아지는 것은 알츠하이머병과 관련이 있다. Ⓑ 노화에 관해 우리가 어떻게 생각하는가가 우리가 어떻게 늙어가는가에 영향을 끼칠 수 있다는 연구 결과가 나온 것은 이번이 처음이 아니다.

39 빈칸 Ⓐ에 가장 적합한 것은 무엇인가? 빈칸 추론

① 활동적인
② 갑작스러운
✓ ③ 앉아 있는(활동하지 않는)
④ 소란스러운

| 분석 | 빈칸 바로 뒤에서 "like sitting all day(하루 종일 앉아 있는 것과 같이)"를 예로 들었기 때문에 이와 동의어인 개념이 빈칸에 들어가야 한다. '몸을 많이 움직이지 않는'이란 의미의 ③ 'sedentary'가 정답으로 적절하다.

40 윗글에 따르면, 다음 중 건강하게 오래 살기 위해 도움이 되는 팁에 해당하지 않는 것은? 내용 파악

① 오랫동안 가만히 앉아 있지 않는 것
✓ ② 과도한 운동을 하는 것
③ 식이요법을 꾸준히 하는 것
④ 낙관적 태도를 갖는 것

| 분석 | 지문에서 나머지는 모두 언급했는데 반면 운동을 과도하게 할 것은 언급한 적이 없으므로 ② '과도한 운동을 하는 것'은 지문에 나온 팁에 해당하지 않는다.

41 다음 중 빈칸 ⓑ에 들어가기에 가장 적절한 것은? 빈칸 추론

✓ ① 노화에 관해 우리가 어떻게 생각하는가가 우리가 어떻게 늙어가는가에 영향을 끼칠 수 있다
② 스트레스와 운동은 서로 관련돼 있다
③ 알츠하이머병은 노화에 대한 긍정적인 태도와 결부돼 있다
④ 분노와 스트레스는 알츠하이머병과 직접적으로 관련 없다

| 분석 | 빈칸은 앞부분에 나온 연구 결과가 처음이 아니라는 문장이므로 빈칸에는 앞부분의 내용이 다시 들어가야 한다. 빈칸 앞부분 내용이 '젊었을 때 노화에 대해 더 부정적인 태도를 가진 사람들의 경우 알츠하이머병에 걸릴 가능성이 더 높았다'는 것이므로 빈칸에는 이러한 내용과 가장 가까운 의미인 ①이 들어가는 것이 적절하다.

[42-43] 2021 중앙대

| 정답 | 42 ① 43 ④

| 어휘 |
immunology ⓝ 면역학　　defense ⓝ 방어　　infection ⓝ 감염
microorganism ⓝ 미생물　　immunity ⓝ 면역　　cellular ⓐ 세포의
molecular ⓐ 분자의　　cowpox ⓝ 우두　　confer ⓥ 제공하다
recipient ⓝ 받은 사람, 수혜자　　inoculate ⓥ 접종하다　　smallpox ⓝ 천연두
pustule ⓝ 농포, 작은 융기　　variolation ⓝ 종두법　　eradicate ⓥ 근절하다

전문해석

면역학은 감염에 대한 인체의 방어에 대한 연구이다. 우리는 미생물에 지속적으로 노출되는데, 그중 다수는 질병을 유발하지만, 드물게 병에 걸린다. 몸은 어떻게 스스로를 방어하는가? 감염이 발생했을 때, 몸은 어떻게 침입자를 제거하고 스스로를 치료할 수 있을까? 그리고 왜 우리는 한 번 마주치고 극복한 많은 전염병에 대해 오래 지속되는 면역력을 발달시킬까? 이것들이 면역학이 다루는 질문들이며, 우리는 세포와 분자 수준에서 감염에 대한 우리 몸의 방어력을 이해하기 위해 면역학을 연구한다.

[B] 과학으로서의 면역학의 시작은 보통 18세기 후반에 에드워드 제너(Edward Jenner)의 업적에 기인한다. 질병에서 살아남는 것이 나중에 그것으로부터 더 큰 보호를 해 준다는 면역의 개념은 고대 그리스 이래로 알려져 왔다. 종두법, 즉 천연두 농포 물질을 흡입하거나 피부의 상처로 옮기는 것은 최소한 1400년대부터 중동과 중국에서 천연두를 막는 보호책으로 실행되어 왔고 제너도 알고 있었다.

[A] 제너는 우두, 즉 종두증이라는 비교적 가벼운 질병이 종종 치명적인 천연두 질병으로부터 보호책을 주는 것 같다는 사실을 관찰했고, 1796년에 우두로 접종하면 접종을 받은 사람이 천연두에 걸리지 않는다는 것을 입증해 보였다. 그의 과학적 증거는 접종 후 두 달 후에 접종자가 천연두 감염 물질에 일부러 노출시키는 방법에 의존했다. 이 과학적 실험은 그의 독창적인 공헌이었다.

[C] 제너는 이 과정을 백신 접종이라 불렀다. 이 용어는 질병으로부터 보호하기 위해 약해지거나 약화된 종류의 질병을 유발하는 물질들을 건강한 사람들이 접종하는 것을 설명하는 데 여전히 사용된다. 제너의 과감한 실험은 성공적이었지만 천연두 예방 접종이

보편화되기까지는 거의 200년이 걸렸다. 이러한 발전으로 인해 1979년 세계보건기구가 천연두가 근절되었다고 선언할 수 있었는데, 이는 거의 틀림없이 현대 의학에서 가장 위대한 승리라고 할 수 있다.

42 윗글의 단락을 논리적 흐름에 맞게 순서대로 배열한 것으로 가장 적절한 것은? 단락 배열
✓① [B] – [A] – [C]
② [B] – [C] – [A]
③ [C] – [A] – [B]
④ [C] – [B] – [A]

| 분석 | [C]에서 제너가 이러한 과정을 백신이라고 불렀다고 했다. 이에 대한 내용은 [A]에 나와 있어 [A] 다음 [C]가 이어져야 하므로 여기에 맞는 것은 ①밖에 없다. 또한 글의 내용은 첫 문단은 면역학 일반에 대한 소개이며 [B] 단락은 면역학의 탄생 이야기이며 [A]는 제너의 백신 접종과 관련된 역사를 다루고 있고 마지막으로 [C]는 제너의 백신 접종의 의의를 다루고 있다.

43 윗글의 내용과 일치하는 것은? 내용 일치
① 에드워드 제너는 천연두 농포의 존재에 대해 모르고 있었다.
② 천연두의 발생은 종두법으로는 막을 수 없다.
③ 우두는 백신 접종을 통해 막을 수 있다.
✓④ 에드워드 제너는 종두법이 과거에 실행되었다는 것을 알고 있었다.

| 분석 | [B] 단락의 마지막 부분에 제너는 종두법을 이미 알고 있었다고 언급하였다. 따라서 ④는 지문과 일치하며 반대로 ①은 지문과 일치하지 않는다.

| 배경 지식 | 제너의 종두법(variolation): 영국의 외과 의사 에드워드 제너는 소에서 전염되는 우두에 감염되었던 사람은 평생 천연두를 앓지 않는다는 사실을 발견하고, 30년의 연구 끝에 1796년 우두를 천연두 환자에게 접종하는 실험에 성공하였다. 제너가 발견한 종두법은 빠르게 보급되어 천연두로 인한 사망률이 급속히 감소하였다.

[44–45] 2022 숭실대

| 정답 | 44 ④ 45 ③

| 어휘 |
proportion ⓝ 비율
population aging 인구 노령화
concerted ⓐ 합심한, 결연한
ageism ⓝ 노인 차별
shift ⓝ 변화
implementation ⓝ 이행, 실행
catalytic ⓐ 촉매의
integrated ⓐ 통합적인
distribution ⓝ 분배, 배급
collaboration ⓝ 협력, 합작, 협조
sustainable ⓐ 지속 가능한

전문해석

전 세계의 사람들이 장수하고 있다. 오늘날 대부분의 사람들은 60세 이상 살 것으로 기대할 수 있다. 세계의 모든 국가는 노인들의 인구 규모와 비율 면에서 성장을 경험하고 있다.

늦어도 2030년에는 세계 인구 6명 중 1명은 60세 이상이 될 것이다. 이때가 되면, 60세 이상 인구의 비율은 2020년 10억에서 14억으로 증가할 것이다. 늦어도 2050년에는 60세 이상이 되는 세계 인구는 두 배(21억 명)로 늘어날 것이다. 80세 이상의 인구는 2020년에서 2050년 사이에 3배가 되어 4억 2,600만 명에 이를 것으로 예상된다. 한 국가의 인구 분포가 고령화되는 것은 인구 노령화로 알려져 있는데, 이러한 변화는 고소득 국가(예를 들면, 일본 인구의 30%가 이미 60세 이상이다)에서 시작되었지만, 현재 가장 큰 변화를 겪고 있는 나라는 중저소득 국가이다. 늦어도 2050년에는 60세 이상이 되는 세계 인구의 2/3가 중저소득 국가에서 살 것이다.

UN총회는 2021~2030년을 "건강한 노화 10년"으로 선포하고 WHO가 이행을 주도할 것을 요청했다. 건강한 노화 10년은 정부, 시민 사회, 국제기구, 전문가, 학계, 언론 및 민간 부문을 단합시켜 더 길고 건강한 삶을 촉진하기 위해 10년간 일치되고 촉매적이고 협력적으로 행동하는 전 세계적인 협업이다.

건강한 노화 10년은 WHO의 국제 전략 및 실행 계획과 UN의 고령화에 관한 국제행동계획(MIPAA: Madrid International Plan of Action on Aging)을 기반으로 하며 지속 가능한 개발과 목표에 관한 UN의제 2030의 실현을 지원한다. 44 ④

건강한 노화 10년은 다음 4가지 영역에서 집단행동을 통해 건강 불평등을 줄이고 노인 가족 및 지역 사회의 삶을 개선하고자 한다. 첫째, 연령과 연령 차별에 대해 생각하고 느끼고 행동하는 방식을 바꾸고, 둘째, 노인의 능력을 육성하는 방식으로 지역 사회를 개발하고, 셋째, 노인들에게 대응하는 사람 중심의 통합 케어 및 1차 의료 서비스를 제공하고, 넷째, 양질의 장기 케어의 이용을 필요로 하는 노인들에 제공하는 것이다. 44 ④

---

44 다음 중 2030년에 일치하는 것은 무엇인가? `내용 파악`

① 세계 인구의 30% 이상이 60세 이상이 될 것이다.
② 60세 이상 노인의 수는 약 21억 명이 될 것이다.
③ 일본은 고령화에 관한 국제행동계획을 시행할 것이다.
✓ 노인들은 양질의 의료 서비스를 더 잘 이용할 수 있게 될 것이다.

| 분석 | 마지막 단락에서, 2021~2030년의 "건강한 노화 10년"을 통해 노인들은 양질의 장기 케어를 제공받게 될 것이라고 하였다. 따라서 ④ '노인들은 양질의 의료 서비스를 더 잘 이용할 수 있게 될 것이다'는 지문과 일치한다.

---

45 2050년에는 어떤 일이 일어날 것으로 예상되는가? `내용 파악`

① 60세 이상의 사람들은 3배가 될 것이다.
② 60세 이상의 사람 중 3분의 2가 고소득 국가에서 살게 될 것이다.
✓ 80세 이상 노인의 수는 4억 2,600만 명이 될 것이다.
④ 노년층과 청년층의 수가 균형을 이룰 것이다.

| 분석 | 두 번째 단락에서 '80세 이상의 인구는 2020년에서 2050년 사이에 3배가 되어 4억 2,600만 명에 이를 것으로 예상된다.'고 직접 언급하였다. 따라서 2050년에 발생할 일로는 ③이 가장 적절하다.

[46-48] 2012 한국외대

| 정답 | 46 ④ 47 ④ 48 ③

| 어휘 |
conception ⓝ 인식, 개념
embrace ⓥ 포용하다, 받아들이다
justify ⓥ 정당화하다
dissolve ⓥ 잃게 하다
corrupt ⓥ 부패시키다
tactic ⓝ 전략
rationality ⓝ 합리성
common sense 상식

human nature 인간 본성
hostile ⓐ 적대적인
inequality ⓝ 불평등
strip ⓥ 박탈하다, 제거하다
defender ⓝ 주창자, 옹호자
discredit ⓥ 무시하다, 짓밟다
disarm ⓥ 무장해제시키다
pertinent ⓐ 적절한

affect ⓥ 영향을 미치다
innate ⓐ 타고난, 천부적인
subvert ⓥ 뒤엎다, 파괴하다
intellectual ⓝ 지식인
desperate ⓐ 처절한
inject ⓥ 주입시키다
menacing ⓐ 골치 아픈

전문해석

인간 본성에 대한 우리의 인식은 아이들을 키우는 방식에서부터 우리가 받아들이는 정치운동에 이르기까지 우리 삶의 모든 측면에 영향을 미친다. 하지만 과학이 우리를 인간 본성에 대한 이해의 황금기로 이끌어 감에 따라, 많은 사람들은 그러한 인식에 적대감을 보인다. 그들은 사고와 감정에 대한 타고난 패턴의 발견이 불평등을 정당화하고, 사회 변화를 뒤엎으며, 개인의 책임을 해제시키며, 삶에서 의미와 목적을 박탈할 것이라고 두려워한다.

'빈 서판'(*The Blank Slate*)에서 스티븐 핑커(Steve Pinker)는 인간 본성에 대한 견해와, 그 견해가 갖는 도덕적·감정적·정치적 영향에 대해 탐구한다. 그는 많은 지식인들이 세 가지 서로 연관된 독단적 교리를 받아들이며, 인간 본성의 존재를 거부하고 있는 방식들을 보여 주고 있다. 그 세 가지는 'Blank Slate'(인간 정신은 선천적인 특성이 없다), 'Noble Savage'(사람은 선하게 태어나 사회에 의해 타락한다), 'Ghost in the Machine'(우리 모두는 선천성과 무관하게 선택할 수 있는 영혼을 지녔다) 등이다. 이 교리들 하나하나는 도덕적 부담을 지니고 있다. 그래서 이들을 옹호하는 사람들은 그들에게 도전하는 과학자들을 짓밟기 위해 필사적 전략에 몰입해 왔다.

핑커는 평등, 진보, 책임, 목적은 풍부한 인간 본성의 발견으로부터 두려워할 것이 전혀 없음을 보임으로써 침착함과 합리성을 이 토론에 불어넣는다. 그는 명료한 사고, 상식, 과학과 역사로부터 얻은 적절한 사실을 가지고 가장 험악한 위협조차도 무장해제시켰다. 20세기에 걸쳐 지식인들 사이에서 유행했지만, 'Blank Slate' 이론은 이득을 주기보다는 피해를 많이 끼쳤다고 그는 주장한다.

46 왜 많은 사람들은 인간 본성을 이해하려는 과학적인 시도를 비난하는가? `내용 파악`
① 사람들은 그들의 이론이 새로운 과학적 발견에 공헌하기를 원한다.
② 사람들은 과학이 인간의 마음을 연구하는 데 적절하지 않다고 생각한다.
③ 사람들은 인간의 마음이 더 엄격하게 연구되어야 하는 것이라고 생각한다.
✓④ 사람들은 그런 노력의 결과가 악용될지도 모른다고 걱정한다.

| 분석 | 첫 번째 문단을 읽어 보면 마지막 문장에서 불평등을 정당화하고, 사회 발전을 뒤엎는 등의 근거를 들면서 사람들은 인간 본성의 선천성에 과학적 설명에 적대감을 느끼게 되었다고 했다. 따라서 정답은 ④ '사람들은 그러한 노력이 남용될 수 있는 결과에 대해 두려워하고 있다.'이다.

47 핑커는 _____ 라고 생각한다. `내용 파악`
① 인간의 마음은 선천적인 특성이 없다
② 사람들은 선하게 태어나지만 사회에 의해 타락한다
③ 'Ghost in the Machine' 이론이 정확하다
✓④ 과학은 인간 본성에 대한 이해를 깊게 한다

| 분석 | 핑커는 세 가지 독단적 교리가 과학자들이 하는 인간 본성 연구에 저해가 되고 있다고 지적하고 있다. 따라서 핑커는 세 가지 교리에 반대하고 있다. 또한 마지막 단락에서 핑커는 '명료한 사고, 상식, 과학과 역사로부터 얻은 적절한 사실을 가지고 가장 험악한 위협조차도 무장해제시켰다.'는 문장을 통해 핑커가 과학을 지지하고 있다는 것을 알 수 있다. 따라서 정답은 ④ '과학은 인간 본성에 대한 이해를 깊게 한다'이다.

48 다음 중 윗글에서 언급되거나 암시되지 않은 것은? `내용 일치`
① 우리가 아이들을 기르는 방식은 인간 본성에 대한 개념에 달려 있다.
② 우리는 현재 타고난 사고의 유형을 잘 이해하고 있다.
✓③ 일부 사상가들은 사람들은 악하게 태어나며 교육을 통해 개선될 수 있다고 생각한다. `언급 안 함`
④ 'Blank Slate' 이론은 20세기에 영향을 미쳤던 인간의 마음에 대한 이론이다.

| 분석 | 지문에서 인간은 선하게 태어나지만 사회에 의해 타락한다는 주장은 'Noble Savage' 이론이다. 지식인들이 믿은 세 가지 교리 중에 '성악설'을 의미하는 ③의 내용은 지문에 언급한 적이 없다.

[49-51] 2018 홍익대

| 정답 | 49 ② 50 ④ 51 ④

| 어휘 |
forensic ⓐ 법의학적인; 법정의
forensic science 범죄과학 수사; 법의학
massacre ⓝ 대학살
reconstruct ⓥ 재구성[재현]하다
magnify ⓥ 확대하다
epidemiology ⓝ 역학, 유행병학
E. coil ⓝ 대장균
contamination ⓝ 오염
strain ⓝ 혈통; 계통; 변종
pivotal ⓐ 중추적인, 매우 중요한
pinpoint ⓥ (원인을) 정확히 설명하다
outbreak ⓝ 발생, 발병
forensic anthropology 법인류학
tissue ⓝ 조직
remains ⓝ 유적; 유골; 잔여물
scanning electron microscope 주사 전자 현미경(SEM)
liquified ⓐ 액화된
deposit ⓝ 퇴적물, 찌꺼기
residue ⓝ 잔류물, 찌꺼기
coat ⓥ 입히다
ailment ⓝ (가벼운) 병, 질환
forensic pathologist 법의학자, 법병리학자

전문해석

법의학은, 어떤 질병의 확산을 연구하는 관점이든, 고대 대량학살 장소를 조사하는 관점이든, 우리가 과거를 이해하는 데 유용하다. 그리고 물론, 법의학은 범죄 해결과 관련하여, 사법제도에도 중요하다. 이 모든 영역을 통틀어서, 현미경은 과거의 사건을 재구성하는 데 유용하고 중요한 도구이다. 현미경은 많은 수사목적에서 필수인데, 왜냐하면 현미경은 물체를 대단히 자세하게 확대할 수 있기 때문이다.

법역학은 질병이 어떻게 전파되는가를 주로 법적인 이유로 조사한다. 예를 들어, 법역학자들은 대장균이나 살모넬라균과 같은 위험한 박테리아의 출처를 발견하는 임무를 맡을지도 모른다. 그렇게 하기 위해(위험한 박테리아의 출처를 발견하기 위해), 법역학자들은 현미경을 이용해 음식이 오염됐는지를 연구할 것이다. 현미경을 통해 보는 경우, 특정 박테리아 변종의 존재는 과학자에게 오염원을 알려 줄 수 있다. 이것은 질병 발생의 원인이 되는 개체나 집단을 정확히 알아내는 데뿐만 아니라, (추가적으로) 더 많은 사람들이 감염되지 않도록 막는 데에도 중심적인 것으로 판명될 수 있다.

법인류학에서, 현미경은 사인을 확인하기 위해 조직, 유골, 또는 다른 유해를 연구하는 데 사용된다. 예를 들어, 주사 전자 현미경(SEM)은 토양의 퇴적물에 남겨져 있는 오래도록 액체 상태로 있어 온 인간의 유해를 식별하는 데 사용될 수 있다. 이 분야(법인류학)에서 현미경은 또한 치아에서 발견된 찌꺼기를 관찰하는 데 사용되기도 한다. 조직, 세포, 또는 다른 잔여물은 사람이 사망한 뒤에 치아에 입혀질 수도 있어서, 연구원들이 사람의 습관, 질병, 심지어 사망의 원인을 규명하는 데도 도움을 줄 수 있다.

법병리학자들은 사람이 사망에 이르게 된 방식을 규명하는 책임을 맡고 있다. 만일 사람이 어떤 질병으로 사망했다면, 법병리학자들은 치명적인 박테리아나 바이러스를 확인하는 데 현미경을 사용할 수 있다. 현미경은 상처 주변의 조직을 보다 면밀하게 조사하는 데 있어 도움을 줄 수 있으며, 총알인지, 칼인지, 그 밖의 다른 것인지 등 어떤 종류의 물체가 그런 손상을 초래했는지를 규명하는 데 도움을 줄지도 모른다.

49 윗글의 가장 적절한 제목은 무엇인가? 제목

① 법의학과 그 법률적 배경 중심 키워드 없음
✓② 법의학에서의 현미경 사용
③ 법의학의 초기 발달 중심 키워드 없음
④ 미래 법의학의 필요성 중심 키워드 없음

| 분석 | 이 글은 법의학과 관련된 다양한 분야에서 현미경이 어떻게 사용되는지, 그리고 법 병리학자가 현미경을 어떻게 사용하는지에 관한 내용을 다루고 있으므로 현미경이라는 핵심 키워드가 제목에서 빠질 수 없다. 따라서 글의 제목으로는 ② '법의학에

서의 현미경 사용'이 적절하다.

50 윗글에 의하면, 다음 중 추론할 수 없는 것은? 내용 추론
① 법의학은 과거의 사건들을 재구성함으로써 과거를 이해하는 것을 다룬다.
② 법역학은 위험한 질병이 전파되는 것을 막는 데 기여한다.
③ 사체의 치아에 남아 있는 물질들은 그 사람의 생활 습관을 암시해 줄 수 있다.
✔ ④ 치명적인 박테리아 및 바이러스는 법병리학자가 조직을 조사하는 데 어려움을 초래한다.

| 분석 | 마지막 단락에서 법병리학자가 현미경을 사용하여 박테리아나 바이러스를 확인한다고 하였는데, 그렇다고 해서 박테리아나 바이러스 때문에 조직을 조사하는 데 어려움을 겪는다고는 할 수 없다. 따라서 ④는 지문에 언급되지 않았으며 지문과 일치하지 않는 진술이다.

51 다음 중 윗글의 구성 방식과 가장 가까운 것은? 글의 구성 방식
① 공간 순서
② 연대순
③ 질문과 응답
✔ ④ 지지하는 목록을 가진 요지

| 분석 | 이 글은 첫 단락에서 '현미경은 과거의 사건을 재구성하는 데 도움을 주기 위해 사용되는 중요한 도구이다'라는 글의 전체 요지를 말한 뒤 이 요지를 지지해 주는 구체적 사례들인 범죄 수사, 법역학, 법인류학, 법병리학 등의 여러 분야에서 제시하고 있으므로, ④가 글의 구성 방식으로 가장 적절하다.

11강 환경 / 동식물

01	①	02	②	03	①	04	②	05	④	06	②	07	①	08	②	09	⑤	10	④
11	③	12	③	13	④	14	②	15	①	16	②	17	③	18	③	19	⑤	20	③
21	⑤	22	③	23	①	24	④	25	④	26	②	27	④	28	④	29	③	30	②
31	③	32	②	33	④	34	②	35	④	36	②	37	④	38	③	39	②	40	①
41	③	42	①	43	④	44	④	45	④	46	①	47	③	48	②	49	③	50	②
51	②	52	③																

[01-03] 2013 고려대

| 정답 | 01 ① 02 ② 03 ①

| 어휘 |
fish school 어군, 물고기 떼
in unison 한결같이, 일제히, 합심하여
align ⓥ 정렬시키다
hydrodynamic ⓐ 유체 역학의, 수력의
wheel ⓥ 회전하다, 방향을 바꾸다
dynamics ⓝ 역학, 동역학, 역학관계
predator ⓝ 약탈자
turbulence ⓝ 교란, 소란, 난류 상태
reverse ⓥ 거꾸로 하다, 반대로 하다
flank ⓝ 옆구리, 측면
spacing ⓝ 간격을 두기, 글자 배열, 공간

전문해석

멀리서 보면 물고기 떼는 큰 유기체와 닮았다. 두세 마리에서 수백만 마리에 달하는 그것의 구성원들은 촘촘한 대형으로 헤엄치고, 거의 일제히 회전하고 거꾸로 간다. 지배적인 체계가 존재하지 않거나 너무 약해서 물고기 떼의 전체적인 역학관계에 거의 영향을 미치지 않는다. 게다가 일관된 리더십은 없다. 물고기 떼가 오른쪽 또는 왼쪽으로 돌 때, 이전에는 측면에 있던 개체들이 주도권을 잡는다. 물고기 떼의 평균 크기는 종에 따라 다르고, 구성원의 간격, 평균 속도 및 3차원적 모양도 마찬가지다. 비록 물고기 떼가 이동하는 동안 보통 군사적 정밀도로 (군대처럼 정확하게) 정렬되지만, 그들은 휴식을 취하거나 먹이를 먹을 때 더욱 거의 무작위적인 방향성을 가진다. 그들의 정렬은 또한 물고기가 포식자들에 의해 공격을 받을 때 특정한 방식으로 바뀐다. 이동하는 무리 내의 간격은 분명히 대체로 유체역학적 힘에 의해 결정된다. 개별 물고기들은 다른 물고기에 의해 생성된 난류로 인해 심각한 효율성 손실을 겪지 않고 가능한 한 다른 물고기들과 가까운 위치를 찾는 경향이 있다.

01 윗글에 따르면, 물고기 떼의 크기에 영향을 미치지 *않는* 것은? 세부 내용 불일치
✔ ① 물고기의 방향
② 물고기의 근접성
③ 물고기의 종류
④ 물고기의 속도

| 분석 | 본문의 6번째 문장에서 물고기 떼의 크기에 영향을 미치는 요인들을 나열했다. 물고기 떼의 크기는 물고기의 '종'에 따라 다르고 구성원은 간격과 속도도 영향을 준다고 서술했다. 보기 ②의 '근접성'은 '간격'을 의미하며 ③의 '종'과 속도'는 언급했지만 보기 ①은 언급하지 않았다.

02 빈칸을 가장 잘 채우는 것을 선택하시오. 빈칸 추론
① 혼자 수영할 기회
✔ ② 일관된 리더십이 없음
③ 자율권의 여지가 거의 없는
④ 발산할 수 있는 강한 감각

| 분석 | 빈칸을 포함한 문장의 앞 문장에서는 물고기 떼에 '지배적인 체계가 존재하지 않거나 너무 약하다'고 했으며 빈칸 뒤 문장에서는 '이전에 측면에 있던 개체들이 방향이 바뀌면 주도권을 잡게 된다'고 했다. 따라서 물고기 떼에 '일관된 리더십'은 없을 것이므로 보기 ②가 빈칸에 가장 적절하다.

---

03 다음 중 "물고기 떼"에 대해 추론할 수 없는 것은 무엇인가? 세부 내용 비추론
  ✓ ① 그것의 주요 역할은 구성원들에게 안전을 제공하는 것이다.
  ② 포식자들은 물고기의 정렬에 영향을 준다.
  ③ 그것은 두 마리 이상의 물고기 무리를 말한다.
  ④ 먹이를 먹는 것은 균일한 대형의 예외다.

| 분석 | 본문 8번째 문장에서 물고기 떼의 정렬은 또한 '물고기가 포식자들에 의해 공격을 받을 때 특정한 방식으로 바뀐다'고 했지만 구성들에게 안전을 제공한다는 언급은 없으므로 보기 ①이 추론할 수 없는 진술이다.

[04-05] 2015 광운대
| 정답 | 04 ② 05 ④
| 어휘 |
prosperity ⓝ 번영, 번성, 번창
priority ⓝ 우선[중요]사항, 우선권
principal ⓐ 주요한, 제1의
pose ⓥ (위협이나 문제를) 제기하다
sweeping ⓐ 전면적인, 포괄적인
avert ⓥ 피하다, 막다
crucially ⓐⓓ 결정적으로
affordable ⓐ 알맞은
in the pipeline (논의·계획·준비 등이) 한창 진행 중인
resilience ⓝ 탄성, 탄력, 회복력
deploy ⓥ 배치하다, 전개하다, 분산하다
commensurate ⓐ (크기나 중요도가) 어울리는, 상응하는

전문해석
우리가 세계의 증가하는 인구에게 안정성과 더 큰 번영을 제공하려면, 우리는 중대한 결정을 내려야 하지만, 그 결정을 내릴 시간이 거의 없다. 가장 우선하는 것은 기후 변화이다. 전 세계적으로, 기후 변화가 일어나고 있고 인간의 활동이 그 주요한 원인이라는 것은 명백하다. 기후 변화는 농업, 수자원, 인류의 건강, 육지와 해양의 생태계에 영향을 미치고 있다. [A] 그것은 경제적 안정과 국가의 안보에 광범위한 위험을 초래한다. [B] 만약 우리가 지금 대담하고 단호한 조치를 취한다면, 우리는 이러한 위험들을 피할 수 있다. 점점 더 많은 정부 지도자, 정책 입안자, 기업, 투자자, 그리고 염려스러운 시민들이 기후 변화에 따른 손실을 이해하기 시작하고 있다. [C] 더 중요한 것은, 그들이 또한 온실가스 배출을 줄이고 회복력을 지원하기 위해 알맞은 해결책들이 존재하거나 진행 중에 있다는 것을 배우고 있다는 것이다. [D] ⟨우리는 이러한 해결책들을 도전과제에 상응하는 규모로 구축해야 한다.⟩ 그것은 투자를 의미하고, 그것은 특별히 금융과 기술 분야에서의 세계적인 협력을 의미한다. [E] 그것이 정부가 가까운 미래에 새로운 보편적인 기후 협약에 대한 그들의 체결을 완료하는 것이 중요한 이유이다.
04 ②

---

04 윗글의 요지로 가장 적절한 것은? 요지
  ① 인간의 활동은 기후 변화의 주요 원인이다.
  ✓ ② 우리는 지체 없이 기후 변화에 대처하기 위해 힘을 합쳐야 한다.
  ③ 기후 변화의 광범위한 영향을 확인하는 것은 중요하다.
  ④ 우선순위에 따라 과업을 나열하는 것은 우리를 안정되고 번영하게 한다.
  ⑤ 온실가스 배출을 줄이기 위해 알맞은 해결책이 개발되었다.

| 분석 | 본문에서 저자는 기후 변화의 주요 원인은 인간의 활동이며 기후 변화로 인한 위험을 막기 위해서는 투자, 금융, 기술에서의 세계적인 협력을 필요로 한다고 주장한다. 따라서 보기 ②가 요지로 가장 적절하다.

05 다음 주어진 문장이 들어가기에 가장 적절한 곳은? 문장 삽입

> 우리는 이러한 해결책들을 도전과제에 상응하는 규모로 구축해야 한다.

① [A]　　　　　　　　② [B]
③ [C]　　　　　　　　✓ [D]
⑤ [E]

| 분석 | 주어진 문장 이후로는 저자가 제시하는 해결책들이 언급될 것을 추론할 수 있다. 본문의 마지막 두 문장이 그 해결책이므로 주어진 문장은 [D]에 삽입해야 한다.

[06-07] 2013 한양대

| 정답 | 06 ② 07 ①

| 어휘 | Antarctica ⓝ 남극대륙　　　　ice pack ⓝ 얼음덩어리　　　　radio wave ⓝ (통신) 전파, 전자파
ice sheet ⓝ 빙상, 대륙빙　　　insulating ⓐ 절연[단열]을 위한　　glaciologist ⓝ 빙하학자, 빙하 연구가
geothermal ⓐ 지구 열학의, 지열의　microbe ⓝ 세균, 미생물　　　contamination ⓝ 오염

전문해석

몇몇 과학자들이 남극대륙의 표면을 탐험하는 동안, 다른 과학자들은 얼음덩어리 4킬로미터 아래에 있는 거대한 물웅덩이에 대해 더 많이 연구하고 있다. 과학자들은 얼음을 관통하는 전파를 사용하여 1970년대에 보스톡 호수를 처음 발견했다. 그 이후로 과학자들은 음파와 심지어 위성을 사용하여 이 거대한 물웅덩이(14,000제곱킬로미터)의 지도를 그렸다. 어떻게 보스톡 호수의 물은 얼음층 아래에서 액체로 남아 있을 수 있을까? 영국 웨일스 대학의 빙하학자인 마틴 시거트(Martin Siegert)는 위의 두꺼운 빙하가 단열 담요와 같은 역할을 해서 물이 얼지 않도록 한다고 말한다. 게다가, 지구 깊은 곳에서 오는 지열은 숨겨진 호수를 따뜻하게 할 수도 있다. 과학자들은 미생물들이 2백만 년 이상 외부 세계와 차단된 보스톡 호수에 살고 있을지도 모른다고 추측한다. 그곳에서 발견된 모든 것은 지구 표면에 있는 것과는 완전히 이질적일 것이라고 시거트는 말한다. 과학자들은 얼음에 구멍을 내고 오염을 일으키지 않고 물 샘플을 채취할 수 있는 방법을 찾으려고 노력하고 있다. 다시, 로봇이 해결책이 될 수 있을지도 모른다. 만약 모든 것이 계획대로 진행된다면, 드릴 모양의 크라이오로봇('cryo'는 추위를 의미한다)이 표면 얼음을 관통해 녹일 것이다. 그것(로봇)이 호수에 도착하면, 그것은 호수에서 수영하고, 사진을 찍고, 생명의 흔적을 찾을 수 있는 하이드로로봇('hydro'는 물을 의미한다)을 방출할 것이다.

06 윗글의 내용과 일치하지 않는 것은? 내용 불일치

① 로봇은 오염 없이 호수에서 물 샘플을 채취하는 데 사용될 수 있다.
✓ 과학자들은 1970년대에 음파를 이용하여 보스톡 호수를 발견할 수 있었다.
③ 보스톡 호수의 물은 2백만 년 이상 외부에 노출되지 않았다.
④ 두꺼운 빙하와 지구의 지열 때문에 보스톡의 물이 얼지 않았다.

| 분석 | 본문 2번째 문장에서 과학자들은 1970년대에 '전파'를 사용하여 보스톡 호수를 처음 발견했다. 따라서 보기 ②는 내용과 일치하지 않는다.

07 윗글의 빈칸에 들어갈 말로 가장 적절한 것은? 빈칸 추론

✓ ① 이질적인
② 친숙한
③ 유사한
④ 위험한

| 분석 | 빈칸이 포함된 문장의 직전 문장에서 '과학자들은 미생물들이 2백만 년 이상 외부 세계와 차단된 보스톡 호수에 살고 있을지도 모른다고 추측'한다. 보스톡 호수에서 발견된 모든 것은 지구 표면에 있는 것과 완전히 '다르거나 차이가 있을' 것이다. 따라서 보기 ①이 빈칸에 가장 적절하다.

[08-09] 2015 성균관대

| 정답 | 08 ② 09 ⑤

| 어휘 |
celtic ⓐ 켈트의, 켈트족의
scrawny ⓐ 야윈, 앙상한
enforcer ⓝ 집행자
insomnia ⓝ 불면증
hefty ⓐ 무거운, 크고 건장한
unchecked ⓐ 저지되지 않은, 억제되지 않은
tab ⓝ 색인표, 식별표
repeal ⓥ 무효로 하다, 폐지하다

전문해석

그들은 스코틀랜드에서 양을 세고 있고 그것은 켈트족의 불면증이 발생했기 때문이 아니다. 지난 수십 년 동안, 연구원들은 스코틀랜드 서부 해안에서 떨어진 세인트킬다 군도에 있는 야생 소이 양을 면밀히 관찰해 왔다. 최근 그들은 이상한 것을 발견했다: 소이 양들의 덩치가 작아졌다는 것이다. 일반적으로 덩치가 큰 것이 양들에게는 좋은 것이라서 이것은 놀라웠다. 그들은 비옥하고 햇볕이 잘 드는 여름 동안 풀을 먹고 살을 찌운다. 혹독한 스코틀랜드의 겨울이 오면, 풀은 사라지고, 가장 작고 마른 양들은 봄에 더 덩치가 크고 건강한 사촌들이 살아남아 번식하는 동안 죽는 경향이 있다.

하지만 런던 임페리얼 대학의 팀 콜슨(Tim Coulson)이 이끈 새로운 연구에 따르면, 불과 25년 만에, 소이 양들은 평균적으로 5% 작아졌다. 그것은 스코틀랜드에서 진화가 무효가 된 것은 아니다. 오히려 지구 온난화가 단지 더 작고, 덜 건강한 소이 양들이 생존하기 쉽게 만들었기 때문이다. 그리고 많은 다른 종들도 비슷한 방식으로 변화하는 기후에 빠르게 적응하고 있다. 한 예측에 따르면, 만약 이대로 방치한다면 21세기 중반까지 전 세계 종의 3분의 1가량을 위협할 수도 있는 지구 온난화가 다윈(진화론)의 새로운 집행자로 떠오르고 있는 것 같다. "우리는 분명히 기후 변화와 관련된 진화론적 변화를 보고 있습니다."라고 토론토 대학의 진화 생물학자인 아서 와이스(Arthur Weis)는 말한다.

08 소이 양의 체중 감소는 _____ 에 의해 발생했다. 세부 내용 일치

① 그들의 불면증
✓ ② 지구 온난화
③ 풀 부족
④ 진화적 변이
⑤ 병의 확산

| 분석 | 본문 2번째 단락의 2번째 문장에서 '지구 온난화가 단지 더 작고, 덜 건강한 소이 양들이 생존하기 쉽게 만들었기 때문'이라는 것이 연구를 통해 밝혀졌다. 따라서 보기 ②가 정답으로 가장 적절하다.

09 야생 소이 양의 경우 "_____"의 아이디어를 지지한다. 세부 내용 일치

① 멸종 위기에 처한 종
② 녹색 혁명
③ 나비 효과
④ 상대성 이론
✓ ⑤ 적자생존

| 분석 | 본문 2번째 단락의 4번째 문장에 따르면 야생 소이 양의 체구를 줄어들게 한 지구 온난화가 '다윈의 새로운 집행자'라고 했다. 다윈 이론은 '진화론'을 의미하며 진화론의 핵심은 '적자생존'이다. '적자생존'이란 환경에 가장 잘 적응하는 생물이나 집단이 살아남는다는 의미를 가진 문구인데 이것이 지구 온난화 상황에서 체구를 줄여 생존한 야생 소이 양의 사례로 증명되었다. 따라서 보기 ⑤가 정답으로 가장 적절하다.

| 배경지식 | 진화론(Evolution): 생물은 진화하는 것이라는 주장으로 1895년에 영국의 생물학자 다윈이 '종의기원'에서 체계화함

[10-11] 2014 홍익대

| 정답 | 10 ④　11 ③

| 어휘 |
swarm ⓝ 떼, 무리　　　　　clog ⓝ 방해물, 장애물　　　　incident ⓝ 사건, 생긴 일
culprit ⓝ 죄인, 범죄자, 피의자　run off 흘러 넘치다　　　　fertiliser ⓝ 비료
desalination ⓝ (바닷물의) 염분 제거, 담수화　　　　　　　fatal ⓐ 치명적인, 생명에 관계되는
take a dip 수영하다　　　　fleet ⓝ 함대　　　　　　　　mush ⓝ 곤죽(같은 덩어리나 반죽)
boom ⓝ (돛의) 아래 활대　　thruster ⓝ (특히 항공기의) 반동 추진 엔진

| 전문해석 |
이달 초 스웨덴의 오스카르스함에 위치한 한 원자력 발전소는, 해파리 떼가 발트해에서 냉각수를 빼내기 위해 사용하는 파이프를 막아서 가동을 멈추어야만 했다. 전 세계 해파리 개체수가 증가하고 있기 때문에 이러한 사건들은 점점 더 흔해지고 있다. 어떤 이들은 기후 변화를 탓한다. 어떤 이들은 해파리를 잡아먹는 종들을 제거하고 먹이에 대한 경쟁을 감소시키는 어류 남획을 탓한다. 어떤 이들은 해파리가 영양분이 많고 산소가 부족한 물에서 진짜 물고기보다 경쟁력이 있기 때문에 비료가 바다로 유출되는 것이 원인이라고 생각한다.
11 ③
이유가 무엇이든지 간에, (그리고 모든 이유가 기여할 수도 있다), 그것들은 발전소에 영향을 미칠 뿐만 아니라 담수화 발전소를 파괴시키고, 어부들을 방해하며, 때때로 치명적인 결과—해변에서 물속에 들어가는 사람들을 쏘는 것—를 초래하기도 한다. 어선을 사용해 해파리를 그물로 걷어내고 제거하는 것은 가능하지만 느리고 비용이 많이 든다. 대전에 있는 한국고등과학기술원의 명현(Myung Hyun) 박사는 더 나은 답이 있다고 생각한다: 해파리를 ⓐ 곤죽으로 만드는 킬러 로봇 함대를 사용하는 것이다. 명 박사와 그의 동료들은 한국의 해안에서 그들의 해파리 사냥 로봇들로 일련의 실험을 해 왔다. 그 기계들은 추진기에 의해 물을 통해 추진되는 한 쌍의 활대 위에서 떠다닌다. 그것들은 선두 로봇을 따르고 대형을 이뤄 함께 작업하도록 설계되었다.

10 ⓐ의 단어를 대체할 수 있는 것은 어느 것인가? | 밑줄 추론 |
① 끈적끈적한 것
② 가혹한 것
③ 살아 있는 것
☑ ④ 부드러운 것

| 분석 | 밑줄 친 ⓐ의 mush는 '곤죽같이 흐물거리는 덩어리나 반죽'을 의미한다. 따라서 보기 ④가 정답으로 가장 적절하다.

11	윗글에 따르면, 다음 중 사실이 <u>아닌</u> 것은? 내용 불일치

① 남획은 해파리를 먹는 종의 수가 줄어드는 결과를 초래한다.
② 해파리 떼는 원자력 발전소나 담수화 발전소뿐만 아니라 해변에 있는 사람들에게도 위험을 노출시킬 수 있다.
✓③ 해파리 개체수가 증가한 것은 기후 변화 때문이다.
④ 한국의 과학자들이 그물을 사용하지 않고 해파리를 죽이는 로봇을 고안했다.

| 분석 | 본문 첫 단락에서 해파리의 개체 수 증가에 대해 제기되는 여러 가지 원인 중 기후 변화가 언급된다. 하지만 여러 원인 중 하나의 가정일 뿐 사실로 언급하지 않았으므로 보기 ③은 사실이 아니다.

[12-13] 2011 한국외대

| 정답 | 12 ③   13 ④

| 어휘 | cliff swallow 삼색제비(북아메리카산)   rock ⓥ 흔들리다, 흔들다   back and forth 전후로, 앞뒤로
well-documented ⓐ 문서[기록]로 충분히 입증된   scout ⓝ 정찰(병)
whereabouts ⓝ 소재, 행방   scent ⓝ 냄새, 향기   waggle ⓥ 흔들리다, 흔들다
waggle dance (꿀벌의) 8자 춤(꿀벌이 꽃 등의 방향과 거리를 동료에게 알리는 동작)
extraordinary ⓐ 대단한, 비상한, 보통이 아닌   precise ⓐ 정밀한, 정확한

전문해석

생물학자 찰스 브라운(Charles Brown)은 몇몇 새들이 실제로 먹이를 찾으러 어디로 가야 하는지 배울 수 있는 "정보 센터(information center)"를 설립한다는 사실을 발견했다. 몇 년 동안 네브래스카의 평원에서 삼색제비를 관찰하면서, 그는 먹이 사냥을 마치고 둥지로 돌아온 새들이 사냥이 성공하면 "(몸을) 앞뒤로 흔든다"는 것에 주목했다. 더 많은 먹이를 찾기 위해 둥지를 떠날 때, 그들의 몸짓이 성공을 나타낼 때만 다른 새들이 따라갔다.
하지만 이 새 춤은 잘 문서화된(이미 많이 연구된) 꿀벌의 춤과는 거의 비교가 되지 않는다. 정찰병들이 음식의 출처를 찾으면, 그들은 벌집으로 돌아와 다른 벌들에게 그것의 위치를 알려 준다. 그들의 냄새는 그들이 찾은 것을 표시한다. 그들의 춤은 방향과 더 많은 것을 알려 준다. 만약 음식이 근처에 있다면, 그들은 "둥근 춤"을 추는데, 이것은 단순히 발견 사실을 알려 준다. 음식의 위치가 멀리 떨어져 있을 때, 그들은 "8자 춤"을 춘다. 8자 춤은 세부적인 면에서 특이하다. 그 움직임은 다른 벌들에게 얼마나 음식이 멀리 있는지, 그것의 정확한 위치, 그리고 심지어 그것이 얼마나 많이 있는지를 말해 준다.

12	다음 중 윗글의 제목으로 가장 좋은 것은 무엇인가? 제목

① 새의 춤
② 정보 센터
✓③ 동물의 의사소통
④ 벌 춤의 두 가지 유형

| 분석 | 본문에서는 새와 꿀벌이 춤을 활용하여 먹이의 존재, 위치, 양 등을 주변에 알린다고 서술했다. 따라서 보기 ③이 제목으로 가장 적절하다.

13 다음 중 윗글에 따르면 사실에 해당하지 <u>않는</u> 것은? 내용 불일치

① 어떤 새들은 먹이 사냥이 성공적일 때 춤을 춘다.
② 꿀벌들은 먹이가 멀리 위치해 있다는 것을 나타내기 위해 몸을 흔든다.
③ 춤을 통해 꿀벌들은 그들이 찾은 음식의 양을 보여 줄 수 있다.
✔ ④ 삼색제비는 먹이를 찾기 위해 둥지를 떠날 때 떼 지어 날아간다.

| 분석 | 본문 첫 단락의 마지막 문장을 통해 삼색제비가 몸짓으로 사냥의 성공을 보여 주면 다른 새들이 따라간다는 것은 알 수 있지만 사냥할 때 무리를 이룬다는 것은 언급하지 않았다. 따라서 ④는 사실이 아니다.

[14-15] 2015 한양대

| 정답 | 14 ②   15 ①

| 어휘 |
extinction ⑪ 멸종
stratum ⑪ 층, 지층 (pl. strata)
iridium ⑪ 이리듐(금속 원소)
astral body 별, 천체
deluge ⑪ 쇄도, 범람
blockage ⑪ 봉쇄, 방해

dinosaur ⑪ 공룡
stellar ⓐ 별의, 별 같은
discount ⓥ 무시하다; 할인하다
suspend ⓥ 매달다, (공중에) 떠 있게 하다
asteroid ⑪ 소행성
food chain ⑪ 먹이사슬

adjacent ⓐ 접근한, 인접한
deposition ⑪ 퇴적, 퇴적물
radioactive isotope 방사성 동위 원소
fallout ⑪ 방사성 낙진
stratosphere ⑪ 성층권

전문해석

과학자들은 지구 기후의 점진적인 변화가 공룡들의 멸종을 일으켰다고 오랫동안 믿었다. 그러나 1979년, 버클리 대학의 한 연구팀이 이탈리아에서 공룡이 사라진 즈음의 점토층을 발견했는데, 인접한 지층에 있는 점토보다 이리듐 수치가 약 30배 더 높았다. 이리듐은 시간이 지나면서 (지층에) 꽤 균일하게 분포하고 그 기원이 외계이기 때문에, 연구자들은 이 점토의 높은 이리듐 수치가 갑작스러운 재앙적인 사건으로부터 비롯되었음이 틀림없다고 결론 내렸다. 과학자들은 이 사건의 정확한 본질에 대해 의견이 다르다. 특정 방사성 동위 원소가 점토에 거의 없기 때문에 항성 폭발이 퇴적을 일으켰을 가능성은 희박해졌다. 만약 이 물질이 태양계 내에서 기원했다면, 지구는 이리듐이 풍부한 물질을 전 세계에 분포시킬 수 있을 만큼 충분히 큰 천체와 충돌했음이 틀림없을 것이다. 그러한 거대한 물체의 충돌에 대한 지질학적 증거는 없지만, 그리브(Grive)는 대기 폭발 이후에 낙진으로부터 점토층이 자리잡을 수 있다고 주장한다. 카이트(Kyte)는 지구의 중력장에 의해 파괴된 혜성이 주요 분화구를 만들지 않고 떨어지는 (혜성) 잔해들의 홍수를 만들어 냈을 것이라고 주장한다. 버클리 대학의 연구팀은 소행성이 바다에 떨어졌을 수도 있다고 제안한다. <mark>사건의 종류가 무엇이든, 버클리 연구팀은 그것이 광대한 물질의 구름을 성층권에 정지시킴으로써 지구의 생태계를 방해했다고 주장한다. 햇빛의 차단이 광합성을 방해하여 전 세계 먹이 사슬의 기초에 거대한 혼란을 일으켰기 때문에 충격의 영향은 증가했을 것이다.</mark>
15 ①

14 저자의 의도로 가장 적절한 것은? 목적

① 전통적인 가정을 반박하기
✔ ② 발견의 의미에 대해 논의하기
③ 새로운 연구 방향 제시하기
④ 다양한 이론을 요약하고 평가하기

| 분석 | 본문은 공룡의 멸종을 '이리듐 수치'와 관련시킨 버클리 대학의 연구를 소개한다. 본문에서는 이 연구의 발견에 대해 논의하고 있으므로 보기 ②가 정답으로 가장 적절하다.

15 "The Berkely Group"의 주장을 뒷받침할 수 있는 근거로 가장 알맞은 것은? 세부 내용 일치

✓① 이탈리아에서 연구된 점토층 위의 지층에서 식물 화석 수 감소
② 이탈리아의 이리듐이 풍부한 점토층보다 오래된 지층에서 발견된 공룡 화석
③ 스페인의 점토층 위와 아래의 암석에서 높은 수준의 이리듐 발견
④ 혜성이 지구와 충돌할 가능성에 대한 과학자들 간의 의견 일치의 진전

| 분석 | 본문 마지막 문장에서 알 수 있듯이 혜성의 충돌과 폭발로 인해 성층권에서 햇빛이 차단되고 광합성을 방해했으므로 식물이 광합성에 실패하고 개체 수가 줄었을 것이다. 그렇다면 폭발 이후의 지층에서는 식물의 화석 수가 감소되었을 것임을 추론할 수 있다. 따라서 보기 ①이 정답이다.

[16-18] 2016 한국외대

| 정답 | 16 ② 17 ③ 18 ③

| 어휘 |
bay ⓝ 만, 산으로 삼면이 둘러싸인 평지
pier ⓝ 부두
abyssal ⓐ 심해의, 심해에 사는
ashore ⓐⓓ 해변으로
iridescent ⓐ 번뜩이는, 무지갯빛의
mosey ⓥ 배회하다, 방황하다

giant squid ⓝ 대왕오징어(심해에 살며 몸길이가 최대 20m까지 되는 연체동물)
juvenile ⓐ 젊은, 어린
feast ⓥ 대접하다, 진수성찬을 먹다
tangle ⓥ 엉키게 하다
lure ⓝ 미끼
recede ⓥ 물러나다, 퇴각하다

specimen ⓝ 견본, 표본
sperm whale 향유고래
wrangle ⓥ 말다툼하다, 다투다, 논쟁하다
unaccustomed ⓐ 익숙하지[숙달되지] 않은

전문해석

일본 도야마 만에서, 바다를 내려다보는 부두에서 빈둥거리는 방문객들은 12피트 길이의 홍백 대왕오징어 한 마리와 마주쳤다. 그것의 거대한 크기에도 불구하고, 이 대왕오징어는 어린 오징어였다. 죽은 표본은 (몸길이가) 43피트까지 측정되었다. 대왕오징어는 심해에서 평생을 보낸다. 이 거대하고 고독한 포식자들은 심해의 다른 물고기나 오징어를 먹어 치우고, 심해의 어둠 속에서 거대한 해양 동물들의 큰 전투로 전개되어야 하는 곳에서는 향유고래의 먹이가 되기도 한다. 그것들은 수 세기 동안 죽은 채로 해변으로 떠밀려오거나 어부들의 그물에 엉켜 죽은 채로 발견되었지만, 그전에는 단지 두 번 살아 있는 채로 화면에 포착되었다. 2004년, 연구자들은 살아 있는 대왕오징어의 첫 사진들을 찍었고, 2012년, 한 탐험대는 최초로 살아 있는 거대 오징어를 촬영했다. 그것은 바다 표면 수천 피트 아래에서 그들(탐사대)의 무지갯빛 미끼와 다투고 있었다. 그러나 도야마 만 방문객의 비디오는 지금까지 살아 있는 대왕오징어를 가장 상세하고 가깝게 촬영한 것이다. 그 동물은 기무라 아키노부(Akinobu Kimura)에 의해 수중 카메라로 촬영되었다. 인간의 상호 작용에 익숙하지 않은 거대한 포식자가 그의 존재에 어떻게 반응할지 알 수 있는 방법이 없다는 것을 고려할 때, 이것(수중 카메라 촬영)은 ⓐ 대담하거나 어리석은 행동이었다. 어린 대왕오징어는 분명히 심해로 후퇴하기 전에 그 만에서 두 시간 동안 어슬렁거렸다.

---

16 다음 중 ⓐ가 의미하는 것은? 밑줄 추론

① 기무라는 자신의 행동방침에 대해 결정을 내리지 못했다.
✓② 그 동물은 기무라를 먹을지도 모른다.
③ 포식자는 도망치고 싶어 할 수도 있다.
④ 위험한 저류가 있을 수 있다.

| 분석 | 밑줄 친 표현이 포함된 문장에서 대왕오징어는 '인간의 상호 작용에 익숙하지 않다'는 내용을 고려한다면 기무라가 수중촬영을 한 것은 대왕오징어의 공격을 받을 수도 있는 행동이었을 것이다. 따라서 보기 ②가 정답으로 가장 적절하다.

17 다음 중 윗글에 명시되거나 암시되지 <u>않은</u> 것은? 내용 불일치 / 내용 비추론

① 향유고래는 대왕오징어와 싸운다.
② 오징어는 빛나는 물체에 이끌린다.
✓ ③ 오징어는 향유고래만을 사냥한다.
④ 도야마 만의 오징어는 완전히 성숙하지 않았다.

| 분석 | 본문 5번째 문장에서 대왕오징어는 향유고래의 먹이가 되기도 하므로 ①은 틀린 진술이다.

18 윗글에 따르면 대왕오징어는 _____. 세부 내용 일치

① 구경꾼들을 자주 즐겁게 한다.
② 깊은 바다에서 해초를 먹는다.
✓ ③ 보통 죽은 채로 발견된다.
④ 일반적으로 수면 근처에서 사냥을 한다.

| 분석 | 본문에서 대왕오징어는 단지 두 번 살아 있는 상태로 화면에 포착되었고 수 세기 동안 죽은 채로 발견되었다. 따라서 보기 ③이 정답으로 적절하다.

[19-21] 2013 성균관대

| 정답 | 19 ⑤ 20 ③ 21 ⑤

| 어휘 |
smart ⓝ 지능, 지성
dabble ⓥ 조금 해 보다, 잠깐 손대다
mollusk ⓝ 연체동물
adept ⓐ 숙련된, 익숙한
rook ⓝ (유럽산) 떼까마귀
tale ⓝ 이야기, 설화

higher thinking 고차원적 사고
smash ⓥ 분쇄하다, 박살내다
corvid ⓝ 까마귀(과)
hook ⓝ 갈고리, 걸쇠
pitcher ⓝ 물 주전자
feat ⓝ 업적, 묘기, 재주

cerebral cortex 대뇌피질
otter ⓝ 수달
jay ⓝ 어치
aptly ⓐⓓ 적절하게
what's more 더욱이, 게다가

전문해석

뇌의 크기는 확실히 지능과 어느 정도 관련이 있지만, 뇌의 구조로부터 훨씬 더 많은 것들을 알 수 있다. <mark>고차원적 사고는 뇌의 가장 진화된 영역이며, 많은 동물들에게는 부족한 대뇌피질에서 발생한다. 포유류는 대뇌피질을 가졌고, 원칙적으로, 그 뇌의 영역(대뇌피질)이 더 크고 복잡할수록, 그 동물은 더 똑똑해진다.</mark> 그러나 그것이 창의적인 사고를 위한 유일한 길은 아니다. 도구 사용을 생각해 보자. 인간은 도구를 가진 마술사이고, 유인원은 그것들을 만지며, 수달은 속에 있는 고기를 먹기 위해 돌로 연체동물(조개)을 깨부수는—원시적이긴 하지만 중요한—일에 숙달했다. 하지만 창의성이 대뇌피질 속에 있다면, 왜 까마귀와 어치를 포함한 새 종류인 까마귓과 동물들이 거의 모든 비인간종보다 더 도구를 잘 사용하는 것일까? ^{19⑤}

예를 들어, 까마귀들은 플라스틱 관의 바닥에 있는 음식 바구니를 낚시하기 위해서 고리를 만들기 위해 철사를 구부리는 데 능숙하다는 것을 증명했다. 더 놀라운 것은, 작년에 케임브리지 대학의 동물학자인—적절한 이름을 가진—크리스토퍼 버드(Christopher Bird)는 까마귓과의 일원인 그 떼까마귀가 물을 마실 수 있을 정도로 수위를 높이기 위해 물이 부분적으로 채워진 물 주전자 속에 돌을 떨어뜨리는 방법을 추론할 수 있다는 것을 발견했다. <u>더욱이</u>, 그것들이 수위를 더 빨리 올릴 것이라는 것을 분명히 깨달으면서, 그 떼까마귀들은 가장 큰 돌들을 먼저 선택했다. 이솝은 2,500년 전에 그런 일을 해낸 새에 대한 이야기를 썼지만, 21세기 과학자들은 그 (새의) 재주가 우화가 아니라는 것을 보여 주었다.

19 윗글에 따르면, 많은 동물들은 _____ 때문에 똑똑하지 않다고 한다. 세부 내용 일치

① 검소한 생활을 하기
② 머리가 매우 작기
③ 도구를 사용할 필요가 없었기
④ 두뇌를 사용하는 훈련을 받은 적이 없기
✓ ⑤ 대뇌피질이 없기

| 분석 | 본문의 두 번째 문장에서 '고차원적 사고는 뇌의 가장 진화된 영역이며, 많은 동물들에게는 부족한 대뇌피질에서 발생한다'고 했다. 많은 동물들이 똑똑하지 않은 이유는 '대뇌피질'과 관련이 있을 것이다. 보기 ⑤가 정답으로 가장 적절하다.

20 빈칸에 가장 적합한 것은 무엇인가? 빈칸 추론

① 반대로
② 그럼에도 불구하고
✓ ③ 더욱이
④ 아이러니컬하게도
⑤ 한편으로

| 분석 | 빈칸 앞 문장에서 떼까마귀들의 도구 사용 능력을 언급했는데 빈칸 뒤로는 그들의 더 고차원적인 추론을 소개했다. 빈칸을 기준으로 앞뒤 내용이 순접으로 연결되며 빈칸 앞보다 고차원적 능력이 언급된 빈칸 뒤 문장을 강조한다면 보기 ③이 정답으로 가장 적절하다.

21 밑줄 친 "재주"는 무엇을 의미하는가? 밑줄 추론

① 동물의 언어 사용
② 수달의 암석 사용
③ 침팬지의 수화 숙달
④ 크리스토퍼 버드의 추론
✓ ⑤ 새들의 목표 달성을 위한 도구 사용

| 분석 | 밑줄 친 부분이 포함된 문장에서는 새의 도구를 사용하는 능력이 사실임을 서술했다. 따라서 밑줄 친 부분은 '새의 재주'나 '새의 도구 사용의 재주'를 지칭할 것이다. 보기 ⑤가 정답으로 가장 적절하다.

[22-24] 2019 성균관대

| 정답 | 22 ③ 23 ① 24 ④

| 어휘 |
per capita ⓐ 1인당의, 머릿수로 나눈
substantial ⓐ 실질적인, 상당한
surpass ⓥ 능가하다, 초월하다
curtailment ⓝ 삭감, 축소
disaster ⓝ 재해, 재난, 참사
carbon dioxide ⓝ 이산화탄소
pledge ⓥ 약속하다, 서약하다
conceivably ⓐⓓ 생각해 보면
catastrophe ⓝ 파국, 대재앙
greenhouse gas ⓝ 온실가스
stride ⓝ 큰 걸음, 진전, 발달
offset ⓥ 상쇄하다, 보완하다
renewable ⓐ 재생 가능한

전문해석

수년 동안, 온실가스의 최대 배출국인 중국과 1인당 최대 배출 국가 중 하나인 미국의 역할에 관심이 집중되어 왔다. 2014년 11월, 두 나라는 처음으로 온실가스 배출에 대한 실질적인 제한을 약속했다. 중국은 2030년 이후 이산화탄소 배출량이 감소할 것이라고 약속한 반면, 미국은 거의 비슷한 시기에 배출량을 4분의 1 이상 줄이겠다고 단언했다. 실제로, 중국의 배출량은 지난 1년 동안 너무 빨리 감소하여 많은 사람들은 중국이 약속한 기간 이전에 그 목표를 달성할지도 모른다고 믿는데, 이것은 지금까지 기후 변화에 대항하는 투쟁에서 가장 큰 진전이다.

<u>대조적으로</u>, 인도의 탄소 배출량은 다른 어떤 나라의 탄소 배출량보다 빠르게 증가하고 있다. 이러한 추세가 계속된다면—그리고 그렇게 될 것이라고 생각할 만한 이유가 있다—<u>인도가 25년 안에 중국을 제치고 세계 최대의 배출국이 될 수도 있을 것이다</u>. 생각해 보면, 인도의 증가하는 배출량은 나머지 전 세계 국가들의 감축 노력을 모두 상쇄하여 재앙으로 이어질 수도 있다. "인도는 가장 큰 퍼즐 조각입니다."라고 시에라 클럽의 국제 기후 캠페인 책임자인 존 코에퀴트(John Coequyt)가 말한다. "이러한 급속한 성장이 빨리 일어나서 이전에 사용되었던 것보다 더 많은 재생 가능한 에너지를 사용하여 사람들을 빈곤에서 벗어나게 할 방법이 있을까요? 그렇지 않으면 그들은 (대기)오염의 통제가 거의 없는 상태에서 <u>그들이 가진 것</u>을 더 많이 만들까요?" 물론 후자는 "모두에게 재앙"이 될 것이라고 그는 말한다.

22 ③

---

22 윗글에 따르면 _____. 세부 내용 일치

① 중국은 미국과의 약속을 지키기를 꺼린다
② 미국은 중국이 세계적인 규칙을 따르도록 압박했다
✓ ③ 인도는 최대 가스 배출국이 될 것이다
④ 미국은 중국과 경쟁해야만 했다
⑤ 인도는 중국의 방식을 따를 것이다

| 분석 | 본문 2번째 단락의 2번째 문장에 따르면 '인도가 25년 안에 중국을 제치고 세계 최대의 배출국이 될 수도 있을 것이다'라고 했다. 따라서 보기 ③은 추론 가능하다.

---

23 빈칸에 가장 적합한 표현은 _____ 이다. 빈칸 추론

✓ ① 대조적으로   ② 그러나
③ 한편으로는   ④ 사실상
⑤ 그런데

| 분석 | 본문 첫 단락에서는 탄소 배출량 감소에 성공한 중국이 소개되고, 빈칸으로 시작되는 2번째 단락에는 빠르게 증가하는 인도의 탄소 배출량을 언급했다. 두 국가의 상황은 대조적이므로 연결표현 중 보기 ①이 정답으로 가장 적절하다.

---

24 어떤 것이 "그들이 가진 것"의 예가 될 것인가? 밑줄 추론

① 태양 에너지
② 풍력 에너지
③ 수소 에너지
✓ ④ 석탄 발전소
⑤ 삼림재건 계획

| 분석 | 밑줄 친 부분에서 'they'는 '인도인'들을 지칭한다. '인도인들이 가진 것'이 다음 문장에서 언급한 '모두에게 재앙'을 일으킨다면 그 재앙은 '탄소 배출량 증가로 인한 재앙'임을 알 수 있다. 따라서 '인도인들이 가진 것'은 탄소 배출량을 증가시키는 것이어야 하며 보기 ④가 정답으로 가장 적절하다.

[25-28] 2020 세종대

| 정답 | 25 ④ 26 ② 27 ④ 28 ④

| 어휘 |
entomologist ⓝ 곤충학자
associate ⓝ 동료 한패, 친구
strike out (방법을) 생각해 내다, (새로운 길을) 개척하다
pursue ⓥ 추적하다, 추구하다
will-o'-the-wisp ⓝ 유령, 도깨비불
toxic ⓐ 독성의 유독한
chemical ⓝ 화학제품, 화학약품
recognize ⓥ 알아보다, 인정하다, 인식하다
ally ⓝ 동맹, 협력자
devise ⓥ 고안하다, 궁리하다
insecticide ⓝ 살충제
dosage ⓝ 투약, 조제; (약의 1회분) 복용[투약]량
pest ⓝ 해충
beneficial ⓐ 유익한, 이익을 가져오는
proper ⓐ 적당한, 타당한
orchardist ⓝ 과수 재배자, 과수원 경영자
proportion ⓝ 비율; 조화, 균형
substantially ⓐⓓ 실체상
do violence to ~을 범하다, ~을 위반하다
abandon ⓥ (계획·습관 등을) 단념하다, 그만두다
attitude ⓝ 태도
superiority ⓝ 우월, 우위, 탁월
organism ⓝ 유기체, 생물
economical ⓐ 경제적인

전문해석

캐나다의 곤충학자인 피켓(Pickett) 박사와 그의 동료들은 독성이 갈수록 더 강해지는 화학물질이라는 도깨비불을 계속 추구하는 다른 곤충학자들과 어울리는 것 대신 새로운 길을 개척했다. 자연에 강한 협력자가 있다고 인식한 그들은 자연이 가진 통제력을 최대한 활용하고 살충제를 최소한으로 사용하는 프로그램을 고안했다. 이 프로그램은 살충제를 살포할 때마다 최소량만을, 즉 이로운 종에게 피할 수 있는 해를 입히지 않으면서 해충을 간신히 박멸할 수 있는 만큼만 사용하는 것이다. 적절한 타이밍 또한 포함된다. 28 ④ [B] 〈따라서 만약에 사과꽃이 분홍색으로 변한 후가 아니라 전에 니코틴 황산염을 살포하게 되면, 중요한 약탈자 중 하나를 살려 주게 되는데, 이는 그것이 아직 알 속에 있는 단계이기 때문일 것이다.〉 이 프로그램은 얼마나 효과가 있었는가? 피켓 박사의 Ⓐ 완화된 살충제 살포 프로그램을 따르고 있는 노바스코샤의 과수업자들은 Ⓑ 강한 화학약품을 살포하는 방법을 사용하고 있는 사람들만큼 높은 비율로 1등급 과일을 생산했다. 그리고 또한 그들은 많은 생산량도 얻었다. 게다가, 그들은 상당히 더 저렴한 비용으로 이 같은 결과를 얻고 있다. 이런 훌륭한 결과보다 중요한 것은 피켓 박사의 프로그램이 자연의 균형에 해를 끼치지 않고 있다는 사실이다. 그것은 G. C. 울리에트(G. C. Ullyett)가 10년 전에 이야기했던 철학을 잘 실현해 나아가는 중에 있다. 울리에트는 "우리는 우리가 가진 철학을 바꿔야 하고 인간이 우월하다는 태도를 버려야 하며, 우리 스스로 할 수 있는 것보다 더 경제적인 방법으로 유기체의 개체를 제한하는 방법을 자연환경의 여러 경우에서 찾아볼 수 있다는 것을 인정해야 합니다."라고 말했다.

25 다음 중 빈칸 Ⓐ와 Ⓑ에 들어가기에 가장 적절한 것은? 빈칸 추론

① 비옥한 – 탄력있는
② 다양하지 않은 – 다양한
③ 사려 깊지 않은 – 사려깊은
✓ ④ 완화된 – 강한

| 분석 | 빈칸 앞에서 살충제를 최소한으로 사용한다고 하였다. 따라서 빈칸 Ⓐ에는 '수정된', '완화된'의 의미를 갖는 'modified'가 적절하다. 빈칸 Ⓑ에는 피켓 박사의 완화된 살충제 살포 방법을 따르는 과수업자들과 그렇지 않은 사람들을 비교하므로 '완화된'의 반대말이 와야 한다. 따라서 빈칸 Ⓑ에는 '강한'의 의미인 'intense'가 적절하다.

26 아래 문장의 가장 적절한 위치는 어디인가? 문장 삽입

> 따라서 만약에 사과꽃이 분홍색으로 변한 후가 아니라 전에 니코틴 황산염을 살포하게 되면, 중요한 약탈자 중 하나를 살려 주게 되는데, 이는 그것이 아직 알 속에 있는 단계이기 때문일 것이다.

① [A]   ✓② [B]
③ [C]   ④ [D]

| 분석 | 주어진 문장을 요약하면 '살충제를 적절한 시기에 살포해야 한다'는 내용이다. 이와 관련된 재진술 부분을 찾아보면 [B]의 앞 문장의 "Proper timing also enters in."이라고 볼 수 있다. 따라서 주어진 문장의 적절한 위치는 [B]이다.

27 피켓 박사의 프로그램에서 살충제를 살포하는 데 가장 중요한 두 가지 요소는 무엇인가? 내용 파악

① 최대한의 양과 적절한 타이밍
② 적절한 양과 빠른 타이밍
③ 충분한 양과 빠른 타이밍
✓④ 최소한의 양과 적절한 타이밍

| 분석 | 첫 번째 단락에서 피켓 박사는 '이로운 종에게는 해를 가하지 않으면서 해충만을 간신히 박멸할 수 있는 양'이라고 하였으며 이어진 문장에서 '적절한 시기'도 중요하다고 하였다. 따라서 피켓 박사 프로그램의 가장 중요한 두 요소는 ④ '최소의 양과 적절한 타이밍'이다.

28 다음 중 윗글로부터 추론할 수 없는 것은? 내용 추론

① 피켓 박사와 그의 동료들은 자연에 강력한 우군이 있다고 믿었다.
② 피켓 박사의 프로그램이 가진 장점 중 하나는 더 적은 비용으로 긍정적인 결과를 만들어 냈다는 것이다
③ G. C. 울리에트와 피켓 박사는 자연을 이용하는 방법에 의견이 일치했다.
✓④ 피켓 박사와 그의 동료들은 유기체의 개체 수를 제한할 필요성을 믿지 않았다.

| 분석 | 피켓 박사와 그의 동료들은 살충제를 해충을 간신히 박멸할 정도만 살포하라고 하였다. 그렇다면 결국 소량이지만 살충제를 사용한다는 것이며 유기체라고 할 수 있는 해충의 개체 수를 제한한다고 볼 수 있다. 따라서 ④는 지문을 통해 추론할 수 없는 진술이다.

| 배경 지식 | 유기체(Organism): 생물체는 무생물과 달리, 형태적으로도 기능적으로도 분화된 여러 부분으로 되어 있고, 부분 상호 사이 및 부분과 전체 사이에 밀접한 관련이 있으며, 전체로서 하나로 정비된 통일체를 이루고 있다. 유기체라는 것은 그러한 구성(유기적 구성)을 갖는 것을 의미하고, 좁은 의미로는 생물을 의미한다. 생물의 개체는 분할되면 통일체로 될 수 없고, 존립할 수도 없다.

[29–30] 2018 한양대

| 정답 | 29 ③   30 ②

| 어휘 | hollow ⓐ (속이) 빈; 공허한   dorsal ⓐ 등에 있는, 등쪽의   nerve cord ⓝ (무척추동물의) 신경색
class ⓝ (생물학 분류에서의) 강(綱)   embryological ⓐ 발생학적인   morphology ⓝ 형태학

spinal cord ⓝ 척수, 등골	peripheral ⓐ 주변적인, 지엽적인	cranial ⓐ 두개(골)의
cardiac ⓐ 심장의	gland ⓝ 선, 분비샘	glial ⓐ 신경교의
irritability ⓝ 피자극성, 흥분	conductivity ⓝ 전도성, 전도율	neuroglia ⓝ 신경교
comparable ⓐ 비슷한, 비교할 만한; 필적하는		neurilemmal ⓐ 신경초의

> **전문해석**
>
> 척추동물 신경계는 속이 빈 등에 있는 신경색으로 특징지을 수 있는데, 신경색은 더 커진 형태로 머리 부위, 즉 뇌에서 끝난다. 가장 원시적인 형태에서도 이 신경색과 그것에 붙어 있는 신경들은 진화적 특수화의 산물인데, 하등 척추동물 강에서 고등 척추동물 강으로의 진화 과정은 아직 완전히 밝혀지지 않았다. 그럼에도 불구하고 기본적인 배열은 모든 척추동물들에서 비슷하므로, 하등 동물들을 연구하는 것이 고등 동물들의 신경계 형태와 구조에 대한 통찰을 준다. 더욱이, ==모든 종에 있어서 신경계의 발생학적 발달에 관한 연구는 성인 형태론을 이해하는 데 필수이다.== 모든 척추동물들에서 신경계는 주요한 두 부분으로 구별된다. 그것들은 뇌와 척수로 구성된 중추 신경계와 뇌신경, 척수신경, 말초신경, 각각의 운동 및 감각 말단으로 구성된 말초 신경계이다. "자율 신경계"라는 용어는 심근, 민무늬근 및 다양한 선들의 활동을 공급하고 제어하는 중추 및 말초 신경계 내의 여러 부분들을 가리킨다. 신경계는 수백만 개의 신경 세포 및 교질 세포, 혈관 및 소량의 결합조직으로 이루어져 있다. "뉴런"이라 불리는 신경 세포는 많은 과정들로 특징지어지고, 고도의 피자극성과 전도성을 보여 준다는 점에서 특화되어 있다. 중추 신경계의 교질 세포는 세포들을 지지하는 역할을 하는데 집합적으로 "신경교"라 불린다. 이들은 신경 세포, 혈관, 결합조직들과 특별한 관계를 갖는 짧은 과정들로 특징지어진다. 말초 신경계에서 비슷한 역할을 하는 세포들을 "신경초" 세포라 부른다.

29 윗글의 주제로 가장 적절한 것은? 주제

① 신경 세포의 진화
② 생명공학의 진보
✓ 척추동물의 신경계
④ 자율 신경계의 기능

| 분석 | 이 글의 중심 키워드는 척추동물의 신경계이다. 척추동물의 신경계를 중추와 말초 신경계로 나누어 설명하고 있다. 따라서 주제로 적합한 것은 ③이다.

30 저자는 태아의 생물학적 구조를 자세히 탐구하는 것이 아마도 _____ 결과로 이어질 것이라고 암시하고 있다. 내용 파악

① 다른 종의 동일 구조 연구를 향상시키는
✓ 완전히 발달된 구조를 더 잘 이해하는
③ 과학자들이 신경 질병을 진단할 수 있는 방법이라는
④ 부족한 발달이 바로잡힐 수 있는 방법을 발견하는

| 분석 | 지문에서 '모든 종에 있어서 신경계의 발생학적 발달에 관한 연구는 성인 형태론을 이해하는 데 필수이다.'라고 한 부분이 단서인데, 단순한 태아의 것을 연구하면 복잡한 성인의 형태도 알 수 있다는 의미이다. 따라서 태아의 생물학적 구조 연구를 통해 아마도 우리는 성인의 생물학적 구조를 알아낼 수 있을 것이다.

[31-32] 2018 명지대

| 정답 | 31 ③ 32 ②

어휘	foe ⓝ 적, 적군	excrement ⓝ 배설물; 대변	repository ⓝ (천연자원 등의) 매장지
human waste 분뇨, 똥오줌	stench ⓝ 악취, 악취를 풍기는 것	heat wave 무더위, 폭염
scorcher ⓝ 모든 것을 태워 버릴 듯이 더운 날		noxious ⓐ 유해한, 유독한

odor ⓝ 냄새, 악취
bill ⓝ 법안
stink ⓝ 악취
thoroughfare ⓝ 주요거리
solely ⓐⓓ 오직, 단지
editorialize ⓥ (~에 대하여) 사설로 논하다; 입장을 밝히다
craft ⓥ (물건·제품을) 정교하게 만들다
a blessing in disguise (문제인 줄 알았던 것이 가져다준) 뜻밖의 좋은 결과, 전화위복
pungency ⓝ (코가) 얼얼함
embankment ⓝ 둑, 제방
congested ⓐ (사람·교통 등이) 혼잡한, 밀집한
embrace ⓥ 기꺼이 받아들이다, 수용하다
airborne ⓐ 공기로 운반되는[전염되는]
rave about ~에 대해 격찬[극찬]하다
figure out 알아내다, 생각해 내다
the Embankment 런던의 템스 강둑길
contagious disease (접촉) 전염병
sewage ⓝ 하수, 오물
get underway 시작하다, 진행 중이다

전문해석

19세기, 영국 정부는 강력한 적에 거의 굴복할 뻔했다—인간 배설물의 냄새. 여름이 되면 이미, 템스강은 인간이 배설한 분뇨의 거대한 매장지가 되어, 그 악취에 런던시 전체가 무릎을 꿇고 말았다.
[C] 이 악취 문제는 수십 년 동안이나 지속된 상태였다. 당시 전문가들은 전염병이 오직 공기로만 전염된다고 믿었기 때문에 템스강에 오물을 버리는 것의 위험성에 대해서는 거의 생각해 보지 않았다. 영국의 타임스(*The Times*)지 같은 언론들은 수년간 템스강을 정화할 필요성에 대해 사설을 통해 입장을 밝혀 왔지만 달라진 것은 아무것도 없었다.
[A] 그러다가 1858년 거대한 폭염이 찾아왔다. 영국의 그해 여름은 엄청 뜨거웠다. 그 엄청난 폭염은 템스강의 분뇨를 끓게 만들었고, 이것은 점점 더 자극적인 유독한 냄새를 뿜어냈다. 상황은 너무나 절망적으로 변했기 때문에 무언가를 해야 한다는 데 모두가 동의했다. 해결책을 생각해 내는 것이 그다음 도전 과제였으며, 수많은 논쟁과 토론을 거친 후 (당시 영국 총리였던) 디즈 레일리(Disraeli)는 마침내 1958년 7월, 오물을 도시 밖으로 보내는 제방과 터널의 건설을 승인하는 법안을 통과시켰다.
[D] 건설공사가 진행됨에 따라 그 공사 프로젝트를 이끌었던 최고 기술자인 조셉 바잘제트(Joseph Bazalgette)는 그 공사의 문제점에 대해 공개적으로 밝혔다. "이 공사는 굉장히 힘든 작업이었어요."라고 바잘제트가 말했다. 많은 어려움에도 불구하고, 제방축조 프로젝트는 점점 현대 도시의 모습을 만드는 데 한 부분이 되었다. 새로운 지하철 시스템도 또한 그 노력의 일환으로 만들어졌다. 제방은 1874년이 되어서야 완공되었지만, 1861년에 이미 주민들은 그 변화에 대해 극찬을 아끼지 않고 있었다.
[B] 그것이 유발한 고통에도 불구하고, 1858년의 대악취(the Great Stink)는 결국 런던에 축복이 되었다. 템스강이 그 후 10년 동안 정화되었을 뿐 아니라 런던시 전체가 템스강둑 덕택에 기간시설 면으로나 시각적으로나 개선이 되었는데, 이 템스강둑은 오물을 흘려보내면서도 동시에 교통이 혼잡한 거리에서 교통체증을 완화하고 새로운 지하철 시스템을 채택하고, 런던의 지상 외관도 더 나아지게 했다.

---

31 박스들 사이에서 적절한 순서를 고르시오. 문장 배열

① [C] – [A] – [B] – [D]
② [B] – [C] – [A] – [D]
✓③ [C] – [A] – [D] – [B]
④ [A] – [C] – [D] – [B]

| 분석 | 이 글은 템스강의 엄청난 악취에 관하여 문제 제기, 문제 해결을 위한 법안과 과정들, 그리고 최종적으로 문제를 해결하고 전화위복하였다는 순으로 구성되어 있다. 주어진 문장은 템스강의 악취 문제에 관하여 문제를 제기하였다. [C] 문장의 내용이 그것을 인지하지 못한 채 수십 년 동안이나 지속되었다는 내용인데 주어진 문장에 대한 부연 설명으로 볼 수 있다. 따라서 [C] 문장이 처음으로 위치해야 한다. 그리고 악취 문제가 더 이상 버틸 수 없을 정도가 되어 해결책을 마련하게 되었다는 [A]가 그다음에 와야 하며, [A]에서 "오물을 도시 밖으로 보내는 제방과 터널의 건설을 승인하는 법안을 통과시켰다."라고 했으므로, [A] 다음에는 오물을 도시 밖으로 보내는 공사에 관련된 내용인 [D]가 와야 한다. 마지막으로 공사를 하면서 문제가 해결되었다는 [B]가 이어져야 자연스럽다.

32 윗글에 대한 가장 적절한 제목을 고르시오. 제목

① 대악취, 영국의 숨겨진 적
② 대악취, 변장한 축복 (전화위복의 개념) ✓
③ 19세기의 어떤 현대적 도시 건설
④ 조셉 바잘제트, 대악취로부터 런던을 구한 남자

| 분석 | 이 글은 분뇨 냄새로 고통받던 런던이 문제를 해결하고 현대 도시로 탈바꿈하게 된 과정을 설명하고 있다. 따라서 제목으로는 ②'대악취, 변장한 축복'이 적절하다.

[33-35] 2021 숭실대

| 정답 | 33 ④ 34 ② 35 ③

| 어휘 |
glacier ⓝ 빙하
fluffy ⓐ 솜털 모양의, 솜털의
pellet ⓝ 단단히 뭉친 알갱이
granular ⓐ 알갱이로 이루어진
firn ⓝ 입상설, 만년설
grainy ⓐ 알갱이가 많은(입상의)
fuse ⓥ 융합되다, 융합시키다
exert ⓥ 가하다
melt ⓥ 녹다
meltwater ⓝ 눈이나 얼음이 녹은 물, 해빙수
slick ⓐ 매끈매끈한
ice sheet 빙상, 대륙 빙하
iceberg ⓝ 빙산
hazard ⓝ 위험
coral ⓝ 산호

전문해석

빙하는 육지 위를 천천히 움직이는 거대한 얼음덩어리이다. "glacier"라는 용어는 프랑스어로 얼음을 의미하는 "glace"에서 유래되었다. 빙하는 종종 "얼음의 강"으로 불린다. 빙하는 매년 ⒶI녹는I 것보다 더 많은 눈이 쌓이는 곳에서 형성되기 시작한다. 눈이 내리고 난 직후에 눈은 압축되기 시작하거나 더 빽빽해지고 꽉 차게 된다. 그것은 가볍고 솜털 같은 결정체로부터 단단하고 둥근 얼음 알갱이로 천천히 변한다. 새 눈이 내려 이 알갱이 같은 눈을 묻어 버린다. 단단한 이 눈은 더욱더 압축된다. 그것은 피른(입상설)이라고 불리는 밀도가 높은 알갱이로 된 얼음이 된다. 눈이 압축되어 빙하의 피른(입상설)이 되는 과정을 피른화라고 한다.

해가 지날수록, 입상설의 층은 겹겹이 쌓인다. 얼음이 충분히 두꺼워지면—약 50미터—전나무 알갱이들은 거대한 고체 얼음덩어리로 융합된다. 빙하는 자체의 무게로 움직이기 시작한다. I빙하는 너무 무겁고 너무 많은 압력이 가해져서 입상설과 눈은 기온의 상승이 전혀 없어도 녹게 된다.I 녹은 물은 무거운 빙하의 바닥을 더 매끄럽게 하여 지대 전역으로 퍼질 수 있게 한다.

빙하는 얼음이 입상설이 축적되는 것보다 더 빨리 녹을 때 녹게 된다. 지구의 평균 기온은 한 세기 이상 동안 급격하게 상승해 왔다. 빙하는 여러 면에서 지구 온난화와 기후 변화의 중요한 지표이다. 녹아내리는 얼음층은 해수면을 상승하게 만든다. 남극대륙과 그린란드의 빙하가 녹으면서, 해수면의 수위를 높이고 있다. 매일 수천 톤의 담수가 바다에 더해지고 있다. 2009년 3월, 160제곱미터에 달하는 윌킨스 빙붕 조각이 남극 반도에서 떨어져 나갔다. 그러한 사건에 의해 만들어진 큰 빙산은 운송에 큰 위험을 초래한다.

많은 양의 담수가 더해지는 것 또한 해양 생태계를 변화시킨다. 많은 종류의 산호와 유기체들은 생존을 위해 소금물에 의존한다. 일부 산호초들은 염분이 덜한 서식지에 적응하지 못할 수도 있다. 빙하 얼음의 상실은 또한 생존하기 위해 담수가 필요한 식물과 동물들에게 이용 가능한 담수의 양을 감소시킨다. 파푸아의 열대 섬이나 남아메리카에 있는 빙하와 같이 적도 근처에 있는 빙하는 특히 위험에 처해 있다.

---

33 빈칸 Ⓐ에 가장 적합한 것은? 빈칸 추론

① 도착하다
② 떨어지다
③ 모으다
④ 녹다 ✓

| 분석 | 빙하가 형성되려면 녹는 것보다 더 많은 눈이 쌓여야 할 것이다. 따라서 빈칸은 눈이 쌓이는 것의 반대의 개념인 ④ 'melt'가 적절하다.

34 다음 중 사실이 아닌 것은? 내용 일치

① 입상설은 눈이 장기적으로 단단해지는 과정의 산물이다.
☑ ② 무거운 빙하는 입상설의 온도를 상승하게 한다.
③ 큰 빙하의 덩어리가 떨어져 나가면 빙산이 생긴다.
④ 일부 산호초는 묽어진 바닷물에 취약하다.

| 분석 | 지문의 두 번째 단락에서 '빙하는 너무 무겁고 너무 많은 압력이 가해져서 입상설과 눈은 기온의 상승이 전혀 없어도 녹게 된다.'고 언급하였다. 빙하는 온도 상승이 없이도 입상설을 녹인다는 것이다. 따라서 ②는 지문과 일치하지 않는 진술이다.

35 다음 중 눈이 피른(입상설)이 되는 과정과 관계없는 것은? 내용 파악

① 추운 날씨　　　　　　　② 쌓인 눈
☑ ③ 빙산　　　　　　　　　④ 알갱이로 된 얼음

| 분석 | ③의 '빙산'은 빙하에서 떨어져 나와 바다에 흘러 다니는 얼음덩어리를 말한다. 따라서 입상설이 되는 과정과 관련이 없다.

[36-38] 2012 이화여대

| 정답 |　36 ②　37 ④　38 ③

| 어휘 |
hydraulic fracturing 수압 파쇄
hard-to-reach ⓐ 접근하기 힘든
fluid ⓝ 유동체, 유체
additive ⓝ 첨가제
provision ⓝ 규정, 조항
dispose of ~을 처분하다, ~을 처리하다
dishevel ⓥ 흩뜨리다
stipulation ⓝ 규정, 조항, 조건
terms ⓝ 조건, 약정, 관계
granular ⓐ 알갱이로 이루어진

fracture ⓥ 부수다
geologic ⓐ 지질의
inject ⓥ 주사하다, 주입하다
leach ⓥ 거르다; 걸러내다
enhance ⓥ 높이다, 더하다
augment ⓥ 늘리다, 증대시키다
animate ⓥ 생기를 주다, 활기를 띠게 하다
directive ⓝ 지령, 명령
void ⓝ 결함, 진공
prop ⓥ 지지하다, 보강하다

trapped ⓐ 갇혀 있는, 묻혀 있는
formation ⓝ (지층의) 계통, 층(層)
a multitude of 다수의, 많은
disclosure ⓝ 발각, 폭로
disarray ⓥ 어지럽히다, 혼란시키다
mitigate ⓥ 누그러뜨리다, 완화하다
dismantle ⓥ 부수다, 분해하다
admonition ⓝ 훈계, 충고
substantial ⓐ 많은, 실질적인

전문해석

수압 파쇄(프랙처어링 공법), 즉 정유사가 접근하기 힘든 지질층에 묻혀 있는 국가의 에너지에 접근할 수 있게끔 해 주는 방식은 최근 들어 환경 및 건강 문제에 있어 점점 더 관심을 끄는 주제가 되고 있다. 수압 파쇄를 이용해 천연가스가 더 많이 매장되어 있는 지대로 접근할 수 있지만, 그 과정에는 매우 많은 물과 파쇄용 액체의 사용을 필요로 하며, 이것들은 높은 압력하에 대량으로 지하로 유입된다. 이 파쇄용 액체들의 성분은 단순한 물과 모래의 혼합물에서 다량의 화학 첨가제가 있는 복잡한 혼합물에 이르기까지 구성에 있어 다양하다. 정유사는 파쇄용 액체의 흐름을 개선시키거나 또는 파쇄 성과를 Ⓐ 줄이는 박테리아를 죽이기 위해 이들 화학 첨가제를 사용할 수 있다. 이러한 화학 첨가제가 안전하게 Ⓑ 처리되지 않거나 걸러지지 않은 채 식수 공급원으로 흘러들게 되면, 환경을 파괴하거나 인간의 건강에 위험을 줄 수 있다. 그러나 연방법에는 수압 파쇄에 관여하고 있는 가스나 석유 개발, 공급사에 대한 공시 ⓐ 규정이 전혀 없고, 주의 공시 규정도 서로 매우 다르다. 업계에서는 조만간 파쇄용 액체의 성분에 대한 공개용 데이터베이스를 구축할 것이라고 최근 발표했지만, 이 데이터베이스에 기록하는 일은 순전히 자발적인 것이므로, 회사가 모든 유정에 대한 정보를 정확하게 알리고 있는지를 확인할 수 있는 방법은 전혀 없다. Ⓒ 이러한 정보의 공백은 대중이 이러한 액체의 사용이 건강에 미칠 수 있는 영향을 알 수 없게 한다.

36 빈칸 Ⓐ와 Ⓑ에 알맞은 적절한 짝은 무엇인가? 빈칸 추론

① 향상시키다 – 무질서한
② 줄이다 – 처리된 ✓
③ 증가시키다 – 박탈된
④ 완화하다 – 흐트러진
⑤ 생명을 불어넣다 – 해체된

| 분석 | 빈칸 Ⓐ 부분의 내용은 회사들이 화학 첨가제를 이용하여 박테리아를 죽이려 한다는 것이다. 박테리아는 회사에 피해를 가하는 것이므로 박테리아는 회사들이 하는 파쇄 행위를 방해할 것이다. 따라서 빈칸 Ⓐ는 reduce, mitigate가 가능하다. 그리고 빈칸 Ⓑ는 화학 제품이 환경을 파괴하는 경우는 안전하게 처리하지 못할 때이므로 disposed of, deprived of, dismantle이 가능하다.

37 ⓐ를 대체할 수 <u>없는</u> 표현은 어느 것인가? 어휘

① 규정
② 명령, 지령
③ 요건
④ 훈계 ✓
⑤ (합의·계약 등의) 조건

| 분석 | 지문에서 provision은 '규정', '조항'이라는 의미로 사용되었다. 나머지 보기들은 전부 규정, 조항, 명령, 조건 등의 의미를 갖는 반면에 ④ 'admonition'은 '훈계', '충고'의 의미이므로 provision을 대체할 수 없다.

38 다음 중 ⓒ에 가장 적합한 것은 무엇인가? 빈칸 추론

① 파쇄용 액체로 인한 환경 및 인간 건강에 대한 위험은 대체로 그 내용물에 따라 달라진다
② 수입 파쇄의 결과로 미국의 천연가스 생산량은 1974년 이래 최고치에 이르렀다
③ 이러한 정보의 공백은 대중이 이러한 액체의 사용이 건강에 미칠 수 있는 영향을 알 수 없게 한다 ✓
④ 일부 파쇄용 액체는 파쇄 과정이 끝날 때 유정에서 제거되지만, 상당량이 땅속에 남게 된다
⑤ 석유 및 가스 회사는 모래나 다른 알갱이로 된 물질을 운반하여 갈라진 틈이 적절하게 열리게 하기 위해 파쇄용 액체를 만든다

| 분석 | 앞 문장에서 회사들이 정보를 공개할 계획은 있지만 자발적이다보니 회사가 모든 유정에 대한 정보를 정확하게 알리고 있는지를 확인할 수 있는 방법은 전혀 없다고 하였다. 즉 그들이 공개하는 정보는 믿을 수 없다는 것이므로 이와 같은 맥락의 문장이 와야 한다. 따라서 ③ '이러한 정보의 공백은 대중이 이러한 액체의 사용이 건강에 미칠 수 있는 영향을 알 수 없게 한다'가 정답으로 적절하다.

[39-41] 2018 숭실대

| 정답 | 39 ② 40 ① 41 ③

| 어휘 | resilient ⓐ 되튀는; 원상으로 돌아가는, 탄력 있는
drought ⓝ 가뭄, 한발
die-off ⓝ 종의 급격한 자연 소멸, 집단사
sustainable ⓐ (환경 파괴 없이) 지속[유지] 가능한, 유지할 수 있는
grassland ⓝ 풀밭, 초원
mortality ⓝ 죽어야 할 운명, 사망
seedling ⓝ 묘목
shrub land 관목지; 키 작은 나무들이 숲을 이룬 지역
withstand ⓥ (곤란 등에) 잘 견디다, 버티다
crank up 시작되다[하다], 늘리다
knock out ~을 쓸 수 없게 하다, 파괴하다

전문해석

새로운 전망에 따르면, 미국 서부의 폰데로사 소나무 숲은 세계가 점점 더 따뜻해지면서 상승하는 기온에 의해 숲이 약해지게 되고, 그때 회복력이 줄어, 점점 빠른 속도로 사라질 것이라고 한다.
이들 숲이 현재의 짧은 기간의 가뭄을 잘 견디고 있다고 할지라도, 온도가 오르면서 숲에 점점 많은 고통을 주고 있다. 이것은 숲이 한동안 견뎌 온 더 짧은 가뭄에서도 더 이상 살아남지 못할 것이라는 것을 의미한다. 그리고 미래의 가뭄은 지구가 따뜻해짐에 따라 더 심해질 것이다.
"우리는 기후가 조금 더 따뜻해지면, 상황은 Ⓐ 조금만 달라지는 것이 아니라 Ⓑ 매우 달라진다는 것을 말하는 것입니다. 사망률이 증가하는 속도가 더 빨라질 것입니다."라고 환경연구저널에 발표된 '온난화 세계에서 나무 사망에 대한 주안점'이라는 새로운 논문의 주요 필자이자 오클라호마 주립 대학교의 식물 생물학자인 헨리 애덤스(Henry Adams)가 말했다.
"나무는 장기간 가뭄이 계속되어야 죽습니다. 하지만 지구가 가열되면, 점점 더 짧은 시간에도 나무는 죽게 될 것입니다."라고 애덤스 박사는 말했다.
이 연구는 한 번의 온도 상승의 영향을 조사하는 것이 아닌 좀 더 현실적인 예측을 제공하는 다양한 증가의 효과를 조사하기 때문에 중요하다.
"우리 산림이 큰 위험에 처해 있다는 것에 대해 우리가 갖게 된 확신은 현재 매우 높습니다. 온난화가 가뭄을 더 치명적이게 만들고 있습니다."라고 애리조나 대학교의 생명자연학과 교수이자 그 논문의 공동 저자인 데이비드 브레시어즈(David D. Breshears)는 말했다.
브레시어즈 박사는 그 연구가 따뜻해지고 있는 기온과 가뭄만으로도 묘목을 죽임으로써 금세기 동안 추가적으로 9개 내지 10개의 숲을 소멸시킬 수 있다는 것을 보여 준다고 말했다. "10년 내지 12년마다 숲이 하나씩 파괴된다면 숲은 지속 불가능합니다. 우리는 많은 숲을 잃을 큰 위험에 처해 있습니다."라고 브레시어즈 박사는 말했다. 연구가들은 또한 이 연구 결과가 세계의 다른 많은 유형의 숲에도 적용될 것으로 생각하고 있다고 말한다.
그와 같은 완전한 소멸은 상태의 변화를 유발할 수 있는데, 그것은 숲이 사라지고 다른 유형의 ⓒ 생태계, 즉 아마도 초지 또는 관목지로 변해 버리는 급격한 변화를 가져올 것이다.

---

39 빈칸 Ⓐ와 Ⓑ에 가장 적합한 짝은 무엇인가? 빈칸 추론

① 매우 – 조금
✓② 조금 – 매우
③ 부분적으로 – 모조리
④ 모조리 – 부분적으로

| 분석 | 빈칸 뒤에서 '사망률이 증가하는 속도가 더 빨라질 것'이라고 언급했다. 이것은 기후 변화가 문제를 더 심각하게 한다는 의미이므로, 빈칸 문장도 같은 맥락의 의미를 만들어야 한다. 따라서 기후가 조금 따뜻해진다면, 결과는 '상황이 조금만 바뀌는 것이 아니라 많이 바뀔 것이다'라고 해야 뒤 문장과도 문맥이 맞게 된다. 또한 심각함의 정도를 말하고 있는 것이지 공간적인 것을 말하는 것이 아니므로 ③과 ④의 '부분적으로', '전체적으로'의 개념은 답이 될 수 없다.

---

40 빈칸 ⓒ에 가장 적합한 것은 무엇인가? 빈칸 추론

✓① 생태계
② 숲
③ 지리
④ 변화

| 분석 | 숲이 사라지고 초지 또는 관목지로 변하게 되는 것은 '지리'나 '숲'이 변하는 것이 아닌 생명체가 살아가는 조건인 '생태계'가 다른 형태로 변하는 것을 의미한다. 따라서 정답으로 ① 'ecosystem'이 적절하다.

41 다음 중 사실인 것은? 내용 일치

① 폰데로사 소나무 숲은 매년 사라지고 있다.
② 브레시어즈 박사는 숲의 지속 가능성에 대해 높은 자신감을 가지고 있다.
✓ ③ 온난화와 가뭄은 산림 손실의 파괴적인 조합이다.
④ 가뭄만으로도 금세기 동안 9~10건의 추가적인 삼림 파괴가 발생할 수 있다.

| 분석 | 이 글은 숲이 가뭄과 지구 온난화로 인해서 완전히 사라져 버릴 위기에 있다고 설명하는 글이다. 따라서 온난화와 가뭄은 소나무 숲을 파괴할 수 있는 파괴적인 조합이라고 진술한 ③은 지문의 전체 내용과 일치한다.

[42-44] 2018 중앙대

| 정답 | 42 ① 43 ③ 44 ④

| 어휘 |
extraction ⓝ 추출, 뽑아냄
imminent ⓐ 금방이라도 닥칠 듯한, 목전의
amidst prep (특히 흥분·공포심이 느껴지는) 가운데에, ~의 한복판에 (amid)
biophysical ⓐ 생물물리학의
affluent ⓐ 부유한
idyllic ⓐ 목가적인
disturbance ⓝ 방해, 혼란, 폐해
erosion ⓝ 부식, 침식
glaring ⓐ (좋지 않은 것이) 두드러진
intensely ⓐⓓ 매우
access ⓝ 접근권, 접근 기회
contentious ⓐ 논쟁을 초래할 만한
controlling agent ⓝ 구제제, 조절제
subsistence ⓝ 생존; 생활 수단; 생계
oversimplify ⓥ 지나치 단순화하다
notably ⓐⓓ 특히
cornucopia ⓝ 풍요, 풍부
exploitation ⓝ 개발; 착취

전문해석

식량 생산은 인간의 모든 요구 가운데 가장 기본적인 것이다. 그것은 자연환경으로부터 물질을 추출하는 데 기반을 둔다. 비록 과잉 생산, 토양의 침식, 물 부족 등으로 인해 특정 조건하에서 농경이 불가능해질 수도 있지만, 원칙적으로 식량 생산은 재생 가능한 활동이다. 식량의 생산과 유통, 소비는 오랜 기간에 걸쳐 상대적으로 큰 변화가 없었지만 지난 40여 년 사이에 변모되었다. 이들 활동은 점점 더 산업화되고 있다. 더욱이, 수백만 명의 사람들에게 생계는 여전히 지상과제이고 기아는 언제나 눈앞에 닥친 문제지만, 다른 수백만 명의 사람들에게 식량은 생존에 관한 문제인 만큼이나 생활양식에 관한 말이 되어 가고 있다. 결핍 속의 풍요는 현대 세계의 두드러진 역설 중 하나이다.

따라서, 어떤 측면에서 현대의 농식품 산업은 다른 제조업들과 별반 다르지 않은 것처럼 보인다. 그러나, 대다수의 식량 생산이 산업화되었다 Ⓐ <u>할지라도</u>, 이런 시각은 대단히 복잡하고 지리적으로 차별화된 활동을 과도하게 단순화한 것이다. 식량 생산이 다른 제조업들과 근본적으로 다른 한 가지 특성, 바로 식량 생산은 생물물리학적 과정에 기반을 두었다는 근본적인 사실에는 변함이 없다.

식량 생산은 대단히 지역적인 과정으로서 특정한 기후, 토양 그리고 종종 사회문화적인 조건에 결부되어 있다. 동시에 특정한 종류의 지역적 생산품들, 특히 Ⓑ <u>고가의</u> 식품들은 그 유통과 소비의 측면에서 점점 더 세계화되고 있다. 대형 할인매장의 진열대에서 넘쳐 나는 온갖 상품들에 접근할 수 있는 부유한 소비자들에게, 계절적 한계점은 영원한 여름철에 의해 사라져 가고 있다(부자들은 사계절 내내 여름을 누릴 수 있다는 의미). 그러나 부유한 소비자들에게는 분명 목가적이라 할 만한 이러한 환경들은 어둡고 논란이 될 만한 한 가지 측면을 지니고 있다.

글로벌 시장을 대상으로 식량을 생산하려면 대규모의 자본 투자가 필수적이므로 다국적 식품회사와 대형 소매업체들은 엄청난 힘을 갖게 된다. 이는 식량 생산자들에게 기회이기도 하지만 다국적 농식품 생산 네트워크 속으로 점점 더 같히게 되는 심각한 문제를 야기한다. 글로벌 식량 생산과 유통은 민감한 자연 생태계에 대한 과도한 개발, 화학 비료와 해충 방제제의 살포, 종자와 식물, 심지어 동물들조차도 유전자를 조작해서 '생명체에 대한 특허를 얻으려는' 시도의 증가, 그리고 지리적으로 동떨어진 곳까지 고가의 식품을 운송하는 문제 등 커다란 환경적 Ⓒ <u>교란</u>을 일으키고 있다. 이러한 과정들은 농식품 산업을 대단히 민감한 산업으로 만들면서, '자연은 누구의 것인가'와 같은 근본적인 의문을 제기한다. 44 ④

42 윗글의 빈칸 Ⓐ, Ⓑ, Ⓒ에 들어가기에 가장 적절한 것은? 빈칸 추론

① ~에도 불구하고 – 고가의 – 교란
② ~ 때문에 – 산업화된 – 혁명
③ ~와 유사한 – 세계적인 – 변화
④ ~에도 불구하고 – 문화적인 – 변화

| 분석 | 빈칸 Ⓐ는 다른 제조업처럼 농업도 산업화되었다고 했는데 이것은 농업이 이제 (다른 제조업처럼) 단순하고, 쉬운 생산업이 되었다는 것을 의미한다. 그런데 주절에서는 이러한 시각은 과도하게 단순화한 것이며 실제로는 복잡하고 하고 있으므로 역접의 전치사가 필요하다. 빈칸 Ⓑ는 '부유한' 소비자들이 전 세제에서 생산된 농식품을 구매하는 것이 가능하게 되었다고 하였으므로 '고가의'가 적절하다. 세 번째 빈칸 Ⓒ는 나열되는 것들이 산업화된 농식품 산업의 영향으로 인한 문제점들을 나열하고 있으므로 '문제'와 관련된 단어인 '교란'이 들어가야 한다.

43 윗글의 내용과 일치하지 않는 것은? 내용 일치

① 현대 농식품 산업 덕분에 부자들은 1년 내내 풍부한 음식을 즐길 수 있다.
② 글로벌 시장은 식품 생산자들이 그들의 제품을 세계적으로 공급하는 것을 더 쉽게 만들어준다.
③ 생태계의 과도한 이용은 효율적인 다국적 네트워크 시스템에 의해 해결될 수 있다. 언급 안 함
④ 식량 생산은 심각한 환경 문제에도 불구하고 재생 가능한 활동이다.

| 분석 | 생태계의 과도한 개발은 현대 농식품 산업이 일으킨 문제점으로 언급하였지만, 그것에 대한 해결책을 언급한 적은 없으므로 ③은 지문을 통해 알 수 없는 진술이다.

44 윗글을 통해 추론할 수 있는 것으로 가장 적절한 것은? 내용 추론

① 식량 생산은 산업화할 수 없다는 점에서 독특하다.
② 농식품 산업은 다른 제조업과 달리 새로운 생태계를 창출하게 되었다.
③ 농산물 산업의 매우 복잡한 활동은 오랜 기간에 걸쳐 생물물리학적 과정으로부터 자유로워졌다.
④ 글로벌 식량의 소비는 어떻게든 민감한 자연 생태계를 악화시키는 데 기여했다.

| 분석 | 마지막 단락에서 '글로벌 식량 생산과 유통은 민감한 자연 생태계에 대한 과도한 개발로 인해 환경적 교란을 일으킨다'고 언급하였다. 따라서 ④는 본문을 통해 추론 가능한 진술이다.

[45-47] 2022 숭실대

| 정답 | 45 ④ 46 ① 47 ③

| 어휘 |
aquarium ⓝ 수족관
blueprint ⓝ 청사진
landmark ⓝ 획기적인 사건
pond ⓝ 연못
assess ⓥ 재다, 평가하다
unprecedented ⓐ 전례 없는

loom ⓥ 어렴풋이 나타나다, 흐릿하게 보이다
rescue ⓝ 구출, 구조
precedent ⓝ 선례, 판례
fluctuating ⓐ 변동이 있는, 동요하는
vertebrate ⓝ 척추동물
extinction ⓝ 멸종

habitat ⓝ 서식지
under way 진행 중인
artificial ⓐ 인공의
parasite ⓝ 기생 동물, 기생충
invertebrate ⓝ 무척추동물
delicate ⓐ 연약한, 취약한

전문해석

야생에서 멸종된 것으로 알려진 "카리스마 있는 작은 물고기"가 체스터 동물원의 수족관에서 길러진 후에 멕시코의 원래 살던 곳으로 재도입되었다. 원래의 서식지에서 북쪽으로 어렴풋이 보이는 테킬라 화산의 이름을 따서 이름 지어진, 테킬라 피쉬는 테우치틀란강에서 1990년에 발견되었다. 최근 연구는 테킬라 피쉬가 테우치틀란강에서 번성하고 이미 새끼를 낳고 있다는 것을 확인했다. 전문가들은 그것이 현재 진행 중인 또 다른 종인 황금 스키피아에 대한 구조 임무와 함께 멸종 위기에 처한 다른 어종의 향후 재도입을 위한 청사진을 만들었다고 말한다. 오마르 도밍게즈(Omar Dominguez)교수는 "멸종된 어종이 멕시코에서 성공적으로 재도입된 것은 이번이 처음이기 때문에 이것은 보존을 위한 진정한 획기적인 사건입니다. 이 프로젝트는 현재 야생에서 멸종 위기에 처해 있거나 심지어 멸종되어 우리의 관심을 거의 끌지 못하는 이 나라의 많은 어종의 미래 보존을 위한 중요한 선례가 되었습니다."라고 말했다. 재도입을 준비하기 위해 군집에서 암수 40쌍을 대학에 있는 커다란 인공 연못에 풀어놓았다. 변동하는 자원, 잠재적인 경쟁자, 기생충, 그리고 새, 거북이, 뱀과 같은 약탈자들을 만날 수 있는 반천연적인 환경에 테킬라 피쉬를 노출시켰다. 4년 후 이 개체군은 10,000여 개의 개체로 증가한 것으로 추정되며 야생으로 재도입되는 원천이 되었다. [46 ①]

수질과 서식지의 질을 평가하는 훈련을 받은 지역 사람들이 참여하는 장기적인 관찰 프로그램이 수립되었다. 체스터 동물원의 하등 척추동물과 무척추동물 큐레이터인 게라르도 가르시아(Gerardo Garcia) 박사는 성공적인 재도입이 종 보존을 위한 싸움에서 중요한 순간이었다고 말했다. "인류 역사상 유례가 없는 속도로 전 세계적으로 자연이 악화되고 멸종 속도가 빨라지는 상황에서 이것은 드문 성공 사례입니다. 우리는 이제 멕시코에서 이 취약한 물고기 종들을 회복시키는 데 무엇이 효과가 있었는지에 대한 청사진을 가지고 있습니다. 그리고 우리는 이미 다음 단계로 나아가고 있는데, 황금 스키피아를 위한 새로운 구조 임무가 이미 잘 진행되고 있습니다." [47 ③]

---

45 다음 중 글의 제목으로 가장 적절한 것은? [제목]

① "카리스마 있는 작은 물고기"의 이름 지엽적
② 새로운 사육 방법의 비용 언급 안 함
③ 황금 스키피아를 되살리는 방법 지엽적
✓ 멸종 위기에 처한 물고기의 재도입

| 분석 | 멸종된 것으로 알려졌던 멕시코의 테킬라 물고기가 연구원들의 성과로 원래 서식지인 테우치틀란강으로 다시 돌아갈 수 있게 되었다는 내용의 글이므로 제목으로 ④가 적절하다.

---

46 다음 중 인공 연못에서 있던 테킬라 피쉬에 관하여 사실이 아닌 것은? [내용 일치]

✓ 테킬라 피쉬는 약탈자로부터 안전했다.
② 테킬라 피쉬는 먹이를 찾기 위해 경쟁했다.
③ 테킬라 피쉬는 번식할 짝을 찾았다.
④ 테킬라 피쉬는 야생으로 방사되었다.

| 분석 | 지문의 중반부에서 테킬라 피쉬를 풀어놓고 "변동하는 자원, 잠재적인 경쟁자, 기생충, 그리고 새, 거북이, 뱀과 같은 약탈자들을 만날 수 있는 반천연적인 환경에 노출시켰다"고 언급하였다. 따라서 테킬라 피쉬는 약탈자에 노출이 되었으므로 ①은 지문과 일치하지 않는 진술이다.

47 다음 중 사실인 것은? 내용 일치

① 테킬라 피쉬는 그 어종을 발견한 사람의 이름을 따서 지어졌다.
② 테킬라 피쉬의 멸종은 사실로 판명되었다.
✓ ③ 재도입 실험은 몇 년 동안 계속되었다.
④ 황금 스키피아의 구조가 완료되었다.

| 분석 | 지문에서 연구팀은 물고기 암수 40쌍을 대학 내 인공 연못에 풀어놓았고, 물고기는 4년 후에 10,000여 개의 개체로 증가하였다고 했으므로 ③ '재도입 실험이 몇 년 동안 지속되었다'는 것은 지문과 일치하는 진술이다.

[48-50] 2016 서울여대

| 정답 | 48 ② 49 ③ 50 ②

| 어휘 |
Komodo dragon 코모도왕도마뱀
specimen ⓝ 견본, 표본
predator ⓝ 포식자
rip ⓥ 잡아 찢다
carnivore ⓝ 육식동물
vomit ⓥ 토하다

lizard ⓝ 도마뱀
snout ⓝ 코, 주둥이
carrion ⓝ 짐승의 썩은 고기
saliva ⓝ 침
hide ⓝ 가죽
nervous ⓐ 흔들리는, 긴장한, 초조해하는; 신경의

expedition ⓝ 탐험, 원정 여행; 탐험대
scaly ⓐ 비늘이 덮인
camouflage ⓝ 위장
blood poisoning 패혈증
throw up 토하다

전문해석

코모도왕도마뱀은 수천 년 동안 인도네시아의 일부 섬에 살아왔다. 한 이야기에 따르면 코모도왕도마뱀은 제1차 세계 대전 기간 동안 코모도 섬 근해에 불시착한 한 비행기로 인해서 처음 발견되었다고 한다. 그 이야기는 코모도 섬까지 헤엄쳐 간 조종사가 그 섬에 살고 있는 무서운 거대한 도마뱀들에 둘러싸여 있었다는 것에 대해서 말하고 있다. 이 이야기는 액션 영화에 나오는 이야기 같은 느낌을 자아낸다. 그러나 이 이야기는 신화에 불과하다. 우리는 코모도왕도마뱀이 발견된 시기를 정확히 알지 못한다. 그러나 코모도왕도마뱀의 존재는 1926년에 처음으로 확인되었다. 이 해에 탐험가 더글러스 버든(Douglas Burden)이 탐험대를 이끌고 코모도 섬에 갔다. 더글러스 버든은 미국 자연사박물관에서 일하고 있었다. 그는 죽은 코모도왕도마뱀 견본 12개와 살아 있는 코모도왕도마뱀 두 마리를 가지고 탐험에서 돌아왔다.

코모도왕도마뱀은 현존하는 세상에서 가장 큰 도마뱀이다. 일부 코모도왕도마뱀은 길이가 3m가량 되기도 하고, 무게가 130kg 이상 나갈 수도 있다. 이는 코모도왕도마뱀이 지구상에서 가장 무게가 나가는 도마뱀이라는 것을 의미한다. 코모도왕도마뱀은 짧은 주둥이를 가지고 있는 긴 머리에, 비늘로 덮인 피부와 짧은 다리 그리고 강력한 꼬리를 가지고 있다. 현재까지 발견된 가장 큰 코모도왕도마뱀은 길이가 3.13m이고, 무게는 무려 166kg이었다! 코모도왕도마뱀은 그들이 살고 있는 코모도 섬에서 최상위 포식자다. 코모도왕도마뱀은 짐승의 썩은 고기, 보다 크기가 작은 도마뱀, 야생말, 돼지, 몸집이 큰 물소, 그리고 때때로 운이 나쁜 인간까지를 포함해서 어떤 것이든 먹어 치운다. 코모도왕도마뱀은 일시적으로 시속 20km로 달릴 수 있긴 하지만, 대개는 인내심과 위장을 이용해서 먹잇감을 사냥한다. 코모도왕도마뱀은 한 장소에서 몇 시간 동안 머무르면서 먹잇감이 나타나기를 기다릴 수도 있다. 그러다가 운이 없는 그들의 먹잇감이 지나가게 되면, 코모도왕도마뱀은 그 먹잇감을 공격한 다음 갈기갈기 찢어 버린다. 코모도왕도마뱀의 침에는 50가지 이상의 박테리아 종(種)들이 들어 있다. 때문에 코모도왕도마뱀에게 물린 상태에서 탈출한 먹잇감 동물은 대개 상당히 빠른 시간 안에 패혈증으로 죽음에 이르게 된다. 만일 이렇게 먹잇감이 패혈증으로 죽게 될 경우, 코모도왕도마뱀은 뛰어난 후각을 이용해 죽었거나 죽어 가는 동물을 추적해서 위치를 알아낸다. 호랑이와 같은 많은 커다란 맹수들은 그들이 잡은 먹잇감의 25~30%는 먹지 않는다. 이들 육식동물들은 위(胃), 가죽, 뼈, 발 등은 먹지 않고 남긴다. 그러나 코모도왕도마뱀은 먹잇감에 대한 낭비를 덜하고, 먹잇감의 약 12%만을 남긴다. 코모도왕도마뱀은 뼈, 발, 털, 그리고 살가죽을 먹고 심지어 위도 먹어 치운다. 코모도왕도마뱀은 자기 체중의 80% 정도를 먹을 수 있다. 그러나 겁을 먹거나 불안을 느낄 경우, 코모도왕도마뱀은 위 속에 있는 내용물을 토하기도 한다. 이것은 코모도왕도마뱀들의 몸을 가볍게 만들어 주기 때문에 코모도왕도마뱀이 보다 쉽게 도망칠 수 있다.

48 코모도왕도마뱀의 존재는 ＿＿＿＿＿＿에 의해서 세상에 알려졌다. 내용 파악

① 비행기가 근해에 추락한 후 코모도 섬으로 헤엄쳐 들어간 비행기 조종사
✓ ② 미국 자연사박물관의 탐험대 리더
③ 코모도 섬에서 실종된 비행사를 수색하러 간 구조팀
④ 코모도 섬에서 거대한 도마뱀을 포획한 어부

| 분석 | 코모도왕도마뱀의 존재가 세상에 알려지게 된 것은 미국 국립 자연사박물관에 재직하고 있던 더글러스 버든에 의해서였다.

49 다음 중 코모도왕도마뱀의 특징은 무엇인가? 내용 파악

① 코모도왕도마뱀은 오랫동안 빨리 달릴 수 있다.
② 코모도왕도마뱀은 음식을 낭비한다.
✓ ③ 코모도왕도마뱀은 필요하면 음식을 토해 낼 수도 있다.
④ 코모도왕도마뱀은 죽은 동물의 고기는 먹지 않는다.

| 분석 | 지문에서 코모도왕도마뱀은 겁을 먹거나 불안을 느낄 경우, 위 속에 있는 내용물을 토하기도 한다고 하였다. 따라서 ③이 코모도왕도마뱀의 특징으로 지문에 언급되었다.

50 어떻게 코모도왕도마뱀은 물리고 나서 도망치는 먹이를 찾는가? 내용 파악

① 먹잇감의 핏방울을 추적함으로써
✓ ② 죽어 가는 먹잇감의 냄새를 따라다니며
③ 위장한 채로 먹이가 죽기를 기다리며
④ 먹이가 오는 길에 침을 떨어뜨려 버림으로써

| 분석 | 코모도왕도마뱀은 뛰어난 후각을 이용해 죽었거나 죽어 가는 동물을 추적해서 위치를 알아낸다고 하였으므로 ②가 정답이다.

[51-52] 2022 중앙대

| 정답 | 51 ② 52 ③

| 어휘 | mercury ⓝ 수은 emission ⓝ 방출, 방출물 gold mining 금 채굴
make one's way to ~로 들어가다 womb ⓝ 자궁 sediment ⓝ 퇴적물, 침전물
food web 먹이사슬 isotope ⓝ 동위 원소(원자 번호는 같으나 질량수가 서로 다른 원소)
watershed ⓝ 강의 분수계(강이 서로 갈라지는 지점) treaty ⓝ 조약, 협정
concentration ⓝ 농도 ecological ⓐ 생태계의

전문해석

수은 오염은 세계적인 문제이다. 금 채굴, 석탄 연소, 또 다른 산업 과정에서 나오는 수은 배출물은 대기 중에서 돌아다니다가 결국 비나 눈에 섞여 땅으로 떨어진다. 수은이라는 독극물은 물고기와 물고기를 먹는 인간에게 들어가, 자궁에서 수은에 노출된 아이의 발달 중인 신경계에 손상을 입혀 기억과 언어의 문제를 일으킬 수 있다.

수은이 습지나 호수의 퇴적층에 가라앉으면 미생물이 그 금속성 원소를 메틸수은이라는 위험한 화합물로 바꾸고, 이 물질은 먹이에 쌓인다. 크고 육식성인 물고기일수록 몸속에 쌓인 메틸수은의 농도가 가장 높다. 공중보건기관들은 많은 호수에서 이러한 물고기를 정기적으로 테스트하고 때로는 이런 생선의 소비를 줄이라고 경고하기도 한다.

[B] 1980년 이후 대기 오염을 통제하려는 규제들이 북미와 유럽의 수은 배출량을 점차 낮추었지만 다른 곳의 수은 원천들은 계속 늘고 있다. 특히 라틴 아메리카의 소규모 금광과 아시아의 석탄 발전소에서 상황이 심각하다. 2013년, 각국은 수은에 관한 미나마타 협약이라는 국제 협약에 합의했다. 협약에 서명한 국가들은 전구와 배터리 같은 상품에 수은을 금지해야 하고 산업 수은 배출량도 감소시켜야 한다.

[C] 하지만 이러한 조치들이 얼마나 빨리 효과를 낼까? 이 질문에 대한 대답을 가로막는 한 가지 장애물은 생태계에서 기능하는 수은의 복잡한 작용이었으며, 이로 인해 생선 내의 수은 농도 감소분 중 어느 정도가 영양분 과다와 침입종들 그리고 또 다른 생태적 변화가 아니라 정말 대기 오염 감소로 인한 것인지 파악하기가 어렵게 된다.

[A] 명확한 파악을 위해 대규모 연구 프로젝트가 2001년에 일종의 화학 추적자인 수은의 농축 안정 동위 원소를 사용하여 실험을 시작했다. 이러한 농축된 형태의 수은 원소는 화학적으로는 일반 수은과 동일한 방식으로 작용하지만 환경에서는 일반 수은과 구별된다. 7년 동안 연구자들은 수은 동위 원소를 Lake 658의 물에 추가했는데, Lake 658은 58개 호수와 분수계를 과학 연구용으로 따로 보존한 실험용 호수 유역이라는, 멀리 떨어진 캐나다 연구 기지다. 연구자들은 또한 서로 다른 동위 원소를 비행기에서 주변 습지와 고지대로 살포해 호수 속으로 어떻게 이동하는지 연구했다.

실험이 시작된 직후, 동위 원소 표를 붙인 메틸수은이 동물성 플랑크톤같이 호수에 서식하는 무척추동물 내부에 축적되기 시작했다. 메틸수은은 동물성 플랑크톤을 먹는 옐로퍼치와 또 다른 작은 물고기 속에서도 수치가 상승했으며, 작은 물고기를 먹는 강꼬치고기 같은 큰 물고기에서도 약 40% 상승했다. 실험 첫 7년이 지나고 연구자들은 동위 원소 수은을 추가하기를 중단하고 호수에 사는 동물들의 농도를 계속 점검했다. 그 후 8년의 연구 기간 동안 동위 원소 수은의 농도는 작은 물고기에서 최대 91%까지 떨어졌다. 농도는 더 큰 물고기 개체군에서도 떨어졌다. 주변의 땅에 추가된 수은의 소량만 물고기에게서 발견되었고 이 수치도 급속히 떨어졌다.

특정 호수에 가져다준 정확한 이익은 예측하기 어려울 것이라고 연구자들은 말한다. 그 이유는 주변 분수계의 규모와 메틸화 비율 같은 지역적 조건이 물고기 속에 쌓이는 수은 수치에 영향을 끼치기 때문이라는 것이다. 그리고 모든 대기 중의 배출량이 멈춘다 해도 일부 수은—과거 대기 오염의 유산—은 계속해서 주변 유역에서 호수로 들어갈 것이다.

51 윗글의 단락을 논리적 흐름에 맞게 순서대로 배열한 것으로 가장 적합한 것은? 〔문장 배열〕

① [B] – [A] – [C]   ✓② [B] – [C] – [A]
③ [C] – [A] – [B]   ④ [C] – [B] – [A]

| 분석 | 수은을 감소시키기 위한 조치라고 할 수 있는 [B]가 가장 먼저 오고 바로 뒤에서 그 조치가 과연 효과가 있는가의 질문을 담은 [C]가 와야 하며, 그 효과를 알아보는 실험을 다루는 [A]가 와야 내용이 자연스럽게 이어진다.

52 윗글의 요지로 가장 적합한 것은? 〔글의 요지〕

① 장기적인 실험은 수은 오염을 예방하기 위해 국제 당국의 지원을 받았다.
② 연구자들은 수은 농도를 증가시키는 요인들을 분석했다.
✓③ 오랜 실험 결과 수은 오염을 줄임으로써 환경이 회복된다는 것이 드러났다.
④ 지역적인 조건들은 수은 농도의 측면에서 각기 다른 결과들을 산출했다.

| 분석 | '수은 감소 조치의 효력이 얼마나 되는가?'라는 질문을 던지고, 연구를 통해 그것을 밝혀내는 글이므로, 연구의 결과가 글의 요지라고 할 수 있다. 마지막 단락에서 연구의 결과가 나오는데 요약하면 장기적 연구의 결과는 성공적이어서 수은 오염이 줄고 환경이 회복되었다는 것이다. 따라서 이 글의 요지로 가장 적합한 것은 ③이다.

여러분의 작은 소리
에듀윌은 크게 듣겠습니다.

본 교재에 대한 여러분의 목소리를 들려주세요.
공부하시면서 어려웠던 점, 궁금한 점,
칭찬하고 싶은 점, 개선할 점, 어떤 것이라도 좋습니다.
에듀윌은 여러분께서 나누어 주신 의견을
통해 끊임없이 발전하고 있습니다.

에듀윌 도서몰 book.eduwill.net
- 부가학습자료 및 정오표: 에듀윌 도서몰 → 도서자료실
- 교재 문의: 에듀윌 도서몰 → 문의하기 → 교재(내용, 출간) / 주문 및 배송

에듀윌 편입 솔루션 독해 Advanced

발 행 일	2023년 11월 1일 초판
편 저 자	에듀윌 편입 LAB
펴 낸 이	양형남
펴 낸 곳	(주)에듀윌
등록번호	제25100-2002-000052호
주 소	08378 서울특별시 구로구 디지털로34길 55 코오롱싸이언스밸리 2차 3층

* 이 책의 무단 인용·전재·복제를 금합니다.

www.eduwill.net
대표전화 1600-6700

독해
ADVANCED

에듀윌
편입 솔루션

독해 ADVANCED 정답과 해설

펴낸곳 (주)에듀윌　**펴낸이** 양형남　**출판총괄** 오용철
개발책임 김진우, 김기임, 윤대권　**개발** 허은지　**디자인** 디자인본부
주소 서울시 구로구 디지털로34길 55 코오롱싸이언스밸리 2차 3층
대표번호 1600-6700　**등록번호** 제25100-2002-000052호
협의 없는 무단 복제는 법으로 금지되어 있습니다.

에듀윌 도서몰 book.eduwill.net
- 부가학습자료 및 정오표: 에듀윌 도서몰 → 도서자료실
- 교재 문의: 에듀윌 도서몰 → 문의하기 → 교재(내용, 출간) / 주문 및 배송

1위 에듀윌만의
체계적인 합격 커리큘럼

원하는 시간과 장소에서, 1:1 관리까지 한번에
온라인 강의

① 최대 500% 환급! 강력한 동기부여 시스템
② 서성한 100% 합격 1타 교수진 강의 무제한 수강
③ 합격 메이커 군단의 1:1 밀착 관리

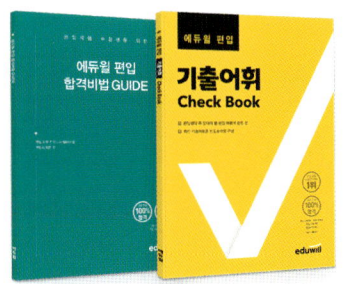

노베이스도 9관왕 합격! **쌩기초 풀패키지 무료** 신청

맞춤 학습과 체계적인 관리 시스템!
직영 학원

① 업계 최고 수준 1타 교수진
② The 'T'쳐 독한 관리 프로그램
③ 넓고 쾌적한 호텔급 학원 시설
④ 복습 동영상 무제한 제공
⑤ 철저한 본사 직영 관리

당일 등록 회원
시크릿 추가 혜택

방문상담 당일 등록 **시크릿 추가 혜택** 제공

친구 추천 이벤트

"친구 추천하고 한 달 만에 920만원 받았어요"

친구 1명 추천할 때마다 현금 10만원 제공
추천 참여 횟수 무제한 반복 가능

※ *a*o*h**** 회원의 2021년 2월 실제 리워드 금액 기준
※ 해당 이벤트는 예고 없이 변경되거나 종료될 수 있습니다.

친구 추천 이벤트
바로가기

* 2023 대한민국 브랜드만족도 편입 교육 1위 (한경비즈니스)

꿈을 현실로 만드는
에듀윌

DREAM

공무원 교육
- 선호도 1위, 신뢰도 1위! 브랜드만족도 1위!
- 합격자 수 2,100% 폭등시킨 독한 커리큘럼

자격증 교육
- 7년간 아무도 깨지 못한 기록 합격자 수 1위
- 가장 많은 합격자를 배출한 최고의 합격 시스템

직영학원
- 직영학원 수 1위, 수강생 규모 1위!
- 표준화된 커리큘럼과 호텔급 시설 자랑하는 전국 44개 학원

종합출판
- 4대 온라인서점 베스트셀러 1위!
- 출제위원급 전문 교수진이 직접 집필한 합격 교재

어학 교육
- 토익 베스트셀러 1위
- 토익 동영상 강의 무료 제공
- 업계 최초 '토익 공식' 추천 AI 앱 서비스

콘텐츠 제휴 · B2B 교육
- 고객 맞춤형 위탁 교육 서비스 제공
- 기업, 기관, 대학 등 각 단체에 최적화된 고객 맞춤형 교육 및 제휴 서비스

부동산 아카데미
- 부동산 실무 교육 1위!
- 상위 1% 고소득 창업/취업 비법
- 부동산 실전 재테크 성공 비법

공기업 · 대기업 취업 교육
- 취업 교육 1위!
- 공기업 NCS, 대기업 직무적성, 자소서, 면접

학점은행제
- 99%의 과목이수율
- 15년 연속 교육부 평가 인정 기관 선정

대학 편입
- 편입 교육 1위!
- 업계 유일 500% 환급 상품 서비스

국비무료 교육
- '5년우수훈련기관' 선정
- K-디지털, 4차 산업 등 특화 훈련과정

에듀윌 교육서비스 **공무원 교육** 9급공무원/7급공무원/경찰공무원/소방공무원/계리직공무원/기술직공무원/군무원 **자격증 교육** 공인중개사/주택관리사/감정평가사/노무사/전기기사/경비지도사/검정고시/소방설비기사/소방시설관리사/사회복지사1급/건축기사/토목기사/직업상담사/전기기능사/산업안전기사/위험물산업기사/위험물기능사/도로교통사고감정사/유통관리사/물류관리사/행정사/한국사능력검정/한경TESAT/매경TEST/KBS한국어능력시험/실용글쓰기/IT자격증/국제무역사/무역영어 **어학 교육** 토익 교재/토익 동영상 강의/인공지능 토익 앱 **세무/회계** 회계사/세무사/전산세무회계/ERP정보관리사/재경관리사 **대학 편입** 편입 교재/편입 영어·수학/경찰대/의치대/편입 컨설팅·면접 **공기업·대기업 취업 교육** 공기업 NCS·전공·상식/대기업 직무적성/자소서·면접 **직영학원** 공무원학원/경찰학원/소방학원/군간부학원/공인중개사 학원/주택관리사 학원/전기기사학원/세무사·회계사 학원/편입학원/취업아카데미 **종합출판** 공무원·자격증 수험교재 및 단행본 **학점은행제** 교육부 평가인정기관 원격평생교육원(사회복지사2급/경영학/CPA)/교육부 평가인정기관 원격 사회교육원(사회복지사2급/심리학) **콘텐츠 제휴·B2B 교육** 교육 콘텐츠 제휴/기업 맞춤 자격증 교육/대학 취업역량 강화 교육 **부동산 아카데미** 부동산 창업CEO과정/실전 경매 과정/디벨로퍼과정 **국비무료 교육 (국비교육원)** 전기기능사/전기(산업)기사/소방설비(산업)기사/IT(빅데이터)/자바프로그램/파이썬)/게임그래픽/3D프린터/실내건축디자인/웹퍼블리셔/그래픽디자인/영상편집(유튜브)디자인/온라인 쇼핑몰광고 및 제작(쿠팡, 스마트스토어)/전산세무회계/컴퓨터활용능력/ITQ/GTQ/직업상담사

교육문의 **1600-6700** www.eduwill.net

- 2022 소비자가 선택한 최고의 브랜드 공무원·자격증 교육 1위 (조선일보) • 2023 대한민국 브랜드만족도 공무원·자격증·취업·학원·편입·부동산 실무 교육 1위 (한경비즈니스)
- 2017/2022 에듀윌 공무원 과정 최종 환급자 수 기준 • 2022년 공인중개사 직영학원 기준 • YES24 공인중개사 부문, 2023 에듀윌 공인중개사 1차 단원별 기출문제집 (2023년 8월 월별 베스트) 그 외 다수 교보문고 취업/수험서 부문, 2020 에듀윌 농협은행 6급 NCS 직무능력평가+실전모의고사 4회 (2020년 1월 27일~2월 5일, 인터넷 주간 베스트) 그 외 다수 알라딘 컴퓨터활용능력 부문, 2023 컴퓨터활용능력 1급 필기 기본서(2022년 9월 5주, 10월 1주 주간 베스트) 그 외 다수 • 인터파크 자격서/수험서 부문, 에듀윌 한국사능력검정시험 2주 끝장 심화 (1, 2, 3급) (2020년 6~8월 월간 베스트) 그 외 다수 • YES24 국어 외국어사전 영어 토익/TOEIC 기출문제/모의고사 분야 베스트셀러 1위 (에듀윌 토익 READING RC 4주끝장 리딩 종합서, 2022년 9월 4주 주별 베스트) • 에듀윌 토익 교재 입문~실전 인강 무료 제공 (2022년 최신 강좌 기준/109강) • 2022년 종강반 중 모든 평가항목 정상 참여자 기준, 99% (평생교육원, 사회교육원 기준) • 2008년~2022년까지 약 206만 누적수강학점으로 과목 운영 (평생교육원 기준) • A사, B사 최대 200% 환급 서비스 (2022년 6월 기준) • 에듀윌 국비교육원 구로센터 고용노동부 지정 '5년우수훈련기관' 선정 (2023~2027) • KRI 한국기록원 2016, 2017, 2019년 공인중개사 최다 합격자 배출 공식 인증 (2023년 현재까지 업계 최고 기록)